Pathways
to Power

Pathways to Power

Political Recruitment and Candidate
Selection in Latin America

Edited by
Peter M. Siavelis
Scott Morgenstern

The Pennsylvania State University Press
University Park, Pennsylvania

Library of Congress
Cataloging-in-Publication Data

Pathways to power: political recruitment and candidate
selection in Latin America/[edited by] Peter M. Siavelis,
Scott Morgenstern.
        p. cm.
Summary: "A cross-national analysis of political
recruitment and candidate selection in six Latin
American countries: Argentina, Brazil, Chile,
Colombia, Mexico and Uruguay. Provides typology
and theoretical insights for other countries in the region
and around the world"—Provided by publisher.
    Includes bibliographical references and index.

ISBN-13: 978-0-271-03375-4 (cloth: alk. paper)
    1. Political candidates—Latin America. 2. Politics,
Practical—Latin America. I. Siavelis, Peter.
II. Morgenstern, Scott.
JL968.P38 2008
324.5098—dc22   2008007418

Contents

PREFACE   vii
PARTY NAMES AND ABBREVIATIONS   xv

Part I   Theoretical Framework   1

Chapter 1   Political Recruitment and Candidate Selection in
Latin America: A Framework for Analysis   3
Peter M. Siavelis and Scott Morgenstern

**Part II   Political Recruitment and Candidate Selection
for the Legislative Branch**   39

Chapter 2   The Recruitment and Selection
of Legislative Candidates in Argentina   41
Mark P. Jones

Chapter 3   Political Ambition, Candidate Recruitment,
and Legislative Politics in Brazil   76
David Samuels

Chapter 4   Legislative Candidate Selection in Chile   92
Patricio Navia

Chapter 5   *Mejor Solo Que Mal Acompañado*: Political *Entrepreneurs*
and List Proliferation in Colombia   119
Erika Moreno and Maria Escobar-Lemmon

Chapter 6   Legislative Recruitment in Mexico   143
Joy Langston

Chapter 7   Why Factions? Candidate Selection and Legislative Politics in
Uruguay   164
Juan Andrés Moraes

**Part III   Political Recruitment and Candidate Selection
for the Executive Branch**   187

Chapter 8   Political Recruitment and Candidate
Selection in Argentina: Presidents and
Governors, 1983 to 2006   189
Miguel De Luca

Chapter 9   Political Recruitment in an
Executive-Centric System: Presidents,
Ministers, and Governors in Brazil   218
Timothy J. Power and Marília G. Mochel

Chapter 10   Political Recruitment and Candidate Selection
in Chile, 1990 to 2006:
The Executive Branch   241
David Altman

Chapter 11 Precandidates, Candidates, and Presidents:
            Paths to the Colombian Presidency   271
            Steven L. Taylor, Felipe Botero Jaramillo, and
            Brian F. Crisp
Chapter 12 Political Recruitment, Governance, and
            Leadership in Mexico: How Democracy
            Has Made a Difference   292
            Roderic Ai Camp
Chapter 13 Presidential Candidate Selection in
            Uruguay, 1942 to 2004   316
            Daniel Buquet and Daniel Chasquetti

Part IV   Gender and Political Recruitment   **343**

Chapter 14 How Do Candidate Recruitment and
            Selection Processes Affect the Representation
            of Women?   345
            Maria Escobar-Lemmon and Michelle M.
            Taylor-Robinson

Part V   Summary and Conclusions   **369**

Chapter 15 Pathways to Power and Democracy in
            Latin America   371
            Scott Morgenstern and Peter M. Siavelis

            REFERENCES   403
            INDEX   423
            ABOUT THE CONTRIBUTORS   437

Preface

With the withdrawal of authoritarian regimes from the political stage of Latin America, the quality of representation and the functioning of democratic institutions have become political scientists' central concerns. These concerns have generated many methodologically sophisticated analyses of presidents, legislatures, election systems, and subnational governments. Nonetheless, these institutionalist accounts of political phenomena in the Americas have sometimes failed in their attempts to explain political outcomes, often, we believe, because they frequently ignore a fundamental influence on politicians' behavior: their pathways to power. Political recruitment and candidate selection—understood as the processes by which candidates are cultivated and chosen for public office—determine who gains political power and empower those who select the candidates. Consequently, these processes underlie the relation between successful candidates and the individuals or groups to whom they owe loyalty, which in turn shapes elected leaders' behavior and decisions. We have assembled this edited volume to explore these themes with reference to Latin America: to analyze, theoretically and empirically, the processes and impacts of political recruitment and candidate selection in Latin America.

The core premise of a representative democracy is that the governed choose those who will govern. These processes, however, are directed by parties and elites who, while almost always professing a commitment to democracy, usually mask the mechanisms by which candidates are recruited and placed on ballots. This lack of transparency and the divergence between the formal rules and the way the processes actually work has seriously hampered the study of recruitment and selection. In fact, we know little about the crucial roles played by party elites, candidates, selectorates, and representatives in emerging democracies.

Though little studied in new and resurgent democracies, the importance of *recruitment and selection* (hereafter R&S) has not escaped the notice of scholars studying European parliamentary governments or the United States. However, this literature is less relevant to Latin America's predominantly multiparty, presidential systems. For Latin America there are only a few theoretically isolated case studies that thoroughly examine questions of recruitment and selection, and there is nothing that is broadly comparative. That body of literature, though of generally high quality, fails to provide an overarching framework for understanding political recruitment and its consequences.

Our volume is a response to this serious lack of knowledge and understanding. *Pathways to Power* analyzes political recruitment and candidate selection as a dependent and independent variable for the executive and legislative branches in Latin America. It does so for six countries—Argentina, Brazil, Chile, Colombia,

Uruguay, and Mexico—chosen for their significance in the region, and with an eye toward providing an optimal mix of cases that are of most interest to students and scholars, but that also vary enough to provide intriguing theoretical insights. For example, we have chosen large and small countries, federal and unitary systems, and countries characterized by different levels of party system institutionalization. For each country we provide one chapter on the legislative branch and one on the executive branch, for a total of twelve country-specific chapters. The legislative branch chapters analyze recruitment and selection for national legislative chambers. The executive branch chapters analyze primarily recruitment and selection of presidents; a few also analyze the recruitment and selection of ministers and, where relevant, provincial or state governors. We have also included a cross-national chapter on gender and political recruitment that assesses the effectiveness of attempts to enhance equity in gender representation in the region's legislative and executive branches. These substantive chapters fit between an introduction that lays out the theoretical framework and a comprehensive conclusion that compares and evaluates the arguments presented in the case-study chapters.

Our introductory chapter, "Political Recruitment and Candidate Selection in Latin America: A Framework for Analysis," provides the justification and theoretical framework for analyzing political recruitment and candidate selection for both executives and legislators in Latin America, which forms the basis for the analyses and discussion in the succeeding chapters. The first section of the chapter begins with a brief discussion of why political recruitment and candidate selection matter. We define political recruitment and candidate selection, exploring the intimate connection between the processes. The second part of the chapter provides an explanation and a defense for understanding R&S as overlapping processes along a continuum rather than as two separate processes. The third section explores how institutional and party system variables interact to produce particular types of legislative candidates with different loyalties, from which we generate a comprehensive typology of four types of legislators: *party loyalists, constituent servants, entrepreneurs*, and *group delegates*. The consequence of candidate type as an independent variable is the next issue. We underscore the different kinds of behavior that should result from different types of candidates. The fourth section discusses how political party and institutional variables related to recruitment and selection condition the behavior of executives (both presidents, and where relevant provincial or state governors), arguing that four roughly parallel types of executive candidates are likely to emerge: *party insiders, party adherents, free-wheeling independents*, and *group agents*. These types are hypothesized to also emerge as a function of to whom candidates owe their loyalty, and can be differentiated as well by the different behaviors they exhibit, in part as a function of their pathways to power.

The subsequent country chapters take up these themes of the different types of candidates and the consequences thereof and employ the volume's framework in individual case studies. In Chapter 2, Mark P. Jones characterizes Argentine legislators as *party loyalists* in the terms used in the volume's framework. However, in an interesting theoretical finding, Jones ties legislators in Argentina to the provincial-, not the national-level, party, as a result of the provincial-parties' control over candidate selection, financing, and ultimately the future careers of legislators. He introduces a variation on the Siavelis and Morgenstern typology to characterize Argentine legislators as primarily *provincial-party loyalists*. He then shows, as a consequence, that this candidate type (as an independent variable) directly affects party discipline and governability (for example, the ability of presidents to implement their legislative agendas) and other aspects of Argentine politics.

David Samuels in Chapter 3 explores the relationship between political ambition, candidate recruitment, and legislative party organization in Brazil. He concludes that we should not expect strong legislative parties in Brazil because party leaders control few resources and individual politicians therefore develop into *entrepreneurs* in the terms set forth in the volume. Samuels points out that in most political systems, national or subnational party leaders exert some degree of control over one or more of the following: nomination to legislative office, distribution of campaign finance, pork-barrel patronage, and postlegislative career advancement. Yet Brazilian party leaders do not control any of these levers over deputies' careers. Consequently, legislative party leaders' influence is comparatively low in Brazil, because leaders cannot brandish these "sticks" at recalcitrant deputies. In terms of legislative behavior, Brazil's *entrepreneurs* engage in largely individualistic or state-based pork-barreling efforts; an organized, "partisan" dynamic does not characterize these efforts, and national political parties have never controlled resource distribution as they have in other countries. Thus, the recruitment process for legislators, as in the Argentine case analyzed by Jones, creates problems for presidents seeking legislative majorities and legislative discipline.

In Chapter 4, Patricio Navia argues that most Chilean legislative candidates conform to the *party loyalist* type. Although party elites do not fully control candidate selection, they exercise an effective veto power in the candidate selection process. However, unlike in other countries covered in the volume, Navia analyzes how coalition formation has been central in affecting the candidate selection process in Chile. This is the case both because party and coalition goals must be reconciled and because a person who successfully builds support for his or her candidacy in a district must prevent a veto by the party elite (perhaps owing to the exigencies of coalition politics) to actually become a candidate representing that party. With respect to behavior, Navia finds that the loyalty of coalition legislators to a large extent depends on the intra-coalition party discipline that exists in the president's coalition. Given that in Chile candidate selection procedures lead to a high degree of party discipline in the legislature, Navia codes most Chilean candidates as *party loyalists*.

Turning to Colombia in Chapter 5, Erika Moreno and Maria Escobar-Lemmon argue that Colombian legislators are clearly *entrepreneurs*. Indeed, the authors argue that Colombia is, in many ways, a textbook case for the emergence of this candidate type. A number of variables conspire to create political *entrepreneurs* in Colombia. The authors argue that electoral norms and the dismantling of the National Front agreement along with the concomitant reaction to the emergence of third-party challenges have enhanced self-selection and the emergence of *entrepreneurs*. The result has been an increasing reliance on one's individual traits to further one's career, which tends to reward those who have distinguished themselves as individuals. Colombian legislators pursue a "go-it-alone" logic, which encourages independence during the campaign and beyond, and benefits the party with the most candidates by rewarding it with seats while exacerbating self-selection norms within the party. In terms of legislative discipline, members of the Colombian Congress clearly see themselves as legislative free agents believing their fate is tied to their own actions and campaign strategies rather than the actions of their party.

In Chapter 6, Joy Langston shows that the three most important Mexican parties, despite operating in a singular institutional environment, deal with the challenges of candidate selection in different ways, leading her to the conclusion that constitutional and electoral institutions alone cannot explain candidate selection in Mexico. Focusing primarily on the Senate, Langston argues that the nomination methods used by the three parties can be largely understood by analyzing the parties' organizational backgrounds before the onset of democratization, the dynamics of electoral competition within the context of Mexico's federal system, and whether the selection in question is for a plurality or proportional seat (within Mexico's mixed electoral system). Despite different pathways to power, Langston argues that *party loyalists* have the upper hand in legislative recruitment and are the most common type of candidate. As hypothesized in the framework chapter and confirmed by material from other cases, this loyalty translates into high party discipline, but executive–legislative relations have been challenging given the tripartite split of the legislature.

When it comes to choosing legislative candidates, the unit of analysis for most of the volume's chapters is the party. In Chapter 7, however, Juan Andrés Moraes points to another theoretically and empirically interesting variation of the *party loyalist* type in Uruguay—just as Jones, writing on Argentina in Chapter 2, adjusts the Siavelis and Morgenstern model to account for *provincial-party loyalists* in that country. Moraes shows that in Uruguay the main candidate selection unit is not the party but different factions within the country's notoriously divided parties. The chapter shows how a set of electoral rules and partisan regulations encourages this dynamic. In particular, the chapter shows how the country's electoral system (which is defined by a combination of a double simultaneous vote with proportional representation and closed lists) shifts control over candidate nomination to faction leaders. The chapter's findings are also intriguing with respect to candidate type as an independent variable. Moraes finds that even though there is a strong incentive for constituency service, he concludes that legislators provide this service in the name of factions. He also finds that the factions display highly disciplined voting patterns, which he ties to legislators ultimately owing their nomination and renomination to faction leaders.

The six chapters in Part III put the recruitment and selection of executives under the microscope. Echoing Jones's findings on legislative recruitment in Argentina, in Chapter 8, Miguel De Luca argues that the recruitment process of presidents and governors is concentrated in the political parties and, within these, in their provincial organizations. This centrality of provincial parties in the recruitment and selection of executives is strongly related to Argentina's particular combination of key party and electoral variables, including an institutionalized party system and moderate levels of party identification among voters. As a result, the political leaders that are selected for these executive offices are mostly *party insiders* or *party adherents*. In an intriguing theoretical finding relating to selection as an independent variable, De Luca shows that there is a good deal of difference between *party insiders* and *party adherents*, especially regarding the organization and style of electoral campaigns, the integration of cabinets, relationships with the party to which they belong, and relationships with Congress.

In Chapter 9, Timothy J. Power and Marilia G. Mochel explore the centrality of executive power in Brazil by analyzing executive power at three levels: the presidency, ministers, and governorships. Although they find the Siavelis and Morgenstern framework quite useful—contemporary Brazilian presidents are easily classifiable according to the Siavelis–Morgenstern taxonomy of executive types—they argue that there are deviations for both governors and ministers. Where governors and ministers fit in the typology varies by party, region, and time period to a much greater extent than other cases in the volume. For ministers, political factors and technocratic qualifications are more important, with the actual weighting of these factors depending largely on timing and on the political challenges of constructing a pro-presidential majority in Congress. Power and Mochel then provide evidence that the postelectoral behavior of these leaders also tends to serve the groups which brought them to power, confirming the hypotheses set out by the editors in the introductory chapter.

The point of departure for David Altman in Chapter 10, on Chile, is that recruitment and selection processes have been conditioned deeply by the context of Chilean postauthoritarian politics, and in particular, the exigencies of coalition building within the context of the "reserved domains" of Chile's 1980 Constitution (elements introduced by outgoing dictator Augusto Pinochet that protected the military and political right). Three of Chile's four presidents since the return of democracy are characterized as *party insiders*, while one better fits the *party adherent* type. Altman's analysis shows the effect of candidate type on presidents' cabinet strategies and eventual ability to build the coalitions necessary to govern and to pass legislation.

In Chapter 11, Steven L. Taylor, Felipe Botero, and Brian F. Crisp find that a variety of selection methods were used to choose Colombian presidential candidates between 1974 and 2002, including primaries, conventions, and caucuses. In all cases, however, candidates were either *party insiders* or *party adherents*. This was the case until 2002, when for the first time a process of self-nomination led to the election of Colombia's first *free-wheeling independent*. They argue that for a variety of reasons, these types of independent candidates are the most likely trend for the future. The chapter analyzes how *free-wheeling independent* candidates face different challenges in promoting their legislative agendas than traditional *party-insider* or *party adherent* presidents, because they cannot naturally rely on party majorities in ways that they had been able to in the past.

The central question Roderic Ai Camp poses and answers in Chapter 12 is how Mexico's democratic transformations in the 1990s, and the introduction of electoral democracy, have affected the processes and outcomes of political recruitment and selection among state and national executive leaders. One might expect that the extent to which leadership characteristics and recruitment and selection patterns had become ingrained since the 1920s would make it difficult, in spite of electoral democracy, to overhaul the process in a relatively short period of time. Contrary to this assumption, Camp argues that Mexico's democratic transformation has led to numerous changes in recruitment and selection processes. He argues that it has done so because competitive pluralism emphasizes skills different from those found in a modified one-party system. President Fox, whom he characterizes as a *party adherent* rather than a traditional PRI *party insider*, was a product of those very changes. Fox himself strengthened the alterations wrought by electoral democracy by selecting ministers and other officials with credentials different from those traditionally valued, but often similar to his own background qualities. Camp argues that this reality partially undermined Fox's legislative success and detracted from his popularity, but concludes that recruitment variables are only partly responsible for these failures.

In Chapter 13, Daniel Buquet and Daniel Chasquetti point to the interaction of institutional and electoral variables and the presence of internal party factions as the keys to understanding political recruitment in the executive branch in Uruguay. Like Moraes (Chapter 7), they note that the distinguishing feature of the main Uruguayan parties is the existence of strongly organized factions with great political autonomy. The authors' central contention is that the highly institutionalized party system produces presidential candidates with long political careers within parties. However, they are situated between the *party-insider* and *party adherent* types. The authors argue that their placement depends on the faction each candidate represents and how central that faction is to controlling the top levels of the party. They note that the Siavelis–Morgenstern model predicts that *party insiders* should be better able to rely on consistent legislative contingents. Buquet and Chasquetti find that this is indeed the case for Uruguay, though they are necessarily tentative about the strength of their conclusions given the few cases on which their statistical analysis leading to these findings is based. Nonetheless, even with the sea change in Uruguayan politics wrought by the 2004 election, the authors argue that factionalism and factional loyalties will continue to be central for the building of presidential coalitions in the legislature.

Maria Escobar-Lemmon and Michelle Taylor-Robinson, in Chapter 14, take up the relationship between candidate type and gender for both the executive and legislative branches. They seek to uncover whether a correlation exists between legislator type and the percentage of women elected to the legislature in the countries covered in the volume. They find that *party loyalist* women legislative candidates tend to be more likely to be nominated and elected than *entrepreneurial* candidates, and are necessarily tentative about the electability of women candidates who are *constituent servants* or *group delegates*. The authors then examine whether a relationship exists between executive type and a propensity to nominate women to cabinet posts. They find that *free-wheeling independent* presidents tend to appoint a higher percentage of women as full cabinet ministers than do *party insiders* or *party adherents*, and when they do, they tend to place them in more prestigious posts.

In Chapter 15, we provide a synthetic analysis of the empirical case studies. We reiterate the value of studying candidate recruitment and selection as a dependent and independent variable and find that studying the process in this way yields important insights into understanding the incentives operating on politicians beyond those that rely on institution-based explanations. The chapter summarizes the key findings of each of the case studies and provides some preliminary conclusions about the significance of the various pairings of legislative and executive types. The authors conclude that recruitment and selection variables have a much more important impact on democratic governability in Latin America than is usually supposed and should be taken into account by would-be institutional reformers.

The chapters that follow demonstrate the exceptional depth of knowledge of the contributors. We thank them for their outstanding work. This book grew out of a conference cosponsored by Wake Forest and Duke Universities in April 2004. Among the participants whose intellectual contributions ultimately contributed to the quality of the volume, we would like to thank in particular John Carey and Lisa Baldez for the crucial insights and contributions to debates during the conference. We also acknowledge the hard work of many individuals who assisted in the organization of the meeting, in particular, Kezia McKeague and Neal Richardson. In addition, we thank the many institutions who provided financial support for the conference and production of this volume, including the offices of the Dean of the College and Provost of Wake Forest University, as well as the Department of Political Science and Center for International Studies. At Duke University, we thank the Office of the Vice Provost, the Center for International Studies, the Latin American Working Group, and the Trent Foundation. We also acknowledge Jorge Domínguez for his very careful and thoughtful comments on the manuscript, Jonathan Hartlyn and Lars Schoultz for suggestions on an early iteration of our framework, and our anonymous reviewers for their helpful suggestions. Finally, we would like to acknowledge the colleagues and graduate students at the University of Pittsburgh who read and offered important comments on several aspects of the project.

PETER M. SIAVELIS

SCOTT MORGENSTERN

Party Names and Abbreviations

Acronym	Party Name in Spanish or Portuguese	Party Name in English
ARGENTINA		
ACh	Acción Chaqueña	Chaqueña Action
ADC	Alianza de Centro	Alliance of the Center
ALIANZA	Alianza para el Trabajo, la Justicia y la Educación	Alliance for Work, Justice and Education
AR	Acción por la República	Action for the Republic
ARI	Afirmación para una República Igualitaria	Affirmation for an Egalitarian Republic
CPC	Compromiso para el Cambio	Commitment to Change
CR	Cruzada Renovadora	Renewal Crusade
FG	Frente Grande	Broad Front
FL	Frente por la Lealtad	Front for Loyalty
FR	Fuerza Republicana	Republican Force
FREPASO	Frente por un País Solidario	Solidary Country Front
FV	Frente para la Victoria	Front for Victory
MODIN	Movimiento por la Dignidad y la Independencia	Movement for Dignity and Independence
MP	Frente Movimiento Popular	Popular Movement Front
MPF	Movimiento Popular Fueguino	Fueguinian People's Movement
MPN	Movimiento Popular Neuquino	Neuquinian People's Movement
PA	Partido Autonomista	Autonomist Party
PANU	Partido Nuevo	New Party
PB	Partido Bloquista	Bloquista Party
PD	Partido Demócrata	Democratic Party
PDP	Partido Demócrata Progresista	Democratic Progressive Party
PI	Partido Intransigente	Intransigent Party
PJ	Partido Justicialista (Peronistas)	Justicialist Party (Peronists)
PL	Partido Liberal	Liberal Party

PRO	Propuesta Republicana	Republican Proposal
PRS	Partido Renovador de Salta	Salta Renewal Party
RECREAR	Recrear el Crecimiento	Recreate for Growth
UCEDE	Unión del Centro Democrático	Union of the Democratic Center
UCR	Unión Cívica Radical (Radicales)	Radical Civic Union (Radicals)

BRAZIL

PCB	Partido Comunista Brasileiro	Communist Party of Brazil
PDS	Partido Democrático Social	Democratic Social Party
PDT	Partido Democrático Trabalhista	Democratic Labor Party
PFL	Partido da Frente Liberal	Liberal Front Party
PL	Partido Liberal	Liberal Party
PMDB	Partido do Movimento Democrático Brasileiro	Brazilian Democratic Movement Party
PP	Partido Progressista	Progressive Party
PPS	Partido Popular Socialista	Popular Socialist Party
PRN	Partido da Reconstrução Nacional	National Reconstruction Party
PSB	Partido Socialista Brasileiro	Brazilian Socialist Party
PSD	Partido Social Democrático	Social Democratic Party
PSDB	Partido da Social Democracia Brasileira	Brazilian Social Democracy Party
PT	Partido dos Trabalhadores	Workers' Party
PTB	Partido Trabalhista Brasileiro	Brazilian Labor Party
PV	Partido Verde	Green Party
UDN	União Democrática Nacional	National Democratic Union

CHILE

PDC	Partido Demócrata Cristiano	Christian Democratic Party
PRSD	Partido Radical Social Demócrata	Radical Social Democratic Party
PS	Partido Socialista	Socialist Party
RN	Renovación Nacional	National Renewal
UCC	Unión de Centro Centro	Union of the Center Center

| UDI | Unión Demócrata Independiente | Independent Democratic Union |

COLOMBIA

AD/M-19	Alianza Democrática M-19	M-19 Democratic Alliance
AICO	Autoridades Indígenas de Colombia	Indigenous Authorities of Colombia
ANAPO	Alianza Nacional Popular	National Popular Alliance
PDA	Polo Democrático Alternativo	Alternative Democratic Pole
PL	Partido Liberal Colombiano	Colombian Liberal Party
PC	Partido Conservador	Conservative Party
MRL	Movimiento Revolucionario Liberal	Revolutionary Liberal Movement
NFD	Nueva Fuerza Democrática	New Democratic Force
NL	Nuevo Liberalismo	New Liberalism
PCC	Partido Comunista de Colombia	Communist Party of Colombia
UP	Union Patriótica	Patriotic Union

MEXICO

FDN	Frente Democrático Nacional	The National Democratic Front
PAN	Partido Acción Nacional	National Action Party
PRI	Partido Revolucionario Institucional	Institutional Revolutionary Party
PRD	Partido de la Revolución Democrática	Party of the Democratic Revolution

URUGUAY

AU	Asamblea Uruguay	Uruguay Assembly
AP	Alianza Progresista	Progressive Alliance
DA	Democracia Avanzada	Advanced Democracy
E90	Espacio 90	90 Space
FA	Frente Amplio	Broad Front
FB	Foro Batllista	Batllista Forum
MPP	Movimiento de Participación Popular	Popular Participation Movement
NE	Nuevo Espacio	New Space
PC	Partido Colorado	Red Party

PGP	Partido por el Gobierno	People's Government Party
PN	Partido Nacional	National Party
PNI	Partido Nacional Independiente del Pueblo	People's Independent National Party
PS	Partido Socialista	Socialist Party
UCB	Unión Colorada y Batllista	Red and Batllista Union
UBD	Unión Blanca y Democrática	White and Democratic Union
VA	Vertiente Artiguista	Artiguist Slant

Part I

Theoretical Framework

Chapter One

Political Recruitment and Candidate Selection in Latin America: A Framework for Analysis

PETER M. SIAVELIS AND SCOTT MORGENSTERN

Legislative campaigning in the United States requires that candidates raise many of their own funds, create advertising, appear on television, organize supporters, target legislation, and send mass mailings. Partisanship influences campaigns and policy positions, but legislators also take district demands into account in determining political postures and strategies. In Colombia and Brazil, legislative candidates and legislators do many of the same things, but there is also a clientelistic aspect. Partisanship is an even less important motivator for legislators in these countries than in the United States. Further, many Brazilian legislators are beholden to state-level politicians, and many more than in the United States retire in favor of state-level political or bureaucratic jobs after a stint in the legislature. Argentine legislative candidates are, by contrast, motivated by partisanship to such an extent that they almost never vote against their party in Congress. Further, their campaigns—which are dominated by newcomers, since so few Argentine legislators are reelected—are very different affairs, as the individual candidates have much less responsibility than their Brazilian counterparts in terms of raising funds or organizing supporters, though many are still involved in meeting local leaders and distributing particularistic goods. Uruguayan legislators share some similarities with the Argentinians, but Uruguay's factionalism leads legislators to simultaneously consider district, factional, and partisan issues in defining their campaigns and political strategies. Some Bolivian legislators represent another distinct type, as they are clearly tied to a particular social group. As a result, these politicians' campaigns and legislative careers are built around meeting the needs of that group, be it rural farmers, members of indigenous organizations, or regional separatists.

Similarly, despite a commonality of basic institutional framework, presidential behavior also varies substantially across contexts. In Chile, longtime party insiders have tended to garner the presidency by campaigning along party ideological lines, and presidents have built cabinets and governed by paying careful attention to partisan and coalition dynamics. Colombia,

Venezuela, and Bolivia stand in direct contrast, presenting striking cases where politicians have created their own partisan vehicles to capture the presidency. Their behavior in office, in turn, has been unrestrained by partisan considerations. Other cases lie between these extremes. In Mexico, Vicente Fox's ambivalent yet important connections to his own party led him to emphasize business ties over partisanship in developing his cabinet and political programs. Once in office, Argentine President Raúl Alfonsín, the undisputed leader of his party, distributed cabinet posts to his copartisans and obtained the support of potential internal rivals through his distribution of party and government posts. By contrast, Alfonsín's successor, Carlos Menem, had more limited partisan ties and, depending on one's viewpoint, worked either against the party or in an effort to remake it. Finally, Brazil's Luiz Inácio "Lula" da Silva provides another model; perhaps because of his defined ideological position, solid position within his party, and minority status, Lula made alliances outside the left, pragmatically cultivating the support of other parties. Colombia's Álvaro Uribe pursued a strategy like Lula's, despite running as an independent and clearly attempting to distance himself from the Liberal Party, where he had built his career.

What explains these different types of legislative and executive candidates and their resultant political behavior? An important determinant is the institutional framework in which the candidates and future officials operate. Institutional theories, however, are incomplete and perhaps flawed, when they expect uniform responses or ignore contextual variables. For example, since the time of Duverger (1951, 1954), analysts have often expected a singular response to incentives stemming from the electoral system. But such a framework, like the framing of a house, can influence without determining the inside layout and architecture. In turn, parties operating under identical institutional frameworks may take many different forms. Tastes and costs determine a house's inside configuration; similarly, goals and opportunities lead parties to react to institutional stimuli in distinct ways. Analyses of presidents, legislatures, parties, or executive-legislative relations, therefore, must consider the factors that combine or interact with the institutional environment to explain political behavior.

Some recent scholarship has moved well beyond Duverger to note that although electoral systems (or other aspects of the institutional framework) operate on all parties in a country, not all parties take the same form. Rather than discarding the value of institutional variables, this recognition has led researchers to begin considering the factors that add to or interact with institutions in their search for understanding. Here we push this type of analysis one step further, discussing how party and legal variables create a framework that produces distinct types of candidates and thereby influences political behavior. By focusing on political recruitment and candidate selection—politicians' pathways to power—this book identifies and describes the framework that bounds political behavior. We explore these pathways and their impacts with a focus on candidates for both executive and legislative positions in Latin America.

The legal framework and formal institutions relating to recruitment and selection clearly create pressures that push political parties in particular ways, but not all parties or their members react similarly. This differentiated response results from the variance in parties' goals, norms, and strategies and those factors' interactions with the institutional environment. For example, one party in a given country could use its closed list electoral rules to assure centralized control of legislative candidate nominations, whereas another could decentralize that power to provincial leaders. Here the electoral system would interact with party organizational variables—which may be dependent on the size, age, and initial development of the party—to determine the process of candidate nominations. Likewise, competitive pressures, a party's regional strength, ideological coherence, and many other factors will influence whether national party leaders, provincial-party leaders, or voters will have the greatest say in naming legislative candidates. Similarly, though party norms may dictate formalized and centralized selection procedures for presidential candidates, and the selection of candidates and presidents with a strong basis in their political parties, second-round elections may provide party dissidents with an incentive to throw their hats into the ring, obviating the importance and necessity of running with a party label. In sum, formal institutional rules (such as electoral systems and federalism) combine and interact with contextual situations (such as structures of party competition) and party-level variables (such as ideological coherence and fractionalization of the leadership) to determine particular selection processes.

Along these lines, this introductory chapter develops two key themes. First we develop an argument about the interaction of specific aspects of the electoral system with party and contextual variables in determining the recruitment and selection process and candidate type. Here we develop the idea of candidates' loyalty to a particular "selectorate," be it constituents or some higher party official. The direction of loyalty determines several candidate types, which in the latter part of the chapter we correlate with campaign and postelectoral behavior to show how candidate type works as an independent variable. We provide a parallel analysis for recruitment and selection in the legislative and executive branches, though we do not expect that the recruitment and selection procedures in the latter will be as significant in shaping subsequent behavior. This leads to our final conclusion about the significant, but often overlooked, impact of recruitment and selection (hereafter R&S) variables on democratic processes and governability.

Why Pathways to Power Matter: The Study of Political Recruitment and Candidate Selection

A key goal of institutionalists has been to establish the relationship between electoral systems and party outcomes, with a particular focus on party discipline in the legislature, executive–legislative relations, and the nature of the party system

(Ames 2001; Carey and Shugart 1995; Morgenstern 2004; Samuels 1999; Shugart 1995; Siavelis 2002). However, because they fail to consider the interaction of the electoral system with recruitment and selection variables, these studies cannot explain the types of candidates, parties, and interbranch relations that emerge within different countries. For example, Brazil's open-list system, where voters choose among multiple intraparty legislative candidates, is said to work against party discipline. However, one party, the *Partido dos Trabalhadores* (PT), has traditionally maintained much more control over nominations than others and consequently has sustained much higher levels of party loyalty. Similarly, analyses of countries employing electoral rules that provide incentives toward party discipline, such as Argentina, fail to explain intrapartisan conflict that can arise from legislators beholden to the regional power brokers that nominated them as candidates. Systemic institutional rules also fail to explain how such disparate presidential candidates can emerge in the same country. The differences (even beyond those related to personality) among recent presidents in Argentina (for example, Raúl Alfonsín, Carlos Menem, Fernando de la Rúa, and Néstor Kirchner), or between highly competitive candidates in Mexico (Felipe Calderón and Andrés Manuel López Obrador) underscore this point. In short, electoral laws do not alone determine the degree to which R&S procedures are centralized; thus electoral laws fail to completely explain candidate types and the resulting behavior of politicians. That explanation, in sum, requires analysis of the R&S processes.

Scholars have generally shied from studying R&S, however, because the associated variables, only some of which are defined in written documents, are overall, notoriously difficult to compare and measure (see Helmke and Levitsky 2004). However, if we are interested in analyzing the effect of political institutions, we must understand the totality of incentives operating on politicians, many of which are rooted in the R&S procedures.

The importance of R&S has not escaped scholars focusing on European parliamentary governments or the United States. Gallaghar and Marsh (1988) build on the early "classic" literature (Black 1972; Czudnowski 1975; Eulau and Czudnowski 1976; Marvick 1968; Prewitt 1970; Seligman 1971) and provide a comprehensive treatment of R&S issues, to which Norris (1997a) and Davis (1988) have made important additional contributions. However, this literature generally ignores Latin America's predominantly multiparty presidential systems. Literature focusing on Latin America has begun to appear, but primarily in the form of individual case studies rather than theoretically oriented comparative studies.[1] A second limitation of the extant literature is that irrespective of the

---

1. For a sampling of this literature see, on the executive branch, Friedenberg and Sánchez López (2001). For particular country studies see Buquet (2001), Camp (1995), Langston (1994), and Siavelis (2002). For an outstanding treatment of the democratization of candidate selection procedures, see a special issue of *Party Politics* edited by Pennings and Hazan (2001).

regional focus, most scholars interested in theory building tend to treat the R&S process primarily as either a dependent variable (analyzing how politicians are recruited and selected) or an independent variable (analyzing the effect of the recruitment processes on subsequent political behavior).[2] We are aware of no study that does both simultaneously, despite the significant insights that can be gleaned by doing so. As such, we lack an overarching framework for understanding political recruitment, candidate selection, and their consequences.

Another shortcoming in the literature is the failure to adequately consider how formal institutions combine with informal institutions and processes to produce outcomes that belie predictions of much of the institutionally based literature. Following Helmke and Levitsky (2004), we distinguish between formal party (and faction and coalition) rules and informal norms or procedures that guide the implementation of the "parchment" rules or laws.[3] Parties develop rules—whether formally inscribed or not—with respect to seniority, incumbency, and the rights to candidacies for militants or outsiders. In some cases, party rules and processes yield centralized control over nomination decisions and tightly guarded campaign finance, whereas others allow primaries and encourage candidates to raise and spend their own funds. Most of these rules and processes are compatible with different types of electoral systems, and all can tighten or loosen the relation of candidates to party leadership. Argentina provides a good example of how the interaction of R&S processes with electoral rules affects behavior. Argentine parties fill closed lists of candidates, giving party leaders (in this case the provincial-party leaders) significant power to name and rank candidates on their lists (see chapter 2, this volume, by Jones). Thus, in line with predictions made by the institutional literature dealing with list type, we would expect legislators who are loyal to be regularly renominated and reelected. However, the *Partido Justicialista* (PJ) has maintained a rule discriminating against incumbents, with the result that only about one-fifth of the legislature is populated by incumbents. In addition, the party's organization reflects the country's federal structure, in that the national hierarchy must contend with significant influence of provincial leaders, who wield tremendous power in the candidate selection process. Thus, Argentine deputies look to and serve the provinces and provincial-party elites, a behavior that in large part is determined by recruitment variables.

2. Some work has been done on the connection between selection procedures and the character of legislators and the composition of legislatures, but less on how the processes affect behavior. See, for example, Loewenberg and Patterson (1979) and Keynes, Tobin, and Danziger (1979).

3. For some cases the level of analysis moves from parties to factions or coalitions. Here we generally refer to parties, but we recognize that at times our analysis also applies to factions or coalitions.

Definitions and Range of Analysis: Recruitment Versus Selection

Political recruitment can be defined as how potential candidates are attracted to compete for political office, whereas candidate selection concerns the processes by which candidates are chosen from among the pool of potential candidates. Although Norris (1996), Hazan (2002), Camp (1995), and others have tried to work within these analytical distinctions, the processes involved are so entangled that it is seldom possible to determine where recruitment ends and selection begins. Norris (1996), for example, usefully divides the legal and party variables that affect how candidates become legislators into three levels: system variables (legal, electoral, and party variables), recruitment structures (party organization, rules, ideology, and nonparty gatekeepers), and recruitment processes (how eligibles become elected, including candidate motivations, party gatekeepers, and electoral choice). These divisions, however, are blurry, as several items could fit into different categories. Furthermore, an explanation of the behavior of politicians before and after elections would be incomplete and perhaps misleading if the processes were separated. Finally, different aspects of the R&S processes take prominence in different countries or even within different parties in a single country.

In addition, because we are interested in where the loyalties of candidates lie, we must consider the long-term process of R&S. It is often the same elites that cultivate, identify, and name candidates, beginning a process that ends with selection and the potential cementing of loyalties. Thus, the process of building loyalty is a long-term one, not located solely at the point of actual selection. It is possible, of course, for candidates to self-recruit and self-nominate, which pushes the recruitment and selection process into the hands of candidates themselves, with important consequences for legislator discipline, executive behavior, and democratic governability.

In sum, recruitment and selection overlap to such an extent that, for our purposes, they are useful to analyze as a single process; the variables that define these processes may be more pertinent to one or the other concept, but the variables are closely tied and do not clearly fit under one rubric or the other. We depict this relation in Figure 1.1, which shows three baskets of variables. On the far left are those that are most closely identified with political recruitment, such as education, political contacts, and career trajectories. On the right are those variables most associated with candidate selection, such as the rules that govern access to the ballot by setting up primaries, endowing governors with powers to choose candidates (in the case of legislative candidates), or allowing candidates to self-nominate. In the middle, finally, are those variables that are pertinent to both processes, such as the party system and the parties' organizational structure. Here we are thinking of parties' decisionmaking structure (hierarchical

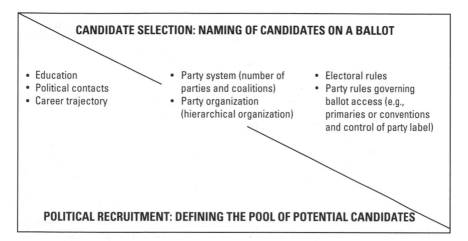

FIGURE 1.1   Overlapping Relation of Political Recruitment and Candidate Selection.

or decentralized), their coalitional calculations, and their ideological bent. The vertical lines in the figure divide these three groups of variables, and the diagonal line differentiates recruitment from selection processes. Overall the figure is meant to show that the variables cannot be bifurcated; some variables are more central to recruitment and others to selection, but even those that are most closely associated with one process also have relevance for the other. As our interest is in political institutions, in this framing chapter we focus primarily on the middle and right boxes, though we also recognize the importance of variables fitting into the left box.

Recruiting and Choosing Legislative Candidates: A Narrow Typology with Wider Implications

We begin with a discussion of legislative candidates. Our goal is to develop a typology based on loyalty as an organizing concept, and then to use that typology to discuss legislator behavior. We will thus focus on how different sets of variables interact to affect the loyalties of candidates, some of whom then become legislators. Because loyalty is a central determinant of behavior, we organize our typology around how R&S processes cement loyalties to party elites, to constituents, to the selfish interests of the candidates themselves, or to particular groups in society. Identifying where loyalties lie is central to differentiation among candidate types and leads to predictions about behavior. Behavior, however, is also predicated on the shape of majorities in congress and executive-legislative relations, which in part result from the existing party

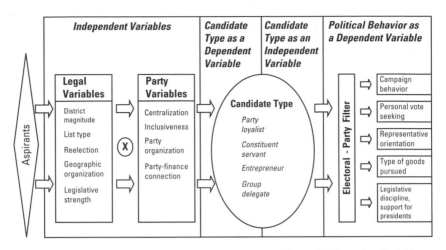

FIGURE 1.2   Legislative Recruitment and Selection as a Dependent and Independent Variable.

system and electoral outcomes. Our model, then, considers the interactive effect of party and legal variables to determine candidate types, but uses an electoral-party filter to predict behavioral outcomes related to campaign styles, candidates' policy promises, party discipline, politicians' use of their time and resources in fulfilling campaign promises, and the ability of parties and presidents to build both governing and opposition coalitions.

Figure 1.2 provides a schematic of our approach to understanding the outcome of legislative R&S. We first treat the emergent candidate's type as a dependent variable, asking about the legal and party variables that determine candidate loyalties and, in turn, candidate type. In the figure we treat legal variables as the basic framework that can predispose a candidate to develop loyalties in certain directions. Party variables then act as an accelerant or a brake—indicated by the multiplicative function between the two boxes—to further shape the evolution and nature of these loyalties, leading in turn to the emergence of four ideal types of candidates (whose genesis we analyze in depth in the following pages): *party loyalists, constituent servants, entrepreneurs*, and *group delegates*.

On the right half of Figure 1.2 we treat the R&S outcome as an independent variable, asking how the types of candidates selected affects political behavior. These behavioral issues include campaign behavior, personal vote seeking, representative orientation, the propensity to engage in patronage politics and logrolling, and legislative discipline and support for the president. Candidate behavior will also depend on the relative party majorities of presidents and legislators that constrain or facilitate resource extraction ("pork," particularistic resources, budgetary influence). For example, the power of legislators to extract resources should be significantly enhanced when they are members of the majority and share the same party as the president. Also, once candidates are victorious, rules regarding reelection and whether candidates have static or progressive ambition continue to affect the extent to which they have to think about reelection and reentering the recruitment arena, which in turn will affect their decisions about policy and behavior and about supporting a president or not. We call this effect the electoral-party filter in Figure 1.2, as it sorts out where candidates find themselves with respect to power relations during campaigns and after elections.

Figure 1.2 schmematizes the generation of candidate types and their impact, but it is deficient in detailing the nuts and bolts of R&S. It is unable to do this because the complexity of variable interactions yields a very large number of potential paths to power. It would therefore be unrealistic (and not very interesting) to generate and test an endless series of hypotheses related to the effect of each variable on candidate loyalties. To solve this problem, in moving forward we rely on a rough form of path analysis to sort out variables and generate our typology of candidates. We consider each significant variable we identify in turn, with each representing a new node on a type of decision tree that charts the pathway to power of different types of candidates. Unlike a game-theoretic choice model, this path analysis does not assume candidates are choosing at each node; rules may be predetermined and inflexible, or parties—or other leaders—may have previously chosen a particular path that legislators must follow. The image that we are trying to evoke is one where these previous turns at each node both affect candidate behavior and restrict options later down the path.

We begin with legal variables because we posit that they predispose parties toward the selection of particular types of candidates, and party variables can then either reinforce or undermine these predispositions. For example, district magnitude (the number of legislative seats per district), makes the emergence of some types of candidates more likely and other types less likely. Small-magnitude systems are more likely to produce candidates with loyalty to constituents than are large-magnitude systems because they facilitate name recognition and identifiably. However, once the list-type variable is introduced, if a closed-list system with moderate magnitude exists, the candidate will have slightly more of an incentive to be loyal to the party to ensure a beneficial list position. With an open-list system this is less likely to be the case because voter recognition rather than list position will be more important to electoral success. This reality pushes candidate loyalty more toward constituents than toward the party because of the parties' increased influence over the electability of the candidate. Subsequently, if parties have very elite-centered and centralized forms of organization and candidate designation, candidate loyalty might be pulled back toward the party.

There is still a problem with this approach. Many variables influence the process, and these variables all interact, so there are an even greater number of potential paths to explore. Even just our five legal and four party-level variables produce forty ($5 \times 4 \times 2$) potential paths, (assuming that each decision node yields binary options, which is clearly an oversimplification). Such a model is scarcely a parsimonious contribution to our ability to understand the origins of different types of candidates.

However, we argue that each of these paths, though distinct, tends to arrive at one of four destinations, which constitute our four ideal types of candidates. This is the case because distinct combinations of variables can interact to push and pull in different directions, but they tend to push and pull candidate loyalty toward or away from four key actors in the R&S process: party elites, constituents, the candidates themselves, or particular corporate or functional groups. From these variations we chart four distinct paths to power, one for each of the four ideal types of candidates we have identified: *party loyalists, constituent servants, entrepreneurs*, and *group delegates*.

More important, we argue that from our multiple paths we can divine four paths where at each decision node all variables align to push candidates toward one of our ideal types. We are not suggesting that all of the variables along each separate path *must* be present to produce each type. Rather, we argue that if all of the variables along each path are present, the types we hypothesize will emerge. However, different combinations of variables can push and pull from the ideal typical path. This is a heuristic exercise that sheds light on the formation of candidate loyalties while at the same time allowing us to explore how departures from the ideal typical path play out empirically so that a candidate still arrives at one of our destinations, albeit via a different route, depending on the strength of the particular combination of variables in each case.

In the following section we explore how each of our major variables affects candidate loyalties. In the section after, we apply this discussion using the type of path analysis we describe to chart the four pathways to power where all of the variables push toward each of our four ideal types.

Building the Legislator-Candidate Typology: Major Variables

To build the legislator-candidate typology, we break independent variables down into legal and party variables. Though not an exhaustive list of all variables (legal or party) affecting R&S, they are the ones most often identified as significant in the candidate selection literature.

Legal Variables

District magnitude and list type. As Carey and Shugart (1995) explain, district magnitude (M) and list type are intimately connected with respect to the incentive structure they produce. Therefore, even though they are separate variables, we discuss them together here for analytical purposes. Carey and Shugart argue that in closed-list systems, candidate qualities lose importance as district magnitude increases and as the party becomes more central to nomination and candidate list placement. In essence, they contend that in closed-list systems, the incentive to cultivate a personal reputation decreases as magnitude increases, whereas in open-list systems the value of personal reputation increases as magnitude increases. In the smallest-magnitude closed-list system—a single-member district would serve as an example—voters can still identify candidates representing the different parties and so the candidates' personal reputations and campaign skills influence the vote. But those same candidates might be anonymous when district magnitude grows, and voters must choose a large team rather than the single players. By contrast, under open-list systems, Carey and Shugart argue, the value of a candidate's personal reputation actually increases as district magnitude increases because voters always have to choose among more individuals, and differentiating oneself by cultivating a personal reputation becomes more important so as to not get lost among a crowded field of candidates. We concur with their findings with respect to the incentives of various systems to cultivate a personal vote in an election at the time of voting.

There is a difference, however, between the value of personal reputation in a single-snapshot election (a personal vote) and the value of cultivating longer-term patterns of loyalty, which is our interest here. This difference in incentives is crucial to understanding the types of candidates that emerge, and prompts us to introduce a variation on the Carey and Shugart argument. Their assertions regarding closed lists apply almost directly to our argument concerning loyalty. In small-magnitude closed-list systems, in spite of the power of the party, there is still an incentive to cultivate the loyalty of constituents, given the identifiably of candidates and the increased influence of voters (as opposed to party elites) in determining electoral outcomes. In closed-list systems, therefore, the value of personal reputation decreases as district magnitude increases, and candidate loyalty should gradually shift from constituents to the party, because as magnitude increases parties increasingly hold the key to election.

With open-list systems, however, we diverge from Carey and Shugart's logic and argue that as magnitude increases, the value of personal reputation in the election may increase as they contend, but the incentive to cultivate the loyalty of constituents for the long term actually decreases. Parties become almost irrelevant in large magnitude open-list systems, because of low thresholds to victory and the decreased importance of a party label. With respect to cultivating constituent loyalty, although the incentives to cultivate a personal reputation are considerable at the time of election, the incentives and the ability to cultivate constituent loyalty over the longer term while serving as a legislator are lower, simply because among a district's many legislators, it is difficult to place credit

or blame on individuals and to hold individual legislators accountable. Therefore, we argue, over time that large- or moderate-magnitude closed-list systems
will provide an incentive to cultivate loyalty to parties, low-magnitude open-
and closed-list systems will provide an incentive to cultivate balanced loyalty to
the party and constituents, and large-magnitude open-list systems generate
little long-term loyalty to constituents or parties.

Reelection. Whether reelection is permitted is central to determining the
loyalty of candidates. If reelection is barred, candidates are likely to cultivate
prospective loyalty toward those who influence their future career destination
rather than retrospective loyalty to those who brought them to power.

Geographic organization. Federalism makes the emergence of decentralized
parties more likely, decreasing the power and influence of national party elites.
Federalism should heighten the influence of governors and perhaps drive competing intra-party loyalties. In addition, localized politics is likely to make the
cultivation of loyalty among local political actors (be they party elites, militants,
or constituents) more central to being designated a candidate.

Legislative strength. We follow Polsby (1968) and argue that the strength of the legislature is crucial in determining the incentives for inducing legislators to channel their
ambition in progressive or static directions. Strong legislatures provide members power
and prestige, and where legislators wield real control over resources, they also provide
individual legislators the power to extract these resources. Though we have placed legislative strength and the resulting desirability of a career in the legislature in the category of legal variables based on the idea that constitutions can create stronger or
weaker legislatures, other factors are also determinative. Also important, for example,
is the number of parties and the legislator's position relative to the legislative majority,
court decisions that can enhance or diminish legislative powers, and the bureaucratization of the legislature, which enhances its policy role. If being a legislator has prestige and the institution has real power over resources, legislators have an incentive to
stay and cultivate the loyalty to whomever brought them to power. Where legislatures
lack power and prestige, on the other hand, legislators with progressive ambitions may
forgo the cultivation of such loyalty because it is not central to their future prospects,
as they look ahead to a more desireable position outside the legislature.

Party Variables

Centralization. Where are candidates chosen? Many writers have stressed the
importance of the degree of centralization in candidate selection processes (see
Gallagher's introduction to Gallagher and Marsh 1988; Norris 1996; Hazan
2002). Where the main actors are national or regional party executives, candidate
loyalty to these party actors will be cemented. In contrast, when the key players
are located in the constituencies and include members, voters, and local party
officers, legislator loyalty will have a local base. Norris (1996) provides a cogent

discussion of the importance of the degree of centralization in candidate designation. However, because she focuses on the institutionalized parties that exist in
most of the countries she analyzes, she does not allow for potentially inchoate or
informal decisionmaking structures. Moreover, in such systems voters may lack
strong partisan identification, thus sharply diminishing the importance of a crucial party prerogative: control over the party label. In other words, when partisan identification is low, party leaders cannot seriously threaten potential
candidates by withholding nominations because recalcitrants can switch parties
without significant costs. As a result, such systems may produce legislators with
local bases of support in spite of centralized nomination rules. It is also possible,
however, that these systems will produce populist presidents whose long coattails
smother locally oriented candidates' independence.

Following Hazan, another alternative is corporate decisionmaking, where the
process is organized along functional rather than geographic lines. He notes that
this may involve a central role for groups such as "trade unions, women,
minorities, etc. . . ." in the designation process (2002, 114).

Consequently, where candidates are chosen can push candidates to curry favor
toward national actors, regional actors, or corporate actors or, indeed, make the
cultivation of regional or national loyalties less relevant once initial selection or
self-selection has taken place. The "where question," however, clearly interacts
with legal and other party variables. For example, decentralized selection is more
likely in federal systems, suggesting yet again the importance of considering the
full model rather than single variables in isolation.

Inclusiveness. Who chooses candidates? Essentially, inclusiveness involves the
number of people involved in candidate choice, which has important implications
for candidate loyalty. Although it may seem redundant to separate inclusiveness
from centralization, candidate choice can be decentralized yet exclusive, with local
notables choosing candidates, or it can be decentralized and inclusive if a local open
primary is employed to choose candidates.[4] Indeed, ultimate control of selection
can even be centralized, yet inclusive. For example, Navia (chapter 4, this volume)
notes that the highly centralized Chilean Christian Democratic Party mandated a
decentralized candidate selection process from the center in an effort to "democratize" the party. Furthermore, there are different forms of exclusivity. A candidate
chosen by a few party elites and one who self-selects both represent exclusive selection procedures, but their incentives for loyalty will be quite different.

Where party elites choose candidates, loyalty to the party will reign supreme,
whereas open primaries will increase the value of cultivating constituent
loyalties. Where self-selection or informality is the norm (for any number of
reasons), self-serving behavior will be the norm especially where reelection is

---

4. Hazan and Voerman (2006) also provide a convincing rationale for analyzing inclusiveness and
centralization separately.

not allowed. Finally, where a corporate or functional group is key to selection, loyalty to that group will follow.

Party organization. How are candidates chosen? Norris (1996) notes the importance of the extent of bureaucratization in the candidate selection process, differentiating between those that rely on highly institutionalized and rule-based patterns of recruitment and those that rely on a patronage formula, based on the activities of power brokers and key gatekeepers that may or may not represent particular factions within political parties. The degree to which key individuals are constrained by organizational rules ultimately determines the leaders' power to demand personal loyalty from prospective candidates. In bureaucratized systems the party follows elaborate rules for candidate designation and can dictate the terms of ballot access and prevent those deemed undesirable from running under a party label. In patronage systems, on the other hand, ultimately the candidate choice emerges from conflicts and compromise between leaders. If other deals become complicated, one possible means of resolution is a primary.

In this sense, it is important to note that bureaucratization is not synonymous with formality; party decisionmaking patterns may be bureaucratized and formal or bureaucratized and informal. In patronage systems, patrons (informal power brokers) may use formal structures to block or promote candidacies. For example, Norris (1996, 205) argues that U.S. parties use patronage-based selection. Therefore, however tempting it is to argue that informal self-selection is the norm (suggesting lack of bureaucratization), U.S. parties use bureaucratized methods (primaries) to resolve conflicts among informal patronage groups such as campaign contributors, campaign volunteers, and PACs (political action committees). Therefore, U.S. parties are patronage-based yet bureaucratized parties.

Some recruitment systems are indeed simply patronage based and are characterized by nonbureaucratized nomination norms, primarily self-nomination. The crucial difference between bureaucratized and nonbureaucratized systems is the extent to which party organizations still matter in resolving conflicts between patronage groups. Where parties and related organizations matter less and nonbureaucratized self-nomination is the norm, we label party organization *inchoate*.

Finally, in some systems functional groups have nomination or veto power over candidacies. These groups can wield power and use methods of selection with varying degrees of bureaucratization and formality, but the significant point is that the corporate or functional group has the last word on nominations.

Highly bureaucratized systems promote candidate loyalty toward the party and its rule enforcers, whereas patronage-based systems push loyalties toward particular party patrons, or toward primary voters who hold the key to resolving conflicts between them. The cultivation of loyalty is a less visible and important force where inchoate selection is the norm, whereas designation by a functional group will create candidate loyalty to that group.

Party finance connection. Who pays the bill for campaigns? Control over financial resources is a central determinant of candidate loyalty. The path of money and the path of loyalty usually run parallel. Where parties control the purse strings (either through private financing or the distribution of state money), loyalty to the party is enhanced. Where party or state money is disbursed and spent at the discretion of individual candidates, or where candidates raise their own money from constituents, loyalty to the party will be relatively less important to the candidates. This should result in more attention to district interests on the part of winning candidates. Similarly, where functional groups or businesses foot the bill for campaigns, candidates will owe relatively less loyalty to parties and more to these patrons. If the candidates themselves are the source of funding, they are likely to act in the name of self-promotion.

The Legislator-Candidate Typology

In Table 1.1 we characterize the ideal typical paths to power taken by each of our four types of candidates, focusing on the five legal variables (district magnitude, list type, possibility of reelection, geographical organization, and legislative strength) and four party variables (centralization, inclusiveness, party organization, and campaign finance) discussed in the previous section. Though there are many potential paths that determine where a candidate's loyalty will lie, we reiterate that the paths charted here are those where the outcomes at each decision node all align to push toward one of the ideal types. There are empirical examples of candidates following slightly different paths, but these usually can be considered subtypes of one of our four major types.

Table 1.1 summarizes the argument set out here with regard to the paths that will produce one of our four ideal typical candidates (indicated at the bottom of each column). Essentially, the table takes the two boxes in the "Independent Variables" section of Figure 1.2 and charts the ideal typical path for candidates that leads to the four ideal types in the center oval of that figure. As these are framework variables through which the candidate must work rather than decision nodes that allow candidate choice, the table does not imply a temporal evolution; still, evoking the vision of a decision tree is meant to suggest that there are multiple possible combinations of the variables, with each direction implying a potentially different outcome. In addition, although we highlight the importance of legal variables for three of our ideal types, the table is supposed to indicate only a minor importance of certain legal variables for the *group delegates* in order to suggest that this candidate type can emerge in a more varied institutional or legal environment. The impact of these legal variables, therefore, are indeterminate. This position does not undermine the importance of institutional variables in the R&S process generally. Instead, the *group delegate's* path provides an example

TABLE 1.1 Ideal Types of Legislative Candidates and Their Ideal Typical Pathways to Power

Legal Variables

District magnitude	Moderate (4–6) or high (7 or over)	Low (1–3)	High (7 or over)	Indeterminate
List type	Closed	Open or closed	Open	Indeterminate
Reelection	Yes	Yes	No	Yes
Geographic organization	Unitary	Federal	Federal	Indeterminate
Legislative strength	Strong	Strong	Weak	Indeterminate

Party Variables

Centralization	Centralized	Localized	Localized	Corporate
Inclusiveness	Elite selection	Primary	Self-selection	Role for functional group in selection
Party organization	Bureaucratized	Patronage based	Inchoate or party identification irrelevant	Group-based
Party-finance connection	Party control or state financing through party	State financing to individuals and independents	Private business or self-financing	Financing by or through functional groups
Candidate Type	*Party Loyalist*	*Constituent Servant*	*Entrepreneur*	*Group Delegate*

that underscores a central thrust of our framework: in certain cases party variables may trump legal/institutional ones, confounding institutionalists and their theoretical propositions regarding the relationship between legal variables and political outcomes. In essence, sometimes institutions matter a lot, and sometimes they matter much less.

Before charting the path of each type of candidate, we offer some additional notes of caution. First, within one country we are likely to find several types of candidates. As noted, this should be expected because even where formal institutions provide the incentive structures within which all parties operate, the parties may vary significantly in their internal characteristics. Second, some but not all nodes represent binary possibilities. Third, for the few categories that are indeterminate, candidates may follow any of the paths on that node, as they have little effect on the type of candidate that ultimately emerges. Fourth, it follows that certain paths are more likely and common than others, as certain combinations of the variables fit together more naturally than others. For example, we are more likely to see decentralized candidate selection in federal systems than in unitary systems and we are more likely to see primaries in decentralized parties. Finally, we reiterate that not every independent variable must be present to produce each type of candidate. Rather, it depends on the relative strength of each of the independent variables that will tend to push toward or away from the type of candidate we expect.

In our analysis of the path of each of the four types of candidates we conclude with a brief summary of the expectations with respect to candidate type as an independent variable (that is to say the behavior we expect from each type as candidates and legislators). These are presented in Table 1.2. We provide the table as a guide to the central thrust of our argument, but it by no means represents a comprehensive summary of the totality of legislative behavior.

Party loyalists. *Party loyalist* candidates demonstrate and maintain loyalty toward party leaders and organizations that hold the key to their political futures. Table 1.1 shows that a fertile institutional environment for the development of a *party loyalist* is a proportional-representation system with moderate or high magnitudes and closed lists. Each of these factors reinforces the power of the party and, thus, the incentives of candidates to toe the party line. Closed lists make party identification important for winning and make optimal party placement on the ballot crucial to victory, prompting loyalty to the party. In Table 1.1 we somewhat arbitrarily define moderate district magnitude as between 4 and 6 and high magnitude as 7 or over. These numbers can vary slightly, but empirically what is important is whether the system produces the incentives related to loyalty described here with relation to list type and magnitude. *Party loyalists* are more likely to emerge where reelection is allowed, in unitary political systems, where centralized parties exist, and where a strong legislature makes a legislative career desirable for reasons of status and control over resources.

TABLE 1.2   Legislative Candidate Type as an Independent Variable and Hypothesized Behavior

Candidate Type	Party Loyalist	Constituent Servant	Entrepreneur	Group Delegate
Campaign Style	Extolling party platform	Appealing to constituents	Personalistic	Extolling group demands
Personal Vote Seeking	Infrequent	Often	Often	Variable, depending on individual's importance to the group
Representative Orientation	Party before constituents	Constituents before party	Individualistic, rewarding supportive groups or individuals	Functional, group before party
Type of Goods Pursued	Collective, programmatic, ideological	Pork and public goods for district	Particularistic pork to reward supporters	Benefits for group
Legislative Discipline, Support for President	High	Moderate, can be bought with targeted pork	Low, self-interested voting	Moderate, can be bought with group rewards

With respect to party variables, *party loyalists* tend to emerge where candidate selection is centralized, is dominated by elites, and is bureaucratized. Where central elites wield control over candidate selection, potential candidates will do everything in their power to cultivate relationships with these elites, and these potential nominees know that party rules will be followed. Thus, this combination of legal and party variables combines to make partisan identification more important to voters than individual candidate qualities, making *loyalists* beholden to the party to achieve their goals.

Turning to behavioral expectations, Table 1.2 shows that, the *party loyalist* will campaign with a concern for presenting the major ideas, ideologies, and programs of the party. One important caveat is, of course, that in a federal system the *party loyalist* may also campaign on issues that are of more concern to the state or provincial-party than to the national-level party (though of course the interests of the state-level and national-level parties are not necessarily mutually exclusive). Personal vote seeking is less important to *loyalists,* and they are likely to demonstrate a preference for the goals of the party over constituents in their representative orientations. In turn, they are likely to seek collective party programmatic goals over individual ones. The implications of *loyalist* behavior for party discipline and governability are clear. *Loyalists* will pursue collective goals related to the ideology and program of the party.

Legislative parties full of *loyalists* are likely to be more disciplined, and presidents from the same party are more likely to be able to rely on reliable majorities of their own party where *loyalists* prevail. Another issue is whether parties of *loyalists* will be more likely to form coalitions with other parties or whether it is easier to buy support from more loosely organized parties when *loyalists* are from a different party than the president. For particular issues it may be easier for a president to seek the support of *entrepreneurial* or *constituent-servant* legislators, but these deals will not bring wide or deep support. Thus, although negotiations with *loyalists* of other parties will require important concessions, such negotiations can yield longer-lasting coalitions that can facilitate governance on a wide range of issues.

Constituent servants. Constituent servants can better achieve their goals through cultivating constituent support rather than through party loyalty. Returning to Table 1.1, the legal variables that contribute to R&S procedures that produce *constituent servants* include majoritarian or low-magnitude PR systems (again, somewhat arbitrarily set at between 1 and 3, bearing in mind the caveats we made regarding district magnitude in our discussion of *party loyalist* legislators) with either closed or open lists. Small-magnitude open-list systems balance the incentives to cultivate party loyalty with additional strong incentives still to cultivate loyalty among constituents. Parties may rank candidates, but voters still retain a good deal of influence in determining electoral outcomes. Small-magnitude open-list systems also enhance the incentives for cultivating constituent loyalty because voters have a good deal of say in determining outcomes. Small-magnitude systems therefore magnify the importance of individual candidacies and personalities irrespective of whether lists are open or closed, and lead potential candidates to cultivate support among constituents. Permissive rules allowing reelection reinforce this tendency. *Constituent servants* should be more common in federal systems, where local decentralized ties are key to election and reelection. Further, a strong, well-institutionalized legislature with established mechanisms for the acquisition and distribution of pork helps legislators develop constituent loyalty.

Thus, *constituent servants* are more likely to emerge where the importance of a party label to election is diluted by legal variables. Party variables may also dilute the value of the party label. Decentralized selection should, for example, reinforce the tendency toward the development of constituent loyalty. The bureaucratized forms of selection in the upper levels of a centralized party that characterized the development of *loyalists* are here displaced by local selection. The likely selectorate is a primary or some sort of decentralized party contest where party elites do not exercise control and parties are patronage based. Sources of independent or state financing dilute the ability of parties to use pecuniary means to induce loyalty.

In campaigns, *constituent-servant* legislators are much more concerned with promoting policies and agendas with more particular significance for their district. Similarly, the primary interest of *constituent servants* when legislating is pleasing the very people who have chosen them; thus they are more likely to attempt to cultivate a personal vote. *Constituent servants* are likely to employ a strategy of patronage aimed at the cultivation of support among local influential groups and political actors as well as constituents. This leads *constituent servants* to pursue pork once in office, but unlike *entrepreneurs*, who may seek pork to benefit friends and those who can advance a later political career beyond congress, *constituent servants* seek benefits for the constituents of their districts in order to curry longer-term constituent favor and gain reelection. With respect to party discipline, we expect relatively less discipline from *constituent servants* than from *loyalists* but more than from either *entrepreneurs* or *group delegates*, because party organization still matters to both legislators and constituents. However, support for the president will ultimately be determined by how particular votes will play in the home district. *Constituent servants* are defined by their weaker ties to parties, but in order to serve constituents they may find that parties afford them the clout to extract the desired resources and gain influence (Cox and McCubbins 1993; Aldrich 1995). The U.S. case suggests that these motivations support some degree of party discipline, and studies of divided government suggest that U.S. presidents often have been able to find the support they need for important legislation (Mayhew 2002; Jones 1994). Again, the number of parties is key, as the lack of a majority or near-majority party would severely hamper the president's ability to find consistent support.

Entrepreneurs. Entrepreneurs have little loyalty to parties or constituents or have at best fleeting and instrumental loyalty to one or the other. These actors are more than simple "independent" candidacies in the traditional sense of the term. *Entrepreneurs* may or may not be elected with a formal party label. In essence, *entrepreneurs* emerge where legal and institutional variables combine to make the selectorate the candidates themselves. However, once they have been chosen as candidates, these politicians' ambition tends to trump other policy or legislative goals.

The legal variables that tend toward recruitment patterns that produce *entrepreneurs* include high-magnitude electoral systems, which we set at 7 or over—with open lists (noting again, our caveats). This combination minimizes the influence of parties and complicates the ability of constituents to place credit or blame, also reducing the importance of the cultivation of long-term constituent loyalty. The nature of ambition is key to defining an *entrepreneur* as well. The ideal-typical *entrepreneur* is little interested in building a long-term career in congress either because reelection is barred or because the legislature is so weak (or lacks routinized methods for resource extraction) that spending a stint as a legislator has little value beyond opening pathways to future positions. *Entrepreneurs* tend to emerge more easily in federal than in unitary systems because local reputation rather than a party label is more likely to be a key to success.

Where parties matter, *entrepreneurs* are more likely to emerge in systems with decentralized party organization, given the lack of central-party enforcement mechanisms. With respect to the decisionmaking structure for selection, informality, and often self-selection, will be the norm rather than a formalized bureaucratized structure or the conflict or negotiation among patronage groups. Financing is undertaken by candidates themselves or is underwritten by individuals or less formal special interests not tied to political parties, such as businesses or other interest groups. All of these variables diminish the influence of parties or, indeed, make them unnecessary for *entrepreneurs* to succeed in getting on the ballot and being elected.

Finally, in terms of behavior the *entrepreneur* is likely to seek any way to cultivate the instrumental and episodic support of voters at election time, rather than to cultivate the deeper loyalty of voters. This type of candidate is more likely to engage in populist rhetoric and discuss few particulars of ideology or policy. Since *entrepreneurs* are extreme independents, presidents will have trouble herding them even if they are of the same party. The presence of too many *entrepreneurs,* thus, harms short-term efficiency, and lacking long-term legislative goals, *entrepreneurs* are unlikely to build the infrastructure that facilitates oversight capabilities and general legislative capacity.

Group delegates. Group delegates owe their primary loyalty to a particular nonparty functional or social group, which may be a trade union, a business association, or a peasant, religious, separatist, or ethnic group. *Group delegates* are the only category in our typology (see Table 1.1) for which four out of our five legal variables are simply "indeterminate." This indeterminacy is a central aspect of our framework and highlights the importance of noninstitutional factors for the emergence of particular kinds of candidates. *Group delegates* may emerge in all sorts of institutional contexts, but the crucial variable is the strength of the functional or corporate group they represent. For example, *group delegates* may perform quite well in large-magnitude systems with closed lists if their party recommends the election of a complete party slate, and there is little to distinguish individual candidates. Alternatively, if party and functional group practice is to build personal followings, we may find that small-magnitude open-list systems are equally likely to encourage *group delegate* candidacies. Similarly, *group delegates* can emerge in unitary, or federal, systems, depending mostly on the geographical organization of the group they represent. Again, sometimes institutions matter a lot, and sometimes they matter much less.

In terms of party variables, it might seem that group interests trump those of the party, making the latter less significant. Nonetheless, parties and party organizations may still be important, where functional groups within the party exert some control over candidate selection either in the place of or in addition to the party (elite, base, or otherwise). Therefore, with respect to centralization, *group delegates* emerge where parties give functional groups rather than geographically oriented elites responsibility for naming and financing candidates.

The *group delegate* will stress the interests of the functional group in campaigns and propose policies that serve that group's interest nationally. Similarly, a *group delegate* more jealously guards the preferences and interests of the associated functional group. The *group delegate* may seek personal votes, but this depends on how central such votes are to the importance of the advancement of the group's agenda. *Group delegates* should be disciplined within their parties, but they may be particularly recalcitrant participants in coalitional bargaining. The consequences for policymaking of the election of *group delegates* are likely to be distinct and depend on whether they represent a governing party or are in the opposition, and whether the president is a member of their group. This is because their membership homogeneity or ideological purity will decrease their propensity to compromise ideals in favor of short term goals.

Recruiting and Choosing Executive Candidates: A Narrow Typology with Narrower Implications

In our consideration of R&S for the executive branch, we are interested in many of the same party and legal variables that we used to study legislative candidates, such as campaign finance, reelection, and primaries. This part of the model has narrower implications, however, because the effects of R&S processes are less constraining for executives than for legislators because presidential races are eminently more personal affairs, which heightens the importance of individual personalities and the candidates' position within discrete historical and political contexts, thus diminishing the role of the R&S process and candidate loyalties to particular persons or groups in explaining behavior. The constraints of loyalty that operate on legislative candidates are also distinct in the case of presidents. Though presidents may be less concerned than legislators about their future careers and thus free of the bonds of cultivated loyalties, they do often think about reelection (where permitted) or their legacies. Finally, in addition to the inherently less constraining impact of laws and rules on presidential candidates, modeling executive behavior has the added complication of the small sample size. The small number of candidates in a given race tends to highlight the importance of personality differences among candidates and limits attempts at generalizations. These modeling hazards are evident from a review of the studies of the U.S. presidency that identify different types of presidential personalities in spite of a (largely) unchanged political system (Barber 1972;

Gergen 2000; Greenstein 2000). Still, our model makes some clear predictions, and the authors of our executive-focused chapters are able to outline clear links between candidate type and executive decisions regarding campaign behavior, cabinet composition, mandate reversals, relations with their own and other parties, and executive–legislative relations generally.

As in the discussion of our legislator model, our executive model assumes that the R&S process produces different types of candidates, who run different types of campaigns, with the eventual winner morphing into a particular type of politician (only in this case, president). Following the organization of the first part of this chapter, we build a typology of executive candidates based on loyalty first, and then later consider the consequences of the types of candidates that emerge for their eventual behavior as presidents.

For analyzing executives we use a group of variables analogous to those we described to explain R&S patterns of legislators (see Figure 1.3). As with the legislators, to explain candidate type we focus on the interaction of party and legal variables, which helps to encompass both informal and formal practices. These yield four stylized ideal typical executives: *party insiders, party adherents, free-wheeling independents*, and *group agents*. The figure also includes a "party/election filter," because the capacity and incentives for presidents to cooperate depends on the outcome of elections—whether or not presidents have workable legislative majorities on which they can rely. As depicted in the figure, we then link the candidate types to behavior (making candidate type an independent variable), asking how the executives' loyalty affects their behavior regarding campaigns, cabinet composition, the tendency for mandate reversals, and relations with their own and other parties in the legislature.

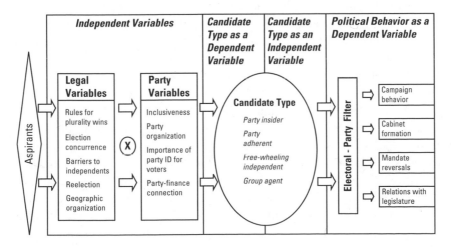

FIGURE 1.3 Executive Recruitment and Selection as a Dependent and Independent Variable.

Building the Executive Candidate Typology: Major Variables

In building our typology of executive types, we begin with legal variables that set the context and then consider how parties adjust their rules to accommodate the context and particular candidates. We continue with the rough style of path analysis we employed for legislative R&S, considering each of these variables as representing a key node with various options that push and pull in certain directions toward one of four types. As for the legislator candidate typology, there are four ideal typical paths where all nodes align to push toward a particular type, and the caveats we mention with respect to building the legislative typology also apply to the executive one.

Legal Variables

Plurality elections. The rules for determining the presidential winner affect the incentives for new candidates to enter as well as the competitive dynamic of elections.[5] Although in several countries legislatures historically decided presidential elections when no candidate garnered a majority, currently all Latin American countries either allow for plurality first-past-the-post presidential elections (Honduras, Mexico, Panama, Paraguay, Venezuela) or have some form of second-round election (every other Latin American presidential system). The latter involves either a simple second round between the first two finishers or some sort of minimum threshold or margin of victory in the first round that obviates the need for a second round (employed in Argentina, Costa Rica, Ecuador, and Nicaragua). The Argentine rule, according to which the leading candidate must win either 45 percent of the vote or 40 percent and at least a 10 percent margin over the nearest competitor, is a useful example. At this node, the rule used can enhance or reduce the power of parties (and thus candidate loyalty to parties) in designating candidates. Where the simple plurality rule is used, Duverger (1954) and later Jones (1995a) show that there are likely to be fewer candidates, so parties' influence in the election may be greater. Where a simple runoff is used, there are likely to be more candidates and less party influence. Systems with a minimum threshold or margin of victory are intermediate in this regard, with still important, but diminished, disincentives for new candidates to enter the race and a corresponding level of party influence in candidate selection.

Election concurrence. Shugart (1995) and Jones (1995a) have shown that when legislative and executive elections are concurrent, the president has a better chance of winning strong legislative support. If concurrent elections tie the fates of executive and legislative candidates, we should expect more party voting and

---

5. We base many of the arguments advanced here on Jones (1995a).

enhanced electability of candidates tied to traditional and institutionalized parties. Nonconcurrent elections break this connection, raising the electoral fortunes of independents and party dissidents, thus increasing the incentives for them to enter the race.

Barriers to independents. Legal or practical impediments to independents or party dissidents logically affect their potential electability. These barriers may be in the form of legal restrictions for independent candidacies or provisions requiring a minimum number of signatures or formal association with a party that has in past elections garnered a significant portion of the vote. Admittedly, there are additional barriers rooted at the party level. The United States is the best example of how the entrenched two-party system deeply affects the electoral prospects of third-party presidential candidates. However, the two-party system is itself rooted in the country's majoritarian institutions, so that ultimately we categorize this variable as a legal rather than party one. Where formal or practical impediments to independent candidates are high, parties will prevail because independent and breakaway candidacies will be difficult. Where barriers are moderate, it is easier for independents or party renegades to enter races and win. Finally, where few practical restrictions to independent candidacies exist, the importance of party endorsements to win may prove minimal.

Reelection. Several countries—including Argentina, Brazil, Colombia, Peru, and Venezuela—have relatively new provisions that allow presidents to serve more than one consecutive term, and all the incumbents that have run for a second term have won (at time of press). Thus, the possibility of reelection plays a clear role in explaining candidate choice and eventual winners, and the behavior of presidents. Seven countries allow reelection after one interim term, one allows reelection after two interim terms, and six ban reelection altogether.[6] The debate on reelection is between those who argue for a ban to prevent *continuismo* (presidents spending too long in office—often through questionably legal measures) and those that hold that the prospect of a second term allows voters to hold presidents accountable—at least once. Recent research by Stokes (2001)—with her counterintuitive findings that it was precisely the presidents who violated mandates that sought and often obtained reelection—sheds new light on this debate. Nonetheless, where the prospect of reelection exists, candidates are more likely to continue to serve the constituencies that brought them to power, and reelection will likely foster the further cultivation of party or group loyalty (depending on the constituency that brought the candidate to power), whereas bans on reelection foster relatively lower levels of loyalty.

Geographic organization. Federal systems not only make the emergence of decentralized parties more likely but also provide an additional subnational level of power to build careers and launch independent or party renegade candidacies.

6. For a breakdown of these countries and an analysis of the reelection debate, see Carey (2003).

Although some unitary systems have produced these types of candidates (most are candidates who have served in municipal offices in capital cities: Tabaré Vázquez, in Uruguay, or Joaquín Lavín, in Chile), federal systems provide more platforms for political outsiders, principally state governors, to launch, cultivate, and build careers. Consequently, in federal systems a role for national political party and centralized party elites as gatekeepers is on the whole less likely than in unitary systems, and candidates are more likely to seek and cultivate the support and loyalty of bases other than the elites of centralized political parties.

Party Variables

Inclusiveness. Who chooses candidates is just as significant for the types of presidential candidates that ultimately emerge as it is for legislative candidates. Experience in Latin America ranges from the Mexican president's now defunct *dedazo* (right to designate his party's next candidate) to open national primaries to candidate self-designation. In recent years at least some parties in many Latin American countries—including Brazil, Mexico, Chile, and Uruguay—have adopted primaries, which are legally mandated in some places but run and organized by parties in others. The effects of primaries have varied.[7] However, in building their careers presidents do cultivate support among their would-be selectors, who may be the party elite, participants in an open primary, or members of a functional group. Where independent candidacies are easy to launch, inclusiveness will be low, and self-selection may be the norm.

Party organization. As is the case for the selection of legislative candidates, the party's basic organizational structure for decisionmaking affects the types of executive candidacies that emerge. We again differentiate parties' decisionmaking and organizational structures on the dimensions discussed in the legislative section: bureaucratized, patronage based, group based, or inchoate.

Importance of party identification. In the literature on U.S. elections, a long-standing debate has raged regarding the importance of party identification for presidential elections. Some argue for the radical decline of the party-motivated vote and the consequential rise of candidate-centered presidential elections (see, for example, Burnham 1970). Others disagree, arguing that partisanship still explains a good measure of voter motivation (Miller and Shanks 1996). For our comparative perspective, variations in the importance to voters of party identification help explain candidate type by affecting the relative importance of a party label to the candidate.

---

7. Freidenberg and Sanchez Lopez (2001) provide tables showing where primaries are used and the rules governing them. Polsby (1983) argues that primaries produce poor candidates in the United States, but Carey and Polga-Hecimovich (2006) report that primaries do not lead to a similar result in Latin America.

Party-finance connection. Though regulated by legislation, campaign finance also fits as a party variable, since parties have varying responsibilities for raising and distributing funds. How this is handled certainly affects the types of candidates able to mount serious campaigns and the influence of party leaders with these candidates. Payne et al. (2002) analyze campaign financing rules for Latin America. They note that systems form a continuum, from Venezuela and Chile, where there is little or no public financing for presidential campaigns, to Mexico, where public funding has predominated since 1996. The actual distribution of the funding is important: where parties control financing (either their own, or that granted by the state) the influence of party elites will be greater (as is the case for legislative candidates). Where public funds are transferred directly to candidates, party endorsements become less important. Where public finance is limited, candidates must be successful fundraisers and may end up with strong ties to moneyed interests. If the candidates are independently wealthy, they may self-finance, cutting loyalty ties completely. Finally, loyalty to a functional or corporate group will be cemented when that group controls financing.

The Executive Candidate Typology

Table 1.3 summarizes the options at each of our nodes that push toward the development of particular types of executive candidates. As in Table 1.1 the goal is to suggest the particular conjunction of variables most likely to produce the ideal typical candidates (listed in the last row of the table).

Table 1.4 summarizes our expectations with respect to candidate type as an independent variable. Once again, this table does not present a comprehensive view of the totality of executive behavior, but should be viewed as shorthand to understand the thrust of our argument. Much more detail about the variables and analysis of these behaviors is provided in the case chapters and the volume's conclusion.

Party insiders. *Party insiders* emerge from long-standing, institutionalized parties. Those parties will have clearly defined ideological bases. Candidates will have been party activists for a considerable period of time, and have held important leadership posts. Many of the legal variables that affect who among the candidates emerges as the eventual winner should, by backward induction, affect the types of candidates that participate in an electoral contest. In legal terms we expect *party insiders* to be more likely to emerge where plurality rules are the norm, rather than runoff elections, because plurality rules discourage independent and dissident candidates from throwing their hats into the ring and thus reinforce the importance and influence of a party label. We do not suggest that runoff systems cannot produce *party insiders*. Rather, a *party insider* will be more likely where the costs are higher for independent and

TABLE 1.3 Ideal Types of Executive Candidates and Their Ideal Typical Pathways to Power

Legal Variables

Rules for plurality wins	Simple plurality victory	Plurality with threshold	Runoff	Runoff
Election concurrence	Concurrent	Concurrent	Nonconcurrent	Nonconcurrent
Barriers to independents	High	Moderate	Low	Low
Reelection	Yes	Yes	No	Yes
Geographic organization	Unitary	Federal	Federal	Indedeterminate

Party Variables

Inclusiveness	Elite-centered or militant primary	Open primary	Self-nomination	Group-based selectorate
Party organization	Bureacratized	Patronage based	Inchoate or no party	Group-based organization
Importance of party ID for voters	High	Moderate	Low, retrospection key to election	Dependent on perceived loyalty to functional group
Party-finance connection	Party-centered	Decentralized or state-financed	Self-financing or particularistic sponsors	Group financing for campaigns
Candidate Type	*Party Insider*	*Party Adherent*	*Free-Wheeling Independent*	*Group Agent*

TABLE 1.4 Executive Candidate Type as an Independent Variable and Hypothesized Behavior

Candidate Type	Party Insider	Party Adherent	Free-Wheeling Independent	Group Agent
Campaign Behavior	Ideological and tied to clearly elaborated party platform	Party-tied, but reform-oriented	Retrospective and prospective orientation with populist appeals	Tailored toward group
Cabinet Composition	Longtime *party-insider* ministers	Party dissidents, personal party confidants, reformers	Based on personal loyalties	Members of functional group
Mandate Reversals	Unlikely, tied to party promises	Likely	Very likely	Unlikely, tied to group promises
Relations with Legislature	Smooth with majority of their own party; minority presidents, contingent on building alliances with other parties	Contingent on reining in their own parties, building coalitions with others	Difficult, especially with *loyalist* legislators of opposition parties	Contingent on skillful ad-hoc coalition building

dissident candidates. Similarly, concurrent elections are likely to help *party insiders* as a result of the more centralized and institutionalized nature of party competition and the effect of reverse coattails. It follows that *party insiders* are more likely to emerge where barriers to independents are high. Finally, *party insiders* are more common where reelection is permitted—because *party insiders* remain *insiders* to attempt to secure renomination—and in unitary systems, where centralized polities tend toward centralized parties and centralized decisionmaking.

With respect to party variables, de facto elite selection (through direct designation, limited-participation conventions, or party central committees) is likely to be the norm. It is possible that these leaders will be chosen in primaries. However, because *party insiders* emerge from long-standing parties, participation in these primaries is more likely to be limited to militants and activists rather than being open to all. Primaries also potentially could be just window dressing to confirm the preferences of party elites. In all of theses cases, party elites likely play a greater de facto role in the designation or nomination of candidates. Highly bureaucratized decisionmaking structures lead to *party insider* candidates, as career paths are more predictable and rules regarding seniority, more respected. These candidates emerge where party identification is important to voters and parties are more likely to control public or private campaign funds.

As Table 1.4 suggests, we expect *party insiders* to wage campaigns on bigger issues related to ideology and the party's record. On the campaign trail the *party insider* will proudly wear the party label. The *insider* will have strong and intimate ties with formal party organizations and will likely appoint ministers with strong party credentials to their cabinets. If other parties are needed for a coalition, *party insider* presidents may be secure enough in their partisan position to facilitate interpartisan negotiations. We expect *insiders*, once they becoming executives, to be more constrained by the party in engineering dramatic policy switches than *party adherents* (or *free-wheeling independents*). *Party insider* presidents should be more likely to have support of legislators from their own parties, particularly when those legislators are of the *party loyalist* type. For minority presidents, *party insider* success in legislating will be contingent on using party leverage to build governing alliances with other parties in the legislature.

Party adherents. These candidates are strong partisans, but differ from *party insiders* in that they are not their parties' undisputed leaders, having perhaps jumped to the national campaign from a provincial or municipal position. We expect *party adherents* to be more likely to emerge where party identification is important but where relatively lower thresholds provide incentives for dissident party members or outsiders to attempt to capture the presidency. We resist electoral system determinism and have repeatedly noted that there is more than one path to each candidate type. Therefore, any system for dealing with plurality winners could yield a *party adherent*, depending on other, principally party, variables. However, we contend that plurality rules with a threshold—where either a particular percentage or a particular margin over the second-place finisher is necessary to win in the first round—provide a fertile institutional environment for a *party adherent*, because of the continued, albeit slightly reduced, importance of a party label and a lower threshold for initial victory. The primary system in the United States, where different states hold primaries on different dates, provides a variant of the threshold arrangement, allowing *adherents* to show support in different electoral markets. Concurrent elections allow *party adherent* candidates to take advantage of their party connections to ride to party victories, although this is a potentially weaker influence than for *party insiders*. *Party adherents* are more likely to emerge where there are moderate barriers to independent candidacies. The possibility of reelection helps prevent *party adherents* from deviating too much from the interests of those who brought them to power, though this variable is certainly less influential than in the case of *party insiders*. The potential to launch an independent candidacy if things go wrong will tempt *party adherents* to defy party elites and facilitate the emergence of challenging *party adherents*, but the continued importance of party identification should prevent the unbridled declaration of independent candidacies of the *free-wheeling independent* type. Finally, the potential for building careers at the subnational level makes federalism a more fertile environment for the development of *party adherent* candidacies.

As suggested in Table 1.3, with respect to party variables, these candidates are more likely than *party insiders* to have to earn their candidacy by competing in an open primary. More decentralized or fractionalized parties with patronage-based forms of decisionmaking are more likely to produce this type of candidate. *Party adherents* are more likely where the importance of party identification is moderate (parties still matter, but party line voting cannot be completely enforced) or loyalties to particular factions (regionally based or otherwise) of parties is the norm. Similarly, financing is less centralized.

For *party adherents*, loyalty to the party is important but in a certain sense instrumental, and this is evident in campaigns (see Table 1.4). *Party adherents* accept the basic tenets of the party but often play down its central ideas and ideology, and advocate the need for reform (both in general and within their parties). Something of an outsider, the *party adherent* is likely to have looser ties with the party organization or to be the leader of a dissident faction within the party. Cabinets reflect this status, with *party adherents* likely to appoint party dissidents, personal confidants, supporters from a particular wing of their party (either from their party faction or region), or reformers. Once in office, the likelihood that these presidents will fail to stick to the party's campaign platform should be relatively high, and they could be expected to try to move their parties in new directions. *Party adherents* are less likely to control majorities in the congress because the likelihood of intraparty factional conflict is higher. Nevertheless, since *party insiders* and *adherents* must by definition come to power as part of a significant party, they will both enjoy significant, though not necessarily majority, support in the legislature. Therefore, key to their relations with the legislature is their ability to form party-level coalitions to generate supportive majorities. Another key issue, though, is whether *party adherents* can be as successful as *party insiders* in forging these coalitions, given that they are less secure in their position as party leaders.

Free-wheeling independents (FWIs). FWIs have no long-term identification with a party—they may be dissidents or they may use a small or new party as an official vehicle for their election. There will not be primaries in this party, since the independent candidate essentially creates a personal vehicle for the contests. FWIs are likely where runoff systems provide ample opportunity for candidates to throw their hats into the ring and see what happens (see Table 1.3). Nonconcurrent elections may help FWIs because they will not require the presidential candidate to build a machine with a full slate of legislative candidates. Low barriers to independent candidacies will facilitate the emergence of FWIs. Reelection bans will likely reinforce independence from the parties or groups that brought the FWIs to power, given the resultant reduced incentive to maintain loyalty. Finally, federalism will provide FWIs with multiple potential career launching pads.

Because FWIs eschew parties, party variables are less significant to how they operate. With respect to inclusiveness, self-nomination is likely to be the norm. An FWI could emerge from an existing party, but only if the party is loosely enough organized for a dissident to be able to gain the nomination. FWIs will generally be more successful in systems where the importance of party identification is low, and retrospective (and prospective) voting is more important to victory than party identification. FWIs rely on the financing of particularistic, non-party-related supporters, and have few ties to the type of functional group that underwrites support for *group agents*.

Campaigns for FWI candidates generally focus more on retrospective evaluations and vague promises for the future (see Table 1.4). For example, constitutional revisions may be a theme, whereas tax or industrial policy will likely be left to the *party adherents* or perhaps the *party insiders*. As candidates with populist tendencies, FWIs should attempt to build multisector coalitions for their campaigns, and perhaps in their cabinets. Cabinets are likely to be ad hoc, made up of outsiders, and based primarily on the president's personal networks of support. This may lead to cabinets full of cronies rather than leaders from different parties. FWIs, possessing loose or nonexistent connections with traditional parties, are likely to lack the luxury of a large disciplined contingent of their own party members in the legislature that they can rely on. Further, these outsiders are likely to have trouble building multiparty coalitions, so their control over patronage resources and their success in building a new legislative party are key to achieving their political and legislative agendas.

Group agents. These candidates are recognized leaders of defined societal groups, such as business organizations, labor unions, indigenous groups, or religious organizations. They may belong to an existing party, but these parties are more homogeneous than those of *party insiders.* They also differ from the *party insiders* in that their supporters come from well-defined, relatively homogeneous social groups (such as labor or peasant organizations).

Legal systems can aid the production of *group agents* by encouraging more candidacies and allowing candidates with regional strength to emerge as viable (see Table 1.3). Consequently, runoff systems are more likely to produce *group agents* than are pure plurality rules or systems with minimum thresholds or margins of victory. *Group agents* will not benefit from concurrent elections, at least initially, unless an institutionalized and regular relationship develops between their functional group and a party. If they have a party, they are more likely to benefit from low barriers to independents, at least in their party's pre-institutionalization stage. Our expectations regarding the effect of reelection are similar to those for *party adherents.* It will be significant only to the extent that candidates feel a need to retain loyalty to the functional group that brought them to power. The territorial organization of the country can matter, but its impact is dependent on the type of group involved. Federalism could be important if the group is regionally concentrated and can elect its leaders to regional posts that can then become springboards to national office. On the other hand, unitary systems may provide *group agents* with a nationally organized functional or corporate group in which they can build a nationally visible career.

Although the inchoate nature of *group agent* parties generally leads them to choose candidates through informal practices, these candidates are much more dependent on an organizational structure of their corporate group than *FWIs* or, at least sometimes, *party adherents.* But if the party becomes a vehicle to promote presidential candidates, the party's institutionalization could possibly include a public and competitive mechanism for choosing among potential leaders. In terms of the party organization, therefore, we are likely to find influential functional groups within parties, and they will determine candidacies either through bureaucratized procedures or through conflict between patronage leaders, depending on the interface between the group and the party. But a *group agent* often is the natural and undisputed leader of a particular functional or corporate group who later casts his or her power and influence into the electoral arena. Therefore, at least in the early stages of development of a *group agent's* party, natural and relatively undisputed candidates may simply emerge. Voters may use party identification to make voting decisions, but at least part of that decision will be based on the candidate's perceived loyalty to the functional group. The functional group is likely to finance and support campaigns, anchoring candidate loyalty to that group.

The ideal typical *group agent's* campaign platform is more explicitly tailored toward a particular group than a *party insider's* and is less inclined toward a pragmatic bending of ideology in order to win an election (see Table 1.4). The cabinet will be made up largely of representatives of the functional group or of those perceived to have strong loyalties to it. This implies that such a candidate will be more trustworthy in office and more likely to implement the policies elaborated in campaign promises than to switch. Like *party insiders, group agents* may be secure enough in their positions to forge interparty alliances in the legislature, but the purity of their platforms and perhaps their status as political outsiders may work against the negotiation process.

Conclusions: Pathways to Power and Democracy in Latin America

Our goal in this introductory chapter has been to provide two schematic models and stylized typologies that together yield theoretical frameworks for understanding and comparatively analyzing both the processes that bring politicians to power and the impact of those processes on the political behavior of the powerful. The emphasis in our model is on the idea that R&S processes are not just a simple response to the institutional framework of the country but, rather, emerge out of the complex interaction of institutional and party variables. What is more, we argue that the behavior of candidates and for the legislature and presidency is shaped by the processes that bring them to power. Here we have not attempted to test the model we develop, but the chapters that follow provide ample application of the model and many examples that demonstrate its utility.

Our findings are theoretically important in at least two ways. First, understanding the real incentives for political behavior in Latin America has crucial implications for institutional analysts and reformers who are concerned with democratic governability. We argue, first, that reformers should consider the effect of R&S procedures when contemplating reforms, as these party-level rules and norms interact with the electoral system and other institutions to determine the behavior of candidates and elected officials. For example, mandating primaries *may*—but will not necessarily—generate more internal party democracy, as some parties could contravene the law's decentralizing intention by crafting creative rules that centralize control of campaign funds or ballot-access rules that are biased in favor of one or another candidate.

Second, Latin America's presidential systems have been criticized as unstable, uninstitutionalized, or possessing tendencies toward "delegative democracy" (O'Donnell 1994) as a result of their structural problems (including the difficulties associated with minority-supported presidents), the type and quality of the leadership the systems have produced, and other factors (Linz and Valenzuela 1994; Mainwaring and Shugart 1997; Mainwaring 1993). Scholars have recognized that presidentialism is much more sustainable where presidents can rely on majorities or near majorities of their own parties. We have argued that legislative behavior and the likelihood that a legislator will support a president is more than just a function of a country's institutional structure or the nature of that legislator's party. Rather, R&S can shape the likelihood that a legislator will support or oppose a president of the same party or, if a member of an opposition party, vote in concert with co-partisans and others in the opposition. The likelihood of interbranch cooperation is enhanced when a president can rely on *party loyalists* of the same party. We must also consider, of course, the possibility that *party loyalists* in the opposition can act as an impediment to the building of such majorities. Whatever the answers to these questions, we have shown that R&S—politicians' pathways to power—have crucial impacts on legislative behavior and the governability of presidential systems. The chapters that follow provide substantial empirical confirmation of this proposition.

Part II

**Political Recruitment and Candidate
Selection for the Legislative Branch**

Chapter Two

The Recruitment and Selection of Legislative Candidates in Argentina

MARK P. JONES

Scholarly understanding of how electoral laws influence elite and mass political behavior has improved dramatically over the past decade. The advances in this area, particularly in Latin America, have magnified, however, the discipline's comparatively weak grasp on the internal functioning of political parties. The lack of information on political career pathways and the candidate recruitment and selection process is especially glaring, and of profound import, since the rules and processes governing candidate recruitment and selection process often are more relevant than the actual electoral laws governing the general elections for understanding legislator behavior.

One of the principal reasons for the lack of scholarly understanding of the vital topic of candidate selection, and especially for the lack of cross-national work, is that the topic is inherently difficult to study. A credible study of candidate recruitment and selection requires both a high level of knowledge of the country and party system under study as well a considerable amount of data and information that are often difficult to obtain. Given the above requisites, the ideal vehicle by which to conduct a comparative study of candidate selection in Latin America is an edited volume, such as this one, where distinct individuals describe and analyze the candidate recruitment and selection process for different countries and political offices. In this chapter I contribute to this overall endeavor by describing and analyzing the key issues surrounding the political career paths as well as the recruitment and selection of candidates for national legislative office in Argentina.

I thank Pablo Ava, Rubén Bambaci, Silvina Danesi, Miguel De Luca, Marcela Durrieu, Alberto Föhrig, Sebastián Galmarini, Ariel Godoy, Ricardo Jaén, Sergio Massa, Scott Morgenstern, Baldomero Rodríguez, Sebastián Saiegh, Peter Siavelis, Ana Suppa, and Rossana Surballe for answering questions and providing helpful assistance, suggestions, and comments.

The chapter begins with a brief overview of Argentine political institutions and the relevant political parties. I then discuss the basic functioning of intra-party politics, highlighting the important role of financial and material resources in enabling a political leader (or leaders) to maintain control over, and influence in, a political party. I continue with an analysis of the candidate selection process, followed by an examination of the political career pathways of national legislators, both prior to and following their term(s) in the national legislature. I then examine the consequences of the nature of candidate recruitment and selection in Argentina for the functioning of the legislative process. I conclude with a discussion of where Argentina is located in terms of the four ideal types of legislators identified by Siavelis and Morgenstern in Chapter 1.

Argentine legislators are closest to the *party loyalist* type. This loyalty however is to the provincial-level party, not to the national party (in contrast to their is Chilean counterparts; see Chapter 4). This chapter provides the most comprehensive evidence to date of the province-based nature of Argentine political career paths. An overwhelming majority of national legislators begin their careers at the provincial level and return to careers in the province following their brief tenure in the national congress. The chapter also refines and extends analysis of the candidate selection process in Argentina, highlighting that different methods of candidate selection employed in the country as well as the ways the decision regarding which selection method is used depends heavily on province-level factors.

Political Institutions and the Party System: 1983–2005

Argentina has a bicameral national legislature (Senate and Chamber of Deputies) as well as a federal system of government in which the twenty-four provincial governors (from twenty-three provinces and one from an autonomous federal capital, Capital Federal) exercise substantial autonomy (Eaton 2002; Sawers 1996; Tommasi 2002). The Argentine Congress, although certainly more of a reactive blunt veto player than a proactive agenda setter, is nevertheless an important actor in the policy process (Corrales 2002; Jones, Saiegh, Spiller, and Tommasi 2002; Llanos 2002).

Argentine deputies are elected to the Chamber of Deputies from closed party lists using proportional representation in multimember districts with a median district magnitude (the number of seats per district) of 3 and a mean of 5. Deputies are allocated to the provinces based on their population, according to the 1980 census; every province receives a minimum of five deputies, and no province receives fewer deputies than it held during the 1973–76 democratic period.

One-half (127 and 130) of the membership of the Chamber of Deputies is renewed every two years, with each of the twenty-four electoral districts (provinces) renewing one-half of its delegation, or the closest approximation.

Prior to 2001 Argentine senators were elected by the provincial legislatures. Between 1983 and 1995 two senators per province were elected for nine-year staggered terms—one-third of the Senate renewed every three years—by plurality rule. In 1995 the number of senators per province increased to three. Between 1995 and 2001 senators were elected by plurality rule as before, with the proviso that one party could not occupy all of the province's senate seats and that the "third" seat be allocated to whichever party had the most seats in the provincial legislature, other than the party that held two seats (Jones 2002). Since 2001, three senators per province have been directly elected for six-year staggered terms, so that one-third of the Senate renews every two years; the Senate renewed completely in 2001. These elections use closed party lists and a limited vote allocation formula, whereby two seats are allocated to the plurality party and one seat is allocated to the first runner-up.

Only political parties may present candidates in elections for the Chamber of Deputies and Senate. The rules governing the formation of new parties are sufficiently flexible though, that it is very easy for any credible political candidate (for example, an "independent") to form a political party on his or her own. To do this the new party must obtain a number of adherents equal to 0.0004 percent of the number of registered voters in the province. Candidates for public office must either be a resident of the province where they are running for a minimum of two years, or else have been born in the province.

During the 1983–2005 period Argentine politics was dominated by two political parties, the Partido Justicialista (PJ, the Peronists) and the Unión Cívica Radical (UCR, Radicals). A few times a "third party" achieved a modest degree of national prominence.[1] To date, however, every single one of these parties has seen its electoral support evaporate after only a few elections. In contrast to the PJ and UCR, these national third parties never established an effective party organization and were overdependent on the popularity of a single leader or small group of leaders. Furthermore, these national third parties have consistently failed to significantly branch out beyond their initial core geographic area of support, the Capital Federal (the city of Buenos Aires) and the portion of the province of Buenos Aires adjacent to the city, Greater Buenos Aires (De Luca, Jones, and Tula 2002).

1. Third parties that achieved this ephemeral national prominence include the Partido Intransigente (PI), Unión del Centro Democrático (UCEDE), Movimiento por la Dignidad y la Independencia (MODIN), Frente País Solidario (FREPASO), Acción por la República (AR), and Afirmación para una República Igualitaria (ARI).

This PJ-UCR dominance can be seen in the substantial control exercised by these two parties, especially the PJ, over the most important political posts in the country: the presidency, the Congress (Senate and Chamber of Deputies), and the governorships. The period 1983–2005 encompasses the presidencies of President Raúl Alfonsín (1983–1989) of the UCR, President Carlos Menem (1989–95, 1995–99) of the PJ, the abbreviated tenure of President Fernando de la Rúa (1999–2001) of the UCR, the term of interim President Eduardo Duhalde (2002–2003) of the PJ, and the term of President Néstor Kirchner (2003–2007) of the PJ.

During this period the PJ held a median of 55.7 percent (ranging from 45.7 to 62.5 percent) of the seats in the Senate and 47.1 percent (37.8 to 54.9 percent) of the seats in the Chamber of Deputies, and the UCR accounted for a median of 39.9 percent (22.9 to 39.1 percent) and 32.7 percent (17.3 to 50.8 percent) of the Senate and Chamber seats respectively (see Tables 2.1 and 2.2). The most successful third party in the Senate during this period was the Movimiento Popular Neuquino (MPN), which held a median of 3.6 percent of the seats (no party other than the PJ or UCR ever held more than two Senate seats during any legislative period).[2] In the Chamber, the most successful third party, Frente por un País Solidario (FREPASO) reached a zenith of 14.8 percent of the seats, with the median percentage of seats occupied by the largest third party in the eleven two-year legislative periods, a status held by five different parties, of only 4.3 percent. Reflective of the apparent fate of all national third parties in Argentina, by the 2003–5 period, FREPASO's Chamber contingent had been reduced to a mere 1.2 percent of the seats, and the party had ceased to exist as a viable political organization (Novaro 2002).

This PJ and UCR dominance extends to the governorships. As Table 2.3 details, the PJ controlled a median of 62.5 percent of the governorships between 1989 and 2003, ranging from 54.6 percent to 77.3 percent, and the UCR placed second with a median of 25.0 percent (9.1 to 31.8 percent). In contrast, no other party ever possessed more than one governorship at any one time during this period, and the highest average for a third party, the MPN, was only 4.3 percent.

2. Argentina has a large number of parties that successfully compete either solely or effectively in only one province (De Luca, Jones, and Tula 2002; Sin and Palanza 1997). This diverse group of parties is collectively referred to as the "provincial-parties." All of the governorships held by parties other than the PJ or UCR have been held by provincial-parties,except that the Frente Grande (FG) held the governorship (Chief of Government) in the city of Buenos Aires during the 1999–2003 and 2003–07 periods. During the past twenty years, the MPN has been the country's most successful provincial-party.

TABLE 2.1 The Composition of the Argentine Senate, 1983–2005 (Percentages)

Political Party	1983–1986	1986–1989	1989–1992[a]	1992–1995[a]	1995–1998[b]	1998–2001[b]	2001–2003[b,c]	2003–2005[b]
Partido Justicialista[d]	45.7	45.7	54.4/54.2	62.5	55.7	55.7	57.1	57.8
Unión Cívica Radical[d]	39.1	39.1	30.4/29.2	22.9	28.6	30.0	32.9	28.2
Provincial-parties	15.2	15.2	15.2/16.7	14.6	15.7	14.3	8.6	9.9
Others	0	0	0/0	0	0	1.4	1.4	4.2
Total number of seats	46	46	46/48	48	70	70	70	71

Source: Honorable Cámara de Diputados de la Nación.

a. The Senate increased from 46 to 48 members in early 1992 when senators from the recently created province of Tierra del Fuego assumed office.

b. During the 1995–2001 period two seats from the province of Catamarca were never occupied due to a political dispute. Because of similar political conflicts during the 2001–2003 period in the Capital Federal and for the 2001–2005 period in Corrientes, two seats were not occupied during the 2001–2003 period and one seat was not occupied during the 2003–2005 period.

c. Beginning in 2001 the Senate partial renovation (previously triennial) became biennial.

d. In at least one three- or two-year legislative period, the party held three or more seats, and is thus listed separately above.

TABLE 2.2 The Composition of the Argentine Chamber of Deputies, 1983–2005 (Percentages)

Political Party	1983–1985	1985–1987	1987–1989	1989–1991	1991–1993	1993–1995	1995–1997	1997–1999	1999–2001	2001–2003	2003–2005
Partido Justicialista[a]	43.7	37.8	38.6	47.2	45.1	49.4	51.0	46.3	38.5	47.1	54.9
Unión Cívica Radical[a]	50.8	50.8	44.9	35.4	32.7	32.7	26.5	25.7	31.9	25.3	17.9
Unión del Centro Democrático[a]	0.8	1.2	2.8	4.3	3.9	1.6	0.8	0.4	0.4	0.4	0.4
Frente País por un Solidario[a]							8.6	14.8	14.4	2.7	1.2
Acción por la República[a]								1.2	4.3	1.6	0.4
Afirmación para una República Igualitaria[a]										6.2	4.3
Provincial-parties	3.1	4.7	6.7	7.5	8.6	9.3	8.6	10.5	9.7	8.6	7.4
Others	1.6	5.5	7.1	5.5	9.7	7.0	4.7	1.2	0.8	8.2	13.5
Total number of seats	254	254	254	254	257	257	257	257	257	257	257

Source: Honorable Cámara de Diputados de la Nación.

a. In at least one two-year legislative period held 3 percent or more of the seats.

TABLE 2.3   Partisan Control of Argentine Provinces (Governorships), 1983–2007 (Percentages)

Political Party	1983–1987	1987–1991	1991–1995[b]	1995–1999[b]	1999–2003[b]	2003–2007[b]
Partido Justicialista[a]	54.6	77.3	60.9	58.3	58.3	66.7
Unión Cívica Radical[a]	31.8	9.1	17.4	25.0	29.2	25.0
Provincial-parties	13.6	13.6	21.7	16.7	8.3	4.2
Others					4.2	4.2
Total number of governorships	22	22	23	24	24	24

Source: Author's compilation.

a. Held more than one governorship in a province during at least one gubernatorial period.

b. The 1993–97 and 1997–2001 gubernatorial periods for Corrientes are included with the 1991–95 and 1995–99 periods, respectively.   The 2001–05 period is included in both the 1999–2003 and 2003–07 periods. The 1996–2000 and 1999–2003 gubernatorial periods for Federal Capital are included with the 1995–99 and 2001–03 periods above.

Intraparty Politics and Campaign Finance

The locus of partisan politics in Argentina is the province (Benton 2002; De Luca, Jones, and Tula 2002; Levitsky 2003). In virtually all Argentine political parties, political careers are generally province based, and the base of political support for politicians and parties is concentrated at the provincial level. Even positions in the national government are often a consequence of provincial factors.

A single person or small group of politicians generally dominates political parties at the provincial level (De Luca, Jones, and Tula 2002; Jones, Saiegh, Spiller, and Tommasi 2002). In provinces where the party controls the governorship, with rare exceptions the governor is the undisputed or at least dominant boss of the provincial-level party. In many other provinces, where the governorship is not held by the party, the party is nonetheless dominated in a comparable manner by a single individual, but there is a greater amount of space for intraparty opponents. Finally, in the remaining provinces where the party does not control the governorship and there is not a single dominant leader, there is generally a small group of influential party leaders who predominate in party life.[3]

This dominance by party leaders is based principally on patronage, pork-barrel politics, and clientelism (Calvo and Murillo 2004; Jones and Hwang 2005; Levitsky 2003). Both primary and general election campaigns are funded primarily via the use of resources gained from patronage, pork-barrel, and clientelistic activities. Government financing of campaigns and party building also exists, although it

---

3. In provinces where the party leadership is fragmented, the role of the national party in provincial-level politics, especially if it is the party of the President, is often more pronounced than is the case where the provincial-level party is united under a single leader (Jones 1997b).

represents only a very modest fraction of the resources used for campaign activity by the relevant parties (see Chapter 8 by De Luca, this volume).

Patronage positions are particularly important for maintaining the support of second- and third-tier party leaders, who in turn possess the ability to mobilize voters, especially for party primaries. The ability to engage in pork-barrel politics improves the party's reputation with key constituents and aids clientelistic practices through the provision of jobs to party supporters and the infusion of money into the party coffers, which in turn is employed to maintain clientelist networks. Some examples of party money sources are kickbacks from contractors and suppliers, skimming off a percentage of the project budget, profits obtained from the granting of government contracts to friends and relatives, and campaign donations by businesses and individuals who wish to curry favor to receive benefits from the government following the election. Clientelism assists party leaders at all levels in maintaining a solid base of supporters.

The province-level party has a large number of positions at its disposal, with the exact portfolio depending on the party's control of national, provincial, and municipal governments (De Luca, Jones, and Tula 2002). All parties control varying numbers of positions in the national, provincial, and municipal legislatures. If the party controls the provincial government, it has further access to positions in the provincial executive branch, and likewise, where it controls municipal governments, it also has access to positions in the municipal executive branch.[4] The degree of this latter control over municipal-level positions varies depending on the province's province–municipality revenue-sharing system. Finally, if their party controls the national government, provincial-party leaders have access to a host of positions in the national government, in both the federal capital and the provincial offices of the national executive branch.

The provincial-party also controls the distribution of national-, provincial-, and municipal-level expenditures, this control varying depending on the party's control over the national, provincial, and municipal governments.[5] These expenditures provide a prime source of the resources needed by party leaders to engage in clientelistic activities. Argentina's federal revenue-sharing system automatically transfers funds to the provinces, which are then mostly utilized at the province's

4. The size of the provincial public sector is quite large in most provinces. For example, in 2000 the ratio of private to provincial employees was above 10 in only three provinces (Buenos Aires, Capital Federal, Córdoba), and as low as 3 in four provinces (Catamarca, Formosa, La Rioja, Santa Cruz), with a median value of 6 (Guido and Lazzari 2001). If one includes all national, provincial, and municipal public employees, public employees account for over 25 percent of the workforce in six provinces, with a median percentage among the twenty-four provinces of 19 percent (Guido 2002). Finally, all but one province spends over 50 percent of its total revenue on provincial public employee salaries, and over half spend more than 67 percent.

5. The control of the government also opens up other potential sources of funding for some unscrupulous politicians, such as payments received to pass certain legislation or to turn a blind eye to or protect illicit activity.

discretion. During the past dozen years the distribution of expenditures in Argentina has been roughly equal between the national government and the provinces (Saiegh and Tommasi 1998; Tommasi 2002) with, for instance in 2000, 52 percent of expenditures being carried out by the national government, 40 percent by the provincial governments, and 8 percent by the municipal governments (Tommasi 2002).

Governors and, to a lesser extent, mayors exercise considerable influence over the execution of public policy, either through their direct control of the provincial budget or their discretionary control over the execution of many national government-funded programs (De Luca, Jones, and Tula 2002). This influence allows them to obtain and maintain the loyalty of their supporters through the granting of privileges in the distribution of material and economic subsidies, low-interest loans, scholarships, and so forth. It also allows them to build relationships with a wide variety of other organized groups. These benefits also accrue in a more limited manner to legislators at the national, provincial, and municipal levels, who are able to allocate resources given to them by the legislature or are able to directly allocate national-, provincial-, or municipal-level resources by working in concert with the respective executive branch.

The result of these patronage, pork-barrel, and clientelistic activities is the dominance of the provincial political party. First and foremost, dominance of the provincial-level party requires that a party leader be able to defeat any rival in an intraparty primary—either to choose candidates for elective office or to elect the provincial-level party leadership.[6] Patronage, pork-barrel activities, and clientelism are important for success in general elections, but they are indispensable for success in party primaries. In a related manner, patronage, pork-barrel, and clientelistic support often has the same anticipated reaction effect on potential intraparty challengers as a large campaign war chest has in U.S. politics; it causes potential challengers to back down from any attempt to defeat the party leader.[7]

Candidate Selection

Legislative candidates are selected via either party primaries or elite arrangement or, in a handful of cases, via competitive party convention votes. Political parties, not the government, run party primaries for both party leadership positions and

6. The party leader, through his or her control of the provincial-level party organization, has a great deal of latitude regarding when and under what conditions primaries are held, which provides incumbent party leaders with an additional advantage vis-à-vis challengers.

7. Challenging the party boss is always an option for intraparty opponents, but it is a decision that is taken with great caution, since a failed challenge often entails serious negative consequences for the challenger. In 2001 and 2003, some potential challengers who realized they had no chance of victory in a primary election opted to run directly in the general election as a candidate of their own party.

candidacies for national, provincial, and municipal public office (De Luca, Jones, and Tula 2002). Primaries involve a considerable amount of mobilization efforts by the competing intraparty lists. The electorate for these contests is either party members alone or party members and independents.[8] Elections for party leadership positions are restricted to party members.

Vital to these mobilization efforts is the support of three groups (De Luca, Jones, and Tula 2002). First, every list needs the support of its own machine, composed of regional and neighborhood-level leaders *(punteros)* who have established ties, normally fostered and maintained via patronage, with the leader or leaders supporting the list. Second, lists seek the support of *punteros* not initially aligned with any of the competing lists. Third, lists seek the support of other organized groups with a strong ability to mobilize large numbers of people such as *piqueteros* (organizations that block roads, bridges, and entrances to businesses, in order to extort funds or consumer goods from the government and private companies), community improvement committees, *barras bravas* (soccer team fan clubs), and others. In addition, to be competitive a list must be able to carry out the following tasks (De Luca, Jones, and Tula 2002): engage in campaign advertising, mobilize voters and then hire a large number of taxis and buses to transport them to the polls, and deploy several election monitors to every precinct *(mesa)* to prevent the list from being the victim of electoral fraud.

To ensure that its list is victorious, a party machine must engage in some campaign advertising. This generally includes painting walls, hanging banners and signs, and distributing campaign literature. The party machine must also be able to mobilize a sufficient number of voters. Some of this mobilization is already guaranteed by the preexisting relationship that exists with individual *punteros* and other groups. However, as the election approaches the machine will generally need to provide financial incentives to these *punteros* who will ensure the turnout of the people under their influence via the distribution of consumer goods, cash, and/or persuasion. The machine also will need to provide transportation, which is generally done through the contracting of taxis in urban areas and buses and vans in rural areas where the polling place is some distance away, or also in urban areas where a large number of individuals from a single location, such as a slum *(villa miseria)* are mobilized at the same time. Finally, since the elections are run by the parties, it is imperative that the party machine have a sufficient number of election monitors to ensure that the election is not stolen from it by a competing party machine via electoral fraud. This may occur

---

8. During the 1989–2003 period, in PJ provincial-level national deputy primaries restricted to party members and those open to independents, the median percentage of registered voters who participated was 7 and 14 percent, respectively. The comparable figures for the UCR were 2 percent and 5 percent, respectively. These estimates are based on partial data, and thus should be treated with some caution. All the same, it is clear that a relatively small percentage of the overall electorate participates in most primaries.

through the removal of ballot papers from the polling booth, switching of ballot boxes, theft and destruction of ballot boxes, bribing or intimidation of "lone" election monitors, or "chain voting" *(voto cadena)*.[9]

In a primary, then, success depends almost entirely on the deployment of financial and material resources. Whether or not a politician will faithfully represent or has faithfully represented the interests of his or her constituents normally has no significant impact on success in the primary contest. As former (1999–2003) Chubut governor José Luis Lizurume stated, "La interna es aparato puro" (The primary is pure machine) (*Diario El Chubut*, July 7, 2003). As a consequence, the use of primaries to select candidates in Argentina does not have the same type of particularistic or ideological effect that primaries in some other countries often have. In Argentina the principal competition is between party machines far more than between individuals, and victory is determined far less by personal characteristics and policy positions than by the amount of material resources that the machine has at its disposal for the primary election contest. Primary election results indicate which party machine has the most resources and makes the most efficient use of them, not which candidate or list of candidates is most popular among the primary electorate.

I now extend an analysis of the determinants of the use of provincial primary elections to select Chamber of Deputies candidates in Argentina (see De Luca, Jones, and Tula 2002). The analysis population consists of the nomination method employed to select the candidates for the biennial Chamber of Deputies elections held between 1983 and 2003 (672 cases total) on the lists presented by the PJ, UCR, the most prominent minor national parties in their bailiwicks during specified periods (see De Luca, Jones, and Tula 2002), and provincial-parties (see Chapter 8, this volume). A case is the method by which a party in a province selected its candidates for the Chamber election. Thus the method the PJ in the province of Neuquén used to choose its candidates for the 2003 Chamber election is considered a case.

Dependent and Independent Variables

I employ two dependent variables. "Primary election—all primaries" codes as 1 all Chamber of Deputies nomination processes carried out using a direct primary and as 0 all nomination processes that were the product of elite arrangement or a party assembly.[10] "Primary election—competitive primaries" codes as 1 all Chamber of Deputies nomination processes carried out using a direct primary

---

9. For a detailed description of the *voto cadena* (a complex form of vote buying), see Tula (2005, 34).

10. The use of party assemblies is so infrequent (2 percent of the cases) that they are not treated as a separate category, and instead are merged with elite arrangement. Excluding the party assembly cases has no substantive effect on the findings.

where the winning list won by a margin of less than 75 percent of the valid vote, and codes as 0 all other nomination processes.

Figure 2.1 details the evolution of the use of primaries ("primary election—all primaries") between 1983 and 2003 by the provincial branches of the PJ, UCR, and all parties combined to choose their candidates for Chamber of Deputies elections. During the 1980s the use of primaries was significantly more common in the UCR than in the PJ, but since 1993 both parties have employed primaries to choose their candidates for national deputy at relatively comparable rates.

De Luca, Jones, and Tula (2002) hypothesize that seven principal factors explain a party's decision to use a primary or an elite arrangement to choose its candidates for Chamber elections. The following paragraphs detail my theoretical expectations for how these variables will affect the propensity of a party to employ primaries and how I have coded them for my statistical analysis that follows.

1. "Provincial opposition party" is coded 0 if the party controls the governorship and 1 if it does not. I expect a positive relationship to exist between this variable and the probability of a primary election being held.
2. "Incumbent governorship/reelection" is coded 1 if the party controls the governorship and the governor is eligible to seek immediate reelection, and 0 otherwise. I expect a party that controls the governorship and whose governor is eligible to seek immediate reelection to have a lower probability of holding a primary to select its Chamber candidates than all other parties (coded 0).

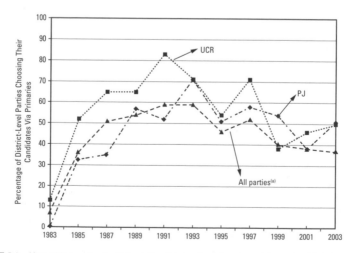

FIGURE 2.1   Use of Primaries to Select Candidates for Chamber of Deputies Elections, 1983–2003.

Source: Author's compilation.

a) All parties includes the PJ, UCR, and all other parties.

3. "National governing party." Instances in which a district-level party was also the party of the president of the Republic (UCR for 1985–1989 and 2001, PJ for 1991–1999 and 2003) are coded 1, whereas all other instances are coded 0. I expect a positive relationship between this variable and the probability that a party uses a primary to select its Chamber candidates.

4. "Contagion." Cases where another relevant party in the province used a primary to select its Chamber candidates for that year are coded 1, whereas all other cases are coded 0. I expect a positive relationship between this variable and the probability that a party holds a primary.

5. "1983 election year" is a variable for which all nomination processes for the 1983 election are coded 1, and all other processes 0. I expect an inverse relationship between this variable and the probability of holding a primary.

6. "UCR in Alianza" means that a UCR candidate was nominated in 1999 and 2001; I coded that 1, and all other cases 0. I expect an inverse relationship between this variable and the likelihood of holding a primary to choose candidates (for information on the UCR-FREPASO alliance, see Chapter 8, this volume, and Novaro 2002).

7. "PJ," "UCR," "minor national party," "provincial-party," "MPN-MPF (Movimiento Popular Neuquino-Movimiento Popular Fueguino)" are five binary variables that I used to control for party fixed effects. All cases of PJ party nomination processes are coded 1, and all other cases 0. I employ a similar coding scheme for the other listed variables. The hypotheses for these party variables are that, first, I expect "provincial-party" to have an inverse effect on the probability of holding a primary, and second, I expect the UCR to be more likely to hold a primary than the historically "verticalist" and uninstitutionalized PJ.

Analysis and Results

Table 2.4 provides the results of a binary probit analysis of the probability that a district-level party employed a primary (as opposed to an elite arrangement or party assembly) to select its Chamber of Deputies candidates in a given election year between 1983 and 2003.[11]

Whether or not a party is in the opposition at the provincial level clearly influences whether it selects its candidates using a primary or an elite arrangement. "Provincial opposition party" has a strong positive effect on the likelihood of a

11. The time-series cross-sectional nature of the data is a potential cause of concern. Methodologies for dealing with this type of data when using maximum likelihood estimation, particularly in unbalanced settings, are relatively undeveloped. However, several diagnostic exercises, such as including temporal fixed-effects variables and running population average and random-effects models, suggest that the results presented here are robust. Given the small number of cases, approximately eighty, that exist for direct senatorial elections, a comparable analysis is not possible for the Senate.

TABLE 2.4 Holding a Primary in Argentina, 1983–2003

Independent Variables	All Primaries Coded 1			Only Competitive Primaries Coded 1		
	Estimated Coefficent	Standard Error (Robust)	Minimum to Maximum	Estimated Coefficent	Standard Error (Robust)	Minimum to Maximum
Provincial opposition party	0.315*	0.139	0.154	0.391**	0.140	0.176
Incumbent governorship/reelection	−0.650**	0.180	−0.205	−0.675**	0.188	−0.188
National governing party	0.220	0.121		0.246*	0.121	0.094
Contagion	0.038	0.115		0.088	0.116	
1983 election year	−1.666**	0.292	−0.417	−1.512**	0.290	−0.368
UCR in Alianza	−0.630**	0.204	−0.249	−0.526*	0.204	−0.204
Provincial-party	−1.365**	0.233	−0.389	−1.326**	0.243	−0.349
UCR	0.210	0.132		0.167	0.131	
Minor national party	−0.617*	0.249	−0.177	−0.523*	0.248	−0.139
MPN–MPF	1.046**	0.362	0.420	1.043**	0.350	0.434
Constant	−0.148	0.162		−0.367*	0.165	
Log likelihood	−381.343			−379.089		
LR CHI2 (10)	108.81			98.97		
Number of observations	672			672		
Method–binary probit						

NOTE: The excluded party is the PJ. The "minimum to maximum" values were calculated with the other variables set to their mean, except where it would be logically impossible for the variable to take on its mean value (e.g., when "incumbent governorship/reelection" equals 1, "provincial opposition party" must equal 0) or where the theoretical comparison requires specific values (e.g., for UCR in Alianza). Clarify (10,000 simulations) was employed to calculate the "minimum to maximum" values (King, Tomz, and Wittenberg 2000).

** Significant at the .01 level for a two-tailed test; * Significant at the .05 level for a two-tailed test.

primary. Holding other values at their mean or zero (if the mean is a logically impossible value), where a party is in the opposition at the provincial level, it is 15 percent (all primaries) and 18 percent (competitive primaries only) more likely to hold a primary than is a party that is in government at the provincial level.

"Incumbent governorship/reelection" has a significant inverse effect on the probability of holding a primary election. Where the incumbent governor is eligible to run for reelection, the likelihood of the incumbent governor's party's holding a primary is 21 percent (all primaries) and 19 percent (competitive primaries) less than when a party is not that of an incumbent governor eligible to run for reelection.

"National governing party" does not have a significant effect on candidate selection at the provincial level when the dependent variable is "primary election—all primaries." It does, however, exercise a significant effect when the dependent variable is "primary election—competitive primaries" (that is, when only competitive primaries are coded 1), and the probability of a primary being held for the latter is 9 percent greater if the party's national leader is the president.

"Contagion" does not have a significant effect on the probability of holding a primary. "1983 election year" has a significant inverse effect on the probability of holding a primary, with parties in 1983 42 percent (all primaries) and 37 percent (competitive primaries only) less likely to choose their candidates using primaries than in other years.[12] In 1999 and 2001 the UCR ("UCR in Alianza") was significantly less likely to hold a primary than in other years. Due in large part to its role in the Alianza, the UCR district-level parties were 25 percent (all primaries) and 20 percent (competitive primaries only) less likely to choose their candidates via a primary in 1999 and 2001 than they were between 1983 and 1997 and in 2003.

Provincial-parties ("provincial-party") were less likely to hold primaries than other parties, with the provincial-parties 39 percent (all primaries) and 35 percent (competitive primaries only) less likely to hold a primary than the other parties. Additional analysis (based on the data used in Table 2.2) indicates the provincial-parties are significantly less likely to hold a primary than all of the other parties or groups of parties. As for the relationships between the four other party variables ("PJ," "UCR," "minor national party," "MPN-MPF"), the only significant differences detected in additional analysis similar to that above are that the MPN-MPF are more likely to hold a primary than the PJ, UCR, and minor national parties, and that the PJ and UCR are more likely to hold a primary than the minor national parties. In spite of the differences in the popular characterization of the UCR (liberal-democratic, institutionalized) and PJ (verticalist, uninstitutionalized), the UCR is not significantly more likely to hold a primary than the PJ.

12. Log likelihood ratio tests indicate that including temporal variables to control for the other election years does not significantly improve the fit of the model. In all instances analysis conducted excluding all data from 1983 provided results not substantively different from those presented here.

To better understand the substantive significance of the results in Table 2.4, I calculated the probability of a primary's being held under six scenarios (see Table 2.5).[13]

1. Where a PJ district-level party is in the opposition at the provincial level and it is not 1983, the probability of its holding a primary is 60 percent (all primaries) and 52 percent (competitive primaries only).

2. Where a PJ district-level party is in government at the provincial level, the incumbent governor is not eligible to run for reelection, and it is not 1983, the probability of its holding a primary is 43 percent and 37 percent.

3. Where a PJ district-level party is in government at the provincial level, the incumbent governor is eligible to run for reelection, and it is not 1983, the probability of its holding a primary is 21 percent and 16 percent.

4. Where a UCR district-level party is in the opposition at the provincial level and it is not 1983, the probability of its holding a primary is 59 percent and 48 percent.

5. Where a UCR district-level party is in government at the provincial level, the incumbent governor is not eligible to run for reelection, and it is not 1983, the probability of its holding a primary is 46 percent and 33 percent.

6. Where a UCR district-level party is in government at the provincial level, the incumbent governor is eligible to run for reelection that year, and it is not 1983, the probability of its holding a primary is 22 percent and 14 percent.

The particular configuration of these partisan and institutional variables has a powerful effect on the probability of holding a primary. These are important substantive differences, and indicate provincial-level factors such as whether or not a party is in the opposition at the provincial level or an incumbent governor is eligible to run for reelection have a salient effect on the likelihood of a district-level party's employing a primary election to choose its Chamber candidates. This analysis underscores the decentralized nature of the Argentine party system and also highlights the prominent influence exercised by provincial-level factors over the nature of the candidate selection process in particular, and over Argentine political career pathways in general.

Profiling the Successful Chamber and Senate Candidates

This discussion suggests that in most instances the reelection decision for members of the Argentine Chamber of Deputies and Senate and the decision regarding their

13. All party variables not explicitly mentioned are set to zero while the mean values for "contagion" and "national governing party" are utilized (for scenarios 1–3, "UCR in Alianza" is set to zero, whereas for scenarios 4–6 its mean value for the UCR is used). The probability is the expected value obtained from the analysis in Table 2.4 using Clarify (King, Tomz, and Wittenberg 2000).

TABLE 2.5 The Probability of a Primary Being Held Under Six Scenarios: All Primaries and Competitive Primaries

Party	Provincial Government Status	Incumbent Governor Eligible for Reelection	All Primaries coded 1 Probability (%) of a Primary Being Held	All Competitive Primaries coded 1 Probability (%) of a Primary Being Held
PJ	Opposition	No	60	52
PJ	Government	No	43	37
PJ	Government	Yes	21	16
UCR	Opposition	No	59	48
UCR	Government	No	46	33
UCR	Government	Yes	22	14

NOTE: "Contagion" and "national governing party" are set at their mean values. "UCR in Alianza" is set to its mean value for the UCR for the UCR predictions. Valid for all years except for 1983. The probability is the expected value obtained using Clarify (10,000 simulations) (King et al. 2000).

TABLE 2.6   Reelection to the Argentine Chamber of Deputies, 1987–2003

Political Party	Percentage of Deputies Running for Reelection	Percentage of Deputies Who Are Reelected	Percentage of Those Running Who Were Reelected
PJ	22	18	90
	(17–33)	(13–28)	(60–100)
UCR	22	17	78
	(11–34)	(4–29)	(33–100)
Provincial-parties	31	25	75
	(10–72)	(10–57)	(50–100)
Others	44	29	60
	(28–62)	(12–43)	(25–100)
Total	24	22	74
	(20–33)	(15–24)	(58–90)

Source: Honorable Cámara de Diputados de la Nación.

NOTE: The first-row cell entries are the median percentage values for the nine elections. The second-row entries in parentheses are the range of the percentage values for the nine elections.

political future lies primarily with the provincial-level party boss(es), and not with the individual deputy. Furthermore, these party bosses practice rotation (Jones, Saiegh, Spiller, and Tommasi 2002), the consequence being very low reelection rates for the Chamber of Deputies and Senate. Table 2.6 provides information on the median percentage and range of deputies who ran for reelection (that is, obtained a position on the party list), were reelected, and, among those who obtained a position on the party list, were reelected between 1987 (the first full-period reelection date) and 2003. During this time period a median of 24 percent (20 to 33 percent) of deputies achieved immediate reelection; the lowest reelection rate I am aware of in democracies that do not prohibit immediate reelection.[14] In the two dominant parties, the median percentage of deputies who achieved immediate reelection during this period was 18 percent for the PJ and 17 percent for the UCR. However, once a deputy obtained a position on the party list, his or her chances of reelection soared to a median of 74 percent for the Chamber of Deputies overall and 90 percent and 78 percent for the PJ and UCR, respectively. These high rates underscore the importance of the control exercised by the provincial-party bosses over the list creation process.

Argentine members of Congress are amateur legislators but professional politicians (Jones, Saiegh, Spiller, and Tommasi 2002). The position of national

14. In 2003, only four, or 17 percent, of the twenty-four senators leaving office were reelected. Calculating reelection rates for the pre-2001 period is complicated by the nine-year terms and the ability of the majority party at the provincial level to replace senators at will, though overall the reelection rates between 1986 and 2003, measured in various ways, were approximately 20 percent.

legislator is merely one station on a lengthy political career path that normally begins and also ends in the legislator's home province. As a consequence, the behavior of deputies and senators is best explained by a modified version of progressive ambition theory, where *progressive* is interpreted in a more flexible manner, with static ambition (where a deputy or senator pursues a career in the Chamber or Senate) and, especially, discrete ambition (where the deputy withdraws from politics after serving his or her term in office) being uncommon (Jones 2002; Morgenstern 2002a; Samuels 2003). Virtually all deputies and senators occupy some type of governmental or party position prior to being elected to Congress. As mentioned above, most of these deputies and senators serve only one term in the Congress. Nonetheless, most deputies and senators, following their tenure in the Congress, do not withdraw from politics but rather occupy a political position at the national, provincial, or municipal level.

In this section I first analyze the position held by deputies elected between 1991 and 1999 and senators elected between 1986 and 2001 immediately prior to being elected to Congress. Second, I review the positions most commonly held at any point during a period of full democracy by deputies and senators prior to their assumption of office. Third, I examine structural (provincial government status), partisan, and individual differences in the types of positions occupied by deputies immediately prior to assuming office during the 1991 and 1999 period. Finally, I provide an overview of the career pathways of deputies and senators following the end of their terms in congress.

The Springboard to the Chamber and Senate

Table 2.7 provides information on the positions held by deputies elected between 1991 and 1999 and senators elected between 1986 and 2001. Three prominent conclusions can be drawn from the table. First, 97 percent of all deputies and all senators occupied either a governmental (82 percent of deputies and 93 percent of senators) or party (15 percent of deputies and 7 percent of senators) position immediately prior to their election. This fact underscores the presence of relatively stable career pathways in Argentine political parties. While these pathways are more complex than those found in many countries (on Chile, see Chapter 4, this volume), as the remaining analysis demonstrates. It is not an accident that a dozen years ago, the people who today are the country's most prominent politicians occupied positions such as mayor, national deputy, and provincial legislator. And it will be no surprise when, in a dozen years, today's mayors, national deputies, and provincial legislators occupy the most prominent political positions in the country.

Second, prior to assuming office, a clear majority of national deputies (62 percent) and senators (54 percent) held governmental or party positions in their home provinces, and an additional 24 percent of deputies and 35 percent of

TABLE 2.7 Positions Held by Argentine Deputies (1991–99) and Senators (1986–2001) Immediately Prior to Elections

General Category and Subcategory	Deputies' Prior Position	Percentage Distribution of the Position Held		
		Post Held by "Prior" Deputies (23%)	Senators' Prior Position	Post Held by "Prior" Senators (16%)
National executive branch, total	**7**	**10**	**11**	**17**
President or vice president	0	0	1	0
Cabinet minister	1	4	2	0
Lower-tier executive branch	6	6	8	17
National legislator, total	**24**	**1**	**35**	**17**
National senator	1	1	16	
National deputy	23		19	17
Provincial executive branch, total	**16**	**14**	**23**	**17**
Governor	2	2	4	3
Vice governor	2	2	4	7
Cabinet minister	6	4	9	7
Lower-tier executive branch	6	6	6	0
Provincial legislator, total	**20**	**24**	**14**	**10**
Provincial legislator	20	24	14	10

| | Percentage Distribution of the Position Held | | | |
General Category and Subcategory	Deputies' Prior Position	Post Held by "Prior" Deputies (23%)	Senators' Prior Position	Post Held by "Prior" Senators (16%)
Mayor, total	**6**	**5**	**7**	**7**
Mayor	6	5	7	7
Other municipal level, total	**7**	**6**	**1**	**7**
Municipal cabinet minister	2	3	0	3
Municipal councilor	5	4	1	3
Party activist, total	**15**	**30**	**7**	**23**
Party activist	13	26	5	23
Legislative staffer	2	4	2	0
Labor leader, total	**2**	**6**	**1**	**3**
Labor leader	2	6	1	3
Nonpartisan background	**3**	**5**	**0**	**0**
Business	2	3	0	0
The arts	1	2	0	0

Source: Author's compilation.

senators represented their province in the Congress. In contrast, only 7 percent of deputies and 11 percent of senators held a position in the national executive branch immediately prior to assuming office. In sum, virtually all relevant candidates for the office of national deputy and national senator are chosen from a pool of governmental and partisan officeholders in the provinces.

Table 2.7 provides a comprehensive review of the distribution of deputies and senators among the different position categories. One important point to be drawn from the table is that the position most commonly held by deputies immediately prior to their being elected as a national deputy was national deputy (23 percent), followed closely by provincial legislator (20 percent); in fact, 24 percent of the former "re-elected" deputies occupied the post of provincial legislator immediately prior to their initial election as deputy. Next in line is the post of provincial executive branch member (16 percent). Among senators, the most popular post held prior to election was national deputy (19 percent), followed by national senator (16 percent), and provincial legislator (14 percent).

Prior Political Experience of Deputies and Senators

Table 2.8 provides information on the percentage of different elective and appointive positions occupied by national deputies and senators at any time during a democratic period prior to their election as national deputy and national senator. Among national deputies, the most common shared position is that of provincial legislator; 35 percent of the deputies had occupied that post prior to being elected as deputy. This is followed by national deputy (28 percent had been national deputies prior to their election as deputy between 1991 and 1999), municipal councilor (23 percent), and a member of the provincial executive branch (21 percent). Only 12 percent had held a position in the national executive branch. Among national senators, the most common previous position is national deputy (33 percent), followed by a member of the provincial executive branch (31 percent), and national senator (21 percent). A total of 17 percent of the national senators had previously held a position in the national executive branch.

Covariates of Deputy's Springboard Position

Table 2.9 displays a summary of a series of nine binary logit analyses, using clustered standard errors, of factors related to the the last post occupied prior to their election by national deputy candidates elected between 1991 and 1999. In the Table 2.9 analysis, the dependent variables are coded according to what type of position the deputy occupied immediately prior to being elected. With one exception, the dependent variables conform exactly to the position categories in

TABLE 2.8   Positions Held Prior to Assuming Office by Argentine Deputies (1991–1999) and Senators (1986–2001), (Democratic Periods Only)[a]

Position	Percentage of Deputies Who Held the Position at One Time	Percentage of Senators Who Held the Position at One Time
Provincial legislator	35	31
National deputy	28	33
Municipal councilor	23	8
Provincial executive branch (appointed)	21	32
National executive branch (appointed)	12	17
Mayor	11	8
Municipal cabinet minister	6	6
National senator	—[b]	21
Governor	—	10
Vice governor	—	8

Source: Author's compilation.

a. Data are provided for positions occupied by 5 percent of deputies or senators.

b. Values less than 5 percent for that column are identified by "—".

Table 2.7.[15] The independent variables are primarily structural (i.e., higher level) and include "party controls governorship" (coded 1 if the party held the governorship at the time of the election and 0 if otherwise) and partisan dummy variables: "UCR," "FREPASO," "center-right/Provincial-party" (coded 1 if the deputy was elected as a member of that party and 0 if otherwise).[16] The partisan dummy variables are measured as differences from the PJ, which is the excluded partisan category.

Two individual-level variables also are included. The first, "sex," is the sex of the deputy elected (1 for women, 0 for men), and the other, "head of list," is whether the deputy occupied the first position on the party list (coded 1) or not (coded 0). In Argentine campaigns the "head of the list" *(cabeza de lista)* is often the most visible "face" of the party list for that election, and the position frequently is used by an ambitious politician as a launching pad to run for a higher political office in the future.

15. Column D, "Provincial Executive Branch I," is restricted to governors, vice governors, and provincial cabinet ministers. Column E, "Provincial Executive Branch II," includes all of the mentioned positions as well lower-tier provincial executive branch officials.

16. The variable "center-right/provincial-party" combines the national-level center-right parties (APR, MODIN, UCEDE) and the provincial-parties. FREPASO includes all center-left deputies that belonged to minor left and center-left parties prior to the creation of FREPASO.

TABLE 2.9 Determinants of the Immediate Prior Career of Argentine Chamber Deputy Candidates, 1991–1999[a]

Independent Variables	A National Legislator	B National Executive Branch	C National Executive Branch-PJ	D Provincial Executive Branch I	E Provincial Executive Branch II	F Provincial Legislator	G Municipal Mayor	H Other Municipal Office	I Party Activist
Party controls governorship		−5.4**	−2.9**	10.6**	15.7**			−2.0**	−2.6**
UCR		−2.4**	NA			1.8**			
FREPASO	1.6*	−2.8**	NA						
Center-right/ provincial-party		−2.4**	NA	2.2*	2.3*				
Head of list		−2.3*			2.0**			−2.2**	−2.7**
Sex	−1.6*				−2.9**		−3.4*	2.4**	2.1**

a. Cell values are the ratio of the maximum to minimum predicted value.

** Difference significant at the .01 level; * Difference significant at the .05 level.

A variety of other variables were examined—for example, previous control of the governorship, midterm elections versus non-midterm elections, list position—but the results either yielded uninteresting results or created serious multicollinearity problems. Hence, these variables are excluded from this exploratory stage of the analysis.

The cell entries indicate the ratio of the predicted value for the variable when it is set at its maximum value (1) to the ratio when it is set at its minimum value (0), with all other values set at their mean, except for the partisan predicted values when calculating the maximum value (King, Tomz, and Wittenberg 2000). Predicted values are included only where the estimated coefficients in the binary logit analysis were significant at the .05 level or greater.

Unsurprisingly, when a party held the governorship in its province, a significantly greater percentage of its candidates occupied posts in the provincial executive branch prior to becoming national deputies (see column B). Of greater interest is the finding that when a party controlled the governorship at the provincial level, its successful candidates were significantly less likely to have occupied positions in the national executive branch (see column B). Conversely, when a party did not control the governorship in the province, its candidates were more likely to be drawn from the national executive branch. Given that the PJ held the national executive branch throughout this period, this analysis is more clearly interpreted when the analysis is restricted to PJ deputies (see column C, "National Executive Branch-PJ"), where a similar significant inverse relationship is detected.

The partisan variables as well as additional analysis where the four different party groups were rotated as the excluded partisan category indicate that there exist relatively few interparty differences in regard to the previous position occupied by their successful national deputy candidates. With the exception of the unsurprising significant lower probability that non-PJ deputies previously occupied a post in the national executive branch, there are relatively few significant partisan differences. FREPASO deputies were significantly more likely than their PJ, their UCR, and their center-right colleagues to have occupied the post of national legislator (column A) immediately prior to assuming office. UCR deputies were significantly more likely than their PJ, FREPASO, and center-right colleagues to have occupied the post of provincial legislator (column F) immediately prior to assuming office. Finally, the center-right national party and provincial-party deputies ("center-right/provincial-party") were significantly more likely than their PJ, FREPASO, and UCR counterparts to have previously occupied a post in the provincial executive branch (columns D and E). This finding is accounted for almost exclusively by the propensity of the provincial-party deputies to come from these provincial executive branch posts.

The results indicate that few positions are significantly more likely to be previously occupied by the head of the party list *(cabeza de lista)* than by those lower down on the list. The only position that was more likely to be occupied by the head of the list was a high-level provincial executive branch official such as governor, vice governor, or provincial cabinet minister (see column D). The head of the list was significantly less likely to be either a nonmayoral municipal official such as a municipal cabinet minister or municipal councilor (column H) or someone who only occupied a party post (column I).

Successful female candidates were significantly less likely than their male counterparts to have been drawn from the position of national legislator (column A), in large part because almost one-half of the analysis population was elected before the first round of beneficiaries of Argentina's pathbreaking gender-quota legislation—in force for all Chamber elections held since 1993—had had the chance to run for reelection. These successful female candidates also are significantly less likely to have held a post in the national executive branch (columns B), in the provincial executive branch (all positions, column E), and as mayor (column G). In contrast, successful female candidates were significantly more likely than successful male candidates to have held only a party post (column I) immediately prior to election or to have held a lower-level municipal post such as municipal cabinet minister or municipal councilor (column H).

Post-Legislative Positions

An adequate understanding of the nature of legislators' political career pathways requires the information presented on the positions occupied prior to assuming office along with information on the positions occupied following the conclusion of a deputy's or senator's tenure in office. In order to better understand the career paths of national legislators, I carried out a study of the position occupied by national deputies in the three years following the end of their term in the Chamber of Deputies. All deputies elected between 1991 and 1999 were included in this analysis.[17]

To determine the position occupied by the deputies upon completion of their term in office, I examined rosters for the national executive branch, national Congress, provincial executive branches, provincial legislative branches, municipal mayors, municipal executive branches of the largest cities in the province, municipal councils of the largest cities in each province, labor union national executive branches, the national judicial branch, and each provincial supreme court only. These rosters were examined in September of the year following the end of the legislative term. The legislative terms end on December 10 of odd years, and I examined the rosters in September of the following even year for five years: 1996, 1998, 2000, 2002, and 2004.

---

17. The combination of the limited number of senators with post-Senate careers during this period, along with space limitations, led me to restrict this analysis to national deputies.

This methodology is not without problems. First, the rosters, particularly for the national and provincial executive branches, generally omit lower-level positions, informal contractual positions, positions that are "off the books," provincial- and municipal-level party leadership positions, and a host of other positions that we know scores of former legislators occupy after their tenure in Congress. Second, the rosters often are out of date or contain inaccurate information. Third, last names are occasionally misspelled in the roster, or different names are employed (the latter is more common for women). Finally, the focus on September of the even-numbered years will lead to the omission of individuals who held positions for a relatively short period of time, which is especially common for appointed positions in the national and provincial executive branches. For instance, even though Domingo Cavallo was the national minister of economy for two-thirds of 2001, his entry indicates he held no identifiable position during the three years following the end of his tenure in office, since in September of 2000 he was still a national deputy and by September of 2002 he was no longer a minister.

In spite of the above limitations, the data presented in Table 2.10 is the most comprehensive review of postcongressional careers of Argentine legislators to date. The table provides convincing additional evidence of the strong provincial based nature of Argentine career pathways.

Table 2.10 provides the distribution of the position occupied by national deputies in the three years following the end of their term in office, the one for which they were first elected in elections held between 1991 and 1999; if more than one position was occupied, the one occupied first is employed here.[18] Columns are provided for all parties, the PJ, the UCR, the combined center-right national parties and provincial parties, and for FREPASO.[19] One point that is immediately apparent is that on average we lack information on the position held by 51 percent, half, of the deputies. This large percentage is due in large part to the methodological limitations previously discussed. In particular, individuals who occupy informal or lower-level positions and prominent positions in the provincial-, municipal-, and county-level party organization are not included here. Earlier, more detailed work that focused on deputies elected in 1991 found that nearly a quarter of deputies (23 percent) occupied these types of positions three years after the end of their terms in office (see Jones, Saiegh, Spiller, and Tommasi 2002; Jones 2002).

18. For deputies elected in 1999, only the position occupied in the first year following the official end of their term, 2004, is examined. If deputies left office prior to the official end of their term, the three-year clock starts from the date of their departure, not the official end of their four-year term. The same categories used in the previous portion of this section are employed here. A partial exception is represented by the "municipal cabinet minister" and "municipal councilor" categories, which only include ministers and councilors from the largest, or in some cases two largest, municipalities in each province. A new "judge" category was also created.

19. For additional information on the coding of center-right national parties and provincial-parties and of FREPASO, see note 16.

TABLE 2.10 Position Held by Argentine National Deputies (Elected between 1991 and 1999) Immediately after the End of Their Term in Office

General Category and Subcategory[a]	Percentage (Holding an Identifiable Position)				
	All Parties	PJ	UCR	CR National or Provincial	FREPASO
National executive branch, total	**10**	**15**	**6**	**3**	**9**
President or vice president	0.3	1	0	0	0
Cabinet minister	1	1	1	0	0
Lower-tier executive branch	9	13	5	3	9
National legislator, total	**51**	**44**	**53**	**45**	**81**
National senator	7	5	12	3	6
National deputy	44	39	41	42	75
Provincial executive branch, total	**13**	**17**	**11**	**12**	**3**
Governor	2	2	4	3	0
Vice governor	1	1	1	3	0
Cabinet minister	3	3	2	6	0
Lower-tier executive branch	7	11	4	0	3
Provincial legislator, total	**17**	**15**	**20**	**36**	**3**
Provincial legislator	17	15	20	36	3

General Category and Subcategory[a]	Percentage (Holding an Identifiable Position)				
	All Parties	PJ	UCR	CR National or Provincial	FREPASO
Mayor, total	**3**	**3**	**4**	**3**	**0**
Mayor	3	3	4	3	0
Other municipal level, total	**2**	**2**	**2**	**0**	**3**
Municipal cabinet minister	1	0	1	0	0
Municipal councilor	1	2	1	0	3
Legislative staff, total	**3**	**3**	**4**	**0**	**0**
National legislative staff	2	3	4	0	0
Labor leader, total	**0**	**1**	**0**	**0**	**0**
Labor leader	0.3	1	0	0	0
Judge, total	**0**	**1**	**0**	**0**	**0**
Judge	0.3	1	0	0	0
No information, total former deputies	51	47	54	62	47

Source: Author's compilation.

a. "Total" = total positions for that category.

Of individuals for whom postcongressional career information was available, an absolute majority (51 percent) continued to represent their province in the national legislature, 44 percent as national deputies and 7 percent as senators. FREPASO deputies were especially likely to continue in the Chamber—albeit not always as FREPASO deputies, especially in 2001 and 2003—which is not particularly surprising, given the limited set of career options open to FREPASO legislators at the provincial level.

Over a third of deputies returned to their province to occupy positions in the provincial executive branch (13 percent), provincial legislative branch (17 percent), and at the municipal level (5 percent). The percentage of legislators who returned to their province ranged from a high of 51 percent among members of the center-right national or provincial-parties to a low of 9 percent among members of FREPASO.

In sum, of those legislators for whom information is available, an average of 86 percent continued in a career that was directly linked to the province: either they continued to represent the province in the national congress or they returned to occupy an elective or appointive position in the province. In contrast, only an average of 10 percent of the deputies went on to hold a position in the national executive branch following their tenure in Congress, positions that in some instances were obtained via "representation" of their province—meaning their provincial-party boss obtained the position for them. There was a PJ president in office in all but one of the five roster years examined in this study, 2000, hence it is unsurprising that a higher percentage of PJ members occupied posts in the national executive branch during this period. All the same, even for the PJ the percentage of former deputies holding national executive branch posts, 15 percent, pales by comparison to the percentage holding posts directly linked to their province, 86 percent.

These data coincide with a more detailed prior analysis of the positions held by major-party (PJ and UCR) deputies of the 1991–95 class as of mid-1998, two and a half years following the end of their term in office (Jones 2002; Jones, Saeigh, Spiller, and Tommasi 2002). This analysis highlighted the percentage, 85 percent, of deputies who continued to occupy a partisan or governmental post following their tenure in office and a large majority, 69 percent, holding a post at the provincial level or representing the province in the national congress (44 and 25 percent, respectively). Two percent were deceased and 2 percent were in prison or fugitives from justice.

This section has provided evidence of the province-based nature of Argentine political careers. Focusing on national legislators, with special attention placed on national deputies, I have shown that a lion's share of political careers begin at the provincial level. Furthermore, most politicians continue these political careers at the provincial level, either by continuing to represent their province in Congress or by returning home to occupy a position at the provincial or municipal level.

Candidate Recruitment, Selection, and Congressional Politics

In the United States (as well as in Brazil and Colombia; see Chapters 3 and 5 in this volume), legislators are considered to be independent entrepreneurs, exercising a great deal of control over their political careers (Finocchiaro and Rohde 2002).[20] Cox and McCubbins (1993) highlight how individual representatives delegate power to the party leadership (especially in the U.S. House) to further their own reelection efforts both generally (party reputation) and specifically (perks of office, pork) as well as to influence public policy. This delegation to the party leadership helps the representatives achieve their collective goals.

As was amply detailed above, Argentine legislators do not possess a level of autonomy comparable to that of U.S. legislators, but most Argentine provincial-party bosses do. Hence, in both legislatures delegation occurs. But whereas delegation is by the representatives to the party leadership (House and Senate) in the United States, delegation is by the provincial-party bosses to the party leadership (Chamber and Senate, but also to the president) in Argentina. These bosses delegate in order to further their collective goal of maintaining control of the provincial-party machine and maintaining (governors) or obtaining (bosses in the opposition at the provincial level) control of the governorship. In terms of the framework outlined in Chapter 1, Argentine deputies are *party loyalists*, but given the decentralized recruitment, nomination, and election process in Argentina, they are loyal to the provincial-level party, not to the national-level party.

In Argentina, majority control of the legislature is based on a distributive, ideological, and reputational logic, but the distributive incentives easily dominate ideology and party reputation. The goals of the provincial-party bosses are best served by distributive policy, since their hold on power is based primarily on patronage, pork, and clientelism.

There is considerable variance in the level of control exercised by Argentine provincial-party bosses over the political careers of deputies and other politicians. At one extreme are situations where a single boss, the governor, is unencumbered by any constraints on his or her immediate reelection and faces no significant intraparty opposition. At the other extreme are situations where the party does not control the governorship and no one person exercises dominance over the provincial-party. Most PJ deputies come from provinces with a PJ governor who in all but a few instances was the undisputed party boss. Between 1989 and 2003, a median of 73 percent (69 to 80 percent) of the PJ delegation came from provinces with a PJ governor, whereas a median of only 24 percent (11 to 38 percent) of the UCR delegation came from provinces where the UCR held the governorship; the median was 34 percent for the period 1999–2001. In the PJ an

---

20. This section draws on Jones and Hwang (2005).

overwhelming majority of delegation was by provincial bosses to the party leadership, and individual legislators most commonly followed orders from the provinces. In the UCR, there was a broader mix in the distribution of legislators for whom provincial bosses were delegating power on their behalf and who themselves were the bosses delegating power, although the former easily represented the majority of the UCR delegation.

In countries like the United States, representatives are the crucial actors who delegate power to the party leadership, while in Argentina provincial-party bosses are the key players who engage in this delegation on behalf of their deputies, to the party leadership in the Chamber of Deputies and Senate. But the end effect on the functioning of the legislature is quite similar. Just as U.S. representatives delegate power to the legislative party leadership to achieve collective goals, so too do the Argentine provincial bosses delegate power to the legislative party leadership (and indirectly to the president in the case of the majority party). The majority-party leadership uses its majority status (especially negative and positive agenda control) to dominate the legislative process, excluding legislation it believes may pass despite its objection, as well as implementing legislation it desires.

The normal operating procedure in Argentina is for the majority-party leadership to manage the functioning of the Chamber and Senate, generally in accordance with presidential directives. In equilibrium, the majority-party leadership, not the provincial bosses, exercises the principal influence over legislators' voting behavior. The decisions made by the majority-party leadership, however, are constantly influenced by the preferences of the provincial bosses, generally on topics that directly affect the provinces, in terms both of what they place on the legislative agenda and of the drafting of the legislation they want to pass.

Of course, provincial bosses reserve the right to dissent, via their legislators, and at times they must also be called on by the party leadership to control their legislators. Nevertheless, serious dissent by the provincial bosses is relatively uncommon, owing to the skill of the majority-party leadership and the president in internalizing their preferences. Thus, the leadership is a good agent of the provincial bosses.

Argentine legislators devote relatively little energy to influencing public policy, developing policy expertise, or providing constituent services. Their main operating principle is satisfying the provincial-party boss, who realizes that the principal value of the member of Congress is his "vote" on the floor and to a lesser extent in committee. Consequently, these deputies' modest level of constituency service and personal vote-seeking behavior—for example, particularistic bill introduction—is marginal in scope and impact compared to the amount of resources the provincial bosses obtain in exchange for the ongoing support of "their" legislators (see Jones, Saiegh, Spiller, and Tommasi 2002).

In sum, the province-centric nature of candidate recruitment and selection in Argentina has profound consequences for the functioning of legislative politics in the country. The substantial control exercised by provincial-party bosses over the candidate recruitment and selection process in Argentina endows these bosses with considerable influence over national politics via the votes and participation of "their" national legislators in the Congress. This in turn signifies that in order to implement their policy agenda, Argentine presidents must concentrate their energies on obtaining the support of the provincial-party bosses to a much greater extent than is the case in the other countries examined in this volume, in which presidents tend to focus their energies on obtaining the support of the indvidual legislators (Brazil, Colombia), national party leaders (Chile), or national-faction leaders (Uruguay).[21]

Conclusion

Of the four types of legislative candidates—*party loyalist, constituent servant, group delegate, entrepreneur*—described in Chapter 1, Argentine legislators most closely resemble the type of *party loyalists*, but the loyalty in question is to the provincial-level party, not the national-level party. The Siavelis–Morgenstern framework predicts this type on the basis of their legal variables, but not of their party variables, which would not necessarily predict the emergence of this type of candidate. The central role played by provincial-level party elites in the designation of candidates explains much of the initial deviation from the Siavelis–Morgenstern framework, but when we take into account the provincial-level party's status as the most important organizational unit of Argentine parties, the Siavelis–Morgenstern framework actually applies quite well to the Argentine case for the party variables as well.

Siavelis and Morgenstern present five legal variables and four party variables that together tend to push any country's legislators toward one of the four legislative candidate ideal types (see Chapter 1, Table 1.1). Argentina most closely fits the *party loyalist* type on four of five legal variables (moderate district magnitude, closed lists, reelection permitted, and a strong legislature). Argentina permits reelection and, although the legislature may not be among the strongest in Latin America with respect to its oversight capabilities, it does give individual legislators the ability to extract resources and bring them back to the provinces—even

21. As Langston (Chapter 6, this volume) persuasively demonstrates, Mexico is currently in a state of flux regarding the key principals with whom the president needs to negotiate, and appears to be slowly evolving from a situation most similar, among the countries in this volume, to that found in Chile toward a situation comparable to that found in Argentina, with the state governors increasingly important actors in the country's legislative process.

though the goal is to satisfy party bosses more than constituents. With respect to federalism, Argentina would be predicted to produce *constituent servants*, but once again, the strength of provincial-parties and their ties to the national party makes this variable function a bit differently than hypothesized by Siavelis and Morgenstern, such that provincial-level party politics actually reinforces party loyalty in a different way.

Regarding the party variables, at first glance Argentina—with localized selection, primaries, and patronage-based decisionmaking—appears to fall squarely into the *constituent servant* category on three of four variables; party-controlled campaign financing is the only variable pushing Argentina into the *party loyalist* category. When we consider the crucial importance of the provincial-level parties, though, candidate selection really shifts into the *party loyalist* category. Though decisionmaking is localized in the provinces, it is actually centralized in the provincial-level parties, which have important ties to the national-level executive branch and which attempt to extract resource transfers back to their province. More important is the fact that even though primaries are used, they are *aparato puro*, "pure machine," and candidate choice is really determined by provincial-level party bosses and their supporters. Contrary to superficial appearances, the selectorate is quite narrow. Therefore, on most accounts Argentina falls most closely into the *party loyalist* category, but provincial-level parties are most significant to the process. (Arguably the only departure is on the bureaucratization variable, resulting from the importance of patronage in candidate designation.) This finding also fits quite well with Siavelis and Morgenstern's overarching contention that loyalty to those responsible for a candidate's selection is one of the most important explanations of legislator behavior.

In sum, Argentine legislators are *party loyalists*, but they are provincial-*party loyalists*, not national-*party loyalists*. Their careers are determined in large part by decisions made by provincial-party bosses. They are recruited from positions within the province as provincial cabinet ministers and legislators and municipal mayors, and following their tenure in Congress most commonly they return to an elected or appointive position in their province. Whether or not they are selected to occupy a viable position on the congressional lists is determined in large part by the provincial-party boss or bosses. Similarly, whether or not they are able to extend their tenure in Congress via reelection or election to the other branch also lies more in the hands of the provincial-party bosses than in their own. Finally, once their tenure in Congress is over—just one term in over three quarters of the cases—it is the provincial-party bosses who primarily determine what position, if any, they will occupy upon their return to the province.

In the Argentine Congress, this party loyalty (to the provincial-level party) results in legislators who behave primarily in accordance with the interests of their principals (i.e., the provincial-party bosses). While some modest level of constituency-based work is expected, the principal role of these legislators is to provide the votes on the floor (and in committee) that the provincial-party bosses employ as a form of currency in their constant negotiation with the national executive branch designed to obtain the maximum amount of resource transfers to their province. These resources are utilized, in turn, to achieve the party bosses' paramount goal of maintaining control of the provincial-party machine and maintaining (governors) or obtaining (opposition provincial bosses) control of the provincial administration.

Chapter Three

Political Ambition, Candidate Recruitment, and Legislative Politics in Brazil

DAVID SAMUELS

In this chapter I discuss how legislative recruitment in Brazil contrasts with that of other countries in Latin America. The purpose of this book is not merely to describe the factors associated with candidate recruitment but to hypothesize about the impact candidate recruitment patterns and the different types of candidates they produce have on larger political processes within and across the countries under study. Thus, using the Siavelis–Morgenstern (Chapter 1) variables, I describe the nature of legislative recruitment in Brazil as well as relate the nature of recruitment patterns to a contentious debate about the nature of Brazilian political parties and thus about the general contours of Brazilian politics. I argue that the institutions and processes that Siavelis and Morgenstern point to as relevant independent variables point away from *party loyalist* candidates and toward *entrepreneurial* candidates.

Given this conclusion, I also suggest that the nature of candidate recruitment in Brazil supports the view that Brazil's parties are organizationally weak. Scholars often describe Brazil's parties as chronically underdeveloped. The party system is highly fragmented, and most of the parties are organizationally weak. Mainwaring and Scully (1995, 17) place Brazil's parties near the bottom in terms of institutionalization across Latin America. Electoral volatility is comparatively high (Roberts and Wibbels 1999), and more than one-third of sitting legislators change parties during a term. On the campaign trail, individualism, clientelism, and personalism rather than programmatic appeals dominate. Within the electorate, levels of identification with a party are below the world average (Samuels 2006). Power (2000, 28) summarizes by stating that "Brazil is an extraordinary case of party weakness." This organizational weakness confirms the contentions of the volume's editors that this type of party organization and its inchoate organizational structure contributes to the development of *entrepreneurial* candidates.

Scholars have suggested that the roots of this weakness lie in Brazil's political institutions: its open-list proportional-representation electoral system (which encourages individualism), large district magnitudes (the number of seats allocated to a district) and a low electoral threshold (which encourages fragmentation), rel- atively weak legislature (which, along with other variables, provides little incentive for the building of a career in the legislature), strong federalism (which encourages politicians to favor local and regional appeals rather than national partisan plat- forms), and the fact that nominations are set at the state and not the national level (separating legislators from national partisan concerns and weakening the power of national party leaders over backbenchers). All these variables are identified in the Siavelis–Morgenstern framework as producing *entrepreneurial* candidates.

Given these circumstances, many scholars suggest that Brazil serves as a good example of how institutional design can contribute to governability problems. For example, although Brazil's president is institutionally powerful (Shugart and Carey 1992), Mainwaring (1997, 107) argues that the president's powers "only partially compensate for the fragmentation created by other institutional arrangements." Power (2000, 31) argues that the productivity of Brazil's Congress is "handicapped by the internal weakness of the larger parties," and Ames (2001, 3) concludes that Brazil's political institutions "create a permanent crisis of governability."

However, other scholars have challenged this image of Brazil as a poster child for the ills of institutional fragmentation. The conventional view of Brazil suggests that governability is sometimes problematic because presidential power is insuffi- cient to overcome inertia generated by the fragmented party system and other insti- tutional roadblocks. Yet some scholars suggest that Brazil's presidents *are* successful and that Brazil's parties *are* cohesive. If this counterclaim is true, then institutions external to the legislature are irrelevant for party strength and government per- formance. The revisionist argument suggests that "individualistic behavior does not thrive" in Brazil's legislature (Figueiredo and Limongi 2000a, 152). Party leaders keep backbenchers in line, which gives presidents the ability to achieve their goals. Figueiredo and Limongi go so far as to suggest that Brazil's presidents "are in a posi- tion to demand support for their entire legislative agenda" (2000a, 165) and that legislative organization "neutralizes . . . representatives' incentives to cultivate 'the personal vote'" (2000a, 152).[1]

Figueiredo and Limongi base their claim that Brazilian legislative party lead- ers can control backbenchers on two empirical phenomena: presidential success rates and party cohesion rates on roll-call votes in the lower chamber of Brazil's legislature, the Chamber of Deputies. Yet as Palermo (2000) and others have noted, one cannot infer presidential success, much less presidential strength,

---

1. See, for example, Figueiredo and Limongi (1994, 1996, 1999); Limongi and Figueiredo (1995). For different views within this debate, see Abranches (1988); Nicolau (2000); Amorim Neto and Santos (2003); Amorim Neto, Cox, and McCubbins (2003); Santos (2003); Meneguello (1998); Pereira and Mueller (2000).

simply from roll-call success rates because roll calls do not account for the process that filters potential proposals to actual proposals that are put to a vote. Ames also analyzed important presidential proposals in Brazil and revealed that many were dead on arrival at Brazil's Congress. In contrast to Figueiredo and Limongi, he thus concluded that Brazil's presidents face "constant, crippling difficulties in moving their agenda through the legislature" (Ames 2001, 222). (Resolving this particular point in the debate hinges on identifying the extent to which presidential proposals are modified both before and after submission, which no scholar has yet done systematically.)

Scholars have also noted that party cohesion scores (in any country) reflect nothing about party leaders' ability to enforce discipline (Krehbiel 2000; Palermo 2000, 539; Power 2000, 24; Ames 2001, 188). That is, parties might exhibit high cohesion because their members share ideological beliefs or because their constituencies share similar characteristics. Cohesion may also be high because the president strategically shapes proposals so that allied deputies will support the proposals without debate (Amorim Neto and Tafner 2002). If this is the case, then Rice cohesion scores indicate nothing about party leaders' capacity to enforce discipline, and thus nothing at all about the strength or weakness of party organization.

I do not dispute the power of Brazil's president to influence the legislative agenda. However, this is a far cry from concluding that the president can get whatever he wants and that legislative party organization neutralizes the incentives of Brazil's other political institutions. In this chapter I relate candidate recruitment patterns to a key aspect of the core necessary condition of the strong-parties hypothesis: Figueiredo and Limongi's (2000a) claim that party leaders can enforce discipline because they control resources that legislators "need for their political survival" (165). If party leaders employ available resources as "carrots and sticks" to keep backbenchers in line, this claim gains support. If we find evidence to the contrary, then we support the conventional wisdom.

To evaluate this point I explore the relationship between political ambition, candidate recruitment, and legislative party organization in Brazil. Given the nature of political ambition and the relevant variables Siavelis and Morgenstern point to in terms of candidate recruitment, I ask whether we should expect strong legislative parties. I conclude that we should not, because Brazilian party leaders control few resources and individual politicians therefore show little loyalty to party elites and develop *entrepreneurial* careers. Anyone reading this volume will be struck by the differences between Brazil's *entrepreneurial* candidates and the nature of candidate recruitment in other countries. If such differences are meaningless, then this book has little use. I argue that such differences do make a difference for broader political processes, and therefore conclude that the revisionist hypothesis is misguided. The nature of political ambition and of candidate recruitment in Brazil suggests comparatively weak legislative parties. Our understanding of Brazilian politics and of comparative legislative politics hinges on debates such as these.

Legislative Recruitment, Political Ambition, and Legislative Party Organization

Legislative parties are endogenous creations of ambitious politicians who work together to solve some sort of collective-action problem. Legislative party structure is therefore a function of the nature of politicians' ambition, which itself is shaped by politicians' particular career goals and the factors that shape their success or failure in achieving those goals (Schlesinger 1966, 1991; Rohde 1991; Cox and McCubbins 1993; Epstein et al. 1997; on the relationship between political ambition and legislative parties in Brazil, see Samuels 2003). In order to understand the nature of party organization and parties' influence over the legislative process, we must therefore explore two questions: the nature of political careers in Brazil and the degree to which career success depends on party elites' control over resources that politicians consider valuable. In other words, to what extent are candidates *party loyalists* or *entrepreneurs*—or some other type? Do leaders control access to the ballot? Do they control access to campaign finance? Do they control other resources that backbenchers consider valuable?

A general way to think about the nature of party influence follows.[2] We can generate a simple fourfold classification of the relationship between political careers, party elites' relative influence, and legislative party strength by dichotomizing the degree of legislative careerism and party leaders' control over political careers into "high" and "low." Figure 3.1 provides the four idealized type outcomes. This scheme holds a great deal constant and assumes that career preferences are exogenously defined, which is reasonable for the exercise at hand, that is, to gain a "snapshot" view of political dynamics.

Follow the "high" careerism branch first. When legislative careerism is relatively high and when party leaders control legislators' careers, then legislative parties will be relatively strong (for example, Japan, Chile). In contrast, when legislative careerism is high but parties offer comparatively fewer payoffs for career-minded incumbents, legislative parties will be relatively weaker and deputies will institutionalize a decentralized system (for example, the U.S. House of Representatives). (These classifications are not fixed in stone but can change over time.) Now let us move to the "low" careerism path. When legislative

2. This discussion derives a great deal from Polsby (1968); Polsby, Gallagher, and Rundquist (1969); Price (1971, 1975, 1977); and especially Epstein et al. (1997).

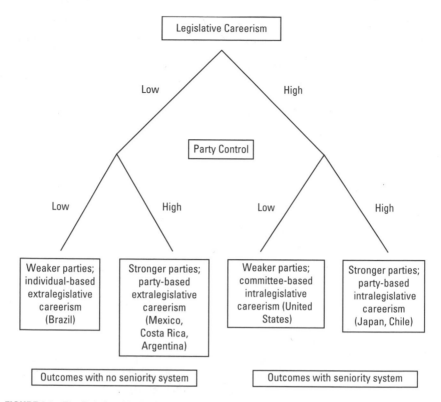

FIGURE 3.1   The Relationship Between Careerism, Party Control, and Legislative Party Strength.

careerism is relatively low but party leaders still control legislators' careers, then legislative parties will be relatively strong.

In contrast, when legislative careerism is relatively low *and* national party leaders do not control legislators' careers, then legislative parties will be relatively weak. What evidence supports my placement of Brazil in Figure 3.1 as a case of comparatively low legislative careerism and comparatively weak parties? To assess legislative party strength, we need to determine the extent to which party leaders control access to the legislature, as well as the more general contours of political careerism in Brazil.

Legislative Recruitment in Brazil

I will first describe the variables that assess the degree to which party leaders control access to the legislature. Morgenstern and Siavelis provide a useful way to classify ideal types of legislative candidates. In Brazil, the variables clearly point away from the *party loyalist* type and toward the *entrepreneurial* type, that is, the most individualist. Both the "legal" and the "party" variables lead to this conclusion.

Brazil's election laws allow for highly individualistic campaigns (see, for example, Mainwaring 1999; Ames 2001), as opposed to a party-coordinated effort. Brazil uses a version of open-list proportional representation whereby the states of the Brazilian federation are the electoral constituencies. Brazil has twenty-seven constituencies with district magnitudes ranging from 8 to 70. A total of 513 seats are at stake in congressional elections, which are held every four years. Following Table 1.1 in Chapter 1, Brazil thus has a "high-magnitude/open-list" system, associated with the *entrepreneurial* type, in contrast to Argentina, for example, which has relatively high magnitudes but has a closed-list system. Under this system, citizens can cast one vote for either an individual legislative candidate or for a party label. Most vote for a candidate (Samuels 1999). The "open" list means that candidates' individual vote totals determine their placement on the list; party leaders do not rank candidates. This system thus promotes both intra- and interparty competition: candidates must compete with their listmates as well as with candidates on other lists to obtain votes. Lists receive seats on the basis of how many total votes all candidates on the list receive, and list seats are then distributed to candidates according to their individual vote totals.

Brazilian law bars independent candidacies. All candidates must run on a party list, must be a member of their party for at least one year prior to the election, and must also have lived within their state or constituency for one year prior to the election. These last two requirements might point toward a *constituent servant* classification of candidate type, but both of these rules are inconsequential. Candidates can and do subvert the residency requirement by purchasing property in the state where they wish to run for office. More important, because constituencies are congruent with entire states (and some of Brazil's states are larger than many countries), the residency requirement is never a contentious issue.

The party affiliation requirement also lacks teeth because of the comparative ease with which Brazilian politicians can (and do) change parties. Over 40 percent of sitting legislators change parties during each legislative session (Schmitt 1999; Desposato 2001), and if we exclude the leftist PT (Partido dos Trabalhadores, or Workers' Party) delegation from this calculation (the PT held about 20 percent of the seats in the 2003–06 legislature), more than half of remaining deputies switch parties during a given legislature! This obviously means that party labels and party organizations possess little value for many Brazilian politicians. Still, the party affiliation requirement does have one visible effect: politicians who are considering running for Congress must declare a party affiliation and refrain from party switching for one year prior to the next election.

As suggested in this volume's organizing framework, both federalism and Brazil's comparatively weak legislature help move the country's legislators toward the *entrepreneurial* type. In the Brazilian case, candidates are chosen at the state level. National-party leaders have little influence over the composition of slates of legislative candidates. And in any case, the ease of party switching makes it impossible for national-party leaders to truly exclude a candidate from competing.

The last "legal" variable is whether reelection is permitted and the degree to which it is pursued. Reelection is allowed in Brazil, and up until 2002 all incumbents were even legally guaranteed a spot on the next election's ballot. This rule made party leaders' preferences about individual candidates' careers wholly irrelevant and made Brazilian politicians' career choices perhaps the most individualistic in the world.

The "automatic renomination" rule is no longer in effect, but "party" variables ensure that Brazilian legislative candidates remain largely *entrepreneurial*. Brazil's electoral code (law number 9504, promulgated initially in 1997 and slightly modified several times since) regulates how parties nominate candidates (see articles 7–10, modified on December 15, 2003). Each national party's statute must contain rules for how the party will choose its candidates and for how it will form electoral coalitions. For legislative elections, all of Brazil's parties' statutes provide for a decentralized system of nomination, and self-selection characterizes the composition of party and coalition lists (confirming the assertions of Siavelis and Morgenstern in Chapter 1). The process is decentralized to the constituency level (that is, to the state level), and state-level politics dominates the party conventions at which lists are generated. However, in contrast to other systems, such as Mexico's or Argentina's, neither national- nor state-level party leaders control the nomination process. Instead, individual candidates have substantial leeway to decide whether to run or not, and for which party label. For all parties, self-selection characterizes this decentralized nomination process.

Few party rules exist regarding who may run for Congress beyond the legal requirements of residence in the state and one-year membership in the party. In seven of Brazil's eight largest parties, which together won 86.2 percent of the seats in the 2002 legislative elections (nineteen parties won at least one seat), the party statutes vaguely state something to the effect that "state-level party conventions shall choose candidates for federal deputy."[3] Only the PT (articles 128–31) has a few additional rules. First, the PT requires that all candidates sign a "commitment to the PT's principles." The party also requires anyone who wishes to run for federal deputy to obtain signatures from one of the following: one-third of the members of the state party executive committee; 5 percent of the municipal committees in the state; 1 percent of all party affiliates in the state;

---

3. These regulations are contained in these respective articles in the party statutes: PMDB (Partido do Movimento Democrático Brasileiro or Party of the Brazilian Democratic Movement) (article 77), PFL (Partido da Frente Liberal or Party of the Liberal Front (currently known as Os Democratas or the Democrats) (article 43), PTB (Partido Trabalhista Brasileiro or Brazilian Labor Party) (article 32), PSDB (Partido da Social Democracia Brasileira or Brazilian Social Democratic Party) (article 77), PP (the Partido Progressista or Progressive Party, formerly the Partido Progressista Brasileiro or Brazilian Progressive Party or PPB) (article 27), PL (Partido Liberal or Liberal Party) (article 14) and PDT (Partido Democrático Trabalhista or Democratic Labor Party) (article 41). All of these are available (in Portuguese) on the web at www.pdt.org.br, www.pmdb.org.br, and so on for each statute.

or approval from a state or national "sectoral" meeting. Finally, the PT requires that all people who fit the above qualifications must obtain at least 20 percent of the votes in the state party convention to make the ballot. These rules may encourage PT candidates to have some minimal connection to the "grass roots" and to the state-level party organization, but they are not as restrictive as one might imagine, nor do they give party leaders as a group at any level of the party particular importance in the candidate selection process.

The legal guidelines that determine the number of candidates a party may nominate are somewhat complex. Parties that run candidates alone—not in a coalition—may nominate up to one and a half times the number of seats in the constituency, in states that have more than twenty seats at stake. In constituencies that contain twenty or fewer seats, each party can run up to two times the number of seats. (Nineteen of Brazil's twenty-seven states have twenty or fewer seats at stake in each election, accounting for 197 of the 513 total seats up for grabs). Coalitions of two or more parties can run two times the number of seats in the states with twenty or fewer seats, and two and a half times the number of seats in the states with more than twenty seats.

As for the formation of electoral coalitions, if the party is not running a presidential candidate, the state party convention can choose its coalition partners for legislative elections. If the party is running a presidential candidate, the national coalition holds for all other levels of elections. Prior to 2002, state parties could decide coalition partners, regardless of the national presidential alliance. In any case, coalitions are not necessary to win a seat. A coalition may boost a list's overall vote total, but it does not help any particular candidate.

On the basis of the number of parties and coalitions in each constituency or state, and given the rules of the electoral law, the maximum number of candidates that parties *could* have nominated in 2002 would have been 10,852 (calculated from Tribunal Superior Eleitoral [Superior Electoral Court] 2002). However, parties "only" nominated a total of 4,296 candidates for the 513 slots (Tribunal Superior Eleitoral 2002), meaning that on average a list filled only slightly more than 40 percent of the slots to which it had a right. For example, in São Paulo, Brazil's largest state, a coalition could nominate up to 175 candidates on its list (the state has seventy deputies). However, the largest multiparty list had only 109 candidates. Overall, 253 parties or coalitions of parties ran candidates in Brazil's twenty-seven state constituencies in 2002, but in only three of these cases did the party or coalition nominate the maximum number of candidates.

Because of the nature of Brazil's open-list system, which provides seats to lists according to the total number of votes each list receives, parties and coalitions prefer to have more rather than fewer competitive candidates, unless competitive candidates on one list find themselves competing over the same geographic space. This happens infrequently. More commonly, especially given the comparative ease with which Brazilian politicians can change parties, a party will seek out candidates to join its list. In fact, parties have a relatively strong interest in swallowing a bitter pill and keeping a popular "troublemaker" on the ballot, because the troublemaker can help boost the total number of candidates the party will elect. After the election, candidates who won election with fewer votes than the troublemaker (and who might not have won election without him or her) stay in office, whether or not the troublemaker stays with the party or switches to another party. Thus, prior to the election, parties always desire to aggregate more votes rather than fewer, and thus always favor having more candidates than fewer. Given this, yet given that parties are *not* actually running the maximum number of candidates, we can conclude that the candidate nomination process is wide open and that candidates self-select.

Why do parties generally fail to recruit enough candidates to fill their lists? Perhaps there simply aren't enough people interested enough to devote the time and energy. Another potential reason is the gender quota, which Brazil established in 1995. Initially the quota was set so that at least 25 percent of all candidates must be women, but it was increased in 1997 to 30 percent for the 2002 elections. According to Brazil's open-list rule, women cannot be ranked on the list, except by voters themselves. Thus, a lack of female candidates may be one reason why so few parties fill their lists. The quota is technically 30 percent of the slots on a list, but parties are penalized for ignoring the gender quota only when they nominate the maximum total number of candidates permitted and still do not meet the quota. In 1994, prior to the law, 6.2 percent of all candidates for federal deputy were women. After the law's promulgation, in 1998, this figure jumped to 10.3 percent of all candidates. But in 2002 the improvement in gender balance slowed, and only 11.4 percent of all candidates were women. Were parties to attempt to fill their lists, they would first have to nearly triple the relative number of female candidates on the lists.

No party has come close to filling the "mandated" gender quota, even without filling the list. The PT, which makes great claim to being inclusive, had the highest proportion of women candidates in 2002, but its proportion was only 13.7 percent. By comparison, of Brazil's largest parties—moving from more conservative to less conservative on the conservative-to-liberal spectrum—the PP had the fewest women candidates (5.7 percent), while the PTB had 12.7 percent, the PMDB 10.9 percent, the PFL 9.1 percent, and the PSDB 12.0 percent (figures calculated from Tribunal Superior Eleitoral 2002). Thus, although there is a slight correlation between a party's position on the conservative-to-liberal spectrum and the percentage of its women candidates, the differences are not that substantial, and in any case no party comes near to meeting the quota "requirement." In short, although a gender quota law exists on paper, de facto there is no quota.

After control over ballot access, control over campaign finance is perhaps the second-most important factor determining the type of candidates that emerge in a given country. If party leaders control the money, and if individual candidates require money to win election, then the party controls the candidates. In Brazil, party organizations are publicly funded through a yearly appropriation, but political campaigns are not. Parties provide very little funding to individual candidates for congressional campaigns. Instead, and in great contrast to most countries in the world and all others in Latin America, individual candidates are largely responsible for raising and spending money for their campaigns. There are no effective limits on campaign contributions in Brazil, and campaigns are quite expensive (Samuels 2001a, 2001b). Not surprisingly, the more a candidate raises and spends, the more likely he or she is to win election (Samuels 2001c).

In sum, the most critical variables—decentralized self-nomination and candidate self-financing—provide an overall picture of *entrepreneurial* legislative candidates in Brazil. Only one variable that Siavelis and Morgenstern point to is ambiguous: "reelection norms." Although reelection is permitted and desired by some incumbents, party leaders do not control access to the ballot, as they do elsewhere. Moreover, reelection is almost never the primary long-term career goal of most incumbents. Instead, incumbents exhibit progressive, extralegislative ambition, which I describe in the next section.

Contours of Careerism in Brazil

We now know that legislative recruitment is a fairly open and decentralized process in Brazil, and that national-party leaders do not act as gatekeepers who can determine whether an individual candidate is nominated or wins legislative office. But once in office, to what extent do national-party leaders influence legislators' choices and success or failure? Do incumbent legislators even desire to stay and build a legislative career?

Brazil's electoral and party institutions appear to encourage incumbency and legislative careerism. That is, even though incumbents are no longer automatically renominated, the decentralized and candidate-centric decision rules for running for reelection leave the decision almost entirely up to the individual candidate. Thus, if deputies wanted to, they could seek to develop legislative careers. However, most of them do not want to. Even though many deputies do run for reelection, almost no deputies seek to build long-term legislative careers. Instead, extralegislative ambition dominates deputies' career goals—deputies focus their energies on seeking positions outside the legislature, typically in state or municipal government, even while they are serving within the legislature (Samuels 2003).

With each election, turnover in the Chamber of Deputies hovers around 50 percent. About two-thirds of incumbents tend to run for reelection, and about two-thirds of these win, accounting for the 50 percent turnover. Two-thirds is not one-third, and indeed some might consider two-thirds a relatively high proportion. Yet although far fewer deputies are returned to the legislature in several other countries where reelection is also permitted, the critical difference is that in many of these countries it is party leaders (provincial or national) who decide not only who gets on the ballot but also the placement of candidates on the ballot. Thus, even if deputies in those countries have static ambition, their own preferences are less important than those of party leaders. That is, in other countries the reason turnover is higher is precisely *because* national-party leaders control incumbents' careers. In Brazil, individual candidates make the decision to run or not, and voters ultimately decide candidates' placement on the list, making the "reelection dynamic" more like what we see in the United States.[4]

More important, several factors point to extralegislative ambition and not legislative careerism. First, the average number of years deputies serve is about seven, about half the average tenure in the U.S. House of Representatives. Yet even this "average length of service" is misleading, as is the percentage of incumbents who run for reelection, because even during a legislature almost 40 percent of sitting deputies exhibit extralegislative ambition by taking a leave of absence to serve in local or state government or by running for municipal mayor (Samuels 2003).[5] That is, many deputies do not consider the legislature their primary goal, even after spending considerable resources to get elected—and they often leave the Chamber of Deputies immediately after winning election. Thus, by the time they run for "reelection" four years later, they may have spent little or no time as a legislator per se. This makes the notion of "legislative careerism" as understood by ambition theory nonsensical for these deputies. And finally, in contrast to the United States, where very few retiring members of the House of Representatives continue in state or local politics (Herrick and Nixon 1996), about two-thirds of Brazilian politicians continue their careers at the subnational level after serving in the Chamber of Deputies (Samuels 2003). Indeed, post-Chamber careers are typically far longer than politicians' legislative "careers" in Brazil, even though legislative terms last four years instead of two, as in the United States.

The high rate of turnover and the evidence of extralegislative ambition also suggest that in contrast to the United States or Japan, for example, Brazil's legislature should lack a career ladder as well as norms for working one's way up that ladder. These are two of the most important indicators of an "institutionalized" legislature, which emerges as a function of the degree to which politicians desire to develop an intralegislative career—one where their career ladder is tied to legislative service. This is indeed the case, for there is no institutionalized career

---

4. Brazilian politicians' extralegislative ambition dominates any ambition they might have to advance within the legislature. Reelection is a second-best option for many incumbent deputies. In contrast, in the United States, far more incumbents see reelection as their best opportunity for consolidating political power. Elsewhere (Samuels 2003) I describe these incentives and their consequences in detail.

5. If a deputy takes a leave of absence, a *suplente*, or substitute deputy, takes his or her place until the incumbent desires to return. Many *suplentes* serve for just a few days or weeks.

ladder within the Brazilian legislature. Legislative agenda-setting and decisionmaking power is concentrated among party leaders and in the hands of the members of the Mesa Diretora (literally, directors' table), a kind of rotating legislative board of directors, over which the president of the Chamber of Deputies (akin to Speaker of the U.S. House) presides. However, a deputy who reaches one of these positions cannot maintain his or her position for an entire legislature (or four-year legislative term), because deputies elect new Mesa Diretora members every two years and reelection to the Mesa is prohibited. Moreover, no institutionalized norms govern access to the Mesa Diretora or to party leadership positions (Figueiredo and Limongi 1996, 23–24). For example, first-term deputies often become party leaders, and level of experience does not determine election to the Mesa. As Figueiredo and Limongi themselves noted (24), the norm of rotating party and Mesa leaders highlights the absence of institutionalized norms of career advancement, and they conclude that "there exist few positions of power that would help establish a congressional career" in the Chamber of Deputies (25).

Service on a legislative committee also does little to advance a deputy's career. The foremost reason for this is that Brazil's president dominates the policy process and often employs the "urgency petition," which allows him to pull proposals out of committee whether the committee has finished its work or not. As a result, legislative committees have a "secondary and imprecise role" within the Chamber of Deputies (Figueiredo and Limongi 1996, 25). Reflecting this, the distribution of committee posts is not institutionalized according to experience (Bernardes 1996, 89) nor even technical expertise (Novaes 1994, 134), and deputies frequently change committee assignments within a legislative period (Figueiredo and Limongi 1996; Santos 1999; Pereira and Mueller 2000). The Chamber of Deputies' internal rules also require selecting new committee chairs every year. Obviously this limits the value of a committee presidency for a career-minded deputy. Thus, unlike in the United States, the committee system does not offer rungs on a career ladder for ambitious politicians.

Party leaders do have firm control over committee assignments, but all evidence suggests that deputies do not really care: as previously discussed, the lack of long-term committee assignments reduces their value as career-building resources. Further, research suggests that legislators ascribe little value to such appointments. Not only can less-experienced deputies obtain committee presidencies, but Figueiredo and Limongi (1994, 19) affirm that "older deputies do not even covet those positions" because the place of committees within the hierarchy of power in the Chamber is ill-defined. Finally, Desposato (2001) shows that the threat of losing a "top" committee assignment does not deter party switchers.

Relatively high turnover, a lack of an internal legislative career ladder, and the lack of institutionalized norms for distributing available posts within the legislature takes us down the "low careerism" path in Figure 3.1. Yet the connection among candidate recruitment, legislative careerism, and legislative party strength remains incomplete. In principle, party leaders in Brazil could still control legislators' political careers, as they do in Mexico and Costa Rica, where party leaders control both intra- and extralegislative careers, even though in those countries reelection is prohibited and thus legislative careers are impossible. Yet in Brazil, in substantial contrast to Mexico and Costa Rica, national-party leaders do not control incumbent deputies' postlegislative careers. In both Costa Rica and Mexico, careers have long been made by working one's way up the ladder within the main national parties (Smith 1979; Carey 1996). This practice may be changing in Mexico, as Langston (Chapter 6, this volume) suggests, as federalism gains importance. Other countries, such as Uruguay and Argentina (Jones et al. 2001; Morgenstern 2004; Jones 2002) also exhibit higher turnover than Brazil. But in Argentina, provincial-party bosses play a tremendous role in determining whether incumbents are renominated or not, and whether and how politicians continue their postlegislative careers (see Chapter 2, this volume, by Jones). In Brazil, in contrast, neither national nor subnational leaders exert such direct influence over deputies' career choices (Samuels 2003).

The Impact of Candidate Type on Politics

If we shift our discussion from candidate type as a dependent variable to candidate type as an independent variable, we then can ask "What impact does the *entrepreneurial* candidate type have on Brazilian politics?" Substantial research already exists on the career backgrounds and socioeconomic makeup of Brazil's legislature. An excellent recent survey of this literature was undertaken by Santos (1998), and the most important recent works are by Marenco dos Santos (2000, 2001a, 2001b) and Martins (2002).[6] There is therefore little need to go into detail about the background of Brazilian legislators. Marenco dos Santos concludes that Brazil's legislature currently manifests slightly greater diversity in terms of deputies' professional backgrounds than it has in the past, with a decline in the number of "professional politicians" and an increase in the number of businessmen and professionals who enter politics somewhat later in life. This is another indicator of the absence of conventional long-term party-oriented careers in Brazil (Marenco dos Santos 2000, 104–5).

However, this relatively small change has had no apparent impact on political outcomes. Brazil is still characterized by seemingly contradictory features: a relatively

---

6. Good work on this subject can also be found in the political anthropology tradition (see, for example, Coradini 2001).

high level of circulation into and out of the legislature (over 50 percent with each election) but relatively little change in the social composition of the legislature itself, which continues to be dominated by members of Brazil's economic and social elites (Marenco dos Santos 2000, 235; see also Rodrigues 2002). This elite also remains largely male: neither the substantial transformation of women's role in Brazilian society nor the quota law has greatly increased the number of women representatives: from 6.0 percent in 1990 to 8.2 percent in 2002, below both the world and regional averages (Tribunal Superior Eleitoral 2002).

It is important to note that the recent growth of the PT (Workers' Party) has not substantially altered this profile of Brazilian legislators as largely elite. Despite massive social change in Brazil over recent decades, including industrialization, modernization, urbanization, and a concurrent rural exodus, and despite the rise of the PT, progressives still make up less than 20 percent of legislative deputies. Brazil therefore remains characterized, as it has been for decades, by a reformist executive and a conservative legislature (Furtado 1971). Brazil's electoral system and nomination procedures have remained constant over all these years. I do not mean to associate the social composition of the legislature with the legal and partisan context, because there is no theoretical reason to expect that substantial differences in social composition should follow from the institutional rules for candidate selection. Legislators are nearly always and everywhere elites of one kind or another, with the notable exceptions to the rule that we all can think of.

Political institutions may have little impact on the social composition of the legislature, but they have a stronger effect on the degree to which party leaders control their delegations. If party leaders do not control access to the pathways to power, and control few resources once politicians are treading that path, we have little reason to believe that Brazilian party leaders are particularly powerful. Figueiredo and Limongi acknowledge that leaders do not control ballot access (these authors do not discuss campaign finance), but they still suggest that "backbenchers who do not follow the party line may have their share of patronage denied" (165) and thus conclude that legislative party leaders possess substantial power.

Yet no scholar has demonstrated that legislative party leaders actually control access to patronage. If it were obvious that party leaders did have such power, we would have better reason to believe that they more generally dominate individual politicians' careers. However, party leaders do not control the primary source of patronage funds, the pork-barrel amendments to Brazil's yearly budget. In general, Congress as a whole has very little influence over the budget: the president prepares the yearly proposal without party input. Congress has a chance to amend the proposal, but the president possesses a line-item veto that permits him to ignore Congress' revisions.

If parties were important to the budget process, we might suppose that they would submit pork-barrel amendments themselves. However, parties themselves do not submit pork-barrel amendments to the budget. Instead, the pork-barrel process serves deputies' individual interests (Ames 2001), as well as the interests of geographically defined *multiparty* groups of deputies, primarily state delegations (Samuels 2003). Highlighting state delegations' importance, Figueiredo and Limongi themselves (2000b, 9) note that "the data show clearly that the amendments presented by state caucuses are now the most important way Congress members influence the budget." Of course, national-party leaders do not control the multiparty state delegations, which are more influenced by state governors' demands and deputies' individual interests.

Party leaders do not control the submission, approval, or funding of pork-barrel budget amendments. Ultimately, the president, not party leaders, has final word on which amendments are funded. This means that neither individual legislators nor party leaders can trade votes for greater shares of pork at the proposal or approval stage of the budget process (Figueiredo and Limongi 2000b). The only opportunity for horse-trading occurs at the execution stage of the budget, which the president controls. Budget amendments are not released to parties, and their release is not celebrated as a partisan event. Rather, they are released to localities—municipalities, states, and even regions—and thus local and state politicians, often in multiparty groups, scramble to take political credit.

In short, like the broader organization of the legislature, politicians have not designed the pork-barreling process in Brazil with parties in mind. The pork-barreling process instead is a function of deputies' individualistic desire to claim credit (Ames 2001) and their need to develop state-level networks to advance their careers (Samuels 2003). This reflects the incentives of deputies' careerist motivations, and also reflects the *entrepreneurial* nature of candidate recruitment: national party organizations are relatively unimportant, but a personal vote base and state-based clientelist connections are key. Brazilian legislators engage in largely individualistic or state-based pork-barreling efforts; an organized, partisan dynamic does not characterize these efforts, and national political parties have never controlled resource distribution, as they have in other countries.

Conclusion

In most political systems, national- or subnational-party leaders exert some degree of control over one or more of the following: nomination to legislative office, distribution of campaign finance, pork-barrel patronage, and postlegislative career advancement. Yet Brazilian party leaders do not control any of these levers over deputies' careers. Consequently, legislative party leaders' influence should be comparatively low in Brazil, because leaders cannot brandish these sticks at recalcitrant deputies. "Vote whipping" and other tools to enforce discipline are only effective when threats by the leadership to withhold valuable resources are credible. Such threats lack credibility in Brazil. Moreover, time horizons are short for both leaders and backbenchers and backbenchers can easily change parties when threatened. When time horizons are short and leaders control few resources, both leaders and backbenchers know that the consequences of defection are going to be minimal (Cox and McCubbins 1993). In short, most of the resources that party leaders use to discipline members are either not available for Brazilian party leaders or not highly valued by deputies.

Despite my argument favoring the weak-parties interpretation, I acknowledge that Brazil is a moving target. The current democratic regime emerged only in 1985, and only three presidents have been directly elected since then. Accepting either the conventional wisdom or the revisionist view of Brazil is in some ways comparable to attempting to generalize about the U.S. party system by studying the U.S. Congress up through the Jefferson administration. We should be willing to adapt and change our views as Brazilian democracy evolves.

Chapter Four

Legislative Candidate Selection in Chile

PATRICIO NAVIA

Since the return of democratic politics two important political coalitions have dominated Chilean politics, the center-left Concertación (Coalition) and the conservative Alianza por Chile (Alliance for Chile). In this chapter I discuss how the Concertación and the Alianza selected their candidates for legislative elections between 1989 and 2001. The parties that make up the Concertación are the Christian Democratic Party (Partido Demócrata Cristiano, or PDC), the Socialist Party (Partido Socialista, or PS), the Party for Democracy (Partido por la Democracia, or PPD), and the Radical Social Democratic Party (Partido Radical Social Demócrata, or PRSD). The Alianza's members are National Renewal (Renovación Nacional, or RN) and the Independent Democratic Union (Union Demócrata Independiente, or UDI).

Party elites in Chile exercise effective veto power in the candidate selection process, but they do not fully control it. Negotiations between parties within each political coalition give party elites additional power to block aspirants from other parties and promote candidacies from their own. Often the preferences of political parties with respect to candidate selection are trumped in the interests of coalition unity. In the cases where internal pro-democracy reforms have resulted in closed or semiopen primaries to select the candidates, party elites have retained power to overrule primary results. So far, though open primaries have been occasionally used to select legislative candidates at the party level, the results can be overruled when parties engage in the process of negotiations with coalition partners, reflecting the strong influence of party elites. For all of these reasons, Chilean legislators fit firmly into the category of *party loyalists* and the Chilean case provides substantial support for the guiding theoretical suppositions of this volume (see Chapter 1). However, despite being the quintessential *party loyalists*, the diffusion of pre-electoral polls, fierce competition that exists between coalition partners, and small district magnitudes have forced parties to pay more and more attention to the personal characteristics and electability of potential Chilean legislative candidates.

After discussing electoral results for the period, I analyze candidate recruitment and selection as a dependent variable. I first explore the legal variables that shape the electoral process for legislative elections and then analyze their interaction with party variables. Next, I discuss the candidate type as an independent variable, exploring how it affects legislative behavior and primarily the current dynamics of executive–legislative relations that have been so central to the success of Concertación governments. I conclude by highlighting that a combination of political tradition and institutional incentives has contributed to make *party loyalists* Chile's primary type of legislator, whose genesis and behavior largely conform to Siavelis and Morgenstern's expectations described in Chapter 1.

The Electoral Results

Chile's national Congress has two chambers, the Chamber of Deputies and the Senate. The Concertación has won all legislative elections between 1989 and 2001 (see Table 4.1), but overall, it gradually lost votes and seats during this period. After a high of 55.4 percent of the votes and seventy seats in the Chamber of Deputies in 1993, the Concertación only managed to obtain 47.9 percent of the votes and sixty-two seats in 2001. The conservative Alianza increased its share of votes and seats during this period. Despite these trends, there has been more continuity than change in Chamber of Deputies elections over this four-election, twelve-year period.

Table 4.2 shows the results for Senate elections for the same period. A growth of electoral support for the left-wing Concertación parties made up for the loss in electoral strength experienced by the PDC. On the right, the Alianza increased its vote share from 34.9 percent in 1989 to 44 percent in 2001. Overall, the Concertación has always won more votes than the Alianza.

In 2001, because it was unlikely that the Concertación could clinch both seats in any district (because of the unique features of Chile's legislative electoral system, which are explained in a later section), the Alianza sought to avoid intracoalition competition. To do so, in seven of the nine Senate districts, that coalition presented only one candidate (or two candidates from the same party, rather than presenting one from each major party). As a result, the Concertación increased its share of votes because it had more candidates but not its share of seats. Although the government coalition, the Concertación, obtained 47.9 percent of the vote in the Chamber of Deputies election, its share of the vote in the Senate election was 51.3 percent.

The Alianza consistently obtained a higher share of seats than its share of votes (see Tables 4.1 and 4.2). Although the Concertación also benefited from obtaining

Table 4.1 Chilean Chamber of Deputies Elections, Percentage of Votes and Number of Seats: 1989–2001

Party	1989		1993		1997		2001	
	Percentage of Votes	Number of Seats	Percentage of Votes	Number of Seats	Percentage of Votes	Number of Seats	Percentage of Votes	Number of Seats
PDC	26.0	38	27.1	37	23.0	38	18.9	23
PPD	11.5	16	11.8	15	3.3	16	12.7	20
PS	—	—	11.9	15	11.1	11	10.0	10
PRSD	3.9	5	3.8	2	12.6	4	4.1	6
Others	10.1	10	0.8	1	0.5	1	2.2	3
Concertación total	51.5	69	55.4	70	50.5	69	47.9	62
RN	18.3	29	16.3	29	16.8	23	13.8	18
UDI	9.8	11	12.1	15	14.5	17	25.2	31
Others	6.1	8	8.3	6	5.0	7	5.3	8
Alianza total	34.2	48	36.7	50	36.3	47	44.3	57
Others	14.3	3	7.9	—	13.2	4	7.8	1
Total	100	120	100	120	100	120	100	120

Source: Author's calculations, based on data from http://www.elecciones.gov.cl.

TABLE 4.2 Chilean Senate Elections, Percentage of Votes and Number of Seats: 1989–2001

Party	1989 Percentage of Votes	1989 Number of Seats	1993 Percentage of Votes	1993 Number of Seats	1997 Percentage of Votes	1997 Number of Seats	2001 Percentage of Votes	2001 Number of Seats
PDC	32.2	13	20.2	4	29.2	10	22.8	2
PPD	12.1	4	14.7	2	14.6	1	12.7	3
PS	—	—	12.7	3	4.3	—	14.7	4
PRSD	2.2	2	6.4	—	1.8	—	1.1	—
Others	8.1	3	1.5	—	—	—	—	—
Concertación total	54.6	22	55.5	9	49.9	11	51.3	9
RN	10.8	5	14.9	5	14.9	2	19.7	4
UDI	5.1	2	10.2	2	17.2	3	15.2	3
Others	19	9	12.2	2	4.5	4	9.1	2
Alianza total	34.9	16	37.3	9	36.6	9	44.0	9
Others	10.5	0	7.2	—	—	—	4.7	—
Total	100	38	100	18	100	20	100	18

Source: Author's calculations, based on data from http://www.elecciones.gov.cl.

a higher share of seats than votes, the Alianza benefited more, successfully preventing the Concertación from transforming its electoral superiority into a safe commanding majority of seats between 1993 and 2001, particularly in the Senate.[1]

Candidate Selection as a Dependent Variable

Legal Variables

There are a number of legal variables that affect the candidate selection process and shape the strategies of candidates, parties, and coalitions. These variables include those set out in Chapter 1 (district magnitude, list type, reelection rules, geographic organization, and legislative power), each of which is analyzed separately here. They all contribute to making *party loyalists* the most common candidate type, in some ways following the ideal typical *party loyalist* path set out by Siavelis and Morgenstern in Chapter 1, and at times diverging slightly. However, this analysis confirms the major thrust of their framework in that all of the variables analyzed tend to push the power of recruitment and selection into the hands of elites, reinforcing candidate loyalty to them. In addition, the exigencies of coalition formation and maintenance push Chilean legislators even more toward the *party loyalist* type, as I explore in detail later.

Chile uses an open-list proportional-representation system for legislative elections, commonly referred to as the binomial system. Senators are elected for staggered and renewable eight-year terms and deputies are elected for renewable four-year terms. Two legislators are elected in each of the nineteen Senate districts and sixty Chamber of Deputies districts using the d'Hondt seat-allocation method. Seats are allocated first to parties, then, within parties or coalitions, seats are allocated to candidates according to the candidates' individual vote share.

The system, which was imposed by the Pinochet government, was created with two objectives in mind: to limit the number of political parties that had existed under Chile's historic PR (proportional representation) system and to maximize the number of seats that conservative parties could obtain, given their minority support (Siavelis 1993; Siavelis and Valenzuela 1997; Rabkin 1996; Fuentes 1999; Navia 2003). Numerous studies attest to the fact that although the system did disproportionately benefit the right, it did little to reduce the number of significant parties in Chile, and the multiparty system in existence before 1973 quickly reemerged after 1990 (Siavelis 1997; Montes, Mainwaring, and Ortega 2000; Scully 1995; Valenzuela and Scully 1997).

---

1. In addition, the existence of nonelected senators tilted heavily in favor of the conservative coalition and gave the Alianza a majority control of the Senate between 1990 and 1998 and between 2002 and 2005.

In fact, the binomial system can be best understood as an insurance mechanism against an electoral defeat for conservative parties (Navia 2005). Given the dynamics of the system described, if a party can secure one-third of the votes in a district, that party will get one of the two seats (50 percent) in the district. This system has helped consolidate an electoral duopoly in legislative elections. Since the threshold to secure the first seat is rather high, about one-third of the vote, parties have incentives to form electoral coalitions to pool their votes to secure half of the seats in every district. The Concertación and Alianza have almost uniformly split the two seats in most districts, largely irrespective of their level of electoral support. In fact, the more competitive the election, the more likely it is that the seats will be split between the two coalitions. Thus, the fact that coalitions are almost guaranteed one seat per district creates strong institutional incentives for candidates to be *party loyalists*. They must curry favor to secure their party's endorsement and to make sure that they remain in the game when their parties sit down to negotiate with the coalition. It also gives elites an incentive to intervene in selection, both to ensure the election of their candidates and to secure a good deal from the coalition.

Therefore, even though Siavelis and Morgenstern posit that low-magnitude and open-list systems push politicians toward the *constituent servant* type, the incentives generated by the election system combined with the centralized organizational characteristics of Chile's parties push more toward the *party loyalist* type. This is the case primarily, and in line with the Siavelis–Morgenstern hypothesis, because this combination of legal variables in Chile unexpectedly gives elites more power (and generates more candidate loyalty toward them) than would be the case in another context of party competition.

As noted in the volume's framework, reelection can push toward either *constituent servants* or *party loyalists*, depending on the variables that precede it with regard to list type and magnitude. In Chile, no reelection restrictions exist for incumbent legislators, again reinforcing the tendency toward *party loyalists*, because renomination largely depends on continuing to secure party endorsements. As Table 4.3 shows, a high number of deputies seek reelection. Between 1993 (the first election with incumbents) and 2001, 73.3 percent of the sitting deputies sought reelection. Their success rate was 82.2 percent. Consequently, about 40 percent of all deputies in each legislative period were serving their first term. Thus, though there are no reelection restrictions, the turnover ratio in the Chamber of Deputies is rather high (Carey 2002). Although the moderately high reelection levels could give way to the emergence of *constituent servants*, *group delegates*, and *entrepreneur* candidates, the fact that parties control the nomination process means that all incumbent deputies have to get their party's consent to gain renomination.

TABLE 4.3   Chilean Deputies Seeking and Losing Reelection Bids: 1993–2001

Election Year	Deputies Seeking Reelection		Deputies Losing Reelection Bids	
	Number	Percentage	Number	Percentage
1993	88	73.3	17	19.3
1997	84	70.0	12	14.3
2001	92	76.6	18	19.6
	264	73.3	47	17.8

Source: Author's calculations, based on data from http://www.elecciones.gov.cl.

Chile's unitary political system also yields the centralized form of candidate selection and party organization predicted in this volume's framework. Political life is largely centered in Santiago and consequently Chile's unitary political system tends to reinforce centralized party organization with weak regional or local parties. Some parties have stronger local organizations than others. Even in these cases, however, national party elites often exercise effective veto power over candidate selection in these local party organizations. This framework further encourages the selection of *party loyalists*.

Furthermore, though Chile's Congress is not nearly as formally strong as some other legislatures on the continent, it wields important informal powers and cannot be counted out of the policy process. Though the president is uniformly considered the most important legislative actor, and members of Congress can extract relatively little pork in comparative regional perspective, the president has actively negotiated with members of both his own coalition and with the opposition in order to extract support for his initiatives. This de facto power has made the Chilean Congress more powerful than it might appear at first glance, and provided a certain power and prestige that goes along with the legislative office.

Thus, in some important ways the Chilean political system provides strong incentives for the emergence of *party loyalists*, sometimes precisely in the way set out in the framework of this volume, and sometimes with slight variations. However, there are additional contextual variables that also push candidates toward the *party loyalist* type. First, one cannot understand the emergence of Chile's *party loyalists* without considering the role of coalition politics, which reinforces the power of party elites, and cements candidate loyalty toward them. Two or more parties can form a nationally binding electoral coalition. For vote-counting and seat-allocation rules, each coalition is treated as one party. Coalitions can also include affiliated independent candidates. Since 1989, two dominant coalitions have emerged, the center-left Concertación and the conservative Alianza por Chile. Since that time they have combined to obtain 98.3 percent of all the seats in the Chamber of Deputies, and an average of 89.2 percent of the vote. Though provisions for coalition formation were originally absent from the electoral law, when the outgoing military dictatorship introduced legislation to establish the binomial electoral system, provisions for coalition formation were also introduced (Allamand 1999a: 125–47, 189–212; 1999b).

Second, although restrictions on independent candidates are somewhat lax, independents have largely failed to win legislative seats. To get their names on the ballot, independents must collect enough signatures to pass a threshold set at 0.5 percent of the votes cast in the corresponding district in the previous election. Independent candidates must have had no party affiliation for at least two months before the registration deadline. In addition, the deadline to register a coalition slate or an independent candidacy for the legislature is 150 days before the election. Such a long registration deadline makes it harder for independents to get their names on the ballot. But because of their high name recognition, incumbents who are not nominated by their parties might find it easier to run as independents.[2] Yet, if their chances of winning a seat are high, it is likely that they will have already been co-opted by a party in the first place, because carrying a party label makes it much easier to win and such a candidate will be an asset to a party.

The incentives to form coalitions create additional pressures on candidates to remain *party loyalists*. Because parties negotiate within their coalitions for the slate of candidates, aspirants who have made careers as *constituent servants*, *group delegates*, or *entrepreneurs* can be easily punished by their parties. Individual parties can readily trade away candidate slates in any given district in exchange for other districts where *party loyalists* are aspirants for their coalition's nomination. Thus, even independent-minded *constituent servants* have incentives to associate with and remain loyal to existing political parties to get their names on the coalition slate.

Party Variables

There has been a good deal of variation in the methods used by Chilean parties to choose legislative candidates. In this section I provide some general background on the nomination process in both coalitions, then provide specific details concerning the evolution of candidate selection methods with respect to the internal dynamics of parties. Each makes reference to the most important party variables set out in the volume's framing chapter, including centralization, inclusiveness, and the different forms of party organization and decisionmaking.

Political parties react to existing electoral rules, strategizing to maximize the number of seats they can get, given their expected electoral support. Parties seek to nominate candidates who will get more votes in a given district than what the party

2. A similar point is tangentially made by Carey and Siavelis (2003).

would otherwise expect. In addition, however, given that the very nature of the coalitions prevents parties from having candidates in all districts, parties seek to identify districts where they can nominate strong candidates and have better chances of transforming those votes into seats. Thus, because parties end up negotiating within their coalitions, strong candidates who are not *party loyalists* can be blocked from running by party elites who cede slates to other parties for any variety of reasons related to coalition maintenance or perceived lack of candidate loyalty.

The parties that make up the two coalitions have experienced different success rates in getting their candidates elected to the Chamber of Deputies (see Table 4.4). To analyze this, I calculate the elected/nominated percentage (the number of elected candidates divided by the total number of candidates). Because of these distortions (differences between the percentage of votes received and the percentages of seats won), the success rates of the Concertación and Alianza coalitions fluctuate around 50 percent. Success rates within coalitions, however, vary from party to party and across elections. For example, in the 2001 election, the PPD did remarkably well by having twenty of its twenty-four candidates elected.

Senate election results also reflect the strategies developed by different political parties to secure safe districts and to get as many of their candidates elected as possible. In the Concertación, there seems to be a zero-sum game. In 1989, the PDC got thirteen of its fifteen Senate candidates elected, but the PPD got only four of its nine. The best PDC performance was in 1997, where that party got its ten candidates elected in each of the ten Senate districts where it ran. Altogether, the other Concertación parties did rather poorly, winning only one seat, despite having candidates in all ten Senate districts. In 2001 the opposite was the case. The PDC only got two of its nine candidates elected in the nine Senate districts up for election.

There is usually a fierce competition among Concertación Senate candidates. That competition is partially moderated in Chamber of Deputies races, where sitting deputies can successfully prevent many strong contenders from running on Concertación slates. But when it comes to Senate races, the Concertación parties tend to present strong aspirants willing to compete for the single seat that the coalition will likely get. Since 1989, there have been only four occasions where the Concertación has clinched two seats in a Senate district, three of those in 1989 and one in 1997. Thus, Concertación parties understand that the seats that go to the PDC are seats lost for the PS-PPD and PRSD, and vice versa. Incumbency also constitutes a strong advantage in the Senate. Most incumbents have chosen to seek reelection, but naturally, as incumbent senators age, the number of open seats increases. In 2001, seven of the nine (77.8 percent) incumbent Concertación senators ran for reelection, and six (85.7 percent) won. In 1997, seven out of ten (70 percent) incumbents ran for reelection, with six succeeding (85.7 percent). However, the success rate of incumbents has not deterred challengers from other Concertación parties.

TABLE 4.4 Chilean Chamber of Deputies Elections, Number of Candidates and Number Elected: 1989–2001

	1989		1993		1997		2001	
Party	Number of Candidates	Percentage of Elected	Number of Candidates	Percentage of Elected	Number of Candidates	Percentage of Elected	Number of Candidates	Percentage of Elected
PDC	45	84.4	48	77.1	55	69.1	54	42.6
PPD	25	64.0	25	60.0	29	55.2	24	83.3
PS	—	—	28	53.6	26	42.3	21	47.6
PRSD	16	31.3	15	13.3	8	50.0	14	42.9
Others	30	33.3	4	25.0	2	50.0	7	42.9
Concertación total	116	59.5	120	58.3	120	57.5	120	51.7
RN	66	43.9	41	70.1	52	44.2	45	40.0
UDI	30	36.7	29	51.7	47	36.2	54	57.4
Others	23	34.8	50	12.0	20	35.0	20	40.0
Alianza total	119	40.3	120	41.7	119	39.5	119	47.9
Others	184	1.6	144	—	203	2.0	142	0.7
Total	419	28.6	384	31.3	442	27.1	381	31.5

Source: Author's calculations, based on data from http://www.elecciones.gov.cl.

The Alianza has employed different strategies from year to year in the Senate candidate selection process. In 1989, RN had fifteen Senate candidates. The UDI had only three and the other twenty candidates were conservative independents. The strong presence of independents continued in 1993, when eight of the eighteen Alianza Senate candidates were independent. But that year their success rate was dismal: only one of the eight independent conservative candidates won a seat. RN got five of its six candidates elected. In 1993, as in 1989, the UDI only succeeded in electing two Senate candidates. Because it was initially focused on increasing its legislative presence in the Chamber of Deputies, the UDI did not focus on Senate elections until 1997. That year, the UDI succeed in electing three of its five Senate candidates. In addition, two independents who were elected joined the UDI in 1998. RN's performance in 1997 was unsatisfactory. Only two of eight candidates won Senate seats. In 2001, as discussed earlier, the negotiations between the UDI and RN allowed for the two parties to exclude independents and divide the nine available districts in the following manner: four districts for RN candidates, three districts for UDI candidates, and two Senate districts with competition between RN and UDI candidates (in the end, those two districts were equally split by RN and UDI winners).

Both in the Concertación and the Alianza, parties punish non-*party loyalists*. Even in cases where aspirants emerge through cultivating a profile of *constituent servants*, *entrepreneurs*, or *group delegates*, party loyalty is still required by political parties to nominate those candidates and defend their bid before the multiparty coalitions. Because parties negotiate their coalition slate of candidates with other coalition partners, party elites can punish candidates who are not *party loyalists* by ceding those districts to other parties in the intracoalition bargaining.

Candidate Selection in the Concertación

Because the electoral system allows only two candidates per coalition in each district, and makes it difficult for coalitions to win more than one seat in every district, party elites have a lot of power to determine which aspirants actually make it onto the coalition slate of candidates. The dynamic negotiation process can be explained succinctly. There are sixty districts where each party can have at most one candidate per district.[3] The PDC has exercised a leading role in the Concertación, with two of the four presidents so far coming from the PDC. Because the PDC will likely present candidates in most districts, the real strategizing occurs among the other Concertación parties.

Siavelis (2002, 424) has explained how the Concertación initially solved the problem of assigning districts to its different members by the formation of two subpacts: one a grouping of parties led by the PDC and the other led by the PS-PPD. The other Concertación parties, which eventually merged into the PRSD after 1993, could bargain with either subpact to maximize the number of

---

3. Only once has that principle been violated, when in 1989 two PDC candidates ran in District 34.

districts where it could field candidates. Because Siavelis (2002) looked primarily at the 1993 and 1997 elections, he tended to treat the PS and PPD interchangeably as one party. Post-1997 political developments have led the PS and PPD to seek distinct identities. They should no longer be treated as two wings of the same party. I discuss in more detail later how each Concertación party has strategized to maximize the number of districts where it can place candidates on Concertación ballots and the number of candidates that actually were elected. Overall, whereas the PDC did fairly well in the first years of this democratic period (84.4 percent of its candidates were elected in 1989 and 77.1 percent in 1993), the PPD did astonishingly well in 2001.

Also, the number of candidate slates that each Concertación party was assigned remained fairly constant from 1993 to 2001 (see Tables 4.4 and 4.5). Again, 1989 is not a good year to evaluate, since the PS was not legally established and many PS members ran as PPD candidates or as independents on the Concertación ticket. The relative weight of independent candidates within the Concertación slate has diminished. But that is as much a reflection of the ban on the PS that was lifted only in mid-1989 as evidence of the consolidation of the four-party nature of the Concertación coalition. Yet, the informal agreement within the Concertación relies on the assumption that there are two subpacts, one composed of the PDC and the other of the PS-PPD. No PPD candidate has faced a PS candidate in any of the sixty districts since 1993. Every time that possibility has arisen, one of the two parties has vehemently opposed it.

Because neither subpact has candidates in all sixty districts (since PRSD candidates must be accommodated), the subpacts negotiate which districts each subpact will keep and which districts will go to the PRSD. In 2001, the PDC secured fifty-four districts, but in additional districts the independent candidates that ran on the PDC subpact were PDC sympathizers.[4] Thus, there were fifty-six districts with PDC candidates in 2001 (93 percent). Logically, there is less strategizing in the PDC on which districts to select than there is in the PS, PPD, and PRSD.

The PPD, PS and PRSD, however, bargained intensively to divide the remaining Concertación slates. From a high of seventy-five available slots (those not taken by PDC candidates) in 1989 to a low of sixty-four in 2001, the other Concertación parties have to identify districts where they stand a good chance of getting more votes than the PDC candidates. Although that strategizing was constrained by the close links that existed between the PPD and PS in 1989 and 1993, much of it occurred within the PS and PPD as the two parties negotiated over which districts each party would keep for its candidates in 1997 and 2001.

The dynamism of this process requires that additional considerations be taken into account. First, all Concertación deputies who seek reelection are almost

---

4. This was the case of Jorge Canals in District 26 and Alejandra Sepúlveda in District 34.

TABLE 4.5 Chilean Senate Elections, Number of Candidates and Number Elected: 1989–2001

Party	1989		1993		1997		2001	
	Number of Candidates	Percentage of Elected	Number of Candidates	Percentage of Elected	Number of Candidates	Percentage of Elected	Number of Candidates	Percentage of Elected
PDC	15	86.7	6	66.6	10	100.0	9	22.2
PPD	9	44.4	4	50.0	4	25.0	4	100.0
PS	—	—	4	75.0	5	—	3	100.0
PRSD	4	50.0	3	—	1	—	2	0.0
Others	8	37.5	1	—	0	—	—	—
Concertación total	36	61.1	18	50.0	20	55.0	18	50.0
RN	15	33.3	6	83.3	8	25.0	6	66.7
UDI	3	66.6	4	50.0	5	60.0	4	75.0
Others	20	45.0	8	25.0	6	66.7	4	50.0
Alianza total	38	42.1	18	50.0	19	47.4	14	64.3
Others	66	0	19	—	—	—	14	—
Total	110	34.5	55	32.7	66	30.3	46	39.1

Source: Author's calculations, based on data from http://www.elecciones.gov.cl.

automatically guaranteed to keep their districts (Siavelis 2002.) Only rarely has a party lost a district where the incumbent deputy seeks reelection. Whenever that was the case, the deputy lost the seat because the party elite chose not to exercise its "holder's-keeper" right, whereby incumbents choosing to run for reelection could not be challenged by others from within the party. Thus, because approximately 75 percent of deputies seek reelection, the actual number of open slots for PS, PPD, and PRSD is lower than sixty. Out of the thirty-one PS-PPD-PRSD deputies elected in 1997, twenty-six sought reelection in 2001. Among them, twenty-three ran in the same districts where they had been elected in 1997. Three others switched districts, and two of these won reelection to the Chamber in their new districts.

The second concern is the potential running mates that PS-PPD candidates will have on the Concertación ticket. Parties often self-select out of districts where there is a strong incumbent from a different Concertación party or where no strong candidate from the party has expressed the intention to run. Again, the process is dynamic in the sense that potentially strong candidates often choose not to pursue a candidacy if they think that the candidate from the other subpact is too strong. Also, because incumbents have a moderately high reelection rate (more than 80 percent between 1993 and 2001), districts where an incumbent from the other subpact seeks reelection are understandably considered difficult districts. Occasionally incumbents do lose. For example, in 2001, twenty-five incumbent PDC candidates sought reelection, but only seventeen won (68 percent). In general, however, candidates have fewer chances of winning when running together with an incumbent from another party from the same coalition.

To be sure, the Concertación occasionally manages to win two seats in some districts, but it is not evident ahead of time in which districts it will be so successful. In most districts where the Concertación has won both seats, the success results from a high concentration of votes for one candidate. The running mate benefits primarily from the trickle-down effect of the d'Hondt seat-allocation rules. Thus, although there is evidence that in 1989 and 1993 the Concertación did place strong candidates in districts where it had good chances of winning the two seats (Siavelis 2002; Carey and Siavelis 2003), in recent years, as politics has become more competitive, fewer two-strong candidate slates are being assembled by the Concertación or the Alianza in Chamber of Deputies elections.

Because all parties will have more aspirants than available slots on the ticket, party leaders can easily punish aspirants who are not *party loyalists* even when they have a good chance of getting elected. True, in order to become strong candidates, aspirants often need to build their bids as *constituent servants*. They are more likely to be nominated by their party if they can show that they are strong candidates in their districts—and they often build personal strength by serving their constituents, usually from government-appointed positions. This is likely an effect confirming Siavelis and Morgenstern's contention that low-magnitude closed-list systems tend to push toward the formation of *constituent servants*. But if being a *constituent servant* helps win a party nomination, party loyalty is what ultimately determines whether the parties will defend that nomination before their coalition partners when they are bargaining over the Concertación slate of candidates. In the next section, I discuss how each of the Concertación's parties has sought to maximize the number of candidacies it receives in the Concertación's internal bargaining process, and how this process reinforces the power of party elites and facilitates the formation of *party loyalists*.

PDC. In 1989, PDC legislative candidates were selected by provincial committees *(juntas provinciales),* which appointed candidates for each of the sixty Chamber of Deputies districts and to fifteen of the nineteen Senate districts (in the remaining four, the PDC had previously agreed to support the candidate from the PR). In Concertación negotiations, the PDC withdrew candidates from several districts to make room for other Concertación parties. The party made concessions to its coalition partners with the expectation that the popularity of the Concertación presidential candidate, the PDC's Patricio Aylwin, would marginally benefit PDC legislative candidates. Despite the use of provincial committees, elites still exercised ultimate control over selection, either through elite veto power, or because the committees simply ratified de facto elite choices. In the end, the PDC did fairly well, succeeding in electing thirty-eight of its forty-five candidates to the Chamber in 1989.

In 1993 and 1997, the PDC held closed primaries to select candidates in districts where more than one aspirant sought to run. Although most strong challengers were dissuaded from running against an incumbent, some primaries were held to select PDC candidates.[5] Most of those primaries were not highly contested. Tellingly, in a few cases the winner of the closed primaries lost the slot when the PDC agreed to cede that district to other Concertación parties. In 1993 and 1997 the PDC ceded districts to make room for candidates from smaller Concertación parties. In both years, Eduardo Frei (Chile's president from 1994 to 2000) intervened to convince the PDC to give up districts in favor of other Concertación parties' candidates, another testament to elite influence. In part because the PDC had more candidates, the percentage of nominated candidates who were elected decreased in 1993 with respect to 1989. That year, thirty-seven of forty-eight candidates nominated by the PDC won Chamber of Deputies seats. The percentage was still higher for the PDC than for the Concertación as a whole (77.1 versus 58.3 percent). In 1997, the percentage was 69.1 percent, slightly lower than in 1997, but still higher than for the entire Concertación (57.5 percent).

In 2001, the PDC experimented with open primaries to select its candidates, and in most cases incumbents were not challenged. But in Senate District 15, an incumbent, Senator Jorge Lavandero, easily defeated a challenger, Deputy

---

5. For example, that was the case in District 10, where Ignacio Walker won a closed PDC primary in 1997.

Francisco Huenchumilla. In Chamber of Deputies district 24, after the results of the open primaries were challenged, the PDC's National Committee (Junta Nacional) exercised elite veto power and ruled that the incumbent deputy, José Jocelyn-Holt, should be the candidate, despite having lost an open primary. In part because of the overall decline in support for the PDC and the stabilization in the electoral strength of the PS and PPD, the percentage of those elected decreased again in 2001 to 42.6 percent (fifty-four candidates nominated, twenty-three elected), lower than the Concertación yield of 51.7 percent.

Overall, the PDC has fostered a process in which militants rather than elites have a growing influence in selecting candidates. However, as several interviewees suggested, the PDC has suffered from unilaterally promoting more participation in the candidate selection process. As a former party president, Gutenberg Martínez, suggested in an interview, when closed primaries (or open primaries with low turnout) are held, a small organized faction of PDC militants can select an aspirant who lacks skills and appeal beyond party militants. When only one party promotes democratizing candidate selection, other parties can benefit by strategically identifying stronger candidates who can then obtain more votes than the less broadly appealing, yet democratically elected, PDC candidate.

PS. The PS has experimented with different mechanisms to select its candidates. In 1989, the then illegal PS managed to present candidates in two different coalitions, the Concertación and the PAIS. Because the party was undergoing a reunification process as the deadline for candidate registration approached, the selection process was particularly convoluted. Indeed, some PS delegates took advantage of dual party militancy to negotiate slates from within the PPD and promote the names of the candidates that the PS Central Committee had agreed upon. Furthermore, only those candidates proposed to the PPD National Council by the PS central committee were selected as PPD candidates. In addition, the PS directly negotiated with the entire Concertación coalition to place some of its members—who were not formally affiliated with the PPD—as independent candidates on the Concertación ticket. Finally, a few PS members opted to run on the PAIS ticket, with the PS making sure that no other PS or PPD candidate could run in the same district on the Concertación ticket.[6]

By 1993, the PS and PPD had formally separated and the two parties competed against each other in the negotiations within the Concertación. The differences between the PS and PPD were increasingly evident in the 1997 negotiations. That year, Santiago's two senate districts were up for election. Initially, the PPD and PS had agreed to assign one district to each party. Yet the PS, under the leadership of deputy and party president Camilo Escalona, offered to trade five Chamber of Deputies districts initially assigned to the PS in exchange

---

6. I thank Jorge Arrate, former PS general secretary, for explaining this point.

for the PPD Senate slate in Santiago. The PPD immediately agreed. In the end, the gamble did not pay off, as both PS candidates lost against PDC candidates. Even worse, the PS lost four seats in the Chamber of Deputies, dropping from fifteen to eleven.

Between 1993 and 2001, the PS used different mechanisms to select its legislative candidates. These mechanisms have ranged from closed party primaries to selection by the party's Central Committee. At first glance it appears that the local party organization had strong influence in selecting the candidates. When the PS has held primaries, only registered party militants have been allowed to vote. Yet, the primary winners have not always gone on to become candidates in the parliamentary election, either because the party has given up that district in negotiations with other Concertación parties or because the party has overruled the primary results on technicalities. Having a Socialist Party primary does not automatically result in the nomination of the winner by the central socialist party leadership.[7]

Although the party has made efforts to introduce more internal democracy in its selection processes, the ability of local party caudillos to exercise control of the small number of party members often results in the nomination of a candidate that is correctly deemed unelectable by the national party leadership. Yet, the PS has not moved to change its system of candidate selection. Instead, the party has passed resolutions to make the system more accountable to the local party organization and reduce the influence of the PS Central Committee in determining the names of the PS candidates.

PPD. Since 1993, the PPD has formally empowered its Directiva Nacional (National Board) with the power to nominate candidates. However, the way the process has actually worked has varied over the years. In some instances, regional councils have made proposals to the Directiva Nacional and on other occasions there have been closed primaries to select the nominee. This was the case in 1997, when Patricio Hales won the closed PPD primaries in District 19 to become the candidate and then win 31.9 percent of the vote. In some instances, when there is more than one person interested in running in a district, the Directiva Nacional has unilaterally chosen the candidate that it perceives has a better chance of winning.[8] Yet, some informal rules can be identified. The "holder's-keeper" principle applies. Incumbent deputies are almost guaranteed their slots, but the party leadership has also convinced some incumbents to switch districts and use their name recognition to successfully run in a new district. That happened in 2001 in Districts 32 and 14, where the incumbent PPD deputies switched districts and won.

The PPD national leadership takes an active role in recruiting potential candidates and securing good districts for them. It actively recruits potential

---

7. I thank the former Chamber of Deputies candidate Álvaro Elizalde for clarifying this point.
8. I thank the former PPD secretary general René Jofré for clarifying this point.

candidates by offering them districts where they stand a good chance of winning. Oftentimes that means that the PPD will not seek as many districts as possible nor will it go after the most populated districts (where a good electoral performance will carry a greater weight in increasing the overall national vote for the party), but instead it selects those districts that can be matched with an electable candidate. Centralized decisionmaking processes have allowed the PPD leadership to successfully use pre-electoral polls to identify winnable districts and effectively name candidates to them. According to PPD leaders and to leaders from other Concertación parties, the ability of the party leadership to name candidates and to negotiate districts without the pressure from candidates who have won closed party primaries has allowed the PPD to achieve the highest elected/nominated yield among all Concertación parties.

PRSD. Because it is the smallest of the four Concertación parties, the Radical Social Democratic Party strives to maximize two objectives when negotiating for seats with other parties. On the one hand, the PRSD wants to get some deputies elected. On the other, the party needs to get enough votes to pass the 5 percent minimum national vote threshold to maintain its status as a legally registered political party. Since the Radical Party merged with the Social Democratic Party after the 1993 elections (thus forming the Radical Social Democratic Party), that party has sought to negotiate concurrently with the PDC and PS-PPD. In 1997, the PRSD obtained eight slots in eight different districts. In 2001, the PRSD got fourteen slots in fourteen different districts, but in most cases those slots were located in districts where the incumbent PDC deputy was widely expected to win reelection. Surprisingly, two PRSD candidates managed to defeat incumbent PDC deputies and another ran in a district where the Concertación managed to gain both seats.

Candidate Selection in the Alianza

There has been less continuity in candidate selection mechanisms in the Alianza coalition. The RN has consistently lost districts since 1989, and the UDI has gained them over the years. In part this is a result of the fact that Alianza had several independents elected in 1989. Most of those districts are now held by UDI deputies, either because previous independent candidates have formally affiliated with the UDI or the party has picked up new seats. In addition, there were always more districts where there was no Alianza incumbent, since the Concertación has historically been more successful in capturing both seats in a larger number of districts. Given that there were more open seats for the Alianza and that challenging an independent Alianza incumbent did not generate intracoalition conflicts, the UDI could initially grow by competing against non-RN incumbents and by having strong candidates in open districts.

Yet, because it has been much less likely for the Alianza than for the Concertación to win two seats (the Alianza has done so three times, only in the Chamber of Deputies and always in district 23), once there is an Alianza legislator seeking reelection, it is highly unlikely that another Alianza candidate can run successfully in that district. Thus, the overall increase in the UDI's legislative contingent simply reflects the party's ability to successfully identify districts where it has a good possibility of winning a seat. Table 4.4 also shows how the UDI evolved from having candidates in only half of the districts in 1989 to having a well-established national presence in 2001, fielding candidates in fifty-four of the nation's sixty districts.[9]

That dynamic has allowed for the emergence of some non–*party loyalists* as candidates among Alianza parties. Because the Alianza has usually allowed for intracoalition competition in Chamber of Deputies elections, RN has sometimes allowed *entrepreneurial* and *constituent servant* aspirants to try to unseat an incumbent UDI deputy. But because RN has also sought to prevent an overtly open confrontation with UDI in all sixty Chamber of Deputies districts, the number of *entrepreneur* and *constituent servant* candidates that actually makes it to the ballot has remained low. Moreover, *entrepreneurial* candidates that do win have a strong incentive to become *party loyalists* in the Chamber so that the party will protect the candidate from open competition from the other coalition partner in the next election.

The candidate selection process in the Alianza has become simplified over the years. As the UDI has grown and consolidated, independent candidates only run in districts where neither the UDI nor RN have a presence. Negotiations within the Alianza follow a two-step process. First, RN and UDI announce in which districts they will present candidates. In selecting districts they consider whether there are conservative incumbents and whether the Concertación has any chance of getting both seats. Second, they complete their party candidate list with independents that need to be aligned with either party and then sit down at the negotiating table.

UDI. The UDI has developed a very centralized candidate selection process, with an electoral commission that works during nonelection years to identify and prepare potential candidates for districts where there is no UDI legislative representation. Similarly, in districts where the incumbent UDI deputy will likely seek a senate seat, or vacate the seat for whatever reason, the UDI works to identify an attractive new candidate.

According to the UDI General Secretariat, the best rationale to take advantage of the electoral rules is that individual legislative careers are less important than the strength of the party. This is telling testament to the preponderance of *party loyalists* in Chile. Be it because weak incumbents are replaced by more

9. For more on the UDI, see Joignant and Navia (2003).

electable candidates or new recruits are assigned into districts years before the election is to take place, the UDI's electoral commission has successfully centralized the candidate selection process with one objective in mind: to get the highest possible nominated/elected yield so that the number of safe UDI districts will constantly increase.[10] This strategy has taken the UDI from a low of thirty districts in 1989 to a high of fifty-four in 2001.

Of all political parties with legislative representation, the UDI has the most centralized and top-down approach to candidate selection. The party leadership controls the entire process. That party does not promote closed or open primaries to select its legislative candidates, nor does it consider them necessary. Because the party has been so successful in increasing its legislative representation, other parties have underlined the apparently negative effects of promoting bottom-up mechanisms in candidate selection.

RN. RN's method for filling candidate slates in negotiations with the UDI has not formally varied over the years. The Consejo General (National Council) ratifies all candidacies. Yet the informal mechanisms used to agree on the list of names to be presented to the Consejo General have varied markedly over time and across districts. Because RN is a party primarily comprising local leaders with very little ideological homogeneity, the Consejo General is highly respectful of local leadership and incumbents. In some instances, where the party does not have local presence, the Consejo General can centrally appoint candidates. These candidates are assigned the district following a franchising rationale. If the candidate wins, he or she will become the RN leader in the district and will join other local leaders in the Consejo General. If the candidate loses, the party will likely not consolidate a presence in the district unless the candidate, or someone else, is willing do it alone without the visibility and attractiveness that comes with begin a deputy.

In that sense, RN is much more an electoral than an ideological party. RN leaders stay together because the RN banner allows them a party structure that can protect them against the growing hegemonic power of the UDI, but the party does not require them to obey the decisions and agreements reached by the national leadership. Because the party is a loose association of local leaders, party elites are more than willing to give up other districts to the UDI if they can be guaranteed that they will not face strong competition from UDI candidates in their own districts.[11]

Candidate Selection as a Dependent Variable: Summary

Chile's leading political parties use different mechanisms to select their legislative candidates (see Table 4.6). Because those internal mechanisms produce candidates who are in turn subject to intracoalition bargaining to determine the coalition

---

10. I am grateful to Juan Antonio Coloma, UDI's general secretary, for clarifying this point.
11. I thank an RN party leader, who preferred to remain anonymous, for his interview.

TABLE 4.6 Chilean Legislative Candidate Selection Mechanism by Party: 1989–2001

	Party	1989	1993	1997	2001
Concertación	PDC	Provincial juntas	Closed primaries	Closed primaries	Open primaries
	PPD	National Board	National Board	National Board	National Board
	PS	Central committee	Central committee or closed primaries	Central committee or closed primaries	Central committee or closed primaries
Alianza	RN	National Council	National Council	National Council	National Council
	UDI	Party leadership	Party leadership	Party leadership	Party leadership

Source: Author's compilation.

slate, the process is not a clear-cut two-step process. A good deal of strategizing goes on within parties and within coalitions without following clearly defined rules. But at the end of the day, because party leaders bargain with other coalition partners, *party loyalists* are privileged over other candidate types. In fact, other types of candidates are often punished by the parties in the negotiations with other coalition partners.

To be sure, only the PDC has made significant strides in promoting internal democracy in its legislative candidate selection process. Other parties have continued to control the selection mechanism at the national, or in some instances, local level. Yet because the PDC suffered a dramatic erosion in its electoral performance and a corresponding loss of legislative seats, the expansion of democratizing practices to select candidates is not likely to occur in other parties.

Thus, although the adoption of reforms that promote the use of open primaries might be desirable, a unilateral adoption of open primaries by a party might not produce positive results for that party. Moreover, given that the final decision over which parties will have candidates in which districts depends on the intracoalition negotiations, the adoption of open primaries will not automatically result in the nomination of candidates who win their party primaries. Unless primaries are held at the coalition level rather than the party level, the adoption of open or closed primaries will not limit the existing power of party elites to influence the candidate selection process in Chile. If primaries are eventually held at the coalition level, then the presence of *party loyalists* will be significantly hindered, since voters—rather than party elites—will make the decision as to who actually makes it on the ballot.

Finally, Table 4.7 depicts the nature of legislative candidates given the candidate selection process. When the transition to democracy first occurred, there were

TABLE 4.7   Chilean Legislative Candidate Types as a Dependent Variable, in Legislative Elections: 1989–2001

Candidate Type	1989	1993	1997	2001
Party loyalists	Concertación/ Alianza	Concertación/ Alianza	Concertación/ Alianza	Concertación/ Alianza
Constituent servants	Few, Concertación/ Alianza	Few, Concertación/ Alianza	Few, Concertación/ Alianza	Few, Concertación/ Alianza
Delegates	—	—	—	—
Entrepreneurs	Few, Alianza	Few, Alianza	Few, Alianza	Few, Alianza

Source: Author's compilation.

some candidates that could be best described as *delegates* or *entrepreneurs*, but as parties consolidated their strength and coalitions were primarily dominated by a few parties, *party loyalists* emerged as the dominant candidate type.

Although some aspirants build up support in their districts as *entrepreneurs* and *constituent servants*—including some incumbents—the ultimate choice as to who can run on coalition tickets is made by party leaders. Thus, party loyalty, more than any other variable, influences decisively the likelihood of an aspirant actually becoming a candidate. However, an aspirant's ability to cultivate personal support in his or her district might have a significant influence in allowing that candidate to defeat a coalition list partner for the only seat that the coalition is likely to garner in the district.

Party Loyalists: Candidate Type as an Independent Variable

The interaction legislators have with the executive and with their own parties is a variable that itself grows out of institutional design and the way parties respond to it. Because Chile has only had presidents that belong to the Concertación coalition, the dynamics of legislative–executive interactions that we have observed so far might be more the result of internal Concertación dynamics than purely a function of institutional design. Several scholars have highlighted the strong nature of Chile's presidential system (Siavelis 2000; Londregan 2002; Aninat et al. 2004), although Siavelis has appropriately described Chile as a strong presidential system with moderate presidents (2000). Yet, despite their moderation, the strong powers granted to the president by the constitution give the executive an enormous influence over the legislative process. For all practical matters, the president exerts agenda control in the legislature (Aninat et al. 2004). Yet presidents still require the legislature to approve the initiatives they send to Congress. Moreover, given that the legislature has the ability to block and delay—although not radically alter—the executive's legislative initiatives, one should not discount Chilean legislators as irrelevant actors. The legislature's ability to position itself as a veto player that can successfully block and delay the executive's legislative initiatives is what induces the president to use some restraint in exercising the enormous constitutional powers granted to the Chilean executive.

Party Discipline and Executive–Legislative Relations

Because the electoral system for legislative elections can be best described as an insurance mechanism against an electoral defeat, the influence a president can have on the legislature does not depend on the president's electoral or popular approval. The president cannot credibly threaten the legislature to use his or her popularity to significantly influence the future composition of either chamber. Because it is highly likely that a large majority of seats will be equally split between the two large coalitions, the president's popularity will not represent a credible threat to legislators from either the opposition or the government coalition. Instead, the loyalty of coalition legislators to a large extent depends on intracoalition party discipline. Similarly, the president's ability to get opposition legislators to support his legislative initiatives depends on the executive's ability to reach agreements with the opposition party leadership. Or, as it has occasionally been the case with RN legislators, the executive can also negotiate with individual RN legislators who are not likely to be penalized by its decentralized party leadership.

Formally, the legal arrangement in the legislature is such that individual legislators are free to vote as they please on any legislative initiative. Yet some institutional arrangements do promote a certain level of discipline within each chamber. Committee appointments are made by party leaders in each chamber and negotiated with other party leaders. Thus, independents have strong incentives to join existing political party delegations (bancadas) to improve their chances of getting into their desired committees. Thus, the formal rules of committee appointment encourage party discipline and make it easy for party leaders to punish entrepreneurial or constituent servant legislators.

Because the legislature is primarily made up of party loyalists, levels of party voting discipline are high (Alemán and Saiegh 2005). In fact, rather than negotiating directly with legislators, presidents are compelled to negotiate their legislative initiatives directly with national party leaders. After reaching an agreement with a national party leader, the president can almost assuredly bank on support from that party's entire legislative delegation. These patterns of discipline reinforce the party-centered nature of political life in Chile, further reinforcing tendencies toward party loyalists, and inducing them to remain disciplined party legislators, with very positive consequences for executive–legislative relations.

Some of the most important legislative initiatives that have been introduced by the three democratically elected presidents since 1990 have been previously negotiated with the opposition parties' leaders. They have been sent to the Congress after an agreement has been reached—and often signed with much fanfare—with opposition parties' leaders (Navia 2004). True, some other pieces of legislation are not agreed upon with the opposition and are sent directly to the legislature, where they are often modified, blocked, or significantly altered. Yet the three Concertación administrations have continuously sought to negotiate their most important legislative initiatives with opposition party leaders before sending them to the legislature. To some extent, something similar has happened between the executive and Concertación parties. Although Concertación presidents have enjoyed considerable legislative support for their initiatives, they cannot automatically count on the support of their coalition allies. Instead, presidents have had to lobby for the support of their coalition partners. In some instances, the initiatives are handled directly with the legislative delegations from the different parties, but whenever symbolic legislative initiatives are discussed, Chilean presidents have opted to negotiate directly with party leaders, both from their own coalitions and those from the opposition.

In this sense, Chile might be considered the ideal combination in Siavelis and Morgenstern's framework in its marriage of *party loyalist* legislators with *party insider* presidents. When deals are negotiated, presidents can count on these deals being carried out. This contention not only applies within the Concertación. Indeed, the existence of *party loyalists* in the opposition assures that deals will be upheld even when they are negotiated across the aisle.

This seemingly unequivocally advantageous combination is not without its drawbacks, however. If the pattern of cross-alliance negotiations breaks down, *loyalists* will remain *loyalists* in the opposition, and they may yield to centrally dictated instructions to vote against presidents. In this sense, without a dynamic of consensus, *constituent servants* might be the more ideal pairing with *insider* presidents, because presidents can attract the support of some from the opposition who may not be so worried about pleasing party elites (see Chapter 15, this volume, for more discussion of pairings of types of candidates).

In addition, this high level of party discipline often undermines one of the legislature's central roles. Because the core components of most legislative initiatives are agreed upon outside the Chamber of Deputies and Senate, legislators have few incentives to spend time in studying legislative initiatives. What is more, for the true *party loyalist*, loyalty and service to the party take the place of loyalty and service to constituents. Because the ability to legislate is not a central determinant in one's chances to win reelection, legislators often overlook their role as lawmakers. Moreover, because party leaders often negotiate the terms of legislative initiatives with the presidents that send them, *party loyalists* will pay a heavy price if they opt to resist their party's political agreements. On the other hand, the fact that party discipline is a central outcome of the candidate selection process means that party leaders can credibly commit their legislative delegations' support. Naturally, leaders cannot automatically force their parties' legislators to go along with any agreement they reach with the executive. Leaders must also take into account the views of their legislative delegations. Thus, in that sense party loyalty is both an asset and a liability. Party leaders can punish legislators who are not *party loyalists*, but party leaders will lose their leadership positions if they alienate their legislative benches.

Because political parties form electoral coalitions, the nomination process often represents a major challenge for coalition unity. The nomination for the coalition presidential candidate raises tensions within the Concertación and the Alianza coalitions because it is an indivisible good. The Concertación has moved over time toward open primaries for the nomination of its presidential candidate. In 1999, in the first fully open presidential primaries—where all registered voters not formally affiliated with opposition parties could cast ballots—the PS-PPD candidate Ricardo Lagos handily defeated the PDC candidate Andrés Zaldívar. The Alianza has continued to trust party leaders to negotiate over the coalition's presidential candidate. Although some voices within the Alianza have asked for open primaries, that coalition has yet to follow the Concertación in granting its adherents the power to choose presidential candidates (see this volume's Chapter 10, by Altman, for a full analysis).

So far, primaries have not been widely adopted to select legislative candidates, but if the trend set by the Concertación for presidential elections is expanded to include legislative nominations, the strong presence of *party loyalists* will undoubtedly diminish. Consequently, the strength of national parties and the solid level of party discipline that we observe in Chile today might also weaken. Thus, although open primaries might in fact be a desirable step toward more participation, transparency, and democracy, they might have an unintended consequence of diminishing the strength and cohesion of political parties.

Conclusion

The candidate selection process reflects and reinforces the strength of existing political parties in Chile. When analyzed as a dependent variable, the candidate selection process for legislative elections signals how the combination of legal arrangements, such as electoral rules, and their interaction with party and coalition variables makes it difficult for aspirants other than *party loyalists* to become successful candidates for the Senate and Chamber of Deputies. Because parties have actively used the incentives provided by the existing electoral rules, aspirants who are not *party loyalists* are often prevented from becoming candidates and incumbents who do not behave like *party loyalists* are easily punished when they seek to win reelection.

When analyzed as an independent variable, the emergence of Chile's model candidate type, the *party loyalist*, is facilitated by the consolidation of political parties as the central legislative actors in negotiating with the executive. Because legislators are primarily *party loyalists*, party leaders can credibly negotiate on behalf of their legislative delegations with the executive. That has facilitated discipline within the government coalition and it has also made it easier for the executive to broker agreements with the opposition. However, because party leaders can directly negotiate with the executive, the role of the legislature as a lawmaking body has been somewhat undermined. Because legislative candidates are primarily *party loyalists*, the strength of political parties continues to be a central component in Chile's democracy. As parties can successfully punish and reward loyal behavior, legislative candidates remain committed *party loyalists*, thus further strengthening already strong Chilean political parties. What is more, much of this loyalty is cultivated by the pathways that bring Chilean legislative candidates to power.

Appendix: Interviews Conducted by the Author

Partido Demócrata Cristiano

Patricio Aylwin, president, 1990–1994; former party president; senator. Interviewed January 6, 2004, in Santiago.

Alejandro Foxley; party president and senator, 1998–2006. Interviewed January 4, 2004, in Santiago.

Eduardo Frei, president, 1994–2000; party president; senator, 1990–94; lifetime senator. Interviewed January 8, 2004, in Santiago.

Gutenberg Martínez, deputy, 1990–2002; former party secretary general. Interviewed January 13, 2004, in Santiago.

Ignacio Walker Prieto, deputy, 1994–2002; senate candidate in 2001. Interviewed on January 5, 2004, in Santiago.

Partido Socialista

Jorge Arrate, former party president and general secretary; Interviewed January 9, 2004, in Santiago.

Álvaro Elizalde, candidate for deputy, 2001; former Socialist Youth president. Interviewed December 31, 2003, in Santiago.

Partido por la Democracia

René Jofré, chief party negotiator in 2001; party secretary. Interviewed January 8, 2004, in Santiago.

Sergio Bitar, senator, 1994–2002; former party president. Interviewed February 20, 2004, in Santiago.

Renovación Nacional

Andrés Allamand, deputy, 1994–98; senate candidate, 1997; former party president. Interviewed January 15, 2004, in Santiago.

Unión Demócrata Independiente

Juan Coloma, deputy, 1990–2002; senator, 2002-10; party general secretary. Interviewed January 22, 2004, in Santiago.

Chapter Five

Mejor Solo Que Mal Acompañado: Political
Entrepreneurs and List Proliferation in Colombia

ERIKA MORENO AND MARIA ESCOBAR-LEMMON

The Colombian political system has long been characterized as
a laboratory of personalized politics. Although the long-
entrenched two-party system has given way to a more plural setting as of late (see Leal Buitrago and Ladrón de Guevara 1990;
Moreno 2005; Pinzón de Lewin 1987; Pizarro 1997), personal
vote seeking (Cain, Ferejohn, and Fiorina 1987; Carey and
Shugart 1994; Crisp and Ingall 2002) and entrepreneurial behavior remain the norm. As Siavelis and Morgenstern (Chapter 1,
this volume) note, recruitment has escaped close scrutiny across
Latin America, in part because it is often conducted out of sight
and, often, informally. The Latin American context is made
more complex by the presence of myriad actors and varying
norms. The Colombian case, however, presents us with a good
opportunity to examine how selection norms developed and
how they affect the pool of successful political aspirants.
Although a great deal of activity occurs informally in Colombia,
national election laws allowing personal-list proportional representation, often referred to as effective SNTV (where parties
present multiple candidate lists in multimember electoral districts but votes are not pooled to the entire party), combined
with decentralized nominations processes have promoted *entrepreneurial* behavior (in the terms used by Siavelis and Morgenstern) among candidates for national legislative bodies. The
presence of a two-party dominant system for most of the country's history also allows us to focus on the development of norms
surrounding nominations in the two largest national parties,
Liberals and Conservatives. Specifically, it allows us to explore
how personal-list PR becomes the key to a broader electoral
strategy, that disproportionately rewards those who engage in
entrepreneurial behavior. "Operation wasp," or *operación avispa*,
takes advantage of personal-list PR—a permissive electoral for-
mat—by rewarding parties that engage in list proliferation.
In fact, parties are often encouraged to exceed the number of

seats available in a district, a tactic that would be counterproductive if votes were pooled to the party. However, since personal-list PR does not require that votes be pooled to the entire party, individual candidate lists function as factional lists, allowing for high levels of intraparty competition. What is more, the manner in which seats are allocated under this electoral system tends to reward large parties that submit multiple lists more so than parties that submit only a few lists. (We illustrate this point in subsequent sections.) Thus, *operación avispa* evokes an image which is not altogether off the mark—a strategy used by large parties that effectively swarm the ballot with lists and overwhelms other, often smaller, parties during the seat allocation process.

We argue that electoral norms and the dismantling of the National Front agreement,[1] along with the emergence of third-party challenges, enhanced self-selection and the emergence of *entrepreneurs*. The result was an increasing reliance on one's individual traits to further one's career, which tends to reward those who have distinguished themselves as individuals at the expense of party loyalty. In Colombia, formal institutions (such as the election law) have reinforced and facilitated the incentives created by informal institutions. This helps explain why even though electoral reforms in 2003 ended the use of personal-list PR (or effective SNTV, single nontransferable vote) and created minimal incentives for party loyalty, prospects for *entrepreneurial* behavior remain. In this chapter we discuss the development of candidate selection norms among the traditionally dominant parties, Liberals and Conservatives, and their effects in enlisting *entrepreneurs*—treating recruitment as a dependent and an independent variable, respectively.

Candidate Selection in the Colombian Context

Candidate selection is understood as resulting from the confluence of party, electoral, and legal variables (see Chapter 1, this volume). The emergence of entrepreneurial agents, as suggested by Siavelis and Morgenstern, is likewise the product of party and legal system variables that both encourage and reward independence. The Colombian context is a textbook case for the emergence of *entrepreneurs*. Party variables, particularly candidate choice, and a specific legal and electoral context—specifically, personal-list PR (or effective SNTV, single nontransferable vote) prior to 2003—fostered extraordinarily high levels of independence across members of the two dominant political parties. The widespread replication of those norms and adept manipulation of the electoral system encouraged *entrepreneurial* behavior

---

1. The National Front (1958–1974) was a pacted agreement between Liberals and Conservatives that required parity in Congress and government offices and alternation for the presidency. Thus, elections determined which representatives of each party were permitted to have a seat at the predivided Liberal–Conservative-only table (see Hoskin 1971).

across nearly every party elected to office in Colombia. We examine this argument using data from the Colombian Chamber of Deputies, 1958 to 2002.[2]

The Contours of Colombian Legislative Elections

Legislative elections in Colombia are conducted every four years in March, two months shy of the first round of presidential elections. For most of the country's history, representatives to both chambers of the Colombian Congress were elected in proportional-representation districts that were congruent with departmental boundaries. Although individuals were elected on closed lists allocated under largest-remainder–Hare (LR-Hare) rules, Colombian law did not limit the number of lists parties could submit. This effectively allowed parties to submit multiple lists, which historically reflected the presence of factions within the Liberal and Conservative parties. Since votes were not pooled to the party, the result is what some have referred to as personal-list PR or, probably more accurately, effective SNTV (Cox and Shugart 1995). This persisted until 1991, when the constitution was amended to create a single nationwide district for Senate elections. Further reforms, enacted in 2003, made significant changes to the electoral system and effectively eliminated the multilist strategy. Although recent electoral reforms have the potential to alter the landscape in Colombia, the emergence of *operación avispa* established the internal logic for candidate selection that guided Colombian parties for most of the modern period. Thus, we begin by exploring *operación avispa* in depth and then address how that logic may impact recent reforms.

The use of *operación avispa* and its implications for candidate selection norms are the direct result of adept manipulation of the electoral rules to resolve internal party conflicts. The seat-allocation formula used in Colombia prior to 2003 was a simple quota and largest-remainders system that first allocates seats to lists that meet the electoral quota. The LR-Hare quota is calculated according to a simple formula, v/s, where v is the total number of votes cast in a district and s is the number of seats to be allocated in the district (or district magnitude).

Table 5.1 shows an example of a district with a magnitude of twenty-six in which 860,240 valid votes were cast, yielding a quota of 33,086. Each list that meets the quota receives seats during the first stage of a two-stage allocation process. For instance, lists with at least twice as many votes as the quota (or 66,172 votes) receive two seats during the first allocation. Lists that meet the quota only once, with between 33,086 and 66,172 votes, receive one seat during the first allocation (e.g. List B in Table 5.1). List A in the table earns the most seats (twenty-one) during the first stage of the allocation process.

---

2. Data are drawn from the Registraduría Nacional del Estado Civil de Colombia.

TABLE 5.1   Hypothetical Allocation of 26 Seats in Colombia's LR-Hare PR Elections[a]

List	Votes	Quota Seats	Remainder	Remainder Seats
A	700,920	21	6,114	0
B	63,720	1	30,364	1
C	31,860	0	31,860	1
D	30,000	0	30,000	1
E	23,740	0	23,740	1
F	10,000	0	10,000	0
Total	860,240	22		4

a. We assume each list is a party list. Quota = 860,240/26 = 33,086.2.

Infrequently all the seats are allocated during the first stage. Some list totals fall far short of the quota, whereas others tend to have some excess votes after the first allocation. Votes left over after list totals are divided into the quota and used in the second stage, and seats go to lists with the largest remainders. So a list with exactly twice as many votes as the quota receives two seats during the first stage and none during the second stage because it has no remainder votes. Meanwhile, lists that did not meet the quota and lists that had votes left over use their remainders to allocate the outstanding seats. As is evident in Table 5.1, List C has the most "remainder" votes and receives a seat during the second stage. The same is true for Lists B, D, and E. Meanwhile List A gets no remainder seats because its leftover votes are so small relative to the other lists. Note that the seat allocated through remainders was "cheaper" than the quota seats. List E's seat cost 23,740 votes, compared to 33,086 votes for a quota seat.

Simple quota and largest-remainders allocation systems are not rare across the universe of PR systems, yet typically each list represents a single partisan effort. Until 2003 Colombia represented a radical departure from the norm, since parties did not submit a single party list and votes were not pooled across the party. The implications of this peculiarity are nontrivial. For one, parties that submitted multiple lists tended to win seats relatively cheaply through remainders allocation, especially in contrast to single party lists. Table 5.2 compares the effects of a party running multiple lists to those running a single list. The first two columns show, using data from the 1990 Chamber of Deputies election in Antioquia, how seats were allocated with multiple lists and no pooling. Liberals submitted fewer lists than Conservatives and won a total of fourteen seats: ten by quota and four through largest-remainders allocation. Conservatives, however, won a total of eleven seats: three by quota and eight remainders seats. Other party lists, in this case, won one seat.

If the Liberals, Conservatives, and other parties each had submitted a single list—as required under the 2003 reforms—and votes were pooled to the party, the

TABLE 5.2   Differences in Allocation across Single and Multiple Lists[a]

List	Votes	Each Party Presents Multiple Lists		Each Party Presents a Single List	
		Quota Seats, Multiple Lists	Remainder Seats, Multiple Lists	Quota Seats, Single Party List	Remainder Seats, Single Party List
Liberal 1	199,540	6	0	—	—
Liberal 2	75,504	2	0	—	—
Liberal 3	47,498	1	0	—	—
Liberal 4	33,380	1	0	—	—
Liberal 5	27,763	0	1	—	—
Liberal 6	25,176	0	1	—	—
Liberal 7	23,032	0	1	—	—
Liberal 8	21,218	0	1	—	—
Total	**453,111**	**10**	**4**	**13**	**2**
Conservative 1	65,796	1	1	—	—
Conservative 2	58,999	1	1	—	—
Conservative 3	44,789	1	0	—	—
Conservative 4	23,441	0	1	—	—
Conservative 5	23,068	0	1	—	—
Conservative 6	21,321	0	1	—	—
Conservative 7	20,836	0	1	—	—
Conservative 8	20,413	0	1	—	—
Conservative 9	17,753	0	0	—	—
Total	**296,416**	**3**	**8**	**8**	**2**
Other 1	18,679	0	1	—	—
Total	**18,679**	**0**	**1**	**0**	**1**
Total	768,206	13	13	21	5

Source: Registraduría Nacional del Estado Civil.

a. Vote totals and seat totals are taken from Antioquia's 1990 lower-house elections. Quota is 33,086. District magnitude is 26.

outcome would have been different (see final two columns in Table 5.2). The party that submitted the most lists, in this case the Conservatives, would earn only ten seats, a loss of one seat by pooling votes. Thus, the multilist strategy tends to give an advantage to the party with the most lists. When votes are pooled to the party level and each party submits a single list, this particular electoral rule tends to work as orig- inally intended: it rewards political minorities with seats in a proportionate manner. However, when votes are not pooled and parties submit multiple lists, some domi- nant party lists get treated as political minorities and earn seats relatively cheaply.

TABLE 5.3 Mean Number of Lists Submitted to Colombian Lower-Chamber Contests, 1958–2002

Year	Liberals	Dissident Liberals	Conservatives	Dissident Conservatives	Others	Total
1958	1.56	0	3.11	0	0	2.63
1964	5.95	0	4.21	0	0	6.03
1966	5.95	0	5.05	0	0	6.53
1968	4.95	0	4.81	0	0	6.72
1970	5.76	1.2	5.20	0.12	0	9.59
1974	4.23	0	2.88	0	2.69	7.97
1978	5.19	0	3.29	0	2.8	11.09
1982	5.94	0	4.13	0	2.31	12.38
1986	4.31	0	3.75	0	3.09	11.16
1990	6.60	0	3.86	0	2.57	11.41
1991	6.91	0	1.91	0	5.82	14.64
1994	8.56	0	2.61	0	7.79	18.97
1998	8.39	0	1.76	0	10.15	20.30
2002	10.12	0	1.72	0	15.61	27.45

Source: Registraduría Nacional del Estado Civil.

Table 5.3 shows the mean number of lists submitted in Chamber of Deputies elections between 1958 and 2002. Although the period between 1958 and 1974 does not represent a period of absolute competitiveness, it is important to note that even during that period we see fluctuations in the number of lists presented by each party. More important, beginning in 1974 we see that the number of lists increased dramatically and that some of the most dramatic increases evident were perpetrated by the Liberal Party in the 1990s. List proliferation, our indicator of entrepreneurial behavior, is not an accidental occurrence; it is a clear indication of the old axiom, *Mejor solo que mal acompañado* (Better alone than in bad company). It suggests that individuals increasingly rely on themselves and their electoral machines for advancement (see Pizarro 1997, 2002). Not only is this suggestive of one of the main characteristics of *entrepreneurship*, list proliferation has unfolded in Colombia in a manner that suggests elected officials are not exclusively beholden to constituents, traditionally defined as voters.

Table 5.3 provides a stark depiction of the dramatic proliferation of lists over time, with the mean number of lists competing in each district rising from one in 1958 to over ten in 2002. This same pattern of list proliferation is evident among "other parties," which submitted a mean of around fifteen lists per district in 2002.[3] This list proliferation is evident in the total number of lists as well. The Liberal Party alone went from a total of twenty-eight lists

3. It is important to note that the increase in other lists is also accompanied by a dramatic increase in the number of new parties that emerge over time, more than eighty by 2002.

TABLE 5.4   Average Number of Winning Lists Submitted to Colombian Lower-Chamber Contests, 1958–2002[a]

Year	Liberals	Conservatives	Others	Total
1974	2.5	1.38	0.54	3.59
1978	3.00	2.32	0.16	4.28
1982	3.35	2.5	0.08	4.81
1986	2.38	2.09	0.50	4.97
1990	4.00	2.29	0.50	5.94
1991	2.60	0.64	1.37	4.61
1994	2.51	1.24	0.88	4.63
1998	2.55	0.82	1.30	4.67
2002	1.67	0.63	2.60	4.91

Source: Registraduría Nacional del Estado Civil.

a. Dissident Liberals and dissident Conservatives are excluded from this table, as they did not compete as such during the 1974–2002 period.

nationally in 1998 to well over three hundred in 2002. The increasing number of lists does not, however, correspond to an increase in the number of seats available in the Chamber of Deputies, since average district magnitude (or M) decreased from about 7 prior to 1991 to about 5.[4] Rather, it reflects intense intraparty competition and the implementation of *operación avispa* as an electoral strategy. It is also clear that Liberals did a better job of winning seats through list proliferation, gaining an average of two seats in each department after 1974, rising to nearly four seats per department in 1990. Meanwhile the Conservatives gained fewer seats per department, dropping to one or less after 1990, primarily because they tended to submit fewer lists than the Liberal Party (see Table 5.4).

List proliferation is at the heart of *operación avispa,* a swarm of lists. Though this strategy may seem counterintuitive, its application was beneficial for dominant parties, particularly the Liberals (Cox and Shugart 1995; Rodriguez-Raza 2002; Ungar Bleier 2003). As Cox and Shugart (1995, 452) note, the Liberal Party has grown increasingly savvy and avoids spreading out its votes in lower-house elections, which would dilute its seat share.

4. The Chamber of Deputies continues to be elected from multimember department-level districts. District magnitude varies from 2 to 18, although the overall number of representatives in the lower chamber fell from 199 to 161 after the adoption of the 1991 national constitution. Not surprisingly, there is some association between the number of seats in a district (district magnitude, or M) and the number of lists. Low-magnitude districts (M = 2) have 3 to 12 lists with an average of 7, whereas high-magnitude districts (M = 17 to 29) contain 18 to 286 lists with an average of 131.

How did list proliferation become such a prominent feature of the Colombian political system? Why do Liberals seem to employ this strategy more than their Conservative counterparts? We examine list proliferation as a function of forces that only began to exert themselves as the National Front ended.

The Effect of Party Strategy on Self-Selection Norms Among Liberals and Conservatives

In this section, we examine the proliferation of lists over time as a function of increased competition following the *desmonte* (dismantling of the National Front). Specifically, we review a series of explanations for the use of the *avispa* strategy by both major parties while focusing our explanations on high rates of list proliferation among Liberals. While we suspect that list proliferation among the Liberals reflects low barriers to entry and the use of decentralized political machines to further vote getting (Archer 1990; Osterling 1989, 164; Ungar Bleier 2003), we focus on the effect that increased competition after the dismantling of the National Front had in creating the *avispa* strategy.

The National Front Period and the Birth of Operación Avispa

Colombia's dominant political parties, the Liberals and Conservatives, both share long histories that are intertwined with the nation's conflicts, most notably during the period of *La Violencia* (1948–1954). Following years of internecine turmoil between the two traditional parties during *La Violencia* and a brief military interregnum, the Colombian political system began a return to democracy in 1957 under a political pact between the two major parties, called the National Front. The pact ensured presidential alternation and legislative parity of representation for Liberals and Conservatives until 1974. Although parity in legislative bodies reduced interparty conflict, it tended to increase intraparty competition, since partisans competed against each other for a limited number of seats.[5] As intraparty competition increased and fissures formed, often along family lines, an increasing number of unofficial party lists competed for congressional seats (Dix 1987; Osterling 1989; Hartlyn 1988). The most notable rupture occurred during the 1970 election, where unofficial lists were recorded as party dissidents (see Table 5.3).

At least initially, the possibility of submitting multiple lists was for both the Liberal and Conservative parties a means to avoid difficult choices at the nomination stage. Until 2003, the electoral system did not discourage or limit the number of lists allowable for each party. It was the combination of party variables and the presence of electoral rules that resulted in list proliferation among the

---

5. The Constitutional Reform of 1968 removed the parity requirement for subnational offices, notably state assembly and municipal council elections.

traditional parties. Access to the party label, at least during the National Front, was largely determined by faction heads, often prominent national-party figures with previous political experience. Rather than choose from among factions representing some of the most prominent families, running official and unofficial lists allowed party leaders to lay responsibility at the voters' doorsteps. It was a compromise position that allowed for a simple democratic solution and converted the general election into an effective primary for both major parties— although it did not mollify critics of those in charge at the national level (Dix 1980, 1987; Giraldo 2003; Martz 1999; Osterling 1989).

The National Front period saw conflicts within the Liberal Party between followers of Julio César Turbay Ayala, Carlos Lleras Restrepo, and Alfonso López Michelson *(lopistas)*, conflicts that often were reproduced at the legislative and subnational levels. Similarly, the Conservatives were split between the *laureanistas* (followers of Laureano Gómez, a former president and ultraconservative) and *ospinistas* (followers of Mariano Ospina Pérez).[6] In both parties, new factions emerged that continued the tradition of intraparty contests. Indeed, some have noted that in both parties, lists that represented different wings of the party were also used as unofficial primaries for aspiring presidential candidates (see Martz 1999). Thus, contests at the legislative and subnational levels were decisive in resolving conflicts at multiple levels of electoral competition.

During the earliest stages of the National Front period, we might consider factions within both parties to be fairly disciplined; they often resorted to kinship ties to enforce loyalty. The extent to which these factions were filled with *entrepreneurs* or populated by faction *loyalists* is unclear, since there were some important ideological and familial divisions that helped create them. Nonetheless, over time the factions lost their ideological and purely familial overtones, and became atomized as their ranks swelled with *entrepreneurs*. This is best illustrated by the fact that factions were clearly distinguishable during the early National Front years, but as time passed, lists became vehicles for individuals who at times lacked a "supporting cast" of copartisans or cofactionalists. The use of the ballot box to settle factional disputes fundamentally reinforced the *entrepreneurial* tendency within the party. By making it clear that popular support was key to success from early on, the party ensured that *entrepreneurs* rather than *group delegates* or true faction *loyalists* (as Moraes describes them in Uruguay in Chapter 7 of this volume) would predominate and emerge because individuals not associated with one of the dominant factions could rise to prominent positions if they could muster sufficient electoral support.

---

6. *Laureanistas* were succeeded by *Alvaristas*, led by Laureano Gómez's son Alvaro Gómez Hurtado. The *Ospinistas* were succeeded by the *Pastranistas-Ospinistas*, which included Andrés Pastrana.

As the country modernized and partisan attachments weakened as a result of the staid parameters of bipartisan rule, the work of turning out voters and electing candidates fell increasingly to local power brokers, also known as *gamonales* (Archer 1990; Dix 1987; Osterling 1989).[7] As it became increasingly clear to aspirants that national-party leaders were willing to allow the voting public a say in deciding internal nomination disputes, especially in presidential contests, by allowing effective primaries to take place during congressional contests among all partisans (see Martz 1999), they turned to mobilizing voters through greater use of local power brokers. The result was a weakening of national-party leaders and a rapid decentralization of the nomination process (Giraldo 2003; Hartlyn 1988; Latorre 1974).

Given the absence of formalized rules regarding nominations, this process gave way to the self-selection process that has guided ballot access. As long as you could gain the support of a *gamonal*, you stood a good chance of winning a seat. Moreover, dependence on *gamonales* weakened the bond between elected official and constituents by placing greater importance on the vote broker as beneficiary of future policy decisions.[8] In other words, the rapid disintegration of the electoral map and increased competition led to the carving out of tiny electoral fiefdoms in each district (this is apparent since seats are earned most cheaply when many lists compete in a single district). These features only made *gamonales* more important because they were the ones that mobilized voters, in some instances physically transporting them to the polls over long distances (Archer 1990). Thus, candidate selection norms emerged from a weakening of internal party rules, which grew more permissive and decentralized over time; this seriously compromised the loyalty of partisans to their party and their factions.

Increased Competition and the Maturation of Operación Avispa

As the National Front drew to a close and restrictions on participation by other actors were loosened, traditional parties faced new challengers. Both parties responded by submitting multiple lists across congressional districts, at least until 2003; the Liberal Party was the more prolific at this. There are myriad explanations for the Liberal Party's penchant for list proliferation. First, *avispa* strategy is largely a function of casual use of the party label by those employing the strategy. Since the Liberal Party did not attempt to vet candidates, it drew on a larger pool of potential

---

7. *Gamonales* were often not elected officials themselves (and rarely held national office) but rather were at the apex of a complex electoral machine reminiscent of those common in the U.S. during the early twentieth century. *Gamonales* "got out the vote" and ensured victory for specific lists and candidates in return for specific, often tangible, benefits. Although this term is usually reserved for vote brokers in rural areas, the political machines built around them are relevant to urban electioneering as well.

8. Voters are not ignored in this exchange, but derive benefits from those closest to them, such as the vote brokers who enlisted them. The kinds of benefits provided to voters need not be material, but may also include a range of cordial or social gestures such as those depicted by Archer (1990).

candidates. Second, beginning with the *desmonte* and continuing to the present day, the Liberal Party has been better connected to electoral machines in crucial urban areas of the country and in key rural districts as well (see Escobar 2002). Thus, the *entrepreneur* is wise to pick the party with the lowest barriers to entry, as well as the one that has some intrinsic appeal across various segments of society. Finally, some suggest that *avispa* was adopted and "perfected" by Liberal Party elites as a strategy to outmaneuver the Conservative Party and new parties (Osterling 1989, 164; Ungar Bleier 2003). Since the Liberals attracted so many good electoral machines, the net result was a strong "party" showing that was due to lots of narrow, individual efforts. We explore the latter explanation empirically.

Some suggest that *operación avispa* is, at best, a reflection of the lack of party discipline (Hartlyn 1988, 161), but others suggest that it is the result of a coordinated strategy (Osterling 1989, 164; Ungar Bleier 2003). Those in the latter camp credit Alfonso López Michelson, the former Liberal president and a national figure, with being its intellectual author (Ungar Bleier 1993). Rather than cede territory to upstart political parties such as the populist ANAPO (Alianza Nacional Popular, or National Popular Alliance), some of which lured defectors from the major parties, the Liberal Party, in particular, left the gates open and fully encouraged aspirants to run on the party label by submitting their own lists. The Conservatives, by contrast, seem far more tentative in their use of *avispa,* presenting far fewer lists per district than their Liberal counterparts, most likely because of a greater desire to control the party message (Ungar Bleier 1993).

We examine the use of *operación avispa* by the Liberal Party in a modest multivariate negative binomial regression model (see Table 5.5). Since we are most interested in the effect of list proliferation by new competitors on the strategies

TABLE 5.5 The Impact of New Actors on List Strategy in Colombian Lower-Chamber Contests, 1958–2002

	Dependent Variable = Number of Liberal Party Lists		Dependent Variable = Number of Conservative Party Lists	
	Model 1	Model 2	Model 3	Model 4
Lists by "other" parties	0.017 (0.00)**	—	−0.008 (0.004)*	—
Lists by "other" parties$_{t-1}$	—	0.011 (0.005)*	—	−0.037 (.009)**
1968 indicator variable	−0.10 (0.11)	−0.23 (0.11)*	0.21 (0.12)*	0.13 (0.12)
1991 indicator variable	0.08 (0.08)	−0.07 (0.09)	−0.59 (0.14)**	−0.62 (0.15)**
Constant	1.15 (0.21)**	1.09 (0.216)**	−0.05 (0.39)	0.27 (0.39)
N	410	374	410	373
Pseudo R^2	0.21	0.22	0.15	0.16

* $p \geq .05$
** $p \geq .01$

NOTE: Models shown employ negative binomial regression. Fixed effects for departments (congressional districts) were also included in all model estimations. Alpha levels exceed the .001 level for all models shown.

of traditional parties over time, we examine the lagged effect of new-party list proliferation on Liberal and Conservative strategies (see Table 5.5). We expect list proliferation by other parties at time $t-1$ to provoke an equal, if not stronger, response by traditional parties at time t. Among traditional parties, we expect the response to be most marked among Liberals. The first two models focus on the effect on Liberal Party strategy, the latter two, on Conservative Party strategy.

When we regress the number of other lists on the number of Liberal lists submitted since 1958, controlling for dramatic drops in the size of the lower chamber in 1968 and 1991, we find a relationship between the rise of challengers and Liberal Party strategy. Specifically, an increase in the number of lists presented by other actors—made possible by the removal of restrictions on party registration and parity under the National Front (legal variables)—tends to spur an increase in the number of Liberal lists that are presented. Model 2 shows that the number of other party lists in the previous election ($t-1$) predicts an increase in the number of Liberal lists. The coefficient for other lists in the previous election is significant beyond the .001 level and the model has notable predictive capability (pseudo R^2 of 0.22).[9]

Simulations leaving control variables at their mode suggest that as other parties increase the number of lists submitted in each district from 0 to 4, we would expect a 0.14 increase in the number of lists submitted by the Liberal Party in each district—or nearly 5 additional lists nationwide.[10] An increase from 4 to 13 other party lists, a one-standard-deviation increase, produces a 0.35 increase in the number of Liberal lists in each district—or 11.2 Liberal lists nationwide. Similarly, an increase from 0 to 131 "other" party lists (the maximum number of "other" party lists seen in Colombia) spurs an increase of 14.88 Liberal lists per district (or 448 lists across the country!). Thus, the results suggest that the increased presence of third-party challengers has a measurable and nontrivial impact on Liberal Party strategy, especially as the number of other parties competing grows.

In contrast, Models 3 and 4, which explore the effect of other party lists on Conservative Party strategy, suggest that the Conservatives did not respond the same way. Rather than encourage list proliferation to crush new actors, Conservatives issued fewer lists in response to prior challenges. The literature suggests conscious discretion in issuing lists within the Conservative Party (see Ungar Bleier 1993). Conservative hesitation to fully promote *avispa* as their Liberal counterparts did may belie an interest in balancing seat gains with maintaining some degree of loyalty. Although Conservatives did not pursue this strategy with the same vigor as Liberals, they did use issue multiple lists, averaging two to five lists per district, though with less effectiveness (see Tables 5.3 and 5.4). The true anomaly is the "new" parties that emerged after the dismantling of the National

9. Several lower-house districts reached statistical significance, including the capital district (Bogotá, D.C.), Antioquia, Bolívar, Boyacá, Caldas, Casanare, Cesar, Cundinamarca, Nariño, Sucre, and Vaupes.
   10. Simulations were obtained by using Clarify software (see King, Tomz, and Wittenberg 2000).

Front, which tended not to engage in list proliferation (with a few notable exceptions), primarily because they lacked the requisite candidate pool.

Even though we refer to *operación avispa* (or list proliferation) as a party strategy, the "go-it-alone" nature of the endeavor means that individuals do not necessarily seek to benefit the party. Although *avispa* originally evolved from a means to avoid tough choices to a concerted strategy to limit gains by new actors, its current perpetrators have less loyalty to the party than their predecessors. When *avispa* was still in its infancy, in the 1970s and early 1980s, many of the lists that appeared were still tied to one of a handful of prominent political families. Dissidents within the parties were still clearly identified with specific leaders, such as Alfonso López Michelson, who headed the long-defunct Movimiento Revolucionario Liberal (Liberal Revolutionary Movement) or Luis Carlos Galán who headed Nuevo Liberalismo (New Liberalism). But as the role of local vote brokers *(gamonales)* became more decisive in securing victory and as national leaders drifted out of the political scene, it has become far less clear, to observers and participants alike, how lists and factions relate to the national directorate or other factions. Most scholars and politicians alike treat individual lists as *microempresas electorales* (electoral micro-enterprises), a complete atomization of electoral efforts, even within the major parties (Pizarro 1997, 2002). Indeed, the rapid acceleration of *operación avispa,* when parties choose not to exert veto power over access to the party label, makes it difficult to see how loyalty among partisans, leaders, and rank-and-file members could be established. To use the categories developed by Siavelis and Morgenstern (see Chapter 1), it is this evolution that leads us to label congress members in Colombia *entrepreneurs.* The reliance on *gamonales* and the potentially weak link between representatives and their voters, especially if the former owe their allegiance to a power broker (Archer 1990), leads us to suspect that although constituency service is important in Colombia, the constituency itself may be a very circumscribed group of citizens. The importance of vote brokers in the process, as well as the often circumscribed nature of representation, means that legislators in Colombia may end up representing a variety of groups who may not be linked in any way. The importance of vote brokers, as opposed to meaningful links between candidates and functional groups, also explains why congress members in Colombia are not *group delegates.*

Thus, the realities facing candidates are reflected in the old proverb "*Mejor solo que mal acompañado*" (Better alone than in bad company). The saying not only reflects the relative lack of concern for the group, in this case the party, but also highlights the individualized nature of the effort. The norms created in the wake of the National Front period structured party politics, but some important changes affecting electoral system variables and, ultimately, party selection norms are occurring. The 2003 political reforms, which require parties to submit a single list (the choice of open or closed is left to the party), have the potential to minimize *entrepreneurial* behavior. In practice, however, the fact that parties can choose to submit open or closed lists suggests this reform is not likely to end *entrepreneurial* action entirely. After all, electoral micro-enterprises will not be eliminated if the party elects to submit an open list. Nonetheless, even under an open-list system, parties that are merely a collection of myriad loose and narrowly focused micro-enterprises are less likely. Sure, malcontents might decide to form their own party and "go it alone," but the 2003 reforms provide a small disincentive for this in the form of a 2 percent electoral threshold which make any parties receiving less than 2 percent of the votes ineligible to earn a seat in Congress. Thus, there are some reasons to expect that the 2003 reforms may shrink the field of *entrepreneurs* within the major parties by forcing them to compete against each other directly, rather than permitting them small electoral fiefdoms as was the case previously. Since there has been only one election under these new rules, it is difficult to say with certainty whether the reforms have had any significant effect on recruitment patterns or the kinds of candidates recruited. Preliminary data suggest that locally the reforms have promoted greater internal party coordination through reduction in the number of lists (Botero 2006).[11] Thus, we expect that the reforms will temper *entrepreneurial* behavior, without necessarily eliminating it. In the following section, we explore exactly what kinds of candidates have fared best in multi-list contests for legislative seats and the resultant implications for behavior.

List Proliferation and Recruitment of *Entrepreneur* Candidates

Multiple lists within a party have reinforced the belief that candidates are on their own. Since success is not tied to partisan efforts and intraparty competition is high, partisan affiliation loses its relevance. The emergence of electoral micro-enterprises *(microempresas electorales)* and the narrow vote totals needed to win a seat through largest remainders (see Tables 5.1 and 5.2) created strong links between legislators and their patrons, but did not necessarily create *constituent servants*. Thus, the nature of electoral competition, resulting from party system variables and legal and electoral rules, produces *entrepreneurs*—politicians with only a fleeting, instrumental sense of loyalty to anyone other than themselves. In this section, we consider how list proliferation, as an independent variable, benefits those with established personal reputations, rewarding *entrepreneurial* behavior.

Members of the Colombian Congress clearly see themselves as legislative free agents. In surveys conducted in 1998 and 2002 by the Universidad de Salamanca, deputies were asked to identify the primary reason they believed they had been elected. An overview of their responses is presented in Table 5.6. In 1998, the most

11. The 2006 presidential elections were characterized by an unusual set of candidacies, including the unprecedented presence of an incumbent, the independent presidential candidate Alvaro Uribe. A large bloc of new movements supporting Uribe (the Partido Social de Unidad Nacional, or Partido de la "U") was able to tap into a strong independent tide. Similarly, an opposition bloc, the leftist Polo Democrático, tapped into another variant of this "independent" sentiment. This combination makes it difficult to establish whether this election will be indicative of future elections.

TABLE 5.6 Colombian Deputies' Beliefs About Why They Were Elected, 1998 and 2002 Surveys[a]

Responses	1998 Survey				2002 Survey		
	PL	PC	Other	Coalition	PL	PC	Others
Individual attributes							
My prior experience in other political or public positions	9 18.8%	10 34.5%	2 25%	1 33.3%	18 30%	9 33.3%	3 37.5%
My personal charm	8 16.7%	2 6.9%	3 37.5%	1 33.3%	19 31.7%	7 25.9%	0 0%
The modern and dynamic style of the campaign I ran	22 45.8%	6 27.6%	0 0%	1 33.3%	11 18.3%	7 25.9%	0 0%
Party attributes							
The party's program	2 4.2%	3 10.3%	1 12.5%	0 0%	6 10%	3 11.1%	3 37.5%
The party's ideology	1 2.1%	1 3.5%	1 12.5%	0 0%	1 1.7%	1 3.7%	0 0%
Family tradition of the voter; bonds to the party	1 2.1%	1 3.5%	0 0%	0 0%	—	—	—
The party leader	2 4.2%	4 13.8%	0 0%	0 0%	5 8.3%	0 0%	2 25%
Don't know	3 6.3%	0 0%	1 12.5%	0 0%	—	—	—
Total Responses[b]	48	29	8	3	60	27	8

Source: Universidad de Salamanca.

a. Question asked: Which of the following do you believe was the principal reason you were elected? Responses in the table include only that identified as the primary reason for electoral success.

b. Includes those surveyed who either did not answer this question or who said they did not know.

common reason Liberal deputies believed they had been elected was the campaign they ran (45.8 percent), followed by prior experience (18.8 percent). Conservative deputies cited prior experience first (34.5 percent) and campaign strategy second (27.6 percent). Meanwhile, other party deputies indicated that personal charm was most important (37.5 percent), with prior experience second (25 percent). Coalition members identified all three individual attributes as equally important for their success (prior experience, personal charm, and campaign strategy each received 33.3 percent). For all parties' candidates involved in the 1998 survey, it is clear that individual attributes were far more important than party attributes.

In 2002, a very similar pattern emerged in both the Liberal and Conservative parties. A plurality of Liberal deputies attributed their success to their personal charm (31.7 percent) while 30 percent believed it was due to prior political experience. Among Conservative candidates, 33.3 percent of deputies selected prior experience as the primary reason for their success and personal charm and campaign strategy fell to second place (25.9 percent for each). Although deputies from "other" parties also identified individual characteristics as key to their success (37.5 percent of respondents selected prior experience), 37.5 percent of deputies also identified the party program as key to their success. It is worth noting that these survey results include members of several minority reformist, civic, indigenous, and leftist parties that have emerged only recently in Colombia as well as Liberals and Conservatives. So the combination of a small sample of other parties and some changes to the party system, by accommodating a number of single-issue parties, may be affecting the 2002 survey. It is nonetheless important that so many individual deputies see their own efforts as most important in securing their election. Thus, while party identification may play a role, by and large deputies believe their actions are primarily responsible for their electoral success—which encourages future *entrepreneurial* behavior in campaigns.

The highly personalizing characteristics of candidate selection and the electoral system encourage and reward personal vote seeking. This rewards and favors candidates with established personal reputations and name recognition among voters. We expect that because of the highly competitive electoral environment, candidates with name recognition should possess electoral advantages and thus should be more likely to seek office. This is not purely an incumbency advantage, since we expect challengers with prior experience as mayor or governor also to possess the name recognition to compete in these elections.

Table 5.7 presents the percentage of candidates for the Chamber of Deputies with various types of prior experience. The percentage of candidates seeking reelection by heading their own list in the Chamber of Deputies has steadily decreased, from about 35 percent in 1986 to 14 percent in 2002.[12] This decline has been driven by the threefold increase in the number of candidates seeking election to the Chamber of Deputies—not by a shift in candidates seeking reelection (reelection rates

---

12. We have chosen to compute reelection seekers including only those who headed their own list.

TABLE 5.7 Prior Experience of Colombian Candidates Heading Lists for the Chamber of Deputies, 1986–2002.

Year	Percentage with Chamber Experience	Percentage with Senate Experience	Percentage with Gubernatorial Experience	Percentage with Mayoral Experience
1986	34.6	8.5	0.0	0.0
1990	43.2	8.9	0.0	0.5
1991	26.4	7.8	0.0	2.5
1994	23.0	4.3	0.0	3.5
1998	17.1	4.3	0.4	4.3
2002	13.9	3.3	1.3	4.7

Source: Author's computation from data obtained from Registraduría Nacional del Estado Civil.

averaged between 50 and 60 percent between 1978 and 1998). Additionally, an increasing, albeit small, percentage of the candidate pool has prior experience at the subnational level as governor or mayor.[13] The absence of control by the party over nominations has removed barriers inexperienced candidates have to placing themselves on the ballot. Thus, it is not necessary to "prove" one's loyalty to the party or to demonstrate support from a given group in order to clinch the nomination. Instead, enterprising individuals with political ambitions are relatively free to self-nominate across almost all parties in Colombia.[14]

In this highly competitive environment, candidates with prior experience should possess an electoral advantage as they have name recognition, patronage resources to distribute, and experience in running a campaign. Given that candidates with past experience should be stronger, or "quality" candidates, we expect that lists headed by candidates with prior elected experience (as mayors or governors as well as in the Chamber of Deputies or the Senate) should be more likely to win election than candidates without that experience. (See Jacobson and Kernell 1981 for a discussion of these effects in the United States.) To test whether this expectation is borne out in Colombia, we examined elections for the Chamber of Deputies between 1986 and 2002. We collected data on all candidates who were heads of lists in elections for the Chamber of Deputies between 1986 and 2002. For each head of list we recorded whether they served in either chamber of Congress (regardless of whether they had been elected as head of list or not) and whether they had been governor or mayor. We controlled for the candidates' party to separate out the value of party label and individual characteristics. We would anticipate that in a system populated by *entrepreneurs*, individual characteristics such as prior elected experience should

13. The first gubernatorial elections were held in 1991 and the first mayoral elections were held in 1988. This explains the absence of candidates with subnational electoral experience prior to these dates.

14. Only a few notable exceptions stand out: the Communist Party of Colombia (Partido Comunista de Colombia, or PCC), Patriotic Union (Unión Patriótica, or UP), and the indigenous parties such as Autoridades Indígenas de Colombia (AICO) that rely on party or community participation for nominations.

TABLE 5.8   The Effect of List Proliferation on Colombian Election Outcomes

	Dependent Variable = Percentage of Vote Received by the List	Dependent Variable = Candidate Elected from List (Y/N)
Conservative party list	-0.677*	0.454***
	(0.381)	(0.109)
"Other" party list	-2.071***	-0.759***
	(0.412)	(0.139)
Number of prior terms in the Chamber	2.548***	0.684***
of Deputies served by head of list	(0.230)	(0.081)
Number of prior terms in the Senate	1.209***	0.367**
served by head of list	(0.459)	(0.184)
Prior service as governor by head of list	8.855	-0.022
	(6.328)	(1.884)
Prior service as mayor by head of list	5.111***	-0.410
	(1.848)	(0.342)
Total number of lists in the district	-0.027***	-0.009***
	(0.007)	(0.0008)
Number of lists × prior Chamber of Deputies	-0.016**	0.006***
experience of head of list	(0.006)	(0.001)
Number of lists × prior Senate experience	-0.011	0.009
of head of list	(0.008)	(0.006)
Number of lists × gubernatorial experience	-0.356	0.031
of head of list	(0.319)	(0.106)
Number of lists × mayoral experience	-0.111*	0.028***
of head of list	(0.067)	(0.008)
Constant	6.763***	-0.748***
	(0.539)	(0.105)
N	3356	33565
F or Wald chi-square	52.43	405.3
Prob F/Prob Chi^2	0	0
R^2/Pseudo R^2	0.223	0.196
Model estimated via:	OLS	Logit

$*$ $p > $ 0.10; $**$ $p > $ 0.05; $***$ $p > $ 0.01.

play an important role.[15] We also control for the total number of lists run by all parties in that department, as this will affect how highly competitive the district is.

Table 5.8 presents two models; the first uses ordinary least squares to estimate the percentage of the vote a list received, and the second estimates the probability of the list electing a candidate, using Logit.[16] We find that similar factors affect both

15. This is one area where *constituent servants* and *entrepreneurs* share similar incentives, as both candidate types benefit from high name recognition to further their electoral careers. After all, both candidate types are forced to compete in a world where party identification is not a decisive factor in determining electoral success.

the votes a list receives and the probability of its electing a candidate with the exception of party affiliation. Not surprisingly, lists from new political parties and movements (the "other" category) are less likely to be elected and are expected to receive a lower percentage of the vote than Liberal lists. Lists from the Conservative Party are expected to receive fewer votes than lists from the Liberal Party, although this variable is only statistically significant at the more permissive 0.10 level. But Conservative lists are more likely to elect someone than Liberal lists, all else being equal. This effect is illustrated in Table 5.9, which presents simulated probabilities and illustrates some of the power of *operación avispa*.[17]

By simulating the probability of a candidate being elected, we demonstrate that across all categories of experience, Conservative Party candidates have a higher probability of being elected than Liberal Party candidates (compare columns 1 and 2 in Table 5.9). For both political neophytes (rows 1–3) and former members of Congress (rows 4–6) there is no overlap in the 90 percent confidence intervals for Liberal and Conservative candidates when the number of lists is at the observed minimum or mean (rows 1 and 2 and 4 and 5). However, as the number of lists increases to the observed maximum (see rows 3 and 6) there is significant overlap in the confidence intervals. These simulations indicate that when the number of lists is small, running fewer lists can be beneficial (which is why the Conservatives do better). But as the number of lists increases to the maximum, there is increasing overlap in the confidence intervals. Essentially, once the number of lists becomes very large, party identification does not become a meaningful way to distinguish candidates. Thus, in highly competitive districts the Liberals do not fare systematically worse than the Conservatives. Part of the power of *operación avispa* is to overwhelm the field and ensure a greater total number of cheaply won seats, although not necessarily a greater percentage of winning lists, because it is here that the overwhelming number of Liberal candidates cancels out any advantage the Conservatives may obtain from pooling their votes in a smaller number of lists.[18]

We expected candidates with prior experience to be more likely to win election because they should better understand how the *entrepreneurial* game is played and because prior experience provides them with a way to distinguish themselves from other candidates, since party identification is not a meaningful distinction. If *entrepreneurial* behavior is in fact rewarded, we would expect to see that all candidates with any kind of prior experience are more likely to be elected than candidates without experience. The different rows within Table 5.9 illustrate the effect of prior experience. Individual characteristics (in

16. Both models were estimated with standard errors adjusted for clustering by department and election to account for correlation resulting from specific factors within that election.

17. This should not be seen as a direct test of the *operacíon avispa* strategy because we are not modeling the effect of party conditional upon the number of lists.

18. We obtained identical results in terms of sign and significance by including the number of Liberal Party lists instead of total lists. The correlation between Liberal lists and total lists is very high (0.99), indicating that it is the Liberals who are driving list proliferation.

the form of past experience) become increasingly salient as competition increases. For instance, the chances for a list headed by a Liberal Party candidate with no experience to be elected declined from 28 to 35 percent when facing three lists (the observed minimum) and from to 2 to 4 percent when facing 286 lists (the maximum observed). Moreover, in those high-competition

TABLE 5.9 Probability a Candidate Is elected to the Colombian Chamber of Deputies[a]

Experience	Liberal Party Candidate	Conservative Party Candidate	"Other" Party Candidate
No prior experience			
Minimum lists	0.32	0.420	0.18
	(0.28–0.35)	(0.37–0.47)	(0.16–0.20)
Average lists	0.21	0.300	0.11
	(0.19–0.24)	(0.26–0.34)	(0.10–0.13)
Maximum lists	0.03	0.05	0.02
	(0.02–0.04)	(0.03–0.07)	(0.01–0.02)
Former congressman			
Minimum lists	0.48	0.59	0.30
	(0.44–0.52)	(0.54–0.65)	(0.26–0.34)
Average lists	0.44	0.55	0.27
	(0.40–0.48)	(0.50–0.61)	(0.23–0.31)
Maximum lists	0.29	0.39	0.16
	(0.19–0.40)	(0.26–0.52)	(0.09–0.24)
Former governor			
Minimum lists	0.69	0.75	0.56
	(0.19–0.98)	(0.26–0.99)	(0.09–0.96)
Average lists	0.68	0.71	0.62
	(0.004–0.99)	(0.01–0.99)	(0.002–0.99)
Maximum lists	0.59	0.60	0.58
	(0–1)	(0–1)	(0–1)
Former mayor			
Minimum lists	0.62	0.62	0.61
	(0–1)	(0–1)	(0–1)
Average lists	0.63	0.64	0.62
	(0–1)	(0–1)	(0–1)
Maximum lists	0.68	0.69	0.67
	(0–1)	(0–1)	(0–1)

a. Ninety percent confidence intervals in parentheses. Probabilities and confidence intervals simulated on basis of Logit model in Table 5.8 using Clarify (see King, Tomz, Wittenberg 2000).

districts (Table 5.9, rows 3, 6, 9 and 12) we observe that candidates with prior experience are far more likely to be elected than those without any experience, indicating that *entrepreneurs* are rewarded.

Candidates without prior experience in elected office are less likely to be elected as competition becomes more intense (compare rows 1 and 3). Moreover, increased competition even hurts candidates with prior congressional experience, although the decline is much less steep (from 0.48 to 0.29 for Liberals with prior congressional experience versus 0.32 to 0.03 for Liberals without prior congressional experience). When faced with 286 competing lists, a Liberal congressman has a 19 to 40 percent chance of winning election, a far cry from the 2 to 4 percent chance a Liberal without experience has in that district. The probability that a list headed by a one-term Conservative will be elected declined from 54–65 percent to 26–52 percent as the number of lists in a district moved from the minimum to the maximum. This points to the ability of *entrepreneurial* behavior to undermine the advantages of incumbency and may encourage Congress members to view elections as a one-shot deal.[19] This may discourage candidates from pursuing long careers in elected politics and may explain the relatively high turnover that has been observed in the Colombian Congress. Implications for behavior include increased incentives to focus on narrowly targeted pork-barrel projects instead of programmatic national bills, to use (or abuse) one's position to promote a future career in the private sector, and to feel less loyalty to any partisan group, including the local vote brokers who proved so instrumental to electoral success in the immediate post–National Front period for both established parties. These findings support the assertions set out by Siavelis and Morgenstern in Chapter 1.

The effect of prior national experience is much stronger than subnational experience. Neither gubernatorial experience nor the interaction of gubernatorial experience with competition affects the probability of a candidate's being elected. But mayoral experience does predict a list's vote share. In fact, former mayors are the only group whose probability of being elected increases as the number of lists grows (see Table 5.9).[20] Thus, the value of name recognition bears out our initial expectations regarding the personalization of politics. The end of the National Front opened the door for increased competition and fostered an environment in

19. This does not mean there is no incumbency advantage as the probability these candidates are elected is well above that for candidates with no experience. More likely this suggests that in districts such as Bogotá, where the number of lists running is typically much higher than anywhere else in the country, it is difficult for any candidate to truly distinguish him- or herself.

20. These results should not be read as implying there is not progressive ambition; more detailed studies of careers are needed. Further, there is reason to suspect that some high-profile mayors are driving these results. For instance, Antonio Navarro-Wolff, a former member of the M-19 guerrillas and the leader of the now-defunct ADM-19 (Alianza Democrática) party, was elected to the mayoralty of Pasto, a municipality bordering Ecuador, in 1994 and a few years later was elected to the Colombian Congress. His position as Pasto's mayor notwithstanding, he is considered a national political figure with extremely high name recognition and is prominent in discussions of political reform.

which successful candidates are those who have some name recognition. The advantage enjoyed by incumbents and especially by former mayors as competition increases points to the importance of being individually identifiable, a characteristic associated with *entrepreneurial* behavior.

Virtually every aspect of the selection and election process benefits those who can distinguish themselves as individuals and dispense with staid partisan labels. The emergence of *entrepreneurs* in Colombia has implications for behavior once the candidates are in office. According to Siavelis and Morgenstern (Chapter 1, p. 23), the *entrepreneur* should "seek any way to cultivate the instrumental and episodic support of voters, . . . engage in more populist rhetoric and discuss few particulars of ideology or policy."

Once candidates are in the legislature, their behavior in terms of bill sponsorship provides further support for our assertion that Colombian politicians engage in *entrepreneurial* behavior in cultivating support "any way" they can. Whereas we might expect the *party loyalist* to initiate predominantly nationally oriented legislation and the *constituent servant* to initiate predominantly locally oriented legislation, expectations regarding *entrepreneurs* are less clear-cut. We expect the *entrepreneur* to initiate some locally focused legislation, as such bills allow them to claim credit and reward supporters. We would also expect the *entrepreneur* to introduce nationally or sectorally oriented legislation, in an effort to gain a reputation and build support that may prove valuable for careers in the public or private sectors—in contrast to the *constituent servant*, who should be expected to focus almost exclusively on local legislation. Since the *entrepreneur's* "patrons" are likely to come from a variety of places, behavior will be far more diverse than it is for *constituent servants* or *party loyalists*.

Bill initiation data from the 1986–1990 and 1994–1998 periods reflect the variety of different bills initiated by members of the Colombian legislature.[21] For both houses of Congress, bills were categorized as targeted at national, regional, sectoral, local, or individual constituencies, following Taylor-Robinson and Díaz (1999). Undeniably, Colombian Congress members pay attention to locally and regionally targeted legislation, since 30.6 percent of the bills in the 1986 Congress and 25.4 percent of the bills in the 1994 session of Congress initiated by members were locally or regionally targeted (Escobar-Lemmon et al., n.d.). Meanwhile, only 2 percent of bills in 1986 and 2.5 percent in 1994 initiated by the executive were locally or regionally targeted. However, Colombian representatives did not focus all their efforts on these bills. In the 1986 and 1994 sessions of Congress, 44.1 and 50.2 percent, respectively, of legislator-initiated bills were nationally focused. Although this is smaller than the percentages of executive-initiated bills for these two sessions of Congress (68 percent and 73 percent, respectively), this is not the pattern of a *constituent servant*. Indeed, in both sessions of Congress the total number of nationally focused bills exceeded the number of regionally, locally, and

---

21. This provides us with data on two complete sessions of Congress, one before and one after the 1991 constitutional reform.

individually focused bills combined. Nevertheless, given what we know of their appraisal of the factors that propelled their success and the *avispa* strategy that dominates the two parties, we would be hard-pressed to conclude that they were *party loyalists.* Thus, the results of aggregate bill initiation data suggest that deputies are paying attention to local issues that are most likely to produce rewards in the short term, but they are also giving attention to national issues.

Avellaneda and Escobar-Lemmon (2006) classified legislators for these two sessions of Congress according to the dominant type of legislation they initiated. Legislators who initiated an equal number of bills of different types or who had no single majority type of bills were classified as mixed. Their classification reveals that 36.6 percent of legislators focus mostly on national legislation; 5.1 percent focus mostly on sectoral issues; 4.1 percent on regional issues; 7 percent on local issues; 1.4 percent on individual issues; and 12.1 percent focus on a combination of categories. This varied pattern confirms our argument that there are few, if any, true *constituent servants* in Colombia, as the mixed strategy is more common than an exclusive focus on regional or local bills. As additional evidence for the prevalence of the *entrepreneur* type we point to the fact that Avellaneda and Escobar-Lemmon find 33.6 percent of legislators do not initiate any bills. They observe that these non-initiators are significantly less likely than any other type to seek to remain in the Congress. This provides further evidence for our argument that Colombian congress members are *entrepreneurs* as they seek to be active in a variety of areas where they believe they have a chance to make their mark.[22] *Entrepreneurs* engage in the type of bill sponsorships they expect to be most "profitable," a behavior that leads to a mixed pattern of initiation where some find locally targeted bills most profitable and others find national bills most profitable.

Conclusions

In Colombia, formal institutional variables created a permissive electoral system that made it easy for potential candidates to get their names onto the ballot without requiring them to obtain the blessing of party leaders. Meanwhile, permissive party rules and decentralized nomination procedures led to the development of informal norms that only exacerbated the tendency for politicians to "go it alone." This combination of formal and informal pathways created a system that until 2003 favored and in many ways necessitated *entrepreneurial* behavior. One of the clearest manifestations of *entrepreneurial* behavior in Colombia is the acceleration of *operación avispa* as a strategy. We trace the development of strategies adopted after the dismantling

22. Avellaneda and Escobar-Lemmon (2006) note that, irrespective of majority type, the average Colombian deputy initiates 2.78 bills per term, of which 1.76 are national, 0.42 are sectoral, and 0.6 are local, regional, and individual, which further suggests that although local issues matter, on average filing locally oriented legislation is not a dominant strategy.

of the National Front. List proliferation was originally adopted as a sort of party solution to the emergence of challenges from within and without, but it morphed into a facilitator of electoral atomization. The informal institutions made it difficult for those elected to change formal electoral rules, and it would be almost thirty years after the informal roots of *entrepreneurship* were laid, in 2003, that political reforms seeking to limit list proliferation and the number of competitors were undertaken. What is more, even in spite of widespread calls to reform the incentive structure in Colombia and the adoption of new rules, informal rules fostering *entrepreneurship* may continue to persist into the future. After all, the new rules provide parties with an opportunity to continue rewarding those who "stand out" from their partisans, since the parties can choose to use open or closed lists. This important escape clause is a manifestation of the persistence of *entrepreneurial* norms that may continue to color the Colombian electoral landscape.

We find that list proliferation (our indicator of *entrepreneurial* behavior) has clear implications for those wishing to compete for office. *Avispa* benefited candidates with prior electoral experience and those who had previously served in high-profile posts. The fact that former mayors tended to do better as competition becomes more intense indicates strong local loyalties, which may be inherent in the system, and reinforced by the personalization of elections. Moreover, *entrepreneurial* norms have shaped the behavior of those elected to national congressional positions. Rather than court party leaders, candidates are resourceful in the ways they court voters through their legislative initiatives. Since voters are not their only constituents, they have sought to benefit a host of actors, including *gamonales*, through targeted legislation. To an extent, this malleability of interests has enabled the Colombian political system to function in the face of extrasystem challenges.

What does the value of individual name recognition in securing election mean when it comes to whom deputies serve or to whom are they loyal? Siavelis and Morgenstern suggest that *entrepreneurs* are loyal only to themselves. Our results are largely consistent with deputies who value their individuality, but also do want to be beholden to the party leadership. This personalistic link, which leads us to classify them as *entrepreneurs*, is firmly rooted in the party system and furthered by the electoral system, at least until 2003. This personal link has resulted in *entrepreneurs* who are dependent upon their own credentials, especially as elections became more competitive. It remains to be seen just how effective recent reforms are in changing these patterns of behavior. Before 2003, deputies in Colombia very much believed that they as individuals represented their supporters (either the country as a whole or the people in their department), without the intermediation of political parties, believing it better to stand alone than in bad company.

Chapter Six

Legislative Recruitment in Mexico

JOY LANGSTON

In this chapter I examine how parties in Mexico choose their candidates and how these methods have changed over time. We find that despite operating in the same institutional environment, the three most important parties—the once-hegemonic Party of the Institutional Revolution (Partido Revolucionario Institucional, or PRI), the center-right National Action Party (Partido Acción Nacional, or PAN), and the center-left Party of the Democratic Revolution (Partido de la Revolución Democrática, or PRD)—deal with the challenges of candidate recruitment and selection in different ways, leading one to believe that constitutional and electoral institutions alone cannot explain candidate selection in Mexico. To understand the changing nomination methods used by the three parties, one should also look at two additional factors: first, the party's organizational background before the onset of democratization, and second, the effects of increasing electoral competition and the dilemmas this creates in a federal system.

Mexico has undergone a prolonged transition in the last decade, and the parties are reacting to their new institutional and competitive context in new ways; thus, the issue of why and how parties change their formal rules is perhaps a more important issue here than in other nations in Latin America, whose parties have not changed selection rules significantly in several years. For this reason, the chapter deals with statutory rules changes more than the problem of the policy consequences of candidate selection and recruitment. In Mexico, little work has been done on why parties change their rules; in fact, there is little recent work on nomination procedures as such.[1] If we assume that statutory rules are valuable resources in that they help determine beneficial outcomes, then we should expect that they would be costly to change (Koelbe 1992, 52). Yet, in the typical literature on candidate selection (Epstein 1980; Gallagher and Marsh 1988; Hazan 2002), we find few testable hypotheses to explain when

---

1. For an important exception, see Bejár (2004).

different kinds of parties in the same institutional settings exhibit different selection techniques, and why party leaders choose to transform these rules. Changes to these selection methods can illustrate how parties react to transformations, such as increasing electoral competition, in the political environment in which they must work.

Candidate selection can be categorized along two important dimensions: the level at which nominations are decided, and the level of openness in who is able to participate in these decisions. One important discussion in the literature revolves around how the level at which nominations are made is related to the type of electoral system. Czudnowski (1975, 221) argues, "The party selection is closely related to the electoral system. When a candidate has to be elected by a local or regular constituency, he will tend to be selected by the local or regional party organization." Gallagher and Marsh (1988) reject this correlation, because they find no empirical support for it, whereas Norris (1997a) declares that owing to a host of new empirical studies, one can safely assert that there is a relation between electoral rules and the level at which nominations take place. However, if this were completely true, then all major parties working within the same set of institutional rules should exhibit similar centralized or decentralized selection methods, which is still not the case in Mexico, most likely because of the seventy-year hegemonic control of the political system by the PRI and the slow evolution of democracy since the end of the hegemonic period in 2000.

One can derive several expectations about how nomination methods can change in a formerly hegemonic political system that has undergone a transition to democracy. We hypothesize that party selection rules under the authoritarian regime often reflected the organizational birth of the party and the political reality of low to nonexistent political competition. As a result, one sees highly centralized and closed informal practices in the case of the hegemonic PRI,[2] and decentralized rules in the case of the opposition PAN, a party that was organizationally based on state affiliates. In the PRD, the demands for internal democracy and the inclusion of all groups and parties that originally made up the center-left party helped dictate open, decentralized nomination methods.

In terms of changing rules or informal practices, one should expect to see that a transformation in the electoral environment affects the ability of each party to win elections, and causes internal ruptures over winning selective benefits. Therefore, in the case of the PRI, as electoral competition rises, party leaders deliver more decisionmaking power to subnational executives who can get out the vote. In the case of the PAN, one finds that far higher probabilities

---

2. For more on the relation between the formal candidate selection rules of the hegemonic PRI and its informal practices, see Langston (2001).

of winning elected posts cause conflict within the party, which leads to even more open and decentralized forms of selection. For the PRD, one sees a surprising evolution of its selection rules: more competitive elections drive the party to maintain its already decentralized selection rules, but party leaders at the national level attempt with greater frequency to impose party outsiders with better chances of electoral success.

Last, the electoral system in Mexico is a mixed form of representation that includes plurality races run in single-member districts with a smaller proportion of members of Congress being elected under proportional representation (PR).[3] The pressures of electoral competition are different for candidates in plurality races than for those in PR districts, and so we should expect to see different nomination forms for these two types of representation.

Although both Chamber and Senate nomination processes have been transformed in each of Mexico's three main parties over the past years, this chapter looks almost exclusively at Senate recruitment and selection for several reasons: first, more is known about the lower chamber of Congress, so this is a good opportunity to concentrate on the upper chamber, relatively unknown territory; second, the Senate is slowly gaining in importance as a center of policymaking; third, we have data on Senate candidates for both the hegemonic (which lasted until the mid-1990s) and competitive periods that does not exist for the Chamber of Deputies; finally, senatorial nominations demonstrate the difficulties and challenges of changing nominations.

In reviewing the literature on candidate selection and its effects on legislative behavior for Mexico's Chamber of Deputies, one finds that selection is largely controlled by the PRI's national leadership, in negotiations with the governors (despite changing formal rules that were supposed to open up selection to registered voters). Electoral competition has driven the PRI to recruit more candidates whose careers are based in local politics and who are close allies with the governors and better known to voters than candidates under hegemonic conditions (Langston 2002). The PAN used district-level nominating conventions, made up of party delegates, and has now instituted what are in effect small closed-party primaries based on votes of registered party members, called militants (Wuhs 2006). The PRD has also moved from a mix of delegate conventions and primaries to open primaries alone to choose lower-house candidates.

The parties have continued to exhibit strong discipline in votes in the lower chamber well into the competitive era (Casar 2000; Nacif 2003; Weldon 2005, 2006). This is usually explained through several variables: the consecutive no-reelection clause of the Mexican constitution, which forces legislators out

---

3. Mexico's Chamber of Deputies has five hundred representatives, three hundred of whom are elected in single-member districts and two hundred from closed lists that are made up of five regional districts that elect forty members each.

after a single three-year term; the national party's control over public campaign financing; the largely party-based vote in plurality districts because of the no-reelection clause; and the continued role of the party in candidate selection. So even though candidates for deputy tend to come from the local political arena, they are still beholden to their party leadership and governors for future career opportunities and thus continue to vote in a disciplined fashion.

Siavelis and Morgenstern have devised a set of categories to clarify the types of candidates that are produced from different recruitment and selection methods (see Chapter 1). The authors hypothesize that closed nomination methods, such as impositions and party conventions, in which candidates are selected by either party leaders or party activists, are more likely to produce *party loyalists*, whereas those chosen by registered voters allow party outsiders or *constituent servants* to capture nominations. One might expect that candidates who are more popular with a wider array of potential voters—those chosen in primaries—to be better able to win elections, whereas those who win nominations as a result of methods where the party controls the vote would be less so. For Mexico, this argument on legislative recruitment and selection must be tempered by the realities created by the no-reelection clause. Senators are elected for six-year terms, and for constitutional reasons they cannot run for the same post in the next electoral cycle. This makes the party vote an especially important element in legislative success, even for the Senate. One way of thinking about the importance of the Senate candidates is to look at split-ticket voting on the state level over time. The state-level Senate vote does not vary significantly from the presidential results in the same state. Although senatorial candidates may not attract voters the way a presidential candidate does, there are only two of them per state and they serve six-year terms. One can place the personal vote for a senator somewhere between the more candidate-driven presidential vote and the more party-driven deputy vote. For this reason, *party insiders* have the upper hand in legislative recruitment, which is less the case for executive, especially gubernatorial, candidates where candidate identity matters more to voters. A candidate's identity does matter, but because the parties still control ballot access to most elected positions, a "good" Senate candidate—that is, one with prior elective or governmental experience—is one who usually has been a member of his particular party for several years.

In this chapter I look first at the electoral system and the specific rules of representation for the Senate; then I discuss each party separately. Within each party section, I present a short organizational history, an assessment of how a Senate seat fits within the typical career path of a party politician, a discussion of the formal rules and informal practices of candidate selection, candidate profiles (if available), and an explanation of both why and how the parties changed their Senate nomination rules and practices.

Mexico's Electoral System

Mexico is a presidential, federal regime with a bicameral legislature and thirty-two states (thirty-one federal entities and the Federal District, encompassing Mexico City, which has similar attributes to a state). Consecutive reelection is constitutionally prohibited for the legislature and mayors, and no president or governor can ever serve in that same position again. To appear on the ballot, a candidate must be registered by a party. Mexico's 128 senators serve six-year terms. Three senators are elected in each state in a closed, two-person ballot. The party that wins the statewide vote places both of its candidates from the closed two-person list (a binomial ticket) in the Senate and the remaining seat goes to the first name of the second-place party. In the electoral reforms of 1993, the PAN and PRI negotiated a reform to allow first minority senators, who were first seated in the 1994 elections. The party that comes in second place in the state is thus able to place the first name from its closed two-person ticket. The remaining thirty-two senators are elected through a closed thirty-two-person national list, the seats roughly distributed according to the national proportion of the vote. Thus, the Mexican Senate necessarily includes minority-party representation. Furthermore, because of the PR aspect of Senate representation, party leaders can enter the Senate on a safer track, just as in the Chamber of Deputies. The full set of 128 senators is elected concurrently with the president and the five hundred members of the lower house of Congress, who serve for three years.

Candidate Selection Rules and Candidate Profiles in the Three Major Parties

This section discusses the candidate selection rules for each party and how they have changed during the competitive era of Mexican politics.

The PRI

For over seventy years the PRI was a hegemonic party that acted as the base of support for an inclusive, authoritarian state. All presidents from 1929 until 2000 were members of the PRI or its organizational predecessors. The party was born as an overarching alliance of almost all local and regional parties that had sprung up after the Mexican Revolution of 1910. One of the greatest struggles of the PRI in its first three decades in power was to centralize power by moving power away from the states and up to the federal level in order to subdue the enormous authority and prerogatives of the governors and local *caudillos*, or bosses (Garrido 1982). The other conflict was to create both formal and informal rules to maintain the unity and coherence of the broad political coalition.

Candidate selection was one of the most important tools for solving both the centralization and control problems. There was little hope of a political future outside the PRI coalition in an institutional context where consecutive reelection for legislative posts was prohibited by the constitution and where PRI leaders could control their ambitious politicians through ballot access.[4] By imposing legislative and executive candidates within a context where politicians had no possibility of a successful "exit" option, party leaders, including the president, could affect party politicians' behavior, since all PRI hopefuls had to continually leave their elected posts and search out new ones, and could gain access to the extremely valuable PRI ballot only with the agreement of the organization's leaders.

Federalism was largely subverted under this system of control. Each president could practically appoint any governor he chose, despite the constitutionally protected elections of state executives, because of the lack of serious opposition challenges and executive control over gubernatorial nominations. Furthermore, PRI presidents had the informal prerogative of deposing governors if their performance in office was found wanting. In terms of resources, the the federal government made a series of tax agreements over time with the states to take away the administrative burden of tax collection from the subnational governments and redistribute these resources via federal transfers. The Senate was not a legislative body designed to represent state interests in federal policymaking under this atrophied federal system.

Although the Senate in particular and the legislative branch in general had little role to play in policymaking in the highly executive-centered regime, ambitious politicians within the PRI had strong incentives to compete for Senate candidacies. Traditionally, senators were the prime candidates to win nominations to gubernatorial posts, and this tradition continues until today. Sitting governors have always had good reasons to attempt to place their allies in Senate candidacies to strengthen their political résumés and groom them as their successors.

Table 6.1 cannot tell us anything about the universe of PRI senators who wished to become governors and failed, but it does speak to how important an upper house seat was to future political advancement. Furthermore, it highlights the importance of the legislative path to the governor's mansion: 52 percent of all governors had been senators prior to winning this office under hegemonic conditions, and almost 70 percent had been deputies. (The legislative experience of gubernatorial nominees of the other two parties will be discussed later).

During the last part of the hegemonic period, the PRI used state nominating conventions with democratically elected delegates to nominate senatorial

---

4. While reelection is prohibited for gubernatorial and presidential posts, politicians for other posts can be reelected to that same position after a term out of office.

TABLE 6.1 Prior Legislative Experience of Mexican Gubernatorial Candidates (Percentages), 1989–1994 and 1995–2005

Prior Position	1989–1994			1995–2005		
	PRI	PAN	PRD	PRI	PAN	PRD
Federal deputy	68	44	59	62	27	39
Senator	52	0	12	47	21	27
Local deputy	34	0	6	38	15	16
N	25	18	17	53	52	51

Source: Author's compilation, based on data taken from newspaper sources and from Grayson (2004).

candidates for plurality formulas.[5] Yet, in the noncompetitive era, informal practices negated the formal rules. In practice, plurality Senate candidates were chosen directly and were imposed on the party by the president and national leadership, although the preferences of the state-level PRI organizations and sectors were taken into account.[6] In the state nominating conventions, delegates were presented with a single two-person formula (called candidates of unity), and it was exceptional to have more than one formula registered.

Once competition for elected posts increased in Mexico during the 1990s, changes began to appear in the informal selection methods for legislative posts. The PRI was the dominant competitor in the Senate until 1988, winning over 80 percent of the national vote in the 1970s, but its electoral strength continued to fall during the 1990s, falling just below 50 percent in 1994, before dropping to less than 40 percent by 1997.[7]

The statutory rules for selecting Senate candidates remained unchanged after the PRI's loss of its Chamber of Deputies majority in 1997, and candidates continued to be imposed through undemocratic state delegate conventions. However, an important transformation occurred in how candidates were chosen *informally*. Because the PRI governors were expected to play a central role in getting out the vote in their respective states in what promised to be a close presidential race, many now had the political weight to demand legislative candidacies for their political allies, and so were able to negotiate with the national leadership.[8] Because

5. In January 2000, the National Political Council (Consejo Político Nacional), the deliberative body of the PRI, decided to hold delegate conventions. The actual prerequisites for the candidates that came out in March were so specific that only one possible candidate could be chosen. In addition, once the candidate had been chosen, the national leadership also had the right to ratify the candidacies, so the National Executive Committee (Comité Ejecutivo Nacional, or CEN) had another means to control candidate selection.

6. Interview with Pedro Ojeda Paullada, former president of the CEN, March 1996, Mexico City. Except for two midterm elections in the 1990s, senators are always chosen concurrently with the president, and so the PRI's presidential nominee was fundamental in the selection process.

7. In 1997, only PR senators were elected.

8. Both former leaders of the PRI, Dulce María Sauri and Humberto Roque Villanueva, report that by 1997, even before the PRI had lost the presidency, PRI governors had a great influence in choosing deputy candidates. Interviews with the author, September 10, 2003, and November 17, 2003, respectively.

the governors were crucial for the PRI vote, they were strengthened in the informal backroom Senate and Chamber of Deputies nomination deals.

In addition to the seventeen PRI governors (out of a total of thirty-two), groups within the state-level PRI, including those not aligned to the sitting PRI governors, were also able to place candidates by 2000. Most state groups within the PRI are formed around either the governor, former governors, or in some cases wealthy businessmen who dominate the landscape of an important city within the state. National-level political figures often make alliances with state groups and their leaders, and in return for political support the state groups can place some Senate and Chamber of Deputies candidates.

Table 6.2 shows the professional profiles of PRI politicians who won the right to compete for a plurality Senate slot both before (1982) and after (2000) the onset of competition. Two types of candidates emerge from the analysis: the first comes from the national level, from posts in the federal bureaucracy, the National Executive Committee (Comité Ejecutivo Nacional or CEN), or national corporatist sectoral leadership positions;[9] the second has spent most of his political career in the state political arena in positions such as mayor or local deputy and in the state government. Even without new decentralized nomination rules, the PRI leaders reacted to the pressures of competition by 2000 and began nominating far more politicians whose careers were rooted in local politics. Because governors were negotiating candidacies by 1997 and because their favored allies were state-based politicians, a higher percentage of PRI candidates in 2000 had prior experience as mayors, local deputies, and state party leaders (as opposed to sectoral leaders or federal bureaucrats) than did their counterparts from the early 1980s.

The local politicians are party loyalists who owe their candidacies to the fact that they have operated within the confines of the party organization for years. These changes to the PRI's Senate recruitment speak to the importance of a federalist system under more democratic conditions. Once electoral competition forces politicians to compete seriously in the states, the PRI turned to more local alternatives, while still reserving these candidacies for party loyalists.

The decisionmaking process and the types of candidates chosen for the closed-list proportional seats are different than they are for the plurality seats, in large part because winning a PR seat depends on the national vote, not on winning a specific statewide district. The candidates for the PR positions in the Senate, which have existed only since 1997, exhibit what one would expect given the lack of direct electoral pressure: party leaders with more national experience in the federal government, party posts, and elected officials who do not wish to chance the turbulent waters of plurality elections. The PR Senate lists are chosen directly by

9. The PRI holds three large peak-level associations: the popular, the peasant, and the workers'. Each of these three sectors is made up of local, state, and national labor unions, depending on the industry or service involved. The lower-level unions are then organized into one of the three peak associations.

TABLE 6. 2 Mexican Candidate Profiles for Plurality PRI and PAN Senators, Pre- and Post-competition (Percentages, Except as Noted)

	PRI, 1982	PRI, 2000	Percentage Difference	PAN, 2000
Federal deputies	64	59	−8	54.5
National positions				
National party	24.5	12.5	−49	10
Federal government	38	10	−74	NA
Party sectors				
National	35	5	−86	NA
Local	11	10	−9	
Total sectors	46	15	−67	
State positions				
State party	16.4	42	+61	59
Local deputies	23	33	+30	34
Mayor	5	20	+75	24
N	61	62		41
Losing candidates	NA	NA		17

Source: Author's compilation, based on data extracted from the *Diccionario biográfico del gobierno mexicano* (Mexico City: Fondo de Cultura Económico, 1994), and communication with party members, including the Secretaria de Capacitación del CEN del PAN. Figures do not add up to 100 percent because candidates could have held more than one post before winning the candidacy.

the party leaders: the PRI's presidential candidate, his closest advisers, and the president of the party. Here again we see party insiders winning candidacies; however, these party politicians are party leaders who operate at the national level, as sectoral leaders and as operators within the party's national bureaucracy and the federal bureaucracy.

After the presidential defeat of 2000, the PRI changed its formal rules for choosing legislative candidates. As of the 2001 National Assembly (party convention) senators could be nominated either by a delegate convention (with one or more names on the slate) or by an open state primary. The changes in legislative statutes appear to be driven by the deputy nominations, which had a spillover effect on the Senate. Primaries weaken the national party leadership, but the party's chief was willing to risk this move to win support from governors, knowing he could finagle the deputy selection rules at a later date. And in fact, in the 2006 selection cycle, because the PRI ran in an alliance with the Green Party, regular selection rules did not apply and a small group around the presidential candidate decided the lists of candidates.

The PRI originally used its centralized control over ballot access to the Senate to control its potentially divisive and ambitious political elite. Party insiders who had demonstrated loyalty and discipline and who had strong connections to a national party faction were rewarded by the president with a Senate nomination and therefore a seat. The national bias of Senate recruitment began to change once competition at the ballot box endangered the PRI's hold over the Senate in the late 1990s, after its loss of the majority in the Chamber of Deputies in 1997. Although the statutory rules did not change until after the 2000 defeat, political realities forced the party to informally decentralize the nomination process to allow governors and state party factions far more influence over candidate selection. Recruitment to the Senate changed as a result: far fewer national politicians were nominated to run for plurality races, though they continued to dominate the high spots of the closed PR list. However, party insiders continue to win Senate nominations for both the plurality and PR slots, as shown by their wide-ranging prior political experience, experience that is won through party-controlled ballot access.

The PAN

The National Action Party survived despite being shut out of elected office for close to forty years. Because it could not participate in national, state, or local government, it developed as a confederation of state parties with weak national leadership (Mizrahi 1997). As such, its candidate selection rules were highly decentralized and were based on the decisions of the party's rank and file, the militants. In this long period in the political wilderness, PAN candidates were without a doubt *party loyalists*: there was so little possibility of winning office and there were so few PAN members that candidate selection often consisted of asking family and friends to sacrifice their time and energy on a losing campaign effort. Because of the rise of electoral competition and, with it, increasing electoral success, the PAN eventually changed its rules for choosing both executive and legislative candidates. The entry of ambitious office seekers with fewer ties to the party's organization into the once-martyred party caused internal conflicts over candidacies that the long delegate conventions were ill equipped to handle. After its excellent showing in the 2000 elections in both the executive and legislative arenas, the PAN decided to open and decentralize its selection rules to an even greater extent, but still based these procedures on adhering to strict controls of party militants.

PAN Senate candidates who are returned from state elections and not the PR lists are *party loyalists*, but loyal to local militants who nominated them, not national party leaders.[10] With decentralizing statutory changes, they have become beholden to a wider group of local militants and it is probable that electoral success will create new incentives to create long-term careers within the

---

10. PAN statutes give the CEN the prerogative to approve or veto any candidate. See Francisco Reveles (2004).

party. PR senators for the PAN are also *party loyalists* in that they are national leaders who enter the Senate through the safety of the closed thirty-two-person national list.

The PAN was formed more than six decades ago by businessmen, professionals, and Catholic activists who were concerned about the growing power of the state over the economy in general and the socialist policies of President Lázaro Cárdenas (1934–1940); see Mabry 1973). In the early days of the party's existence, it had little or no chance of winning elections on a PRI-dominated playing field, and so the party leadership took as its central objective to "educate" Mexico's electorate. The party's ideology as the loyal opposition in a one-party hegemonic regime was crucial to its survival outside of public or elected office. Especially before the semi-proportional reforms to the Chamber of Deputies in 1963, the party was incapable of delivering almost any selective material benefits to its members and activists, as it rarely won elections in the single-member-district deputy elections and for this reason almost never participated in government, in any branch, at any level.[11] The PAN won its first gubernatorial race in 1989 but did not win a Senate seat until 1991.

Mizrahi argues (1997, 2) that as the PAN's electoral fortunes improved from the late 1980s and especially into the 1990s, it has been confronted with a dilemma: increased opportunities to win selective office benefits have created tensions within the party as an influx of ambitious politicians has placed pressures on an organization accustomed to losing, not winning. Furthermore, now that the party has a chance to win on Election Day, there is more tension among the many loyalists who feel that they deserve a candidacy. During the 1980s and 1990s, many ambitious office seekers who had never participated in the PAN when it could not win stormed the party's gates, a process which began especially in the northern and central parts of the country after the bank nationalization of 1982, and continues to this day. Many of these new *panistas* (from "PAN") are businessmen who are more concerned with good government—understood as producing and delivering public goods and services to the constituents without recourse to clientelist exchange—than with organization building or the party's traditional ideology of Catholic social action and civic education. The result is that the party's candidates do not spend much time or resources on the party, either before or after winning office (Mizrahi 1997).

So ambitious office seekers with business backgrounds—called *neopanistas*—began to win party nominations for mayoral and gubernatorial posts, but they were less interested in legislative positions. Many of them wanted to effect change directly in their cities and states, and believed local executive posts provided a better means

---

11. The 1963 electoral reforms were designed to give the opposition parties representation up to twenty seats in the Chamber of Deputies, even if they did not win a single SMD (single-member district) race (there was no proportional representation at this time). In the 1958 federal deputy elections, the PAN won just 6 seats in Congress (of 171 seats), and in 1961 it won 5 of 178 (Sartori 1976, 233).

to do so. Legislative posts were not seen as desirable during the 1980s and much of the 1990s and Senate nominations were still largely reserved for party loyalists with careers in their respective state parties and with experience in elected office.

Before 2001, the statutory rule for choosing candidates for governor and senator was a state nominating convention with delegates.[12] To be a delegate it was necessary to be a militant of the party, to register with the local municipal committee as a delegate, and to travel to a central convention. This type of selection process was highly decentralized, especially compared to that of the PRI, and also democratic because it was difficult for national-party leaders to impose candidates. If a party militant was interested enough in participating, he had the right to be a delegate; they were not elected (as in the case of the PRI)—they were self-selected.[13] It was, however, relatively difficult to become a rank-and-file member (militant) of the PAN, in part because the party wanted to make sure its ranks were not filled with *priístas* (from "PRI") trying to subvert the party and in part because the educational mission of the party required well-indoctrinated members. The rules to become a PAN militant have changed over time, but in general, an interested citizen must be sponsored by a party member, must take a series of training classes, and must wait at least six months before being admitted to the PAN. Once he has done so, he must also keep current in his dues and attend party meetings to maintain his rights as a militant. The PAN also keeps close tabs on members through their local organizations, and the states' membership lists are considered largely accurate (unlike those of the PRI or PRD). Thus, party nominations are based on the militants' choices, but this rank-and-file membership is closed and closely monitored.

The reasons a PAN politician would wish to win a candidacy can vary. First, the Senate is now a more serious policymaking body than it was, which gives a senator greater exposure; second, there is a governor-to-senator dimension in the PAN. As in the PRI, the Senate is used as a stepping stone to the governor's mansion (see Table 6.1); but it is also the case that an unsuccessful but well-fought run in a state executive race that raises the party's vote share above its historic average can lead to a run for the Senate, especially for a plurality seat, because it denotes that the PAN politician is popular among state voters.

Under competitive conditions in the 1990s and onward, a seat in the upper house of Congress for a *panista* has meant one of three things: first, if the candidate is running in a state in which the party has no electoral possibility, the politician is committing a strategic sacrifice, knowing he will lose the race, and he will expect future benefits for having helped the party fill a candidacy. Second, politicians competing in plurality races in states that are competitive for the

---

12. The statutory rules for choosing the presidential candidate had been changed prior to the 2000 race from a vote of the party's National Council to a closed-party primary (Reveles 2004).

13. Wuhs (2006) reports that the party has instituted rule changes to make it more difficult to become a convention delegate since 2003.

PAN are ambitious up-and-comers at the state level, but probably are not national-level party leaders. Finally, *panistas* high on the PR lists are most likely to be ranking members of the National Executive Committee or distinguished legislative leaders. A position at the bottom of the PR list is either punishment for irresponsible or undisciplined behavior or a sacrifice.

The electoral situation in which the party was situated for so many decades goes a long way toward explaining the "localist" nature of PAN Senate candidates for plurality races up to 2000. By localist careers, we mean those that are based in experience as a mayor, local deputy, or in municipal and state government. Unfortunately, we do not have professional background data on PAN candidates for the Senate from before the competitive period as we do for the PRI, but one could expect to see candidates with far less prior electoral experience than their PRI counterparts, as the party could barely win access to the lower house of Congress, municipal posts, or state government positions before the 1990s.

The information in Table 6.2 highlights the importance for PAN senators of loyalty to the party and a dedication to a state political career.[14] The loyalty is evident in the high number of senators who have lost elections for the party's cause. Because losing was a constant for the party in many areas, having run for a post with almost no hope of winning was considered a crucial aspect of party service. Almost 60 percent (58.5) have been members of the state party organizations. This too bespeaks the "*loyalist*" nature of the Senate candidates for the PAN. Very few politicians except for *party loyalists* would have been interested in holding such a post (especially up to the mid-1990s) except for those most interested in the party's long-term mission.

The table not only highlights the importance of party loyalty and a state-level career, but it also shows that, as in the PRI, the legislative route is highly important, with 54.5 percent of all Senate candidates in the 2000–2006 period having been a federal deputy prior to becoming senator. Many senators (34 percent) have been local deputies. What is most interesting is that there do not appear to be two separate career paths, one from the local level and the other from the federal, as in the PRI. Rather, even many national figures within the party begin their careers at the state level. This is no doubt true because of the historic lack of electoral opportunities in the federal government, owing to the PRI's continued control of the presidency between 1930 and 2000.

If one compares these PAN background figures to those of the PRI for 2000, it becomes clear that despite radically different nomination methods, the two parties' candidates are similar in their localist experience and their close ties to their party organization. The PRI sought out better candidates from local politics to run for the Senate, much like those the PAN chose.

14. Only forty-one of sixty-four plurality candidates were found.

The PR Senate lists contain a different set of political actors, especially, of course, those who are placed in the ten to thirteen highest spots on the closed thirty-two-person list—meaning that they are expected to win a spot. The formal statutory rules again admit the participation of the state conventions— each chooses a single name to be included on the PR list, according to the PAN Statutes and rules (*reglamentos*; see www.pan.org.mx). These thirty-two names, listed alphabetically, are sent up to the National Council—the three-hundred-member oversight body of the party's CEN. Then, each council member votes for ten different names. The top thirty-two vote-winners are placed in order of the number of votes received, except for three positions in the top ten places that are reserved for the CEN's preferences, which usually means that the best-known party leaders are chosen. There is no doubt but that the PAN leaders winning high-level positions in the PR list are *party loyalists* and they will go on to lead the PAN's delegation in the Senate, as some have already done in the Chamber of Deputies. Of the top ten names in the 2000 list, eight had been federal deputies and seven had been or became members of the CEN that year, higher percentages than those found in the plurality candidacies. Similar types of national leaders entered the PR lists in 2006.

Even during the 2000 candidate selection process, there were indications that certain party leaders were interested in "opening" the candidate selection processes of different elected posts. The president of the CEN of the PAN, Luis Felipe Bravo Mena, announced that the party should modernize itself via candidate selection reform after the 2000 selection cycle. Delegate nominating conventions became a problem for the PAN during the 1990s. First, more militants were interested in participating in choosing a candidate for governor or senator who might actually go on to win the election, and this caused the number of delegates to grow, making conventions more difficult to manage. Second, as mentioned above, party outsiders began to interest themselves in PAN candidacies—candidates for the PAN do not have to be militants, even though voting delegates do.[15] As noted, this began to cause a far greater amount of conflict within the party as *neopanistas* flooded the party in the 1990s, in the hopes of being named a candidate in an election that was now possible to win.

Although no party likes to admit to factional infighting among its ranks, in the PAN internal groupings began to form, and these groups began to compete fiercely to place candidates in the Senate. Combating this problem was a final reason why party leaders contemplated candidate selection reform, with the goal of dissipating some of this local feuding and placing the onus of selection on a majority of militants in each state. The local groups have been more active in selecting Senate plurality candidates than their national counterparts. These state groups

---

15. The party's CEN has the right to approve all outsider candidates.

were once defined by similar ideological splits as those on the national level, and later by their willingness to negotiate with the PRI-dominated regime under Carlos Salinas de Gortari or to support Vicente Fox as a presidential candidate. It now appears that present-day local groups are formed not on an ideological basis but rather around personalities and the search for posts and political space within the party.

Because these local groups have incentives to fight over candidacies, opening up nomination procedures was seen as a way of damping down conflicts by taking the choice away from the most dedicated militants in the convention setting that was more easily manipulated by different group leaders and involving more of the state's rank and file in an atomistic closed-party primary. Party statutes must be changed in a party assembly, and eighteen months after the PAN's stupendous series of victories in July 2000, the party's leadership and a part of the rank and file met to revise the statutes. However, candidate selection was not the only problem on the table, and one should understand these specific reforms in light of a larger drive to bring the party closer to the population without falling into the traditional patron-client practices of the PRI.[16]

In the 2001 party assembly the PAN chose to reform its rules moderately: militants can still vote in the internal elections for legislative candidates, but there were several important changes. First, militants do not have to register as delegates with their municipal committees. Second, the state or national party has the option to establish either one voting station or several; in the former case, the militants do not have to preregister, but still have to travel; if the party sets up several voting stations instead of a single convention location, the internal selection is run as a closed-party primary. Finally, party sympathizers (called adherents) are sometimes allowed to participate in primaries, as was the case in the 2006 presidential primary.

The multiple reforms show that the PAN has reformed its statutes in response to the exigencies of competing in elections and holding government office. The decision base of the party continues to be the militants, but the practical impediment to participation have been eased. The new dilemma for the party under nonconsecutive reelection laws is to choose candidates who not only are popular with the electorate but also identify with and will act in accord with the party's principles. In terms of types of candidates, clearly the PAN's candidates must be loyal to the party's rank and file in order to sustain a political career. As Mexico's democracy develops, long-term political careers within the PAN are increasingly possible and attractive, which should lead to more refinement in the selection processes and also enhance politicians' loyalty.

16. In the National Assembly (the deliberative assembly of the party) of December 2001, the PAN set up a commission to present a reform agenda, which was presented by the CEN and approved by the National Council (Béjar 2004).

The PRD

The Party of the Democratic Revolution (Partido Democrática de la Revolución) is a center-left party born of a split in the PRI and the marriage of the former PRI faction with several small left parties at the end of the 1980s. It had very little opportunity to win Senate seats, except for those from the PR list (first introduced in the 1997 elections). In practice, plurality Senate seats were seen as impossible to win, so these types of selections during the 1990s did not cause internal ruptures (as did nominations for mayor in certain PRD states or candidacies to the PR lists for the Chamber of Deputies). During this same period, the party used both conventions and party primaries to choose candidates for Senate seats. After the 2000 electoral disappointment, the PRD chose to reduce the number of nomination options to one: party primaries in which all registered voters can participate. Of the three parties, the PRD candidates are most closely identified with their constituents because of open primaries, but it is the party least likely to win Senate races. The PRD is also very willing to bring in "external" candidates, especially exiles from the PRI, to win states in which the PRD has been traditionally weak.

The Party of the Democratic Revolution was born out of a rupture of the PRI-regime during the presidential succession of the 1986–1988 period, and achieved an electoral miracle by almost defeating the PRI candidate, Carlos Salinas, in the 1988 presidential elections. Cuauhtémoc Cárdenas, together with other distinguished members of the regime, left the party his father helped build, and ran for the 1988 presidential election under a coalition banner, the National Democratic Front (Frente Democrático Nacional, or FDN), which included a number of small parties on the left and leaders of social movements (Garrido 1993). A good number of these organizations went on to form the PRD in 1989. The manner in which the PRD was born—from a coalition of leftist parties and ex-PRI members, in a battle in the electoral arena against the giant official party—is believed to have marked the PRD as an organization (Bruhn 1997; Prud'homme 1995). Because of the massive fraud that distinguished the 1988 presidential battle, successive PRD leaders had to negotiate between using the electoral arena to gain political space and automatically questioning the validity of negative electoral results in postelectoral street protests (Eisenstadt 2003; Meyenberg 2004). Elections were both a means to win political objectives, such as the control of government office and legislative weight, and a means to mobilize supporters against the authoritarian regime (Prud'homme 1995). Vote winning was not the only measure of support for the PRD, as it would be for parties operating in more democratic nations. Furthermore, the enormous popularity and charisma of the PRD's perennial presidential candidate tended to outshine the party's electoral and organizational efforts at other levels of government (Meyenberg 2004, 53).

The coalition that formed the ranks of the PRD created a propitious environment for internal group formation (Bruhn 1997, 136). For the first few years after the birth of the PRD, three groups circulated within the party's leadership: former members of the PRI, social activists whose base was in social organizations, and members of leftist parties that had joined the new party. Leadership posts and candidacies were given to each of these groups in the first stage of party consolidation; in subsequent years the constellation of forces within leadership posts changed as different groups grew stronger (Prud'homme 1995, 24–31).

Finally, the fact that the PRD was born of a rejection of the extremely "vertical" decisionmaking structure of the PRI would lead to a search for democratic rule-making procedures, which on one hand allowed for a great deal of internal democracy but on the other resulted in a party that is difficult to lead. Bruhn (1997) has written, "The PRD's attempts to develop internal democracy, while they brought many benefits to the party, also lay at the heart of some of its most serious weaknesses, including its inability to cope with internal divisions and its difficulty in institutionalizing or legitimating party rules" (169). During the early stages of party development in the 1990s, nomination rules provided for two ways to choose candidates for elected posts: the direct vote of the militants, or a convention of democratically elected delegates. Internal party primaries, although by far the most "democratic" decisionmaking method, caused as many problems as they solved. First, it was difficult and expensive to set up voting booths, even at the state level. Second, party primaries tended to cause serious splits in the organization because (much like the case of the PRI) it was difficult to assure compliance with internal procedures that regulated the primaries, so candidate hopefuls had strong incentives to subvert these internal elections. But conventions of elected delegates were also divisive, especially in a party characterized by such strong group identification. Bruhn argues that conventions allowed leaders more influence, as they were able to organize voting blocks, which then gave all group leaders incentives to do the same.

In 1997, Cárdenas won the first elections ever held for head of government (*jefe de gobierno*) for the Federal District. Not only did Cárdenas do well, he was so strong in the national media outlets that his city-level campaign helped elect *peredistas* (members of the PRD) from all over the country to Congress. After the victory of 1997, the PRD was an electorally viable party. This fact made candidate selection and office winning ambition within the party a far greater problem—much as it was for the PAN—than it had been when there was little hope of victory at the ballot box. However, because the PRD continues to be weaker in many states than the PAN, many of its battles among Senate candidates over who would win a high spot on the PR list took place among the national factions. Since 1997, the factions have become even more antagonistic, as there are more selective benefits to fight over. Increased office-seeking ambition seems to have been channeled through the already-existing party factions. These groups are not divided by ideology, and many of the leaders come from the groups formed within the party in the early 1990s.[17] The response to the internal competition marked the Senate selection cycle in 2000, as some leaders and militants became more wary of the price (literally and figuratively) of internal democracy and the party's leadership began to impose some Senate candidates for reasons of political expediency.

The no-consecutive-reelection clause means that for the PRD, as for all parties in Mexico, the route to power is a series of jumps among different elected, leadership, and government posts. Some of those who have been senators would rather return to the Chamber of Deputies than remain out of office (*Proceso*, April 2, 2000). Many established party leaders have come up through the Chamber of Deputies, while maintaining seats in the CEN. Younger members of the party are now winning posts in local congresses, especially the Assembly of the Federal District—in large part because the party is so strong in the Federal District—and then attempting to win candidacies in the Chamber of Deputies. Candidacies are usually won because of one's membership in a faction.

Table 6.1 shows that that having been a senator was an important springboard to winning a gubernatorial nomination for almost a third of those *peredistas* who ran for governor after 1995. Having been a federal deputy was even more helpful, probably because Senate posts were so difficult to win, and because so many of these PRD gubernatorial candidates had little chance of being elected. Nonetheless, when one compares the importance of a legislative seat to becoming a gubernatorial candidate, there are many similarities between the PRD and the PAN: 16 percent of the PRD candidates and 15 percent of the PAN had been local deputies. Twenty-seven percent of the PRD and 21 percent of the PAN candidates for governor had been senators in the competitive era. More PRD state candidates had been federal deputies (39 percent) before running for governor than in the PAN (27 percent) but in a data point not shown in the table, more PAN nominees had been mayors (37 percent) than those in the PRD (16 percent).

Until the late 1990s, Senate plurality seats were seen as largely unobtainable for the PRD. This is a large difference from the PAN, a party that was able to place twenty-four of thirty-two first minority positions in the Senate in 1994, when the first minority seats were instituted. Because the PRD was the most likely third-place finisher in many states, the state party organizations could fight over their senatorial candidacies without the outcome making a large difference for the party in terms of overall votes won. After the 1997 midterm elections, however, the PRD rose to become the second electoral force in some states, as measured by results of the 1997 elections for federal deputy.[18] This put the once-unreachable Senate on the map in terms of career paths of PRD party members.

---

17. Meyenberg (2004) argues that only once Cárdenas's power began to wane after the 2000 electoral disaster did true factions begin to emerge that were not beholden to his overarching leadership.

18. After the poor electoral results of 2000, the PRD lost its advantage in many states.

The hope of either winning the state and placing both names from the closed two-person list in the Senate or being the first minority and placing one person in the Senate generated conflict over candidate selection, as evidenced in Campeche, the Federal District, Estado de Mexico, Michoacán, and Morelos. In response to the internal tension and a concern with choosing popular candidates, the CEN of the PRD has imposed some candidates, sometimes even ignoring the preferences of the state-party affiliates in particularly competitive states.[19] It has done this through its National Council, which maintains a party-level statutory right to place external candidates in up to 20 percent of all candidacies. Furthermore, when the National Council decides that the party should enter into an electoral alliance with another party in a specific state, the internal selection process is suspended, even if a candidate has already been chosen.[20] Electoral demands can drive the party leadership to centralize selection.

Like the PAN, the PRD has different nomination strategies for the binomial plurality races and for the PR list. The PR lists for the Senate demonstrate a similar tendency to those of the PAN and the PRI: the party's leaders (and the strongest *party loyalists*) win high positions on the list (in the case of the PRD, in the top eight). In both the federal deputy and Senate PR lists, the four most important *corrientes*, or groups, fought over the final distribution of what is considered the true prize of the PRD, the plurinominal closed PR list. Because the PRD often runs in electoral alliances with other parties, it must give up a good number of PR seats to alliance partners.

The PRD's changing patterns of candidate selection since the creation of the party in 1989 until the 2000 elections demonstrate how both the organizational realities of factionalism and the opportunities and challenges presented by electoral competition have affected the type of party politicians who win nominations to the Senate. As the PRI dominance over the ballot box weakened, long-term political careers became possible for members of the left-leaning PRD and a place on the ballot gained greater value. In the case of the Senate, candidate selection is differentiated between the binomial plurality and PR forms of electoral representation. Both local and national factions fight to place their allies into the first spot of the two-person ticket because the PRD still cannot win the statewide vote in most states.[21] As the party has become more viable in electoral terms, the national leadership has stepped in to impose some external candidates on state-party affiliates. This raises a difficult dilemma for the PRD: mobilize supporters or win elections. In the mid- to late 1990s the two main-party leaders made a specific decision to dedicate more of the party's energies to the second goal. As a part of

---

19. See *El Universal*, April 4, 2000; *Expediente Político*, April 1, 2000; *La Union de Morelos*, April 1, 2000; and *Notimex*, March 20, 2000.

20. Article 15 of the PRD's statutes; see www.prd.org.mx.

21. For more on the local factions, see Bruhn (1997) and Sánchez (1999); on national factions see Meyenberg (2004, 59) and Sánchez (1999).

this strategic turn, the PRD has welcomed politicians from other parties, normally from the PRI, as candidates, and has been successful in strengthening the party's electoral fortunes in many states. This has led some party loyalists to complain bitterly when they were passed over for nominations.

Since the questioned 2006 presidential election results, which went against the PRD's popular presidential candidate, Andrés Manuel López Obrador, this dilemma has once again caused problems for the PRD's party organization. López Obrador has pressured his party not to negotiate with the new PAN president, and has had himself proclaimed the "legitimate president of Mexico." These moves have caused the PRD's popularity to drop, which could put its midterm legislative seat totals in jeopardy. What is good for keeping López Obrador in the news might not be good for the PRD as a whole.

Conclusions

In this chapter, in which I have focused almost exclusively on candidate type as a dependent variable, I have tried to explain why the parties' candidate selection rules were formulated in different ways. I have shown that there is a strong link between the organizational life of the party under hegemonic conditions and the specific forms that nominations took within the three parties. Second, because of Mexico's democratic transformation, I have explored the issue of why parties (and their leaders) change statutory rules or informal practices over time and have argued that the external electoral environment has had a great influence on changes to rules and practices. In particular, the PRI was forced by the possibility of losing its seventy-year majority in the Senate to allow its governors and state groups to place party politicians with state based careers in candidacies for federal office. Although the party did not change its formal statutory rules until after the 2000 defeat, it has continued to impose legislative candidates with the help of governors. The PAN, a party with decentralized nomination rules and strict controls over membership, saw internal conflict over selective benefits rise with its increasing success at the ballot box. In reaction, the party chose to decentralize further, instituting closed party primaries, while maintaining high barriers to entry into the party. Finally, the PRD is still buffeted by the winds of competition and change, unveiling a conflict between party ideals and the winning of elections; internal democracy, one of the party's bases, has cost the organization dearly, in terms of both finances and internal unity, and as the center-left party has become more viable in certain states, the leadership group within the National Executive Committee, the National Council, has been willing to impose candidates to assure a better electoral outcome.

Siavelis and Morgenstern hypothesize in Chapter 1 that different kinds of selection mechanisms produce different types of candidates, and thus the process affects politicians' behavior. The Mexican case sheds light on these relationships and also emphasizes the importance of candidate type on success at the ballot box. For the PRI, *party loyalists* with career paths based in national politics are no longer considered good contenders for Senate plurality races. National-party and sectoral leaders do continue to win high-level spots on the thirty-two-person personal closed list, however. In 2000, the governors and state-party factions negotiated Senate candidacies with the national-party leadership, which they also did for single-member-district deputy candidates in the 2000, 2003, and 2006 elections. This informal decentralization of nominations still produced candidates who were *party loyalists*, as evidenced by their career backgrounds. Party careers based in the state political arena give Senate candidates enough exposure to do well in statewide districts.

For the center-right PAN, decentralized democratic state nominating conventions, whose electors have been devoted party militants, have by and large chosen *party loyalists* to fill their Senate plurality candidacies. The 2006 Senate candidates were chosen in closed party primaries, forcing Senate hopefuls to lobby state-party militants in order to win a first- or second-place spot on the binomial ticket. The PRD has been willing to use external candidates to raise its senatorial profiles in certain states, despite complaints from its state-party affiliates, leading one to infer that the national leadership has serious concerns about the electoral viability of its state *party loyalists*, at least in more competitive states in which the party does not hold the governorship.

Chapter Seven

Why Factions? Candidate Selection and Legislative
Politics in Uruguay

JUAN ANDRÉS MORAES

Since the mid-1990s there has been a proliferation of studies
analyzing the determinants of candidate selection processes in
industrial democracies and the consequences of these processes for
the internal dynamics of parties (Gallagher and Marsh 1988;
Norris 1997; Davis 1998). The unit of analysis for these important
contributions has been almost invariably the party as a unified
actor. In other words, the predominant view has been that
political parties have primary authority to select their candidates
for different governmental offices (see Cox and Rosenbluth 1996;
McCubbins and Rosenbluth 1995 for exceptions). The major
question guiding this chapter is what occurs when the unit of
selection is not the party but a set of factions within the party.
In particular, this chapter examines the determinants of a faction-
centered selectorate and the consequences of this for the behavior of parties in the Uruguayan legislature.

I first show how a set of electoral rules and partisan regulations
structure the process for selecting representatives around factions
rather than parties as unified actors. In particular, the study shows
how the combination of the double simultaneous vote (DSV)
with closed-list proportional representation (PR) has stimulated
an organizational form in which faction leaders have discretion to
select who can be nominated for a seat in Congress. The particularities of the system, however, allocate this power to faction
leaders, thus creating *faction loyalists*, rather than *party loyalists* in
the terms set out by Siavelis and Morgenstern (see Chapter 1).

I also examine the effect of the nomination process on
legislative behavior. Others have documented the relationship
between the very high voting discipline of Uruguayan factions

I am indebted to Fran Hagopian, Michael Coppedge, Scott Mainwaring,
Daniel Chasquetti, Daniel Buquet, Lucas González and Annabella España for
their helpful comments and suggestions on earlier drafts of this paper. Funding
for this research was provided by the Kellogg Institute for International Relations
and the Department of Political Science at the University of Notre Dame.

and the electoral system and the nomination process. High discipline, I find, does not necessarily imply a lack of involvement of the legislators in individualistic behavior. In particular, while institutional analysis would suggest that individual legislators would lack incentives to provide constituent services (Carey and Shugart 1995), I show that Uruguayan legislators do provide such services, allocating a significant amount of personalized attention to voters (an average of about thirty hours per week). What are the incentives to provide those services? I argue that despite the negative incentives produced by the nomination system for the provision of services to particular groups, the internal party competition among factions, the career ambitions of individual legislators, and the ideological positioning in the left-right scale create incentives to provide those services. The analysis thus shows legislators can be simultaneously loyal to their factions and still provide constituency service. This service is provided to enhance individual candidate reputation and the reputations of factions to which candidates belong—meaning that constituency service serves the needs of both candidates and those who control candidates' futures: faction leaders.

The chapter has four sections. First, I review how factions have been understated as institutionalized units of selection within parties and how study of the Uruguayan case can fill this lacuna in the literature. Next, I show how the electoral system and party statutes and primaries shape the candidate selection process around factions, generating strong faction leadership control over nominations. In the third section I discuss the results of tests of the incentives to provide constituent services based on a survey conducted with a representative sample of fifty-eight Uruguayan legislators in 2002. In the last section I discuss the empirical evidence and spell out some conclusions.

Where Is the Faction?

The literature on candidate selection is not new in comparative politics. During the mid-1970s, a generation of pioneering studies (Eulau and Czudnowski 1976; Putnam 1976) largely dealt with the broader issue of the recruitment of elites in industrialized democracies. These studies analyzed the different roles played by politicians, their political socialization, as well as differences in access to political power across different demographic categories such as sex, income, race, education, and other personal attributes. However, within this sociological approach political parties and the formal candidate selection procedures were not an area of interest. Only more recently have parties assumed a central place in studies of candidate selection, where electoral rules and partisan regulations come to the fore as determining factors in the ways candidates are selected and the strategies followed by politicians to remain in office or move on to a different post (Gallagher and Marsh 1988; Norris 1997).

This shift in attention to political parties and the different types of rules governing candidate selection processes has been largely positive for theory development. However, there remains one striking gap in the literature: by focusing solely on parties as the units of analysis, it has neglected cases where different party subunits are in charge of candidate selection. In other words, parties have been largely observed as complex organizations using different procedures (more or less centralized and more or less democratic) to nominate their candidates in a relatively unified fashion, yet some political parties are organically structured around factions, and this organizational model has different implications for the internal dynamics of parties and their behavior in legislatures.

Case studies of the candidate selection process in most industrialized democracies use parties as their the unit of analysis (Gallagher and Marsh 1988; Norris 1997). For instance, in analyzing the Australian case, McCallister (1997) argues that parties determine recruitment, and "in common with other advanced industrial democracies with strong party systems, legislative recruitment depends on a party label" (p. 17). The same is true for Canadian parties, where Erickson (1997) argues that despite Canada's candidate-oriented electoral system, "parties monopolize" and "determine who will run under the party label" (34). Furthermore, in cases such as Finland and Germany, where nomination procedures are highly decentralized at the district level, local party elites have to negotiate the specific location of their candidates on the national list with national party leaders (Wessels 1997, 79; Helander 1997, 97). Even in the United States, where party leaders do not have control over the nomination process, party primaries have been the most important device for the supply of candidates in a unified or partisan fashion.

The fact that parties have been the predominant unit of analysis in most case studies does not mean that they have been viewed solely as monolithic organizations. Indeed, different authors have pointed out the presence of "factions" or "tendencies" such as Panebianco's (1988) "governing coalitions" or the different competing groups within parties described by Kitschelt (1989). However, these "factions" or "tendencies" in the literature have been very diffuse agents in determining not only the nomination of candidates but also the behavior of politicians once elected. One important exception in the literature is the study of Japanese parties. As some authors clearly show for this case, factions dominate the Liberal Democratic Party, although they have no legal status within or outside the party (McCubbins and Rosenluth 1995; Cox and Rosenbluth 1996).

In this context, I argue that the Uruguayan case demonstrates how factions may dominate parties and control the nomination procedures. In particular, I show how the unique Uruguayan electoral system and partisan regulations create factions as selectorates within parties. Unlike other countries where factions may exist, Uruguayan factions are institutionalized and stable agents within parties, with their own legal status and mechanisms to nominate candidates for parliament. In turn, this faction-centered selectorate has important consequences for the internal behavior of parties and the behavior of candidates once they become legislators.

Using Siavelis and Morgenstern's typology to classify candidates and legislators, I argue that Uruguayan legislators can be classified as *faction loyalists* because this particular type is characterized by centralized selection procedures (see Chapter 1 of this volume). In this case, I take factions as units of analysis rather than parties, because it is factions rather than parties that are key to recruitment and selection processes in Uruguay. I find that the Morgenstern and Siavelis argument holds up quite well when factions, the main organizational unit of Uruguayan politics, are analyzed under the same theoretical lens as parties within the framework of this volume. Changing the unit of analysis allows me to demonstrate that where faction leaders have control over nominations, legislators owe their seats and future renomination to those leaders whom they systematically repay with loyalty. This loyalty is expressed in terms of legislative discipline and in providing service to constituents to enhance the reputation of the factions to which candidates belong (Morgenstern 2001).

Legislative Recruitment

The Uruguayan electoral system has been traditionally considered as a case of complex legal engineering. Indeed, it is so complex that a prominent politician, Juan Vicente Chiarino, noted with irony that outcomes were "so secret that even Uruguayans didn't know for whom they were voting" (Solari 1991). In this section, I review both the legal and partisan rules (as independent variables) governing the candidate selection process (as a dependent variable) for the lower house, the Chamber of Deputies. In particular, I show how factions are the units of selection within parties and how faction leaders control the whole nomination process. Neither the recent changes to the electoral system, which forced primaries for the presidential contest, nor party rules mandating that conventions choose legislative candidates have limited the faction leaders' control. Institutions are thus a crucial determinant of the nomination process, but their influence here lies in their creating the framework in which nominations take place, not automatically inducing a particular selection method. This notion reinforces Siavelis and Morgenstern's (Chapter 1 of this volume) argument that institutions form the basic framework of incentives for the adoption of particular selection methods, and party systems act as accelerant or brakes on the general tendencies exerted by the institutional framework.

Two Basic Electoral Rules

The Uruguayan electoral system is structured around two main characteristics. The first is the double simultaneous vote (DSV), which fundamentally amounts to a simultaneous intraparty and general election. It was originally introduced in 1910 with the clear intention of preventing major splits within the two traditional parties. The main traditional parties are the National Party (Partido Nacional, or PN), also known as the White Party (Partido Blanco), and the Colorado Party (Partido Colorado), also known as the Reds. Uruguay's third party the Broad Front (Frente Amplio FA) is newer, having been founded as a coalition of previously fractured leftist parties in 1971. It first won the presidency in 2004 with the election of FA president Tabaré Vázquez. Basically, the two historic parties adopted the election system because DSV restrains defections that could hurt the electoral performance of parties by allowing intraparty competition. In other words, it allows national elections to operate as party primaries where different factions within parties compete for the executive and legislative seats in parliament. In essence, and as is often noted, the system provides something of a simultaneous primary and general election. Thus, the DSV can be considered as a variant of the intraparty preferential vote (see Katz 1986): on the ballots, citizens are allowed to select among parties (lemas) and then among factions (sublemas) within parties (Botinelli 1991; González 1991; Buquet et al. 1998; Morgenstern 2001).[1]

The DSV compels voters to choose parties before factions. The ballot is structured such that votes are primarily cast for a party, with diminishing concerns for the presidential candidate, the list of candidates for the Senate, and finally the list for the Chamber of Deputies (See Chapter 13, this volume, for a more complete explanation of the system).[2] In this way, factions are hierarchies with national leaders at the top (presidential candidates and senators elected on a national basis), followed by deputies elected with a mix of national and local bases (see Figure 7.1). Arguably, the most visible dimension of a Uruguayan faction (or sublema) is a list for the national Senate, which is usually shown below the names of presidential candidates on the ballot. (Botinelli 1991; Buquet et al. 1998; Morgenstern 2001; Piñeiro 2002).

Uruguayan factions are institutionalized agents within parties. This basically implies that not only are Uruguayan parties stable, but also that factions are stable groupings within parties across time and elections. Indeed, if a Senate list is the most accurate unit representing a faction, an *effective number of factions* (ENF) can be easily calculated to show that these agents are stable across time.[3]

---

1. Regarding legislative elections, one could argue that the system works with a triple simultaneous vote (TSV), given that voters vote for parties, a particular presidential candidate, and a list of candidates for the Senate and the Chamber of Deputies. For simplicity I will use DSV as a synonym of the TSV.

2. Buquet and Chasquetti (Chapter 13, this volume) present the ballot structure and discuss the way votes are allocated within parties.

3. The effective number of factions (Buquet, Chasquetti, and Moraes 1998) is calculated using Laakso and Taagapera's (1979) formula to calculate the effective number of parties. In this case, party votes are replaced by faction votes, or *sublemas*, as national Senate lists. That is: $ENF = 1/\Sigma(v^2_j)$.

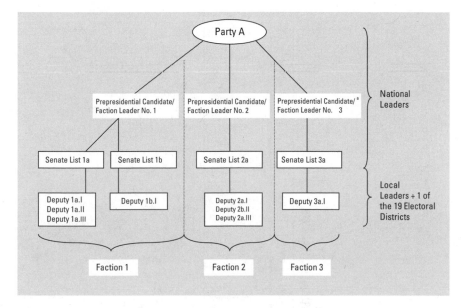

FIGURE 7.1 Party Organization and the Structure of Factions in Uruguay.

a. Presidents are elected for a five-year term in runoff elections since the constitutional reform held in 1996. Previously, presumptive or "pre-presidential" candidates had to compete in open primaries before the first electoral round. Before this reform, parties were allowed to offer multiple presidential candidates running under plurality rule.

Table 7.1 shows the *effective number of parties* (ENP) and the ENF from 1942 through the 2004 national elections. While the ENP and ENF have varied a bit, the range of values suggests a continuity of three parties, two key factions for each of the Blanco and Colorado Parties, and three or four factions in the Frente Amplio. The variation in these numbers is more indicative of shifts in the balance of power among the parties and factions rather than a shift in the number or identity of the competitors. Furthermore, as described in more detail by Buquet and Chasquetti (Chapter 13, this volume), since the mid-1920s certain factions have been dominant in each party, but several vie for power (the *herreristas,* named for Luis Alberto de Herrera, make up the dominant faction in the Blanco party, and the *batllistas,* named for Jorge Batlle, form the major faction in the Colorado Party). Some of the alternative factions have become stable and successful over time, such as the Foro Batllista (Batllista Forum) led by the former president (and then senator) Julio María Sanguinetti. Other minor factions frequently coalesce to campaign against major factions, as has been the case of the Movimiento Nacional de Rocha (National Movement of Rocha, or MNR), which joined with the Alianza Nacionalista (Nationalist Alliance, or AN), in order to survive in the electoral arena. This merger helped MNR leader Luis Alberto Larrañaga defeat former President Luis Alberto Lacalle and leader of the *herreristas* in the party primary of 2004.

TABLE 7.1 Effective Number of Parties (ENP) and Effective Number of Factions (ENF), Uruguay, 1942–2004

	1942	1946	1950	1954	1958	1962	1966	1971	1984	1989	1994	1999	2004	Mean
ENP	2.3	2.9	2.5	2.5	2.4	2.3	2.3	2.7	2.9	3.4	3.3	3.1	2.4	2.7
ENF—Colorado	2.2	3.0	3.0	2.1	2.3	2.5	3.9	2.7	2.3	2.5	1.9	2.0	1.8	2.5
ENF—National	1.6	1.4	1.4	2.7	2.0	2.5	4.6	3.8	1.8	2.9	4.2	1.5	1.6	2.5
ENF—Frente Amplio	—	—	—	—	—	—	—	3.6	2.6	2.3	3.5	3.8	4.2	3.3

Source: Buquet, Chasquetti, and Moraes (1998) and Piñeiro (2002).

A second central feature of the Uruguayan electoral rules is a closed-list PR (D'Hondt formula) system for electing the ninety-nine representatives and thirty senators. These features ensure that the distribution of seats is extremely proportional among parties in comparative terms because votes are primarily assigned on a single national district for both chambers. Once the distribution of seats among parties has been set, a second key step is the distribution of seats among factions within each party across the nineteen districts into which the country is geographically divided (also using PR with closed lists).[4] It is at this level where competition among factions takes place, because those groups have to compete within districts (ranging in magnitude -or seats per district-from 2 to 44) for the seats that the whole party won in the election.[5] I will develop this important point later in the chapter. For now, what is important here is that the distribution of votes within parties takes place among factions and across districts.

Clarifying the concept of a faction is necessary to understand what makes a faction the effective unit of candidate selection—but the concept of a faction is elusive. For instance, one critical view of the role played by factions in Uruguayan politics defines factions as "lists," and focuses on the party supply of deputy lists to show an important proliferation during the last decades (Vernazza 1989; González 1991; Monestier 1999). The core of this position implicitly assumes that deputies are self-selected and that faction leaders have no control over the nomination process. Thus, since parties are observed "from below," this perspective undermines the ability of faction leaders to select who can be nominated for the lower chamber. An important problem with this literature is that although one can agree that there are legal incentives for self-selection, running alone is electorally inefficient for most ambitious politicians without a national faction sponsoring the candidacy for a seat in the lower chamber. Arguably, the fact that national factions perform the electoral coordination explains the fact that the ENF has been relatively low and stable over time (see Table 7.1).[6]

Moreover, this view has been fairly criticized for ignoring the fact that representatives are vertically integrated: presidential candidates, national senators, and representatives are all elected in simultaneous elections (Botinelli 1991; Buquet et al. 1998; Piñeiro 2002). Looked at this way, factions are national groups that coordinate the supply of candidates for the lower chamber because aspirants have to be linked to national senators and presidential

---

4. The Senate remains as a single national district (M = 30).

5. More specifically (figures in parentheses indicate the number of districts with these size magnitudes): M = 2(11); M = 3(4); M = 4(2); M = 13(1); M = 44(1).

6. Note the difference with the Colombian case where until constitutional reform, self-selection was electorally efficient for individual politicians (see Pizarro Leongómez 2002; Escobar-Lemmon and Moreno, Chapter 5, this volume).

candidates on the same ticket.[7] Thus, faction leaders have control over ballot access, deciding who can be nominated under the faction label, which is the only level that really matters if we consider that parties as unitary agents actually do not present candidates for elective offices. In sum, this view "from above" largely supports Panebianco's (1988) argument that factions are groups with a clear vertical cut within parties.[8] The electoral system does not provide incentives for self-selection at the deputy level, but rather it promotes a highly hierarchical structure of national factions with powerful leadership.

Party Statutes and Primaries

The basic organizational features of Uruguayan parties have remained stable for more than one hundred fifty years. Indeed, there is a large body of evidence suggesting that Uruguayan parties had factions before the DSV was adopted in 1910, and DSV became the legal expression and solution for an organizational model of parties already in place. This is just one example of how political elites shape the rules by which they play, and this maxim applies not only to the electoral rules governing elections but also to partisan statutes. These types of rules in turn affect party organizations, the distribution of power within parties, and internal party competition among groups or factions.

As we have seen, Uruguayan electoral rules promote an organizational structure where factional leaders amass tremendous power through their control of access to elective (and some nonelective) posts in government. In this context, most Uruguayan parties have only weak mechanisms to counterbalance the power of faction leaders. Those limitations can take the form of party statutes or regulations that may cut across parties, such as party primaries. These types of statutes and regulations, however, are not sufficient to counterbalance or weaken the control that faction leaders have over nominations.

Party statutes differ for the three largest Uruguayan parties. Both the Blanco and Colorado parties stipulate in their statutes (approved in 1983 and 1999, respectively) that the national and local (departmental) conventions will nominate

---

7. Faction leaders also largely centralize campaign financing, since the Banco de la República distributes funds according to the number of votes won by each *sublema*, or faction, in the previous election. Deputies and individual candidates also contribute to their own campaigns.

8. Uruguayan factions have been relatively stable over time, as can be observed by noting the main leaders within the two traditional parties, the Blancos and Colorados. For instance, the current president, Jorge Batlle, has been a presidential candidate since 1966, leading a faction, Lista 15, originally formed by his own father, the former president Luis Batlle. Former President Julio María Sanguinetti (1985–1989 and 1995–1999) has been leading a faction, Foro Batllista, for over twenty years. A similar picture can be found in the National Party. Former President Luis Alberto Lacalle (1990–1994) leads a faction *(herrerismo)* founded by his grandfather during the early twenties.

the party lists for the national Senate and the Chamber of Deputies. These conventions also reflect the distribution of power within the party, as the size of the factional delegations is based on the previous electoral results. However, the party statutes allow for the nomination of different lists of candidates for both chambers, which implies that factions will provide those lists. Further, party conventions always endorse the lists of candidates provided by the factions, thus allowing the general elections to determine the distribution of votes and seats in parliament. The effective power of factions, is thus, also central to the functional weakness of party rules. The factions all benefit from allowing multiple lists and so, given the DSV, party rules about nominations become almost irrelevant. Further, because the factions have no statutes, the faction leaders have almost complete discretion.

The third main party, the Broad Front (Frente Amplio or FA), presents a somewhat different and more mixed picture. This party can be considered a coalition of leftist factions (Yaffé 2005), some of which used to be independent parties before the FA's inception in 1971, such as the Communist (Partido Comunista del Uruguay, or PCU) and Socialist parties (Partido Socialista del Uruguay, or PSU). In these cases, factions authorize their local and national conventions to select candidates for both chambers of parliament. The power of the convention is more de jure than de facto, however, as the factions' leaders—generally senators, representatives or local council members *(ediles)*—traditionally manipulate the nomination process. In other cases, such as that of the Uruguayan Assembly (Asamblea Uruguay, or AU) and the Movement of Popular Participation (Movimiento de Participación Popular, or MPP, the former Tupamaros), the statutes stipulate democratic procedures for the nomination of candidates. But these factions are also dominated by strong national leaders: Senators Danilo Astori and José Mujica, respectively.

AU was formed by Danilo Astori, a former senator and the current finance minister, in 1994. Since its foundation, this faction has had a strongly personalistic style, despite the fact that it has national and departmental authorities. According to interviews I conducted with party members and militants, even if Astori does not impose his preferences over the nomination process, he can nonetheless veto alternative candidates. Since party lists are closed, the challenge for potential candidates is not merely gaining access to the list but also gaining a position on the list that is propitious for winning a seat. The leader exercises tremendous power through the ability to impose the order of the names on the list. The same is true for the MPP, led by José Mujica, the current minister of agriculture and a former guerrilla leader. In this case, despite the fact that the faction has a strong democratic and participative outlook, my interviews and national electoral results show that the MPP has a centralized procedure whereby Mujica simply decides who gets the competitive spots on the list.

Arguably, what distinguishes the FA from the Blancos and Colorados is not the greater level of participation by or influence of militants in the nomination process. Rather, as Buquet and Chasquetti document (Chapter 13), whereas the Blancos and Colorados present multiple presidential candidates, the Frente Amplio has always had a single candidate. All factions within the Frente Amplio have national and local leaders, but the party has always united under a single presidential candidate. The leaders who have played that role, Liber Seregni from 1971 to 1989 and Tabaré Vázquez since 1989, have not been all-powerful. Although they have played relevant roles in the programmatic or ideological positioning of the party and the determination of the party's overall strategies, they have had no influence over the factions' nomination processes.

The central role of factions in the nomination of legislative candidates has not changed with the imposition of the new electoral law in 1996. In that year a coalition of Blancos and Colorados approved a constitutional reform stipulating that there should be open party primaries before national elections. This reform has had a tremendous impact in Uruguayan politics (Buquet and Chasquetti, Chapter 13, this volume; Buquet 2000), but it has in no way diminished the importance of factions within parties.

The reform has influenced the process of candidate selection in two ways. First, it forced the parties to select single presidential candidates through the use of primaries. But it did not mandate primaries for legislative candidates, so it allowed factions to continue controlling legislative nominations. Second, and perhaps more important, the reform prohibited parties (or factions) from presenting multiple lists for a single deputy seat in a given district. This actually had the effect of centralizing power with the faction leaders even more, since they now have the power to effectively force the choice of a particular candidate. A former candidate within a Colorado faction in a small district explained how his faction leader wielded power: "Senator Hierro came here and said that we had to support deputy Pérez, by unifying lists. . . . In this way, [national leaders] use their economic power, the force of their career trajectory, and a well structured organization to influence choice of candidates. The key point is that they put into balance potential votes with the cost of those votes" (Luna 2004, 180). In other words, in choosing a particular candidate, Senator Hierro solves a coordination problem, by drastically reducing the supply of candidates. In choosing the candidate with the highest probability of winning at the lowest cost, he effectively diminishes the electoral inefficiencies of the party in general and the faction in particular.

In a few exceptional cases the faction leaders have ceded their nominating powers to the party or the voters. The Foro Batllista, for example, used the presidential primary to decide the order of the list for deputies. Leaders who do not expect to do well in such primaries, however, are unlikely to submit to such procedures very often. As the former candidate quoted above clearly implies, the party primary for the lower chamber is not an open primary with free

TABLE 7.2 Influences on Legislative Candidate Selection in Uruguay—Means Comparison[a]

Party	Faction Leader Influence	Personal Reputation	Business Sector Influence	Labor Movement Influence
FA	3.73	2.88	1.36	2.20
PC	4.00	3.12	1.88	1.35
PN	4.09	3.36	1.60	1.40
Total	3.89	3.06	1.58	1.77

Source: Author's survey data for 2002. The question was phrased, "How would you characterize the level of importance of the following factors in your election as deputy during the last election?"

a. **Scale**: 1 = of little importance; 2 = somewhat important; 3 = of average importance; 4 = very important; 5 = enormously important.

competition for a spot on the list. Rather, the primary is an endorsement of the preferences or the results of the coordination game played by faction leaders.

Table 7.2 shows that legislators acknowledge the faction leaders' tremendous control over the nomination process. In a survey of fifty-eight legislators, the average respondent gave faction leaders' influence over candidate selection a score of almost 4 on a scale of 1 to 5, where 5 indicated "enormous" influence. Tellingly, this number is much greater than the scores for the influences of personal reputations, the business sector, or the labor movement.

In sum, neither the presidential primaries nor the party statutes governing the legislative candidate selection process has had a significant impact on nomination procedures because these rules have not counteracted the factionalized nature of the system. The conclusion, however, is not that institutions are irrelevant, as it is precisely electoral institutions that drive and underwrite the maintenance of the factional system. The impact of the electoral system on the nomination process is both direct and indirect. It operates indirectly by cultivating (or maintaining) the factions, and directly by allowing the factions to nominate multiple intraparty candidates. The overriding result, then, is that the faction leaders dominate the process, thus creating legislators (and in particular, deputies) who are loyal to factions rather than parties.

Behavioral Incentives

Given the features of the candidate selection process, what kind of political incentives act on individual legislators? The primary consequence of Uruguayan electoral rules is that party organizations are structured around factions whose leaders exert a great deal of control over the entire nomination process. Internally, these factions are very hierarchical, since until the 2000 election voters cast their ballots simultaneously for a party, a presidential candidate, a list of candidates for the Senate, and a list of candidates for the Chamber of Deputies. Since the reform, the presidential candidate has been elected separately, but each party's main candidate has continued to act as a faction leader. In this chain of authority, deputies are always subordinated to presidential candidates and Senate leaders, who have control over nominations. This suggests that two factors contribute to the distinctive form of factional organization.

Influence of intraparty competition. First, the intraparty competition among factions creates incentives to cultivate a "factional vote." The factional competition provides a collective incentive for faction members to differentiate their group from others within the party. This generates a tension within the party, similar to that which the U.S. congressional literature shows between individuals and collective bodies, like parties and committees. (Cox and McCubbins 1993; Carey 1996; Crisp et al. 2004). Second, despite faction leaders' centralization of the nomination process, the career ambitions of individual legislators create incentives to cultivate personal reputations. This is reinforced by the advantages that a personal reputation among constituents can have when faction leaders are choosing candidates. In this section, I focus my analysis on the future career perspectives of legislators to show this game of dual interests for legislators.

The preferential vote system within parties, inherent in the DSV, promotes internal competition among factions, creating a strategic dilemma: whether to privilege the party or the faction. Parties have the incentive to gain electoral support and there is a clear collective interest for all factions to win the election as a party. But at the same time, factions have to differentiate among each other to obtain the highest number of seats in both chambers and win the presidency (Morgenstern 2001). Thus, electoral rules simultaneously create the collective incentive to win the election as a party and a clear collective dilemma centered on the competition for votes among factions. Since the intraparty competition takes place among factions rather than individuals, I argue that legislators have incentives to cultivate a "factional vote." This point implicitly assumes that legislators are agents and principals of factions in a prototypical principal-agent model.

Furthermore, in electoral systems with an intraparty preferential vote such as the DSV, the incentives to compete within parties (arguably among factions) increase as the district size increases (Carey and Shugart 1995). This is clearly the case in Brazil and Colombia (Pizarro Leongómez 2002; Samuels 2003; Chapter 5, this volume). Uruguay has nineteen districts, two of which have much larger magnitudes than the others. In those districts—Montevideo and Canelones, which elect forty-four and thirteen members, respectively, to the Chamber of Deputies (out of a total of ninety-nine)—there is both inter- and intrapartisan competition. That style of competition stands in contrast to the fourteen districts that elect just two or three legislators. In these districts the competition is concentrated among intrapartisan factions, as the party division of the seats is generally a foregone conclusion. In other words, with three large parties competing for two or three open seats, each party competes with intrapartisan factional rivals as if the district magnitude were just 1, because the probability of winning more than one seat is very low.

Legislators' career ambitions. The second factor that contributes to the distinctive form of factional organization is the pattern of legislators' career ambitions (Mayhew 1974; Samuels 2003; Morgenstern 2004). Even beyond the mechanisms of candidate selection stressed before, different career aspirations (besides reelection) have important consequences for the behavior strategies pursued by legislators. As Siavelis and Morgenstern (Chapter 1, this volume) argue, cultivating loyalty and support among those who hold the key to future career aspirations is crucial. For instance, legislators concerned with running for local office in the future should have a particular interest in maintaining good ties to the district. According to my own interviews, Uruguayan legislators vary on their desired career paths: 48 percent stated that they would pursue reelection, 18 percent said they would run for mayor *(intendente)*, 9 percent, for the national Senate, 12 percent planned to seek an executive post in the administration, and 5 percent intended to retire at the end of the legislative term.

There appears to be a relationship between these alternative career paths, the level of leadership control over nominations, and the incentives to cultivate personal reputations. Reelection seekers are more reliant on faction leaders when the lists are drawn up than those who seek election to the local mayoralties *(intendencias)* or the national Senate. In the case of mayors, some important legal factors intervene in the nomination process since a constitutional reform was passed in 1996 that staggers national and local elections. One of the main by-products of this reform has been that mayors have gained some power within parties and their links with factional leaders have been progressively diluted. Indeed, mayors have become such an important group of political figures within parties that some of them now stand an excellent chance of making the leap to the presidency, and there is evidence that they are also starting to influence the nomination process in several small districts.[9] This type of locally oriented career implies that legislators will be more interested in ensuring votes at the district level, resulting in a greater tendency for them to cultivate a personal reputation.

Access to the Senate is more restrictive than the local mayoralties, because deputies have to have national name recognition or reputation within and outside the faction in order to be nominated by current senators or presidential candidates. Indeed, this is one of the most important reasons why there are more deputies running for the local mayoralties than for the Senate (18 and 9 percent, respectively).

9. This was the case for two out of three presidential candidates in the 2004 national elections won by the Frente Amplio. In this case, Tabaré Vázquez and Jorge Larrañaga were former mayors of Montevideo and Paysandú respectively.

The cost of creating a new faction (or Senate list) is extremely high both in terms of labor and resources and most of the time yields electoral inefficiencies. In other words, it is cheaper and more efficient for an incumbent deputy to run for a local mayor's office than to create a national faction.

In sum, legislators face different, and many times, contradictory incentives. The system promotes strong leadership control over nominations for deputies and other future career paths. As we have seen before, the combination of DSV and closed-list PR structures parties around factions with leaders controlling the nomination process. In this context, factions have incentives to compete with each other; by extension, their members are induced to cultivate a "factional vote."[10] Beyond this, individual legislators have incentives to cultivate their own personal vote, depending on their career ambitions.

I now look at provision of constituent services as a way to explore the extent to which legislators cultivate a factional and personal reputation in a context where the whole candidate selection process is concentrated in the hands of faction leaders.

Constituent Services

Traditionally, constituent service has been viewed as a type of legislative behavior oriented to cultivate support among particular voters or targeted groups within the electorate (Cain, Ferejohn, and Fiorina 1987). Basically, it has been linked to electoral systems where legislators have incentives to cultivate a personal reputation or systems where nomination control is highly decentralized or is not in the hands of party leaders (Norris 1997, 2004; Ingall and Crisp 2001; Crisp and Ingall 2002). In other words, constituent service has been an indicator of how legislators compete for votes when the electoral system clearly provides incentives to cultivate a personal reputation. *Prima facie* the candidate selection process does not give Uruguayan legislators strong incentives to provide services to constituents. There are, however, some collective and individual incentives to do so.

This discussion is based on data I gathered from a survey I conducted in 2003 among a representative sample of fifty-eight (out of ninety-nine) Uruguayan deputies. This section tests the how intraparty competition and the career preferences of individual legislators affect their propensity to provide constituency service. More concretely I test three basic hypotheses that arise from my previous discussion of the behavioral incentives of individual legislators.

Hypothesis 1 is that the higher the level of intraparty competition, the larger the effect on the provision of service to constituents. Since it is expected that the level

10. Divisions among factions within parties can be so deep that some voters whose candidate's chances to win the election are low will always prefer to cast their votes for the ideologically closest faction of the "other party" instead of any other candidate within their own party.

of intraparty competition varies with the district magnitude (M), Hypothesis 2 is that the larger the district magnitude the greater the provision of service to constituents.[11] Hypothesis 3 is structured around four subhypotheses concerning the impact of different career ambitions: reelection; election to a subnational executive government or mayoralty; election to a Senate seat; obtaining an executive post in cabinets and the state apparatus. In this case, although all the career preferences may be positively associated with the provision of service to constituents, reelection seekers have fewer incentives than those who have other career ambitions, because their political fate is more dependent on faction leaders.

The dependent variable to be tested is the number of hours per week deputies and their staff members spend with individual constituents (see the Appendix to this chapter for the questionnaire text). With respect to the number of hours spent, the question was open-ended, assuring an important level of variation in the number of hours reported. One of the implicit risks of this type of question and particularly the type of information that is being requested is that legislators can inflate the real number of hours. However, informal conversations with members of the administrative staff of legislators and permanent staff of the Uruguayan parliament indicated that the reported values are relatively reliable. On average, deputies allocate twenty-seven hours a week to constituent services, a surprisingly high number even when compared to countries where the incentives for personal vote seeking are relatively strong. Hagopian's (2002) survey shows that Brazilian deputies allocate an average of thirty hours per week and Chileans about twenty-five hours to constituency service.[12]

To test my expectations, I employ a negative binomial regression model (NBR).[13] This type of model is more suitable than a linear regression for two basic reasons dealing with the dependent variable, hours. First, OLS (ordinary least squares) leads to erroneous estimates when the values of the dependent variable are only positive integers (count data). Second, given that a precondition for using a Poisson model is that the mean must be equal to the variance, and this is a difficult condition to fulfill, NBR is the only alternative.

The model that I run regresses the number of hours a deputy allocates to constituent services (CS) on the district and candidate characteristics discussed earlier. The regression is specified as follows:

$$CS = \alpha + \beta_1 ENF + \beta_2 M + \beta_3 Resk + \beta_4 Amb1 + \beta_5 Amb2 + \beta_6 Amb3$$
$$+ \beta_7 Rel_{t-1} + \beta_8 NL + \beta_9 FA + \beta_{10} PN + \beta_{11} PC + \varepsilon,$$

11. Note that the correlation between the district magnitude and, respectively, the number of lists per party and the total number of lists is about 0.4 and 0.9. However, the correlation between the ENF and the district magnitude is only 0.2.

12. Thanks to Frances Hagopian for providing this useful data.

13. Here I use a methodological procedure very similar to that used by Ingall and Crisp (2001).

where

> ENF = Effective Number of Factions
> M = District magnitude
> Resk = Reelection seeker
> Amb1 = Seek intendencia
> Amb2 = Seek Senate
> Amb3 = Seek executive appointment
> Rel_{t-1} = Reelected in previous period
> NL = Number/place on the list
> FA = Frente Amplio
> PN = Partido Nacional (Blanco Party)
> PC = Colorado Party

In this model, the effect of the level of intraparty competition is measured with the ENF per party, at the district level (Piñeiro 2002). The effect of the district magnitude is captured by the district magnitude where the legislator was elected. Career preferences of deputies are captured by a set of dummy variables (see the Appendix to this chapter), including reelection; mayoralties or local government executive posts; Senate seats; executive appointments; and retirement. Given the marginality of results for retirement, this option was omitted in the estimation order to compare all other career patterns.

The model takes into account three control variables. First, since seniority has been systematically found to be a meaningful factor in the U.S. literature on congressional behavior, I included a dummy variable to capture the effect of this factor. In this case, it is expected that senior members work less than new members of parliament because those seats are perceived as safe by those who hold them (Cain, Ferejohn, and Fiorina 1987). Second, it also has been argued that the incentives to provide service in closed-list PR systems vary depending on the person's position on the list. The farther down a deputy is on the list, the greater the incentives to provide service. The intuition is that the effort required to gain better positions on the list or to gain access to other posts is costly for those with a less known reputation within the list. Third, the regression also controls for partisanship with dummy variables for each of the three main parties. There are two reasons to do so. First, the Frente Amplio has been a programmatic coalition oriented toward promoting public policies and reforms since it was formed in 1971 (Yaffé 2005). This has been evident during the last three mayors' administrations of the capital, Montevideo, where the FA has become a predominant party. In general terms, the Frente Amplio was born as and remains a programmatic party with a very critical discourse against the historical clientelistic practices of Blancos and Colorados. The second reason, though plausible, is more controversial: since traditional parties have been historically attached to the state, it is reasonable to expect that access to public resources may constitute an important strategic tool

TABLE 7.3 Negative Binomial Regression; Dependent Variable = Hours Devoted to Individual Citizens by Uruguayan Deputies

	Coefficient	$P > |z|$
Effective number of factions	0.116	0.000
District magnitude	0.000	0.900
Seek reelection	0.662	0.000
Seek intendencia	0.813	0.000
Seek Senate	0.712	0.002
Seek executive appointment	0.652	0.001
Reelected$_{t-1}$	−0.114	0.123
Number/place on list	−0.017	0.483
Frente Amplio	−1.111	0.002
Blanco Party	−0.213	0.329
Colorado Party	0.017	0.931
Constant	2.308	0.000
N	58	
Prob > chi^2	0.0000	
Pseudo R^2	0.0974	

Likelihood-ratio test of alpha 5 0: chibar2 (01) 5 6.09, Prob > 5 chibar2 5 0.007.

for political competition. The historical condition of the Frente Amplio as an opposition party without access to resources and power within the bureaucratic structure limited legislators' capacity to provide service to constituents.

Results: Table 7.3 provides evidence for Hypotheses 1 and 3. First, time allocation is clearly affected by the ENF (Hypothesis 1), which is my indicator of the degree of intraparty competition. Hypothesis 3, regarding future career ambitions of deputies is also substantiated, as deputies seeking reelection, a mayor's post, or a Senate post worked with their constituents significantly more than the legislators who indicated that they planned to retire.

There is no evidence in this regression, however, for Hypothesis 2, as the district-magnitude variable failed to reach standard levels of significance.[14] This suggests that some of the party and informal variables, rather than the electoral system, take predominant roles in driving legislative behavior. Importantly, these variables seem to be more closely related to factionalism and career ambitions than partisanship or seniority, as these latter variables were also insignificant in the regression.

Raw NBR regression results are not clear in terms of providing concrete measures or expected values. I thus analyzed the data using Clarify software (King, Tomz, and Wittenberg 2000), which works on the basis of Montecarlo simulation to multiply the number of cases without changing the original results.

14. In this explanation, the necessity of traveling to the Uruguayan parliament in the capital is not a competing argument, since representatives elected in small districts spend on average only two days a week in Montevideo.

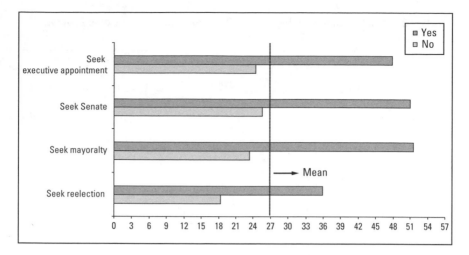

FIGURE 7.2 Political Careers and Expected Weekly Hours of Constituency Service for Uruguayan Deputies.

The advantage of this program is that it allows us to display concrete expected values measured in the units of our dependent variable (hours).

Holding all other variables at their means, the Clarify program suggests that whereas an average deputy allocates twenty-seven hours a week in service to constituents, those elected in districts with the higher ENF spend fifty-six hours (106 percent more than the average) in service and a deputy elected in a district with the minimum ENF invests just twenty-one hours (23 percent less). These results are statistically significant.

The set of hypotheses testing career ambitions shows that all of them are statistically significant, with the expected sign. Importantly, deputies simply seeking reelection, though their hours are above average, put less time into constituent services than those pursuing executive appointments, Senate careers, or a mayorality (Figure 7.2).

The table shows that deputies hoping to pursue any of these other offices allocate at least twenty-four hours a week more to constituent services than the average deputy. It is important to note that the nonelective career in the executive branch is dependent on the electoral performance of the party and faction with which the legislator is associated. As in most European parliamentary systems, cabinet ministers and many other nonelective posts (embassies, public firms, and so on) in Uruguay are selected from among members of the legislature, so those who seek those jobs usually compete in elections. Further, the party needs to win the presidency to control the bureaucracy, and the better the legislator's faction performs, the more posts to which the faction can lay claim.

Finally, partisanship deserves a separate comment. The expectation was that the Frente Amplio would have depressed constituency service because it is considered a more programmatic party and perhaps because the other parties are more tied into the largesse of the state, and the regression did return a statistically significant p-value supporting this hypothesis. Furthermore, the substantive effect is significant, as the Clarify analysis suggests that deputies from the Blanco and Colorado parties allocate 63 percent more time to constituency service than an average deputy, and deputies from the Frente Amplio allocate on average fifteen hours or (44 percent) less than the mean.

In sum, although Uruguayan legislators largely depend on their faction leaders to gain the nomination for a seat in the lower chamber, the system has important incentives to cultivate a factional and personal vote, though this varies with the level of intraparty competition among factions and the type of career desired by individual legislators. Concomitantly, although nomination procedures are centralized, factionalism and ambition give Uruguayan legislators incentives to provide constituent services.

What are the theoretical implications of classifying Uruguayan candidates as *faction loyalists*? On the one hand, the nomination process leads us to conclude that there is a clearly centralized procedure where faction leaders have control over the nominations. Given the particular constellation of party and electoral system variables one would predict that Uruguayan legislators should be disciplined and loyal to faction leaders and not oriented to providing services to constituents. *Prima facie,* there appear few incentives to provide such service. Nonetheless, they do so. We are left with a seemingly contradictory type of legislator with many features of a *faction-loyalist* and some of the behaviors of a *constituent servant.* But a second view suggests coincident interests of the legislators and faction leaders in providing these services. In sum, since the legislators represent factions, and the factions compete with one another, all have incentives to provide constituency service to cultivate the support of voters individually with an eye to improving a faction's reputation.

Concluding Remarks

The Uruguayan case shows how factions, rather than parties as unitary actors, can be the key units in candidate selection processes. The main explanatory factor facilitating this internal structure of parties rests upon the combination of the DSV with a closed-list PR system. As we saw, a direct consequence of these rules is that faction leaders have tremendous control over nominations for the Chamber of Deputies and influence over legislators' future careers as well. In this context, party statutes and primaries are mostly formal procedures that systematically serve to endorse the preferences of faction leaders. In other words, party politics in Uruguay is factional and so is the candidate selection process.

One of the main political consequences of a factionalized party system is that factions have to compete for votes both within and among parties. The by-product of this intraparty competition is that legislators, as agents of those factions, have incentives to cultivate a reputation within a faction and to advance the reputation of the faction as a whole. Beyond this, the career ambitions of individual legislators also affect the extent to which legislators may cultivate a personal reputation, even in a context where the whole candidate selection process is centralized in the hands of faction leaders. This chapter shows that the cultivation of factional and personal reputations can simultaneously be achieved through the provision of constituency service.

The major puzzle is, of course, why do individual legislators provide constituent services if faction leaders centralize nominations? What does this say about the all-important variable of loyalty set out in the Siavelis and Morgenstern framework (see Chapter 1)? This chapter has shown that what is seemingly a contradiction really is not. Most studies cast constituency service as a set of actions that detracts, from politicians' interests in public policies and loyalty to their party or faction leaders. This view compels us to see legislators either as providers of public policies or as providers of services to particular groups and constituents, but not both simultaneously. For instance, it is assumed that politicians who protect their individual political fortunes will provide more constituent services than those who are loyal to their leaders and value the party label. Thus, the consensus in the literature is that the provision of services entails a zero-sum game, given that those services can hurt the party (or faction) label.

However, Uruguayan legislators are comparatively high providers of constituency service and yet remain tremendously loyal to their faction leaders. The fact that they strongly depend on faction leaders to gain nomination or advance in their career ambitions guarantees a positive sum game where constituency service simultaneously benefits factions and candidates.

The arguments presented here do not definitively allow us to answer the question of under what conditions faction leaders promote or inhibit the provision of constituency service. We know that they are powerful agents because they control nominations for the election and reelection of legislators. In this context, leaders do not face important challenges in passing legislation or pursuing relevant public policies because they are able to discipline their members in parliament (Buquet et al. 1998). Indeed, the evidence shows that Uruguayan factions are extremely disciplined when voting in parliament (Morgenstern 2004), and parties taken as units have been very disciplined at least since the democratic restoration in 1985 (Buquet et al. 1998). Control over nominations gives faction leaders what they want: discipline. Thus, it is possible that faction leaders do not care about the activities of individual legislators who provide constituency service, given that they get what they want—loyalty—from their legislators in parliament. Furthermore, it is also possible that faction leaders actually promote the provision of constituent services among legislators, given that the effect can be positive (enhancing faction reputation), or neutral in the worst of cases. Thus, representatives perform the double function of gaining or retaining votes through the provision of constituency service while remaining disciplined in their voting, in order to support faction leaders' political strategies and ensure their political futures.

Appendix: Career Plans and Constituency Service Questionnaire

The questionnaire was designed by Professor Frances Hagopian for a comparative study of political representation in Latin America. For my research I used two of its questions:

1. In thinking about your professional career, what position would you like to exercise in your next appointment?

    1. President of the Republic
    2. Intendente
    3. Senator
    4. An appointment in the Executive Branch
    5. A position in the private sector
    6. Reelection to the same position
    7. Retirement
    8. Other (specify) _____
    9. NA

2. Considering your public activities, how many hours per week do you and your staff employ in attending to complaints and requests from individual citizens? _____ hours.

Part III

Political Recruitment and Candidate Selection for the Executive Branch

Chapter Eight

Political Recruitment and Candidate Selection in Argentina: Presidents and Governors, 1983 to 2006

MIGUEL DE LUCA

While the military has often played a central role in Argentine politics, presidents and governors have been cast in that position since the return to democracy in 1983. The importance of presidents and governors makes it essential to unravel their paths to power, because, as this volume makes clear, the processes of political recruitment and candidate selection (R&S) for the presidency and provincial governments deeply affect postelectoral behavior. There is little empirical research, however, that explores who in Argentina aspires to executive positions, where the aspirants come from, how the aspirants are selected, or the consequences of selection methods for later political behavior.[1] This chapter addresses these questions by paying special attention to both winners (presidents and governors) and defeated candidates in the traditional Argentine parties—the Partido Justicialista (PJ, the Peronists) and the Unión Cívica Radical (UCR, Radicals)—as well as other relevant parties, at both the national and provincial levels.

The central argument of this chapter is that in Argentina, the R&S process of presidents and governors is controlled by political parties—specifically, the parties' provincial branches. In terms of R&S as a dependent variable, the process functions this way because of a particular combination of key electoral and party variables: plurality electoral rules, concurrent elections, a moderately institutionalized party system (see Mainwaring and Scully 1995), a medium to low degree of electoral competitiveness at the national and provincial levels, and a decentralized party organization based on patronage, pork-barrel politics, and clientelism.

I wish to thank Mark P. Jones, Marcelo Leiras, Andrés Malamud, Juan Pablo Micozzi, Ana María Mustapic, and Javier Zelaznik for providing many helpful comments and suggestions. Any errors remain my responsibility alone.

1. For exceptions, see Jones (2002), Molinelli, Palanza, and Sin (1999, 519–35), and Serrafero (1997, 1999).

Considering candidate type as an independent variable, Argentina's R&S process produces leaders who have already established political careers that are built within the party and are generally centered in their province. However, there are variations with respect to how intimately candidates are related to their formal party structures, and the level of formal party institutionalization is the main factor that explains this difference. In consequence, the political leaders that are elected for these executive offices are mostly *party insiders* or *party adherents*, to use Siavelis and Morgenstern's terms (see Chapter 1, this volume), or a hybrid of these two ideal types. The evidence from Argentina also confirms Siavelis and Morgenstern's speculation that though the framework for analyzing R&S at the presidential level cannot be directly applied to R&S for gubernatorial candidates, it does provide important insights for understanding subnational politics.

I begin with a brief description of the rules that govern the election of presidents and governors and the relations of power between them, and follow with a portrayal of the main features of the Argentine party system and its constituent parties. The second section describes and analyzes intraparty relations, the different types of Argentine parties, and the selection process of presidential and gubernatorial contenders. In the third section, I review the various types of executive candidates. In the fourth section, I analyze presidential campaigns and the behavior of different types of presidents. Though my sample is small (four of the presidents since 1983: Raúl Alfonsín, Carlos Menem, Fernando de la Rúa, and Néstor Kirchner—I exclude Adolfo Rodríguez Saá and Eduardo Duhalde who were interim presidents very briefly), I link the presidential types as described by Siavelis and Morgenstern to the behavior of these leaders, considering especially campaign style, cabinet integration, and the candidates' relationship to their party. I then extend the analysis derived from small-N presidential politics to gubernatorial politics. Conclusions are presented in the fifth section.

Presidents, Governors, and Parties in Argentina

Since 1983 Argentine politics has undergone some important changes, though there remains continuity with respect to its principal actors and rules of the game. A brief review of these continuities and changes is crucial to understanding their effects on the R&S process.

Presidents and Governors

The Argentine presidency is quite powerful. In addition to extensive executive powers, the president also has important legislative powers (the ability to initiate laws, a total and partial veto, and the authority to issue decrees), the right to designate ministers and other top governmental executives, and the power to intervene in any of the twenty-four provinces of the Argentine federation.[2]

In 1983 and 1989 the president of Argentina was elected via an Electoral College (requiring a majority vote of its members), held the position for six years, and could not be immediately reelected. The president was chosen with a vice president on the same single-party "ticket," called a *fórmula presidencial*. The 1994 constitutional reform established three important changes. First, the president is now chosen directly by a two-round system, requiring 45 percent of the valid votes or 40 percent with a margin of at least 10 percent for first-round victory. Second, the presidential term was shortened from six to four years. Third, one consecutive presidential reelection is now allowed.

Every Argentine province has its own constitution and a directly elected governor and legislature. Each elects its governor for a four-year term, with all but a few (three in 1983, two in 1987, three in 1991, three in 1995, and four in 1999 and 2003) employing a simple plurality formula. The rules on gubernatorial reelection vary by province and have undergone considerable reform since 1983 (Serrafero 1997). In 1983 no provincial constitution allowed immediate gubernatorial reelection. As of 2006, all but four of the twenty-four provinces (Corrientes, Entre Ríos, Mendoza, and Santa Fe) allowed the immediate reelection of the governor and all but five of the other twenty (Catamarca, Formosa, La Rioja, San Luis, Santa Cruz) limited the governor to two consecutive terms. Elections for president and governor were and are, with very few exceptions, concurrent with the elections for the federal Chamber of Deputies or the provincial legislatures.[3]

Several authors underscore the important role that the Argentine governors play at both the provincial and national levels (De Luca, Jones, and Tula 2002; Jones 1997b; Spiller and Tommasi 2000). Governors' power derives from an important group of institutional and political resources, including their control over jobs in the provincial public sector, the provincial budget, and the provincial party organization. The governors' power is based on patronage, pork-barrel politics, and clientelism, and since these processes or forces operate at both the provincial and national levels, there exists a two-way relationship between provincial and national political influences. On the one hand, because the principal nucleus of electoral competition is at the provincial level, the governors exercise strong control over the selection of their party's candidates for the Senate and the Chamber of Deputies (De Luca, Jones, and Tula 2002; Jones 1997b; Jones, Chapter 2, this volume), thus affording the governors influence over the representatives who, of

2. The federal capital, the city of Buenos Aires, achieved a semiautonomous status in 1994. Here it is considered one of the provinces and its directly elected head of government is treated as a governor.

3. Elections for the national legislature are held every two years with approximately one-half of the seats at stake (see Chapter 2).

course, are of concern to the presidents. In turn, presidents can influence (or pressure) governors by distributing positions in the national government, influencing provincial budgets with discretionary federal funds, threatening federal intervention in the province in certain situations, or backing a rival candidate in the next gubernatorial election.

Parties and the Party System

In the last several years, Argentine political parties have suffered deep political and electoral shocks. First, the 2001 legislative elections had the lowest turnout and highest vote-spoiling rate ever. Second, the country experienced an unprecedented institutional crisis in 2001–2002, when a wave of popular protest provoked the resignation of president Fernando de la Rúa and his successor, interim president Adolfo Rodríguez Saá. Nevertheless, the 2003 and 2005 elections showed a reconstitution of parties and the party system to a pattern resembling that before the 2001–2002 shock. The Argentine party system remains, therefore, "moderately institutionalized," according to Mainwaring and Scully's criteria (1995).

In the post-1983 era, two major groups of political parties stand out: the traditional parties (Peronists and Radicals) and minor national and provincial parties.

Peronists and Radicals. The PJ and the UCR have dominated Argentine politics since the 1940s and have had a national presence (more extended in the case of the Peronists than the Radicals) backed by a dense network of provincial political machines based on clientelism and patronage relationships (Calvo and Murillo 2004; Jones, Chapter 2, this volume; Levitsky 2003). These parties' organizational structures mirror the country's federal system in that the parties' provincial units have significant autonomy from the national-party organizations. In its sixty years of existence, the PJ has been characterized by a strong collective identity, yet low levels of formal institutionalization, with few established rules for selecting leaders and candidates and a lack of stable and routinized career paths (Levitsky 2003; McGuire 1997; Mustapic 1988). The UCR, by contrast, is characterized by a relatively high level of organizational institutionalization, a party apparatus that operates relatively well with a considerable level of internal competition for selecting party leaders and candidates, and well-established rules in recruiting and promoting leaders. Therefore, in the terms set out by Siavelis and Morgenstern, the PJ employs more patronage-based selection norms, while the UCR tends more toward bureaucratized forms.

Minor national parties. There are several minor parties (known as *terceras fuerzas*, or "third forces," in political vernacular) that have achieved a national presence at some point since 1983, but with the exception of two current minor national parties, all turned out to be flashes in the pan. After obtaining a substantial number of votes in one or two elections, a majority of these parties failed to consolidate an important base of support and, eventually, effectively disappeared from the electoral map. Principally, the evaporation of these *terceras fuerzas* is due to their inability to extend their initial electoral support, strongly concentrated in the populous Buenos Aires region (BA, the province of Buenos Aires and the federal capital), to the interior region (INT, the other twenty-two provinces).[4] Further, all the *terceras fuerzas* have been extremely dependent on the electoral success of a single leader and all of them have lacked an organizational party structure with national presence similar to those of the PJ or the UCR.[5]

Provincial parties. Argentina has a large number of parties that either solely or effectively compete in only one province (always in INT), where they often are the dominant or main opposition party.[6] With only two exceptions, the Neuquino People's Movement (Movimiento Popular Neuquino, or MPN, in the province of Neuquén), and the Fueguino People's Movement (Movimiento Popular Fueguino, or MPF), they have two general characteristics: a lack of organizational structure (small membership and little physical presence at the neighborhood level), particularly compared to Peronists and Radicals, and a tendency to be dominated by a single person or small clique, reinforced by the fact that the party competes in only one province.[7]

In postauthoritarian Argentina, the PJ and the UCR are the only two parties whose candidates have reached the presidency, either alone or in coalition with another party. In the struggle for this office, there has been intense competition

4. Forty-six percent of the country's population lives in the Buenos Aires region (16.5 out of 36 million, according to the 2001 national census), and it is the country's economic nucleus.

5. The parties in this category (with the period they achieved some electoral success in parentheses) are Partido Intransigente (PI, 1983–1991), Unión del Centro Democrático (UCeDé, 1983–1993), Movimiento por la Dignidad y la Independencia (MODIN, 1991–1995), Acción por la República (AR, 1997–2001), Frente Grande/Frente por un País Solidario (FG/FREPASO, 1993–2003), Afirmación para una República Igualitaria (ARI, 2001–2005), and Recrear/Compromiso para el Cambio/Propuesta Republicana (RECREAR/CPC/PRO, 2003–2005).

6. The most relevant parties of this type are the "provincial parties" that have held the governorship in their respective province at some point in time since 1983: Acción Chaqueña (ACh), Cruzada Renovadora (CR), Fuerza Republicana (FR), Movimiento Popular Fueguino (MPF), Movimiento Popular Neuquino (MPN), Partido Autonomista (PA), Partido Liberal (PL), Partido Bloquista (PB), Partido Nuevo (PANU), and Partido Renovador de Salta (PRS). I also include in the analysis the most prominent provincial party that failed to win the governorship during this period, the Partido Demócrata de Mendoza (PD).

7. MPN, the country's most successful provincial party since 1983, is the only provincial party with an important mass base, perhaps stemming from its Peronist origins. The MPF is also distinct from any of the other provincial party because its leadership is not concentrated in the hands of one prominent leader or a clique. Its elite is divided, for a whole series of historical and geographic reasons (Tula and De Luca 1999).

TABLE 8.1   Votes in Argentine Presidential Elections, by Party or Coalition, 1983–2003 (Percentages)

Party or Coalition	1983	1989	1995	1999	2003
Partido Justicialista (PJ)[a]	40.2	49.4	49.9	38.7	60.8
Unión Cívica Radical (UCR)[b]	51.7	37.2	17.0	48.4	2.3
"Tercera fuerza"[c]	2.3	6.9	29.3	9.8	16.4
Other parties	5.8	6.5	3.8	3.1	20.5
Total[d]	100.0	100.0	100.0	100.0	100.0

Source: Author, based on data provided by the Dirección Nacional Electoral, República Argentina.

a. In 2003, PJ percentage totals include votes won by three candidates who ran separately.

b. In 1999, this alliance included the UCR-FREPASO and several provincial parties such as CR, PB, and the PRS (Alianza).

c. In 1983: PI; in 1989: Alianza de Centro (ADC, including the UCEDÉ–PDP); in 1995: FREPASO; in 1999: AR; in 2003: RECREAR.

d. The percentage totals include votes won by candidates on lists other than those of their respective parties.

between both parties, but minor national parties have not seriously threatened the victory of Peronists or Radicals (see Table 8.1).

Likewise, the Peronists and Radicals have taken control of an overwhelming majority of the twenty-four provincial governments since 1983 (see Figure 8.1), converting some of them into important electoral bastions.[8] In these cases, above all in the PJ bailiwicks, nomination by the party in the government is frequently synonymous with election.

The combination of an unconventional presidential runoff, the election of an overwhelming majority of governors under the plurality formula, and frequent concurrence of executive and legislative elections at the national and the provincial levels had allowed electoral competition with a low number of candidates between 1983 and 2006. Furthermore the clause allowing immediate presidential reelection and the rising number of provinces that allow the immediate reelection of governors (sometimes without limits on the number of reelections) had created a political context very favorable for incumbents. The effects of these electoral rules, combined with a party-based system that exhibits a medium to low degree of competitiveness at both the national and provincial levels, has effectively worked as a funnel for candidates into the presidency and provincial governorships.

In effect, although the rules governing the formation of new parties are very flexible and it has been very easy to create one's own party under which to run for election, no presidential candidate has been viable without the PJ or the UCR label, and practically no gubernatorial candidate has had a real chance to win without the support of Peronists, Radicals, or the related provincial party. The support of these party machines was and is vital to get

8. During this whole period, the Peronists maintained uninterrupted control of the governorship in seven provinces, the UCR in one, and the MPN in one.

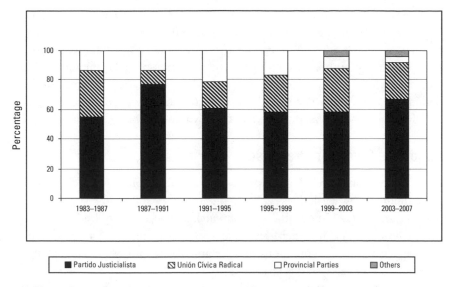

FIGURE 8.1 Partisan Control of Argentine Governorships, 1983–2007 (Percentages)
Source: Based on data from the Dirección Nacional Electoral de la República Argentina.

elected to relevant executive posts and so the potential pool of successful candidates is rather small.

Party Organization and Candidate Selection Processes

In addition to the crucial party and electoral variables already mentioned which act as filters for potential competitors in defining the profile of presidential and gubernatorial candidates, there are two additional factors that determine the types of candidates that emerge: the characteristics of party organizations and the parties' processes of candidate selection.

Party Organization

Because the principal nucleus of electoral competition is at the provincial level, party provincial branches play a preeminent role in the activities of candidate promotion, campaign, and voter mobilization. These provincial-party organizations are often dominated by a single person or a small number of people. Dominance of the provincial-party organization requires that a party leader be able to defeat any rival in an intraparty primary (either to choose candidates for elective office or to elect the provincial-level party leadership). Patronage, pork-barrel activities, and clientelism are indispensable for success in party primary elections (De Luca, Jones, and Tula 2002; Jones, Chapter 2, this volume). For this reason, the leadership type in these provincial party organizations is, by general rule, directly associated with the control over provincial government resources. In provinces where the party controls the governorship, with rare exceptions the governor is *el jefe* ("the chief")—the undisputed (or at least dominant) boss of the provincial-party organization.[9] In the provinces where the governorship is not held by the party, the locus of party dominance varies between control by a single person and control by a small group of influential party leaders. In both cases there is ample space for intraparty conflict.

Candidate Selection Processes

In Argentina, candidate selection procedures are not explicitly mandated by the constitution or by legal statutes. Party organizations follow the stipulations of their internal party statutes (the *carta orgánica*). However, party leaders, through their control of the provincial-level party organization, have a great deal of latitude regarding the conditions and details of the process, giving them an additional advantage vis-à-vis challengers.

From 1983 to 2006 political parties employed three methods of candidate selection for presidential and gubernatorial elections: elite-centered choice, direct primaries, and party splitting. A fourth method of candidate choice, the double simultaneous vote (DVS), was employed only for gubernatorial elections.

Elite-centered choice. This method includes a variety of elite arrangements, ranging from the nomination of an undisputed leader (a *candidato natural*) or the imposition of a candidate by a national-party leader or a provincial-level caudillo such as a powerful governor to a contender who emerges from negotiations among national- or provincial-party leaders.

Primary. This second category includes cases where two or more candidates compete in a direct primary election. The electorate for these contests is either the party members alone or party members and those not affiliated with any party (referred to as independents in Argentina). Political parties rather than the government run primaries, and they involve a considerable amount of mobilization (get out the vote) efforts by the competing intraparty candidates. Presidential and gubernatorial primaries are open confrontations between the candidates' party machines, backed in turn by networks of provincial or local party machines; success depends almost entirely on financial and material resources (for more details about Argentine primaries, see De Luca, Jones, and Tula 2002, 2003; Jones, Chapter 2, this volume).

Party splitting. This method allows opposing leaders within a party to present more than one presidential or gubernatorial candidate to the general electorate. Party splitting is infrequent except in the uninstitutionalized PJ, where it is not formally accepted—nor is it usually desired, owing to its risks—but is tolerated.

---

9. This is the typical case for several PJ governors, such as Adolfo Rodríguez Saá in San Luis (1983–2001), Gildo Insfrán in Formosa (1995–present), and Rubén Marín in La Pampa (1983–1987 and 1991–2003).

In effect, party splitting fits well with the PJ's tradition of considering the party as an electoral vehicle and minor appendage of the broader Movimiento Justicialista. Unlike other parties, PJ candidates can break with the official party leadership and present a nonofficial candidacy without being expelled, because loyalty to the movement is what matters (Malamud 2005). Nevertheless, this method has not been used by Peronists in all elections, and tends to be employed during periods of power struggles—for example, during the conflict between the *Ortodoxos* and *Renovadores* in the 1980s, and the division between Menemists and non-Menemists in 2003.

Double simultaneous vote. Since 1987 several provinces have employed the DSV (also known as the *Ley de Lemas*, or law of "party banners") to elect governors.[10] This method entails a simultaneous intraparty and general election. Under DSV, parties may present more than one candidate. Votes are pooled by party and the governor is the highest-polling candidate of the party with the most votes.

The DSV, like party splitting, has been adopted by several provinces as a means for the PJ to avoid severe intraparty conflict—so severe that intraparty primaries were not considered an acceptable mechanism of dispute resolution by one or more of the factions. At first glance the method proved successful for Peronists: of the twenty-three gubernatorial elections held using the DSV, the PJ has only lost two. However, because the DSV encouraged intraparty conflict and provided little incentive for consensus among disparate factions, governors were faced with factionalized PJ delegations in provincial legislatures, which created considerable problems of governance. Over time, Peronists recognized that the costs of the DSV outweighed its benefits, and its use has declined precipitously. The *Ley de Lemas* was eliminated in province after province during the mid- to late 1990s, normally with the support of the UCR and other opposition parties.[11]

As noted, of the four methods of presidential and gubernatorial candidate selection, elite choice and primaries are the most common. The decision regarding which of these two methods will be employed is based principally on three factors: whether the party is in the opposition or in the government (national or provincial), whether the president or governor is allowed to seek reelection, and the size of the party (De Luca, Jones, and Tula 2002, 2003). This generalization is applicable to both the presidential and gubernatorial candidate selection processes. Since 1983 the party that occupies the presidency is more inclined to choose its candidate via an elite agreement or via not-very-competitive primaries, whereas the major opposition parties have generally used primaries to choose their presidential candidate (see Table 8.2). In the cases where the

10. For a discussion of the DSV in Argentina, see Tula (1995, 1997). See Moraes (Chapter 7, this volume) and Daniel Buquet and Daniel Chasquetti (Chapter 13, this volume) for an assessment of the similar Uruguayan system.

11. The percentage of provinces that used the DSV for gubernatorial elections in 1987 was 5 percent; in 1991, 40 percent; 1995, 38 percent; 1999, 17 percent; and 2003, 8 percent.

TABLE 8.2 Presidential Candidate Selection in Argentina, 1983–2003

Year	Party or Coalition	Status (Government or Opposition)	Candidate Choice	Candidate	Candidate Type	Post	Votes (Percentage)	Primary Challenger	Post	Votes (Percentage)	Voters (in Thousands)
1983	PJ	—	Elite-centered	Luder	*Party insider*	—					
	UCR	—	Elite-centered[a]	**Alfonsín**	*Party insider*	—					
	PI	—	Elite-centered	Alende	*Party insider*	—					
1989	PJ	Opposition	Closed primary	**Menem**	*Hybrid insider-adherent*	Gov	54	Cafiero	Gov	46	1,544
	UCR	Government	Closed primary	Angeloz	*Party insider*	Gov	89	León	Sen	11	713
	ADC	Opposition	Elite-centered	Alsogaray	*Party insider*	Dep					
1995	PJ	Government	Elite-centered	**Menem**	*Party insider*	Pres					
	UCR	Opposition	Closed primary	Massaccesi	*Party insider*	Gov	65	Storani	Dep	35	642
	FREPASO	Opposition	Open primary[b]	Bordón	*Free-wheeling independent*	Sen	51	Alvarez	Dep	49	530
1999	PJ	Government	Elite-centered	Duhalde	*Party insider*	Gov					
	Alianza[c]	Opposition	Semiopen primary	**De la Rúa**	*Party insider*	Gov	64	Fernández Meijide	Dep	36	2,327
	AR	Opposition	Elite-centered	Cavallo	*Free-wheeling independent*	Dep					
2003	PJ (FL)	Opposition[d]	Party splitting	Menem	*Party insider*	Dep					
	PJ (FV)	Government[d]	Party splitting	**Kirchner**	*Party adherent*	Gov					
	PJ (MNP)	Opposition[d]	Party splitting	Rodríguez Saá	*Hybrid insider-adherent*	Gov					

Year	Party or Coalition	Status (Government or Opposition)	Candidate Choice	Candidate	Candidate Type	Post	Votes (Percentage)	Primary Challenger	Post	Votes (Percentage)	Voters (in Thousands)
	UCR	Opposition	Semiopen primary	Moreau	*Party insider*	Dep	53	Terragno	Sen	47	496
	RECREAR	Opposition	Elite-centered	López Murphy	*Free-wheeling independent*						
	ARI	Opposition	Elite-centered	Carrió	*Free-wheeling independent*	Dep					

Source: Author, based on information from national newspapers, biographical collections, and interviews with political leaders.

NOTE: The year corresponds to the presidential election year. Some of the selection processes took place during this year and others occurred in the preceding year. "Post" is the position the candidate held when running of office. Pres = president, Gov = governor, Sen = national senator, Dep = national deputy. The period prior to the selection was a dictatorship as indicated by — . Presidents are in bold.

a. Alfonsín had easily won the party leadership primary held earlier in 1983. This victory was determinant for an elite-centered presidential candidate choice in 1983.

b. All of the data listed for this primary are estimates, as the final results were never released.

c. The Alianza was an alliance between the UCR, FREPASO, and several provincial parties. Both de la Rúa and Fernández Meijide were selected as their respective party's candidate by an elite arrangement.

d. Three PJ candidates ran separately. President Duhalde only backed Kirchner.

incumbent president was prevented from seeking reelection (Alfonsín in 1989 and Menem in 1999), or decided not to run (Duhalde in 2003), that person played a key role in the designation of his successor, either by promoting the nomination of his choice (an heir apparent) or by blocking the candidacy of his main rival.

Whichever selection method is used to put together the *fórmula presidencial*, Peronists, Radicals, and the *tercera fuerza* parties attempt to balance their presidential–vice-presidential ticket by naming one candidate from each of the two traditional regions, BA and INT (see Table 8.3). This practice is aimed at motivating the party base in both regions, but party leaders principally consider it a useful mechanism to build successful intraparty alliances between regional machines in the primary season, as do party or coalition leaders in national elections.[12] The importance of regional balance for the *fórmula presidencial* and the effect of provincial-level factors on decisions regarding which of the two methods (elite-centered choice or primaries) is employed by the party organizations to select its governor candidates reveal the decentralized character of the Argentine party system and the influence exercised by provincial-level factors over the R&S process.

Whether a party controls the state government or is in the opposition is the first provincial factor influencing the selection process for governor. If the party has a governor in power, the probability of a provincial elite division is decreased, making a primary less likely. Powerful governors, who control the provincial administration, can impose their successors, co-opt potential opponents, or successfully negotiate an agreement with other party factions. Because governors bear a disproportionate share of the costs of divisive primaries, they have the incentive and means to arrange a negotiated choice of candidate. Governors' only challenge comes from copartisans who have access to the kind of resources necessary to construct and maintain their own machines and to withstand the governor's efforts to co-opt supporters.

Potential challengers with such resources are scarce but could include mayors of large cities, some national senators and deputies, and particularly members of theses groups supported by the party president, especially if the party president is also President of the Republic. In contrast, where the district-level party is in the opposition at the provincial level, it is much less likely to have an undisputed leader or the kind of resources controlled by the governor. Opposition parties, instead, are generally characterized by several high-profile leaders who control important, but limited, machines.

Given their strong position, of the forty-six times since 1983 that an incumbent governor was eligible to seek immediate reelection, the governor did so in all but

---

12. Coalition building and intraparty ideological equilibrium are also often considerations in composing lists. For an extended discussion of the *fórmula presidencial* in Argentina, see Serrafero (1999).

TABLE 8.3 Political Experience, Party Leadership Posts, and Regional Source of Presidential Tickets in Argentina, 1983–2005[a]

Year	Party or Coalition	Presidential Ticket (Fórmula Presidencial)	Executive Offices				Legislative Offices				Total Years in Office	Party Posts	Source Region (Interior or Buenos Aires)
			Pres	Min	Gov	May	Sen	Dep	Leg	Cou			
1983	PJ	Italo Luder					3				3	PLn	INT
		Deolindo Bittel			6						6	Pp, VPn	INT
	UCR	**Raúl Alfonsín**						3	4		11	Pp, Pn	BA
		Víctor Martínez				3			1	4	4	VPn	INT
	PI	Oscar Alende			4			3	4		11	Pn	BA
		Lisandro Viale									4	Pp, VPn	INT
1989	PJ	**Carlos Menem**			9						9	Pp, VPn	INT
		Eduardo Duhalde				5		2		1	8		BA
	UCR	Eduardo Angeloz			6		3		3		12	Pp	INT
		Juan Casella		1				1	3		5	Pp	BA
	ADC	Alvaro Alsogaray		2				6			8	Pn	BA
		Alberto Natale						4		3	7	Pp	INT
1995	PJ	**Carlos Menem**	6		9						15	Pp, VPn, Pn	INT
		Carlos Ruckauf		2				4			6	Pp	BA
	UCR	Horacio Massaccesi			8			2	1		11	Pp, VPn	INT
		Antonio Hernández						4	4		8		INT
	FREPASO	José Bordón			4		3	4			11	Pn	INT
		Carlos Alvarez						6			6	Pn	BA

(Continued)

TABLE 8.3 *(Continued)*

Year	Party or Coalition	Presidential Ticket (Fórmula Presidencial)	Executive Offices				Legislative Offices				Total Years in Office	Party Posts	Source Region (Interior or Buenos Aires)
			Pres	Min	Gov	May	Sen	Dep	Leg	Cou			
1999	PJ	Eduardo Duhalde			8	5				1	14	Pp	BA
		Ramón Ortega			4		1				5		INT
	Alianza	**Fernando De la Rúa**			3		10	1			14	Pp, PLn, Pn	BA
		Carlos Alvarez						10			10	Pn	BA
	APR	Domingo Cavallo		7				4			11		INT and BA
		Armando Caro Figueroa		4							4		INT
2003	PJ (FL)[b]	Carlos Menem	10		9		9				19	Pp, VPn, Pn	INT
		Juan C. Romero			8						17	Pp	INT
	PJ (FV)[b]	**Néstor Kirchner**			12	4					16	Pp	INT
		Daniel Scioli						6			6		BA
	PJ (MNP)[b]	Adolfo Rodríguez Saá			20				3		23	Pp, VPn	INT
		Melchor Posse				20		2			22		BA
	UCR	Leopoldo Moreau					6	14			20	Pp	BA
		Mario Losada					12	2	2		16	Pp, Pn	INT
	RECREAR	Ricardo López Murphy		2							2		BA
		Ricardo Gómez Diez					2	6	4		12	P	INT
	ARI	Elisa Carrió						8			8		INT
		Gustavo Gutiérrez						8	6		14	P	INT

a. Only experience under constitutional governments and with more than four months of duration are included. Presidents and vice presidents are in bold. Pres = president, Gov = governor, May = mayor, Min = minister, Sen = national senator, Dep = national deputy, Leg = provincial legislator, Cou = municipal councilor, Pn = national-party president, VPn = national-party vice president, PLn = national parliamentary leader, Pp = provincial-level party president, P = president of a provincial party.

b. These tickets represent factions of the Peronist Party (PJ).

Source: Author, based on information from national newspapers, biographical collections, and interviews with political leaders.

eight instances.[13] In thirty-two of these thirty-eight elections the incumbent was victorious. This success rate increases the governors' influence, because not only do they control the provincial administration but it is also likely that they will continue to control it for the next four years. These governors should be able to avoid the risks of primary elections to a much greater extent than nonincumbent gubernatorial candidates. Party size is the final relevant factor in a party's decision whether to choose presidential and gubernatorial candidates via an elite agreement or via primaries. Given their national scope and their predominance in a considerable number of provinces, the PJ and the UCR have had more space for intraparty conflict and consequently have been more inclined to choose candidates through primaries. In contrast to this, the small size and cliquish leadership of the *terceras fuerzas* make maintaining control of the organization much easier, allowing them to undertake candidate selection by elite-centered methods. In provincial parties, these same characteristics of small size and cliquish leadership, plus their limited geographical scope, tend to produce the same outcome as with the *terceras fuerzas*, with the notable exceptions of the MPN and the MPF.

In sum, incumbency and party size largely determine whether a party holds a primary or elects its leader via an elite closed-door process. This implies, as has been pointed out in connection with legislative candidates (De Luca, Jones, and Tula 2002; Jones, Chapter 2, this volume), that despite differences in the popular characterizations of the UCR (liberal-democratic, institutionalized) and PJ (vertical, uninstitutionalized), the UCR is not significantly more likely to hold a primary than the PJ.

Profiles of Presidential and Gubernatorial Candidates

Who are presidential and gubernatorial candidates? What experience do they have? What relationship do they have with the political party that backs them? My analysis indicates that the majority of the relevant presidential and gubernatorial candidates have accumulated significant party-oriented political experience.[14]

Presidential Candidates

Given the very small number of presidents since 1983, it is not possible to delineate a "typical" path to power. Nonetheless, one can make some important generalizations concerning the characteristics of presidential candidates.

First, by whatever means selected, all the PJ's, UCR's, and minor national parties' presidential candidates have previously occupied an elected legislative

13. Of the eight governors who declined to run, two did so primarily because of their advanced age (eighty-two and seventy-seven; the seventy-seven-year-old's son ran in his place), while three others successfully ran for president. If the latter had lost the presidency, they would have run for reelection as governor.

14. This analysis is based on information from national newspapers, from biographical collections, and from interviews with political leaders.

position (municipal councilor, provincial legislator, national deputy, national senator), an elected executive position (mayor, governor, or president), or have held a post to which they were appointed by the president (minister). In several cases, the candidates have held at least two of these three types of positions (see Table 8.3). Relatedly and second, the candidates have been involved in politics for a significant period of time, with most of them having spent ten to fifteen years or more running for or serving in significant political positions (see Table 8.3).

Third, serious presidential candidates tend to follow a political career with a fairly well-defined direction. This career has generally been tightly linked to their respective political party and built on a territorial basis, which is later projected on the national level, as shown in Table 8.3. In the PJ and the UCR the positions of governor have been the most frequent launching pads for a run for the presidency, confirming the importance of a strong provincial base for electoral success at the national level. For the *terceras fuerzas*, these launching pads tend to be a seat in the Chamber of Deputies or Senate.

Fourth, during the whole period analyzed, all the Peronist and Radical presidential candidates have characteristics of both *party insiders* and *party adherents*, to use Siavelis and Morgenstern's terms. In contrast, while the presidential candidates of the minor national parties were *party insiders* in the 1980s, they have been *free-wheeling independents* (*FWIs*) in more recent elections. However, all these *FWIs* exhibit political credentials linked with Peronists or Radicals: in effect, they obtained their previous elective posts running for these parties after a well-defined party-based career (José Bordón for FREPASO in 1995 and Elisa Carrió for ARI in 2003), or they were national cabinet ministers of the PJ (Domingo Cavallo for AR in 1999) or UCR administrations (Ricardo López Murphy for RECREAR in 2003).

Fifth, almost all the PJ, UCR, and minor national parties' *compañeros de fórmula* (the vice-presidential candidates) have also held similar positions to the presidential candidates following the same fairly well-defined directions, serving as either a deputy, national senator, or national minister (see Table 8.3).

Gubernatorial Candidates

Virtually all the gubernatorial candidates in the 1987–2006 period had previously held or were holding an elective or appointive post or a party office when they became candidates. For example, 79 percent of the PJ's candidates had been or were governor, national senator, national deputy, provincial legislator, or mayor. In the UCR, 88 percent of the candidates occupied or had occupied one of these positions, and 75 percent of the provincial party candidates had done so (see Table 8.4).

Table 8.5 shows previous political experience of the 140 governors elected between 1983 and 2006. Most of the 140 governors had previously held an elected, appointive, or party position, or several of these, though there are a few

TABLE 8.4 Percentage Distribution of PJ, UCR, Provincial-Party, and National Minor-Party Gubernatorial Candidates in Argentina, by Position Held When Running for Office, 1987–2006

Position Held	PJ %	UCR %	Provincial Parties %	National Minor Parties %
Governor	30	12	9	14
National senator	22	17	21	
National deputy	14	33	36	43
Mayor	9	16	9	
Party activist	6	6	15	14
Provincial legislator	4	10		14
Amateur[a]	4	1	3	14
National executive branch (second-tier)	4			
Provincial minister or secretary	2	2	6	
Vice governor	2	1		
Vice president	2			
National minister	1			
Municipal councilor		1		
Number of Candidates	133	126	33	7

Source: Author, based on information from national newspapers, biographical collections, and interviews with political leaders.

a. This includes people with no prior partisan political experience in an elective, partisan, or appointive post.

TABLE 8.5 Percentage Distribution of PJ, UCR, Provincial-Party, and National Minor-Party Governors in Argentina, by All Previous Positions Held When They Ran for Office, 1983–2006[a]

Position Held	PJ %	UCR %	Provincial Parties %	National Minor Parties%
National deputy	31	28	5	
Governor	26	19	30	50
Provincial minister or secretary	25	28	15	
Provincial-party president	23	34	22	
National senator	18	22	22	
Mayor	17	25	50	
Provincial legislator	12	41	11	100
Vice governor	9	12		
Municipal councilor	6	12		100
Amateur[b]	3			
National secretary	2			
National minister	2			
Vice president	2			
Number of Candidates	88	32	18	2

Source: Author, based on information from national newspapers, biographical collections, and interviews with political leaders.

a. Included are all the candidates who won a gubernatorial election between 1983 and 2006. Percentages do not add to 100 because some candidates held more than one post.

b. Includes people with no prior partisan political experience in an elective, partisan, or appointive post.

exceptions.[15] Consequently, following Siavelis and Morgenstern's typology, nearly all serious candidates for governor and all governors in Argentina are either *party insiders* or *party adherents*.

The political experience of both the successful candidates for president and governor—those who won—and defeated candidates of the PJ, the UCR, minor national, and provincial parties makes clear that in Argentina the particular combination of intraparty politics and the more usual candidate selection methods (elite-centered choice and primaries) also establishes a recruitment funnel through which some types of candidates pass more easily than others. Clearly, the kinds of candidates who make it through this funnel are those who have access to the type of resources necessary to construct and maintain their own machine or have the possibility to obtain the support of this kind of party machine: governors, some national senators and deputies, or mayors of large cities.

Candidate Choice, Campaigns, and Postelectoral Behavior: *Party Insiders* or *Party Adherents*—Does It Make a Difference?

In this section I first provide a preliminary answer to this question, analyzing an admittedly limited number of cases. I focus on how selection variables and candidate types affect campaigns and presidential behavior once a person is in office for the four popularly elected presidents between 1983 and 2003: Presidents Alfonsín and de la Rúa of the UCR and the PJ Presidents Menem and Kirchner. Then I extend some hypotheses derived from the anaylsis of small-N presidential politics to gubernatorial politics.

Analyses of Adolfo Rodríguez Saá's (2001) and Eduardo Duhalde's (2002–2003) presidencies are not included because of their atypical path to power via appointment by Congress. Following the resignation of De la Rúa in December of 2001 in the context of severe economic crisis and massive popular protests, Rodríguez Saá was designated interim president for three months, with the idea that he would convene new presidential elections. He was then forced to resign after one week and was replaced by Duhalde. These atypical paths to power make drawing conclusions based on these cases quite difficult.

Presidents

Raúl Alfonsín, 1983–1989. Alfonsín's career molded him perfectly into the *party insider* type. Step by step, from 1954 to 1983, he pursued a thirty-year political career as a UCR leader in Argentina's most important electoral district, the province of Buenos Aires.

15. Some of those who did succeed were the businessman Jorge Escobar, the singer Ramón "Palito" Ortega, and the F-1 car racer Carlos Reutemann. All three were PJ candidates and relied on strong personal support from President Menem to win.

In 1983 Alfonsín obtained an overwhelming victory in the elections for the leadership of the UCR, defeating Fernando de la Rúa, then leader of the traditional internal faction that had dominated the party for thirty years. This triumph immediately provoked the suspension of the UCR's planned presidential primary and established Alfonsín as the undisputed UCR presidential candidate. Despite this overwhelming victory, Alfonsín assured himself the backing of his internal party adversaries in the electoral campaign through the distribution of positions in the UCR party hierarchy and the awarding of legislative candidacies to cultivate support (Malamud 2005).

In the campaign, Alfonsín maintained the UCR's programmatic lines as predicted for *party insiders* under the Siavelis and Morgenstern framework, but at the same time he gave the party more fighting spirit and mobilization, which attracted a significant number of supporters who traditionally did not vote for Radicals. This new orientation helped break the hitherto iron law of Argentine politics: the impossibility of defeating the PJ in competitive and completely open elections—something that had not occurred since Peronism appeared on the scene in the 1940s.

Alfonsín's unprecedented defeat of the Peronists provided him significant room to maneuver within the UCR and to govern as he wished. Alfonsín's initial cabinet was completely filled with UCR members, but following his campaign strategy he appointed both his own followers and former internal rivals. He established a standard of partisan equilibrium for practically all cabinet, secretariat, and subsecretariat posts, even within the more technical ministries such as the Ministry of Economy.

Throughout his presidency, Alfonsín maintained de facto and de jure party leadership with little dissent. In 1984 the UCR modified the party statutes prohibiting simultaneous occupation of the presidency of the party and presidency of the Republic to allow Alfonsín to serve in both positions. He maintained the post of party president after the UCR's defeat in the 1989 presidential elections and during the subsequent hyperinflationary crisis.

Though this dual role broke the UCR's traditional rules, the party did not undergo a generalized process of reform of its internal rules or structure. Nor did its programmatic orientations change. What is more, despite Alfonsín's efforts to formalize reforms in order to provide wider party input into governing—as would be expected from the *party insider* model—constant economic crisis prevented him from doing so. As a result, the government ruled in crisis mode and he ultimately ended up performing precisely within the mold of a *party insider*. From the arrival of Juan Sourrouille as minister of the economy in 1985 until his departure at the beginning of 1989, major economic decisions were taken by a small group of ministerial officials in consultation with the president, and other UCR leaders had very little to say about these decisions (De Riz and Feldman 1991).

Fernando de la Rúa, 1999–2001. Like Alfonsín, Fernando de la Rúa built an extensive political and party career in the federal capital, occupying leadership positions, which made him a *party insider* as well. Nevertheless his leadership never threatened Alfonsín's power, who as noted had remarkable success in maintaining control of the party during the post-1983 era until the end of the period covered by this study (2006).

For the 1999 presidential elections, the UCR and FREPASO (Frente por un País Solidario, or Front for National Solidarity) teamed up to form the Alianza, and agreed to support a common presidential candidate selected in a semiopen primary. De la Rúa ran in a coalition primary as the uncontested leader of the UCR, defeating Graciela Fernández Meijide, a FREPASO national deputy. Pitting the UCR's national party machine against FREPASO's more modest one, de la Rúa scored a substantial victory, with very high levels of voter participation. Despite his overwhelming victory over his Alianza colleague, de la Rúa respected previous coalition agreements regarding the distribution of candidacies for governors and national deputies and did not horde them for the UCR.

The presidential campaign was centered on de la Rúa's personal character, but also on the promotion of the Alianza as a novel electoral force in Argentine politics. In October 1999 the Alianza obtained an overwhelming victory over the PJ and de la Rúa was proclaimed president of the republic.

Fernando de la Rúa's first cabinet showed his recognition that his victory was a win for the Alianza electoral coalition as a whole. He maintained a delicate equilibrium in the distribution of ministerial posts between the UCR and the FREPASO, trying to replicate the model of the Chile's Concertación cabinets (see Altman, Chapter 10, this volume). Nevertheless, after a short period, de la Rúa broke away from this formula and established a more personalistic style of government, promoting relatives (in particular, his son), personal friends, technocrats, and second-tier party leaders as key government players. This style contributed to the progressive abandonment of the original Alianza program and led to a distancing between the president and the coalition of parties that had backed him.

The first large cabinet reorganization, which was undertaken by de la Rúa in 2000 without consulting with FREPASO leaders, resulted in the resignation of Vice President Carlos "Chacho" Alvarez and provoked a serious crisis in the Alianza. De la Rúa also acted with great autonomy in the second reorganization of the cabinet, in 2001, appointing as economics minister first Ricardo López Murphy and later Domingo Cavallo. This provoked an open conflict with his own party, still headed by Alfonsín. The departure of de la Rúa, a *party insider*, from the party-oriented strategy we expect from this type of candidate, is explained by a combination of circumstances: the fractious and conflictive rather than homogeneous coalition he led, his lack of leadership skills, and the severe economic and political crisis over which he presided that eroded his initial support.

Carlos Menem, 1989–1999. Before Menem reached the presidency, almost his entire political career was centered in La Rioja, one of Argentina's least electorally important provinces (Cerruti 1993; Leuco and Díaz 1989). Menem first attained national prominence in the 1980s when he confronted PJ party leadership, which consisted of a group of union leaders called the *Ortodoxos*, and transformed himself into a principal leader of a reform sector that became known as the *Renovadores*. After a series of intraparty but nationwide struggles, the *Renovadores* gained the upper hand in the party 1988, and its two most important leaders, Antonio Cafiero, then the governor of the province of Buenos Aires, and Menem became the PJ party's president and vice president, respectively.

A short time later, in 1988, Menem and Cafiero competed for the PJ candidacy in the first presidential primary in the party's fifty-year history. At the time of the primary, Cafiero formally had the overwhelming support of PJ governors and legislators and the principal party bosses aligned with the *Renovadores* majority. Menem relied on a heterogeneous support base made up largely of union forces, the *Ortodoxo* faction, and a conglomerate of small groups of left- and right-wing Peronists (Leuco and Díaz 1989). Thus supported—and brandishing a proselytizing, markedly personal, and antiparty style—Menem won a hard-fought victory.

After this intraparty triumph, Menem relied once again on a proselytizing strategy to develop a clearly plebiscitary presidential campaign, in which he presented himself as a quasi-religious figure making personalistic appeals to voters. (Palermo and Novaro 1996; Waisbord 1995). With this campaign he achieved an overwhelming victory over Eduardo Angeloz in the 1989 presidential election.

During his ten-and-a-half-year administration, Menem pursued an ambitious state reform policy and oversaw economic deregulation and the privatization of state-owned companies, flouting the traditional statist and nationalistic orientation of Peronism. In all these areas, Menem governed unilaterally, sidestepping the Congress and using and abusing emergency decrees and partial vetoes in times of both crisis and stability (Ferreira Rubio and Goretti 1998; Mustapic 1995).

Menem's strategy in dealing with his party falls into two discernible periods, the first, from 1989 to 1991, characterized by neglect of the PJ, and the second, 1991 to 1999, by his moves toward a strategy of accommodation with the party (Corrales 2002). Between 1989 and 1991, in putting together his cabinet, Menem partnered with three actors that could be considered at worst hostile and at best foreign to the Peronist tradition: top executives from the business conglomerate Bunge & Born, the free market–oriented technocrat Domingo Cavallo, and a group of neoliberal and

decidedly anti-Peronist Unión del Centro Democrático (UCeDé) party leaders. The pro-market reforms coupled with this cabinet strategy provoked a
severe crisis within the PJ, which began to behave like an opposition party,
causing delays and setbacks to Menem's programs.

Beginning in 1991 Menem changed course and managed to obtain PJ
cooperation and support in Congress for his policies. Menem achieved this
objective by calling on the PJ to be the standard-bearer of the state and market-
oriented reform process, adopting a Peronist-friendly criterion for cabinet
appointments, and above all granting substantial autonomy and power resources
to PJ governors. These harmonious Menem–PJ relations facilitated his smooth
reelection in 1995. However, another major conflict erupted in 1999 when
Menem sought a third term, which was viewed as an abusive act aimed at per-
petuating his personal power. The conflict between Menem and the PJ formally
ended with the nomination of Eduardo Duhalde, the governor of the province
of Buenos Aires, as the PJ's presidential candidate.

Judging by his party career and national notoriety as candidate, Menem
could be considered a *party insider* in the Siavelis–Morgenstern typology. But his
provincial-peripheral origins, his victory against the formal national party leadership, and his populist campaign style in the primary and the national election
in 1989 suggest a *party adherent* classification. As president, during the two first
years Menem ignored the party to a greater extent than one would expect even
from a *party adherent*. Yet throughout his tenure he maintained leadership of the
party and made efforts to transform it from within as one would expect from an
adherent. Somewhat ironically, he is also credited with remaking the electoral
viability of the party by transforming it from a union-based one to a political
machine–based party (Levitsky 1998, 2001). For these reasons the hybrid *insider-
adherent* label describes Menem better in 1989 and the *party insider* category fits
him as unchallenged PJ leader and candidate in 1995.

Néstor Kirchner, 2003–2007. Until his election as president, Néstor Kirchner's
political trajectory was that of a peripheral Peronist leader. His career had strayed
little from the limited reach of the relatively electorally irrelevant province of
Santa Cruz, in the southern Patagonian region. Kirchner's ascension to the presidency was similar to that of governors elected in provinces administered by the
PJ where there was a divided party leadership. Thus, Kirchner, much better than
Menem in 1989, fits the mold of a *party adherent*.

Kirchner's political ascendancy was determined by intraparty struggles, specifically a deep rivalry between President Eduardo Duhalde of the PJ and Menem.
This rivalry, already described, fundamentally grew from Menem's earlier efforts
to stymie the candidacy of Duhalde in 1999. During his short time in office in
2002–2003, Duhalde used all the tools of the presidency to impede Menem's
return to power after his 1999 defeat. Powerless to designate his own successor

and conscious of the difficulty of winning a primary against Menem, Duhalde promoted the presentation of multiple PJ presidential candidates in the general election. The PJ thus went to the polls in a party-splitting mode with three candidates: Menem and two contenders with anti-neoliberal platforms: Adolfo Rodríguez Saá, a traditional populist, and Kirchner, a progressive center-left candidate who was backed by Duhalde.

In the first round, Menem finished first, with 24 percent of the vote. Nonetheless, his certain defeat by Kirchner, predicted by public opinion polls, led to Menem's withdrawal from the second round. Kirchner thus became the new president in an election in which he obtained 22 percent of the vote and in which the three Peronist candidates combined won more than 60 percent.

In appointing his cabinet, Kirchner attempted above all to reflect the party agreement that had brought him to the presidency rather than hiring the long-standing party officials. As could be predicted for a *party adherent*, an ad hoc combination of ministers was appointed to shore up his support. Four cabinet posts were awarded to members of the president's intimate circle, three posts were reserved for functionaries of the Duhalde administration (all linked to the province of Buenos Aires PJ), and an equal number were distributed among other leaders with strong Peronist credentials. Posts were denied to cabinet candidates from northern districts, as nearly all these, though Peronist bastions, had been aligned with Menem in the presidential election, and to leaders who did not specifically back Kirchner; the latter group would have permitted Kirchner to extend his meager base of support.

Kirchner followed and deepened the policy program of President Duhalde, which had been a significant programmatic course change from Menem's neoliberal policies; this is the reformist bent that the Siavelis–Morgenstern typology would predict for a *party adherent*. This change of course signified the reorientation of the PJ toward its traditional statist tendencies, a reorientation perhaps made possible by the fluid internal structure of Peronism that allowed it to adapt to changing circumstances. In effect, once Menem was defeated, PJ provincial leaders quickly abandoned support for his policies, even though they had previously backed them.

Much like Menem in 1989, Kirchner enjoyed substantial autonomy and started his administration by concentrating power and governing unilaterally. Unlike what occurred in Menem's case, this time these strategies did not provoke a severe crisis within the PJ. On the contrary, after breaking with Duhalde, Kirchner was still backed by Duhalde's supporters in the Peronist landslide victory in the legislative elections of 2005, thus establishing Kirchner as the undisputed new leader of the Peronists. Ultimately, pragmatism and opportunism combined with the fluidity in the structure of the PJ allowed this almost immediate transfer of personal loyalties from one leader to another.

Governors

The Argentine case shows that the presidents' and governors' political careers are strongly underwritten by the political parties that back them. As underscored by Siavelis and Morgenstern, though the lessons from the presidential R&S process do not seamlessly apply to R&S for governors, they do manifest the same general tendencies and provide important insights.

At the national level, presidential candidates who were hybrid *insider-adherents* and *party adherents* have successfully emerged from outside a party's inner circle or from within a divided party leadership to challenge the formal leadership party core. This has been the case in the formally uninstitutionalized PJ, in contrast to the formally institutionalized UCR, which since 1983 has invariably chosen *party insiders* as presidential candidates. Does party institutionalization matter to the type of executive candidates that party choose? Is the PJ more likely than the UCR to choose as candidates hybrid *insiders-adherents* or *party adherents*? Can this question, derived from small-N presidential politics, be converted to a hypothesis and survive a test at the level of gubernatorial candidates?

In the UCR, well-established rules in recruiting and promoting leaders consistently resulted in *party insiders'* (*candidatos naturales*) running for the governorship. This is not the case in the PJ, where open career paths and changing methods of leadership selection facilitate the emergence of *party adherent* or hybrid *insider-adherent* candidates. This is particularly the case for Peronist governors elected in provinces administered by the PJ but with a divided party leadership (where there are disputes within the party over leadership). However, variations in how closely integrated the governors are with their provincial party structures seems not to have had significant effects on the propensity of the governors to work within party structures. This may be a function of the limited differences in the level of integration, suggesting that many candidates fit between the ideal typical *insider* and *adherent* categories.

This generalization can be appreciated by examining the postgubernatorial political careers of former governors (see Table 8.6). An important number of governors have run for reelection and obtained a second mandate (or up to a third and fourth mandate, if the provincial constitution allows for it), and many have obtained a post as a national deputy or have been active solely as party leaders. At the same time, Argentina is notable for the significant number of governors who, after completing their terms of office, have obtained a seat in the national Senate and aspired to return to provincial government (see Table 8.7). In this sense Argentina parallels the Brazilian case (see Samuels, Chapter 3, this volume), in that state or provincial positions are plum jobs. In any case, the common denominator for all these governors is that to actively continue their political careers they must maintain a good relationship with the party, which means observing party rules and practices. As a result, it seems that the *adherent* candidates move toward *insider* governors and thus there is little difference in the behavior of PJ and UCR governors, or between Peronists *insiders* and *adherents*. For example, once elected as governors, notorious outsiders co-opted by the PJ such as Ramón "Palito" Ortega or Carlos Reutemann have engaged in party-oriented behavior and pursued a traditional party-oriented career in a form similar to indubitable PJ *party insiders* such as Jorge Busti, Rubén Marín, or Carlos Juárez, and UCR *insiders* such as Eduardo Angeloz or Horacio Massaccesi (see Table 8.7).

Just as at national level, the success of *adherents* or hybrid *insider-adherents* in pursuing a successful careers is explained by the virtually unchallenged authority that Argentine governors exercise within provincial borders, a nonprogrammatic tradition, the tendency of *party insiders* to bandwagon toward office-holding leaders (where losers and their loyalists rapidly change positions and join groups led by victorious leaders), and the flexible party organization exhibited by the PJ (Levitsky 2003; McGuire 1997).

TABLE 8.6 Position Held by Argentine Governors after Term of Office, 1983–1999 (Percentage)

Position Held	PJ %	UCR %	Provincial Parties %	National Minor Parties %
Governor	31	27	12	100
National deputy	18	19	25	
National senator	17	12	19	
Party activist	11	8	19	
Private activity[a]	9		12	
National executive branch (second-tier)	4	8		
President	3	4		
Mayor	3			
Provincial legislator	1		6	
National minister	1	8		
Ambassador	1			
Deceased	1			
National-party president		4		
Provincial-party president (only post)[b]		8		
Number	72	26	16	1

Source: Author, based on information from national newspapers, biographical collections, and interviews with political leaders.

a. The person was not engaged in any noteworthy partisan activity and did not hold any elective or appointive position.

b. Only position held. Where a provincial-party president held an elective or appointive office, that post is counted.

TABLE 8.7 From Argentine Governor to National Senator and Vice Versa, 1983–2006

| Party | Name | Province | From | | To | |
			Governor	Senator	Governor	Senator
PJ	Antonio Cafiero	Buenos Aires	1987–91			1992–2001
	Eduardo Duhalde	Buenos Aires	1991–99			2001
	Ramón Saadi	Catamarca	1983–87			1987–88
	Ramón Saadi	Catamarca		1987–88	1988–91	
	Ramón Saadi	Catamarca	1983–87, 1988–91			2003–present
	Vicente L. Saadi	Catamarca		1983–87	1987–88	
	José M. de la Sota	Córdoba		1995–98	1998–present	
	Jorge Busti	Entre Ríos	1987–91, 1995–99			2001–03
	Jorge Busti	Entre Ríos		2001–03	2003–present	
	Carlos Snopek	Jujuy	1983–87			1989–91
	Guillermo Snopek	Jujuy		1992–95	1995–96	
	Rubén Marín	La Pampa	1983–87			1989–91
	Rubén Marín	La Pampa		1989–91	1991–2003	
	Rubén Marín	La Pampa	1983–87, 1991–2003			2003–present
	Carlos Verna	La Pampa		1993–2003	2003–present	
	Carlos Menem	La Rioja	1987–89			2005–present
	José O. Bordón	Mendoza	1987–91			1992–96
	Julio C. Humada	Misiones	1987–91			1992–2001
	Ramón Puerta	Misiones	1991–99			2001–05
	Juan Carlos Romero	Salta		1986–95	1995–present	
	José Luis Gioja	San Juan		1995–2003	2003–present	
	Adolfo Rodríguez Saá	San Luis	1983–2001			2005–present
	Alberto Rodríguez Saá	San Luis		1983–94, 1998–2001	2003–present	
	Carlos Reutemann	Santa Fe	1991–95			1995–99
	Carlos Reutemann	Santa Fe		1995–99	1999–2003	

Party	Name	Province	From		To	
			Governor	Senator	Governor	Senator
	Carlos Reutemann	Santa Fe	1991–95, 1999–2003			2003–present
	Carlos Juárez	Santiago del Estero	1983–87			1987–95
	Carlos Juárez	Santiago del Estero		1987–95	1995–2001	
	Carlos Juárez	Santiago del Estero	1983–87, 1995–2001			2001
	Carlos Manfredotti	Tierra del Fuego		1995–99	1999–2003	
	José Alperovich	Tucumán		2001–03	2003–present	
	Julio Miranda	Tucumán		1992–99	1999–2003	
	Julio Miranda	Tucumán	1999–2003			2003–present
	Ramón Ortega	Tucumán	1991–95			1998–2001
UCR	Fernando de la Rúa	Capital Federal		1983–89, 1992–96	1996–99	
	Eduardo Brizuela del Moral	Catamarca		2001–03	2003–present	
	Oscar Castillo	Catamarca	1999–2003			2003–present
	Carlos Maestro	Chubut	1991–99			2001–03
	Eduardo Angeloz	Córdoba	1983–95			1995–2001
	Horacio Massaccesi	Río Negro	1987–95			1995–2001
	Jorge Colazo	Tierra del Fuego		2001–03		2003–05
PB	Leopoldo Bravo	San Juan	1983–86			1986–2001
	Carlos Gómez Centurión	San Juan		1983–87	1987–91	
PL	Ricardo Leconte	Corrientes		1983–87	1987–91	
PA	José Romero Feris	Corrientes	1983–87			1987–2001
MPN	Pedro Salvatori	Neuquén	1987–91			2001–present
PRS	Roberto Ulloa	Salta	1991–95			1995–2001
CR	Alfredo Avelín	San Juan		1992–99	1999–2002	

Source: Author, based on information from national newspapers, biographical collections, and interviews with political leaders.

Conclusion

In Argentina, the R&S process for choosing candidates for president and governor is centered in political parties, and within them, in the parties' respective provincial branches. The centrality of parties in R&S is related to the combination of a key group of electoral and party variables: plurality electoral rules, congruent elections, a moderately institutionalized party system with medium to low degrees of electoral competitiveness at the national and provincial levels, and a decentralized party organization based on patronage, pork-barrel politics, and clientelism. As a consequence, the leaders that are elected to executive offices are mostly *party insiders* and *party adherents* or a hybrid of these two ideal types. The evidence presented here concerning the behavior of the presidents in the post-1983 period shows, in some contrast to what was previously noted about governors, notable differences in the behavior of *party insiders* and hybrid *party insider-adherents*.

As a *party insider* Alfonsín mobilized his party behind his presidential candidacy in the 1983 campaign, and afterwards he was inclined to integrate his cabinet with UCR members, making sure to maintain smooth relations with the party and to structure positive relations with the UCR contingent in Congress. Somewhat contrary to the hypothesis set out by Siavelis and Morgenstern, the *party insider* de la Rúa experienced serious difficulties in coordinating relations between his administration and the party coalition that supported it. However, the key difference between him and Alfonsín was that he relied on a coalition of parties and could rely less than Alfonsín on his party contacts to build these legislative contingents.

On the other hand, a PJ hybrid *insider-adherent* such as Menem in 1989 or a *party adherent* such as Kirchner—who built almost their entire careers on the party periphery and reached the presidency by challenging the inner circle (Menem) and as a result of divided party leadership (Kirchner)—are eloquent cases of attempts to move the incumbent party in a new direction without paying much attention to internal debate. Both managed to fill cabinet positions without considering major-party issues and to resolve coordination problems between the president and his legislative support base through mechanisms other than their party.

The Argentine case gives us interesting empirical material to deepen the study of the relationships between different types of parties and the types of candidates they produce, and the performance of presidents. As expected, the more formally institutionalized UCR has had presidents of the *party insider* type, whereas the PJ has produced hybrid *insider-adherents* or *party adherents* because of low levels of formal institutionalization and the lack of formalized rules that characterize the PJ. What is intriguing, however, is that a hybrid *insider-adherent* such as Menem in 1989 or a *party adherent* such as Kirchner in 2003 were more successful in carrying out their policies than the *party insiders* commanding institutionalized parties—Alfonsín and de la Rúa. The likely reason for this is that, as noted in Chapter 15 of this volume, Menem and Kirchner demonstrated the type of authoritarian efficiency that often exacts a cost on representation. The nonprogrammatic tradition of the party, the tendency of members to bandwagon toward office-holding leaders, and the flexible party organization exhibited by the PJ in large part explain the career success of PJ governors who are *party adherents* or hybrid *insider-adherents*. The virtually unchallenged authority that Argentine governors exercise within provincial borders also determines how successful politicians will be in pursuing a successful career. However, for the long term, the disaster that befell Argentine politics after the Menem period suggests that his type of authoritarian efficiency, while potentially effective from a policy perspective in the short term, may not be optimal for the long-term consolidation of democracy.

Chapter Nine

Political Recruitment in an Executive-Centric
System: Presidents, Ministers, and Governors
in Brazil

TIMOTHY J. POWER AND MARÍLIA G. MOCHEL

Brazil's enormous size, its status as the world's third-largest
democracy, and its permissive, high-magnitude electoral system
make it a world leader in the production of candidates for elective office. But many of those candidates seek offices that they
neither care for nor plan to hold for very long. Life as a legislator is often disdained, and executive office is supremely valued. This simple observation is confirmed by both behavioral
and attitudinal data.

In terms of politicians' behavior, the preferred pathways
to power in Brazil can be inferred from the strategic choices
that politicians make. In the quadrennial municipal elections, typically 20 to 25 percent of the membership of the
Chamber of Deputies will choose to run for the mayoralty of
one of Brazil's more than 5,500 municipalities. Compare this
to the United States, where in the entire country there are
probably fewer than five cities that might attract a sitting
member of Congress to throw his or her hat into a mayor's
race. The scramble for mayoralties is a revealing datum for
political scientists: even without being asked which office
they prefer, a quarter of federal deputies are obviously voting
with their feet.

Judging by their attitudes, when politicians do respond to
surveys, a similar pattern emerges. The survey statement "In
general, it is better to hold a position in the executive branch
than a seat in Congress" was agreed to by 73 percent of a
sample of 158 federal legislators in 1997. When the question
was repeated in the subsequent legislature, in 2001, 66 percent

The authors would like to thank Joy Langston, Scott Morgenstern, Edson
Nunes, and Peter Siavelis for helpful comments on an earlier version of this
chapter.

of 137 respondents agreed.[1] In unstructured interviews about career preferences, it usually does not take long to uncover the reasoning behind these views. "Politics is all about hiring and firing," legislators say. "Every politician wants to control a budget" is another typically wistful comment about life in the executive branch. "The deputy is forever asking someone else to do something for his strongholds. His dream is not to have to ask anymore." In a political system characterized by poverty, inequality, patron–client relations, and a strong sense of *imediatismo político*—the idea that problems must be solved yesterday—"you can't even compare" political service in the legislative and executive branches.[2] Executives—not legislators—can make a difference in the lives of ordinary voters, and politicians know this. The bottom line is that political ambition in the Brazilian political system reflects the strongly executive-centric nature of politics in Brazil (Samuels 2003).

At the pinnacle of executive power stands the President of the Republic, the dominant figure in Brazilian politics. Arrayed behind the president in Brasília are the two dozen or so *ministros de estado*, ministers of state, who control policy and purse strings in various domains of government output: health, transportation, agriculture, finance. At the subnational level, executive power accrues to the twenty-seven state governors (until 1930, they were, revealingly, called presidents) who are the chief executives of what are essentially hyperpresidential mini-political systems. The governors are surrounded by their own "ministers," known as *secretários estaduais*, many of whom are technocrats who will eventually use their state-level executive portfolios to launch political careers. At the municipal level, the pattern is replicated identically with *prefeitos* (mayors) and *secretários municipais*. There is a clear hierarchy in the more than five thousand mayoralties: the chief executives of the twenty-six state capitals are powerful political figures in their states, second only to their governors, and there are close to two hundred other large cities in Brazil whose mayors also exert great influence. This hierarchy of power is reflected in the Constitution: only cities with more than 200,000 voters have mayoral runoff elections, whereas the others, considered less politically important, use first-past-the-post rules. Moreover, in another nod to executive power, any federal legislator who is invited to serve as a *secretário estadual* (state secretary) or as a *secretário municipal* (municipal secretary) of a capital city is allowed to take a leave from Congress and later return to his or her seat; at any given moment, two or three dozen members of Congress are enjoying this

1. The statement was worded "*Em geral, ocupar um cargo executivo é melhor do que ter um mandato parlamentar.*" In each survey, about half of the respondents had held executive office and half had not, and there was no statistically significant difference in the rates of agreement—in fact, agreement was almost identical across the two groups. From a survey of members of both houses of the National Congress carried out by Power in 1997 and 2001.

2. From interviews conducted by Power with federal legislators in 1990 and 1993. For a list of names of interviewees and dates, see Power (2000, chapter 6).

privilege. This roster of executive positions largely corresponds to what politicians aspire to achieve (Samuels 2003, 16–23). Arguably, we could also add to this list the "number twos"—the vice president, the vice governors, and the vice mayors—since under Brazilian law the vices will almost always have a chance to exercise executive power—some for up to six months in a four-year term.[3]

Given the critical importance of executives in Brazilian politics, it is essential to uncover their pathways to power—who are they, where do they come from, and how are they chosen? For the greater part of this chapter, executive candidate type is treated as a dependent variable. But the type of candidate should also be conceived of as an independent variable. To avoid consigning recruitment to the category of "a cause in search of an effect," we try to identify some political consequences of distinct pathways to power. We examine three types of executive office: the presidency, ministerial portfolios, and state governorships. Municipal mayors are excluded not for lack of relevance but owing simply to a lack of data: there is no central information source on the more than 5,500 territorial units and executive incumbents. Exclusion of municipal executives is a shortcoming that we and others should endeavor to rectify soon, given the centrality of *prefeitos* in Brazilian political life.

Our main arguments can be summarized briefly. As the editors of this volume point out, the presidency presents an obvious analytical problem due to the small-N nature of the office. However, despite personal idiosyncrasies of presidents and some caveats relating to partisan factors, we find that a number of contemporary Brazilian presidents can be adequately classified according to the taxonomy of executive types devised by Siavelis and Morgenstern (Chapter 1, this volume). Turning to cabinet ministers, we find that *ministros* are recruited in accordance with political factors and technocratic qualifications, the actual weighting of these factors depending largely on time and on the political challenges of constructing a pro-presidential majority in Congress. Finally, with regard to state governors, we find that several of the institutional variables identified by Siavelis and Morgenstern—particularly electoral rules and the timing and sequencing of elections—shape recruitment to the governorship in important ways. The sequencing of elections in Brazil's transition to democracy magnified the power of governors; the use of double-ballot majoritarian rules encourages a large number of candidacies; and the concurrence of gubernatorial and presidential elections means that governors are critical to coalition building and governability. Partisan variables matter as well, but we argue that the editors' taxonomy of executive types needs to be "stretched" in order to accommodate the critical distinction between catchall and ideological parties in the races for governor (Mainwaring 1999) as well as the remarkable regional diversity of Brazil's subnational units (Soares 1967; Cintra

---

3. The seconds-in-command formally assume power whenever the chief executive travels outside the jurisdiction. Also, some incumbent executives (although not the president or vice president) are required to temporarily stand down while seeking reelection or election to other offices.

1979). Regional factors are often as important as partisan variables in shaping overall patterns of recruitment to the governorship.

We deal with presidents, ministers, and governors in turn, with the majority of the analysis given over to the enormously important state governors. We then proceed to our conclusions.

Recruitment to the Presidency

Brazil became a republic in 1889. Since then, eleven individuals have held the title of president under democratic conditions. Of these, only ten have actually served (one died before assuming office) and only eight were actually elected to the presidency (three acceded from the vice presidency). As of 2007, only three democratically elected presidents have successfully concluded their terms and handed over power to a successor also chosen in free elections. The first two times this happened, in 1950 and 1960, the successor himself did not complete his term; but the third attempt, begun with the transition from Fernando Henrique Cardoso to Luiz Inácio Lula da Silva in 2002, made history when Lula completed his first term in office in 2006. Since the modern period of presidential elections began in 1989, there have been fewer than twenty serious candidacies across the five electoral cycles, and only nine men have ever won more than 10 percent of the first-round vote for president.[4] Clearly, the Brazilian presidency has not had patterns of candidate selection and succession that would allow us to derive empirically based generalizations about pathways to the office. Nonetheless, some general observations can be made.

First, prior executive experience matters in presidential recruitment. As Table 9.1 shows, all modern presidents but one have previously served as minister, governor, or mayor. João Goulart made his name during a brief stint at the Labor Ministry under Getúlio Vargas, and Cardoso launched his successful presidential campaign from the Finance Ministry. Many have been governors of important states (Vargas, Jânio Quadros, Tancredo Neves), although governors of less developed states have also projected themselves politically (Fernando Collor, José Sarney). Excepting Eurico Gaspar Dutra, who was war minister during the Second World War, all modern presidents have served in the National Congress—but it would be difficult to make the case that legislative service was decisive as a springboard for any of them. Cardoso is the only *party loyalist* legislator to have been elected president, but this occurred only after he was magnified by the Finance portfolio in 1993–1994. The only modern president with no prior executive experience in government is the incumbent as of spring 2008, Lula.

---

4. The nine individuals are Fernando Collor (PRN, 1989), Inácio Lula da Silva (PT, 1989, 1994, 1998, 2002, 2006), Leonel Brizola (PDT, 1989), Mário Covas (PSDB, 1989), Fernando Henrique Cardoso (PSDB, 1994, 1998), Ciro Gomes (PPS, 1998, 2002), Anthony Garotinho (PSB, 2002), José Serra (PSDB, 2002), and Geraldo Alckmin (PSDB, 2006). See next note.

TABLE 9.1 Prior Political Experience of Brazilian Presidents in the Two Democratic Periods, 1946–1964 and 1985–2003 (Number of Terms)

President	City Council	Mayor or Vice Mayor	State Legislator	Governor or Vice Governor	Federal Deputy	Senator	Minister	Prime Minister	Vice President	Total Years in Office
Dutra							1			9
Vargas[a]			2	1	2		1			40
Kubitschek		1	1	1	2					15
Quadros	1	1	1	1	1					12
Goulart			1		1		1		2	12
Neves[b]			1	1	5	1	1	1		33
Sarney				1	2	2			1	26
Collor		1		1	1					10
Franco		2				2			1	19
Cardoso						2	2			11
Lula da Silva[c]					1					4

a. Total years in office prior to being elected president. Vargas occupied the presidency from 1930 to 1945, but after the 1934 elections were not held. Vargas became president through democratic channels only in 1950.

b. Neves was elected to the presidency in 1985 but died prior to taking office. Earlier, he was one of the two prime ministers during Brazil's brief experiment with semipresidentialism, from September 1961 to January 1963.

c. As of December 31, 2006, when Lula completed his first term in office. He was reelected to a second four-year term in 2006.

Second, electoral rules governing presidential nomination are lenient. Although Brazilian law does not permit independent candidacies, it has been very permissive regarding the creation of new parties. The successful candidacy of Fernando Collor in 1989 is perhaps the best-known example of a party's (the Partido da Reconstrução Nacional, National Reconstruction Party, or PRN) being created uniquely for the purpose of a single presidential bid. Candidates are usually selected in national conventions in which both federal legislators and regional elites (governors and mayors) have influence. Of the major parties, only the PT has used a presidential primary—once, in 2002.[5] But since the only such primary was won by Lula with more than 80 percent of the vote, we cannot say that primaries have had any impact yet on presidential candidate selection in Brazil.

In the current democracy, the permissiveness of nomination rules has led to twenty-three candidacies in 1989, eight in 1994, twelve in 1998, six in 2002, and seven in 2006, although only a third of these candidacies could generously be considered realistic. The unusually high number of candidates in 1989 is explained by two factors: first, pent-up demand in the context of a "founding election" (this was the first direct presidential contest since 1960), and second, the lack of concurrence with other races. Beginning in 1994, presidential and legislative elections were made concurrent, and they also coincide with gubernatorial and state assembly elections. This has forced major parties to coordinate their alliance formation with greater care, leading to a smaller effective number of presidential candidates, and the magnification of the importance of party ties.

Whereas in 1989 each of the major parties ran its own candidate, each of the subsequent four contests saw some large parties stepping aside and supplying vice-presidential candidates to other parties. In 1994, 1998, and 2006, the Partido da Frente Liberal (PFL or Liberal Front Party)[6] clearly believed that it was better to join a viable alliance and have power in the subsequent administration than to run a candidate with no real chance of winning—thus it allied with Cardoso's Brazilian Social Democratic Party (Partido da Social Democracia Brasileira, or PSDB). The same logic led to a PSDB–PMDB alliance in 2002. Thus the effective number of presidential candidacies cannot be inferred automatically from electoral rules. Both the permissiveness of nomination procedures (Mainwaring 1999) and the existence of a double-ballot majoritarian system (Jones 1999) should predict a very high number of candidacies in Brazil. But the need for parties to coordinate alliances has led to frequent ticket balancing.

Most of the postwar presidential candidates can be classified using the typology developed by Siavelis and Morgenstern. Despite Brazil's reputation for loose

---

5. A list of party abbreviations with Portuguese and English names appears in the preface to this volume.
6. In March 2007, the PFL changed its name to Democratas (DEM). For consistency, in this chapter we refer to the party as the PFL.

parties, a surprisingly large number of aspirants can be viewed as *party insiders*. In the 1950s, both Juscelino Kubitschek (PSD) and Goulart (PTB) fit the mold, although the latter never actually ran for president. We add to the editors' framework the hypothesis that *party insiders* are particularly prone to compete in "founding elections." Thus the first round in 1989 was overcrowded with *party insiders*: Inácio Lula da Silva (PT), Leonel Brizola (PDT), Ulysses Guimarães (PMDB), Paulo Maluf (PDS), Aureliano Chaves (PFL), Mário Covas (PSDB), and Roberto Freire (PCB) were the dominant figures in their parties at the time. *Party adherents* have also been common. In 1998, Ciro Gomes, a new recruit to the PPS (formerly PCB), became a star vote getter for a previously marginal party, and in 2002, the same occurred with Anthony Garotinho, a recent *adherent* to the PSB who went on to win an impressive 18 percent for a party that had traditionally been a minor satellite of the PT. Again in contrast to Brazil's reputation in the literature, the number of *free-wheeling independents* (*FWIs*) has been rather small at the presidential level. Jânio Quadros in 1960 and Fernando Collor in 1989 both ran as antiparty populists, with Quadros borrowing the UDN label and Collor creating his own party, the PRN.

Consistent with its long history of corporatist representation (Power and Doctor 2004), Brazil has also seen its fair share of *group agents*. In 1989, Ronaldo Caiado, a conservative landowner, ran on the PSD label as the candidate of the Rural Democratic Union (UDR), a hard-line group representing a social movement opposed to agrarian reform (Payne 2000). The same year, Fernando Gabeira competed as the candidate of the tiny Green Party (Partido Verde or PV). Gabeira's was not a partisan campaign but rather a proxy candidacy for the environmental movement, which hoped only to influence the larger parties. Finally, in both 1994 and 1998, two retired military officers, Admiral-Ret. Hernani Fortuna and General-Ret. Ivan Frota, ran as corporate representatives of the armed forces and symbols of authoritarian nostalgia. None of these *group agents* had much difficulty in securing a party nomination and filing for candidacy. Having done so, they were able to take advantage of the legal provision that guarantees free television time for all candidates. Even the most resource-poor special interest groups in Brazil can gain some media visibility by running *group agents* in elections.

We now reverse our focus and examine presidential recruitment as an independent variable, as suggested by this volume's editors. How well do these candidate types work as predictors of electoral and postelectoral behavior in Brazil? *FWIs*, whose campaigns are usually assaults on established parties, should be expected to be erratic and unpredictable after election, and this corresponds to the reality of Quadros and Collor. Both ran on the same main issue: corruption. Neither finished his term, leaving Brazil with two unelected presidents, Goulart and Itamar Franco. *Group agents* in Brazil have not proved viable, perhaps because of Brazil's federal structure and regional diversity. *Party adherents* have campaigned in ways that would be predicted by Siavelis and Morgenstern, downplaying ideology and stressing vague and broad themes.

We offer a caveat regarding the predictive capacity of the *party insider* in Brazil: the need to forge electoral and governing alliances implies that partisanship will be a poor predictor of behavior both on the campaign trail and in government. In 1994, Cardoso's preelection alliance with the conservative PFL marked a sharp break with the historical social democratic identity of the PSDB (Power 2001). Lula's 2002 campaign was the first in which the PT made alliances outside the left, and it was also the first election that the party won. His remarkable pragmatism after 2003 moved the PT rightward, much as occurred with the PSDB in the 1990s and the PMDB in the 1980s. Thus, the political requisites of coalition building severely limit the extent to which partisanship and ideology can be used to predict the behavior of aspirants and presidents.

Recruitment to Ministerial Office

In his study of the political ambition of Brazilian legislators, Samuels (2003) discusses the country's political "opportunity structure." He outlines a career ladder where ministerial and gubernatorial offices are perceived as the most attractive positions. In this section we examine ministers, and in the next section we give more extended attention to governors.

Samuels notes that "a governorship offers more benefits than a seat in the Chamber (or the Senate), but it remains unclear whether it ranks higher than a ministry" (2003, 20). The evidence in Table 9.2 suggests that federal legislators attach wildly different values to ministries. When asked in 1990 to name the most important ministry for their state or region, about half of legislators cited either the Agriculture or Interior Ministry—neither of which has the sort of prestige associated with Finance or Foreign Relations and both of which are routinely filled by forgettable ministers. The Agriculture, Interior, Education, and Transportation portfolios are all ideal as the locus of public works and for distributing favors and pork, but many other ministries have little value to individual deputies (though they may have more perceived value to parties).[7] Not all ministries are created equal, but more research is necessary to devise a precise weighting of their political worth.

Recruitment to the federal cabinet has changed in important ways in the postwar period. Here we build on the excellent study by Nunes (1978), who collected data on 227 ministers in civilian portfolios between 1946 and 1977. His intent was to compare ministerial recruitment in the democracy of 1946 to 1964

7. See Ames (2001) for a discussion of the relationship between individual deputies and cabinet ministers.

TABLE 9.2 Perceived Importance of Ministerial Portfolios among Brazilian Federal Legislators, 1990[a]

Ministry	Spontaneous Mentions	Percent
Agriculture	54	24.4
Interior[b]	53	24.0
Finance	32	14.5
Education	27	12.2
Transportation	14	6.3
Mines and Energy	11	5.0
Industry and Commerce	8	3.6
Health	5	2.3
Social Security	4	1.8
SEPLAN (Planning)	3	1.4
Communications	2	0.9
Science and Technology	1	0.5
Justice	1	0.5
Total	221	100.0

Source: Mail survey conducted by Timothy Power, 1990. Open-ended question for write-in answers: *Se o Sr. tivesse que escolher um Minisério federal que é da maior importancia para seu estado ou região, qual seria? (Por favor escreva o nome de um dos 23 ministérios que existiram durante o governo Sarney).* "If you had to choose a federal ministry that is of the highest importance for your state or region, which one would it be? (Please write in the name of one of the 23 ministries that existed during the Sarney administration)".

a. $N = 249$. Some twenty-two did not answer, and six gave invalid responses. Only valid responses shown. Respondents cited thirteen of twenty-three possible ministries.
b. Known today as the Ministry of Regional Integration.

with the post-1964 military dictatorship. Updating his work, we have added data on 109 ministers in the Cardoso and Lula administrations, from 1995 to 2004. The results are presented in Table 9.3.

The most important change in the postwar period has been the fluctuation in the percentage of ministers with "political" backgrounds. Here we define a political background as prior service in the National Congress or a state legislature. In the 1946–1964 democracy, about 60 percent of ministers were recruited from legislative backgrounds. As Nunes pointed out in 1978, this percentage fell by half during the military regime (Table 9.3). The sharp drop illustrated both the military's technocratic approach to development and its mistrust of professional politicians. Our extension of Nunes' analysis shows that since the return of democracy in the 1980s, the percentage of ministers drawn from legislative life has indeed increased, although not to the levels preceding the 1964 coup. Only 44 percent of 109 ministers between 1995 and 2003 could be classified as having a legislative background, although this figure conceals a major difference between the cabinets of Lula (more political) and Cardoso (more technocratic). More than one-third of all Cardoso ministers (thirty-four of eighty-eight) came from technical or bureaucratic backgrounds.

TABLE 9.3 Legislative Experience of Nonmilitary Permanent Brazilian Ministers per Administration in 1946–1964, 1965–1978, and 1995–2004 (Percentages)

Origin Administration	Legislative Experience	Military[a] Experience	Other[b]	Technical Bureaucracy	No Info	N
Dutra	52	4	20	4	20	25
Vargas	75	—	25	—	—	20
Café Filho	50	4.5	36.5	4.5	4.5	22
Kubitschek	65	4.4	30.4	—	—	23
Quadros	60	—	10	—	30	10
Goulart	59.7	—	25	5.7	9.6	52
Totals 1945–1964	**59.9**	**2.0**	**25.7**	**3.3**	**9.2**	**152**
Castelo Branco	35.7	3.6	42.8	10.7	7.2	28
Costa e Silva	37.5	12.5	50	—	—	16
Médici	18.7	12.5	68.7	—	—	16
Geisel	20	20	53.3	6.7	—	15
Totals 1965–1978	**29.3**	**10.7**	**52.0**	**5.3**	**2.7**	**75**
Cardoso 1	44.4	—	13.8	41.7	—	36
Cardoso 2	32.7	—	13.5	36.5	17.3	52
Lula	62.5	—	25	12.5	—	24
Totals 1995–2004	**44.1**	—	**16.5**	**32.1**	**7.3**	**109**

Source: First and second periods from Nunes (1978). Third period calculated by authors.

a. This column refers to ministers in nonmilitary portfolios who had military experience. Ministers of the army, navy, and air force are excluded.
b. The category "other" includes businessmen, diplomats, mayors, and union leaders.

Our first point about ministerial recruitment is therefore that politicians may have less automatic access to the cabinet than they did in the past. Admittedly, this could be an artifact of the Cardoso period (Lula's 62.5 percent political cabinet is on par with precoup levels),[8] but there are persuasive reasons why presidents may be increasingly tempted to employ technocrats in the future. One is an older, secular trend toward specialization of state functions and the growing importance of "technocratic roles" in government (O'Donnell 1973). Another is a newer trend: the intense pressures of economic globalization. Latin American presidents increasingly make policy and appointments with an eye focused externally on "the markets" rather than internally on party politics: this favors apolitical *técnicos* for key jobs. Conversely, when state reforms are urgently prescribed, professional politicians may actually prefer that these reforms be carried out by technocrats rather than assume the responsibility for themselves or their parties.[9]

Our second point about ministerial recruitment concerns what happens to the ministries that do remain within the domain of party politics. Given one of the most fragmented party systems in the world, Brazilian presidents must behave like European prime ministers: they must fashion multiparty cabinets and multiparty voting blocs on the floor of the legislature.[10] Abranches (1988) gave this system an apt name: *presidencialismo de coalizão*, or coalitional presidentialism. The game of *presidencialismo de coalizão* means that ministries are awarded to parties— and withdrawn from them—on the basis of loyalty to the president. Large parties that can deliver lots of floor votes are particularly demanding, as Lula discovered when he invited the PMDB to join his government in 2003. Amorim Neto (2002) has shown empirically that from the president's perspective, *presidencialismo de coalizão* actually "works" in the sense that executives can indeed expect higher coalition discipline when they compose their cabinets wisely.

Amorim Neto's cogent analysis of cabinet management leads us to hypothesize that the candidate type, as outlined in Chapter 1 of this volume, is an important intervening variable in coalitional presidentialism. *Party insiders*, on becoming president—for example, Cardoso—will instinctively seek out legislative interlocutors with similar *insider* backgrounds, thus facilitating the negotiations that lead to mutually satisfactory cabinets. Cardoso's choice of another consummate

8. The large number of ex-legislators in Lula's first cabinet is understandable, given the PT's history. Founded in 1980, the PT did not win the presidency until 2002. By the time it came to power, it had a long political "waiting list"—more than a hundred former deputies and senators who had never held a cabinet portfolio and who formed the initial talent pool for Lula.

9. Political concerns often tie the hands of presidents in this regard. One interpretation of Brazil's severe electricity crisis in 2001 was that the Ministry of Mines and Energy had become ineffective during its long period of partisan control by the PFL, which stretched back through several administrations. When the crisis hit in mid-2001, Cardoso maintained the PFL minister, Rodolpho Tourinho, in office, but transferred effective control of the energy portfolio to a technocrat, Pedro Parente.

10. Cardoso's PSDB never held more than 21 percent of the seats in the Chamber of Deputies in the 1995–2002 period. Lula's PT won only 18 percent of the seats in 2002 and 16 percent in 2006.

insider, Marco Maciel (member of the PFL, former senator and president of the Chamber of Deputies), as his vice president was no accident: their joint capacity for interpartisan deal making was unparalleled in recent Brazilian history. But *free-wheeling independents* do not speak the same language as *party insiders*: FWIs are unlikely to have much prior experience or subsequent success in the complex negotiations necessary to maintain a functioning coalition in Congress. Collor's studied disdain for party leaders in his 1989 campaign was maintained throughout his short and disastrous presidency, and even his ostensible supporters in Congress abandoned him when he ran afoul of the law in 1992 (Weyland 1993).[11] Revealingly, Collor's terminal cabinet had to be padded with technocrats and nonpartisans because he was facing impeachment and no one serious would sign up for his cabinet any more. Candidate type matters, but the fluid, improvisational nature of *presidencialismo de coalizão* makes it difficult to develop a predictive theory of ministerial recruitment in Brazil.

Therefore, the most we can say about ministerial recruitment at present is that it seems to respond partly to mounting technocratic pressures and more clearly to presidents' short-term need to keep their coalitions intact. But when we view ministerial office as an independent variable, it is clear that a well-placed ministry is an excellent launching pad to a presidential bid, as Cardoso, Serra, and Ciro Gomes have shown in recent years.

Recruitment to the Governorship

Of the three executive offices we are examining here, the governorship is the most promising for analytical purposes. Governors provide us with a far higher N (number of cases) than presidents, and the position of governors as intermediaries between presidents and legislators is a key facet of political life (Abrucio 1998). We begin this section with a simple assumption: the post of governor is extraordinarily attractive in Brazil, and virtually all politicians except active presidential candidates want to be governor. We then introduce two key variables that explain the selection of gubernatorial candidates. First, characteristics of the political party system in Brazil shape the recruitment process. The differentiation between left-wing, ideological parties and right-wing, catchall parties is paramount (Mainwaring 1999). Second, environmental characteristics of subnational political systems are also critical. Recruitment of gubernatorial candidates can be starkly different between oligarchic states and more pluralistic ones. After

---

11. We believe that Collor's status as an *FWI* is the dominant factor explaining his poor management of executive–legislative relations. However, an institutional factor was also at work: Collor's victory in a nonconcurrent election in 1989 may have led him to claim a stronger mandate than he would otherwise have done.

discussing these two variables, we turn to the consequences of the selection processes for politicians' behavior. What are the recurrent patterns of candidate selection across state borders in a very decentralized political system? Adapting the Siavelis–Morgenstern framework, we develop four ideal types of politicians who win nominations for governor: *party insiders*, proxies of party bosses, oligarchical proxies, and independents searching for a party label.

The Nature of State Governorships

In Brazil, the attractiveness of the governorship could almost be described as a constant rather than a variable—except that the mode of democratic transition in the 1980s actually increased the importance of subnational politics (Samuels and Abrucio 2000). The first free gubernatorial elections, in 1982 and 1986, took place before the first direct presidential elections in Brazil, in 1989. Therefore, other races, and the political system more generally, had already been organized around the state-level contests. Mayors and state deputies became highly dependent on gubernatorial support in elections. The weakness of political parties is both a cause and a consequence of this phenomenon.

Samuels (2003) argues that gubernatorial coattails are more important than are the dynamics of the presidential contest for federal deputies. Consequently, federal deputies become dependent on the state-level executive for their career opportunities, and therefore display a great deal of allegiance to the governor while in Congress, underscoring the relevance of Siavelis and Morgenstern's focus on loyalty as a central organizing concept. Since gubernatorial coattails drive elections, parties have an incentive to nominate strong political candidates for governorships. Or, as we shall see, established bosses sometimes try to transfer their political prestige to more obscure nominees.

Recall that gubernatorial contests are majoritarian elections. Unlike the pattern under open-list PR, majoritarian contests require that candidates have broad appeal in order to carry the state. Gubernatorial aspirants normally have to construct multiparty coalitions, and should also possess statewide name recognition. Thus, over time the percentage of *insider* governors has remained high. Our extension of Nunes (1978) shows that ex-legislators provided 69 percent of governors in the democratic 1946–1962 period, 64 percent under the military regime from 1965 to 1974, and an astounding 78 percent in the democratic elections from 1986 through 2002 (Table 9.4). A comparison of Tables 9.3 and 9.4 illustrates a key point made by Nunes about the military regime: although the generals downgraded the importance of professional politicians in the national cabinet, they did not do so in state-level politics. The military needed established elites to help it govern the provinces. In today's democracy, four out of five governors have served in the state assembly or national legislature, making them political insiders and familiar faces to voters.

TABLE 9.4 Pathways to Brazilian Gubernatorial Office in Three Periods[a]

Pathways	First Period 1946–1962		Second Period 1965–1974		Third Period 1986–2002		Total	
	N	%	N	%	N	%	N	%
Legislatures[b]	66	69	42	64	106	77.9	213	72
Other channels	16	17	21	33	30	22.1	68	23
No info	13	14	2	3	—	—	15	5
Total	95	100	65	100	136	100	296	100

Source: First and second periods from Nunes (1978). Third period calculated by authors.

a. All governors who were elected plus the vice governors who took office because of death of the elected governor are included. Owing to reelection, some governors were included more than once. Consecutive reelection was prohibited prior to 1998.

b. Includes both state assemblies and the national legislature.

Partisan Factors in Recruitment

The underinstitutionalization of the Brazilian party system is amply documented, and we will not revisit those arguments here.[12] For our purposes here, we need borrow only two propositions from this literature: the crucial differences between catchall and ideological parties (Mainwaring 1999) and the overall decentralization of the party system.

Mainwaring (1999) finds that politicians in catchall parties believe that their electoral success rests more on their individual efforts than on the party label. As a consequence, Abrucio notes, "Oftentimes the parties depend more on the candidates than the candidates on the parties" (1998, 176). Given the dynamics of open-list PR (see Samuels, Chapter 3, this volume), parties work to recruit politicians who are proven vote getters (*puxadores de votos*). As a precaution, in legislative elections catchall parties may also recruit minor figures to provide descriptive and corporatist representation to different social groups: in the language of Siavelis and Morgenstern, these are often *group delegates* whose role is to "vacuum up" whatever votes remain unclaimed. Gubernatorial coattails serve to line up politicians according to intrastate cleavages instead of national, programmatic party agendas (Samuels and Abrucio 2000).

Mainwaring (1999) shows that leftist parties behave quite differently. First, politicians in left-wing organizations see the party label as more important than their personal efforts in the campaign. In stark contrast to catchall parties, leftist parties have been able to mobilize grassroots groups to keep the party organization running between elections. These features strengthen the party to the detriment of

12. For a discussion of institutionalization and underinstitutionalization of political parties in Brazil, see Mainwaring (1999) and Ames (2001).

TABLE 9.5 Partisan Affiliations of Brazilian Gubernatorial Candidates, 1990–2002

Party[a]	N	Percentage
Right microparties	151	24.8
PT	81	13.3
PMDB	71	11.6
PSDB	48	7.9
PDS/PPR/PPB	48	7.9
Left microparties	42	6.9
PDT	42	6.9
PFL	38	6.2
PSB	34	5.6
PTB	20	3.3
PCB/PPS	11	1.8
PRN	11	1.8
PL	7	1.1
PDC	5	0.8
PC do B	1	0.2
Total	610	100.0

Source: Author's compilation, based on TSE data.

a. See the list of political parties by country that appears in the preface to this volume for full names.

the personalism that characterizes catchall organizations, meaning that left-wing candidates are more likely to be *party loyalists* in Siavelis and Morgenstern's terms.

The PT is the best example of an ideological party, and it is also the only large party of this type.[13] Unlike the catchall parties, the PT does not have an "open admissions" policy and therefore does not attract politicians looking for a "party for rent" *(legenda de aluguel)*. The party requires that candidates be members of the organization since December 15 of the year prior to the election, make the appropriate financial contributions to the organization, and sign the party principles agreement (Guzmán and Oliveira 2001). The PT has traditionally nominated gubernatorial candidates by consensus within the state-level *diretórios*. Reflecting its commitment to internal democracy, when consensus has not proved possible the PT has begun to use primary elections. In 2002, PT primaries were held in five states.

Given the PT's uniqueness as an ideological and nationally organized party, we would expect that the PT would be the party most likely to nominate its own candidates rather than back the names offered by others. Table 9.5 presents the partisan affiliations of all 610 candidates for state governorships in Brazil between 1990 and 2002. In 81 of the 108 elections (75 percent of the time), the PT nominated its own candidate for governor. Only the PMDB comes close to this total,

13. The PT became notably less ideological after winning national power in 2002. See Samuels (2004b) and Hunter (2006).

and the PMDB was considerably larger than the PT for most of this period. All of the other major catchall parties nominated gubernatorial candidates at less than half the opportunities, mostly because their alliances are fluid and shifting within and across states. Another clear pattern is that the small parties of the left largely abstained from nominations in favor of the PT, but nondescript small parties of the right supplied fully one-quarter of all gubernatorial candidates in Brazil. Ideology matters because personalism, party switching, and "open-admissions policies" are rampant on the right.

Apart from ideology, the other aspect of the party system that impacts gubernatorial candidate selection is the decentralization of parties. Although the national organizations of the catchall parties have some power on paper, the truth is that they barely intervene on state-level issues. Catchall parties generally do not enforce party discipline because politicians can easily switch parties. Moreover, gubernatorial candidates are granted wide latitude to construct whatever type of alliance that can get them elected. This has created, as Samuels (2003) puts it, "a near-total absence of partisan congruence across states." Presidential candidates are frequently "disinvited" to gubernatorial campaign rallies within the states because they may aggravate state-level feuds between their national-level supporters.

Once again the PT is the exception. Party principles delegate a good deal of decisionmaking autonomy to local PT organizations, but the party also possesses a strong, centralized national executive that is unafraid to overrule subnational party selectorates. In 1998, the state convention of the PT of Rio de Janeiro, then dominated by radicals, nominated Vladimir Palmeira for governor. However, the requirements of the PT's presidential-level alliance with the PDT required the PT to withdraw its candidate for governor in Rio and supply only a running mate (eventually Benedita da Silva) for the PDT gubernatorial nominee (Anthony Garotinho). The PT of Rio balked. Unflinchingly, the PT national organization intervened in the Rio directorate, overturned the results of the state convention, and quashed Palmeira's candidacy. Such an action would be unthinkable in any of the other major parties.

In sum, recruitment to the governorship varies widely, depending on whether candidates emerge within catchall or disciplined parties. Moreover, the behavior of governors in office is partly a reflection of their partisan affiliation. Governors in catchall parties are unlikely to answer consistently to their parties. Thus, catchall parties are continually instrumentalized by *free-wheeling independents* (*FWIs*).

Oligarchical Versus Pluralistic States

If looking at differences across parties is one useful way to examine gubernatorial recruitment, another is to look at differences among states. A helpful thought experiment is to conceive of states as approximating one of two ideal types: oligarchical and pluralistic systems. We do not claim that there are pure examples of either type of state, only that characteristics of each ideal type help us to understand dimensions of gubernatorial recruitment.

Hagopian (1996) describes "traditional politics" in Brazil as characterized by clientelist bargains, corruption, personalism, and regionalism. Power is concentrated in the hands of a few, access to decisionmaking is restricted, channels of political representation are hierarchically arranged, and political competition is strictly regulated. Political parties are weak; they are merely instruments of oligarchical power. Abrucio's study of the governorship dovetails with Hagopian's claims. He warns that rather than view state-level machine politics in partisan terms, it would be more appropriate to see state machines as based on the distribution of favors. Political demands are generally channeled through the executive rather than through political parties.

One could argue that traditional politics has a foothold in *all* Brazilian states, but what we term *oligarchical states* is the group of states whose politics is overwhelmingly controlled by one personal clique. There might be opposition groups in electoral contests, but politics revolves around allegiances to the dominant clan, once again demonstrating the importance of loyalty central to understanding candidate type and behavior. Even when they lose gubernatorial races, oligarchs are usually able to maintain their political power. A classic example of a system like this would be Bahia, where politics is organized either in support of or in opposition to the family machine of the late Antônio Carlos Magalhães (Dantas Neto 2006). The same pivotal role is played by the Sarney family in Maranhão politics, or the Siqueira Campos clan in Tocantins. In oligarchical states, the use of the state machine and the overwhelming concentration of economic and media power cast doubts on the fairness of the electoral game. As in the old Solid South in the United States, nomination by the machine is often tantamount to election. In more pluralistic states, in contrast, the electoral game is not centered on one group. Examples are Rio de Janeiro, São Paulo, and Rio Grande do Sul. Even in these states, bosses can control party machines, but the overall system is more competitive.

Candidate Types

We have discussed how the attractiveness of the position, differences between the parties, and differences across states shape candidate selection for the Brazilian governorship. Turning to outcomes of this process, we adapt the Siavelis–Morgenstern taxonomy of candidate types. Their taxonomy is best suited to presidential candidates, who operate in fully nationalized elections in a single electoral district, and key differences across subnational units in Brazil require some modifications before the typology can be applied to governors. We thus propose four ideal types of politicians emerging from gubernatorial selection processes: *party insiders, insider proxies, oligarchy proxies,* and *free-wheeling independents.* Our focus on proxy candidacies is intended to complement rather than challenge the Siavelis–Morgenstern framework, and it reflects our view that political "stand-ins" have traditionally played a major role in subnational politics in Brazil.

Party insiders. Siavelis and Morgenstern depict *party insiders* as politicians who built their careers in the party organization and typically belong to long-standing and institutionalized parties. They add that the party usually has a strong ideological base and therefore its label is important to voters and candidates, thus favoring loyalty. The PT of course will always generate such nominees, but even allowing for the overall low levels of party identification in Brazil, it is still possible to identify *party insiders* in catchall organizations as well. For example, even though it became a catchall party in the 1990s, the PSDB was still nominating key *insiders* such as Aécio Neves (Minas Gerais), José Serra (São Paulo), and Yeda Crusius (Rio Grande do Sul) to the governorship in 2006. We note that due to the decentralization of parties in Brazil, being a *party insider* at the gubernatorial level does not necessarily mean that the candidate is influential within the national party. It merely means that he or she has control of his or her state party. Some *insiders*, like Neves, are *insiders* at both the national and subnational levels, whereas others, like Crusius, are more oriented toward state politics.

A good example of a *party insider* at both the national and subnational levels is José Genoíno (PT), a candidate for the governorship of São Paulo in 2002. Genoíno was first elected to the Chamber of Deputies in 1982, in the first elections in which the PT participated, and was reelected at every opportunity through 1998. As Samuels (2003, 65) notes, he had been elected to Congress solely on the basis of what Brazilians, in a revealing phrase, term the *voto de opinião* (ideological or issue voting). Loyal and unfailingly adaptable to his party's needs, Genoíno lost the 2002 race for governor, but went to the runoff against the incumbent, Geraldo Alckmin (PSDB), another candidate of the same type. Confirming his status as *insider*, Genoíno later became president of the national PT.[14]

Party bosses and their proxies. Control of gubernatorial nominations is dependent on the control of state-party delegates. Leaders who control the majority of delegates can make the nominations; they are party bosses. In general, politicians who control party machines have previously held important political positions, are owed many favors, and are skillful negotiators.

Until 1998, governors were not permitted consecutive reelection, leaving incumbents in the uncomfortable position of having to find a loyal successor whom they could get elected. Oftentimes the proposed successor was supposed

---

14. Genoíno served as party president until 2005, when he fell victim to a corruption scandal surrounding the Lula administration. However, he was reelected as a deputy in 2006, albeit much lower on the list.

just to "keep the seat warm" until the incumbent governor could return four years later, usually after a stint in Congress (typically in the Senate, which uses majoritarian rules that favor ex-governors). Although consecutive reelection became possible after 1998, this has not entirely solved the problem of succession, since powerhouse incumbents are still term-limited after one reelection (they can return for a third term after sitting out for four years). Therefore, party bosses at times have picked unknown candidates to run who radiated some reflected glory from the personal prestige of their patron. These are proxy candidacies. When proxy candidates substitute for party bosses, we call them *insider proxies*, and when they substitute for ruling clans, we call them *oligarchy proxies*. Both result from a process of political grooming and sponsorship known as *apadrinhamento* (from the word for godfather, *padrinho*).

Abrucio (1998, 145) discusses the interesting case of Orestes Quércia, a PMDB vice governor of São Paulo who succeeded to the governorship in 1986. In office from 1987 to 1990, Quércia acted like all other governors, cultivating the support of local authorities and assemblymen via the distribution of patronage. Quércia became the undisputed master of the São Paulo PMDB and hand-picked the next gubernatorial candidate, Luiz Antônio Fleury Filho, a political unknown who had served as secretary of security. After forcing the PMDB convention to ratify Fleury, Quércia wanted to be sure to *eleger seu sucessor* ("elect his successor," the ultimate test of political prestige for any executive in Brazil), so the governor put the state machine to work in favor of his protégé.

The problems emerged when Fleury became governor. Fleury attempted to take over control of the party from Quércia's loyalists. Quércia successfully blocked Fleury's offensive, but the two men had a severe falling out, and Fleury quit the party. His political career after leaving office was reduced to a less prestigious congressional seat for the PTB, which he lost in 2006. This conflictual pattern has occurred again and again whenever *insider* proxies become too comfortable with power and attempt to supplant their political godfathers. When Anthony Garotinho, a proxy for the PDT's Leonel Brizola in Rio de Janeiro, won the governorship and then tried to wrest control of the state party machine, he too was forced out by Brizola. But Garotinho had the last laugh, switching to the PSB and becoming a powerful, popular governor, in office from 1998 to 2002. Politically, he eclipsed his legendary mentor, who died in 2004. In 2002, when he stepped down to run for president, Garotinho was able to find a more reliable *insider proxy* for himself than he had been for Brizola, nominating his wife, Rosinha, to the governorship, which she won easily. He then joined her cabinet.

Oligarchy proxies. This type of candidate, common in the oligarchical states, is distinguished from the *insider proxy* by the fact that successful *oligarchy-proxy* candidates have less incentive to defect than do *insider proxies*, that is, to turn against their *padrinhos*. As discussed earlier, party machine bosses have tight control of a party machine so that one person dominates the selectorate. In oligarchical states, the criterion for gubernatorial nomination is often membership in the clan—but when blood is unavailable, loyalty will have to do.

Like *insider proxies, oligarchy proxies* are chosen primarily for their trustworthiness, and sometimes they lack notable political careers. The main difference comes from the *oligarchy-proxy* candidate's incentives to comply with the wishes of the oligarchical leader who appointed him or her. Subservience is a key job qualification. As discussed, in oligarchical states one personal or familial clique controls the state apparatus, its power based on clientelistic relationships. Even when the ruling oligarch loses elections, he manages to keep control of important political resources because of the personal sway he holds over many congress members, mayors, and allies whom he has infiltrated throughout the state apparatus.[15] Typically, his group enjoys significant economic power in the state, too. Therefore, other things being equal, proxies of oligarchs are more pliant than proxies of *party insiders. Oligarchy proxies* have few incentives to defy the ruling clan, although it occasionally happens.

Souza (1997) labels this kind of nominee "technocrats-turned-politicians." She recounts the emergence of Antônio Carlos Magalhães (ACM) as the preeminent *coronel,* or local political boss, of Bahian politics.[16] For the past two decades, the vast majority of the federal legislators elected by the PFL of Bahia have been former cabinet secretaries in Magalhães's various administrations. Yet, Souza recounts instances when Magalhães's appointees tried to undermine his power. In all cases, they failed and were relegated to second-rank political careers. The political influence of oligarchical leaders is perhaps best summarized by the 1998 campaign motto of Paulo Souto, a technocrat-turned-politician, in his successful run for the governorship of Bahia. His slogan was comically descriptive: "Paulo Souto, ACM's candidate!"

Free-wheeling independents at the state level. Nomination processes can be very contentious. In many cases, gubernatorial hopefuls are denied a spot on the ticket; this often results from a clash of local heavyweights. Since electoral rules in Brazil are permissive regarding party switching, politicians who are denied nomination are inclined to search for another party that will sponsor their candidacy.

Thus, many *FWIs* at the state level in Brazil are former governors, mayors, or senators longing to return to executive office. When their old pathway to power is blocked, they seek an alternative nomination. The case of Garotinho in Rio de Janeiro is emblematic; knowing he could not be renominated by his own party, he simply moved to another. Hélio Garcia, a former governor of Minas Gerais, lost control of his own party, the PMDB, and formed a new party,

---

15. The use of masculine pronouns is intentional.

16. The use of the term *coronel* to designate a local political boss evolved from the practice of granting local oligarchs courtesy appointments in the National Guard.

TABLE 9.6   Other Characteristics of Brazilian Gubernatorial Candidates, 1990–2002

Candidate Characteristics	N	Percentage
Had previously served as governor	94	15.4
Won victory outright in first round	51	8.4 .
Advanced to a runoff election[a]	116	19.0
Female	53	8.7
Totals	610	100.0

Source: Author's compilation, based on data from the Tribunal Superior Electoral (2002).

a. Of the 108 gubernatorial races analyzed here, 58 cases (54 percent) went to a second round.

the PRS (existing only in Minas), which lasted just long enough to get him reelected to the governorship in 1990. Perennial candidates such as Álvaro Dias, Jaime Lerner, and Affonso Camargo have all changed parties several times in bids to recapture the governorship of Paraná, which they have all held at one time or another. A former governor of the Federal District, Joaquim Roriz, has changed parties five times over the past fifteen years and has been elected to the governorship three times on three different party labels. In cases like these, what matters is not the party label but the existence of an established political machine organized around an ex-governor.

The experience of *FWIs* at the state level shows that getting elected to a governorship only once is a transformative experience. Politicians are elevated into a new caste. From that point onward, they are likely to remain players in their states for a long time. As Table 9.6 shows, fully 15 percent of all gubernatorial candidates are ex-governors, but this is misleading because the universe includes many hopeless candidacies. If we were to consider only politically viable candidacies, the proportion of ex-governors would be somewhere from one-third to one-half. The experience of executive power is one that ex-governors want to repeat. From that point on, the party systems of their states are likely to adapt to their necessities, and not the other way around.

In sum, the governorship is enormously magnetic. Several Brazilian presidents—Quadros, Collor, and Franco—have chosen to run for their state governorships *after* leaving the president's Palácio do Planalto. Of the three, none had any strong ties to a political party, and only Franco was successful.

Discussion and Conclusions

Brazil is a political system dominated by executives from top to bottom. In national politics, the president and his ministers predominate; in the states, power is centered on the state governor; within the municipalities, the *prefeito* reigns supreme (our exclusion of municipal executives leaves out an important part of the picture here). This is not to say that legislators are unimportant: recent scholarship, especially that of Figueiredo and Limongi (1999), has shown the opposite to be true. But it also true that most legislators would prefer to be executives.

Here we have turned our attention to presidents, ministers, and governors. The study of presidents was hampered by the fact that there have been only eleven modern presidents under democratic conditions, and of these, three (Goulart, Sarney, and Franco) were elected only to the vice presidency. Two of the others were a former dictator, Vargas, and his minister of war, Dutra. One president, Neves, was not elected directly and never served. This leaves us only five individuals (Kubitschek, Quadros, Collor, Cardoso, and Lula) who were recruited by normal procedures of candidate selection and went on to win the presidency in direct elections. Clearly, the sample does not allow for much inference. But of the five normally recruited and elected presidents, Kubitschek, Quadros, and Collor had served both as the governor of their state and earlier as the mayor of its capital city. Cardoso had held two cabinet portfolios. Executives beget executives.

Lula is the first president with legislative experience and no prior executive experience, but this does not mean that Lula is or was a "congressional insider." He has run in seven elections, six times for executive positions, and ran for Congress only once—in 1986, against his wishes. The career choices of prominent Brazilian politicians illustrate a clear career ladder, and all the important rungs on the ladder are executive posts.

Cabinet ministries are an important stop along the way. Five modern Brazilian presidents have previously been ministers. The revolving door of the cabinet provides hope to many politicians, since there is a large number of ministries and a lot of public money to spend. For example, Sarney had a cabinet of twenty-three ministries in which more than seventy individuals served. Assuming that most of those individuals left on good terms with the president, that is a lot of political IOUs that can be called in later. Not surprisingly, Sarney was estimated to have controlled more than fifty votes in Congress after leaving the presidency. But several factors make recruitment to the cabinet somewhat ad hoc and randomized. Presidents are under increasing pressure to award key ministries to technocrats and apolitical professionals. Moreover, the pattern of shifting legislative alliances under *presidencialismo de coalizão* means that no one's tenure is ever secure. In 2007, eleven parties in Congress support Lula, and the presidential chief of staff—Dilma Rousseff, a longtime party insider—is given the task of doling out appointments and keeping those who get them all in line. A good deal of Brazilian macropolitics is explained by this single allocative function: an executive doling out executive power.

Governorships are perhaps the most interesting executive posts in Brazil, since they reveal so much about the crucial role of state-level and local politics. We privileged two recruitment variables. First, crucial differences between ideological and catchall parties in Brazil mean that different types of candidacies are favored in each type of party. Gubernatorial nominees of ideological parties are always *party insiders*, but under certain conditions nominees of catchall parties can be *insiders* as well. A key observation is that *free-wheeling independents* are only viable in the catchall type of party. Second, the uneven development of Brazil has created states with vastly different environmental characteristics. By definition, oligarchical states have a predictably narrow range of viable gubernatorial candidates. In more pluralistic, competitive states, politicians can make their careers by attaching themselves to parties rather than to clans.

After discussing these two institutional variables, we turned to the construction of four ideal types of gubernatorial nominee. We find that proxy candidacies in Brazil are common. Of the two types, the *insider proxy* is a riskier bet than the *oligarchy proxy*. Living in a relatively freer political market, the *insider proxy* may attempt either to take over an existing party or to move to a new one. Sometimes this strategy fails (Fleury) and sometimes it succeeds (Garotinho). In contrast, the *oligarchy proxy* is less likely to defect. The reason for this is that the oligarchy is quasi-totalizing, in the sense that the ruling clique dominates not only political power but also economic power and media access. In such a state, it is very unpleasant to have a falling out with the dominant oligarch: one can be frozen out of public life altogether. As Leal wrote about *coronelismo* more than 50 years ago, "The position of the local leader in opposition is so uncomfortable that, as a general rule, he only remains in opposition when he is unable to attach himself to the government" (Leal 1949/1977, 19).

Our analysis of the Brazilian selection processes reveals mostly elitist practices. The recent adoption of primaries by the PT is the exception that proves the rule: Brazilian political parties remain distinctly unenthusiastic about internal democracy. Nor has there been much popular or journalistic pressure for the adoption of primaries, despite the widespread suspicion of parties and politicians in Brazil. The weakness of the Brazilian party system results in part from hyperpresidentialism at the state level: the existence of powerful governorships (Abrucio 1998). The independence that governors have in relation to any higher authority, be it the president or state-level mechanisms of checks and balances, perpetuates the dynamics of traditional politics in Brazil.

Chapter Ten

Political Recruitment and Candidate Selection in Chile, 1990 to 2006: The Executive Branch

DAVID ALTMAN

Patterns of executive-branch candidate recruitment have had significant impacts on Chilean politics and policy since democratic reinstallation in 1990. Generally speaking, within the ruling coalition, the Concertación, candidate selection or recruitment has evolved from being extremely informal (albeit constrained) to a more formalized process. The first postauthoritarian president, Patricio Aylwin (1990–1994), was chosen by a pact within the political elite, but his successors, Eduardo Frei (1994–2000) and Ricardo Lagos (2000–2006), were elected in closed and open primaries, respectively. Michele Bachelet (2006–2010) was nominated by her coalition only after her adversary dropped out of the presidential race, thus obviating the planned primaries. This process of increasing openness has important practical and theoretical consequences that will be explored in further depth in the following pages.

The central challenge in postauthoritarian Chile has been reconciling the goals of many parties in one coalition. Over the last fourteen years, one of the most critical elements which has held the coalition together has been power sharing, tied to a cross-party, coalitional nomination process and distribution of candidate slates (see Chapter 4, this volume). Power-sharing agreements have also been central at the presidential level. Although primaries are obviously important, and "natural" leaders emerged, in the first years of the transition there has also been a feeling of "whose turn it was" at the time. Some scholars, including Siavelis, have even argued that the primaries that have been held were forgone conclusions—everyone knew

I thank Rossana Castiglioni, Tomás Chuaqui, Roberto Durán, Jael Goldsmith, Juan Pablo Luna, Scott Morgenstern, Patricio Navia, and Peter Siavelis for their comments and suggestions along the way. I also thank Andrés Madrid and Enrique Morales, who provided precious research assistance. This research fits within the scope of the Fondo Nacional de Desarrollo Científico y Tecnológico de Chile (FONDECYT) project 1060749.

who would win before the actual election. During the 1999 elections, committed *Concertaciónistas* "knew" it was a Socialist's turn, and accordingly supported Lagos (Siavelis, personal communication, 2004). In the opposition camp it is hard to see a pattern or evolution toward the democratization of the nomination process of presidential candidates. On the contrary, the right has relied on elite-centered mechanisms, which might be one of the reasons it has consistently lost elections.

The overall argument of this chapter is centered on three major points. First, presidential candidate selection is moving toward formality in the ruling center-left Concertación coalition but remains informal in the right's Alianza coalition. Second, following Siavelis and Morgenstern's arguments (see Chapter 1), I contend that the type of candidate chosen has a bearing on campaigns, coalition relations, and cabinet structure. Finally, I conclude that the distribution of cabinet posts depends on proportionality in elections, levels of horizontal integration, and the general type of presidential candidate. From this perspective, Chile most resembles Brazil's "coalition presidentialism" (see Chapter 9, this volume).

This chapter first tackles candidate selection as a dependent variable and then approaches it as an independent variable. The first section includes a basic description of how candidate selection for the presidency has evolved since the democratic reinstallation in both the Concertación and the Alianza. I discuss how the types of candidates chosen fit in the typology established by Siavelis and Morgenstern in Chapter 1 (this volume). In the second section I treat candidate type as an independent variable tying the types to cabinet structure and behavior. I then quantitatively analyze how the distribution of executive offices (ministers, undersecretaries, *intendentes*, governors,[1] and ambassadors) is related to patterns of proportionality, the electoral calendar, and levels of horizontal integration.

Candidate Selection as a Dependent Variable in Presidential Elections Since 1990

Siavelis and Morgenstern argue in Chapter 1 that context matters to R&S and at times overrides institutional variables. The processes of selection and nomination for the executive branch in Chile must be understood in the context of the restraints imposed by the country's transition to democracy and the "reserved domains" (certain institutional and political guarantees granted the right and the military) inherited from the authoritarian regime, circumstances unique to Chile in the region. The end of the authoritarian period and the delicacy of the transition warranted a consensus-centrist candidate and the need

---

1. *Intendentes* are appointed by the president to serve as regional representatives. Governors are appointed by the president and serve below the *intendentes*, representing each municipality.

to use an elite-centered method of selection. Democratization, then, pushed the Concertación, the governing coalition since 1990, to use more open systems in the next two elections (1993 and 1999) and was ready to do so in 2005. However, as noted, the right, which operated under a different logic, continued to rely on elite-centered mechanisms.

Before the military regime there was a single round of election for the presidency, and the candidate who obtained the plurality of votes was usually elected.[2] However, if no candidate obtained an absolute majority of votes, Congress chose between the two top candidates in a joint session. Congress always chose the candidate with the most votes (unlike Bolivia where Congress sometimes chose the second- or even the third-most voted candidate). From 1990 until the constitutional reforms of August 2005, presidents were elected for a single six-year term using a majority runoff method *(ballotage)* when no candidate obtained more than 50 percent of the valid vote (Dow 1998, 63). Currently, presidents are elected for a four-year term and a second round of elections is prescribed for contests where no candidate wins majority support. Presidents cannot be reelected to consecutive terms and executive and legislative elections are now concurrent.

Chile's Law 18.700 (Articles 13 and 14) spells out the process for nominating presidential candidates. Independent candidates can be nominated if they demonstrate they have the support of at least the 0.5 percent of voters who cast ballots in the previous election for deputies through the collection of signatures. Parties who wish to nominate candidates can do so if the party is legally registered and recognized by the electoral authorities in all regions of the country. If not, the party must fulfill the same requirements as independent candidates in the regions where it does not legally exist.

In Chile there are no legally mandated internal party or coalition rules for choosing presidential candidates, as there are in other Latin American countries. Also, the organization and financing of the presidential selection process is the sole responsibility of each party and coalition, leaving an open door for potential corruption.[3] When elections for the legislature and the executive were concurrent—as happened in 1989 and 1993 and since 2005—the presidential nomination and the distribution of legislative slates were all part of the same negotiating equation.

Beyond these general similarities, the government and opposition blocs differ in their handling of presidential nominations. In the governing coalition there is a clear and explicit intention to democratize the process. It moved from a *conclave* style of nomination in 1989, which placed power exclusively in the hands of party

---

2. In this chapter I look at only the national executive offices and consequently I do not consider subnational executives, given Chile's unitary system, and the lesser importance of provincial-level governments.

3. Comisión de Reforma del Estado (2000; 2003).

elites, to indirect or closed primaries in 1993, also known as a *convención de orígen mixto* (a mixed-origin convention), where only militants and adherents in the coalition's constituent parties had a say in the election process. For the 1999 elections the governing coalition opted for open primaries. Finally, in 2005, the Concertación resolved its internal divisions regarding the formula for choosing a president by adopting an institutionalized, internal, and democratic process, despite Lagos's undue influence in tagging an early favorite. Table 10.1 summarizes the selection method for each presidential candidate in Chile since 1989, using the framework established by Siavelis and Morgenstern for the designation of presidential candidates.

In the Alianza, partisan elites nominate candidates, a process that emphasizes personal charisma, popularity in public-opinion surveys, and previous electoral accomplishments. During the eighteen years of democracy since 1989 the right has shown a clear tendency toward *independentismo*, where candidates assert their

TABLE 10.1 Candidates, Parties, and Selection Methods for Chilean Presidential Elections, 1989–2005

Elections	Candidate	Party or Coalition	Selection Method
1989	Patricio Aylwin	Concertación (PDC)	Elite-centered
1989	Hernán Büchi	Independent (Right)[d]	Elite-centered
1989	Francisco Javier Errázuriz	Unión de Centro Centro	Self-nomination
1993	Eduardo Frei	Concertación (PDC)	Closed primaries[a]
1993	Arturo Alessandri	Independent (Right)[d]	Elite-centered
1993	José Piñera	Independent	Self-nomination
1993	Manfred Max Neef	Independent	Elite-centered
1993	Eugenio Pizarro	Communist	Elite-centered
1993	Cristián Reitze	Humanist and Green	Elite-centered
1999	Ricardo Lagos	Concertación (PS)	Open coalition primaries[b]
1999	Joaquín Lavín	Alianza por Chile (UDI)	Elite-centered
1999	Gladys Marín	Communist	Elite-centered
1999	Tomás Hirsch	Humanist	Elite-centered
1999	Sara María Larraín	Independent	Self-nomination
1999	Arturo Frei	Independent	Self-nomination
2005	Michele Bachelet	Concertación (PS)	Open coalition primaries[c]
2005	Joaquín Lavín	Alianza por Chile (UDI)	Elite-centered
2005	Sebastián Piñera	Alianza por Chile (RN)	Elite-centered
2005	Tomás Hirsch	Juntos Podemos Más (Communist + Humanist)	Elite-centered

a. Only for affiliated citizens.

b. All citizens permitted to vote with the exception of those affiliated with parties other than Concertación.

c. Open primaries were scheduled but Soledad Alvear, Bachelet's Concertación contender, pulled out before the primary could be held.

d. "Right" denotes a de facto candidacy for the RN-UDI coalition (later known as the Alianza) despite an Independent label.

independence from party machines or even claim they are not politicians. The candidates Hernán Büchi and Joaquín Lavín were nominated in this way; the nominations of Arturo Alessandri by a party convention in 1993 and Sebastián Piñera in 2005 are partial exceptions to this tendency.

Birth of the Concertación and the 1989 Presidential Election

After the formation of the first organized resistance to the military regime in August 1983 (the Alianza Democrática), two types of leaders emerged in the opposition that would shape presidential candidate selection processes further down the road: disruptive and adaptive, exemplified, respectively, by the Christian Democratic Party (Partido Demócrata Cristiano or PDC) leaders Gabriel Valdés and Patricio Aylwin. Whereas Valdés advocated constant social mobilization and a radical democratic transition, Aylwin had a strong commitment to negotiate with the military regime (Cañas 1994, 51), asserting that Valdés's disruptive style would damage the chances for a democratic transition and strengthen the support for the military regime. On August 2, 1987, Aylwin assumed the leadership of the PDC while simultaneously another adaptive and nondisruptive leader, Ricardo Lagos, emerged from the left. In response to Pinochet's planned October 1988 plebiscite, Aylwin and Lagos agreed on an important project that came to life in February of 1988: *La Concertación de Partidos por el No*—the Coalition of Parties for the "No." "No" referred to these leaders' stand on how citizens should vote in the plebiscite on Pinochet's continued rule. As Cavallo (1992, 48–49) makes clear, from the moment Aylwin was appointed official spokesman of the Concertación, he was accepted as its leader. Nonetheless, his tenure as the leader of the coalition and his party was far from tranquil. Few expected the internal fissures that soon emerged (Otano 1995, 70–71).

Despite Aylwin's success in managing leadership of the Concertación, new PDC leaders challenged Aylwin's position. In addition to Valdés, Eduardo Frei entered the political scene and has maintained a central position ever since. Frei was the most popular candidate in public opinion surveys, no small issue to a coalition preparing for elections. Valdés's faction pushed for internal elections and, following the internal party statutes approved in 1987, forced the party to form a National Council (*Junta Nacional*) to decide on a mechanism for selecting a candidate. Finally, Aylwin was chosen by the majority of the delegates (156 to 129 votes) and was recognized unanimously as the presidential candidate.[4]

The Concertación appears to have been waiting for the PDC to sort out its messy internal politics before undertaking further negotiations on presidential candidacies. The period from October 5, 1988, to July 6, 1989, was marked by two

---

4. This national council was integrated by delegates and provincial presidents elected in the past internal election.

events of great significance for the democratic transition and the Concertación: an agreement within the Concertación to support a single presidential candidate, and an agreement to compensate all the parties of the coalition for their participation through eventual cabinet posts and shared lists for congressional elections.[5] Intraelite pacts continued to characterize the process, and on January 6, 1989, the PDC and Socialist Party (Partido Socialista, or PS) leadership reached a solid agreement that Aylwin would be the candidate (Siavelis 2001).

On the right, the presidential nomination process was more inchoate. The National Party (Partido Nacional, PN), the preauthoritarian expression of the political right, had dissolved itself immediately after Pinochet's coup d'etat— bowing to his antipolitical discourse. Pinochet's stance translated into a non-ideological, antiparty, technocratic orientation toward politics on the right during the dictatorship. Nonetheless, as Agüero et al. (1998) note, the 1980 constitution breathed new political life to the parties of right as the authoritarian regime drew to a close. Constitutional provisions and new laws regulating parties and elections provided the right with a very positive competitive landscape. This new scenario, coupled with growing divisions within the regime and among its adherents, yielded additional impetus for the right's political reorganization. Finally, two parties emerged: National Renewal (Renovación Nacional, or RN) and the Independent Democratic Union (Unión Demócrata Independiente, UDI). The UDI positioned itself as the most loyal to the military regime and its legacy. Renovación Nacional, with roots in the former Partido Nacional, had a more liberal tradition. After the defeat suffered in the plebiscite of 1988, the political right attempted to fill the leadership void left by Pinochet by looking for a presidential candidate for the elections of 1989, but finding a common candidate for the right was no easy task. RN tried to distance itself from Pinochet while simultaneously defending the substance of the military regime's program, especially its neoliberal economic policies.

RN favored a candidate from one of the party machines, and proposed the nomination of party activists who had been former ministers of the Pinochet regime: Arturo Fontaine, Sebastián Piñera, Enrique Barros, and Andrés Alla-mand. However, the UDI was convinced that these candidates would not attract sufficient support from the more antiparty business sector, yet its support was fundamental for success. The UDI, therefore, decided on a candidate who seemed to satisfy both those who wanted a less partisan "new face" and those who wanted continuity with the military regime: Hernán Büchi. Büchi's approach was fine-tuned by the UDI and its style of populist "antipolitics" (a trend that has continued on the right in every election). For the UDI this translates into a technocratic orientation aimed at solving the problems of every-day people through practical rather than political solutions. However, this style of

5. See Navia, Chapter 4, this volume.

TABLE 10.2 Chilean Presidential Elections of 1989

Presidential Candidate	Number of Votes	Percentage
Patricio Aylwin	3,850,571	55.17
Hernán Büchi	2,052,116	29.40
Francisco Javier Errázuriz	1,077,172	15.43
Total votes	6,979,859	100.0

Source: www.elecciones.gov.cl/indexf.html.

politics also tended to increase the gap between the parties of the right because RN advocated a more traditionally partisan approach. Though all counterfactuals involved are necessarily speculative, it is likely that division on the right negatively influenced the coalition's electoral performance in the 1989 elections. However, even if the sector had supported a common candidate right from the beginning, it is still unlikely that the right would have beat Aylwin. The actual vote, as summarized in Table 10.2, yielded 29.4 percent for Büchi, 15.4 for Francisco Javier Errázuriz of the Unión de Centro Centro (Union of the Centrist Center or UCC; an unaligned center-right party), and 55.2 for Aylwin.

The 1993 Presidential Election

The 1993 presidential race demonstrated that even after four years of government the PDC had not resolved its internal divisions, and three candidates threw their hats into the ring: Andrés Zaldívar, Alejandro Foxley, and Eduardo Frei. Zaldívar asserted that he represented a larger share of activists and militants than the others and at the same time was more loyal to traditional party institutions. As a successful businessman, Frei was less tied to traditional party institutions and had the advantage of name recognition as a member of one of Chile's most important political families (Godoy 1994). He was, once again, one of the favorites in opinion polls. The best bet for Alejandro Foxley, Aylwin's successful and popular minister of finance, was to cast himself as the guarantor of stability. Among all of Aylwin's ministers, Foxley received the highest approval ratings and was one of the best-known political leaders at the time.[6]

In terms of choosing the Concertación's standard-bearer, this election was more complex than the founding election. The results of the 1992 municipal elections were used by the PDC as a bargaining chip. The PDC argued that it was the strongest party within the Concertación, having received more than 30 percent of the votes, whereas the combined parties of the left, the Socialist Party and the Party for Democracy (PS-PPD) had garnered less than 18 percent. The left, on the other hand, contended that in the interests of coalition maintenance all parties should be

6. See Centro de Estudios Públicos, "Estudio Nacional de Opinión Pública, Junio 2007", at http://www.cepchile.cl/dms/lang_1/cat_443_inicio.html.

represented and that it "was their turn to have the presidential candidate." But the parties of the left had few electoral arguments with which to defend their position.

The PDC continued to advocate an interelite settlement to choose a candidate, because primary elections would introduce a significant element of chance (Genaro Arriagada, *La Época*, January 20, 1993). The PDC proposed an interparty convention similar to the one used for the 1989 elections. The other significant partners of the PDC in the Concertación, specifically the PS-PPD, argued that a convention was not really participative and would only produce a predetermined result. After several weeks of deliberations, the PS-PPD candidate, Lagos, proposed an alternative plan for a "mixed convention." Such a convention would include delegates elected through some sort of primary election and another group reflecting each party's proportion of votes in the 1992 municipal elections. The PDC said that only the second part of Lagos's plan should be adopted. With the opportunity for an agreement fading away, the PDC agreed to accept an open primary with the condition that parliamentary lists would proportionally reflect the relative power of parties in the 1992 elections (Carrasco, *El Mercurio*, February 6, 1993).

Finally, the parties agreed on the participation of 400,000 party members and adherents who would elect 1,800 delegates to the convention. The caveat that the outcome of this system would be predictable and predetermined proved true, as Lagos obtained 37 percent of the vote to Frei's 63 percent (see Table 10.3). More than 430,000 people participated.

On the right, this election was marked from the beginning by a scandal nicknamed "Piñeragate," a case of telephone espionage that involved two potential presidential candidates: Sebastián Piñera and Evelyn Matthei. A recorded conversation was made public in which Piñera gave tips to a friend—Pedro Pablo Díaz—on how to discredit Piñera's potential adversary, Matthei. What could have been a small internal affair escalated to career-damaging proportions, because of the harsh words used in the conversation, which revealed serious intracoalitional competition and avid strategizing. The fallout of this affair destroyed the presidential prospects of both Piñera and Matthei, and again made the right appear divided and disorderly.

As expected, some new names also appeared: on the UDI's side, Jovino Novoa, and Manuel Feliú from RN. Simultaneously, José Piñera, brother of Sebastián Piñera, who had resigned from the UDI, ran in the election as an independent while also trying to gain the support of the UDI. Meanwhile, the UDI had

TABLE 10.3   1993 Chilean Presidential Primary Results, May 23, 1993

Type of Voter	Eduardo Frei Votes	Percentage	Ricardo Lagos Votes	Percentage	Total Votes	Percentage
Militants	68,100	60.7	44,054	39.3	112,154	100.0
Adherents	204,455	63.9	115,318	36.1	319,773	100.0
Total	275,555	63.4	159,372	36.6	434,927	100.0

Source: Navia (2005), based on *El Mercurio*, May 29, 1993.

TABLE 10.4   Chilean Presidential Elections of 1993

Presidential Candidate	Number of Votes	Percentage
Eduardo Frei	4,040,497	57.98
Arturo Alessandri	1,701,324	24.41
José Piñera	430,950	6.18
Manfred Max Neef	387,102	5.55
Eugenio Pizarro	327,402	4.70
Cristián Reitze	81,675	1.17
Total votes	6,968,950	100.0

Source: http://www.elecciones.gov.cl/index.html.

also successfully managed to get a new ally: the Union of the Center Center, the right-leaning populist party that had garnered 8 percent of the votes in the 1992 municipal elections. The mechanism chosen for the presidential nomination was a convention scheduled for August 8, 1993. Although José Piñera did not approve, representatives to the convention were assigned in proportion to the party's showing in the 1992 elections. With 1,847 members participating, the RN received 547 votes; the UDI, 449; the UCC, 391; and independents, 370 (20 percent of the total). The Partido Nacional and the Partido del Sur garnered the other 90 votes.

Once convened, this convention was far from straightforward. At the convention, Novoa, the UDI's candidate, withdrew his candidacy in favor of a man who had barely registered previously on anyone's radar screen: Arturo Alessandri. Alessandri, an independent who collected over 33,000 signatures in record time, was privileged with a historical Chilean last name, and could count on the support of the diminished Partido Nacional and important sectors of the business community.[7] Though Novoa's reasons for pulling out of the race are uncertain, he likely reached this decision in reaction to the overwhelming electoral machine that quickly turned its support to one of the most the most powerful *apellidos* (last names, i.e., Alessandri) in Chilean politics. The results of the convention were decisive: 56.48 percent voted for Alessandri and 38.74 percent for Feliú. In spite of not obtaining the required two-thirds support, Alessandri was proclaimed victor as soon as Feliú recognized his defeat. However, José Piñera refused to recognize the result and continued as an independent candidate into the general election. Thus, the right's first convention provided new lessons and, once again, divided its ranks, causing it to appear disorganized. It looked as though the right was coming up with a last-minute candidate who, to add insult to injury, would have to compete for votes with an independent candidate on the right. Table 10.4 shows the results of the 1993 elections.

7. Arturo Alessandri was grandson of Arturo Alessandri Palma (twice President of the Republic 1920–1925, 1932–1938) and nephew of Jorge Alessandri Rodríguez (President of the Republic between 1958 and 1964).

The Presidential Elections of 1999

In the presidential elections of 1999 the figure of Ricardo Lagos emerged with a force comparable to that of Aylwin ten years before. Lagos had vast political experience. There was also a sense that it was definitely his turn, both with regard to his personal trajectory as a politician and that it was time for an alternation of power within the coalition. Lagos represented both parties on the left (the PS and PPD) and though he is formally a Socialist (PS), his relation with the PPD goes beyond mere instrumentality. The parties tended to act as a unit, at least for the purposes of the presidential election. During the primaries of 1993 Lagos had shown a strong commitment to the maintenance of the Concertación. After two PDC administrations, however, there was a general consensus within the Concertación that the alliance needed some revitalization. In 1993 Lagos had to demonstrate the strength of his support in "indirect primaries"; in 1999 he faced "open primaries" against Zaldívar, the PDC candidate. Participation in the primaries was open to any enfranchised Chilean, meaning registered at the national electoral commission, with the important exception of voters formally affiliated with parties not belonging to the Concertación. The results of the primary are summarized in Table 10.5. It shows Lagos's overwhelming victory, implying a shift to the leftist parties of the Concertación.

On the right Joaquín Lavín emerged as the most popular candidate. Given his experience as a mayor, and perhaps due to his previous candidacy for the Chamber of Deputies, Lavín showed a significant inclination toward local politics. Analysts note his tendency to "municipalize" problems, which are cast in terms of immediacy with technocratic rather than political solutions. Lavín was an *alcalde* (mayor) who during elections took on the problems of everyday people, instituting programs while taking noticeable populist shortcuts. Many UDI leaders welcomed Lavín's style, accepting even some of the extravagant measures he took as mayor of Las Condes and Santiago.[8] The endless contradictions between his proposed policies and the ideological positions of the political and business elites that supported him can only be understood within a populist frame of reference.

Despite Lavín's leadership on the right, the sector is still marked by the ghost of *independentismo* (Allamand 1999b). In its search for presidential candidates since the return of democracy, this *independentismo* has forced the right to look to candidates with a well-known family name, a technocratic profile, or associations with a successful personal ministerial performance. The nomination of Büchi and Alessandri certainly fit this pattern, whereas Lavín's ascendancy, after a very long career within the UDI, really represents an insider playing the "outsider's" game. Ultimately, he enhanced the performance and popularity of the right, as the Alianza's very narrow loss in the 1999 elections suggests (Lavín got 47.51 percent of the vote to the Lagos's 47.96 percent). Table 10.6 summarizes these results.

8. These include an attempt to make rain to clean polluted air, a beach on the banks of the polluted Mapocho River, and a proposed ski resort in downtown Santiago.

TABLE 10.5   Chilean Presidential Primary Results for the Concertación, 1999

Candidate	Women's Votes	Women's Percentage	Men's Votes	Men's Percentage	Total Votes	Total Percentage
Ricardo Lagos	479,342	69.7	511,708	73.1	991,050	71.4
Andrés Zaldívar	208,862	30.3	188,572	26.9	397,434	28.6
Total	688,204	100.0	700,280	100.0	1,388,484	100.0

Source: Navia (2005).

TABLE 10.6   Chilean Presidential Elections of 1999 (First and Second Rounds)

Presidential Candidate	Number of Votes, First Round	Percentage, First Round	Number of Votes, Second Round	Percentage, Second Round
Ricardo Lagos	3,383,339	47.96	3,677,968	51.31
Joaquín Lavín	3,352,199	47.51	3,490,561	48.69
Gladys Marín	225,224	3.19		
Tomás Hirsch	36,235	0.51		
Sara María Larraín	31,319	0.44		
Arturo Frei	26,812	0.38		
Total votes	7,055,128	100.0	7,168,529	100.0

Source: http://www.elecciones.gov.cl/index.html.

The presidential elections of 1999 were the first nonconcurrent elections since democratic reinstallation in 1990. Thus, the electoral calendar played a significant role in determining the competitors' electoral prospects and strategies. Lavín's near victory in the first round was clearly helped by the nonconcurrence of other races. Because Lavín was not tied to congressional races on the right, he could more forcefully assert his independent status.

The Presidential Elections of 2005

An encouraging economic atmosphere and an outgoing president who enjoyed unprecedented levels of popular support presented a very promising electoral landscape for the Concertación in 2005. The question, therefore, was who would be chosen to continue the Concertación legacy, carrying the governing coalition to its twentieth year of continuous government, and leading Chile toward a significant and highly symbolic date, the bicentennial of independence, 2010.

As frequently is the case where reelection is not permitted, when a party or coalition is led by a strong and popular leader, it is difficult to find a candidate that can fill the shoes of the outgoing president. Within this context, presidents often use their informal powers to designate a successor. Following this pattern, President Lagos backed his minister of defense, Michele Bachelet, as the presidential candidate of the PRSD-PPD-PS subpact of the left within the Concertación.

Though the extent of Lagos's support was unusually strong, it is true that Bachelet was one of his most successful and popular cabinet ministers (Gamboa and Segovia 2006). Lagos's support for her was nonetheless openly criticized by Soledad Alvear, the presidential candidate of the PDC, who was elected by its National Council on January 2005. At that time it was clear to all actors that the process established to choose the 1999 candidate would again be used in 2005. The Concertación planned and expected a primary. However, trailing in the opinion polls, Alvear opted out before the primary could be held, but it likely would have gone forward had Alvear chosen to continue as a candidate.

As usual, the nomination process within the Alianza was filled with tensions and divisions. As in the election of 1999, the UDI nominated Lavín as its candidate and it was expected that RN would simply ratify his candidacy at its general council meeting in May 2005. Instead, however, unexpected disagreements arose during the council meeting and Sebastián Piñera began promoting his own candidacy. Finally, the council of RN decided to support Piñera, by more than 70 percent of the vote. Negotiations between the Alianza's parties bore little fruit and no agreement was reached, leaving both candidates in the presidential race. Thus, although it might appear that Piñera's candidacy was determined through the coalition's ballot box, this was not a democratic internal party or coalition process. It was rather, as Siavelis explains (personal communication), a sign of the malfunction of internal party processes and rules, and a case where elites faced a coordination problem that they simply failed to resolve. Table 10.7 show the results of the 2005 elections that Bachelet won with 53.5 percent in the second round. This was not a foregone victory for the Concertación, however, as the sum of the vote for the two rightist candidates, Lavín and Piñera, exceeded that of Bachelet in the first round.

Types of Candidates

Table 10.8 summarizes all of Chile's presidential candidates since 1989, their type according to the Siavelis–Morgenstern typology, and electoral returns. It shows, in particular, that there have been ten *party insiders*, three *party adherents*, and

TABLE 10.7   Chilean Presidential Elections of 2005 (First and Second Rounds)

Presidential Candidate	Number of Votes, First Round	Percentage, First Round	Number of Votes, Second Round	Percentage, Second Round
Michelle Bachelet	3,190,691	45.9	3,712,902	53.49
Sebastián Piñera	1,763,694	25.4	3,227,658	46.50
Tomás Hirsch	375,048	5.4		
Joaquín Lavín	1,612,608	23.2		
Total votes	6,942,041	100.0	6,940,560	100.0

Source: http://www.elecciones.gov.cl/index.html.

three relatively minor *free-wheeling independents*. In part this pattern is the result of the return of elites who had dominated the political scene during the pre-authoritarian period (Agüero et al. 1998, 161). Three of Chile's four presidents since the democratic transition, Patricio Aylwin, Ricardo Lagos, and Michele Bachelet, have strong relationships with the Chilean political establishment and they all fit the category of *party insiders* that Siavelis and Morgenstern identify in Chapter 1. Though Frei certainly comes from one of the most pedigreed families of Chilean politics, his business background and semi-outsider status really make him more of a *party adherent*. However, it is important, as noted by Navia (Chapter 4, this volume) to understand the centrality of coalitions to postauthoritarian Chilean politics. In light of this, Frei's behavior and room to maneuver as an *adherent* was constrained by the exigencies of coalition politics. Without these constraints, we may have seen more behavioral characteristics of an *adherent*. What is more, the three *party insiders* as well as the *party adherent* emerged from ideological parties with established roots in society (see Mainwaring and Scully 1995). Moreover, their parties, the Socialist and the Christian Democratic, have consistently been central to the Chilean political process and were key actors during the period between 1958 and 1973, a period of party politics characterized as the "three thirds," an allusion to the relatively uniform strength of the three traditional ideological pillars of Chilean politics: the left, the center, and the right.[9]

All four presidents since 1990 had held important leadership positions in traditional parties and proudly wore the party label. Their high regard for their political cadres, party militancy, and internal discipline is evidenced by their long history as leaders of institutionalized parties. They clearly accepted the mechanisms of candidate selection decided at the coalition level, even though they tried to change them for their own benefit on occasion. Their political visions were largely attuned to the parties they represented, perhaps suggesting that all were examples of *party insiders* as Siavelis and Morgenstern conceive of them.

Despite these circumstances, I categorize Frei as a *party adherent* because of his relative outsider status when compared to those of other Chilean presidential candidates. Of *party adherents*, Siavelis and Morgenstern note, "These candidates are strong partisans, but differ from *party insiders* in that they are not their parties' undisputed leaders. . . . [T]hese candidates are more likely than *party insiders* to have to earn their candidacy by competing in an open primary" (Chapter 1, pp. 32–33). Eduardo Frei fits this pattern.

With respect to careers, it is hard to pinpoint any obvious cursus honorum for the presidency in Chile, unlike in Argentina (see De Luca, Chapter 8, this

9. For different interpretations of the Chilean "three-thirds" see Carey (2002); Flisfisch (1992); Montes, Mainwaring, and Ortega (2000); Ortega (2003); Scully (1992, 1995); Torcal and Mainwaring (2003).

TABLE 10.8 Chilean Presidential Candidates and Their Types

President	Percentage of Votes	Election	Type of Candidate	Party or Coalition	Previous Political Career	
Patricio Aylwin	55.2	1989	*Party insider*	Concertación–PDC	Senator	1964–1973
Hernán Büchi	29.4	1989	*Party adherent*	Independent (Right)[a]	Undersecretary, minister	1979: Economy / 1981: Health / 1985–89: Interior
Francisco Javier Errázuriz	15.4	1989	*Free-wheeling independent*	Unión de Centro Centro	None	
Eduardo Frei	57.9	1993	*Party adherent*	Concertación–PDC	Senator	1990–94
Arturo Alessandri	24.4	1993	*Party adherent*	Independent (Right)[a]	Deputy, senator	1972–73 / 1990–94
José Piñera	6.2	1993	*Free-wheeling independent*	Independent (Right)	Minister	1978–81: Labor / 1981: Mining
Manfred Max Neef	5.5	1993	*Group agent*	Independent	None	
Eugenio Pizarro	4.7	1993		Movement of Democratic Allendeist Left	None	
Cristián Reitze	1.2	1993	*Party insider*	Humanist	None	
Ricardo Lagos	47.9	1999	*Party insider*	Concertación–PS	Minister	1990–93: Education / 1994–98: Public Works
Joaquín Lavín	47.5	1999	*Party insider*	Independent (Right)[a]	Mayor	1992–99: Las Condes / 2000: Santiago
Gladys Marín	3.2	1999	*Party insider*	Communist	Deputy	1965–1973

President	Percentage of Votes	Election	Type of Candidate	Party or Coalition	Previous Political Career	
Tomas Hirsch	0.5	1999	*Party insider*	Humanist	None	
Sara Ma. Larraín	0.4	1999	*Group agent*	Green Party	None	
Arturo Frei	0.4	1999	*Free-wheeling independent*	Independent	Deputy, senator	1969–1973 1990–1998
Michele Bachelet	45.9	2005	*Party insider*	Concertación–PS	Minister	2000–2002: Health 2002–2004: Defense
Joaquín Lavín	23.2	2005	*Party insider*	Independent (Right–UDI)	Mayor	1992–99: Las Condes 2000–2004: Santiago
Sebastián Piñera	25.4	2005	*Party insider*	Alianza por Chile (Renovación Nacional)	Senator	1990–98
Tomas Hirsch	5.4	2005	*Party insider*	Juntos Podemos Más (Communist + Humanist)	Ambassador	1990–92: New Zealand

Source: Author's compilation.

a. Right denotes a de facto candidacy for the RN–UDI Coalition (Later known as the Alianza) despite an Independent label.

volume). Nonetheless, some general observations can be made. An account of the thirteen presidents Chile had between 1932 and 2007 tells us that 94 percent of presidents were male and had an average age of sixty, and 50 percent were lawyers. Most started as deputies and then moved to the Senate or held a cabinet position before reaching the presidency. Table 10.9, which shows the path to power taken by these thirteen presidents of Chile, does not suggest significant changes in the postauthoritarian period.

Candidate Type as an Independent Variable

As demonstrated throughout this volume, the procedures used to choose candidates and the types of candidates who ultimately emerge, have a profound impact on campaigns and on the behavior of politicians once they assume office. I now analyze the campaigns of each of the major candidates in presidential elections, tying campaign style to candidate type (always recognizing the additional constraints imposed by coalition politics). Next I attempt to find connections between candidate type and the behavior of presidents once they assume office. The *party insider* mold has best described three presidents in Chile since 1990—Aylwin, Lagos, and Bachelet—and we should expect them to exhibit similar patterns of executive behavior. We would also expect some differences between these three and the one president who was closer to the *party adherent* type, Eduardo Frei. Frei, however, was also constrained by the overwhelming inertia of coalition politics, and thus the differences should be subtle. (It is too early to evaluate Bachelet's government, so analysis of her behavior focuses only on her campaign.) The differences, however, are evident in how he approached campaigning, coalition formation, cabinet formation, and policy orientation. When Lagos won, he reintroduced a pattern more similar to Aylwin's, suggesting that their origins as *party insiders* might explain some of this similarity.

Campaigns

During the 1989 presidential campaign, Aylwin faced five significant challenges:

1. Cultivating support on the left, portions of which opposed him because of his past position as leader of the opposition to the Unidad Popular (Socialist Salvador Allende's government, 1970–1973).
2. Incorporating the interests of a heterogeneous coalition into his campaign.
3. Maintaining support of conservative Christian Democrats, who might be disaffected by the alliance with the left.
4. Avoiding outright confrontations among coalition parties.
5. Challenging a candidate from the center of the political spectrum, Francisco Javier Errázuriz.

TABLE 10.9   Chilean Presidents and Their Backgrounds in Executive or Legislative Offices

President	Years	Party	Year of Birth	First Degree	University	Posts
Arturo Alessandri	1932–1938	PL	1868	Lawyer	University of Chile	1897: Deputy 1915: Senator
Pedro Aguirre	1938–1941	PR	1879	Lawyer and Spanish professor	Pedagogical Institute	1915: Deputy 1918: Minister of Education and Justice 1920: Minister of Interior 1921 Senator
Juan Antonio Ríos	1942–1946	PR	1888	Lawyer	—	1924: Deputy
Gabriel González	1946–1952	PR	1898	Lawyer	University of Chile	1933: Deputy 1939: Ambassador 1945: Senator
Carlos Ibáñez	1952–1958	—	1877	Military	—	1925: Minister of Defense
Jorge Alessandri	1958–1964	PL	1896	Civil engineer	University of Chile	1947: Minister of Finance 1957: Senator
Eduardo Frei	1964–1970	PDC	1911	Lawyer	Catholic University of Chile	1946: Minister of Public Works 1949: Senator
Salvador Allende	1970–1973	PS	1908	Surgeon	University of Chile	1937: Deputy 1939: Minister of Health and Social Welfare 1945: Senator
Augusto Pinochet	1973–1990	—	1915	Military	—	—
Patricio Aylwin	1990–1994	PDC	1918	Lawyer	University of Chile	1964: Senator 1971: President of Senate
Eduardo Frei	1994–2000	PDC	1942	Civil engineer	University of Chile	1989: Senator
Ricardo Lagos	2000–2006	PS-PPD	1938	Lawyer	University of Chile	1972: Ambassador to USSR[a] 1990: Minister of Education 1994: Minister of Public Works
Michele Bachelet	2006–	PS	1951	Surgeon	University of Chile	2000: Minister of Health 2002: Minister of Defense

Source: Author's compilation.

Notes: See the list in the preface for a complete list of party signa.

a. Never ratified by Congress.

His key strategy was to depersonalize the campaign and, as predicted by his *party insider* status, to focus not only on the big ideas and the ideology of his party but also, and more important, on the big ideas and ideology and program of the Concertación. This was recognized as key to holding the transition together. The Concertación's slogan for the campaign, "*Gana la gente*" ("The people win"), expressed the idea that Aylwin was merely the leader of a coalition that had succeeded in transferring decisionmaking power to the citizenry. This image allowed him to downplay his personal past. He managed to capitalize on his political performance in his fight against the military regime and position himself as a democratic statesman concerned with big ideas above petty partisan politics. His participation as spokesman of the "No" in the plebiscite of 1988 broadened his support, and his plan for governing reflected the common understanding of the need for a peaceful transition.[10] He successfully managed to maintain the rhetoric of the 1988 plebiscite, capturing antidictatorship votes while simultaneously incorporating new issues into the campaign.

The most delicate issue was human rights, not because Aylwin lacked support within the Concertación for a human rights agenda but because the coalition parties all had different proposals. Aylwin had to balance maximalist positions with moderate ones. He struck this balance with a proposal for *justicia dentro de lo possible*—justice within the realm of the possible. Another difficulty for Aylwin was his age—he was seventy-two at the time of the election. The Alianza's candidate, Hernán Büchi, age 40, was clearly a candidate with whom Chilean youth could identify. However, Aylwin's perceived age handicap was effectively managed, again, by the depersonalization of the campaign and, as had occurred during the "No" campaign, through the Concertación's use of young politicians and popular TV personalities to cultivate support among the young. Also working against Büchi was his status as a *party adherent*, which took him down the less dramatic and appealing road of technocratic politics at a time when Chileans were drawn to big ideas and lofty ideals.

Aylwin oriented his campaign toward the twin goals of reconnecting citizens with democracy—including making special efforts to reconnect with forgotten sectors like trade unions—while simultaneously marketing the *concertacionista* coalition as a viable and capable governing force. In this sense, the electoral campaign helped form a collective identity, a solid and visible coalition, and consequently, a real alternative. Aylwin's status as a *party insider* added coherence to the campaign, aiding the preservation of a continuous base of support that maintained the nexus between civil society and politicians and between politicians and the coalition's program. The depersonalization of the campaign was also most easily accomplished for a *party insider* because ideas mattered more than individuals. Finally, Aylwin and the Concertación constructed and maintained this nexus of

10. The 1988 plebiscite was called by Pinochet to determine whether or not he would remain in power until 1997.

ideas while avoiding the maximalist tendencies of the pre-1973 era. Citizens understood the transitional logic and provided Aylwin with a significant electoral support for an agenda of democratization through gradual change and *justicia dentro de lo posible*.

The right's campaign tried to break the image of continuity between the right and the military regime. In accordance with Büchi's status as a *party adherent* rather than a *party insider*, his campaign stressed three themes that related strongly to the candidate as a person:

1. Büchi as representing a sharp change of leadership from the Pinochet regime.
2. Büchi's outstanding performance as finance minister.
3. Büchi's apolitical nature, differing from those traditional politicians who were often said to be filled with *mucho ruido y pocas nueces* (a lot of noise and few results).

The Alianza also stressed nonpolitical issues, spotlighting instead the concrete problems of real people in an effort to differentiate itself from the "idealistic" and "ideological" focus of the Concertación. However, the right failed to recognize that there is a difference between the "essential" and the "concrete" problems of citizens. Furthermore, the solutions to concrete and on-the-ground questions grew out of broader questions related to the political and economic models inherited from the military regime and the ideology on which they were based. The right also called for a solution to these problems, while simultaneously and timidly trying to erase its old loyalties to the military regime. This led to a campaign that looked ahead to the modernization of the country as its leitmotiv, ignoring items on the current political agenda and some pressing political problems (such as unemployment, poverty, and exclusion, among others). Ultimately, Büchi's campaign was a dissonant reaction to the political agenda proposed by Aylwin. Also, unfortunately for Büchi, his service in the Pinochet government prevented him from effectively distancing himself from the military regime.

For the elections of 1994, Frei could count on a more consolidated Concertación, more in sync with the business world, and with a proven track record in managing the economy. He also could rely on a more advanced democratic transition, with agreements on the basics of macroeconomic policies, prudent handling of civil–military relations, and a policy of reconciliation based on the principle of justice within the realm of the possible. The cornerstone of his campaign was the slogan "*Para los nuevos tiempos*" ("For new times") that, without breaking the unity and continuity of the Concertación, would allow it to project the idea of a future government dedicated to helping the poor, the young, and women, in accordance with the values of democracy, justice, and fairness (Godoy 1994). Frei campaigned in support of a market economy but one that included a political technocracy whose expertise would bolster the effectiveness and the efficiency of public policies. Frei's status as a *party adherent* and his very technocratic and business orientation led him to shy away from big ideas and ideology in the campaign and to focus more on the importance of basic economic management and technocratic solutions. He may have gone even further in this direction if he hadn't been constrained by a wider dynamic of a coalition still steeped in Aylwin's *party insider* campaign style.

The right's candidate, Arturo Alessandri, combined the Alianza's tendency toward *independentismo* with some of the characteristics of a traditional politician, to make him a classic *party adherent*. Although he was a conservative, his self-proclaimed "independent" status suggested an ambivalent relationship with the traditional parties of the right. He was neither young nor dynamic. A crucial strategic error he made—but one that was understandable, given his status as an *adherent*—was to separate his campaign from the legislative campaigns in order paint himself as an independent, even though the presidential and legislative elections were concurrent in that year. This hurt both the presidential and the legislative campaigns because it seemed the right was, again, tending toward division and incoherence. This perception was further confirmed by the existence of another independent candidate from the right, José Piñera, who managed to snatch some votes from Alessandri.

In the 1999 elections the electoral clash between traditional politics and antipolitics came to a head. The Concertación candidate, Ricardo Lagos, had to achieve the difficult task of appealing to both the still-politicized voter and the new depoliticized voter. The Concertación sought to attract both types of voters with a new focus on social policies. "*Crecer con igualdad*" ("Growth with equality") was the slogan of the first round, which suggested maintaining the basic rules of the market economy while making adjustments to it to better deal with the inequality it created. Whereas Frei was a somewhat colorless proponent of technocratic efficiency, Lagos represented a return to big ideas, and the promotion of an overarching party platform in classic *party insider* style. On the right, Lavín also focused on social issues but emphasized depoliticization and reinforcing the power of the individual. Though Lavín's long career in the UDI categorizes him as a *party insider*, it is important to reiterate that he was an insider playing an outsider's game, which pushed his campaign style more toward the *party adherent* type. This was the case in his self-declared "independent" status and in his focus on the need for reform in the way the right did politics. Lavín did break new ground in this campaign in the up-to-date communication standards he set. His modern and effective campaign forced Lagos to change his own style during the campaign in response to Lavín's success. Following Lagos's narrow victory in the first round, in the second round the Concertación refocused the campaign to widen its appeal to all Chileans, with the slogan "*Chile mucho mejor*" ("A much better Chile").

For the 2005 elections, Bachelet counted on a strong coalition and was both a party and a coalition *insider*. In addition, Constitutional reforms in 2005 eliminated "designated" senators (constitutionally mandated appointed senators who generally supported the right), meaning the Concertación would presumably enjoy a comfortable majority in both chambers of Congress. Even though most opinion polls predicted that Bachelet would be the next president of Chile, her campaign suffered as virulent attacks were launched against her from both right and left. From the right, Piñera and Lavín accused her of indecisiveness—a traditionally chauvinist criticism. From the left, Tomás Hirsh, who led a non-Concertación leftist coalition called Juntos Podemos Más (Together We Can Do More) attacked with an antiestablishment message, arguing that the "Chilean model" was unfair to most citizens. These three male candidates all stressed the need for a change in the way politics was done, and Bachelet's campaign struggled to maintain a delicate balance between change (to revitalize the coalition) and continuity (to build on the success of previous administrations).

During her campaign, Bachelet promised a new style of administration, increasing popular participation and calling for a "citizens' government." Along these lines, Bachelet's campaign slogan "*Estoy contigo*" ("I am with you") suggested a personalized way of doing politics, showing that she represented the "real" change. She also made a commitment to a gender-balanced cabinet with equal numbers of men and women. Ultimately, success depended on turning the old into the "new," as the coalition Bachelet led would be two decades old by the time she stepped down as president. Her true colors as a *party insider* were soon evident, however. The expectations generated during the campaign about instituting a government with greater social participation were frustrated the moment she began building her cabinet, and parties began to struggle to claim their "piece." The mathematical distribution of cabinet posts among coalitional parties had always characterized the Concertación, and this time, again, "old politics" won the battle of cabinet posts, notwithstanding the "newness" of the formula for cabinet distribution with respect to gender. On the societal front, protests and student mobilizations of May and June of 2006 challenged the capacity of the state to face a civil society mobilized for the first time since the democratic transition.

In search of this "new style" of engaged government, Bachelet created citizen commissions to discuss critical reforms to the electoral system, to pension politics, and education. Unfortunately, these commissions combined three potentially contradictory sets of membership: technocrats and academics, party elites (generally following a strict quota), and, for the last two commissions, citizens (integrating different social sectors involved with the reforms). Because the commissions served simply an advisory role, recommendations from these commissions often had limited or no influence, and after months of work the emerging proposals were usually rejected by the parties. Even worse, the rejections could occur within hours, as was the case with the Boeninger Commission's report on electoral reform.[11]

11. The author was a member of the Boeninger Commission.

Cabinet Structure and the Behavior of Aylwin, Frei, and Lagos

The general rule for postauthoritarian presidents was to appoint cabinets proportional to the relative power of the coalition's constituent parties. When it comes to presidents' cabinet-related actions, the Siavelis–Morgenstern framework, although applicable, needs some adjustment. For purposes of coalition formation, even a quintessential *party insider* such as Aylwin was bound by the informal agreement of the Concertación to respect party quotas in the distribution of cabinet posts among the coalition's member parties. Thus we can consider Aylwin (and for that matter Lagos) *coalition insiders*. Respecting the Concertación cabinet distribution agreement amounted to toeing the party line, so we can consider those who respected agreements to be simultaneously party and coalition *insiders*. The evidence is that Frei, less of a *party insider*, was also less of a coalition *insider*.

The transitional situation that Aylwin's government faced forced him to be extremely careful to not rock the boat in any way that would alter the basic political consensus created between the military and civilian authorities and, perhaps more important, among the partners of the Concertación. So it is no surprise that his cabinet was one of the most stable in Chilean history, and that the distribution of offices reflected almost mathematically perfect proportions. Aylwin used what Rehren calls a mechanism of *horizontal integration* to distribute portfolios (Rehren 1992, 71), where a minister of one party is paired with an undersecretary from a different party in the coalition. In this manner, Aylwin avoided the creation of administrative and executive reserved domains or power niches. The horizontal integration mechanism facilitated cooperation among the parties of the Concertación in a way that resembles the power-sharing typical of a consociational democratic model (see Lijphart 1999; Lijphart and Waisman 1996). (This mechanism resembles Brazil's "coalition presidentialism"; see Chapter 9, this volume).

The basis for distributing offices was the percentage of votes received in the 1989 legislative elections; in that election the PDC got about 26 percent of the votes, so it got a commensurate piece of the pie in the distribution of power and offices and also received a larger share of the political ministries than other parties. Even so, relations among coalition allies remained smooth. The key institution that helped to smooth relations between parties, and especially between the executive branch and the legislature, was the Secretary General of the Presidency (Secretaría General de la Presidencia, or SEGPRES), an administrative cabinet post that has ministerial status. All proposals for legislation from each of the ministries pass through SEGPRES, which acts as both a clearinghouse and a "filter" for legislation (Siavelis 2000, 56). The rule for Aylwin's legislative style followed a model of gradualism predicated on widespread agreement within his own coalition, and between it and the opposition.

Whatever the cause of Aylwin's success, Frei was its beneficiary, though there were some differences in the way he structured his cabinet. Frei, less of a party and coalition *insider*, respected less the notion of horizontal integration and was willing to rely more on a close inner circle of advisers and a more personalist cabinet, especially in the political ministries. If Aylwin progressively looked to depersonalize his administration, Frei surrounded himself with what became known as his personal "iron circle," as we would expect from a *party adherent*. As already noted, Frei was not a strong party activist and was more connected to the business world. After the tragic death in 1982 of his father, Eduardo Frei Montalva, a former president of Chile who was presumably assassinated by the military regime because he was a member of the opposition, the son became a member of the board of directors of Radio Cooperativa. His colleagues there were Genaro Arriagada, Edmundo Pérez Yoma, and Carlos Figueroa (Cavallo 1998, 237), and these three men became known as Frei's "iron circle." Later, Gutenberg Martínez, Juan Villarzú, and Francisco Frei would complete his circle of confidants. Half a year after assuming office, Frei reshuffled his political cabinet and decided to give preference to his own party by placing the whole "iron circle" in the key political offices (Garretón 2001). Although the consensualism inherited from the Aylwin administration was under severe stress (Siavelis 2000, 54), Frei altered but did not destroy the horizontal integration he inherited. Frei also gave his administration a much more technocratic element than Aylwin's. Frei's status as a *party adherent* helps to explain his more personalist orientation, greater technocratic tendencies, and willingness to bend party rules.

Lagos, a *party insider*, extended the overall horizontal integration that dominated the executive branch during the entirety of Aylwin's administration and the first months of Frei's. Lagos also introduced an informal affirmative action policy for his cabinet posts and for other executive offices (ambassadorships, undersecretariates of ministries, directors of publicly owned companies, etc.). Five women were appointed ministers: Michelle Bachelet (Health), Soledad Alvear (Foreign Affairs), Mariana Aylwin (Education), Josefina Bilbao (Women's Affairs), and Alejandra Krauss (Planning). María Antonieta Morales was appointed to the Supreme Court. Interestingly, all of these appointees were from the PDC, with the exception of Bachelet, who, like Lagos, is a Socialist. The success of this experiment in affirmative action was evident as the two major contenders for the Concertación's presidential nomination for the 2005 elections were women: Bachelet and Alvear.

Executive Offices: Proportionality, Electoral Calendar, and Horizontal Integration

A key issue in considering presidential appointments is the degree to which there is balance between the parties' electoral strength and their cabinet representation. What is the effect of candidate types and other variables on maintaining this balance? The expectation is that party and coalition *insiders* will be particularly attuned to coalitional dynamics and thus worry about balancing their appointments.

TABLE 10.10   Frequencies of Political Offices and Gender in Chile (1990–2006)[a]

	Total	Women	Percentage Women	Men	Percentage Men
President	3	0	0.0	3	100.0
Candidate Presidency	12	2	16.7	10	83.3
Minister (Type I: Political)	70	6	8.6	64	91.4
Minister (Type II: Economic)	94	3	3.2	91	96.8
Minister (Type III: Social)	94	30	31.9	64	68.1
Undersecretary (Type I: Political)	140	4	2.9	136	97.1
Undersecretary (Type II: Economic)	126	9	7.1	117	92.9
Undersecretary (Type III: Social)	98	22	22.4	76	77.6
Ambassador (Type I: USA, Argentina, Brazil, Spain)	203	0	0.0	203	100.0
Ambassador (Type II: Peru, Venezuela, Colombia, Australia)	244	5	2.0	239	98.0
Ambassador (Type III: All the rest)	453	41	9.1	412	90.9
Mayor (*intendente*)	182	17	9.3	165	90.7
Governor	702	99	14.1	603	85.9
Total	2,421	238	16.1	2,183	83.9

Source: Author's compilation.

a. Does not include Bachelet's administration.

Presidents who are less integrated into the party or coalition should worry less about maintaining such balance. There are at least two other issues that may affect presidents' appointments, however. (1) As elections approach, pressures mount for cabinet shuffles, and the president may work to concentrate his or her own forces. (2) While electoral exigencies may point presidents in one direction, presidents in Chile have also concerned themselves with an unwritten law that pushes them to avoid generating a party monopoly in any given specific policy area (see Rehren 1992, 1998). The analysis below suggests that the party and coalition *insiders* fend off the electoral pressures better than did the one party and coalitional *adherent* in our sample. The result, therefore, was better proportionality and balance in the *insiders'* appointments.

This analysis relies on a database detailing the executive posts appointed by the president (ministers, undersecretaries, *intendentes*, governors, and ambassadors) and the party affiliation of the politicians appointed to these offices. Table 10.10 shows the frequencies of each office in the database. Not all ministries are equal in public visibility and resources. Therefore, I divided all cabinet positions as follows: (1) the "political ministries" (Foreign Affairs, Defense, Interior, Secretary of the Presidency, and Secretary of Government), which are physically located at the presidential palace; (2) "economic ministries" (Budget, Agriculture, Transport, Mining, Economy and Energy, Public Works, Planning and Cooperation); and (3) "social

TABLE 10.11 Bivariate Correlations Between Percentage of Votes and Share of Executive Offices in Chile[a]

	Ministries	Subsecretaries	Intendancies
Aylwin	0.965	0.975	0.894
Frei	0.963	0.962	0.961
Lagos	0.927	0.969	0.955

a. All coefficients significant at 0.001 level.

ministries" (Justice, Education, Health, National Patrimony, Women, Housing, Work and Social Welfare). Like ministers and undersecretaries, ambassadors were also divided into three groups according to their perceived importance.[12]

Before turning to the conclusions relating presidents' types to their propensity for balancing their appointments, given this volume's concern with gender issues it is worth noting the extreme gender chauvinism of Chilean politics at all levels and offices evident in Table 10.10. Strikingly, women have a tougher time trying to enter the system at the municipal level than at the ministerial level. But this male domination has been drastically reduced, at least at the ministerial level, by Bachelet's appointment of a cabinet made up of one-half women (see Escobar-Lemmon and Taylor-Robinson, Chapter 14, for a full analysis of candidate type and gender).

Distribution of Executive Offices Through a Principle of Proportional Representation

As noted, Aylwin and Lagos were extremely careful in sharing their executive offices among the Concertación parties in a manner consistent with the parties' electoral strength. Frei tried to adhere to the same strategy during much of his administration, but at the very beginning and end of his presidency fairness in the distribution of ministries among coalition allies was blurred. As I showed in previous work (Altman 2001), in multiparty presidential regimes, once a governing coalition is formed, the type and number of executive offices received by each coalition member follows the principle of proportional representation and reflects the electoral results of each member of the governing coalition. His *adherent* (rather than outsider) status led Frei to concern himself with coalitional proportionality in the appointment of ministers, but being an *adherent* rather than an *insider* might explain why he eventually strayed from proportionality and appointed members of his inside circle to the most important cabinet posts.

Table 10.11 shows the results of bivariate correlations between the share of the vote that each Concertación party received in the last election and its respective

12. I thank Roberto Durán for his help in determining the criteria to rate the importance of different ambassadorial appointments.

share of executive offices (ministers, undersecretaries, and mayors). Although the number of cases is relatively small, the results are impressive. The nine correlations are significant at the 0.001 level and there are no major differences among the three analyzed administrations

Electoral Calendar and Distribution of Executive Offices

From the section above we know that in Chile a principle of proportionality is applied to distribute executive offices. Nonetheless, this distribution can change, as Frei's cabinet reshuffle shows. In Latin America the balance of executive appointments among members of a governing coalition changes as each administration approaches new elections (see Altman 2000, 2001). In other words, the closer the elections are, the more offices the party of the president concentrates in its favor, and consequently, the fewer offices the coalition allies have to share. If this proves correct in Chile, it would represent a violation of the principle of horizontal integration described earlier.

Figure 10.1 shows the percentage of portfolios received by parties in Chile since 1990. Two interesting phenomena can be observed: The first is the remarkable stability of the cabinet during the Aylwin administration (almost flat lines in both figures) and the fluctuation of the distribution of these offices during the Frei and Lagos administrations. The second is the "mirror" effects of these lines during the last two administrations. Thus, in the ten years from 1994 to 2005 there is a clear zero-sum game in the distribution of cabinet posts to the PDC and the PS-PPD subpact. The growth in the number of ministers of the PS-PPD subpact reflects the improving electoral performance of the left, given the principle of proportional distribution of portfolios based on electoral performance.

As a matter of fact, there is no statistical evidence that the president's party tends to appoint more of its own members as time goes by, as happens in most of Latin America (Altman 2001). In other words, the distribution of cabinet positions is not contingent on the electoral calendar. In Chile, this is probably because presidents know that the probability of the coalition's survival is extremely high, though there is uncertainty about the next president's party affiliation.

Division of ministries, however, is only one way that presidents balance coalitional powers. Ministerial portfolios are not "equal," in public visibility and in the resources they command, so it is possible that presidents weight their appointments by these other factors. Further, presidents may use second-level appointments to appease coalition members. To consider this possibility, Figure 10.2 analyzes "partisan congruence," which is defined by whether the minister and undersecretary are of the same party. High congruence thus implies less attention to coalitional politics. The figure breaks these statistics according to the type of portfolio and uncovers some very different patterns than were evident in the aggregate statistics.

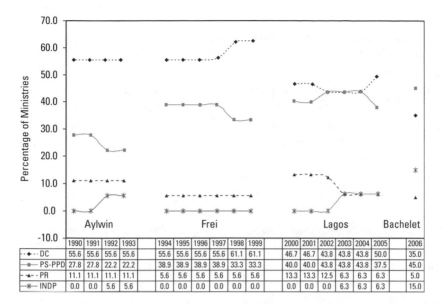

FIGURE 10.1 Distribution of Ministries by Party, 1990–2006.

NOTE: DC = Christian Democratic Party; PS–PPD = Socialist Party and the Party for Democracy.

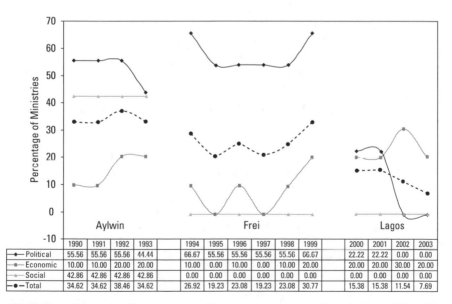

FIGURE 10.2 Ministers' and Undersecretaries' Partisan Congruence, by Type of Ministry, 1990–2003.

Note: Partisan congruence refers to whether the minister and under secretary are of the same party. Excessive cabinet turnover in the Bachelet government makes analysis of her administration difficult for this measure at time of press.

The first and perhaps most obvious phenomenon is the very high degree of partisan congruency in the "political" ministries during the PDC administrations (1990–1999). The second observation is the absolute lack of partisan congruency in the social portfolios during the Frei and Lagos administrations. In other words, the principle of horizontal integration reaches its maximum in this group of ministries. The Lagos administration has the overall lowest degree of partisan congruency of the three. Finally, Frei's administration is characterized by a concentration of PDC members in the political portfolios at the level of ministers and undersecretaries, thus violating the principle of horizontal integration in this cabinet subgroup. In accord with predictions for an *adherent*, he violates this principle more than the *insiders* Aylwin and Lagos, but Aylwin also failed to balance many of these ministries.

To confirm the patterns evident in the figures, I conducted a statistical test which also considers the importance of the electoral calendar. Table 10.12 shows the result of a logistic regression that tests whether congruency changes with the proximity or distance to the next election, the administration, or type of ministry. These tests confirm the impressions drawn from the figures. The type of ministry does have an effect on the degree of partisan congruency, as do the dummies controlling for administration. What is interesting is that the electoral calendar has no effect whatsoever on the overall degree of partisan congruency. The lack of significance of this variable is consistent with my (2001) study of coalition formation and survival in multiparty presidential regimes and could be explained by the extremely powerful influence the Chilean electoral system has on parties' behavior.

The logistic regression on Table 10.12 shows that the Aylwin and Frei administrations had a statistically significant higher degree of partisan congruency than Lagos's (the reference group in the model). It also shows the importance of having included a variable dealing with the different types of ministries coexisting in

TABLE 10.12 Partisan Congruency in the Chilean Cabinet, 1990–2003

	B	S.E.
Electoral calendar	−.026	0.396
Dummy AYLWIN	1.435**	0.389
Dummy FREI	0.787*	0.375
Type Ministry (1 = political, 2 = economic, 3 = social)	−1.048**	0.192
Constant	−.098	0.500
N	356	
Nagelkerke R^2	0.191	
Cox & Snell R^2	0.128	

* $p < 0.05$; ** $p < 0.001$.

a given cabinet. The preponderance of Frei's "iron circle" in his political ministries made his average congruency higher than during the Lagos administration, suggesting a different strategy of cabinet appointments reflecting his status as a *party adherent*. In other words, Lagos's administration could be characterized as the government that took the horizontal integration to its maximum expression since the transition to democracy in 1990.

When it comes to the overall pattern of congruity in cabinet appointments, however, Aylwin and Frei look much more similar than Aylwin and Lagos. Because both the latter were *party insiders*, we would expect a similar pattern in coalition formation. What explains the divergence? It might be a result of the point analyzed earlier: the principle of proportional distribution of offices based on electoral results that has been very important to coalitional politics. The PDC was clearly the most important party in the coalition in the immediate transition period, but its performance eroded with the passage of time, eventually yielding its dominant role to the combined parties of the left. This reality and the perceived inviolability of the deal struck by the coalition in the initial election may explain the similarity of Aylwin's and Frei's overall pattern of cabinet appointments, despite their being different types of candidates.

Conclusions

This chapter analyzed how presidents become presidents in Chile and the consequences of the process for parties, policies, legislation, and representative government. As a dependent variable the chapter explored how recruitment for the presidency has evolved since the democratic reinstallation, underscoring different types of candidates and campaigns. It is clear that the two majority blocs (government and opposition) differ greatly in their handling of presidential nominations. In the Concertación, candidate recruitment and selection have evolved with time from being extremely informal (albeit constrained) to being a more formalized process. On the right, elite-centered mechanisms continue to be the norm. Of course, since there are only four cases to analyze, these are tentative hypotheses about trends.

Four presidents that Chile has had since the transition—Patricio Aylwin, Eduardo Frei, Ricardo Lagos, and Michele Bachelet—all have strong ties to the Chilean political establishment, and fit in the *party insider* category. Yet Frei's greater personalism, strong technocratic orientation, and long trajectory in the business world gave him many characteristics of the *party adherent* rather than the *party insider* type.

As an independent variable this chapter statistically analyzed whether the factors that influence patterns of distribution of executive offices that usually hold historically (proportionality, electoral calendar, and horizontal integration) apply today. The conclusion is that presidents have been quite careful in building and sustaining their coalitions by sharing and carefully distributing offices among coalition allies. At times, this distribution approached perfect mathematical proportions. Of course, this was not a law, but rather an informal institution all members were expected to respect and defend. Moreover, the institutions of horizontal integration were basically maintained since the return of formal democracy in 1990. If different categories of ministries (political, economic, and social) are considered, during the Frei administration horizontal integration was undermined the most within the political ministries. I suggest that this difference is in part explained by Frei's status as a *party adherent* type. Still, his adherence to the coalition yielded a pattern of cabinet appointments relatively similar to that of one of the *insiders*, Aylwin. At least in the early years of the transition, then, coalition dynamics appear to have trumped the difference that might have been caused by candidate types in this particular behavior. Lagos's administration, however, divided ministries and vice-ministries much more evenly, perhaps suggesting that *insiders* more concerned with coalitional politics may behave in a distinct manner. It appears that Bachelet's cabinets will confirm this hypothesis, as her first appointments have emphasized a concern with both gender and partisan equity.

Chapter Eleven

Precandidates, Candidates, and Presidents:
Paths to the Colombian Presidency

STEVEN L. TAYLOR, FELIPE BOTERO, AND
BRIAN F. CRISP

The institutional procedures that would-be public officials must
face to win office should, by backward induction, exert influence on the types of candidates who emerge. For example, if
the process of becoming president informally entails careful
public scrutiny of one's private life, individuals with morally
checkered pasts will not seek the nomination. More formally, if
the candidate selection process requires one to be endorsed at
an elite-dominated party summit, party "black sheep" or otherwise independent-minded individuals need not apply.

However, in the race for the Colombian presidency, the institutional rules adopted by parties to name candidates are not
important as independent variables in the equation to explain the
types of precandidates who emerge. Instead, the organizational
looseness of Colombian parties means that precandidates of
various types can emerge and that they will struggle to impose
selection procedures that favor their own candidacies. Clearly,
selection institutions matter for explaining who receives the nomination. If they did not, precandidates would not bother to fight
over which ones are used. However, it is selection procedures'
unusual malleability in the context of Colombian political parties
that makes them a dependent rather than independent variable.

The Race for the Colombian Presidency

In Colombia when there is a precandidate for president without any serious challenger, any selection method will lead to his
nomination—thus, no struggle over procedures. However, it is
often the case that precandidates with very different political
backgrounds and very different connections to the leaderships

An earlier draft of this chapter was presented at the 2004 Meeting of the Latin
American Studies Association, Las Vegas, Nevada, October 7–9, 2004.

within their parties contest for the nomination. Employing the terms of the Siavelis-Morgenstern framework (Chapter 1, this volume), *party insiders* have histories of capitalizing on machine politics and prominent family ties to gain control over the party and previous presidential nominees. *Party adherents*, on the other hand, are not as centrally located within the national leaderships of the party and tend to have risen to the national stage by serving at the local and state level. *Party insiders* espouse themes traditionally associated with their parties, whereas *adherents* frequently, though not always, talk about the need for reforms—including reforms to their own party. When a *party insider* (tradition-oriented) precandidate faces a *party adherent* precandidate, the *insider* will seek to impose a centralized candidate selection procedure, whereby his standing as a party elite and his close ties with other party elites will prevail. On the other hand, the *adherent* will seek more participatory procedures in order to neutralize the power of the *insider's* supporters and to capitalize on his broader appeal.

Historically, failure to obtain designation as the official candidate of the Liberal or Conservative party ended one's prospects of achieving the presidency (at least for the immediate term). Losing precandidates could permanently give up their pursuit of the office, wait until the next term, or announce their intention to seek the office as an independent in the current race—and lose. For example, Luis Carlos Galán's loss of the Liberal nomination to Alfonso López, an *insider*, in 1982 led him to break from the party and run as the head of his own independent movement—arguably costing the Liberals the presidency. Recently, however, the increasing urbanization of the Colombian population and the concomitant decline in importance of patron–client networks for delivering votes to presidential candidates has increased independent candidates' probability of winning. This increased electoral opportunity for independents makes the defection of strong candidates from the traditional parties more likely, and as a result it should put pressure on party elites to adopt candidate selection processes more to the liking of the *adherents* on the verge of becoming independents. *Insider* candidates, given their loyalty to the party, are unlikely to become independents. However, the tension between the local patron–client networks used to earn votes for election to Congress and the broader, more urban base of support sought by candidates for the executive mean that parties have been constrained in their ability to adapt to the new reality of presidential politics. That is, parties have to simultaneously satisfy the interests of rural constituencies, mostly clientelistic, and the interest of urban electorates, more programmatic. We show that *insider* candidates for the presidency are much more dependent on rural voters whereas *adherents* have relatively more urban bases of support, which further distances them from the traditional bases of power within the Conservative and Liberal parties.

Given the historic importance in Colombia of patron–client ties and the ability to deliver the rural vote, which is still central for election to the Chamber of Representatives, the traditional parties themselves are declining in importance in the race for the presidency, in which urban voters are the key to victory. An open question is how this dynamic between increasingly urban and nationally oriented presidents on the one side and rural and locally oriented members of Congress on the other affects presidential behavior and interbranch relations. If these tensions are significant in the race for the nomination and eventual election, they should be reflected in how sitting presidents interact with members of their own party, with opposition parties and their members, and with Congress more generally. We will examine these relations by looking at bill initiation patterns and cabinet composition.

Our chapter is structured as followed. In the next section we detail the struggles for the presidential nomination of the Liberal and Conservative parties since the end of the National Front in 1974. An examination of career paths prior to competition for the nomination helps us distinguish between *party insiders* and *party adherents* in the terms set out by Siavelis and Morgenstern in Chapter 1. We show how changes in legal variables, including the way in which ballots were printed and changes in the electoral calendar, interacted with party variables to determine the type of candidate selection process chosen and therefore the type of candidate to receive the official nomination. In the third section of the chapter we show that candidate type is related to campaign style and the geographic bases of support for winning and losing candidates. Traditional *party insiders* who achieved the nomination through centralized processes are more likely to get their support in the general election from rural areas. Conversely, *party adherents* and *free-wheeling independents* who achieve their party's nomination through relatively more participatory procedures focus on urban residents less likely to be bound by patron–client ties in their bids to win the general election. Finally, we examine how the selection process, candidate type, and electoral base (or campaign style) influence presidential behavior. We will examine where presidents turn for their cabinet members and the balance between branches in pursuing their preferences through bill initiation to determine whether the requisites of seeking the office continue to influence behavior even after the general election. We will conclude by making the argument that the decreasing importance of being the official candidate of one of the traditional parties for actually winning the presidency is a symptom of the larger disjuncture between the Colombian party system and the reality of electoral politics.

Career Paths and Candidate Types

In Colombia, using the typology set out by Siavelis and Morgenstern in Chapter 1, three types of candidates have aspired to the presidency: *party insiders*, *party adherents*, and *free-wheeling independents*. For our purposes, *party insiders* have enduring identification with a party that is more than their personal vehicle, and prior to seeking that party's nomination *insiders* have attained a clear leadership position among the group's elite. *Party adherents* too have enduring identification with a particular party, but their position among its leadership is less obvious. While clearly having a partisan identification, *adherents*, in the Colombian context, are often associated with efforts to reform the party from within. A *free-wheeling independent*, as the label implies, either has no experience within a long-standing party or after some association makes a very clear break from the party's ideology and organizational structure to seek the presidency. Looking at the nineteen major candidacies to contest the race for the presidency since the end of the power-sharing National Front in 1974, we identified seven *party insiders*, nine *party adherents*, and three *free-wheeling independents* (Table 11.1).

How does one arrive at these positions relative to the leadership of the major parties? We traced the political biographies of the nineteen major candidates, breaking previous experience (elected and appointed) into prior service in the

TABLE 11.1 Colombian Presidential Candidate Type and Selection Method, by Party and Election: 1974–2002

Candidates	Selection Method	Candidate Type
1974 **Alfonso López** (PL)[a]	National convention	*Party insider*
Álvaro Gómez (PC)	National convention	*Party insider*
1978 **Julio César Turbay** (PL)	Quasi primary	*Party insider*
Belisario Betancur ("Candidato Nacional"/PC)	National convention	*Party adherent*
1982 Alfonso López (PL)	National convention	*Party insider*
Belisario Betancur (Moviemento Nacional/PC)	National convention	*Party adherent*
Luis Carlos Galán (NL)	Self-nomination	*Free-wheeling ind.*
1986 **Virgilio Barco** (PL)	Quasi primary	*Party adherent*
Álvaro Gómez (PC)	National convention	*Party insider*
1990 **César Gaviria** (PL)	Open primary	*Party adherent*
Rodrigo Lloreda (PC)[c]	National convention	*Party adherent*
Álvaro Gómez (MSN)	Self-nomination	*Free-wheeling ind.*
1994 **Ernesto Samper** (PL)	Open primary	*Party adherent*
Andrés Pastrana ("Andrés presidente"/PC)	National convention	*Party adherent*
1998 Horacio Serpa (PL)	National convention	*Party insider*
Andrés Pastrana ("El cambio es Andrés"/PC)	Closed caucus	*Party adherent*
2002 Horacio Serpa (PL)	National convention	*Party insider*
Juan Camilo Restrepo (PC)[b]	Closed caucus	*Party adherent*
Álvaro Uribe (Primero Colombia)	Self-nomination	*Free-wheeling ind.*

Source: Author's compilation.

NOTE: PC = Partido Conservador; PL = Partido Liberal Colombiano
NL = Nuevo Liberalismo; MSN = Movimiento de Salvación Nacional.

a. **Winners** in boldface type.
b. The conservative candidate withdrew from the race and the PC supported Uribe's candidacy.
c. In 1990 the PC was officially known as the Partido Social Conservador.

national executive, in the national legislature, in subnational executive posts, and in local legislative posts. There was one characteristic shared by all nineteen candidates: prior service in the national legislature. Some candidates had repeated terms in both houses while others had served only once, but all of them had been elected to the national legislature at some point in their careers. Even candidates bent on changing the form of Colombian politics recognize the importance of clientelisticic practices, and a seat in Congress (where there are no restrictions on reelection) has always been the best perch from which to orchestrate the use of such largesse for constructing political followings. What is more, the limited powers and resources allotted to state and local government historically meant that it was difficult to claim that experience at those levels was preparation for leading the country.

Gubernatorial posts were appointed until 1991, and mayoral races were first contested in 1988 (the 1991 constitution mandated substantial revenue transfers to these levels). Thus, most of the candidates under study here could not use the races for subnational executive posts as a means of honing their electoral skills and proving their suitability to lead. However, this may be changing. The two most recent presidents served as subnational executives. Andrés Pastrana was the first elected mayor of Bogotá in 1988 and Álvaro Uribe was elected governor of Antioquia for the 1995–1997 period. It remains to be seen, but it is possible that subnational executive posts may supplant or at least serve as an alternate route to the presidency beyond service in Congress. Despite a process of decentralization, Colombia remains essentially a unitary state. Still, the high-profile nature of gubernatorial and mayoral posts, coupled with the electoral might associated with winning such posts, may present a new route to the presidency.

The candidacies of *party insiders* have frequently shared an important informal piece of political experience. More than half the time since 1974, *insider* candidacies could tout the service of the candidate's father as president. In other words, these sons were virtually earmarked as likely precandidates at birth. Another feature shared by *party insiders* was their ability to receive their party's nomination a second time after having lost the race for the presidency previously (presidents cannot be reelected). This emphasizes "the lock" one can achieve on the nomination by rising to the central hierarchy of the party apparatus.

Party adherents are less likely to have fathers who served as president. Rather than having a natural entrée to presidential politics, they were more likely to have earned their base of support in local and department assemblies. Whereas only 14 percent of post-1974 *insider* candidates had served in a local assembly, the percentage was four times as great among *adherent* candidacies. *Party adherent* candidates were more than twice as likely to be able to point to service in a local assembly as *insider* candidates. In order to make a mark on the national stage, *adherents* were more likely than others to have served in (subcabinet) bureaucratic positions at the national level. In sum, compared to *insiders*, *adherents* seem more likely to have taken a tough and circuitous route to the nomination, having earned their way to the nomination by building bases of support through subnational elected posts and national appointed posts.

We have fewer *free-wheeling independent* candidacies to observe. As noted, like all others they had previous experience in the national legislature, but all three were senators with no experience in the Chamber of Representatives. Given the relatively low district magnitudes for Senate races prior to the adoption of the 1991 constitution and the use of a nationwide district after 1991, Senate candidates typically had to earn more votes than representatives. The propensity that leads one to launch a candidacy for the presidency without the support of a major party may be the same propensity that encourages one to seek a seat in the Senate without having served in the lower house first. In a sense, *FWIs* would like to be on a fast track to building a broad constituency and are less interested in being associated with the parochial politics of the lower house and subnational assemblies.

Given their diverse career trajectories, the three types of precandidates vary in their sources of political strength, defined primarily by their relationship to the central leadership of the major parties. Thus, a precandidate's prior career experience influences the type of candidate selection process through which he or she is most likely to achieve the nomination. *Party insiders* prefer centralized processes where their position among the party elite can work to their advantage. *Party adherents*, with a looser grip on the reins of the party, prefer a less centralized process, where the *insiders'* high level supporters are counterbalanced by rank-and-file members. *Free-wheeling independents*, on the other hand, as their title would imply, opt out of the party candidate selection process altogether and declare themselves candidates of their own movements. In the next section, we examine the relationship between the candidate selection process and candidate type.

Candidate Types and Selection Procedures

The Siavelis and Morgenstern framework posits that the selection process is an independent variable that influences candidate type. In the Colombian case, we have found that the selection process is a dependent variable. Yes, the selection process is a filter through which one type of candidate passes more easily than others, but the malleability of political-party institutions in Colombia means, especially in the case of the Liberal Party (Partido Liberal Colombiano, PL), that precandidates have fought for a preferred selection process from a menu of institutional options that have evolved over the past three decades. Thus, the key turning point in the race for the nomination is not the kind of candidates who emerge because they are favored by institutionalized selection processes but the battle that diverse types of precandidates wage to impose the process of their choice. The ability to force a fight depends very much of the type of aspirants seeking nomination and on the degree to which the party is fractured over whom to nominate in a given cycle. Rather than a specific process dominating the system, or even a particular party's settling on a certain process over time, the parties have selected from a menu of options, changing selection processes from election to election, often as a means of settling factional disputes (or as the results of such a dispute). The PL has been more prone to selection from the menu, whereas the Conservatives (Partido Conservador Colombiano, PC) have largely stuck to some form of internal elite consensus or convention process.

This recalcitrance on the part of the PC to reform its selection process has resulted in serious fragmentation and desertions from the party. With limited policy and process preferences represented within the party, the use of relatively centralized candidate selection processes has been agreed upon to settle more or less personalistic differences in the struggle for the nomination. Thus, factions are usually designated by the surnames of their champions—for example, the Ospinista–Pastranista wing versus the Laureanista–Alvarista wing. Belisario Betancur, an *adherent* of the Conservative Party rather than an *insider*, was somewhat of an exception to this personalistic infighting and a stalemate among the *insiders* allowed him to capture the nomination in 1978, despite the use of a relatively centralized candidate selection process (a national convention). His strong showing in the elections assured him a second nomination in 1982. The return to dominance of the Ospinista–Pastranista faction allowed them to use the national convention to make official the candidacy of Rodrigo Lloreda in 1990, and the reemergence of the faction encouraged Álvaro Gómez to break from the party and run as an *FWI*—the last time he would appear on the ballot. The peculiar relationship of Pastrana with the PC should be noted. Although his close ties with the party are undeniable, in his political career he seems to have avoided being identified as a *party insider*. For all of the elected posts he ran for, Pastrana ran under personal electoral vehicles other than the PC: Gran Alianza por el Cambio (Grand Alliance for Change) in the 1988 mayoral race in Bogotá, Nueva Fuerza Democrática (New Democratic Force) in the 1991 senatorial race, Andrés Presidente (Andrés for President) in the 1994 presidential bout, and Gran Alianza Democrática (Grand Democratic Alliance) in the 1998 presidential race. Despite having the explicit support of the PC in all his political ventures, Pastrana promoted himself as a member of *movimientos suprapartidistas*—supraparty movements.

Where the PC has used a centralized process to select candidates (forcing disgruntled members to consider the *free-wheeling independent* route), the PL has employed virtually every possible process option. A clear elite consensus gave a Liberal *party insider*, López, the nomination in 1974. When two strong candidates, Julio César Turbay Ayala and Carlos Lleras Restrepo, emerged prior to the 1978 elections, the party had to choose a process through which to resolve the struggle. An agreement, the Consenso de San Carlos (San Carlos Accord), was reached to use congressional elections, held in March, to help select the party's nominee for the May presidential contest (Martz 1999). When elite agreements were not reached, party factions tried to show their electoral strength as a means to secure nominations. Party factions printed their own ballots for congressional elections and the ballot itself indicated not only the congressional (and other) candidates on the subparty list, but also which intraparty faction the lists adhered to. For example, a ballot in the 1978 election might have been marked "Liberal Llerista" (Llerista Liberal) at the top and state, elsewhere on the ballot, "*Esta lista respalda la candidatura presidencial de Carlos Lleras Restrepo*" (This list endorses the presidential candidacy of Carlos Lleras Restrepo). The split electoral calendar combined with clearly marked factional lists made it possible to assess the basic strength of a candidate among the party's voters—in essence, a closed primary—in advance of the presidential elections.

In 1982 López, a Liberal *party insider*, returned and was able to prevent the use of the congressional elections as a way of assessing party voters' preferences. The son of a former president and a former president himself, he struggled to impose the use of a national convention where his position as the foremost leader within the party could best be used to leverage support among other party leaders. López's ability to impose a process that favored a candidate with his career path and current standing within the party led Galán, who had favored a more open process for selecting the Liberal nominee, to break from the party and run as a *free-wheeling independent*. This split in the party made clear the need to adopt a candidate selection process that resulted in a legitimate winner of the nomination. The eventual solution was to use congressional elections as a quasi–closed-primary process to select the party's 1986 nominee (McDonald and Ruhl 1989, 88). Virgilio Barco, a *party adherent*, won the nomination and went on to win the presidency.

That the *adherents* in the party seemed to be gaining the upper hand over the *insiders* was evidenced by the use of an even more participatory process in 1990. An open primary, called the *consulta popular,* led to the choice of a *party adherent*, César Gaviria, in 1990. Gaviria went on to win the election and to champion a referendum that resulted in the election of a constituent assembly and political reforms that were institutionalized in a new constitution.

During these years, not only party variables influenced the selection process; numerous legal changes also affected it. One of these reforms somewhat inadvertently made the use of congressional elections as a closed primary for selecting a party's presidential nominee impossible. The national government began to produce electoral ballots in 1991, and, as a result, intraparty factions no long printed individualized lists readily identifiable with a given presidential candidate. With this option off the table, the open primary was used again prior to the 1994 elections to choose *party adherent* Ernesto Samper as the Liberal's nominee. The open-primary process was codified into law in 1994 with the passage of Law 130, which detailed, in Title III, Section 10, that the state would pay for the cost of such an event at the national, departmental, district, or municipal level, as well as count the votes. But just when it appeared that the open-primary process favorable to *adherents* had become the norm within the party, Liberal *party insiders* were able to impose the use of acclamation at the party convention in January 1998 as the means of selecting the party's nominee. This relatively closed process privileged the party's elite, and they selected one of their own—the *party insider* Horacio Serpa (Semana 1997; *El Tiempo* 1997, 1998). Serpa lost to Patrana, a Conservative *party adherent*, in 1998. In 2001, the National Election Council (Consejo Nacional Electoral, or CNE) approved the use of a closed primary, a *consulta interna,* by the PL.[1] In 2002, Serpa's domination of the Liberal Party allowed him to impose the use of an internal caucus to select the party's candidate, securing his own renomination. This allowed for a closed caucus type of process in which PL members of various elected bodies (and others approved by the party) could vote to select the party's candidate.

Serpa's ability to recentralize the candidate selection process and to foreclose the opportunities of *party adherents* undoubtedly helped create the phenomenon of the *free-wheeling independent* Álvaro Uribe. Also facilitating such a viable independent candidacy was the 1991 adoption of majority runoff rules for the selection of presidents, because now candidates not advocated by one of the major parties could hope to gain votes in a second round if they could poll more strongly than a weak major-party nominee had done in the first round. The malleability of party variables related to the selection process and the permissibility of renomination meant that neither *insiders* nor *adherents* could rest assured that they would consistently have the upper hand in seeking the party's nomination. With *adherents* apparently on the wane, Serpa leading the traditionalist *insiders*, and the potential of only needing to do well enough in the initial voting to make it to the runoff, Uribe broke from the party and pursued the presidency as a *free-wheeling independent*. He declared himself the candidate of Primero Colombia (Colombia First), his own movement, and disavowed several party positions and practices. With this strategy he won election in 2002. Midway through his term, in 2004, his supporters tried to amend the constitution to allow for his reelection, and the battle over how the Liberal Party would choose its nominee was already heating up—with Serpa still championing traditional *party insider* processes and positions.

In sum, legal variables, such as majority runoff rules or privately printed ballots and nonconcurrent elections, have played a role in the dynamics among candidate types. More important, the inability especially in the Liberal Party, to institutionalize a single set of candidate selection procedures has meant that candidates of various types have fought with one another to impose their preferred processes on the party. This oscillation of party processes makes rational forecasting by precandidates with diverse career paths and sources of strength difficult, if not impossible. The persistent flip-flopping of party structures may lead to a lack of certainty on the part of possible candidates, but that uncertainty is a double-edged sword: current winners cannot use institutionalized party processes to insulate themselves from challengers and current losers are never fully convinced that the institutional "deck" is

---

1. See Consejo Nacional Electoral, Resolución 0091 (February 2001).

permanently stacked against them. As a result, likely losers in the candidate selection process always have the option to opt out for the *free-wheeling independent* route but to later return (directly or indirectly) to regain control of party procedures.

Candidate Type and Bases of Electoral Support

The internal dynamics within traditional parties show a struggle between identifiable factions, and these factions have distinct relationships to the party as an institution. That is, factions led by *insiders* and factions led by *adherents* value the party label differently. As our account of changes in candidate selection processes makes clear, this struggle has been less explicitly taken up by the Conservative Party. The PC has been divided around powerful leaders who have worried more about their dominance of the party than about redefining it vis-à-vis the electorate. The party has failed to incorporate the splinter movements that emerge as a challenge to the party leadership and the attempts to reform the party to broaden its appeal to voters are lost when the spin-off movements disappear after a couple of elections. The Liberals, by contrast, show an explicit schism between reformist and traditionalist factions and the party has been far more successful at incorporating dissidents. *Party adherents* who champion the reformist faction have been more concerned with defining national policy positions for their party and with bringing about social and political reforms. Reformists tried to respond to the changing political dynamics in the country during the 1960s, 1970s, and 1980s, catering to the urban electorates (with little success, in part because of the opposition of the traditionalist faction within their own party). As Archer and Shugart (1997) suggest, the urban constituents were more sophisticated than their rural counterparts in the sense that they had weaker partisan identification and were willing to vote on issues rather than on partisan cues. Conversely, *insiders* who represented the traditionalist faction were more attached to the rural constituents and therefore to personal exchanges of favors for votes. In contrast to the PC, the rivalry between reformists and traditionalist in the PL was not as harmful for the party because *adherents* were occasionally successful in imposing relatively participatory candidate selection processes and thus achieving the party's nomination. The ability to modify candidate selection processes served as a pressure valve of sorts and kept unhappy factions from deserting the party entirely (the incorporation of spin-off movements such as López's Revolutionary Liberal Movement [Movimiento Revolucionario Liberal, or MRL] and Galán's New Liberalism [Nuevo Liberalismo], for example).

If it is the case that the struggles between *insider* and *adherent* precandidates entail differences in the grounds on which candidates appeal for votes, then campaign styles should lead to differences in the geographical support that candidates receive. The argument suggests that PL *insiders* have more clientelistic campaign styles, which should be reflected in strong electoral support in rural areas.

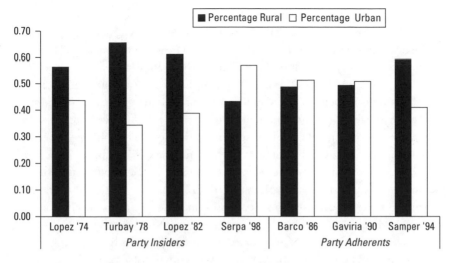

FIGURE 11.1 Colombian *Party Insiders'* and *Party Adherents'* Bases of Support.

Source: Author's compilation from data obtained from the Registraduriá Nacional del Estado Civil.

Adherents should be stronger in urban centers. For the PC, our argument implies that the geographical patterns of support should remain stable and mostly rural. Support for candidates breaking from the PC to run under separate labels, by contrast, will seek broader constituencies, and thus show a more urban focus.

The increasing pressure on *insiders* from *adherents* has taken place in the context of increasing urbanization—thus, within the Liberal Party, demographic trends should be on the side of *adherents*. We defined as urban the votes cast in municipalities where the total number of votes cast was greater than 20,000. The Conservative Party exhibits a marked reliance on rural votes. Not once between 1974 and 2002 did the PC's rural vote percentage dip below the national percentage of rural votes.[2] The share of the PC vote from rural municipalities was smaller than 55 percent on only two occasions—both times for *adherents*, not *insiders*: 54 percent of Lloreda's support in 1990 was from rural municipalities and 46 percent of Pastrana's support in 1998 came from rural municipalities.

The geographic patterns of support for the PL vary considerably from one election to the next and reflect whether an *insider* or *adherent* secured the presidential nomination at a given time. On average, *party adherent* candidates such as Barco, Gaviria, and Samper, who are typically closer to the reformist faction of the party (Samper is an exception) get relatively more (48 percent) of their votes from urban municipalities than *insider* candidates such as López, Julio César Turbay, and Serpa, who are closer to the traditionalist camp (43 percent). Figure 11.1 plots the rural–urban breakdown of the vote for these candidates, by election.

2. We performed comparisons of proportions of rural votes obtained by the parties with the national proportion of rural votes. All differences are statistically significant at conventional levels.

The first three elections shown in Figure 11.1—1974, 1978, 1982—show the predicted pattern of support. The party fielded *insiders* as candidates and their machineries produced electoral support in rural areas predominantly. The 1982 election is interesting as well because of the participation of a *free-wheeling independent* in the dispute over the presidency. Galán defected from the PL ranks, created his own movement, and launched his presidential campaign on an anti-corruption platform. He lost miserably, garnering a little over 700,000 votes. Regardless of how small his base of support, it was overwhelmingly—nearly 75 percent—urban. Had Galán's supporters voted for the *insider* Liberal, López, the latter would have overtaken the *adherent* Conservative, Betancur, and won the election. Losses like this may explain why the Liberal Party has been more flexible in the struggle over selection processes and the prospects of choosing an *adherent* candidate.

The elections of 1986 and 1990 drive home the different bases of support by candidate type. The PL ran two reformists consecutively, Barco and Gaviria, both of whom obtained a greater share of their support from urban rather than rural municipalities. In the same two elections, the PC ran two *party insiders*, Gómez and Lloreda, both of whom obtained a greater share of their votes from rural municipalities. Interestingly, Gómez ran again in 1990, but this time as a *free-wheeling independent* with his own party, the National Salvation Movement (Movimiento de Salvación Nacional, or MSN). As an independent Gómez was able to appeal to more urban voters and he finished second in the election, behind the winning Liberal *adherent*, Gaviria.

In 1994 *adherents* were nominated by both parties, the Liberals' Samper and the Conservatives' Pastrana. As hypothesized, the support for Pastrana was predominantly rural—something quite remarkable considering that the majority of the population by then already lived in urban centers. Surprisingly, given our hypotheses and the patterns just described, the Liberal Samper, who won, also had a relatively more rural base than we would have expected for a Liberal *adherent*. The 1998 election also showed some puzzling results. The Samper administration suffered a severe crisis because of its links to illegal drug money that lasted almost the entire presidential term. The generalized dissatisfaction with the president and Congress (which exonerated Samper, despite incriminating evidence) may have led citizens to realize the importance of taking part in the political process. In the run-up to the 1998 election, levels of participation were more than twice those of four years earlier, and more than 8 million people voted in the presidential election, 5 million in urban areas. With such an elevated participation rate, it is not surprising to see both candidates amassing a majority of their votes in cities rather than in the countryside.

This cursory analysis of electoral data reveals interesting variations in the patterns of support that the traditional parties obtain. Traditionalist candidates of both parties, embodied mostly by *party insiders*, tend to get most of their support in rural areas. Reformist candidates, better characterized by *party adherents*, tend to obtain their support mainly in large cities. Furthermore, reformists seem to put a premium on their political agendas even if that means defecting from the party, as Gómez and Pastrana did with the PC, and Galán with the PL.

Candidate Type and Presidential Behavior

Three of the candidate types identified by Siavelis and Morgenstern have won the Colombian presidency: *party insiders*, *party adherents*, and *free-wheeling independents*. Does it make any difference for how the country is governed? Given the novelty of the executive political recruitment project, there is very little literature from which to glean formal hypotheses. Efforts to test hypotheses will always be made difficult by the relatively small numbers with which we are working and the difficulty of constructing measures of behavior that can be meaningfully applied across countries (and national cases). Our intuition was that candidate type (career path, selection procedures, and base of electoral support) should continue to affect a president's relations with members of his own party and with members of other parties even after he takes office. In general, we know that *party insiders* are confident in their standing within their own parties. Will this give them the leeway to seek the cooperation of others or does it mean that they will remain dependent on their traditional base of support? *Adherents*, on the other hand, have relatively tenuous relations with the traditional power base of their parties. Does this mean that in order to govern they will need to shore up relations with their own parties or does it mean that they will be forced to look for support elsewhere? Finally, *free-wheeling independents* have already shown their desire to distinguish themselves from traditional parties, but how does one govern without their support? Do *FWIs* surround themselves with other independents and hope to "go it alone"—perhaps through extraconstitutional means or by intimidating others with their personal popularity?

The confidence we can have in our answers to these questions will, as noted above, always be limited by the few administrations on which our observations are based. With eight presidents chosen since the end of the formal agreement to restrict participation and alternate control over the office (the National Front) in 1974, Colombia provides one of the longest uninterrupted time series of democratic governance in Latin America. But, even if eight administrations is a relatively large number, we are still hampered by the lack of comparable data for the entire period. First we look at the partisan composition of cabinets. We are fortunate to have data beginning in 1974 with the Liberal administration of López. Our data set currently ends in 2000 midway through the "suprapartisan/Conservative Gran Alianza" administration of Andrés Pastrana. We also examine bill initiation patterns, but there are no data before 1986, so we examine data beginning

TABLE 11.2 Partisan Composition of Colombian Cabinets, by Presidential Candidate Type: 1974–2000

Candidate Type	Copartisans	Primary Opposition	Other Partisans	Independents	Others	Total
Party insiders	50.00	46.67	0.00	0.00	3.33	60
Party adherents	65.53	24.27	2.91	3.88	3.40	206
Party insiders With majority support[a]	50.00	46.67	0.00	0.00	3.33	60
Party adherents With majority support	74.81	13.74	4.58	3.82	3.05	131

Source: Author's calculations.

a. In another instance of the problem of a small number of cases, we have no cases of a *party insider* president facing a congress where his copartisans are not in the majority.

with the Liberal administration of Virgilio Barco (1986–1990) and ending approximately midway through the independent first administration of Álvaro Uribe (2002–2006). With these caveats in order (and more to come), let us look at differences in political behavior across presidential administrations.

First we examine the composition of presidential cabinets. Constitutionally, Colombian presidents have the right to appoint and dismiss members of their cabinets at will. When a president has the opportunity to select a minister, does he choose a copartisan, a member of the primary opposition party, a member of some third party, or an independent? The choice of whom to appoint is important for several reasons. First, the choice of a minister can signal a president's desire to reach out to parties in the legislature. The appointment of a member of the opposition signals a desire to gain that party's support for the president's legislative agenda. The appointment of an independent signals that the president desires to keep his agenda above the traditional political fray or at least to avoid offending one partisan bloc or the other. Second, it can signal the policy direction of the administration, at least vaguely, given the marginal role that ideology plays in Colombian parties. For example, a Liberal president who appoints only Liberal ministers is likely to adopt policy further to the left of center than a Liberal president whose administration contains a large proportion of ministers from the Conservative Party. Ministers can directly submit bills for legislative consideration.

Looking at cabinets between 1974 and 2000, we present data on the percentage of appointments made by presidents of different candidate types.[3] As the figures in Table 11.2 indicate, perhaps contrary to expectations, *party adherents* work very hard to signal their faithfulness to the party, whereas *insiders* appear

3. The analysis examines all cabinet appointments for the years in question.

TABLE 11.3 Bill Initiation Patterns in Colombia, by Presidential Candidate Type: 1986–2004

Percentage of Bills Initiated . . .	During the Administrations of *Party Adherents*	During the Administrations of *Free-Wheeling Independents*
Only by members of the legislature	79.96	84.81
Only by members of the executive	17.61	15.19
Jointly by members of the executive and legislature	1.57	0.00
All others	0.86	1.58

Source: Gaceta del Congreso.

NOTE: Again, we stress caution, given the small number of observations for the *free-wheeling independent* category and the complete lack of observations in the *party insider* category.

freer to reach out to members of the opposition.[4] This difference is magnified when we control for partisan support in congress. *Party adherents* whose party holds a legislative majority are particularly like to appoint copartisan ministers. If they can shore up the support of their own party, they will have the numbers necessary to implement their programs.

Party insiders have the luxury of being able to reach out to the opposition. They are relatively assured of the support of their copartisans in Congress, because of their central role in the party leadership—and they can pick up additional support in Congress by naming members of the opposition. As a result, they use their solid power base in their own party as an anchor while co-opting the opposition, making it jointly responsible for the government's program. *Adherents*, with their more tenuous hold on their own party, may fear that success in reaching out to the opposition would be offset from defections by the more traditional sectors of their own party.

When we look at bill initiation patterns, again, they may indicate that candidate type has a small effect on which branch initiates legislation (see Table 11.3). Legislators apparently feel that bills initiated by an independent president less accurately

4. Early presidents, *insiders* and *adherents* alike, were "bound" by the 1968 Lleras reform to offer positions in their cabinets to members of the opposition. The reform initiated a process of dismantling the National Front but preserved some elements of the original agreement and extended others. In particular, it stated that most administrative positions, including ministries, governors, and mayors, were to be divided equally between the PL and the PC until 1978. This agreement was still honored in the Turbay and Betancur administrations, although at that point it was not a formal, constitutional, requirement (Martz 1997). This agreement undoubtedly plays a part in our finding that *insiders* named relatively few copartisans to their cabinets. But it is hard to know how much weight to give this agreement and how much weight to give to candidate type: the agreement was honored by *insiders* from both parties but broke down the first time an *adherent* was elected to the presidency.

reflect their own agendas. The proportion of bills initiated only by members of the legislature is almost 5 percent higher during *free-wheeling independent* administrations than during *party adherent* administrations. What the percentages in the table do not reveal is that the number of bills initiated—by both the executive and the legislature—has jumped dramatically during the administration of a *free-wheeling independent*, Uribe. If trends hold in the Uribe administration, legislators will initiate something approaching 1,400 bills, or 20 percent more than under any other previous administration. Concomitantly, the cosponsorship of legislation by members of the executive branch and members of the legislative branch dropped from infrequent to never. Only under the Pastrana administration, which had minority support in Congress, was cross-branch cosponsorship nonexistent while in some administrations it reached as high as fifty bills. Thus, the distance between *free-wheeling independents* and legislators resulting from their paths to office seems to carry into the process of governing.[5]

Unlike bill initiation data, bill passage rates are dramatically distinguishable from one another across presidential candidate types. The *free-wheeling independent* administration of Álvaro Uribe started its second consecutive term in 2006, and we had only collected data up to 2004, a little more than the middle point of his first term in office. At that point, the vast majority of bills initiated were still pending a final outcome. However, the very preliminary evidence regarding which bills actually become law profoundly contradicts the expanding gap in initiation rates and previous relative rates of bill approval. Legislators initiated far more bills than members of the executive branch in every administration and this gap was slightly exaggerated when the president was a *FWI*. In terms of passage rates, during *party adherent* administrations, bills initiated by members of the legislature led to between 43 percent and 50 percent of the laws adopted. The success rate of *party adherent* presidents with and without majority copartisan support was equal in terms of bill adoption. However, two years into the *free-wheeling independent* administration of Álvaro Uribe, in 2004, only 24 percent of the bills that had been adopted as law were initiated solely by members of the legislature. In other words, the *free-wheeling independent* president had a relatively high percentage of his bills successfully navigate congressional shoals. His lack of partisan support was apparently more than compensated for by his popularity. If this is the explanation, interbranch relations may be particularly volatile during *free-wheeling independent* administrations. Independents may be able to use their personal popularity to persuade legislators to back their programs of government, but if they are unpopular, their lack of ties to either traditional party may lead to the stymying of their legislative agendas.

In sum, candidate type helps predict behavior in office. *Adherents* appoint cabinet members from their own parties and fare equally well in bill adoption with

---

5. Our bill initiation data begin with the Barco administration, so we have no information on *party insider* administrations.

or without a copartisan majority. *Insiders* appointed relatively more members of the opposition to their cabinets, but we do not have data to determine the impact of this on bill initiation and adoption. Preliminary evidence indicates that independents picked other independents to staff their cabinets and fared very well in bill adoption—when they were popular.

Persistently Impermanent Party Procedures

During the National Front, when the two major parties agreed to alternate the presidency, all competition for the office was by definition intraparty. Once the party whose turn it was to occupy the presidency had made its official selection, the identity of the next president was a foregone conclusion. Alternation forced competition out of the general election stage and into the candidate selection stage. The finality of the candidate selection process meant party leaders worked very hard to contain conflict by remaining in control of candidate selection processes. It is the reintroduction of competition at the general election stage in 1974 that introduces variability into the candidate selection stage. Given that deciding on the nominee was no longer tantamount to selecting the president, the need of party leaders to control the candidate selection process and of disgruntled precandidates to remain a loyal member of one of the major parties to capture the office was diminished.

Internally institutionalized parties have the ability to adopt and maintain candidate selection (and other) processes that would homogenize their members by diminishing the prospects of candidates of any other type. Colombian parties have been unable to adopt such rules. The central tension driving the oscillation in internal processes seems to be the breakdown of clientelistic networks as a result of urbanization combined with the disjuncture between what it takes to be elected a member of Congress and what it takes to be elected president. When the country was largely rural, clientelistic networks were the unchallenged means of attaining both executive and legislative offices. As demographics changed, apportionment of legislative seats continued to favor relatively less populated areas and thus to promote the continued use of patron–client ties for winning a seat in Congress. Another option presented itself for presidential candidates. *Party adherents* and potential independents could appeal directly to urban voters, over the heads of *party insiders*. However, parties have never been able to settle on executive candidate selection procedures that would favor these candidates (and their urban supporters) because the parties are also competing for seats in the disproportionately rural legislative races. Rules for election to Congress serve to strengthen traditional *party insiders* and to generate precandidates, predominantly from the Chamber of Representatives, who want to maintain centralized procedures that favor their career ambitions.

The Conservative Party's resistance to pressure to oscillate in its selection procedures has led it to pick a single candidate type—*insiders*—who are generally weak contestants. Further, the decline in the party's competitiveness for the presidency may be hurting the party's prospects in the legislative races, to which, ironically, their internal procedures are designed to cater. By contrast, the variation in Liberal Party procedures has led to variation in that party's candidate types: *insider, adherents*, and even *adherents* turned *FWIs*. This variation has helped them to choose stronger candidates.

Demographic trends seem to be on the side of reformist *party adherents* or *FWIs*, and the inability of *adherents* to permanently reform their own parties may signal an increased likelihood of more Uribe-like *FWIs*.[6] The prospects of successful governance by such *FWIs* is still questionable. Since they cannot rely on a party's support as *insiders* can, they must either build coalitions or rely on their personal popularity to shepherd their bills through the legislature. Building coalitions by means of distributing cabinet posts is, however, difficult because these presidents have at best a strained relation with their former party and an oppositional relation with the other party. *Free-wheeling independents*, therefore, are left to rely on their personal popularity. Uribe's experience has shown that popular *free-wheeling independents* lead legislators of all stripes to flock to them. When they are unpopular, however, will those legislators scatter in multiple directions?

Appendix: Summarizing the Independent Process Variables

The independent process variables for Colombia, broken down into party and legal variables, are described and summarized below. Discussion of the variables follows the table.

Legal Variables

Rules for Plurality

> Two-round system for president
> Plurality for governors

Election Concurrence

> Congress: every four years in March
> President: every four years in May–June
> Governors: every three years in October

---

6. If *adherents* continue to be willing to remain in or rejoin traditional parties when they think they can control their internal procedures, the oscillation described in this analysis may continue without escalation.

Barriers to Independents

> Quite low

Reelection

> Reelection prohibited until 2003
> After 2003, a constitutional reform allowed for immediate reelection

Geographic organization

> Unitary

Party Variables

Inclusiveness

> No established norm; instead, a menu
>
> • Elite selection
> • National convention
> • Internal consultation (closed-party caucus)
> • Quasi-closed primary (factional success in congressional elections)
> • Popular consultation (national open primary)

Party Organization

> Ranging from formally bureaucratized to inchoate

Importance of Party ID

> High, but weakening over time

Party–Finance Connection

> Private–public mix (candidate-centric)

Discussion

Rules for plurality wins. From 1974 to 1991, the system was one of plurality winners. From 1991 to the present, the system has been a two-round absolute-majority system. Governors and mayors are still elected on a plurality system.

Election concurrence. Since 1978 the presidential and congressional elections have been separate, with congressional elections preceding presidential elections by approximately two months. Gubernatorial elections are on a three-year cycle and are held at the end of October.

Barriers to independents. According to Law 130 of 1994, all legally recognized parties have the right to control their labels and symbols, and to name candidates to office. Forming a new party or getting onto the ballot as an independent is not difficult, requiring getting signatures on petitions and putting up a small amount of money to prove financial capacity to run. On August 22, 2003, the National Registry published a document listing seventy-four parties, social movements, and candidate groups—an indication of the relative ease with which candidates can access the ballot.

Reelection. Under the 1886 constitution, consecutive (but not nonconsecutive) reelection was prohibited, and under the 1991 constitution presidents were limited to one term, but we see a pattern in which losers are often given a second bite at the apple. In the eight elections during the 1974–2002 period, two Liberals, López and Serpa, were nominated twice and three Conservatives ran twice: Álvaro Gómez—he ran a third time as a member of the National Salvation Movement— Betancur, and Pastrana.[7]

The constitutional prohibition against consecutive reelection of presidents was eliminated in 2003, which allowed Álvaro Uribe to successfully seek a second term in 2006.

Geographic organization. While Colombia is subdivided into thirty-two departments for administrative purposes, the state is unitary in nature. Historically this has produced candidates and presidents whose career paths were primarily constructed of central government experience. As noted above, decentralization policies, especially the popular election of governors and mayors, has opened a potential new route to political prominence. Both Pastrana (1998–2002) and Uribe (2002–2006, 2006–2010) held elected executive office at the local level prior to ascending to the presidency.

Inclusiveness. No legal requirements exist which dictate the selection process to be employed. Instead, a menu of options has evolved. The Liberals have frequently shifted the process from contest to contest, while the Conservatives have been more prone to conventions and elite selection.

Party organization. Using Scott Mainwaring and Timothy R. Scully's (1995, 5) measures of institutionalization, it is clear that Colombia's traditional parties should be considered well institutionalized, but as Archer (1995) notes, they have never been especially strong organizationally. As noted above, the processes used to choose candidates have often been the result of specific power negotiations in a given electoral cycle. Indeed, this has been increasingly true because the establishment of the new constitution in 1991 made it easier for new parties to form. Further, the quest to capture the presidency has been one of the few remaining glues that holds the institutional structure of the traditional parties together, and that has been eroding for some time—as exemplified by the Gómez break from the PC in 1990 with the formation of the National Salvation Movement, not to mention the pluripartisan campaigns of Betancur and Pastrana. The ultimate schism between the presidency and the traditional parties came in 2002 with the

7. López was also a candidate in 1962, under the Revolutionary Liberal Movement. When he ran in 1982 he was taking advantage of the fact that under the 1886 constitution a person could serve nonconsecutive terms.

election of Álvaro Uribe. Although he had once been a Liberal, he adopted his own label and defeated the Liberal Horacio Serpa in the election rather handily.[8] Thus, not only did Uribe defeat the PL, but the PC's candidate, Juan Camilo Restrepo, quit the race before the elections, and did not even appear on the ballot. The 2006 election continued to show the increasing inability of the traditional parties to dominate the electoral arena. Uribe ran again on an independent label and again won the election handily. The PC, for a second term in a row, declined to present a candidate of its own and instead, as decided by an overwhelming majority in a national party convention, supported Uribe's candidacy. The PL failed even to finish in the second place, which was taken by the relatively new left-of-center Alternative Democratic Pole (Polo Democrático Alternativo). This is the first time in recent history that the PL did not finish a presidential race as either victor or runner-up.

The lingering question, brought on by the PC's political anemia and the victory of Uribe, is how much longer the party system will last in its current incarnation. Further, the new political actors have demonstrated both bureaucratized behavior in terms of candidate selection (the PDA) and inchoate ones (such as displayed by Uribe).

Importance of party ID. There was a time when partisan identification was the be-all and end-all of Colombian politics, but the significance of the traditional parties has been waning in the last decade or so. A 1988 survey found that 52.7 percent of respondents thought that the quality of the political parties was "bad" and only 15.6 percent thought them "good"; a 1989 survey found that only 15.9 percent of the respondents had confidence in the parties (Dugas 2000, 94). Surveys in 1994 and 1995 found similar confidence levels, 22 percent and 16 percent, respectively (Pizarro 1997, 208). Both parties have continued to capture the lion's share of the vote—with the exception of Uribe in 2002—but since the early 1990s there has been steady evidence of the willingness of voters to go elsewhere.

Party-finance connection. Campaign finance in Colombia is a mix of public and private. Title IV of Law 130, passed in 1994, spells out the process. In presidential elections candidates are paid a sum for each valid vote they receive. This means that campaign finance is largely in the hands of individual candidates, who raise their own funds and also receive some recompense from the state after the election is over.

---

8. Uribe served as a council member and mayor of Medellín and senator and governor of Antioquia, all as a Liberal. He bested Serpa 5,862,655 to 3,514,779 votes in 2002.

Chapter Twelve

Political Recruitment, Governance, and Leadership
in Mexico: How Democracy Has Made a Difference

RODERIC AI CAMP

Mexico underwent a remarkable transformation in its political
model in 2000, with the electoral victory of the National
Action Party (Partido Acción Nacional, PAN), the
inauguration of President Vicente Fox, and the removal of a
political party and leadership that had governed Mexico for
some seven decades. To what extent has the democratic
transformation in the 1990s, and the introduction of electoral
democracy, affected the processes and outcome of political
recruitment and selection among state and national executive
leaders? Intuitively one might expect equally remarkable
transformations in leadership characteristics as both the political process and origins of that leadership were altered. On the
other hand, an equally compelling case might be made that
the degree to which those processes had become ingrained
since the 1920s would make it difficult to modify recruitment
and selection patterns in a short period of time.

Regardless of the failures of Fox to address numerous
policy issues, his administration produced influential consequences for numerous aspects of political recruitment and
selection. Within months of his election, alterations in political
structures and behavior began to occur in response to the
emergence of different leadership from competitive elections.
Democracy functioned as an independent variable in producing new types of leaders who achieved electoral success. At the
same time, the background characteristics of these new leaders
also produced policy consequences, highlighting the importance of recruitment processes functioning as independent variables, as Siavelis and Morgenstern argue in Chapter 1 of this
volume.

The impact of electoral democracy and specifically Fox's
administration on political recruitment and selection can only be
understood in broad terms if we understand why Mexicans actually voted for Mr. Fox, and what they appeared to expect from

his leadership. We cannot divine his own leadership selections if we do not assume a connection between those selections and Fox's perceptions of citizen policy concerns, as well as similar linkages that have occurred at the state level among gubernatorial candidates.

A comprehensive panel survey, repeated among the same random group of voters, sponsored by a National Science Foundation grant led by Chappell Lawson, captures citizen views in 2000 (Lawson 2003). This study is valuable because it provides insights as to how Mexicans viewed the leading presidential candidates over time, particularly the leadership qualities of the two leading contenders, Francisco Labastida from the incumbent Institutional Revolutionary Party (Partido Revolucionario Institucional, or PRI) and the National Action Party's Vicente Fox.

Why did Mexicans vote for Vicente Fox, who were those Mexican voters, and what were they seeking in a leader? The fundamental issues that were of greatest concern to the Mexican voter were personal security, the economy, and poverty. It is ironic, therefore, that of the voters who said they voted for a candidate because they thought he could solve these problems, only 22 percent based their choice on their candidate's actual policy proposals. So voters did not choose Fox because he offered specific policy solutions. Of all the reasons given for voting for a particular candidate, by far the leading reason was change (Camp 2003, 25–41). Forty-three percent of Mexican voters listed change as their number one reason for voting for Fox.

Among the voters who considered change the most important issue, about 66 percent voted for Fox and only 15 percent for the PRI's candidate. By contrast, of those Mexicans who voted for a candidate based on personal qualities, only 9 percent of all voters, half voted for Labastida, the PRI candidate, compared to 28 percent for Fox. These figures clearly suggest that voters were not choosing specific leadership qualities such as experience, skill, integrity, but were choosing someone who represented characteristics consistent with changing the political model of 2000. Fox was perceived as someone outside the traditional party system. He clearly fits Siavelis and Morgenstern's label of a *party adherent*, in sharp contrast to Labastida, who is the perfect embodiment of a *party insider*. Analysts have long pointed to PAN's restricted membership, and the obstacles the party has placed in the way of expanding membership. The original leadership hoped to keep the party ideology consistent by relying on a small, homogeneous membership. This attitude contradicts a political party's mission in a highly competitive process. In 2001, the party returned to a more restrictive candidate selection process, limiting voting in primary elections to active members only. This is exacerbating differences between the PAN rank and file and the leadership, because new members more sympathetic to the *neopanistas,* such as Vicente Fox, are slow to be accepted into the active party ranks (Mizrahi 2003, 56–57). Ironically, Labastida actually won the nomination in an open primary. But the party was in the throes of internal divisions and transformation, and his candidacy was viewed by many as having the support of President Ernesto Zedillo, who nevertheless neither participated in the process nor publicly advocated any of the candidates. All of the potential leading PRI presidential candidates, however, were examples of *party insiders*. Fox brought different personal qualities to the forefront as president, qualities that were atypical of his executive-branch predecessors in the presidency, the cabinet, and state governorships.

Mexico presents a fascinating example of a political transformation from a semiauthoritarian to a democratic model, in which democracy is wrapped up perceptually as change in the minds of the voters. Thus a democratic political model, defined as political change, produced the presidential victory of Vicente Fox, who qualitatively also represented leadership characteristics that were atypical. Numerous voters equated change and democracy as one and the same, and they contributed significantly to Fox's recruitment, his selection as his party's presidential candidate, and his election to the presidency.

Fox and his cabinet choices represent a significant change in certain respects from past Mexican politicians, but this change by no means was intentional. In other words, voters did not identify any personal or professional qualities specifically as important to their decision. Most of the characteristics that affected executive-branch recruitment were a reflection of Fox's career experiences. The argument can be made, however, that Fox's *adherent* status, with no ties to the incumbent party or federal government, and few ties to his own National Action Party, guaranteed that he would bring associated leadership qualities not found among the pre-2000 *priístas* and, to a lesser extent, *panistas*. Yet Fox would never have been recruited and selected as the PAN candidate, and his achieving the presidency would have been even less likely, if the presidential campaign had not focused on changing the political model, which he personified in the minds of many voters. Furthermore, a case can be made that Fox's popularity with the voters encouraged him, when proposing major policy reforms, to reinforce his personal connection to voters after taking office instead of focusing on the necessary details of executive–legislative relations, resulting in significant administration failures, a variable raised by Siavelis and Morgenstern's analysis of U.S. executive–legislative relations.

Changes in political recruitment in the recent past, of which the most notable was a shift from the generalist to the technocrat in the 1980s and 1990s, were definitive, intentional changes made by Mexico's leading executive-branch politicians, changes reflected in significant leadership qualities and policy preferences. The introduction and dominance of an economically trained elite, which contributed to the internal political transformation toward a democratic model, clearly illustrated this shift (Camp 1997). In Mexico, democratization did not produce technocratic leadership or democracy, nor were most technocrats actively promoting democracy. Nevertheless, their opening of the economy to outside influences did generate other pressures favoring a democratic transformation. These earlier recruitment patterns were not, of course, a reflection of citizen preferences expressed in the electoral process, but were largely determined by an elite-controlled candidate selection process.

A second variable that played an important role in the 2000 election was the predominance of urban voters, who constituted 70 percent of the electorate; nearly half of them supported Fox. The other distinguishing feature of Fox voters was their youth; many were first-time voters. Sixty percent of all the voters were under thirty-nine, and Fox received nearly half of their votes. Urban and younger voters are among the best educated in Mexico. This best-educated group, too, supported Fox. Of the voters with a high school or better education—representing 58 percent of the electorate—more than half also voted for him.

The age of the voter is significant because it can be linked to the age of Mexican leadership in 2000. The most astounding figures illustrating this point can be found in the makeup of the 2000–2003 Congress, where a comparison of PAN with PRI deputies reveals that 70 percent of the *priístas* were *over* forty-nine and 70 percent of the *panistas* were *under* forty-nine. This suggests a significant generational difference, which I would argue was translated into policy preferences and explains in part the stalemate in Congress. The congressional delegations from these two parties represent entirely different generations. Further exploration of the composition of these legislative groupings in greater detail is likely to reveal substantial differences, many of which can be explained by the collective age of the politicians in each group.

The age of the voters may also determine the age of future politicians, thus introducing a structural component in the selection and recruitment process. In other words, parties, may purposely select younger candidates so as to appeal to younger voters, as PRI did in 2003. In so doing they automatically altered some of their legislative representatives' characteristics, which not only differ from their older counterparts within the party, especially plurinominal deputies (those chosen from party lists rather than in single-member districts), but who may actually share more in common with similar age cohorts from the National Action Party than with their own older PRI colleagues.[1]

Having offered these brief observations about why Mexican citizens were voting for Fox, let us explore what he accomplished in relation to the overriding reason for his election, change, and, if possible, explore links to executive-

1. Mexico is represented by two types of deputies in the federal congress, three hundred elected from single-member districts and two hundred from party lists. The latter, called plurinomial deputies, are designated by party leadership, are often older, well-established political figures with strong ties to the party organization, and therefore do not share the characteristics of deputies who have fought heated electoral contests, regardless of the party. This is a structural characteristic that produces a significant divide in legislative recruitment and candidate selection.

branch recruitment and selection. His accomplishments through 2005 can be measured in three steps: the immediate impact of his election as a preeminent test of democracy, his taking office, and the selection of his ministers and other executives.

A Democratic Election and Expectations of an Altered Leadership

Of the three steps, Fox's election has, perhaps, had the most significant long-term consequences. Why? First, the removal of the incumbent party from control over the federal executive branch automatically set in motion a plethora of consequences for leadership recruitment and selection, resulting from President Fox's own career background in the private sector, his status as an outsider in his own party, and the specific leadership qualities of prominent *panistas*. Second, prior to the election, most Mexicans continued to believe that their country was not a democracy. Immediately after the election, 63 percent stated that they believed Mexico was a democracy.

What are the implications of voter perceptions of electoral democracy? The congressional elections in 2003 provide an answer to this question. Significantly, 54 percent of the voters who voted for Fox in 2000 were dissatisfied with democracy in 2003. Fewer voters believed in the possibility of radical change, or believed that change was the answer to Mexico's problems. The view that Fox's policy failures were associated with his outsider status helped the *panista insider* Felipe Calderón win the nomination in 2006.

Presidential Selection and Political Recruitment

The second way we can measure Fox's impact on the democratic transformation is through his taking office and in his choice of government colleagues. These choices presage a much broader impact on recruitment and selection in the executive branch because they go beyond the voters' choice of one individual, even though the president is responsible for the cabinet makeup, and indirectly the top executive branch leaders. In Fox's case, his personal influence on his initial cabinet selections may well have been moderated by his reliance, in some cases, on using headhunters, rather than choosing candidates himself (Grayson 2003, 13).

I argue here that Mexico's democratic transformation led to numerous changes in recruitment and selection processes, thus democracy became the independent variable affecting these processes. It did so because competitive pluralism emphasizes skills different from those found in a modified one-party system. President Fox's victory was a product of those very changes, yet Fox himself complemented the alterations wrought by electoral democracy by emphasizing different facets of political recruitment and by selecting as his ministers and advisers national executives with different credentials from past office holders, but often similar to his own. Thus, it can be argued that democracy as a causal variable produced changes in recruitment that in turn, also as a causal variable, produced changes in leaders. It is the democratic setting and a new president, as well as their interactions, that recharacterize the recruitment and selection processes. The altered recruitment process led to changes in leadership selection criteria, too.

There are two broad categories of political recruitment patterns, formal and informal. The formal credentialing process is much easier to identify and measure, and is critical to informal characteristics that mold the process. A detailed survey of top leaders in the executive branch reveals trends set in motion by Fox's victory, by his appointments, and by the democratic setting. Fox's outsider status, atypical of the pattern followed by *panistas* throughout the national-party leadership, responded to a set of specific political circumstances in Mexico and to PAN's unusually narrow partisan base. Therefore Fox's outsider status, while definitely affecting some of his choices, did not replicate itself among any contenders for the presidency in 2006.

PRI's candidate in 2000, Francisco Labastida, had emerged as the winner of an open primary in 1999. The PRI is the first and only party as of 2006 to have held an open presidential primary. The PRI also used statewide primaries to select its gubernatorial candidates until 2003, when it replaced this procedure at the state level with a convention of party delegates. The party replaced the open primary because it was costly, and it also allowed losing primary candidates to obtain recognition, declare the elections to be fraudulent, and then leave the party and become a candidate from one of the other parties. Such splits occurred in Baja California del Sur, Tlaxcala, and Zacatecas. The PRI returned to the convention method of allowing party *delegates* to select its presidential candidate in 2006, which favored the candidacy of a *party insider*, Roberto Madrazo, the party president (Varela 2004, 221).

In contrast, Fox in 2000 was selected through a closed, democratic ballot among PAN delegates, a long-established party tradition. After 2000, however, at the state level, PAN actually moved away from party delegates electing its candidates, instead allowing a larger pool of party activists to participate in the selection process. In 2006 it chose a similar method for its presidential candidate, allowing party activists in regional elections to select PAN's presidential candidate. They chose a *party insider*, Felipe Calderón, the party's former president, in a surprise victory over Fox's choice, who had been favored.

In 2000, the Party of the Democratic Revolution's (Partido de la Revolución Democrática, or PRD) candidate, Cuauhtémoc Cárdenas, was self-imposed, as he had been in 1994. The PRD's nominee in 2006 was the elected head of the Federal District (Mexico City), Manuel Andrés López Obrador, also a former party president. But the PRD has developed no clear process for selecting its candidates at the state level, typically relying on a decision by delegate conventions combined with national or state leadership. In fact, it often takes advantage of splits in the PRI, and nominates the losing contender as its own candidate. The PRD won six gubernatorial races in 2003 and 2004 relying on this unorthodox technique. It can be argued that these victories help to reinforce recruitment patterns that are more typical of PRI politicians, since these individuals are selected by the PRD typically after long public careers as *priístas*.

By the mid-1990s, most national politicians in Mexico came from upper-middle-class backgrounds, from urban settings, specifically Mexico City, and from public careers, especially in the national bureaucracy. They were highly educated, they increasingly were products of Mexico's leading secular private institutions of higher education, they often boasted graduate degrees, including a high percentage of Ph.D.s. Many had studied abroad, typically in the United States, and increasingly they were from technical fields, especially economics (Camp 1995, 99). Furthermore, they were disciples of similar individuals, career politicians who recruited them into national bureaucratic politics. This recruitment occurred through various channels, including kinship ties and shared career experiences, but education proved to be a major determinant of recruitment, accounting for more than six out of ten linkages.[2] Thus, it was no accident that most top members of Mexico's executive branch were college professors as well as politicians. Many of these traits played a crucial role in the selection process. Typically, their contacts at the highest levels of the national bureaucracy and in many cases their shared educational experiences in college led to their being selected for the cabinet. This in turn made them visible to the incumbent president as presidential material.

Electoral democracy, by allowing a candidate from another party to win the presidential race in 2000, instantly altered recruitment and selection processes. Fox shared few of the typical characteristics of his presidential predecessors or cabinet members. For decades, Mexican presidential leadership had been drawn from the incumbent president's cabinet, so the potential pool of successful contenders was small. It also established national bureaucratic politics as the place to be and the skill to learn. But the entrance of democracy through the door of the 2000 election changed that condition dramatically, opening up the pool of candidates: the three leading candidates were state governors, and only Labastida, the PRI candidate, had served in the cabinet. By changing the presidential candidate pool, Fox and Cárdenas,

---

2. The exact figures are educational institutions, 61 percent; career positions, 28 percent; family, 7 percent; social engagements, 2 percent; and civic organizations, 2 percent (Camp 2002, 43).

products of electoral pluralism, altered a long-established structural boundary that had given the federal bureaucracy and specific cabinet agencies a commanding role in the recruitment and selection of future presidents and cabinet members. In effect, democracy reduced the impact of traditionally important political institutions on recruitment and selection processes, and reinforced the influence of other institutions.

Will democratic pluralism continue to alter those processes? We cannot say with assurance whom President Calderón will select for top executive-branch positions, but given his close electoral victory and his need to incorporate figures from the two losing parties, especially the PRD, the pool from which executive leadership is drawn will continue to be diverse. Calderón served briefly in Fox's cabinet, but his primary career trajectory is electoral, and within the PAN party leadership he represents the traditional, non-Fox wing. Governors have become the most important pool for future national leadership selections, and democratic elections since 1997 have significantly altered their qualities too.

Fox's credentials can be distinguished from his predecessors' in numerous respects. First, he came from a provincial background. Nearly all of Fox's adult life was spent outside Mexico City, so that he not only was distant from the halls of political power but lacked links with elite governmental institutions and traditional paths through which he might have been recruited to politics. Fox lived and worked for much of his career in Guanajuato State. This experience highlighted his provincial credentials and, more important, for the first time in decades revived regionalism as a variable in explaining national political leadership.

Throughout the twentieth century, since the establishment of the PRI's antecedent, the National Revolutionary Party, in 1929, Mexican political leadership has sought to centralize decisionmaking and leadership in the hands of a federal bureaucracy. As the postrevolutionary elites' exclusive political control grew, the importance of the national bureaucracy became paramount. Proximity to the physical location of the governmental apparatus in Mexico City facilitated access to that bureaucracy in several ways. First, kinship or social connections to established political elites were much more likely to occur in Mexico City, where retired and active elites lived. Second, since many of these active elites taught in local public institutions—notably the National Autonomous University (Universidad Nacional Autónoma de México, or UNAM) and National Preparatory School (Escuela Nacional Preparatoria), and in later years the private Mexico Autonomous Institute of Technology (Instituto Tecnológico Autónomo de México, or ITAM)—attendance at these institutions often was tantamount to establishing a mentor–disciple relationship.[3] Third, individuals professing an interest in politics who resided

---

3. Ninety-six percent of Mexico's leading politicians in the three decades between 1970 and 2000 were mentored by members of Mexico's political power elite. Forty-five percent of mentors' contacts occurred in an educational setting, followed by 42 percent through a career post (Camp 2002, 23–24, 29).

in areas outside the capital were much more likely to enter politics through other institutional doorways, specifically elective positions on the state and local level, eventually allowing them entrance to national politics through Congress.

What democratic elections have accomplished in Mexico is to place a greater emphasis on the third of these patterns, and its characteristics are likely to continue (note Calderón's career). Fox illustrates this pattern personally as did his cabinet. He was not a member of PAN until 1988, just twelve years before becoming president. That same year he became a victorious PAN candidate for Congress from his home state, Guanajuato. Encouraged by the relative opening up of electoral politics, Fox obtained his party's nomination as a gubernatorial candidate in 1991. He lost in a decidedly fraudulent election, after which he ran a second time, six years later, and won overwhelmingly. He used his Guanajuato political base to achieve national prominence and to make his race for the PAN presidential nomination in 2000. What is important is that both of his prior positions originated in Guanajuato, not the capital.[4]

Equally important, the only way to achieve a national office from a provincial background is to obtain a nomination for elective office, representing your home state in the Chamber of Deputies or the Senate. Successful governors also have found themselves recruited to cabinet posts by various presidents. Regardless, to achieve adequate recognition without the Mexico City connection, one typically must have served in elective office, either in the national legislative branch or as governor. Thus, because democratization has decreased geographic centralization, it has increased the number of prominent national executives with backgrounds incorporating elective careers.

This pattern can be seen in the fact that a third of Fox's cabinet members had held elective office, many of them as governors and mayors, and several of them as members of Congress. Of his four new appointees in 2004, two were governors and the other two had run unsuccessfully for the state house. Several cabinet figures, such as Felipe Calderón, a *party insider*, can be viewed as influential former members of Congress. Calderón twice served in the Chamber of Deputies and coordinated the PAN delegation in the 2000–2003 Congress. The numbers with legislative experience in the Fox cabinet represent a significant increase over the cabinets of President Miguel de la Madrid (1982–1988) and President Carlos Salinas (1988–1994), where only 5 and 20 percent, respectively, had been members of Congress (Camp 1995, 140). More telling, among all executive-branch leaders under de la Madrid and Salinas, only 5 and 2 percent, respectively, had held local political office. Zedillo (1994–2000) maintained the presence of executive-branch leaders with elective political experience at the level of his predecessor (see Table 12.1), but Fox increased that by 39 percent. Experience in elective office is becoming a more common route to positions in

4. Calderón also started his electoral career in 1988, as a member of the local assembly in the Federal District of Mexico City. But unlike Fox, he had already had held several national posts in PAN.

the national executives, and competitive elections are likely to increase the value of this experience in the next administration.

The geographic anomaly in presidential leadership that Fox represents, after seven decades of the country's moving in the opposing direction, from 1929–2000, reflects a historic pattern common to the governing elite in the 1940s through the 1960s, during which large numbers of leading national politicians still pursued careers more similar to that of Fox, establishing their reputations locally. All of Mexico's presidents through 1970 had state or local political experience. Fox's election, and the competitive electoral setting that made it possible, has encouraged a return to political credentials characteristic of this earlier era.

Fox, however, introduces a different version of the traditional PRI regional politician, and this difference is crucial. Not only is he an outsider by virtue of his regional credentials, but he is truly an outsider for not having been a professional politician. Most successful national politicians prior to 2000 spent fifteen years or more in the government. Fox was a Johnny-come-lately to politics, having spent his entire career in the private sector before becoming a congressman. His personal experiences, his social world, his institutional culture, and his political attitudes and values could be expected to be different from those of a professional politician, regardless of his party label.

One of the truly dramatic differences between Fox's and Zedillo's advisers and cabinet members, one that has the potential for altering politics' institutional culture, is that only one-third of Fox's cabinet pursued careers in government service, as compared to every member of the preceding cabinet (see Table 12.1). Three of four new appointees in 2004 also had pursued careers in the private sector. The lack of public-sector experience in the Fox cabinet is notable, and in the opinion of many analysts helps to explain his disappointing failures in the policymaking process and in his poor relations with Congress.

TABLE 12.1 Significant Differences in Background Characteristics of Vicente Fox's and Ernesto Zedillo's Cabinets (Number of Officials and Percentage Change)

General Characteristic	Zedillo Cabinet	Fox Cabinet	Percentage Change
University attended			
Private	18	44	+144
Graduate work			
Mexico only	18	33	+83
Career			
Private sector	0	68	
Public sector	100	32	−68
Electoral experience			
Elective office	23	32	+39

Source: Roderic Ai Camp, *Politics in Mexico: The Democratic Transformation* (New York: Oxford University Press, 2003), 112, and a complete sample of Fox's twenty-eight cabinet members and chiefs of staff from 2000 to April 2004.

Another distinctive quality that Fox brought to Mexican national leadership is that he is a product of the private sector, not of politics. Fox joined Coca-Cola of Mexico immediately following his graduation from Ibero-American University, in Mexico City in 1965, and left the company as its CEO in 1979, to manage his own frozen-foods export firm. He became the first president of Mexico since 1929 to have emerged from the private sector. Indeed, only one other cabinet member could claim his level of managerial experience before 2000. Among Fox's own cabinet, two-thirds had pursued careers in the private sector, as businessmen or professionals (see Table 12.1).

These altered patterns reflected in the president's background signify a dramatic change in regional focus and career orientation and an end to the technocrats' dominance at the cabinet level. Only two of Fox's original cabinet-level ministers—one was his treasury secretary—could be described as orthodox technocrats, and only four had pursued national bureaucratic careers typical of the technocrats in prior administrations.

Consequences of Political Recruitment in a Democratic Transformation

Political recruitment may operate as an independent variable in explaining other influential patterns. Fox's appointments have introduced several significant features that I believe have long-term implications for governance and political leadership in Mexico. Those qualities are a reflection of Fox's own leadership preferences in the narrow sense, but, equally important, they reflect the pluralistic setting that made possible his victory. What are those patterns and what consequences might they generate for the political model and recruitment and selection?

One of the noteworthy differences between the Fox government and its predecessors is the overt and increased collaboration with the private sector, represented by prominent career managers from the private sector taking over major portfolios in his administration. As Mizrahi (2003) has shown at the state level, "Where entrepreneurs have run as party candidates and won elections, they have had a decisive influence in the integration of their cabinets. Usually first-level positions in PANista administrations (secretaries and deputy secretaries) have been held either by businessmen who worked closely with the candidate during the campaign or by professionals who do not necessarily belong to the PAN" (94).

The same pattern can be found at the national level. This was the first time since 1946 that individuals from Mexico's capitalist elite influenced an administration directly, and that a CEO from a top company served in the cabinet.[5] Forty percent of the cabinet members in Fox's administration owned their own firms or held high-level management posts prior to their appointments. Fox relied equally heavily on prominent entrepreneurial figures in his campaign, some of whom he knew from his career with Coca-Cola or his studies at Ibero-American University, a Jesuit higher-education institution where Fox studied business administration.[6] Fox stated publicly that he would apply what he learned at Coca-Cola to administering public institutions. If his colleagues from the private sector also attempted to introduce their entrepreneurial "institutional culture" to a public-sector setting, they might have initiated long-term consequences on the way government agencies make decisions. Fox's choices increased the importance of two new institutions in the selection process of prominent executive-branch leadership, the campaign itself and private-sector careers. The latter change was tempered by the fact that Fox eventually removed the two leading businessmen from his cabinet.

From a political perspective, Fox's initial cabinet appointments also legitimized the private sector's open role in politics. In effect, it made it acceptable for prominent businessmen to accept cabinet-level appointments or to run for elective office as governors or presidents. This pattern had been rare in Mexican politics, but the older pattern began to break down in the 1990s, as some individual businessmen began to risk their own entrepreneurial activities to support PAN or to run for office (Mizrahi 1994).

The most influential institution promoting the legitimation of active business political interests is unquestionably the Mexican Association of Employers (Confederación Patronal de la República Mexicana, or Coparmex). Coparmex, unlike most business groups in Mexico, long encouraged its members to be interested in and informed about political and social issues, and to take an active role in their communities in promoting policies reflecting their knowledge (Camp 1986, 164). A recent history of the PAN confirms that one of the "key social institutions contributing to the rise of the *neopanistas*" was Coparmex (Ard 2003, 99). This linkage can be detected in our own data at the state level. It is not surprising, therefore, that of the thirty governors elected between 1997 and 2004, over half of the *panistas* about whom we have information were local or national leaders of Coparmex and other business organizations. In the cabinet, the figures are not nearly as dramatic; nevertheless, 16 percent led business organizations.[7] Most

---

5. Ernesto Martens Rebolledo served as the director general of Vitro, a company he joined in 1977. *Expansión*, June 10, 1992, 60.

6. For example, Fox resided at the Five Star Fiesta Americana in Mexico City from 1999 to 2000, courtesy of Gastón Azcárraga Andrade, leader of the Grupo Posadas and a member of one of Mexico's leading capitalist families (Martín 2001; Irene Rodríguez 2000).

7. http://www.cddhcu.gob.mx, Secretaria General, Secretaria de Servicios Parlamentarios, December 12, 2001.

significant is that Emilio Goicochea Luna, who as President of Concanaco, Mexico's Confederation of the National Chambers of Commerce (Confederación de Cámaras Nacionales de Comercio, Servicios, y Turismo), from 1983 to 1984 who advocated business involvement in politics, took over as Fox's chief of staff in the middle of his term, in 2004.[8] Fox himself also affirms that he first met his political mentor, Manuel Clouthier, the PAN presidential candidate, in 1988, when the latter was president of Coparmex (Gonzalez Ruiz 2001, 175).

Fox not only expanded the pool of future political elites by integrating people from the private sector and state and local government, but also brought in representatives of the international community, appointing as his first economic development secretary Luis Ernesto Derbez, a two-decade veteran of the World Bank, who then became secretary of foreign relations. Fox in a sense carried globalization to a new level. Instead of only appointing prominent figures who were educated in the United States or Europe, he incorporated individuals with extensive credentials in international bureaucracies. One could make the argument that democratization, as part of a global trend in the 1990s, introduced and emphasized the importance of international institutions, language, and culture and certified a new type of career credential as ideal for national executive leadership.

These fresh experiences, along with Fox's own career in a multinational corporate setting, raise an interesting issue. To what extent are such politicians products of international cultures, sharing institutional values and international vocabularies different from those of Mexicans who have spent most of their careers in domestic organizations? The global character of their experiences may well be more important than whether or not they emerge from private-sector backgrounds.[9]

Fox represents a third pattern distinct from those of his immediate predecessors in the presidency and in the executive branch. At the time of his presidential bid, Fox did not have a college degree. He completed his business administration studies in 1964, but never wrote a thesis—he allegedly completed it during the presidential campaign. Thus, although Fox technically could claim to hold a degree when he became president, in no way does he represent the highly educated pattern characterizing recent executive-branch figures. Both Salinas and Zedillo, and the majority of their cabinet appointees, had earned Ph.D.s.

The level of education per se is not the influential component of this credentialing process but, rather, the fact that academia played a significant role in the careers of former presidents and cabinet figures. Zedillo, who had received his doctorate in economics at Yale, could accurately be described as a budding

---

8. Emilio Goicochea Luna, author interview, Mexico City, August 24, 1983.

9. In fact, there is no question that it has affected the behavior of Mexican capitalists, including changing the actual corporate structure of their firms. See Thacker (2000, 99–100).

academic before he entered the Mexican economic bureaucracy. Many prominent figures from the 1990s, including Pedro Aspe, treasury secretary and architect of Salinas's neoliberal economic program, were university administrators and professors.[10] Academia exerted an important influence over recruitment and, later in their careers, selection processes, and of course was crucial to elite socialization. Fox, on the other hand, had had little contact with academia and the intellectual community.

The democratic setting, by opening up political competition from the grassroots upward, created a need for different skills than the incumbent semiauthoritarian system. The politicians boasting the new skills emphasized career backgrounds different from those of their predemocratic peers. Electoral democracy, in allowing Fox to win the presidency fairly, also influenced the recruitment and selection processes introduced by the new president. Presidents, in playing a decisive role in the designation of their cabinets, often choose individuals in their own image, valuing their own credentials highly.

The case can be made that a private university graduate such as Fox would introduce more diversity in the recruitment process, but in the long run such a shift will only increase the socioeconomic homogeneity of Mexican politicians. Restricting the pool of candidates for executive government posts to private universities means narrowing the field to members of the upper-middle class, eliminating an important source of working-class Mexicans among political leaders, public universities. Indeed, not a single member of Fox's cabinet is known to have come from the working class, and over a third came from wealthy families. This is an unexpected recruitment consequence of democracy.

Fox's educational patterns differed in two significant respects from those of his two immediate predecessors. First, Fox introduced the dominance of one of Mexico's most prestigious universities, an institution with long ties to PAN, the Escuela Libre de Derecho (Free School of Law). Three cabinet members were graduates of this small institution, as is the president elected in 2006, Calderón. Second, although national public institutions continue to be important sources of political leaders, a significant group of politicians are the products of provincial public institutions.

Another element of diversity introduced in recent years is the changing professional emphasis—as disciplinary interests change they have the potential for changing both the level and location of education. Traditionally, in Mexico as in the United States, law predominated as the most common academic background for university-educated politicians, but this fell from a high of 75 percent in 1910 to only 23 percent among Salinas's colleagues. Only three out of ten of Fox's

10. *Proceso*, August 31, 1992, 15.

cabinet members had law degrees, continuing a reduction in the centrality of legal training. For the first time among Mexican politicians, under Salinas the number of economics graduates equaled the number of law graduates, and graduates from disciplines other than law and economics formed the largest single group, accounting for half of all graduates among top government officials.

Another change in the educational backgrounds of Mexican politicians can be found in the advanced levels of education achieved. Typically, graduate education among Mexican cabinet members exceeds that of U.S. cabinet officers. The emphasis on graduate education began with President Luis Echeverría (1970–76), increased to nearly half under de la Madrid, and under Zedillo rose dramatically to seven out of ten. Under Fox, just slightly fewer collaborators, 64 percent, also completed graduate work. These figures are more important because of where the education is obtained, not necessarily their level.

The most dramatic educational change in the recruitment process is the globalization of education among not only politicians but all leadership groups in Mexico. Of the five most important groups—politicians, Catholic bishops, intellectuals, capitalists, and the officer corps—50 percent of those born since 1945 had studied in the United States and 20 percent in Europe. Indeed, only 28 percent of Mexico's influential leaders had studied only in Mexico. Even among older figures prominent since 1970, 53 percent studied abroad.

These remarkable statistics clearly establish beyond any doubt that the majority of Mexico's most recent leadership has been exposed to cultural influences from abroad. Among Fox's cabinet members, half studied abroad, 85 percent in the United States. Of those cabinet members who studied in the States, half studied economics.

The central issue of this leadership pattern is the extent to which foreign students are socialized by their experiences in U.S. classrooms.[11] On the basis of letters and interviews with numerous students and their former professors, I have concluded that the impact is substantial, although it varies considerably by elite profession and discipline studied. For example, many economists who became Mexico's leading decisionmakers in the 1980s and 1990s had picked up American graduate school views of macroeconomic policymaking and they encouraged Mexicans to pursue those policy strategies in their own country, beginning with President Salinas in 1989. Individuals well-versed in the language of international, Western economics controlled the three leading financial institutions in Mexico: the Federal Reserve, the Ministry of the Treasury, and the Ministry of Budget and Planning. Today, Treasury and the Banco de México continue to be controlled by the same group who emerged under the prominent economist Leopoldo Solís in the 1970s, providing continuity in economic policy for nearly twenty years.

11. For one of the few exceptions to the general dearth of work on this subject in Latin America see Montesinos and Markoff (2000, 48).

In short, numerous leadership groups, for different but complementary reasons, came away from their educational experiences abroad with a new approach to intellectual discussion and debate, and with fresh ideas about political and economic development, all of which contributed to elite-led change that ultimately produced the Fox presidential victory. These attitudes and interpretations, learned in educational environments, are both the cause of as well as a direct result of changing recruitment processes brought on by the democratic transformation and the victory of an opposition-party candidate. The recruitment process has reinforced the importance of these international educational experiences. Under the past three presidents—De la Madrid, Salinas, and Zedillo—international educational experiences also contributed to the selection process by bringing together individuals in U.S. graduate schools who would later appoint each other to influential political positions. Under Fox, this has not occurred, largely because such educational experiences are more dispersed than previously.

Finally, as I have argued elsewhere, the importance of teaching and the location of one's teaching career in the backgrounds of Mexican politicians have been crucial to initial political recruitment for more than a century, but this point continues to be ignored in the literature on elites. Theoretically, this may be the most important point. Most prominent figures in politics, and in all other leadership groups in Mexico, are the disciples of mentors, who themselves were equally prominent in a previous generation. These linkages are important to recruitment patterns, including the changing pattern of education.

The members of the first generation of politicians who studied in the United States were more likely to have been disciples of mentors who also had studied there. That can be seen most clearly among Mexico's technocrats. This issue needs to be addressed because most leaders in Mexico are mentored by other prominent elites, and those same elites often established their connection to their disciples through education. Equally important, they were responsible for the shift in patterns of education from public institutions to private institutions and from graduate study in Mexico to graduate study abroad at elite American colleges.

College professors play a critical role because they serve: as a stimulus for a career in public life, as a source of recruitment, often the most important source of initial political recruitment in Mexico, and as a means of forming or enhancing the teacher's own political group in politics and sometimes in cultural life. Under Fox, what is remarkable is that two individuals Jorge Castañeda and Santiago Levy Algazi, taught full-time at New York University and Boston University, respectively, and both received their undergraduate degrees from American colleges, thus extending this academic pattern abroad. Fox was also the first recent president who had not taught. Nevertheless, more than two-thirds of his collaborators had taught, and a fifth of them could be described as important educators, including even the secretary of national defense, who directed the armed forces' elite Colegio de Defensa Nacional.

Because mentors are crucial to the Mexican recruitment and selection process, and because many of them have come in contact with future leaders in their classrooms, any alteration in the educational system, or in the percentage of political mentors who are university professors, alters the political mentoring process. In other words, it redirects political mentoring away from educational institutions and away from part-time educators toward other types of individuals, in different institutional settings, such as managers in large corporations.

What sets Mexico apart from many other countries is that education has been used not only to train future leaders in the skills necessary to fulfill their responsibilities but also to recruit the best and brightest into public office. Education performs this function in some other countries, such as Japan, France, and England, but Mexico differs in that politicians themselves played a role in skill development, recruitment, and a third function, socialization. The educational institutions that have been strongly represented in the backgrounds of Fox's cabinet-level colleagues who could provide opportunities for mentoring and recruitment, in addition to UNAM, are the ITAM, Ibero-American University, the Universidad de las Americas, the Escuela Libre de Derecho, and Opus Dei's IPADE (Pan American Institute for Higher Management, whose management course is increasingly found on the résumés of top Mexican officials).

The consequences of changes in political recruitment paths for Mexican leadership have been explored mainly at the national executive level.[12] Because democratic changes first occurred at the state level, and because governors have increasingly become major political actors on the national scene, we can obtain a deeper and broader sense of changing recruitment patterns by examining recent governors, especially because they represent all three political parties, suggesting influential trends that may well extend beyond 2008.

In the 1990s, pluralism and competition first got a toehold in state and local politics, spurring Mexico's democratic transformation by increasing control and influence by the opposition to half the population in less than ten years. Consequently, it makes sense to analyze governors elected during the period of electoral transparency as a reflection of top executive leadership (see Table 12.2). Furthermore, two of the three presidential candidates in 2006 were governors, confirming Siavelis and Morgenstern's strong argument for their inclusion as components of the pathway to power. As was the case for the presidency in 2000, the democratic setting influenced the recruitment and selection

---

12. The exception is Rodríguez (2005).

TABLE 12.2   Background Characteristics of Recent Mexican Governors (Percentages)

Characteristic	All Governors	PAN Governors Only
Precollege studies locally	90	89
Held elective office	77	56
Graduated from provincial university	64	33
Elective federal office	63	33
Middle-class origins	63	50
Professional politician	55	0
Born in small town	43	33
Developmental post in state bureaucracy	40	22
Born in state capital	37	63
State party leader	33	33
Mayor	33	44
Nontraditional college degree	33	44
Law degree	32	11
Business career	29	56
Attended private university	21	30
Led business organization	20	44
Graduate degree	20	22
No college degree	20	33
Working-class origins	25	25
Graduate work abroad	17	22
No governmental experience	10	33

Source: Author survey of a sample of thirty four governors who took office between 1997 and 2004. Only one governor is excluded from the sample, that of Tabasco (PRI), for insufficient information.

process of state governors, foreshadowing many of the new directions Vicente Fox represents.

The backgrounds of recent governors suggest some changing patterns in executive-branch leadership at the state level. First and foremost, the majority of new governors began their careers locally, whether they entered politics as student activists in high school, as college students, or during their professional careers. The fact that nine out of ten governors remain in their home towns or in a local community for their secondary education is significant for two reasons. First, they do not come in contact with future national elites educated at leading public and, more recently, private preparatory schools in the nation's capital. There are only four exceptions to this pattern. Second, recent governors are not given the opportunity to form mentor–disciple relationships at such institutions with peers or teachers.

Additionally, two-thirds of governors remain in their home states or nearby states for their tertiary education. This pattern prevents even more significant networking from occurring with influential future national-level politicians at Mexico City institutions. It also contributes to the decentralization of education, and a move away from the more homogeneous socializing experiences shared by the majority of national politicians who were previously educated in a small number of institutions. Among the college-educated governors in the provinces, twelve different schools in eleven states were represented. The National Autonomous University is still responsible for the largest pool of alumni among governors: 30 percent were graduates, followed by 13 percent from the Monterrey Institute of Higher Studies (Instituto Tecnológico y de Estudios Superiores de Monterrey, ITESM), one of Mexico's most prestigious and increasingly influential universities. It is the only regional university that produces a significant number of prominent national-level politicians in the executive branch.

It is worth noting that a significant proportion of governors, one-fifth, have not graduated from any college. Not having such a credential would basically preclude such an individual from holding a cabinet-level post. Finally, although governors have begun to reflect the national-level increase in graduate education, only 20 percent have obtained such training, most of them abroad. From a recruitment angle, that 20 percent is insignificant because governors are not attending the elite American Ivy League institutions preferred by prominent national figures.

A second important trend in governors' backgrounds, with influential consequences for political recruitment patterns generally, is that several career experiences stand out. First, elective office is becoming a valued and common quality among chief executives before they reach their top posts. Two-thirds of governors have previously been elected as congressmen or senators, and a third have served as mayors, often of capital cities. Indeed, nearly 80 percent have held elective office.[13] In contrast, only 8 percent of executive-branch administrators from director general through the cabinet in the 1990s shared similar electoral experiences. Increasing numbers of governors use their posts to achieve national prominence, yielding many candidacies for president and, increasingly, cabinet posts.

The other quality that stands out about governors is that over half were professional politicians, having made their livelihood from holding governmental positions, often in the state bureaucracy. Many of these politicians held two types of positions, economic and political oriented experiences. Interestingly, with state administrative agencies, an increasing number of governors (two-fifths) enhanced their careers and obtained experience in departments and institutions devoted to state economic development or finance. This pattern suggests that financial skills in the public sector are as important as or even more important than prior experience in sensitive political posts. Governors do have direct political administrative experiences, but the most common such experience is as a leader of their political party. Local-party leadership increasingly determines who will be the gubernatorial candidate, so local-party ties are essential for political success.

13. Significantly, among PRI gubernatorial candidates, local career experience was not statistically correlated with victorious governors. Instead, it may well have been their private-sector experience that was influential (Díaz 2005, 46).

The three presidential candidates in 2006 all were national-party presidents, experience that, as Siavelis and Morgenstern predict, should influence their behavior.

Finally, several demographic variables combine to alter the backgrounds of younger governors, variables that may be translated into national-level executives in the next decade. The birthplaces of recent governors are small, provincial cities. This is an important finding because since 1970 national politicians in the executive branch have not emerged from small towns and villages.

Traditional institutions have played a dominant role in Mexican political recruitment, including academia, the federal bureaucracy, the Congress, the state executive, and local elective offices. But Fox's recruitment and selection patterns suggest the role new institutions are playing in Mexico as sources of new talent, a phenomenon that is directly attributable to the democratic transformation and to Fox's electoral campaign (de la Torre Castellanos and Ramirez Saíz 2001). Among the most important new sources are civic organizations, or NGOs, which have not produced top leadership in prior administrations, with the possible exception of Zedillo's environment secretary (Diez-Mendez 2004). The clearest example of this tapping of new blood in the Fox administration is the influential San Angel Group, an informal civic organization. In this group Fox met many of his future top advisers and cabinet appointees, including Jorge Castañeda, his first foreign relations secretary; Adolfo Aguilar Zinser, his national security adviser and ambassador to the United Nations; and Santiago Creel, his secretary of government.[14]

Provincial grassroots organizations are likely to produce more significant sources for political recruitment. A casual connection exists between rural backgrounds and parents' socioeconomic status among Mexican politicians. Governors come from working-class origins in numbers higher than presidents, representing a shift away from the complete dominance of middle-class backgrounds. Among executive-branch administrators from the department level on up in the mid-1990s, only 2 percent came from working class origins.

I have argued that the democratic setting, beginning in the late 1990s, has contributed to the altering of Mexican recruitment and selection patterns. Thus, all parties and their representatives have been affected by these environmental changes. In particular, the PAN's increased presence in gubernatorial posts allows us to make the case that this newly incumbent party either has accounted for some significant changes or has contributed disproportionately to altered recruitment characteristics.

The most remarkable distinctive quality that PAN governors bring to Mexican leadership is their lack of life-time governmental experiences. PAN governors are not professional politicians (see Table 12.2). Not one has made

---

14. "Tensiones, diferencias y recelos entre Fox y el PAN" *Proceso*, July 16, 2000, available at www.proceso.com.mx.

governmental service a career. Of course the reason for this is structural, since prior to 1989, active *panistas* would not have been able to hold state offices, since all of those positions were controlled by PRI governors. The fact that these individuals have made a living through some other activity also explains why they have held few posts in the state bureaucracies and have not been well represented in federal, elective offices. On the other hand, unlike their PRI and PRD peers, they are much more likely to have served in local elective offices as mayors.

What really distinguishes PAN state executives is their business backgrounds. Over half have worked in the private sector, and many have owned their own businesses. They have pursued political interests through business organizations, and many of them have served as the presidents of local and state business interest groups, most commonly Coparmex. They are also the most likely to have only a secondary-level education, having gone into a family business directly after preparatory school, a pattern seen also among Mexico's leading capitalists.

Public Policy and Political Recruitment

Can Fox's policy failures, illustrated by his inability to achieve his major proposals, such as private investment in the energy sector, be attributed to his leadership choices, and therefore, to these new political recruitment and selection trends, which unquestionably are linked to the democratic transformation? Not entirely, but a connection exists. He fired his energy and environmental secretaries in 2003. What did these two secretaries, Ernesto Martens and Víctor Lichtinger, represent? Martens was a prominent businessman, and his firing, in terms of policy impact, obviously represents a dramatic failure, one that reduces the likelihood of more top businessmen taking over cabinet portfolios. One explanation for his dismissal was his inability to acquire support from the opposition parties, which some analysts attributed to his lack of political experience. Apparently Fox had not completely rejected prominent business leaders, since one of his cabinet appointments in 2004 was a top manager of a major corporation with strong ties to leading capitalists. The failure of a business leader, turned politician was reinforced dramatically in a recent gubernatorial race, where, according to a leading entrepreneur, PAN "lost overwhelmingly in Nuevo León because the people are disillusioned with business-style governments" (Grayson 2003, 25). Lichtinger, too, represents a failure, not of a businessman but of an international NGO leader, also new to the political process.

Their replacements brought with them a new emphasis, political party skills, and the importance of negotiating with Congress. Calderón, whose experience comes from the Chamber of Deputies and PAN leadership, replaced Martens, and

Alberto Cárdenas, the former governor of Jalisco, replaced Lichtinger. Fox's press secretary openly admitted that these two individuals had been chosen because of their known political skills, useful in executive–legislative policy battles.

Trends in political recruitment within the PAN, at both the national and state executive levels, have produced a bifurcated leadership. This leadership is made up of *neopanistas*, many of whom come from the business community, who began exerting considerable influence in 1982 (Martínez Vázquez 2002, 124), and established *party insiders*, who spent years in the party bureaucracy, and have made their political careers in the national legislative branch. This shared leadership, common to state leadership, has produced numerous tensions, which have been translated into significant policy failures (Mizrahi 2003, 94). Fox replicated this pattern at the national level, with a divided cabinet and poor relations between his cabinet and his own party in Congress, especially from 2000 to 2003—which Siavelis and Morgenstern predicted would be the case of a *party adherent* (See Chapter 1).

What policy successes, if any, can we identify that are affected by or even determined to a large extent by Fox's leadership choices? One of the most significant actual accomplishments of his administration because of its long-term structural implications was his willingness to weather criticism while pushing significant political disputes into legal channels for a permanent resolution. The most important political consequences that Fox's presidency originally set into motion were widespread conflicts on the state and local levels among the various political parties. Yucatán witnessed such a conflict involving the Federal Electoral Institute's decision to seat its choice of commissioners on the state board. Instead of intervening to neutralize locally controlled intransigence, Fox publicly advocated going through legal channels for a solution. The Supreme Court ruled in favor of the Federal Electoral Institute, the newly independent quasi-judicial, quasi-executive body tasked with the job of holding elections and certifying the electoral results.

Fox's posture toward the legal system is the product of two influences. First, he campaigned in support of accountability and the culture of law, a position the business community strongly supported. Second, in order to guarantee a fair electoral outcome, he and other opposition leaders strongly supported the Federal Electoral Institute, a body that became a critical actor in the contested election of 2006.[15] Because many of Fox's collaborators came from the opposition party or from business backgrounds, and both sets of institutions repeatedly expressed the desire to establish a credible legal system, both to improve the business environment and to provide accountability politically, their dominance in the new administration helped Fox push this issue.[16]

Fox's decision in Yucatán, and others like it, established three important precedents: first, the independent role of the judiciary in solving highly charged

15. This is the only political institution in Mexico that generates high levels of public confidence.
16. Interestingly, Fox submitted a major judicial reform bill in March 2004 (Boudreaux 2004).

legal disputes; second, the real and symbolic importance of the rule of law, or, more broadly, the culture of law; and third, the willingness of the executive branch to reduce its decisionmaking authority. As the president of the Supreme Court noted, the Court is the institution of last resort in defending Mexicans against the abuse of public power. Some observers considered the Fox administration's use of the legal system as a political means to block the candidacy of the PRD candidate, Andrés Manuel López Obrador (technically, he broke the law by violating a court order in 2006), for the president, but ultimately vociferous public pressure dissuaded the government from continuing its questionable legal case. The legitimacy of public institutions, notably the Federal Electoral Institute (Instituto Federal Electoral, IFE) and the Federal Electoral Tribunal (Tribunal Federal Electoral, TRIFE), played a crucial role in the outcome of the 2006 presidential race, legally confirming Calderón's narrow victory over his PRD opponent. Following their controversial decisions, both electoral institutions actually increased their levels of support to two-thirds of the population.[17]

A second accomplishment of his administration, which also can be linked to the type of leadership he recruited, is the passage and recent implementation of the transparency law in June 2003, making all federal executive branch agencies more transparent. This new law is tied to a much larger fundamental issue of democratic transformation: accountability. The sharing of governmental information, while still imperfect, is nothing short of astounding compared to the pre-2000 situation. This law, which has widespread implications, requires a fundamental change in attitude among political leaders, that is, being responsive to their constituents and knowing how to respond to those constituents.

The third consequence of his administration that has serious implications for the democratic process is that legislation before Congress, in order to obtain a simple majority of votes, must have the support of at least two of the three major parties. This has been the case since 1997 and continues to be the case in Calderón's presidency. This means that democratic compromise must dominate presidential and legislative behavior if the government hopes to function successfully. From a recruitment perspective, the lack of a single-party majority in congress suggests that individuals with skills in negotiating will become highly valued in the legislative process. Nine cabinet members have held elective office, an all-time high in the last twenty years. Calderón is the first president since 1964 with extensive legislative experience and the only president with leadership experience in the legislative branch since 1930.

The final aspect of the legacy of Fox's administration and his new directions is the emphasis on the importance of local politics, both city and state. The divided

---

17. "El tribunal electoral pasó la prueba y aumentó la confianza en el IFE," www.parametria.com.mx.

support for the various parties has produced a situation that rewards political leaders for their performance, not for their party affiliation. This is demonstrated conclusively through statistics on repeat victories in municipal elections. In 2001, PAN only won 35 percent of the elections where it was the incumbent party (Mizrahi 2003, 29). Politicians with strong grassroots support and ties to their communities will increasingly dominate state and local positions, the same positions with growing importance as feeders for national political office.

In conclusion, then, many of Fox's accomplishments, while not visible in the policy process itself, have significant implications for future political behavior, institutions, and structures in Mexico, implications that will mold the Mexican model for years to come and will impact importantly on political recruitment and selection patterns. Thus the consequences of Fox's administration have been largely political in terms of their impact on democratic behavior and decision-making.

Whether the political process can result in the implementation of substantive policies that deal with citizen concerns still remains to be seen. The policy issues that dominated the 2000 presidential race remained in 2006, with poverty being a central, intensely held concern. Calderón will need to implement influential economic and social programs, not only to satisfy citizen demands but, equally important, to legitimize and sustain this new democratic process and these recruitment and selection patterns. His first year in office suggests much greater success than his predecessor in achieving policy compromises, notably with the PRI. The failure of the executive- and legislative-branch leadership to reach compromises on major legislation in the remaining five years will adversely affect all the parties and could have an even more important negative impact on democracy's health and on some of the recruitment and selection trends introduced in 2000.

Chapter Thirteen

Presidential Candidate Selection in Uruguay, 1942 to 2004

DANIEL BUQUET AND DANIEL CHASQUETTI

This chapter analyzes the presidential candidate selection process in Uruguay before and after the constitutional reforms of 1996. In light of the peculiar features of the Uruguayan political system—internally factionalized parties and a double simultaneous vote (DSV) electoral system—we analyze presidential candidate selection processes from the perspective of parties and their factions. In particular, we focus on the impact of institutional variables on the candidate selection process as well as the political consequences of the types of presidential candidates and the ensuing behavior of the person elected.

The ways presidential candidates compete is directly shaped by the national electoral system. Before the 1996 electoral reform, Uruguayan electoral rules allowed party factions to present their own candidates, who competed with other intra-party rivals knowing that the intraparty competitors' votes would be summed to determine the outcome of the interparty contest. As a result, Uruguay is unique with respect to the visibility of internal party competition in the electoral arena. This allows us to study factional systems with a lens similar to that used to study the relationship between electoral systems and party systems in other countries.

Our study suggests (as outlined by Siavelis and Morgenstern in Chapter 1) that electoral institutions create the context that has defined candidate selection in Uruguay, but do not ultimately determine the processes. In the Uruguayan case, the DSV (described later) has fostered the development and maintenance of factions, but party- and faction-level factors such as the organization, leadership, and competitiveness of the factions must enter the analysis to explain the choice of candidates and the subsequent behavior of elected officials.

In this chapter we argue that Uruguayan presidential candidates have been *party insiders* and *party adherents* (see Chapter 1). However, given that they usually represent factions, we contend that most should be considered as *faction insiders* or *faction adherents* (though they exhibit the predicted behavior of the *insider* and *adherent* types, this behavior is tied and directed to the party faction rather than the party as a whole, a perspective we share with Moraes (see Chapter 7, this volume). Further, we find that the electoral path to power helps to determine whether *factional insiders* or *factional adherents* emerge. DSV encourages the natural leaders of the main national factions to become presidential candidates, whereas the plurality rule for presidential elections creates incentives for minor factions to build agreements among themselves to designate common candidates. We refer to the former type of candidates as *natural* and the latter as *designated*. Natural candidates tend to be *faction insiders* and the designated candidates are more likely to be and act like *faction adherents*.

The next two sections of this chapter briefly describe the most significant institutional features of the Uruguayan political system, and especially the party and electoral systems. The following section explains how the electoral and party systems influence the type and number of presidential candidates. The last section analyzes the influence of candidate type on the political process, focusing on the size of presidents' legislative contingents, legislative discipline, and types of cabinets. We show that the type of candidate has a weak influence over the size of legislative contingents and does not seem to have a substantive effect on legislative discipline. Candidate type, however, does tend to affect the characteristics of the cabinet. Although the presidents who were natural candidates (and tended to be *party insiders*) had more stable and lasting cabinets than the presidents who were designated candidates (and were more likely *party adherents*), the latter showed more care in building cabinets congruent with their legislative support.

The Uruguayan Party System

The Uruguayan party system is one of the most stable and persistent in Latin America. In their foundational work, Mainwaring and Scully (1995) recognize Uruguay, along with Venezuela, Costa Rica, Chile, and Colombia, as having a particularly institutionalized and competitive party system.

The Uruguayan party system has three important parties. On the center-right are the two "traditional parties," the Colorado (Red) Party (Partido Colorado, or PC) and the National or Blanco (White) Party (Partido Nacional, or PN), and on the left is the Broad Front (Frente Amplio, or FA). The two traditional parties are as old as the country itself, and have always held governing positions. During most of the twentieth century, however, they have coexisted with a group of minor parties, called "parties of ideas." In 1971 these parties joined to form a third relevant party, the Frente Amplio. This party has governed the capital city of the country for three consecutive five-year electoral cycles and in 2004 captured the presidency.

The most outstanding feature of the major parties is the existence of strongly organized autonomous factions. Though it is common for political parties to be internally divided, the peculiarity of the Uruguayan case is that these factions show great political visibility, to such an extent that they have been considered parties within parties (Lindahl 1977). Nevertheless, national parties still matter, and thus, as many scholars have argued (González 1993; Mieres 1992), Uruguayan parties are best described as "factionalized parties" (Buquet, Chasquetti, and Moraes 1998).

Although both traditional parties have had a large and diverse number of factions throughout history, the factions have generally been grouped around two main competitive blocs. The Colorado Party is divided between the *batllistas*,[1] who in general have constituted the progressive wing of the party, and the non-*batllista* sectors,[2] who are generally more conservative. At present, the non-*batllistas* factions have practically disappeared in the Colorado Party and all its factions are thus considered *batllistas*. In the National Party the *herreristas* are more conservative,[3] with solid roots in the rural areas, whereas non-*herreristas* have a more urban base and a more centrist ideology.

Batllismo and *herrerismo* have been the dominant factions of traditional Uruguayan parties to such an extent that throughout the whole twentieth century there was never an elected government that excluded both of these factions. Occasionally another faction has won the internal competition, but these victors have always required support from dissident *batllistas* or *herreristas*.

At the party level, the first three decades of the century were dominated by the Colorado Party and the charismatic José Batlle y Ordóñez, the leader who gave his name to the long-lived faction. Within the party, Batlle's sector was dominant, winning an average of 70 percent of the party votes during the 1920s. After Batlle's death, Gabriel Terra, a Batlle follower, was elected president in 1931. Two years later he carried out a coup d'etat in agreement with Luis Alberto de Herrera, the leader of the main faction of the National Party. This interparty coalition ruled the country until 1942. Then, with the return of competition, the *batllista* faction of the Colorado Party again claimed the presidential mansion between 1942 and 1958, led during much of this time by Luis Batlle Berres, a nephew of the elder Batlle.

After a long absence from power, the Blancos won the elections in 1958 and 1962. The *herrerista* faction was the majority during the first government, but the non-*herrerista* wing (Unión Blanca Democrática, or UBD) dominated the second

---

1. Followers of José Batlle y Ordóñez, who was president twice (1903–1907 and 1911–1915), initially adopted this name, which was reinforced with the presidency of Batlle's nephew Luis Batlle Berres (1947–1951).

2. They have gone by different names such as the *riveristas*, *blancoacevedistas*, *catorcistas*, *pachequistas*, or just Colorados.

3. Named for Luis Alberto de Herrera, the main Blanco leader of the twentieth century.

government. The Colorados returned to office following the 1966 election, and remained there until the military coup of 1973. Significant social unrest combined with an awkward election in 1971 brought to power a president with dubious party ties to the Colorados, Juan María Bordaberry;[4] his election led to the 1973 coup and military government that lasted for twelve years.

The dictatorship did little to change the country's electoral map at the party level. The Partido Colorado's (PC's) Julio María Sanguinetti won the 1984 election that ended the military government. Then after sitting out the required term, he was reelected in 1994 and continues to lead his own faction, the Foro Batllista (Batllista Forum). The Colorados also won in 1999, when Jorge Batlle Ibáñez, the son of Luis Batlle, was elected under a new rule that forced the country's only runoff. The Blancos have only won once since the return to democratic rule, in 1989, under the *herrerista* Luis Alberto Lacalle, a grandson of Luis Alberto de Herrera.

At the faction level, there have also been only limited changes. The main Colorado intraparty conflict has been between the Sanguinetti's Foro Batllista and Jorge Batlle's Lista 15. Among the Blancos, the conflict has been between *herrerismo*, led by Lacalle, and a variety of non-*herrerista* groups that came together under the leadership of Jorge Larrañanga.

Though the first postdictatorship election yielded a result for the Frente Amplio similar to what they had experience prior to the dictatorship, winning about 20 percent, the party grew rapidly and won its first presidency in 2004 under Tabaré Vázquez. Unlike in the other parties, however, there is not a clear bipolar division, though there are "moderates" and "radicals." Currently the FA has seven main factions. Three groups formed prior to the founding of the FA: Democracia Avanzada (Advanced Democracy, or AD—led by the communist party), Espacio 90 (Space 90, or E90—led by the socialist party), and Movimiento de Participación Popular (Popular Participation Movement, or MPP—the former Tupamaros),[5] and two other large factions developed subsequent to the party's formation: Vertiente Artiguista (Artiguist Slant, or VA), which is headed by the former mayor of Montevideo, Mariano Arana, and Asamblea Uruguay (Uruguayan Assembly, or AU), which is headed by the current economics minister, Danilo Astori. A sixth sector is Alianza Progresista (Progressive Alliance, or AP), which comprises former Blancos, Christian Democrats, and former Communists, among others. Finally, Nuevo Espacio (New Space, or NE), is a last crucial piece of the puzzle. Its membership has origins in the Colorado Party, and though it joined the Frente Amplio in 1971, it operated independently between 1989 and 2004. In the 2004 election, Nuevo Espacio, along with the other six FA affiliates, rode Vázquez's coattails to obtain legislative representation.

4. Juan María Bordaberry came from a traditional non-*batllista* Colorado family but he was elected senator for the National Party in 1962 as a result of the agreement between the ruralist movement and the National Party.

5. The Tupamaros are a former guerrilla movement that was active during the 1960s and 1970s.

The Presidential Electoral System in Uruguay

Between 1966 and 1994, Uruguayan elections were held concurrently every five years to elect the president and vice president,[6] all thirty members of the Senate, and all ninety-nine members of the House of Representatives. In the republic's nineteen departments, mayors *(intendentes municipales)* and the members of the departmental assemblies (city councils) were also elected simultaneously.[7]

Until the 1996 reform (discussed in the next section), elections for the three national offices of government—Presidency, Senate, and House—were connected by means of a block vote. Voters selected one among a large assortment of *voting sheets*, or ballots, which identified the lists of candidates for all offices. These voting sheets—containing the names of the candidates supported by each political group for every position in play—were printed by each political group in every department and registered with the Electoral Court. All candidates appearing on a voting sheet had to belong to the same party, so voters could not choose different parties for different offices. The voter had to choose one from different "combinations" for the different offices, as follows: For each party, one or more presidential–vice presidential tickets (called *formulas*) was accompanied by different Senate lists; once the voter chose a candidate for president, he or she would have to choose one of the Senate and House lists that supported that particular candidate (see Morgenstern 2001; Moraes, Chapter 7, this volume). The voting sheets, however, were created by the political groups and were nonseparable; voters, therefore, had to choose among preestablished combinations of formulas and lists and could not create their own combinations of candidates at the different levels.

The president and vice president were elected on a list that included both candidates based on a plurality system and using double simultaneous vote (DSV), a system whereby a primary and a general election are conducted simultaneously. The elected president was the candidate who received the most votes in the party that received the most votes. Traditional parties presented many candidates, hoping that the sum of their votes would bring victory, whereas the minor parties and the FA generally unified under a single presidential formula.

After the 1996 constitutional reform, the DSV was eliminated for the presidential election and the majority runoff method *(ballotage)* was introduced. Political parties were forced to present single presidential candidates by establishing mandatory open primary elections. Under the new rules, all parties that want to participate in the electoral process must have "internal" elections (primaries),

---

6. Between 1954 and 1962 a nine-member collegial executive, called the National Council of Government (Consejo Nacional de Gobierno), was elected instead of a president and vice president.

7. Following the 1996 constitutional reforms, municipal authorities are now elected on a different date.

which are held on the same day.[8] Internal elections serve two purposes, to select the presidential candidate in each party and to elect delegates to the national and nineteen local-party conventions. The national party conventions have five hundred delegates elected by proportional representation. Delegates select the presidential candidate if none receives more than 50 percent of the vote (or more than 40 percent with at least a ten percentage–point margin over the second front runner), and they select the vice-presidential candidate.

The National Factions' Candidate Selection Processes

The pre-1996 Uruguayan electoral system established a set of rules for candidate selection that allowed self-selection as a general criterion. There were few formal requirements for running candidates, and political parties were very permissive about the use of their labels. Therefore, anybody who seriously wanted to run for any elective post was able to do so. Despite this informality, the main national factions virtually monopolized the elective positions. The previous section mentioned the great diversity in sheet options available to voters, especially until 1994. In spite of the great number of options, almost no minor electoral *entrepreneur* succeeded in winning an elective position. While nonrestrictive formal and informal norms ruled the presentation of candidacies, quite restrictive rules governed the ultimate allocation of seats.

The main national factions, which have won practically all elective offices, control their own candidates' selection (Morgenstern 2001; Moraes, Chapter 7, this volume). Further, most Uruguayan factions have a strongly individualist slant, concentrating most decisionmaking power as well as the economic resources of the faction under a highly visible leader.[9] Although they cannot defend against the creation of multiple lists, the leaders do work to maintain control over who will win seats, sometimes by designating "official lists," which are promoted by the faction and the presidential candidate (Morgenstern 2001). Some national factions also build alliances at the national or local level which are crucial to electoral outcomes, thus again limiting the chances of outsider candidates. These two systems combine to provide power to faction leaders because they can rely on the vast majority of citizens to vote for these official lists, which generally have the better-known personalities, the support of strong political organizations, and major economic

8. Citizens may vote in any party primary, but may only participate in one. Part of the reasoning behind holding primaries on the same day for all parties was to prevent voters from intervening in the affairs of more than one party.

9. The public financial contribution to any political group is determined by the total percentage of the vote received by each voting sheet and is distributed in the following way: 20 percent for the presidential candidate, 40 percent for the Senate list, and 40 percent for the House list. As the presidential formula (the ticket) and the Senate list are presented in every constituency, the factional leadership controls most of the public economic resources for campaigning.

resources. As a result, candidate self-selection and the wide diversity of the electoral options hide what is really a faction-centered process of candidate selection in Uruguay. As in many other countries, the key difference is between "real" and "formal" candidates, and only the former have serious electoral potential.

The following section describes the presidential selection methods used by national factions of the three main Uruguayan parties. In keeping with the framework we have followed, we first present the pre-1996 process, separating the traditional parties and the FA. In those two sections we also consider how the system has affected the number of presidential candidates. We then consider the changes introduced by the 1996 constitutional reform and their impacts.

Presidential Candidate Selection in the Traditional Parties

The incentive structure of the DSV system prompted both traditional parties to always run multiple presidential candidates between 1942 and 1994. As long as parties were not forced to present single presidential candidates, and multiple candidacies enhanced potential success, it was less costly to have more than one candidate than to reach an agreement on a single one. By the same token, presidential candidacies emerged in preexisting rather than new parties because running under an extant party banner was less costly than creating a new party. In this way the DSV had a double impact, on the one hand stimulating factionalized parties and on the other sustaining the already established parties (González 1993; Buquet, Chasquetti, and Moraes 1998).

As noted, until the reform, the selection of presidential candidates in the traditional parties was a faction-level decision. The main ambition of faction leaders was to reach the presidency, and their decisions and strategies were oriented toward that goal—but they had to compete with copartisans. Within the factions, the designation of the presidential candidates was dominated by elites.[10] Even though elite selection was the predominant method, some distinctions were important. First, most presidential candidates had been the undisputed leaders of their own factions, so there was no "selection process," and nomination was taken as a given by party elites and the public. These candidates best fit the *party insiders* category, but could be better termed *faction insiders*. Most of these leaders either had run previously for the presidency or had held privileged governmental or legislative positions that placed them in a leading political role. By allowing each faction to present its leader as a candidate, the DSV promoted "natural candidates" who were able to build new movements to challenge old leaders.

---

10. The only exceptions were in 1966 and in 1989, when the *batllistas* used primary elections to designate their presidential candidate.

Although faction leaders were clearly the most common type of presidential nominee, in three situations other types of candidates emerged. The first was where a faction lacked an undisputed leader. Such a situation was exceptional, because personalist factions were the norm. The situation did arise, however, when a faction leader died without leaving a clear heir. The second situation arose when different factions built an alliance to present a common candidate. When presidential races began, leaders of different factions who by themselves had little chance of winning often joined with other copartisan factions in order to challenge the party's front-runner. The goal of these intraparty coalitions was almost always to select a single presidential candidate (chosen by the collective of elites) that two or more factions could support in order to displace the rival factions' leader as the party's top vote getter. In these cases the pool of possible candidates extended beyond the natural faction leaders and included "neutral" personalities, thus yielding some *faction-adherent* candidates. Third and finally, a nonnatural leader emerged when the faction's leader was also the current president and was thus constitutionally banned from immediate reelection. In these cases, presidents tended to designate a trusted heir with a low profile, thus allowing the president to maintain his leadership.

The process of designating the nonnatural candidates often promoted the creation of new factions and presidential candidates as well. Elite agreements and the coalition compromises did not generally satisfy all groups and leaders, and those who were disenchanted often created new factions with their own presidential candidates.

As noted here, the predominant type of presidential candidate in Uruguay has been the *faction insider*. Though Uruguayan parties are far from having a "clearly defined ideological base," as Siavelis and Morgenstern put it, *party insider* "emerg[e] from long-standing, institutionalized parties . . . where party identification is important to voters" (Chapter 1, pp. 29, 32). We analyzed seventy-eight presidential candidates who in the thirteen elections during the period from 1942 to 2004 obtained more than 5 percent of the votes. Seventy-three of them (94 percent) were *party* or *faction insiders* and only five (6 percent) *party* or *faction adherents* (see Appendix Tables 13.1A and 13.2A at the end of this chapter).[11] Neither *free-wheeling independents* nor *group agents* have ever existed in Uruguay (a testament to the strength, influence, and institutionalization of parties). In light of this reality our natural focus must be on the distinction between natural and designated presidential candidates.

Table 13.1 shows the distribution of natural and designated candidacies for the traditional parties. The table suggests that natural candidates (who tend to be

---

11. For the period of the Nacional Colegiado Gobierno (National Council of Government) (the 1954, 1958, and 1962 elections), we use the head of the council list as the "presidential candidate."

TABLE 13.1   Types of Presidential Candidates in Traditional Uruguayan Parties: 1942–2004

	Natural		Designated		Total	
	N	Percentage	N	Percentage	N	Percentage
Partido Colorado	22	63	13	37	35	100
Batllista factions	8	62	5	38	13	100
Non-batllista factions	14	64	8	36	22	100
Partido Nacional	17	57	13	43	30	100
Herrerista factions	9	69	4	31	13	100
Non-herrerista factions	8	47	9	53	17	100
Other parties	6	46	7	54	13	100
Total candidates	45	58	33	42	78	100
1942–1971	20	44	25	56	45	100
1984–2004	25	76	8	24	33	100
Winning candidates	6	46	7	54	13	100

Source: Author's compilation of data from the Area de Política y Relaciones Internacionales del Banco de Datos de la Facultad de Ciencias Sociales de la Universidad de la República (ICP-UDELAR).

faction insiders) are the dominant type, but designated leaders (who tend to be *faction insiders*) are also common. In part there is a bias in the results, however, in that designated candidates tend not to endure more than one election, because they either lose and fade away or parlay their exposure to convert themselves into natural candidates.[12] Still, it is notable that the candidate's type does not seem to act as a predictor of electoral success, as seven of the thirteen winners were natural candidates and the remaining six, designated.

Dividing the studied period into two parts highlights an important change: whereas natural candidates predominated in the postdictatorship period, in the precoup years (1942–1971) somewhat fewer than one-half of the candidates could be considered natural. The other interesting pattern here is the separation of the *herrerista* and non-*herrerista* factions, the former having a greater preference for the natural candidates than the latter. This phenomenon reflects the quasi-hegemonic position of *herrerismo* within the party, which has obliged the other factions to make alliances and, as a result, look for presidential candidates by negotiating. Apart from this, the independent nationalist sectors have always questioned Herrera's *personalismo,* perhaps thereby inciting the faction to avoid creating and choosing its own natural candidates.

Effect of the Electoral System on the Number of Candidates

Though under the pre-1996 system voters had access to numerous electoral sheets, there were several aspects of the electoral system that reduced the number

12. Martín Echegoyen (1958–1966), Oscar Gestido (1962–1966), Alberto Zumarán (1984–1989), and Alberto Volonté (1994–1999) were *faction insiders* who became faction leaders.

TABLE 13.2 Effective Number of Presidential Candidates in Traditional Uruguayan Parties: 1942–2004

	1942	1946	1950	1954	1958	1962	1966	1971	1984	1989	1994	1999	2004	Average
Colorado Party	1.78	2.23	2.96	2.03	2.04	2.46	2.99	2.26	1.57	2.11	1.63	2.01	1.20	2.10
National Party	1.03	1.02	1.01	2.41	2.22	1.96	2.72	1.82	1.39	2.29	2.43	2.81	1.82	1.92

Source: Author's compilation of data from the Area de Política y Relaciones Internacionales del Banco de Datos de la Facultad de Ciencias Sociales de la Universidad de la República (ICP-UDELAR).

of sheets open to voters and kept the number of significant presidential candidates at around two per party. First, although every faction could present its own presidential candidate, in many cases minor factions in the traditional parties abstained from doing so, either because they sought a common candidate with other factions or directly supported the presidential candidate of a larger faction. As noted, this was partly the result of strategic considerations of the minor factions. The fused vote for the two legislative houses and the presidency prior to 1996 also reinforced this pattern. Given this system, minor factions that failed to field a serious presidential candidate had little chance of winning a Senate seat, because voters would not waste their votes on a presidential candidate with no chance of winning just to support a favored senatorial candidate. The linkage of competition for the presidency, the Senate, and the House thus reduced the number of sheets and, in a manner consistent with Duverger's law, helped to reduce the number of each party's presidential candidates.[13] Table 13.2 shows the "effective number" of presidential candidates for both traditional parties in the period from 1942 to 2004.[14] It clearly shows the persistence of a "two-faction" competitive scheme at the presidential level.

Within the parties, the presidential contest is decided by a plurality of votes, which according to Duverger's law should lead the parties toward two-candidate competition. Before the constitutional reform of 1996, the DSV simultaneously resolved both the competition between parties and the competition between candidates of the same party. As Morgenstern (2001) claims, the system created a prisoners' dilemma for the factions, because they had to cooperate with each other in order to win the election, but at the same time they were forced to compete among themselves. Within the parties, however, the factions seemed to resolve the conflict, generally putting into play cooperative campaign strategies, perhaps because the factions frequently fit Pancbianco's (1990) description of opponents rather than competitors (owing to their diverse ideological tendencies).

13. Maurice Duverger (1951) maintains that the plurality electoral system favors the formation of a two-party system.

14. The effective number of presidential candidates is calculated in a similar way to the effective number of parties proposed by Laakso and Taagepera (1979): $1/\sum pi^2$ where p represents the share of votes obtained by each presidential candidate divided by the total party vote.

Presidential Candidate Selection in the Frente Amplio

The most evident difference between the traditional parties and the FA is that the latter has always presented a single presidential candidate for each election. Moreover, only three different people have fulfilled this role since the party's foundation in 1971. Líber Seregni, known for his independence and commitment to consensus building, was nominated as the group's first candidate. After his nomination he played what most observers consider an outstanding role during the last stretch of democratic transition and thus became a natural leader of the party. After the return to democracy in 1984 he would still have been the party's standard-bearer, but the military prohibited his candidacy. The party then chose Juan J. Crottoggini, who had been Seregni's vice-presidential candidate in 1971. Seregni was the FA candidate again for 1989. In that year, however, the FA suffered a political crisis when two founding groups seceded. Seregni's leadership deteriorated and Tabaré Vázquez, a charismatic member of the Socialist Party who was elected that year as Montevideo's mayor, emerged as the party's new leader. He became the party's presidential candidate for the 1994 election, ran again in 1999, and won the presidency in 2004.

Being the natural leader, however, did not guarantee Vázquez's claim to the party's candidacy after the electoral reform. Under the new rules, even though the Frente Amplio chose its candidates in a convention, the party had to run a primary for the 1999 election. Danilo Astori, leader of a moderate faction of the FA, took advantage of this situation to present himself as a candidate, formally competing against Vázquez. Astori did not have much hope of actually winning in 1999, but it raised his profile and popularity. Still, much of the party's base saw this challenge as unfortunate and divisive for the party.

The process used by the FA clearly shows the importance of informality within the context of formal laws and rules. A convention of delegates elected by FA adherents formally designates the candidate, and FA statutes suggest that the selection of the presidential candidate does not emerge from the elite but from the membership of the party. However, convention members are almost all tied to one of the factions and vote in a disciplined manner in the convention, thus simply ratifying the elite's resolutions. The FA, then, is not an exception to the predominant model of selection by elites, which tends to benefit the natural candidates. The most important difference is that the FA has had natural candidates representing the entire party, whereas the traditional parties have only had natural candidates representing certain factions.

The Effects of New Internal Party Elections

At first sight the electoral reform would not seem to have had much effect because, as before, factions designate precandidates. There are numerous forces at work, however, that will likely change competition within and among the parties. First, the rules to select the party presidential candidates have changed; under the new rules, candidates must win a primary by gaining either 50 percent of the vote or at least 40 percent with an advantage of ten percentage points over the second-place finisher. If no candidate meets these requirements, a party convention chooses the candidate. This threshold for winning the primary provides an impetus toward a two-person race in the primary, but the possibility of having the candidate chosen through the convention could yield a more fragmented scheme, as tends to happen in two-round electoral systems (Mainwaring and Shugart 1997).

Second, holding primaries independent of the general election lengthens political campaigns and increases the costs of the electoral process. These changes have political implications, including public discussions about costs and legitimacy. At least one important advantage of the DSV system was its shorter campaign season with its concurrent primary and general elections. The result of debates regarding cost and timing did lead the legislature to move the primaries from April to June, thus shortening the campaign period.

Separating the primary and general elections has another impact that could carry even greater weight. Primary elections force candidates belonging to the same party to compete among themselves, highlighting their differences and potentially generating internal confrontations. Here the prisoner's dilemma structure of incentives is clear, as cooperative solutions are difficult to find. Most analysts accept that parties that avoid internal conflict perform better in general elections. For the U.S. system, "all studies point toward divisive nomination campaigns contributing a negative effect in general election outcomes" (Atkeson 1998, 257). Kenney and Rice concur, finding that "when one party has a divisive primary season while the other party's nominee is essentially uncontested, the divided party will be adversely affected in November" (1984, 31). Uruguayan evidence fails to conclusively confirm these findings. Rather it suggests that a moderate level of competitiveness is the best, whereas either too much or too little competition damages the party.

The three main parties have chosen different strategies to deal with the new primary system, and each party dealt with the situation differently in 1999 than it did in 2004. The general trend, however, is toward less internal competitiveness. The FA had some symbolic internal competition in 1999, but put forth a single candidate in 2004. Primaries in the PC were characterized by well-balanced competition between two candidates in 1999, but the party ran a hegemonic candidate in 2004. The PN, which in 1999 had been excessively fragmented, ran just two main candidates in the last election, who competed without high levels of vitriol. Whether cause or consequence, if we link the degree of competitiveness of each primary contest to the electoral performance of each traditional party at the general election, we see that when the effective number of candidates was close to two, the party did well and when this number moved away from two,

TABLE 13.3 Effective Number of Presidential Candidates in the Traditional-Parties' Primaries in Uruguay 1999 & 2004

	Partido Colorado		Partido Nacional	
	Effective Number of Candidates[a]	Electoral Growth[b]	Effective Number of Candidates[a]	Electoral Growth[b]
1999	2.0	0.4%	2.8	−8.9%
2004	1.2	−22.2%	1.8	12.8%

Source: Author's compilation of data from the Area de Política y Relaciones Internacionales del Banco de Datos de la Facultad de Ciencias Sociales de la Universidad de la República (ICP-UDELAR).

a. Effective number of presidential candidates in the primary contest.

b. Percentage of electoral growth related to the previous election.

either up or down, the performance in the general election worsened (see Table 13.3). This does not seem to be true for the FA, which had a very low level of competitiveness in both elections while its electoral growth continued an upward trend that started in 1971.

Although there have not been enough elections under the new system to test a hypothesis, it seems that running two main candidates has helped the parties present a balanced image and minimize internal confrontation. This seems to have been important in presenting the voters with both choice and unity. Importantly, it also seems that too little conflict—or perhaps attempts to manipulate the outcome in order to avoid confrontation—has also been harmful for the traditional parties. In 2004 the major factions of the PC unified behind a single candidate, thus distorting the primary process. The result proved disastrous, as the party lost badly in the general election.

These problems point to the advantages of the DSV system. In addition to the benefits with respect to cost and timing noted earlier, the DSV also encouraged faction rivals to limit their intrapartisan fights in order to focus their energies on interpartisan rivalries. Overall, then, the DSV, encourages party building, whereas primaries may damage parties. The DSV final virtue over primaries helps both parties and voters. Colomer (2002) argues that "candidates selected in primaries tend not to be very popular or to lose in the general election" (119). This occurs because of the differences in who participates in the two rounds. According to Colomer, "The more widespread mass participation in the primary elections, within certain limits, the less influence for party leaders whose ultimate goal is to win elections, the more influence for activists and voters with extreme or minority political-ideological preferences, and the greater the distance between the winner of the primary election and the preference of the median voter preference within the whole electorate" (119–20).

Colomer's reasoning can be clearly illustrated in spatial terms. A primary winner should be the one who is closest to the median voter within a party. However, a centrist within a party may be an extremist for the whole electorate. A leftist party, therefore, would do better in the general election by choosing a candidate who is to the right of its median member and a rightist party should do the opposite. The DSV resolves this problem for parties by allowing the presentation of a wide array of options to the whole electorate, therefore benefiting both the citizenry and the party.

Only two elections have been held under the new system, and only one of these supports Colomer's claims. In 1999 the PN's primary winner, Lacalle, was without a doubt closer to the median Blanco voter, though his defeated adversary within the party, Ramírez, was much closer to the whole electorate's center. Something similar could be said of the FA, where the winner, Vázquez, clearly showed a more radical profile than Astori. The winner in the Colorado internal election, Batlle, however, was ideologically further to the right than the defeated candidate, Luis Hierro, but Batlle was still in a much better position with the entire electorate because of Hierro's relation with the outgoing government. In 1999, then, the Colorados chose the best candidate for the general election and were ultimately successful. In 2004, the only party with a true primary was the PN, choosing Larrañaga over Lacalle. In this case Larrañaga was closer to the electorate's median than Lacalle, and thus this case does not conform to Colomer's hypothesis that party militants will choose the more extreme candidate. Furthermore, even though the Blancos chose a centrist, the FA won the general election in a landslide, despite Vasquez's position on the left of the ideological scale. In sum, primaries have not always yielded winners who are more representative of their parties than the full electorate, and it is also unclear that these relatively extreme candidates are poor general election competitors (see Carey and Polga-Hecimovich 2006). More data is necessary to test whether this is a result of the other parties simply choosing poor candidates (though the 2004 election does not support this assertion).

Candidate Type as an Independent Variable

In this section we analyze candidate type as an independent variable to explore how it affects political behavior. Siavelis and Morgenstern recognize in Chapter 1 that recruitment patterns tend to affect the electoral campaigns and the prospects for presidents to build majorities and to develop stable relationships with the legislature. They also recognize that there are numerous problems with a direct tie between recruitment and selection processes and the behavior of executives. Still, we propose to test their hypothesis that *party insiders* will be more likely to have support of their own parties, especially if the legislators from the president's party are *loyalists*.

With the aim of testing this hypothesis, we analyze four variables that may be affected by the type of candidate: the electoral campaign of the main presidential candidates for the period from 1985 to 2004; the presidents' legislative support; the president parties' discipline in the legislative arena; and the types of cabinets built by presidents. Though our data is limited, we find, overall, support for Siavelis and Morgenstern's hypotheses.

Campaigns

Following Siavelis and Morgenstern, we expect *party insider* candidates to have ideological party-based campaigns and the natural-*faction insiders* to act in a similar fashion. Thus, since all main presidential candidates between 1984 and 2004 were *party* or *faction insiders*, we should not expect to find important differences in the candidates' or parties' campaign styles.

In 1984, Sanguinetti won the presidency by mounting a campaign centered on the problems related to the transition to democracy. The slogan of his campaign was *"El cambio en paz"* ("A peaceful change"), which was intended to communicate confidence to the electorate that he and his party would be the most appropriate options to conduct the transition. The main candidate of the PN, Alberto Zumarán, by contrast, carried out a campaign centered on the political defects of the transition. José Crottoggini of the FA ran on updating the party's electoral program of 1971 and stressing solutions to the problems left over from the military dictatorship (Gillespie 1995).

In 1989, the winning candidate, Lacalle, anchored his campaign in a structural reforms–based program geared to decrease the size of the state with the slogan *"Respuesta nacional"* ("The national answer"), while he introduced himself in the media as "Presidente Lacalle." His main opponent, Jorge Batlle, developed a campaign based on policies similar to Lacalle's. His slogan was *"Para volver a vivir"* ("To live again")—aimed at making the citizenry aware of the prosperous past associated with the Partido Colorado and, in particular, presidents with last the name Batlle.[15] The FA's candidate, Liber Seregni, focused his campaign on economic and social problems, a platform very similar to that in the last election.

In the following election, Sanguinetti returned to government with a social democratic program untitled *"El Uruguay entre todos"* ("Uruguay for everyone"). As a response to the reforms promoted by Lacalle's government, the PC proposed a campaign intending to transform the state and the economy based on gradual reforms that could attract widespread social support. The main candidate of the PN, Alberto Volonté, proposed the program *"Manos a la obra"* ("Let's get to work"), whose thrust was very similar to the one presented by Sanguinetti. The FA presented Tabaré Vázquez as its candidate and its program contained political proposals fitting for the moderate left (Garcé and Yaffé 2004).

In 1999 Uruguay used its new electoral system, which forced every party to present only one candidate for the first time. The PCs' candidate, Jorge Batlle,

15. By then there had been three presidents with the last name Batlle who were associated with prosperous periods: Lorenzo Batlle (1868–1872), José Batlle y Ordoñez (1903–1907 and 1911–1915), and Luis Batlle Berres (1947–1951 and 1955–1959).

distanced himself from the programmatic style developed in previous elections. The main slogan of his campaign—*"Un sentimiento que está en la gente"* ("What the people feel")—was developed as a two-round strategy. For the primaries this slogan was meant to create an image of the candidate as a sensitive person, representative of the whole party, whereas for the general election it was meant to facilitate a programmatic alliance with the PN (De Armas and Cardarello 2000). The candidate of the PN, Luis Alberto Lacalle, launched a campaign based on his achievements while in office, using a strategy similar to the one developed in 1989, which had had "Presidente Lacalle" as its slogan. Tabaré Vázquez, already acknowledged as the leader of the left, was the candidate of the FA again. The outlines of his program, *"El otro programa"* ("The other program") was similar to that of the previous election. The second round had an important programmatic slant, because the debate centered on the tax reform proposed by the FA (Garcé and Yaffé 2004).

Finally, in 2004, the candidate who ultimately won, Tabaré Vázquez, developed a campaign based on the idea of *"El Uruguay productivo"* ("A productive Uruguay"). His program was more moderate than that of the previous election, and it was meant to call attention to proposals for overcoming the economic and social consequences of the deep 2002 financial crisis. The candidate of the PN, Jorge Larrañaga, carried out a campaign with similar programmatic contents. His slogan *"Un nuevo país"* ("A new country") also mentioned the necessity of overcoming the consequences of the crisis. The candidate of PC, Guillermo Stirling, presented a program called *"La revolución del centro"* ("The revolution of the center") that suggested his proposed reforms for guaranteeing the growth of the country in the medium term (Chasquetti and Garcé 2005).

To sum up, the competition in these four presidential elections was dominated by *insiders*, and there are no significant differences between natural and designated candidates. The campaigns confirm Siavelis and Morgenstern's expectation that "*insiders* [should] wage campaigns on bigger issues related to ideology and the party's record" (Chapter 1, p.32). Although the programmatic positions of parties and candidates tended to moderate in the course of time, the intensity of ideological debate between left and right has remained a constant, and the *insider* candidates have always presented significant campaign issues and proudly worn the party label.

Legislative Support

Using the Siavelis–Morgenstern framework (see Chapter 1), we consider the president's legislative contingent as a dependent variable, with the expectation that *insider* presidents will have larger and more loyal support. Thirteen heads of government were elected in the period under consideration, ten as presidents and three as heads of the National Council of Government (Consejo Nacional de

TABLE 13.4   Types of Uruguayan Presidential Candidates, Candidates' Average Level of Party Support and Effective Number of Parties

Type of Candidate	Number of Candidates	Winning Candidates	Presidents' Party Support	Effective Number of Parties[a]
Designated *faction insider*	24	6	51.5%	2.50
Natural *faction insider*	39	5	39.6%	3.07
Natural *party insider*	6	1	52.5%	2.39
Designated *faction adherent*	3	1	41.4%	2.72

Source: Data Bank ICP—UDELAR.

a. Chamber of Representatives.

Gobierno, or NCG), a nine-member collegial executive that was elected instead of a president and vice president between 1954 and 1962. With the two exceptions of Juan María Bordaberry, who was classified as a *faction adherent*, and Tabaré Vázquez (2005), who is a *party insider*, all other winning candidates were *faction insiders*. The main difference among the *faction insiders* is how they were selected—whether they were natural or designated candidates. However, there are no theoretical reasons to expect differences in the size of the party's congressional contingent.[16] The only expectation, then, is that the *faction insiders* will have greater and more stable support than *faction adherents*.

Of the thirteen presidents, five were natural *faction insiders*: Luis Batlle Berres (1955–1959), Julio María Sanguinetti (1985-1990 and 1995–2000), Luis A. Lacalle (1990–1995), and Jorge Batlle (2000–2005). Designated *faction insiders* were Juan José de Amézaga (1943–47), Tomás Berreta (1947–47), Andrés Martínez Trueba (1951–52), Martín Echegoyen (1959–59), Daniel·Fernández Crespo (1963–63), and Oscar Gestido (1967–67).[17] Table 13.4 illustrates the average number of the presidents' supporters in the legislature, and the effective number of parties (ENP) according to the type of politician. It shows that the designated candidates have had considerably larger partisan contingents than have the natural candidates: 51.5 percent in comparison with 39.6 percent.

This association is less clear than it appears, however, since the ENP also comes into play. Jones (1995b) has shown that there is a strong inverse association between the ENP and the size of the legislative contingent of the president.

In addition, almost all the designated candidates are concentrated in the period from 1943 to 1973, when Uruguay had a two-party system. The natural candidates

16. We count as part of the presidential legislative contingent all seats held by the president's party not considering that there are factions of the president's party that do not support him, and factions of other parties that do support him.

17. Some of these terms are so short because the leaders served during the period of Uruguay's collegial executive (1952-1967) and they were presidents of the governing council, which rotated (Echegoyen and Crespo). Trueba resigned office to join the new collegial executive. Others died in office.

emerged in the postauthoritarian period (with the exception of Batlle Berres), when the party system became more fragmented. As a result, the average ENP for the designated candidates is 2.5, whereas for the natural candidates it is 3.1, and there was a strong correlation between the ENP and a president's party support in the legislature (−0.83), which confirms Jones's hypothesis.

The move to a multiparty system has also had other effects. During the long two-party era there was strong intraparty competition among many factions, though as we have explained, that competition was generally structured between two main political blocks inside each party, because minor factions built agreements to maintain their viability. As a result of these negotiations, designated candidates were common. This changed after the dictatorship, and the proportion of designated candidates dropped from 56 percent to 24 percent (see Table 13.1). Furthermore, in the earlier period six designated candidates were successful in their electoral bids, but none have won election since the return to democracy. Thus, changes in the party system dramatically affected the nature of intraparty competition, and in the current period, factions with a natural candidate have had more electoral success than those without such candidates.

To sum up, the legislative contingent of the president was larger when Uruguay had a two-party system, and there were more designated candidates than there are currently, in part because larger parties had more space for strong intraparty competition. Thus, although the level of the party system fragmentation (ENP) is still the best independent variable for explaining the size of the legislative contingent of the president, there is a clear link between the type of candidate, the ENP, and the legislative support of the president's party.

Legislative Discipline

According to Siavelis and Morgenstern we should expect *insiders* to enjoy more loyal legislative support than *adherents* or *free-wheeling independents*. Unfortunately, there are no data to measure party discipline for the predictatorship period, but we can consider the post-1985 period, when a succession of natural *faction insiders* won election. Table 13.5 shows the average Rice Index for the discipline of the president's party in successfully passing the most important pieces of legislation in each legislative term (Buquet, Chasquetti, and Moraes 1998).[18]

Parties have maintained extremely high discipline for each president, indicating a possible relationship between *faction-insider* presidents and the level of discipline of his partisan supporters. Nevertheless, these four cases do not allow

---

18. Daniel Buquet, Daniel Chasquetti, and Juan Andres Moraes (1998) created an index of legislation's importance. The Rice Index is the difference in the percentage of yes and no votes for the legislation divided by the total number of votes of the president's supporters in the legislature. A score of 100, then, implies perfect discipline and a score of 0 implies the party was divided equally.

TABLE 13.5   Measures of Legislative Discipline of Uruguayan Presidential Parties (Averages): 1985–2006

Period	President	President's Party Rice Index	Number of Laws Voted, on in Senate
1985–1990	Julio Ma. Sanguinetti	94	40
1990–1995	Luis A. Lacalle	90	33
1995–2000	Julio Ma. Sanguinetti	99	34
2000–2005	Jorge Batlle Ibáñez	100	18
2005–2006	Tabaré Vázquez	98	12

Source: Buquet, Chasquetti, and Moraes (1998); Lanzaro et al. (2001); Koolhas (2003).

categorical conclusions, since we do not have information for the other cases. For an explanation of these high levels of party discipline, Moraes (Chapter 7, this volume) argues that the highly hierarchical structure of factions ensures low transaction costs for presidents within their parties, because they have to negotiate with a small number of faction leaders—just two to three.

Cabinets

Finally, we examine the influence of candidate type on cabinet structure. Specialized literature on parliamentary cabinets affirms that the fragmentation of the party system and the degree of ideological polarization are related to cabinet duration (Laver and Schofield 1990; Strom 1990). These features should come into play in Uruguay, as presidents have the power to appoint and dismiss their ministers, but the legislature has the power of censure. Thus, weak legislative support risks cabinet instability. Here, our concern is to test Siavelis and Morgenstern's suggestion that *insider* presidents should have more stable and lasting cabinets than *adherents*.

For this study we analyzed presidential cabinets for the period from 1943 to 2000, taking into account the type of candidate, the effective number of parties, the size of the president's faction in the legislature, and the degree of congruence between shares of cabinet positions held by different parties and the legislative weight of the parties represented in the cabinet. We could not include an analysis of ideological polarization because of the lack of information for the period from 1943 to 1973.

Tables 13.6 and 13.7 show data about the duration and stability of cabinets, the Cabinet-Party Congruence Index,[19] and the ENP. We can see that natural *faction insiders* have almost two cabinets per government, lasting an average of

19. The Cabinet-Party Congruence Index measures the relationship between parties' share of cabinet seats and their legislative weight. The formula is $C = 1 - 1/2 \Sigma (|S_i - M_i|)$, where M_i is the percentage of ministries party i receives when the cabinet is formed; S_i is the percentage of legislative seats party i holds of the total of seats held by the parties joining the cabinet when the cabinet is formed (see Amorim Neto 1998).

TABLE 13.6   Type of Uruguayan Presidential Candidate and Cabinet Stability: 1943–2005

Cabinet	Date	Type of Candidate	Average Duration in Months	Number of Cabinets[a]	Cabinet-Party Congruence Index (Average)[b]	ENP[c]
Amézaga	1943	DFI	16	3	0.80	2.43
Berreta[d]	1947	DFI	10	1	0.92	2.97
Martínez Trueba	1951	DFI	19	2	0.76	2.55
Batllismo (Batlle Berres)	1955	NFI	24	2	0.96	2.53
Herrerismo (Echegoyen)	1959	DFI	48	1	0.69	2.41
UBD (F.Crespo)	1963	DFI	24	2	0.76	2.35
Gestido[d]	1967	DFI	5	2	0.83	2.33
Bordaberry	1971	DFA	5	3	0.84	2.72
Sanguinetti	1985	NFI	60	1	0.85	2.93
Lacalle	1990	NFI	20	3	0.83	3.33
Sanguinetti	1995	NFI	60	1	0.74	3.30
Batlle Ibáñez	2000	NFI	30	2	0.86	3.07

Source: Compiled and calculated by the authors from Data Bank ICP—UDELAR.

a. We applied three criteria to distinguish a new presidential cabinet: (1) the inauguration of a new president; (2) a change in the party membership of the cabinet; and (3) a change of more than 50 percent in the identity of individual ministers. See Amorim Neto (1998).

b. Cabinet-Party Congruence Index is a mathematical indicator proposed by Amorim Neto (1998).

c. Effective number of parties.

d. Berreta passed away in October 1947 and Gestido in December 1967.

TABLE 13.7   Summary of Types of Uruguayan Presidential Candidates and Cabinet Duration: 1943–2005

Type of Cabinet	N	Duration in Months	Number of Cabinets	Coalescence Index	ENP[a]
Designated *faction adherent*	1	5	3.0	0.86	2.72
Designated *faction insider*	6	20	1.8	0.81	2.52
Natural *faction insider*	5	28	1.8	0.83	3.03

Source: Compiled and calculated by the authors from Data Bank ICP—UDELAR.

a. Effective number of parties.

twenty-eight months, and the designated *faction insiders* also have an average of about two cabinets each, though with an average of only twenty months' duration.[20] In particular, Sanguinetti, a natural *faction insider*, maintained a single cabinet for each of his two terms in office, whereas Batlle Ibáñez, Batlle Berres, and Fernández Crespo were forced to make multiple changes. The only designated *faction adherent*, Juan María Bordaberry, had an even more unstable cabinet—three

20. From 1943 to 1967 the presidential term was four years, and since 1967 it has been five years.

cabinet shuffles resulting in cabinets that lasted an average of just five months each. This was a period of high political unrest and many have suggested that the selection of Bordaberry contributed to the process that eventually ended in a coup.

There is also some difference in the care that the two types of winning candidates put into building their cabinets. This is demonstrated with the Cabinet-Party Congruence Index, which measures the relationship between parties' share of cabinet seats and their legislative weight. It yields a slightly higher number for designated *faction-insider* presidents (0.86) than that of the natural *faction-insider* presidents (0.81). Even though the difference is slight, the figures suggest that designated candidates put more care into maintaining intracabinet equilibrium than natural candidates, by appointing faction ministers in proportion to the legislative size of each allied party. Regardless of the difference between the two types, the evidence is consistent with conclusions presented in this volume about Chile (see Chapter 10) and Brazil (see Chapter 9), both of which show that *party insiders* tend to build more proportional cabinets than other types of candidates.[21]

Thus, the analysis shows that natural *faction insiders* have somewhat more stable cabinets than designated *insiders*, though the latter type appoints slightly more representative cabinets. Still, we cannot validate Siavelis and Morgenstern's prediction, since there are no data on other presidential types and there is significant variance in the stability levels for the two subtypes with which Uruguay has had significant experience.

Conclusions

Candidate selection in Uruguay is and has been deeply influenced by its electoral system. The age and institutionalization of the party system have assured that almost all presidential candidates have been leaders with long political careers within their parties and factions, yielding candidates who are situated between the *party insider* and *party-adherent* categories, though they are usually (and almost exclusively in the traditional parties) *faction insiders* or *faction adherents*. Although DSV allows self-nomination, in practice a few internal factions of the main parties monopolize the elective positions, making them the true agents of candidate nomination.

The candidates of large national factions either emerge naturally or result from a negotiated settlement among different faction elites. Even when the designation is formalized by means of a convention or primary, participants tend to ratify a previous elite decision. The most important exception to this rule has been the designation of the Frente Amplio's presidential candidate, where the party has

---

21. Notice that we all reach similar conclusions in spite of using different methodological strategies.

played a greater role. All parties must now hold primary elections, but the previous forms of designation continue beneath the surface.

The effects of the electoral system and party variables on candidate type are clear, but we have had less success in delineating the effects of executive type on the political behavior of presidents. We found that there were more designated candidates, but this was related to changes in the number of parties. We also showed that natural faction leaders had won the last five elections, and that internal competition did affect electoral outcomes. The clarity of the results is clouded by other factors, however, including the number of parties and the type of candidates chosen by each party. Finally, we found that natural candidates produced somewhat more stable cabinets, though upon becoming president, designated candidates were a bit more careful in appointing cabinets congruent with legislative support.

The 1996 constitutional reform introduced significant changes in the electoral system—elimination of the DSV for the presidential election and mandatory primaries—which were intended to produce important changes in the parties. The parties have embarked on a learning process, as they have used very different selection systems in the two elections since these changes went into effect. It is already clear, however, that the party and faction leaders are finding ways to accommodate the changes while retaining the most crucial aspects of Uruguay's presidential candidate selection process: factional politics and elite decisionmaking.

Appendix to Chapter 13

TABLE 13.1A Uruguayan Presidential Candidates by Party, Faction, Type and Career: 1943–2005

Election	Candidate	Party	Faction	Type of Candidate	Previous Political Career
1942	Juan J. de Amézaga	PC	Batllismo–PSP	Designated *faction insider*	1908–14 Representative/1914–18 Minister/1921–31 Public Enterprise Director BPS
1942	Eduardo Blanco Acevedo	PC	LS	Natural *faction insider*	1934–38 Senator
1942	Eugenio Lagarmilla	PC	Riverismo	Designated *faction insider*	1908–14; 1920–23 Representative/Minister
1942	Luis A. de Herrera	PN	Herrerismo	Natural *faction insider*	1905–08; 1914–17 Representative/1925–30 CNA/1934–42 Senator/1919, 1925, 1930 Presidential Candidate
1942	Martín C. Martínez	PNI		Designated *party insider*	1899–1902; 1905–08; 1914–16 Representative/1917–25 Senator
1946	Tomás Berreta	PC	Batllismo	Designated *faction insider*	1923–30 Representative/1931–33 CNA/1943–46 Minister of Public Works
1946	Rafael Schiaffino	PC	LS	Designated *faction insider*	1945–46 Minister
1946	Alfredo Baldomir	PC	PSP	Natural *faction insider*	1938–43 President
1946	Luis A. de Herrera	PN	Herrerismo	Natural *faction insider*	1942 Presidential Candidate
1946	Alfredo García Morales	PNI		Designated *party insider*	1920–23; 1926–29; 1943–45 Representative/1929–31 Senator/1931–33 ANC
1950	César Mayo Gutiérrez	PC	Batllismo 14	Designated *faction insider*	1920–25; 1927–31 Representative/1943–50 Senator
1950	Andrés Martínez Trueba	PC	Batllismo 15	Designated *faction insider*	1920–29 Representative/1943 Senator/1947–1951 Mayor of Montevideo
1950	Eduardo Blanco Acevedo	PC	LS	Natural *faction insider*	1942 Presidential Candidate/1947–51 Senator
1950	Luis A. de Herrera	PN	Herrerismo	Natural *faction insider*	1946 Presidential Candidate
1950	Asdrúbal Delgado	PNI		Designated *party adherent*	None
1954	Orestes Lanza	PC	Batllismo 14	Designated *faction insider*	1932–33 Representative/1951–54 Senator
1954	Luis Batlle Berres	PC	Batllismo 15	Natural *faction insider*	1926–33; 1943–47 Representative/1947 Vice President/1947–51 President
1954	César Charlone	PC	LS	Natural *faction insider*	1932–33 Representative/1934–38; 1940–54 Senator /1938–1943 Vice President
1954	Luis A. de Herrera	PN	Herrerismo	Natural *faction insider*	1950 Presidential Candidate
1954	Daniel Fernández Crespo	PN	MPN	Designated *faction insider*	1932–51 Representative/1951–54 Senator
1954	Pantaleón Astiazarán	PN	Reconstrucción	Designated *faction insider*	1932–33; 1943–54 Representative
1954	Arturo Lussich	PNI		Designated *faction insider*	1905–08; 1917–27; 1943–47 Representative

TABLE 13.1A (Continued)

Election	Candidate	Party	Faction	Type of Candidate	Previous Political Career
1958	César Batlle Pacheco	PC	14-LS	Designated *faction insider*	1951–58 Representative
1958	Manuel Rodríguez Correa	PC	Batllismo 15	Designated *faction insider*	1947–52 Representative
1958	Martín Echegoyen	PN	Herrero-Ruralismo	Designated *faction insider*	1943–58 Senator
1958	Angel María Cusano	PN	Intransigentes	Designated *faction insider*	1934–42 Representative/1943–58 Senator
1958	Salvador Ferrer Serra	PN	UBD	Designated *faction insider*	1947–55 Representative/1955–58 Senator
1962	Luis Batlle Berres	PC	Batllismo 14	Natural *faction insider*	1947–51 President/1955–59 NCG
1962	Zelmar Michelini	PC	PGP 99	Natural *faction insider*	Representative 1955–62
1962	Oscar Gestido	PC	UCB	Designated *faction insider*	Military/1955–1962 Public Enterprise Director PLUNA and AFE
1962	Alberto Arocena	PN	Herrero-Ruralismo	Designated *faction insider*	None
1962	Daniel Fernández Crespo	PN	UBD-Herrer. Ortodoxo	Designated *faction insider*	1954 NCG Candidate/1955–59 NCG
1966	Jorge Batlle Ibañez	PC	Batllismo 15	Natural *faction insider*	1959–66 Representative
1966	Amilcar Vasconcellos	PC	Defensa Batllista	Natural *faction insider*	1951–59 Representative/1962–66 NCG
1966	Zelmar Michelini	PC	PGP 99	Natural *faction insider*	1962 NCG Candidate/1963–66 Representative
1966	Oscar Gestido	PC	UCB	Natural *faction insider*	1963–67 NCG
1966	Martín Echegoyen	PN	Alianza Nacionalista	Natural *faction insider*	1959–62 NCG/1963–66 Senator
1966	Alberto Heber	PN	Herrerismo Ortodoxo	Natural *faction insider*	1959–63 Representative/1963–66 NCG
1966	Alberto Gallinal Heber	PN	Reforma y Desarrollo	Designated *faction insider*	1958 NCG Candidate
1971	Liber Seregni	FA	Independent	Designated *party adherent*	Military
1971	Jorge Batlle Ibañez	PC	Batllismo 15	Natural *faction insider*	1966 Presidential Candidate
1971	Juan Ma. Bordaberry	PC	UCB	Designated *faction adherent*	1963–67 Senator PN/1970 Minister

(Continued)

TABLE 13.1A *(Continued)*

Election	Candidate	Party	Faction	Type of Candidate	Previous Political Career
1971	Amilcar Vasconcellos	PC	Unión del Partido	Natural *faction insider*	1966 Presidential Candidate
1971	Mario Aguerrondo	PN	Herrerismo	Designated *faction adherent*	Military
1971	Wilson Ferreira Aldunate	PN	PLP-MNR	Natural *faction insider*	1954–62 Representative/1963–67 Minister
1984	Juan José Crottogini	FA	Independent	Designated *party insider*	1971 Vice-presidential Candidate
1984	Julio Ma. Sanguinetti	PC	Batllismo	Natural *faction insider*	1963–73 Representative/1970 and 1972 Minister
1984	Jorge Pacheco Areco	PC	UCB	Natural *faction insider*	1967–72 President
1984	Dardo Ortiz	PN	Herrerismo	Natural *faction insider*	1955–1972 Representative/1972–73 Senator/1966 Vice-presidential Candidate/1966 Minister
1984	Alberto Zumarán	PN	PLP-MNR	Designated *faction adherent*	None
1989	Liber Seregni	FA	Independent	Natural *party insider*	1971 Presidential Candidate/since 1971 FA's President
1989	Hugo Batalla	NE	PGP 99	Natural *party insider*	1960–71 Representative/1985–89 Senator
1989	Jorge Batlle Ibañez	PC	Batllismo	Natural *faction insider*	1971 Presidential Candidate/1985–89 Senator
1989	Jorge Pacheco Areco	PC	UCB	Natural *faction insider*	1967–72 President/1984 Presidential Candidate
1989	Luis A. Lacalle	PN	Herrerismo	Natural *faction insider*	1972–73 Representative/1985–90 Senator
1989	Carlos J. Pereyra	PN	MNR	Natural *faction insider*	1971 Vice-presidential Candidate 1963–67 Representative/1967–73 Representative/1967–73 Senator/1985–89 Senator
1989	Alberto Zumarán	PN	PLP	Natural *faction insider*	1984 Presidential Candidate/1985–89 Senator
1994	Tabaré Vázquez	FA	PS*	Designated *party insider*	1990–95 Mayor of Montevideo
1994	Rafael Michelini	NE		Natural *party insider*	1990–94 Representative
1994	Jorge Batlle Ibañez	PC	Batllismo 15	Natural *faction insider*	1989 Presidential Candidate
1994	Julio Ma. Sanguinetti	PC	Foro Batllista	Natural *faction insider*	1985–90 President
1994	Jorge Pacheco Areco	PC	UCB	Natural *faction insider*	1989 Presidential Candidate
1994	Juan Andrés Ramírez	PN	Herrerismo	Designated *faction insider*	1990–92 Minister of Interior/1992–94 Senator
1994	Alberto Volonté	PN	Manos a la Obra	Designated *faction insider*	1988–1993 Public Enterprise Director UTE
1994	Carlos J. Pereyra	PN	MNR	Natural *faction insider*	1989 Presidential Candidate/1990–94 Senator

TABLE 13.1A *(Continued)*

Election	Candidate	Party	Faction	Type of Candidate	Previous Political Career
1999	Tabaré Vázquez	FA	PS*	Natural *party insider*	1994 Presidential Candidate/since 1996 FA's President
1999	Rafael Michelini	NE		Natural *party insider*	1994 Presidential Candidate/1995–99 Senator
1999	Jorge Batlle Ibañez	PC	Batllismo 15	Natural *faction insider*	1959–67 Representative/1985–00 and 1995–00 Senator/1966–71–89–94 Presidential Candidate
1999	Luis Hierro López	PC	Foro Batllista	Designated *faction insider*	1985–89 Representative/1990–98 Senator/1998 Minister of Interior
1999	Juan Andrés Ramírez	PN	Desafío Nacional	Designated *faction insider*	1994 Presidential Candidate
1999	Luis A. Lacalle	PN	Herrerismo	Natural *faction insider*	1990–95 President
1999	Alberto Volonté	PN	Manos a la Obra	Natural *faction insider*	1994 Presidential Candidate/since 1995 PN's President
1999	Álvaro Ramos	PN	Propuesta Nacional	Natural *faction insider*	1994 Vice-presidential Candidate/1995–97 Minister of Foreign Affairs
2004	Tabaré Vázquez	FA	PS*	Natural *party insider*	1999 Presidential Candidate/since 1996 FA's President
2004	Guillermo Stirling	PC	Batllismo	Designated *faction insider*	1985–98 Representative/1998–2003 Minister of Interior
2004	Alberto Iglesias	PC	UCB	Natural *faction insider*	2000–04 Public Enterprise Director BSE
2004	Jorge Larrañaga	PN	Alianza Nacional	Natural *faction insider*	1990–99 Mayor of Paysandú/2000–04 Senator
2004	Luis A. Lacalle	PN	Herrerismo	Natural *faction insider*	1990–95 President/1999 Presidential Candidate

★ Tabaré Vázquez is a member of the Socialist Party but he is not the faction leader

Notes: The ANC—Administrative National Council (CAN—Consejo Administrativo Nacional) which lasted from 1919 to 1933 and NCG—National Council of Government (CNG—Consejo Nacional de Gobierno) which lasted from 1952 to 1966 were collegial bodies that governed Uruguay rather than an individual President. The PNI and NE parties have no faction indicated in the table because they were actually factions acting as parties.

Abbreviations: BPS - Banco de Previsión Social (Social Security Bank), PLUNA - Primeras Líneas Uruguayas de Navegación Aérea (Uruguayan National Airways), AFE - Administración de Ferrocarriles de Estado (National Railroad), UTE - Usinas y Transmisiones Eléctricas (Uruguayan State Electricity Company), BSE - Banco de Seguros del Estado (Uruguayan State Insurance Company).

TABLE 13.2A Characteristics of Uruguayan Presents: 1943–2005

Presidents	Years	Type of Candidate	Party	Year of Birth	Age	Years in Public Posts	First Degree
Juan J de Amézaga	1943–47	Designated *faction insider*	PC	1881	62	18	Lawyer
Tomás Berreta	1947*	Designated *faction insider*	PC	1875	77	14	Farmer
Andrés Martínez Trueba	1951–55	Designated *faction insider*	PC	1884	67	25	Lawyer
Luis Batlle Berres	1955–59	Natural *faction insider*	PC	1897	58	15	None
Martín Echegoyen	1959–63	Designated *faction insider*	PN	1891	68	18	Lawyer
Daniel Fernández Crespo	1963–67	Designated *faction insider*	PN	1901	62	31	None
Oscar Gestido	1967*	Designated *faction insider*	PC	1901	66	12	Military
Juan Ma. Bordaberry	1972–73	Designated *faction insider*	PC	1928	44	5	Farmer
Julio Ma. Sanguinetti	1985–90	Natural *faction insider*	PC	1936	49	10	Lawyer
Luis A. Lacalle	1990–95	Natural *faction insider*	PN	1941	49	7	Lawyer
Julio Ma. Sanguinetti	1995–00	Natural *faction insider*	PC	1936	59	15	Lawyer
Jorge Batlle Ibañez	2000–05	Natural *faction insider*	PC	1927	73	18	Lawyer
Tabaré Vázquez	2005	Natural *party insider*	FA	1940	65	5	Medical doctor

Source: Author's compilation.

* Died in Office.

Part IV

Gender and Political Recruitment

Chapter Fourteen

How Do Candidate Recruitment and Selection
Processes Affect the Representation of Women?

MARIA ESCOBAR-LEMMON AND MICHELLE
M. TAYLOR-ROBINSON

An extensive literature has developed in the study of women and politics exploring how institutions affect the representation of women. However, this analysis has focused most often on formal institutions, in particular ballot type (open versus closed list), district magnitude, and quota laws. The women-in-politics literature also theorizes that recruitment processes should affect representation of women, as female political aspirants must be willing to throw their hats into the ring in order to receive a nomination (see Norris 1987, 1997c; Matland 2006). To date it has been more feasible to explore how formal rules affect representation of women because of the availability of data for coding election rules used in a country and the percentage of women found in the legislature or cabinet. This volume's focus on recruitment and selection processes makes it possible to explore whether norms for selecting candidates for the legislature and recruitment patterns for presidents affect representation of women in the legislative and executive branches of national government.

In this chapter we apply the findings from the country-study chapters to explore how candidate types found in the executive and legislative branch affect representation of women. Siavelis and Morgenstern theorize how formal and informal institutions prompt parties to select different types of candidates for president and the congress. The country-specific chapters clearly show that institutions matter, but that they are not determinant (Morgenstern and Siavelis, Chapter 15, this volume). Institutions mold the environment, but working within that environment, parties still must decide what types of candidates to select (and how), in order to maximize their chances of winning elections. Institutions such as electoral rules and gender quotas, party nomination procedures and federalism, as well as the nature of parties and the party system (for example, whether parties are coalitions of factions or united units, whether two parties dominate the party system or there are multiple important parties) affect the types of presidential and legislative candidates parties recruit and select. Here we explore whether this effect is gender-neutral, or whether women are more likely to obtain representation in the executive and legislative branches, where certain types of candidates predominate.

First we explore whether there is a correlation between Siavelis and Morgenstern's four legislative candidate types and the percentage of women in the legislature. Then we examine whether there is a relationship between the four presidential candidate types proposed in their theory and the propensity of presidents to nominate women to their cabinet, and whether women receive high-prestige cabinet posts. We also examine whether other factors that have been found to be important in earlier studies of representation of women appear to complement or mitigate the effect of candidate recruitment and selection procedures.

Literature and Hypotheses

The candidate recruitment and selection theory developed by Siavelis and Morgenstern offers a felicitous new perspective on how institutions may affect representation of women. Norris (1987, 1997c) explains that both supply and demand for women in government, as viewed by party nomination gatekeepers, impact representation of women.[1] On the supply side, women are needed who meet the unofficial but expected qualifications for a legislator or cabinet minister—for example, a pool of women with the academic, professional, and party credentials to be credible candidates or appointees (also Davis 1997). But the supply side is also affected by the willingness of female potential candidates to "throw their hats into the ring." This is where we expect party norms for candidate recruitment and selection to affect representation of women in the legislature.

We expect that parties that recruit *party loyalist* legislators will bring more women into the legislature than parties that recruit *entrepreneurs*. This expectation is derived from the women-in-politics literature (worldwide, not limited to Latin America) indicating that women are more likely to try to obtain their party's nomination when a *loyalist* is the type of deputy the party commonly wants. *Party loyalist* legislators are expected to emerge in countries where party leaders have control over nominations, such as in closed-list PR systems. However, there is a debate in the literature as to whether women are likely to be represented in greater numbers in open- or closed-list PR electoral systems. Some scholars argue that women can do better in open-list systems, because an open-list ballot gives

---

1. Richard E. Matland (2006) develops a theory of how different types of affirmative action programs for women (from quota laws to party quota rules to nominations) can affect the propensity of women to run.

voters an opportunity to vote for women (moving them up the list) when party leaders do not place women candidates in "electable" slots (Rule 1994; Shugart 1994; Taagepera 1994; Rule and Shugart 1995; Schmidt, n.d.). Others expect that women will do better in closed-list systems, provided that party leaders have concluded there is an electoral advantage to nominating women, for example, to reach out to the female vote in a political system with a gender gap in voting. Thus, parties can use the composition of their list to send a cue to voters, particularly female voters, that the party is pro-women (Jones 1998; Reynolds 1999; Ellis 2002). In addition, some scholars argue that women candidates will be less successful in open- than closed-list systems because open-list (or preferential vote) systems tend to rely on a clientelistic strategy to get votes, and such a system advantages incumbents. Since women are still represented in most legislatures in substantially lower numbers than men, women candidates are less likely to be incumbents and thus are less likely to have access to the pork and patronage resources that are often important for winning elections in those systems. Women are also thought to prefer taking part in a campaign strategy that focuses on cross-party competition and constructive ideas, rather than intraparty competition that directly pits copartisans against each other (Ellis 2002; Shugart 1994, 38).

These debates provide several reasons for us to anticipate that more women should want to throw their hats into the political ring when candidates are *party loyalists* rather than *entrepreneurs*. Although we do not have data to measure women's interest in running for congress, it is at the self-selection phase of the recruitment process that we anticipate party recruitment and selection processes to have an important impact on representation of women. Thus, our first hypothesis:

Hypothesis 1: More women will be elected to Congress when parties recruit and select *party loyalists* than if parties favor *entrepreneur* types.

Recruitment and selection processes may also affect the demand side of the equation for female candidates. Gatekeepers must perceive women candidates to be the "type" of candidate their party wants, or they will not actively recruit women. The power of a party's nomination gatekeepers will be particularly strong in closed-list PR electoral systems, where party leaders have the power to virtually guarantee the election of highly valued candidates by placing them in "safe" slots on the party's lists. Thus, we expect ballot type to interact with legislator type:

Hypothesis 2: More women will be elected to the legislature where ballot type is closed list and when parties recruit and select *party loyalists* than when ballot type is open list.

The ability of gatekeepers to select the candidates they want for the legislature is also affected by quota laws, or by a party's quota rule. The most straightforward case is where a country has adopted a quota law that stipulates a party must nominate at least a certain percentage of women in electable positions on all party slates or the party lists are thrown out. Where a "quota law with teeth" exists, we expect representation of women to increase, regardless of the type of legislator parties want to recruit, as parties will not want their lists to be thrown out by the elections tribunal (Jones 1996, 1998; Htun and Jones 2001; Norris 2004; Baldez 2007). Therefore:

> Hypothesis 3: In the presence of a quota law, we expect more women to be elected to the legislature across all legislator types.

The literature about appointment of women to cabinets is fairly small (see Davis 1997; Escobar-Lemmon and Taylor-Robinson 2005; Moon and Fountain 1997; Reynolds 1999; Siaroff 2000). In part this is because women have only recently begun to obtain full ministerial-rank appointments (with the notable exception of the Scandinavian countries, where they have had this rank for several decades), and because only very recently have presidents been criticized for not appointing any women to their cabinets. Some of the general literature about cabinet appointments, not specifically about gender, does provides a basis for expectations about how president type might affect appointment of women to the cabinet. In parliamentary systems, the cabinet must obtain majority support from the parliament, so the prime minister must form a coalition, unless his or her party won a clear majority in the parliament. Thus, prime ministers are often constrained in their cabinet appointments by the need to satisfy coalition partners. In presidential systems, presidents do not have to receive congressional approval of cabinet appointments, though in some countries the congress can censure or impeach ministers once they are in office.[2] Thus, since presidents are, at least in principal, free to select anybody they want to serve in their cabinet (Blondel 1985, Chapter 3), president type may exert a strong effect on the propensity of a president to appoint women.

Different types of presidents may perceive greater or lesser political advantage to appointing women to their cabinets. For example, *party insiders* may feel a strong need to balance party factions in order to maintain party unity, as in Argentina, where President Alfonsín gave cabinet posts to potential rivals within the party, and Chile, where Presidents Aylwin and Lagos distributed cabinet posts among the parties making up the Concertación to maintain the coalition (De Luca, Chapter 8, and Altman, Chapter 10, this volume). Such a constraint may mean that *party insiders* appoint faction leaders to their cabinet, and unless those faction leaders happen to be women, there may be little or no space left

2. One of the characteristics of a presidential, as compared to a parliamentary, system is separate selection of each branch. Thus the U.S. rule that the Senate confirm cabinet appointments is a violation of the pure presidential type (Shugart and Carey 1992).

to appoint women to posts of full cabinet rank. On the other hand, *party adherent* types may feel less beholden to their party. As De Luca showed in the chapter on Argentina (Chapter 8), and Altman in the chapter on Chile (Chapter 10), *party adherent* presidents tend to appoint personal confidants, with little regard for their party ties. In Colombia, however, *party adherents* focused on shoring up their support in their party, whereas *party insiders* reached out to the opposition (see Taylor, Botero, and Crisp, Chapter 11, this volume). On the whole, however, we expect that the more "open" appointment style of *party adherents* may be advantageous to women (provided the president has female confidants) because *party adherent* types are not limited to women who have achieved a leadership rank within their party. *Free-wheeling independent* presidents also presumably are not shackled by party expectations about whom they should appoint to their cabinet. For example, Colombia's President Álvaro Uribe named ministers from outside the traditional parties (see Chapter 11, this volume). Thus, *free-wheeling independents* may be the most likely type of presidents to appoint more than the minimum percentage of women to their cabinet. In fact, promotion of women might be yet another way for such a president to exhibit his or her independent style and to show that his or her administration is a break from the past. Thus:

Hypothesis 4: *Party insiders* will appoint a lower percentage of women to their cabinets than other types of presidents.

Hypothesis 5: *Free-wheeling independents* will appoint a higher percentage of women to their cabinets than other types of presidents.

Not all ministerial portfolios are equally valuable or prestigious, and women commonly receive less prestigious posts such as culture, education, environment, family, women's affairs (Davis 1997; Inter-Parliamentary Union 1999; Escobar-Lemmon and Taylor-Robinson 2005). Some cabinet posts make a politician a policy leader on the national or even international stage and can make him or her a *presidenciable* (politician with the potential to run for president), whereas other posts confer little prestige, policy influence, or control over pork-barrel resources. Since women have only recently become an expected part of the cabinet in Latin American countries, the number of women who have received the highest-prestige posts is still very small and not distributed evenly across countries (see Escobar-Lemmon and Taylor-Robinson 2005 for a detailed explanation of the differing prestige levels of cabinet posts). But the rarity of women in top cabinet posts—finance, foreign affairs, defense, interior—means that a president can make a real statement—that he is bringing new faces into government or that he promotes equal rights for women—by appointing a woman to these posts. We thus expect that the *free-wheeling independent* type of president will be the most likely to appoint a woman to one of the highest-prestige posts.

> Hypothesis 6: *Free-wheeling independents* will be more likely than other types of presidents to appoint a woman to a high-prestige cabinet post.

Some factors may constrain the appointments made by all types of presidents. A president whose party lacks a secure majority in the congress may need to use cabinet appointments to try to build a coalition for passing his or her legislation (Reynolds 1999; Amorim Neto 2002; Kellam 2007). Party leaders from the coalition parties are most likely to receive these coalition-building cabinet posts, and party leaders are still not likely to be women (Shvedova 1997). This suggests we would expect women to fare worst in terms of cabinet appointments when coalition building is most important.

Left parties have for quite some time made an effort to reach out to women, by adopting women-friendly policy platforms, nominating more female candidates, and often even adopting party gender quota rules (Davis 1997; Lovenduski and Norris 1993; Norris 1987, 1997d; Rule 1987; Studlar and Moncrief 1999; Thiébault 1991; Caul 2001; Htun 2003). Thus, we would expect a president whose party was to the left of the party of his closest challenger to appoint more women to his cabinet, and to be more inclined to appoint a woman to a high-prestige cabinet post, than a president from a right party, regardless of the president's type.

Methodology and Data

Ideally we would like to ask, and answer, the following questions in this chapter: All else being equal, do parties that recruit and select candidates of one type tend to elect more women to the legislature than parties that recruit and select candidates of another type? All else being equal, do some types of presidents have a greater propensity to appoint women to cabinet posts? The best way to ask these questions and produce findings that would be most comparable to other studies would be to add a variable for "legislator type" or "president type" to a standard model used to predict representation of women in the legislature or the cabinet (for example, Matland 1998; Escobar-Lemmon and Taylor-Robinson 2005, 2006). However, a multivariate regression analysis is not feasible owing to the small number of cases available and insufficient variance within cases.

Legislator Types and the Representation of Women in the Congress

Theoretically each party that wins seats in a chamber of the legislature is a case for analyzing how legislator type affects representation of women in the legislative branch. Each chamber would constitute a distinct case because, though a party's "legislator type" should be the same across chambers, other electoral factors expected to affect election of women vary across the chambers (for example, in Argentina, until 1998, senators were appointed by state legislatures whereas deputies are elected on closed party lists). However, an obstacle to conducting such fine-grained analysis is that over time data about representation of women in the legislature is available for the entire chamber, but not broken down by party.[3] Another obstacle, as can be seen in Table 15.4 (Chapter 15, this volume) is that most parties in a country have the same legislator type, despite other differences across parties such as ideological differences or differences in the party's age or electoral success. For example, in Argentina all parties recruit and select provincial *party loyalists*, in Chile *party loyalists*, and in Uruguay party faction *loyalists*. In Brazil, with the exception of the Workers' Party (PT), all parties recruit and select *entrepreneurs*, and in Colombia, both major parties recruit and select *entrepreneurs*. Only in Mexico do major parties recruit and select different legislator types—either *party loyalists* or *constituent servants*. Finally, with the partial exception of Brazil's PT, which recruits *party loyalist* or *group delegate* types, no parties in the countries studied in this book have deputies of the *group delegate* type, and only Mexico's PRD (Partido de la Revolución Democrática), and possibly the PAN (Partido Acción Nacional) have deputies of the *constituent servant* type.

Our analysis of how legislator types affect the election of women to the congress must thus be preliminary, yet it produces interesting findings that point to the utility for women and politics scholars of collecting data about legislator type for more countries. In the next section we assess the effect of legislator type on the election of women to both chambers of the six congresses discussed in this volume (Argentina, Brazil, Chile, Colombia, Mexico, and Uruguay), examining all elections since the installation of democracy, or since 1980.[4] Additional tables explore whether other factors help explain the variance in election of women within legislator type categories.

President Type and the Composition of Cabinets

Each presidency is a case in the cabinet composition analysis. While cabinet composition changes frequently in Latin American countries (Escobar-Lemmon

3. Data on the representation of women in each legislative chamber for each election going back to 1945 are available from the Inter-Parliamentary Union, Women in National Parliaments Statistical Archive (www.ipu.org/wmn-e/classif-arc.htm).

4. Data for Argentina begin with the Congress elected in 1983 (including the Senate, which was indirectly selected by the state legislatures until 1998). Data for Brazil begin with the Congress elected in 1985, in Chile with the 1990 Congress, and in Uruguay with the 1985 Congress. Colombia and Mexico have held regular elections for their legislatures for a much longer span of time, but to prevent the number of cases from those countries' being far greater than the number of cases from the other countries, we begin with the Congresses elected in 1978 in Colombia and Mexico.

and Taylor-Robinson 2005; Blondel 1985), our key independent variable of interest is "president type" based on the recruitment and selection processes used by the party that wins the presidency. President type does not change during a term, since the recruitment mechanism occurs before a president is elected so presidential term becomes our unit of analysis. Most of the presidential types that actually occur in the six countries studied in this volume are *party insiders* or *party adherents*, with two cases of *free-wheeling independents*. No *group agents* actually won the presidency. In addition, many countries repeatedly elect presidents of the same type, even when they come from different parties. For example, three of the four presidents since Uruguay installed democracy in 1985 are *party adherents*, and all Mexican presidents before Vicente Fox were *party insiders*. Colombia is the case that provides the greatest variance in president type, with four *party insiders*, two *party adherents,* and one *free-wheeling independent*. Brazil appears to have a broad array of president types, but the two *group agents* and two *party adherents* were unsuccessful candidates, and one of the *party insiders* was from the Second Republic, as was one of the *free-wheeling independents*, and we lack information about cabinet gender composition from that period.

Thus, as with our analysis of legislatures, our analysis of how president type affects appointment of women to cabinets is by necessity preliminary. Nonetheless, it produces interesting findings that point to the utility for women and politics scholars of collecting data about president type for more countries. Below we assess the effect of president type on appointment of women to the cabinet, and appointment of women to high prestige cabinet posts.[5]

Data

Our analysis of how candidate recruitment and selection processes affect representation of women covers the period of the Third Wave of democracy in Latin America (Huntington 1991). For the countries examined in this volume, that means Argentina beginning with the administration of Raúl Alfonsín that was installed in 1983; Brazil beginning with the administration of Fernando Collor, who took office in 1990; Chile starting with the administration of Patricio Aylwin in 1989; Colombia beginning with the presidency of Julio César Turbay Ayala, who took office in 1978; Mexico beginning with the presidency of Jose López Portillo, whose term began in 1976; and Uruguay starting with the administration of Julio María Sanguinetti, who took office in 1985. Start dates for our analysis of Colombia and Mexico are more difficult to select than for the countries that made a transition from military-led authoritarian rule to

---

5. We count each presidential term for which president type is presented in the country chapters as a case, so Carlos Menem of Argentina, Fernando Cardoso of Brazil, and Julio Sanguinetti of Uruguay contribute two cases each.

civilian-led democracy during the 1980s. Colombia's democratic regime began with the National Front agreement, which was installed in 1957 and ended in 1974. In Mexico, the PRI governed continuously since the 1930s, but when the regime made a transition to democracy is difficult to pin down. In the interest of balancing the time frame covered in all cases, we begin study of Colombia and Mexico with the presidential term that began closest to 1980, plus or minus a few years. To make representation of women in these six countries comparable with the entire Latin American region, we also present data for all eighteen countries, and again we use the rule of including a country in the analysis in the year it made a transition to democracy, or with the presidential administration that began closest to 1980.[6]

Women in the legislature. We measure representation of women by the percentage of women in a legislative chamber after each election, using data from the Inter-Parliamentary Union (1995; see also the IPU's Women in National Parliaments Statistical Archive www.ipu.org/wmn-e/classif-arc.htm). Each election is an observation, and if a country has a bicameral legislature, each chamber is a separate observation.

Women in the cabinet. Representation of women in presidents' cabinets is measured in two ways: the percentage of women holding the post of minister in a cabinet and whether any women hold high-prestige cabinet posts.[7] Cabinet membership changes frequently in Latin American countries: 45 percent of ministers serve only one year, and only 16 percent of ministers serve four years or more. This is problematic because our main explanatory variable of interest is presidential recruitment and selection type, which is a constant throughout a president's term. To address this issue we utilize the average percentage of females across all years of a president's term.

To determine the percentage of females in a cabinet, we coded the gender of all cabinet members based on minister names. Both authors and a native Spanish speaker independently coded all minister names in the eighteen-country data set. In cases of disagreement we contacted country experts and conducted web searches for information about the ministers. To determine whether women receive high-prestige cabinet posts, we divided all cabinet portfolios into three categories. *High-prestige* ministries are those that exercise significant control over

6. Analysis of both the legislative and presidential type includes all eighteen countries: Argentina, Brazil, Chile, Colombia, Mexico, Uruguay, plus Bolivia, Costa Rica, Dominican Republic, Ecuador, El Salvador, Guatemala, Honduras, Nicaragua, Panama, Paraguay, Peru, and Venezuela.

7. Our data about cabinet composition is assembled from data compiled by the U.S. Department of State and the CIA in Countries of the World and Their Leaders Yearbooks, which is published annually and lists the name and portfolios of all ministers. As in Escobar-Lemmon and Taylor-Robinson (2005), we include only individuals whose position had full cabinet rank. This means we exclude central bank presidents, heads of decentralized agencies, and planning corporations, as well as deputy or assistant ministers.

policy and are highly visible and prestigious: finance and economy, foreign affairs, government or interior, and public security and defense. *Medium-prestige* ministries are in charge of less high-profile policy areas and lack the prestige of top posts, but control significant financial resources: agriculture, construction and public works, education, environment and natural resources, health and social welfare, industry and commerce, justice, labor, transportation, communications and information, and planning and development. *Low-prestige* is a residual category that includes all other ministries. These portfolios lack large budgets or patronage resources and typically receive little media coverage: children and the family, culture, science and technology, sports, tourism, women's affairs, ministers for reform of the state, temporary and transient ministries, and ministers without portfolio.[8] We coded a cabinet as positive for a woman holding a high-prestige post if a female minister held a high-prestige post in any year during the administration.

A final point to clarify is that each presidential term is a separate observation, even if a president was reelected. The reason for this decision is twofold. First, at least in theory, candidate recruitment and selection processes could change from one term to the next. Second, other factors that have been found to predict representation of women in Latin American president's cabinets can vary across president's terms.

Candidate recruitment and selection types. Data about the types of candidates parties recruit and select for the legislature and for president comes from the country chapters in this volume, and are summarized in Table 15.4 (Executive and Legislator Types in Latin America) in Chapter 15. In some of the country chapters, authors defined a subtype of the basic types of candidates presented by Siavelis and Morgenstern in Chapter 1. For example, Jones designates the *party loyalist* legislators of Argentina as "provincial" *party loyalists*, and Moraes designates the *party loyalist* legislators of Uruguay as "faction" *loyalists*. Due to the small number of cases available for analysis here (each country is a case for the reasons just discussed), we use only the major legislator candidate types. We make the same decision for presidential types, as in Uruguay, even though Buquet and Chasquetti (Chapter 13) designated *party adherent* presidents as *faction insiders*.

Legislative chambers in a country, rather than individual parties, are cases for our analysis of representation of women in legislatures because data on the percentage of women in the legislature is for the entire chamber, and is not broken down by party. For Argentina, Chile, Colombia, and Uruguay this is not

---

8. See Escobar-Lemmon and Taylor-Robinson (2005) for more detailed information about coding the prestige level of ministries.

a problem, as all major parties within a country recruit and select the same type of candidates. In Brazil and Mexico, however, parties differ in the types of candidates they recruit and select. For those countries, we code the chamber's legislator type as the type of the party(s) that holds the majority of seats in the chamber. In Brazil, since the Workers' Party is the only party with a distinct type of legislator, and it has always been a minority party, Brazil is coded as having *entrepreneur* legislators, because that is the type of legislator recruited and selected by all other major parties. In Mexico, for the terms where the PRI held a majority of seats in either chamber of Congress, Mexico is coded as a *party loyalist* case. After 1997, when the PRI lost its majority in the Chamber of Deputies, we continued to treat Mexican deputies as *party loyalists* because Joy Langston (Chapter 6, this volume) classifies the PAN as being both *constituent servant* and *party loyalist*, leading us to believe the median legislator in this case is a *party loyalist*.

Two presidents covered in this analysis, Carlos Menem and Néstor Kirchner in Argentina, are described as fitting into two presidential types. To resolve these cases we carefully read the country chapters and coded each president according to the focus of the cabinet discussion provided, which led us to code Menem and Kirchner as *party adherents*.

Electoral system. The literature about election of women has long contended that women are better served by PR (proportional representation) electoral rules than by SMD (single member district) rules, but it is less clear how different types of PR ballots affect the election of women. Latin America does not have any legislatures elected by pure-SMD rules, but different types of PR elections are used. The six countries that are the focus of our analysis here use open lists (Brazil, Chile), closed lists (Argentina, Uruguay), and mixed-member majoritarian (Mexico) systems. Before 2006, Colombia elected the members of its congress via closed-list elections, but owing to the multiplicity of lists that ran under each party's label, it has been dubbed a "personal-list system." Still, for all but the 2006 election, which was officially open-list, we coded Colombia as closed-list. To code electoral rules for all eighteen Latin American countries, we obtained information from Jones (1995a, 1995b), Alcántara and Freidenberg (2001), and Willis Otero and Pérez-Liñan (2005).

Gender quota law. In some countries that have adopted a quota law mandating that women receive at least a certain percentage of the positions on the ballot, representation of women has increased dramatically. However, the impact of a quota law is thought to depend largely on whether it stipulates that women must be in "electable" slots on party lists and whether courts can sanction parties or throw out lists that do not comply with the law. Owing to the small number of cases for which we have data about legislator type, we simply examine whether a country had a gender quota law in effect at the time a particular chamber was elected.[9]

Seats the president's party holds in the legislature. To account for how constrained a president is likely to be by the need to build a coalition in the legislature, we devised a three-category coding scheme: A president's party has a *secure majority* if it controls 55 percent or more of the seats in a unicameral congress or both chambers of a bicameral congress. A president's party has a *near majority/narrow minority* if it holds 45 to 54.9 percent of the seats in a unicameral congress or in the chamber in which the party is least well represented of a bicameral congress. A *minority* president's party is one that holds less than 45 percent of the seats in a unicameral congress or in the chamber in which the party is least well represented in a bicameral congress.[10]

President on the left or right of the political spectrum. Left parties have a history of promoting women and women's issues, but what is considered a party of the left and what is considered a party of the right can vary from country to country, depending on the location of the center of the country's ideological spectrum. To capture these country-based differences, we measure whether a president is to the right or left of the second closest finisher in the presidential contest. This allows us to examine how a president whose party is perceived as liberal or conservative in a particular country affects representation of women. Data about the ideological placement of parties are from Coppedge (1997) and Alcántara and Freidenberg (2001).

Legislator Type and the Representation of Women in the Legislature

Between 1980 and 2006 the percentage of the legislature that is female consistently increased. After the most recent elections in Argentina and Costa Rica, 41.7 percent and 38.6 percent, respectively, of their legislatures are female. This is an impressive change from past years, when often less than 5 percent of legislators were female. One common argument in the literature is that the richer, more developed countries will have higher levels of women's representation (Matland 1998; Kenworthy and Malami 1999; Reynolds 1999; Norris 2004). To indicate simultaneously how the six countries discussed in this volume compare with the region as a whole and to observe the effect of development upon women's representation, we graphed the percentage of women in the legislature by a country's score on the UN Human Development Index (HDI) using different markers for

---

9. Information about quota laws is from the International Institute for Democracy and Electoral Assistance (IDEA) Global Database of Quotas for Women (www.quotaproject.org/).

10. See Escobar-Lemmon and Taylor-Robinson (2005, 834) for a detailed discussion of why this trichotomous measure is preferable to a simple count of the percentage of seats the president's party holds in a chamber.

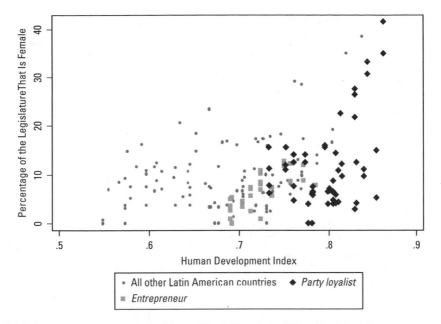

FIGURE 14.1 Percentage of the Legislature That Is Female, by HDI and Legislator Type.

each legislator type (see Figure 14.1). Although the countries discussed in the other chapters in this volume tend to fall at the upper end of the observed range of HDI, they display significant variation in the percentage of women in the legislature, with some observed instances of zero percent and also the highest observed value in the region. Thus, although, regionwide, there is a positive association between higher levels of HDI and the percentage of women in the legislature (correlation = 0.33), the variation across the six countries covered in this volume indicates our conclusions are not determined by HDI.

Table 14.1 shows how the percentage of women in the legislature compares across the different legislator types and across the specific countries in our sample. Comparison with the regional average of 9.8 percent women in the legislature (the average for eighteen countries across the entire period of the Third Wave of democracy) shows that where most legislators are *party loyalist* types there tends to be a higher than average percentage of women in the legislature (11.5 percent) and when legislators are *entrepreneurs* there tends to be a lower than average percentage of women (6.7 percent). As there is significant variation within each legislator type, we tested statistically to see whether the average percentage of women in the legislature was higher for *party loyalist* types than for *entrepreneur* types, as predicted by Hypothesis 1. A two-sample *t*-test with unequal variances yields a *t*-statistic of 3.4. The

TABLE 14.1   Percentage of Women in the Legislature by Deputy Type

	Party Loyalist **Deputies**	*Entrepreneur* **Deputies**
Average percentage of women in the legislature (observed range)	11.48 (0–41.67)	6.69 (0–12.75)
Average by country	Argentina: 13.2 (2.8–41.7) Chile: 7.8 (4.1–15) Mexico: 12.5 (4.7–22.6) Uruguay: 6.6 (0–12.1)	Brazil: 6.2 (0–12.4) Colombia: 7.0 (0.9–12.8)

Source: Author's compilation.

NOTE: Regional average using all eighteen Latin American countries is 9.7 percent with a range of 0–41.7 percent. The average for countries not included in this analysis is 9.6 percent with a range of 0–38.6 percent.

probability the two have equal means is 0.001 and that *party loyalists* have a higher mean than *entrepreneurs*, 0.0005. This provides strong support for our Hypothesis 1. It also provides interesting new support for a long-held idea in the women and politics literature that some types of political arenas are better for women because they are more *appealing* to women and thus are likely to generate more female candidates.

Hypothesis 2 was that whether legislators are selected via open- or closed-list PR should interact with a candidate's type. Specifically, a *party loyalist* recruitment and selection method should advantage women even more in closed-list elections than in elections that promote direct competition among individual candidates. A test for the equality of the means between *party loyalist* legislators from closed-list PR and those from all other systems offers the most direct comparison; however, in this case we find reasonable evidence that how *party loyalists* are selected does not affect the percentage of women in the legislature (t-statistic −1.15, 0.26 probability of equality and 0.13 probability closed-list is larger than others). If we limit the comparison to open- versus closed-lists by excluding Mexico (the only country of the six to use a mixed-member system and also the only country whose legislators may not be pure *party loyalists*, but may be *constituent servants*), then we do observe a difference in the means. When *party loyalists* are elected via closed-list PR, an average of 12.7 percent of the legislature is female compared with 7.8 percent when they are elected in open-list PR. This difference is significant, as the t-statistic is −2.18 with a 0.04 probability that the means are equal and a 0.02 probability that the mean for closed-list is higher (using a test for unequal variances). Our results provide qualified support for Hypothesis 2, prompting us to consider

TABLE 14.2   Effect of Electoral System and Deputy Type on the Percentage of Women in the Legislature

	Open-List PR	Closed-List PR	Mixed Member
Party loyalist	7.8	12.7	13.1
	(4.1–15)	(10–41.7)	(7.6–22.6)
Entrepreneur	6.3	6.9	
	(0–12.3)	(0.9–12.7)	
Regional average	8.8	9.7	13.2
	(0–29.2)	(0–41.7)	(5.9–22.6)

Source: Author's compilation.

how the electoral system affects *entrepreneurs* and how both types compare with the regional average.

Table 14.2 reveals that electing *party loyalists* via closed-list PR tends to produce a higher percentage of women than does open-list PR, and in fact the closed-list PR elections used in Argentina and Costa Rica have produced the region's highest percentages of women. However, it is not clear that closed-list is unambiguously better than mixed-member elections for women, as the averages for these two categories are close among *party loyalists*. Moreover, it appears that across the region, the mixed-member system produces a higher percentage of women in the legislature than either pure open- or closed-list PR.[11] Interestingly, among legislatures characterized by *entrepreneur*-type legislators, there is not a noticeable difference in the percentage of women when open-list PR is used (Brazil and Colombia post-2006) versus when closed-list is in effect (Colombia pre-2006) since the means and ranges are nearly identical.[12]

Quota laws can dramatically increase the percentage of women in the legislature. Of the six countries studied in this volume, three have adopted a gender quota law, though none has been in effect the entire period. Argentina adopted the pioneering *Ley de Cupos* (law of quotas) prior to the 1993 election for the Chamber of Deputies; in Brazil a quota affected both Senate and Chamber elections in 1998 and 2002; and Mexico's quota law for the Chamber of Deputies went into effect for the 2003 election. Of these only the Argentine quota law can

11. Caution is in order regarding any conclusions based on these results, as only three Latin American countries—Bolivia, Mexico, and Venezuela—have adopted a mixed-member system. Moreover, Mexico, which contributes the bulk of the observations used to compute the regional mean for mixed-member systems, has had a quota law in effect for part of the period as well (see Baldez 2004). Additionally, it is not clear whether under this system women fare equally well under both SMD and closed-list PR or if the large number of women is simply due to their success in the closed-list PR elections.

12. These countries, however, do not offer the ideal test because prior to the adoption of open-list ballots in 2006, Colombia was known as having a "personal-list" system. The electoral law called for closed-list ballots, but parties were allowed to run multiple lists, and for the major parties, lists proliferated to the point of becoming "personal lists" that were essentially electoral vehicles for the top candidate on each list (Moreno and Escobar-Lemmon, Chapter 5, this volume).

TABLE 14.3   Effect of Quota Laws and Candidate Type on Percentage of Women in the Legislature

	No Quota Law	Quota Law
Party loyalist	8.2	28.2
	(0–16)	(14.4–41.7)
Entrepreneur	6.4	8.5
	(0–12.7)	(5.7–12.3)
Regional average	7.6	17.9
	(0–20.7)	(2.5–41.7)

Source: Author's compilation.

really be described as a quota law "with teeth"; thus, we look at the effect of simply having a quota law, regardless of how it is written or whether it contains enforcement mechanisms.[13]

Table 14.3 reports the percentage of women elected in countries that do and do not have a quota law, for both *party loyalists* and *entrepreneurs*. The differences are striking. Regionwide, in countries that do not have a quota law, the average percentage of the legislature that is female is only 7.6 percent, compared with 17.9 percent in countries with a quota law. The variation is also noticeable in that the maximum observed percentage of women in the legislature without a quota law (20.7 percent) exceeds the average observed in countries with a quota law. Interestingly, quota laws only have an impact in legislatures characterized by recruitment and selection of *party loyalists*, not legislatures known for *entrepreneurs*. In countries where there is a quota law and legislators tend to be *party loyalists*, the average percentage of women in the legislature is 28.2 percent; when there is no quota law, *party loyalist* legislatures have on average only 8.2 percent women. This obviously large difference is statistically significant as well, with a *t*-statistic of −7.2 with an associated probability of 0.0001 that they are equal and a 0.00005 probability that the percentage of women in a country with a quota law is larger than in countries without. However, we do not see the same strength of association among *entrepreneurs*, where we see an increase of only about two percentage points (from 6.4 percent to 8.5 percent) when the country has a quota law. Not surprisingly, this difference is statistically insignificant with a *t*-statistic of −1.3 with an associated probability of 0.25 that the two are different.

In sum, women do better at achieving representation in legislatures when parties recruit and select *party loyalists* to be their candidates. Women also do better

13. This is a strong test of the hypothesis and if we find results even in this case, we would be certain to find stronger confirmation for the hypothesis if we limited our analysis to quota laws "with teeth." Even though the quota law in Mexico has teeth with regard to the percentage and placement of women, the effectiveness of the law is diminished by the "escape clause," that parties do not have to comply with the quota if they select candidates via a primary, particularly since the Federal Electoral Institute (IFE) did not verify whether the primaries were legitimate. See Lisa Baldez (2007) for a thorough analysis of the effect of the interaction of primaries and gender quotas on the election of women.

with closed-list elections than with open-list, and where there are quota laws. Of the six countries covered in this volume, this combination is found in Argentina, and Argentina is a world leader in representation of women in the legislative branch. We cautiously conclude that part of the reason for the success of Argentina's quota law is not only its teeth and the country's closed-list ballot type (Jones 1996; Htun and Jones 2001), but also the type of candidates the major Argentine parties desire to recruit. In addition, the *party loyalist* type is predicted to be most appealing to potential women candidates, and they are likely to prefer the enhanced issue and party orientation characteristic of the *party loyalist* type.

Presidential Type and the Representation of Women in Cabinets

From previous research (Escobar-Lemmon and Taylor-Robinson 2005) we know that countries with higher HDI tend to have a larger percentage of the cabinet that is female (correlation = 0.26). A plot of HDI against the percentage of the cabinet that is female for the three observed types of presidents and the other countries in the region (Figure 14.2) again shows that the cases selected for analysis in this volume fall near the upper end of the development range for Latin America. There is not, however, a strong relationship between higher levels of HDI and type of president, and the percentage of women in the cabinet varies across all levels of HDI. Thus, HDI alone does not allow an accurate prediction of the percentage of women in the cabinet, so we do not believe this relationship drives our analysis.

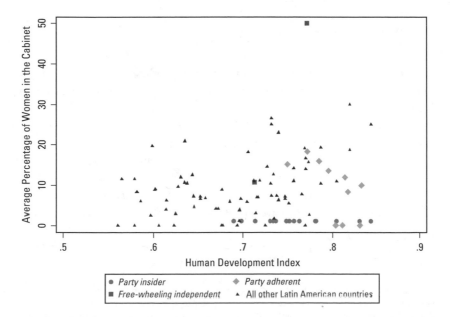

FIGURE 14.2 HDI and Average Percentage of Women in the Cabinet, by Presidential Type.

TABLE 14.4 Percentage of Cabinet That Is Female, by Presidential Type and Country

Presidential Type	Party Insiders	Party Adherents	Free-Wheeling Independents
Average percentage of cabinet that is female (range)	7.5 (0–30.5)	9.3 (0–18.4)	30.4 (10.7–50)
Average by presidential term	*Argentina* Alfonsín: 0 de la Rua: 10 *Brazil* Cardoso 1: 1.7 Cardoso 2: 0 Lula: 13.0 *Chile* Alwyin: 0 Lagos: 30.5 *Colombia* Turbay: 5.1 Betancur: 9.5 Barco: 13.5 Gaviria: 10.8 *Mexico* López Portillo: 4.3 de la Madrid: 0 Salinas: 1.9 Zedillo: 11.8	*Argentina* Menem 1: 0 Menem 2: 10 *Chile* Frei: 12 *Colombia* Samper: 15.2 Pastrana: 18.3 *Mexico* Fox: 13.6 *Uruguay* Sanguinetti 1: 15.9 Lacalle: 0 Sanguinetti 2: 8.3 Batlle: 0	*Brazil* Collor: 10.7 *Colombia* Uribe: 50.0

Source: Author's compilation.

NOTE: Regional average using all eighteen countries is 9.4 percent with a range of 0–50 percent. The average for countries not included in this analysis is 9.3 percent with a range of 0–30 percent.

Figure 14.2 provides preliminary support for Hypotheses 4 and 5 regarding the lower chance that *party insiders* appoint women to their cabinet and the greater chance that *free-wheeling independents* do. Only two presidents—Collor and Uribe—are classified by the authors in this volume as *free-wheeling independents*. One of them, Colombia's President Uribe, has the highest female percentage of his cabinet of any president in Latin America—almost 50 percent.[14] Though Collor, the other *free-wheeling independent* president, was not such a crusader for equality, the overall average percentage of women in the cabinet was highest for *free-wheeling independent* type presidents (see Table 14.4). On average, the two *free-wheeling independents* appointed cabinets where about 30 percent of the members were female. In contrast, cabinets of *party insiders* and *party adherents* averaged 7.5 percent and 9.3 percent female, respectively.

14. In 2000, Colombia adopted a quota of 30 percent women in appointed posts in the executive branch, which may help explain why Colombian presidents have a large number of women in the cabinet; President Uribe went above the minimum required by this law with his appointments.

Table 14.4 thus provides support for Hypothesis 5, that *free-wheeling independents* will appoint more women to their cabinets than other presidents. However, it provides at best weak support for Hypothesis 4. Although *party insiders* average the lowest percentage of the cabinet that is female, their average is not significantly different from that of *party adherents*, and both *party adherents* and *party insiders* appoint fewer women than the regional average of 9.4 percent. Statistical testing confirms the absence of this difference. Using one-way ANOVA (analysis of variance) to permit a comparison of the three presidential types and all other countries in the region, we tested whether the average percentage of the cabinet that is female is the same for *party insiders*, *party adherents*, *free-wheeling independents*, and all other cases. Not surprisingly, we do not observe statistically significant differences between the means for *party insiders* and *party adherents* nor for either *party insiders* or *adherents* and the other cases. The only statistically distinguishable group is the *free-wheeling independents*. The differences between *party insiders* and *free-wheeling independents* of 22.9 ($p = 0.003$), *party adherents* and *free-wheeling independents* of 21.0 ($p = 0.01$), and *free-wheeling independents* and other cases of 21.1 (P = 0.004) are all statistically distinguishable from zero. If we restrict our analysis to presidents whose term begins after 1990 we find consistent results, although the average percentage of women is slightly higher for *party insiders* and slightly lower for *party adherents*. It remains constant for *free-wheeling independents*—who both won office after 1990. This is consistent with the diffusion effect and increasing acceptance of women in leadership positions noted by Escobar-Lemmon and Taylor-Robinson (2005). Overall, this provides relatively compelling evidence in support of Hypothesis 5, that *free-wheeling independents* really are independent and do behave differently from other presidents, although given the small number of cases in this category caution must be exercised in generalizing from these conclusions. The absence of differences between *party insiders* and *party adherents* may be due to other factors such as the president's partisan support in the legislature or left–right orientation.

Before exploring how these other factors interact with presidential type, we examine whether the pattern observed regarding the president's willingness to appoint women also extends to high-prestige cabinet positions (foreign affairs, defense, finance, and interior). Table 14.5 presents, by type, data on presidents who appoint women to high-prestige ministries. Both *free-wheeling independents* appointed at least one woman to a high-prestige ministry, whereas only 20 percent of *party insiders* and 10 percent of *party adherents* did. The average for *party insiders* is close to the regional average, but *party adherents* are noticeably lower, so they appear less disposed to appoint women to these visible high-powered posts. Table 14.5 provides strong support for Hypothesis 6, though again the small number of presidents who can be classified as *free-wheeling independents* suggests caution in generalizing these results without additional data.

Having established that, as their name implies, *free-wheeling independents* behave differently from other kinds of presidents in terms of their propensity to appoint

TABLE 14.5 Effect of Presidential Type on the Appointment of Women to High-Prestige Ministries

	Party Insiders	Party Adherents	Free-Wheeling Independents
Appointed women to high-prestige ministerial position	3 (20%)	1 (10.0%)	2 (100%)
	Lagos, Chile Gaviria, Colombia Zedillo, Mexico	Samper, Colombia	Uribe, Colombia Collor, Brazil
Did not appoint women to high-prestige ministerial position	12 (80%)	9 (90.0%)	0 (0%)

Source: Author's compilation.

NOTE: Across all eighteen Latin American countries, twenty-one of ninety-nine presidents (21.2 percent) appointed at least one women to a high-prestige post and seventy-eight (78.8 percent) did not. Among the twelve countries not discussed in this volume, fifteen of seventy-two presidents (20.8 percent) appointed a women to a high-prestige post and the remaining fifty-seven (79 percent) did not.

TABLE 14.6 Effect of Presidential Type and President's Support in the Legislature on the Percentage of Women Appointed to the Cabinet

	Secure Majority	Near Majority or Narrow Majority	Certain Minority
Party insider	2.1 (0–4.3)	10.1 (0–30.5)	6.2 (0–13.0)
Party adherent		9.3 (0–15.3)	9.4 (0–18.4)
Free-wheeling independent			30.4 (10.7–50.0)
Regional average (18 countries)	3.5 (0–7)	9.2 (0–30.5)	10.5 (0–50)

Source: Author's compilation.

women to the cabinet and to give them high-prestige posts, we now consider whether the president's support base in the legislature may constrain his ability to include women in the cabinet, if these positions must be used either to shore up support with faction leaders or to build coalitions with other parties, either of which is likely to place women at a disadvantage.

Table 14.6 classifies presidents on the basis of their support in the legislature (secure majority, near majority/narrow minority, certain minority) and by presidential type and reports the average percentage of women in the cabinet. Three things are noteworthy in Table 14.6. First, both *free-wheeling independent* presidents lacked a support base in the legislature, which prevents us from drawing any conclusion regarding what effect a president's support base in the legislature has upon the appointment of women by *free-wheeling independents.* Second, only in cases where the president was a *party insider* did the president possess a secure majority. The few cases in this category are all from pre-1997 Mexico (José Lopez Portillo, Miguel de la Madrid, and Carlos Salinas), and these presidents were among those least likely to include women—averaging only about 2 percent female cabinet members between them. All three may have been secure enough in their position that they did not try to "reach out" to women, preferring instead to use their appointments for other purposes. Among *party insiders,* presidents with a near majority or a narrow minority tended to appoint the largest percentage of female cabinet ministers (10.1 percent). However, this difference is not statistically significantly from the percentage appointed by minority (or majority) presidents. Third, there is little observable difference between *party adherents* who are certain to have a minority and those with somewhat more partisan support in congress. The lack of variance in terms of presidential support in congress within president types makes it difficult to draw conclusions about whether partisan support in congress affects the cabinet appointment patterns of any type of president. For now, what is possibly of greatest interest is that the pattern for *party insider* presidents resembles that for all Latin American presidents, with the higher percentage of women appointed to cabinets of presidents who lack a clear majority in the legislature. President type will need to be determined for more countries and parties before strong conclusions can be made about how president type and the seat share of the president's party in the legislature interact to affect representation of women.

Lastly, we explore whether presidential ideology affects the appointment of women to presidential cabinets after controlling for presidential type. Table 14.7 compares the percentage of women in the cabinet for presidents who were to the left of the runner-up with those to the right of the runner-up across

TABLE 14.7   Effect of Ideology and Presidential Type on the Percentage of Female Ministers

	President to the Left of Runner-up	President to the Right of Runner-up
Party insider	10.5	2.6
	(0–30.5)	(0 9.5)
Party adherent	12.9	7.0
	(8.3–15.9)	(0–18.4)
Free-wheeling		30.4
independent		(10.7–50)
Regional average	8.8	10.2
(18 countries)	(0–30.5)	(0–50)

Source: Author's compilation.

presidential types. Regionwide averages might lead to a conclusion that there is little difference in the willingness of presidents of the left or right to appoint women to their cabinet, which is contrary to the expectation in the literature that parties of the left promote representation of women. However, among both *party insiders* and *party adherents* we find the expected pattern that presidents of the left promote women more than presidents of the right. Moreover, although the differences in means between left and right presidents are not meaningful in the regional sample, they are among *party insiders* and to a lesser degree among *party adherents*. The almost eight-percentage-point difference between left- and right-leaning *party insiders* is statistically different from zero (t-stat $= -1.82$, $p = 0.09$) and with higher certainty ($p = 0.05$) is greater for left presidents. Among *party adherents* the difference only approaches statistical significance when testing if the mean is greater for presidents of the left than those of the right ($p = 0.11$). Since all *free-wheeling independent* presidents covered in this volume were to the right of their closest competitor for office, we cannot examine how ideology interacts with the *free-wheeling independents* type. Still, these findings indicate that when parties recruit and select *party insider* types of presidential candidates, presidents who are to the left of their nearest challenger are statistically more likely than right presidents to appoint women to their cabinets (t-stat $= -1.8$, $p < 0.05$). The difference, among *party adherents* is not statistically significant (t-stat $= -1.34$, $p < 0.11$), although it is in the expected direction.

In sum, president type makes a difference for representation of women in the executive branch. *Free-wheeling independents* appoint a greater percentage of women as full cabinet ministers than do *party insiders* or *party adherents*, and they also put a woman in one of the most prestigious posts. More detailed analysis indicates that a *party insider* president who is to the left of his closest competitor advantages women, and that women fare better when a *party insider* lacks a strong majority in the congress.

Conclusion

This chapter shows quite clearly that candidate recruitment and selection processes matter for representation of women in both the legislative and executive branches of Latin American governments. Although six countries is a small group of cases from which to make generalizations, and the six countries studied in this volume tend to cluster at the high end of the development spectrum for the region, the cases vary on candidate types, and also on key factors that have been found to influence election and appointment of women (ballot type, gender quotas, the left–right position of candidates). Thus, even though the number of cases we are able to study here is small, the findings are very important for the study of women in politics in Latin America.

Information about candidate recruitment and selection processes can help explain the variance within types of institutional or socioeconomic factors that the literature expects to have a significant impact on representation of women. For example, women are expected to be advantaged in electoral systems that use closed-list ballots with high district magnitude and that have a gender quota. But we know that even within the subset of Latin American countries that use closed-list ballots or that have adopted a gender quota for legislative elections, there is great variation in the percentage of seats held by women. This chapter shows that the types of candidates major parties tend to recruit and select can help explain which countries with closed-list PR elections or a gender quota law are likely to do especially well in terms of representation of women.

The type of presidential candidate parties recruit and select impacts the likelihood that women will have respectable representation in the cabinet. We cannot talk about "equal representation" of women in the cabinets of Latin American presidents, as few cabinets even come close to gender parity, and not all cabinet portfolios are equally valuable in terms of their importance in the cabinet or the resources or policy areas that they control. But still, we find interesting variance across president types in terms of the percentage of cabinet posts held by women and the propensity of presidents to appoint a woman to a high-prestige cabinet post. Factors such as a country's level of development, whether the president is from the left or right of a country's political spectrum, and the level of the president's partisan support in the legislature have been found to help predict representation of women in cabinets. There is also an international diffusion effect at work, and a time effect, and representation of women has increased throughout the region with the passage of time since the Third Wave of democracy began (Escobar-Lemmon and Taylor-Robinson 2005). Our findings here indicate that president type is another factor that predicts how well women will be represented in the top ranks of the executive branch.

These provocative findings about how candidate recruitment and selection processes affect representation of women prompt us to encourage scholars to study recruitment and selection in other countries. With information about recruitment and selection processes in more parties and more countries, it will be possible to control for candidate type in cross-national, time-serial empirical analysis of factors that affect the election and appointment of women. The analysis conducted here indicates that candidate type will be a valuable variable for better understanding the varying success of women in Latin American politics. Increasing the number of countries for which candidate type is known would be useful because some of the theoretical types of legislators and presidents presented by Siavelis and Morgenstern are not represented in the actual cases studied in this volume. None of the legislatures had a majority of *constituent servant* or *group delegate* type legislators, and none of the presidential candidates who were actually elected fit the *group agent* type, so we cannot evaluate how these types of legislators and presidents effect representation of women. However, given the clear differences across the types found in these six countries, it would probably be a fruitful topic for exploration. Future research should also disaggregate legislatures into party delegations, to determine whether parties within the same country with different recruitment and selection processes produce different results for women. Such disaggregated analysis was not possible here, owing to our lack of data about the partisan breakdown of the women in these legislatures, and also owing to the lack of variance in legislator type within four of the six legislatures. Future study of countries where major parties tend to recruit and select different types of legislators would allow a laboratory-like test of how candidate type, as opposed to institutional factors that often do not vary within one country, affect representation of women.

We end with the guarded conclusion that the processes parties use for recruiting and selecting candidates may benefit women, even when they may create challenges for governability and accountability. Siavelis and Morgenstern (Chapter 15, this volume) assess how different combinations of president and legislator types are likely to affect executive/legislative relations. Their analysis suggests that the combination of *free-wheeling independent* presidents and *party loyalist* legislators should produce sub-optimal outcomes. Our findings, however, indicate that representation of women in the legislature and the cabinet is likely to be highest with exactly those types of presidents and legislators. This underscores the many layers to the concept of representation (Pitkin 1967), and highlights that potentially problematic executive–legislative relations, and the governability challenges that result, may have a silver lining—enhanced representation of the historically underrepresented gender.

Part V

Summary and Conclusions

Chapter Fifteen

Pathways to Power and Democracy in Latin America

SCOTT MORGENSTERN AND PETER M. SIAVELIS

At its core, this book evaluates the role of institutions in explaining political processes. The substantive chapters support our general conclusion that institutions matter, but the chapters equally demonstrate that they are not determinant; institutions create the environment that molds outcomes and behavior. At a second level, we have explored the role of specific institutions, including party and electoral systems, in explaining a specific type of outcome, namely the procedures for choosing the types of executive and legislative candidates that emerge in different countries in Latin America. Again, we have emphasized the importance of these institutions, but also found that party-level factors, such as organization, degree of centralization, and control of financing, plus noninstitutional contextual factors such as the degree of partisanship in the electorate are necessary for understanding the origin of different types of candidates. Third, we have asked how these institutions and noninstitutional factors affect executive–legislative relations, campaigns, and intra- and interparty relations through their effects on the types of politicians that different recruitment and selection (R&S) systems produce. In this concluding chapter we aggregate the lessons of the preceding chapters to explore these issues in a comparative framework.

R&S as a Dependent Variable: Laws, Rules, and Other Factors

In Chapter 1 we generated a framework from which we hypothesized that electoral laws, geographic organization, legislative strength, and other institutions would create a context within which party rules and informal processes—including primaries, deference to leaders, party control over career paths, and other factors that could be considered part of a party's organizational and decisionmaking norms or culture—would determine candidate types. We now turn to an empirical evaluation of that proposition, beginning with the legislators and then turning to the executives.

Legislators

Table 15.1 summarizes the legislative candidate types identified by our authors. Of course, in coding candidates or countries the authors faced numerous difficulties, not least of which are the multiple types of legislative candidates within most countries, and potentially within each party. Nonetheless, we identify the modal type of candidate for each country and party according to the evaluation the substantive country-chapter authors.

The table makes evident both inter- and intracountry variance. The authors place legislators from these six countries mostly in the *party loyalist* and *entrepreneurial* columns, though the *loyalist* category produced important subtypes in Argentina and Uruguay and there are examples of legislators of the other types as well. The authors identified Brazil's PT (Partido dos Trabalhadores or Workers' Party) as a partial fit for our *group delegate* category, but it seems that Bolivia's MAS (Movimieto al Socialismo or Movement Towards Socialism) and Ecuador's Pachakutik, as well as the representatives of the special seats set aside for minority groups in Colombia, would also fall into this category. Importantly, then, the distribution across legislator types and the seeming emptiness of certain categories of legislators is the result of our case selection. If we had chosen Ecuador or Bolivia we would have had more *group agents*, and since the peasant, workers, and "popular" sectors

TABLE 15.1   Legislator Types

	Party Loyalist	Constituent Servant	Entrepreneur	Group Delegate
Argentina	Provincial-party loyalists PJ, UCR			
Brazil	PT[a]		PP, PTB, PMDB, PFL, PSDB	PT[a]
Chile	PS, PPD, PDC, UDI, RN			
Colombia			PL, PC	
Mexico	PRI, PAN[a]	PRD, PAN[a]		
Uruguay	Faction loyalists PC, PN, FA			

Source: Author's compilation.

a. In more than one category.

of Mexico's PRI (Partido Revolucionario Institucional or Institutional Revolutionary Party) were always given an important number of legislative seats, that party could also land in the *group agent* category. Further, traditional work on U.S. legislators (for example, Fenno 1978; Mayhew 1974) suggests that they would fit into the *constituent servant* category, as would Chile's legislators prior to the dictatorship, according to the description in Agor (1971) and Shugart and Carey (1992).

These patterns lead to two clear conclusions. First, the multiple categories suggest that legislator types are not a country-level phenomenon, and the intra-country variance indicates that political institutions generally and electoral institutions specifically are insufficient as explanations for candidate types. This is not to say that institutions are unimportant: each chapter specifically underlines how politicians react to the institutional framework. Still, the chapters make clear that party-level factors are often the final determinants that explain the type of candidates that emerge in each system. A key theoretical question, then, is the degree to which different types of institutions are restrictive in the sense that they channel all politicians toward a particular behavioral pattern. Most of our cases show that the particular electoral laws do yield behavioral responses, but the politicians' differing goals, strategies, and contextual situations lead them on multiple paths, often even in their responses to similar institutional stimuli.

This combined role of the electoral system and other factors is first evident in the four countries that generate *party loyalists*: Chile, Mexico, Argentina, and Uruguay. Two of these four countries, Argentina and Uruguay, produce subtypes of our category, but in all cases the authors describe the electoral rules creating a context in which other factors, such as federalism, the parties' organizational arrangements, and decisionmaking norms determine if legislators are leaders at the national, faction, or regional levels.

Chile and Mexico provide our clearest examples of *party loyalists*. For Chile, the two-member open-list electoral system would be expected to point legislators toward constituent service, according to our framework in Chapter 1. The logic was that the open list would encourage the candidates or legislators to pursue personal votes, but given the low district magnitude the party would still maintain important control over nominations. The parties have experimented with primaries to name candidates, which should decrease legislators' need to maintain loyalty to the parties. Navia, however, pointing to the centrality of the urgency of coalition maintenance, claims that the party elite have pulled the potential *constituent servants* into the *party loyalist* box by maintaining control over nominations in spite of primaries. He also cites the elites' control over legislative perquisites and committee membership to secure loyalty. The electoral laws also help the party leaders by discouraging independent candidacies, primarily through the combination of small district magnitude, and as Navia notes, the overwhelming need for elite intervention to structure alliances that have been central to the success of

Chile's democratic transitions. The conclusion, then, is not that the electoral laws are unimportant; instead we see some direct effects as well as an indirect effect of leading the parties to adapt to the incentives inherent in the system.

A different set of variables generates Mexico's *party loyalists*, but a similar broad conclusion is reached about the importance of electoral laws. Langston argues in Chapter 6 that selection strategies take place along two dimensions: the degree of openness and the level at which the decisions are made. Institutions— including the prohibition on immediate reelection, federalism, and the electoral system under which some legislators are elected by proportional representation and some by plurality in single-member districts—affect these two dimensions of candidate selection. At the same time, Langston notes the important differences among parties (including the labeling of PRD legislators as *constituent servants*) as a reason to focus on noninstitutional factors. That is, given that the election system is common to all the parties, it cannot explain differences across parties in their R&S procedures. Among the noninstitutional variables, she focuses on the parties' predemocratization organizational form and their response to increased competition. Specifically, since the PAN (Partido Acción Nacional or National Action Party) was organized at the state level, it initially implemented a decentralized candidate selection system, while the PRI used a centralized process that reflected its predemocratic organizational form. The PRD (Partido de la Revolución Democrática or Party of the Democratic Revolution) was formed in order to push for democratization, and these pressures led that party to allow more internal democracy in candidate selection during the party's early years. Explanations that rely on environment to explain behavior often border on tautology, but Langston explains that an important shift in environment led to a behavioral change. In this case the change was the increasing competitiveness of the electoral playing field. The electoral system did not change, but each of the parties adopted new candidate selection procedures. The PRI responded to the new environment by devolving some of its recruitment power to the states, the PAN increased its decentralization, and the PRD, in spite of similar pressures, moved in the opposite way, sometimes imposing candidates from the center who leaders thought could enhance their party's chances of victory.

Several of Langston's findings point away from an important role for the electoral system or other institutions in determining R&S processes, but other evidence points in the opposite direction. The most important piece of evidence against the role of the electoral system is the parties' changing R&S methods absent a change in the electoral system. She also shows that the parties have created different structures to deal with the federalist system, ranging from the PRI's centralized system to the PAN's state-based organizations. A third piece of evidence against an institutional hypothesis could be gleaned by comparing Mexico's Senate with the Chamber of Deputies, which we suspect would show similar methods in spite of dissimilar electoral rules. Langston does provide a key countervailing piece of evidence, however, when she discusses the two senatorial tiers. One-fourth of the senate is elected by a national PR list, and these politicians have different profiles and are chosen by different processes than their colleagues. The electoral system, therefore, does play a role. The plurality system is apparently an unrestrictive institution, allowing parties to choose among multiple strategies.

Argentina (Chapter 2) provides the first subtype of *party loyalist*: the provincial-*party loyalist* (though Jones also argues that some variables push the legislators toward the *constituent servant* category). From the institutionalist perspective, Jones describes a context based on a closed-list electoral system operating within a federalist system with two primary parties that sometimes must share the political playing field with provincial parties and occasional important third parties at the national level. Where in some countries (for example, pre-Chavez Venezuela) these rules could yield national-party elite control, in Argentina informal processes instill candidate loyalty to provincial rather than national leaders. These informal processes include the provincial-party elites' power to nominate candidates, control campaign financing, and influence ex-legislators' careers, as well as other aspects of patronage politics. Formal and informal variables have other influences as well. The lack of formal barriers to forming new parties and limited residency requirements for candidates and (on the informal side) voters who are willing to vote against the traditional parties allow disgruntled politicians to leave the party fold, thereby limiting the degree of discipline leaders can compel. An important aspect of Jones's study is the decision by parties to implement primaries. Though the primaries are party-level events rather than mandates of federal law, Jones's discussion shows how the primaries create a context to which the parties and candidates react; winners are those who better control the party machinery, and financial resources are key.

Uruguay yields another *loyalist* subtype, the faction *loyalist*. Again the electoral system plays a central role, as Moraes explains how the double simultaneous vote fosters a unique style of factionalized politics where the factions compete with both intra- and interpartisan rivals in the general election. A key component of this analysis, however, is the source of the institutions. In this case, there is an answer to the chicken-and-egg conundrum: factionalism among the parties led politicians to design Uruguay's unique electoral system to accommodate the prevailing factionalism. Since that decision in 1910, the electoral system has helped to reify and sustain the factions. Moraes's analysis shows that factionalism defines the R&S processes, but it is also clear that these processes are only sustainable in an accommodating electoral system.

Moraes goes beyond the institutions and also investigates the role of party statutes in explaining R&S processes. Again he finds, however, that the reified factions override other factors in explanatory power. Specifically he looks at how the parties created rules under which their convention would approve candidate lists. But, since the parties are factionalized, the rules allow the conventions to approve the multiple lists of factional candidates. He concludes, therefore, that the pulls of the electoral system are so influential in sustaining factionalized system that the party statutes are almost inconsequential. Even with the Frente Amplio, where party statutes dictate internal democracy, Moraes's interviews showed leaders imposing their will on party lists. Uruguay recently undertook an important reform of its system, which forced factions—but not parties—to limit themselves to a single list in a district. This reconcentrated power in the hands of national factional leaders, but provided further evidence of the marriage of factionalism and the electoral system.

Next, both Colombia—at least prior to its 2006 electoral reform—and Brazil have generated *entrepreneurial* legislators. For both Samuels (Chapter 3) and Moreno and Escobar-Lemmon (Chapter 5), this legislator type is strongly tied to the electoral system. The Brazilian system and the pre-2006 Colombian system allow virtual self-nomination of candidates, thus limiting leaders' abilities to assure loyalty of the rank and file. Leaders of Brazil's PT, however, have found a mechanism to counteract the electoral-system incentives. By requiring candidates to pass through a careful screening process, the party has largely eliminated self-nomination and thus produces legislators that are much closer to *party loyalists* (or perhaps *group delegates*, given the party's ties to the labor unions) than other parties. Important to this effort, Samuels notes, is the deep-rooted support for the party (rather than the politicians) in the electorate. The Brazilian case thus illustrates two central points: First, the finding that most Brazilian parties produce *entrepreneurs* is evidence of an institutional effect, which our authors trace to the electoral laws. Second, the experience of the PT's employing a different strategy and producing a different type of legislator illustrates the lack of determinacy or restrictiveness of at least this particular electoral law and the importance of party-level variables.

The Colombian case gives particular emphasis to the first of these conclusions. Moreno and Escobar-Lemmon argue that conclude, the personalism that characterizes the Colombian political system is a result of a combination of electoral and party system variables, but the key party system variable in their analysis was a direct result of a legal change. First, the authors explain that by allowing multiple lists, by withholding the right of central-party authorities to approve candidacies, and by not providing a vote pooling mechanism which gives some incentives for a party's candidates to work together, the pre-2006 electoral system not only sustained but "encourage[d] and reward[ed] independence" (p. 120) thus generating *entrepreneurial* legislators. Still, since the system permitted multiple lists without prohibiting parties from limiting their number, a party could adapt its internal regulations in an attempt to generate *loyalist* legislators. Moreno and Escobar-Lemmon point to some of the newer parties' taking control of the nomination process and rejecting some proposed lists. This shows, again, that permissive laws allow multiple R&S strategies, thus producing multiple types of legislators from one electoral system.

The Colombian case also shows the tremendous influence of a particular electoral law that is unlike those generally discussed in a comparative context. The authors explain that the heightened personal-vote seeking and factionalism that still characterizes Colombian politics was jump-started from legal provisions limiting interparty competition during the National Front period (1958–1974). These behaviors are encouraged by the multiple-list system that was already in place at that time, but because the National Front pact predetermined the number of seats for the two main parties, it led legislators to turn their attention to intraparty rivals. The previous system also produced intraparty competition, but with the National Front *all* of the competition was internal. This, the authors argue, led to heightened factionalism and disunity.

Starting with the election in 2006, Colombia implemented a new electoral law requiring that the parties present only a single list, and many of the impacts will require more time to be discernible. Still, the 2006 electoral results provide more evidence about the influence of the electoral system and contextual variables on R&S. The large number of parties in the election (no party won even one-quarter of the 163 seats in the legislature and seven parties won at least seven seats) suggests that the old factions simply formed themselves into parties rather than submitting themselves to party leaders who may or may not have given them a slot on the party list. These changes also suggest two conclusions about the role of electoral institutions. The increased number of parties shows not only that politicians do react to changed institutional formats but also that the political context interacts with the institutions in determining the legislators' behavior. The Colombian candidates in 2006 were not limited to traditional party labels in their attempt to attract voters—evidence that the voters' low level of partisan identification limits the potential impact of the electoral system. As a result, we can conclude that the new electoral system did lead to changed strategies, but at least in this foundational election it did not accomplish the goal of consolidating the political groupings.

The new system also implies an important lesson about loyalty. Under the old system, factions did not need to worry about loyalty to party leaders, because leaders approved virtually all lists submitted to them. The new system, however, forces the leaders to choose among potential candidates because only as many candidates are allowed as there are seats available from that district. Given the party leaders' discretion over who gets a slot on the list, a legislator wannabe has to have some loyalty to the party. The system allows the parties to use open lists, and consequently, as we know from the Brazilian case, the party cannot always demand strict discipline. Still, especially in small-magnitude districts, party loyalty should be higher than it was under the old system—though that discipline will likely occur within smaller party units. A key question, however, is whether the less-loyal members will simply move to other parties or submit to the discipline of the traditional parties. The answer will depend on whether the candidates' electoral fates are dependent on the traditional party labels, which they do not appear to be, given the 2006 electoral results.

Finally, Langston labels PRD legislators and some *panistas* as typifying *constituent servants*. Concerned with choosing "good" candidates, these two parties have experimented with primaries to select legislative candidates with better ties to the electorate. The party-level decision as to what type of selection system is thus a key variable, as primaries push the candidate type from *loyalists* toward *constituent servants*. As noted earlier, however, the electoral system and the no-reelection clause in the constitution are also central concerns. First, the single-member district electoral system (covering three hundred of the five hundred seats) sets up the possibility of primaries. But counteracting the independence that primaries could have is the ban on reelection which leads legislators to immediately look to their parties (or others) for aid in their postlegislative careers. This could generate more party loyalty than would be expected in a system where candidates self-nominate for primaries and tie themselves to constituents to assure future electoral success. The resulting candidates are not *entrepreneurs* but are more tied to party and district concerns.

In sum, a conjunction of contextual variables, institutions, and party-level rules and practices combines to explain the type of legislators a system produces. Given that the electoral laws only create a context (the first node in the tree suggested in Chapter 1), different parties pursue different strategies, given their different organizational arrangements, electoral challenges, and policy goals. The result is different types of candidates, even within a single country. Note also that since the party-level rules and processes change frequently in response to changes in the political environment, candidate types can change over time, even when institutional systems remain unchanged. For example, democratization in Mexico led parties to adapt their rules in a direction that produced candidates who may still be loyal to their parties but are clearly more independent than their predecessors. The United States also shows how changes in party rules can bring about changes in the types of legislators; in recent years the U.S. parties' greater use of campaign support to individual legislators has perhaps helped move the *constituent servants* somewhat toward the *party loyalist* category.

It is also evident from the chapters that party system characteristics that are not necessarily derivatives of the electoral system also influence the R&S patterns and resulting candidate types. A prime example here is the voters' identification with existing parties. Jones explains how disgruntled Argentine politicians who fail to win the nomination from one of the large parties can often win election as a member of a provincial party, and from Samuels's chapter on the Brazilian legislature we can conclude that the weak partisanship in the country contributes to the development of *entrepreneurial* legislators. As noted earlier,

Colombia provides another example: when all voters were forced to choose between the two main parties but the number of seats for the parties was pre-determined, competition turned inward. Then, after the National Front, the system sustained itself as politicians took advantage of voters' ties to the traditional parties and continued competing as loose amalgams of factions. But when the electoral system changed for the 2006 contest in a way that would not allow factional competition, and politicians sensed more limited ties of voters to the traditional parties, new parties arose. Similarly, the formation of Chile's coalitions was encouraged by its two-member-district electoral system, but the shape of those coalitions was certainly influenced by societal divisions demarcated by beliefs about Pinochet. Thus, Chile's R&S process, which entails bargaining within the coalitions about candidacies in particular districts, cannot be understood without taking into account the importance to the parties of maintaining coalition unity. Likewise, although Mexico's two-tiered electoral system for its Senate clearly influenced the R&S processes,[1] Langston explains that the nature of competition drives the degree of decentralization in those processes. Specifically, when the PRI was unconcerned about competition, its leaders maintained centralized control. But when choosing quality candidates became imperative, the party decentralized the nomination procedure. As further evidence in support of this theory, Langston notes that the process is more centralized in the states where competition is less significant and the Senate candidates chosen for the PR seats (where local ties are less important to electoral success) are still selected by central-party leadership.

In sum, the chapters all point to the role of context, institutions, and party-level rules in determining to whom candidates are loyal, which is the basis of the candidate types. At times the institutions have taken center stage, which suggests that the first node in the path gives a strong push to all politicians (as described by Moraes for Uruguay). At other times party arrangements help to define whether the candidates owe loyalty to party elites (see Jones on the provincial party ties in Argentina), militants (as Langston explains for the PAN in Mexico), constituents (PRI and PRD legislators in Mexico), outside groups (such as the coca growers in Bolivia), or just themselves (like some Brazilian legislators, according to Samuels).

In addition to the broad conclusion about the interactive role of institutions and less-formal factors, this review illustrates an important direction for future research about the restrictiveness of the particular institutions. Cox (1997) suggests that the restrictiveness of institutions interacts with social cleavages to determine the number of parties, but we have not yet been able to define the

---

1. In each of the thirty-two states, two senators from the top party plus one from the first minority win seats. Another thirty-two seats are distributed in a nationwide PR district, based on the aggregated vote for the other senators.

restrictiveness of institutions beyond Cox's finding about low district magnitude and the number of parties (see Morgenstern and Vázquez-D'Elía 2007). Here the Argentine and Chilean cases suggest that their electoral systems have not determined party strategies, which supports a hypothesis that these systems are nonrestrictive. The Uruguayan case, in contrast, suggests that its electoral system has had a clearer role in explaining R&S processes, thus leading to a conclusion that its system is more restrictive. That conclusion, however, must be tempered with the knowledge that the electoral system first accommodated rather than created the country's factionalism.

Executives

Institutions still create a framework for the executive R&S processes, but here party organization and context are even more influential than in legislative R&S. Among the institutional variables that the authors found influential were primaries, two-round electoral systems, party systems, and federalism. But the institutions appear even more malleable than when discussed in connection with the legislative processes, suggesting that, as a whole, rules are less restraining to executive than legislative candidates.

When dealing with executives, the science of politics is challenged with the greater importance of contextual variables and the much smaller number of cases than when studying legislators. Still, our contributors described executive candidates as fitting all four of our ideal types, with no country exclusively producing just one type of president or candidate. Table 15.2 summarizes this result (the table includes some candidates who are only coded in the authors' tables and adds a few candidates and presidents who were not explicitly detailed in the chapters).[2] Authors identified *party insiders* in all six of our countries. In four countries (Brazil, Chile, Mexico, and Uruguay) *party insiders* held the presidency as of 2007, but in another, Colombia, *insiders* have not held the presidency since the 1980s. In our final case, Argentina, *insiders* have twice held the presidency since the return of democracy in 1983, and a third president moved from the *adherent* to the *insider* category for reelection. The authors did identify a few *group agents*, but none of these were elected. Eight *free-wheeling independents* (*FWIs*) were identified in four countries, nowhere near the number of *party insiders* or *party adherents*. Again, as was the case in our findings concerning types of legislators, part of the reason so few *FWIs* were identified was the result of case selection. Indeed, with the emergence of Hugo Chavez, a quintessential *FWI*, and other candidates of his ilk, the *FWI* seems to be a type of candidate that is growing in importance.

2. For illustrative purposes, the table includes Salvador Allende, in Chile, and Ernesto Zedillo and predemocratic presidents in Mexico, coded as *insiders*. These designations seem uncontroversial, though Zedillo's academic and bureaucratic career point somewhat toward the *adherent* category.

Table 15.2 oversimplifies the detailed analysis in the preceding chapters: for example, although the Uruguayan candidates and presidents are coded as *party insiders* or *adherents*, Buquet and Chasquetti (Chapter 13) explain that most are better identified as *faction insiders*. De Luca describes Menem, in Argentina, as

TABLE 15.2   President Types

Country	Party Insider	Party Adherent	FWI	Group Agent
Argentina	Alfonsín	Menem[a]	Bordón	
	Alende	Kirchner	Cavallo	
	Luder		Carrió	
	Alsogaray			
	Angeloz			
	Menem[a]			
	Massaccesi			
	de la Rúa			
	Duhalde			
Brazil	Kubitschek	Gomes	Quadros	Caiado
	Goulart	Garotinho	Collor	Gabeira
	Cardoso			
	Lula			
Chile	Allende	Büchi	Errázuriz	Neef
	Aylwin	Alessandri	J. Piñera	
	Frei			
	Lagos			
	Lavín			
	Bachelet			
	Hirsch			
	S.Piñera			
Colombia	Lopez	Betancur	Uribe	
	Turbay	Gaviria		
	Barco	Samper		
	Serpa	Pastrana		
Mexico	Labastida	Fox		
	Madrazo			
	Calderón			
	López Obrador[b]			
	Cárdenas[b]			
Uruguay	Vazquez	Sanguinetti[c]		
		Lacalle[c]		
		Batlle[c]		

a. De Luca argues that Menem is a hybrid *adherent/insider.*

b. López Obrador and Cárdenas are not explicitly coded in Chapter 12, and as noted, Cárdenas, at least in his early campaigns, fits better into the *FWI* category.

c. Or *faction insiders*

fitting between or having moved from the *party adherent* to the *insider* category. In Chile, coalition dynamics complicate the coding; recent candidates are identified as *party insiders*, but they have served as candidates of the coalition. Mexico presents further complications. Although Camp describes recent and historical PRI candidates as *insiders*, Vicente Fox as a *party adherent*, and Felipe Calderón as an *insider*, the PRD candidates are not easily categorized. In spite of his antisystem posturing after losing his legal challenge in the 2006 election, the PRD flag-bearer for 2006, Lopéz Obrador, should get the *insider* label, given that he rose from positions as mayor of Mexico City and party president. The problem arises with Cuauhtémoc Cárdenas, who created the PRD and ran as its self-anointed presidential candidate between 1988 and 2000. The PRD is now a central player in Mexican politics, but it is perhaps somewhat misleading to code the founder of a new party as an *insider* rather than an *FWI*. Further, at the governor level, the PRD's candidates could hardly be considered *party insiders*, as Camp describes the party's strategy of recruiting failed PRI candidates.

In addition to oversimplifying the analysis, the table ignores the important insights that several of the chapters make with regard to executives other than the president. Explaining the types of governors and ministers—which helps analysts overcome the problem of low sample sizes in studying executives—was a key concern to the chapters on Argentina and Brazil, and the chapter on gender used the presidential types to explain the R&S of females to ministerial positions. For Argentina, De Luca explains how *party adherents* and *insiders* dominate the gubernatorial contests. Power and Mochel describe the increasing importance in Brazil of a technocratic career for ministers, though a majority of President Fernando Henrique Cardoso's ministers also had legislative experience. For governors, Power and Mochel add to our framework by describing the difference between "oligarchic" and "plural" states, and they argue that the combination of variables produces four types of gubernatorial candidates: "*party insiders*, proxies of party bosses, oligarchical proxies, and independents searching for a party label" (p. 230).

The Impact of Institutions on Executive Type

In Chapter 1 we identified five institutional variables with potential influence on executive type: the concurrence of executive and legislative elections, barriers to independents, geographic organization, the possibility of reelection, and whether countries used plurality or majoritarian rules in selecting their executives. Perhaps because the chapters were focused on either the executive or the legislature, the concurrence of the elections in the two branches did not receive much attention in the studies (though the issue is discussed in several chapters). Geographic centralization plays an important role in several chapters, but the discussion is closely linked to two party variables, inclusiveness and party organization, and thus we discuss those issues in the following section. Barriers to candidacy also failed to capture attention in the chapters, probably because the candidates they studied had overcome any barriers. Next, though its impact on candidate types was not a central concern, the possibility of reelection has certainly been influential in the selection of candidates and in their behaviors. For example, the no-reelection clause in Mexico led the sitting president, Vicente Fox, to use his sway to support an heir rather than position himself for reelection, as did Ricardo Lagos with Michele Bachelet in Chile in 2005. By contrast, Carlos Menem in Argentina, Luiz Inácio Lula da Silva in Brazil, and Álvaro Uribe in Colombia could work to maintain themselves in their positions and it seems uncontroversial to presume that the prospect of reelection led these presidents to pursue different strategies with respect to coalition partners than would have been the case if they had been lame ducks. In fact, in Menem's case, reelection probably led him to move (at least for a time) from the *adherent* toward the *insider* category.

The country studies allow a more complete review of the theory about plurality versus two-round electoral systems, an issue that interacts to some degree with barriers to entry for independents. Our general conclusion is that while the two-round systems can permit the rise of *FWIs*, these candidate types have not arisen where existing parties continue to hold the attention of voters. One case, Colombia, does suggest, however, that two-round systems could contribute to factionalization of a party system. As suggested in Chapter 1, institutional variables create a context from which party or contextual variables determine a path toward candidate types.

Our extension of the standard electoral-system hypothesis—that plurality elections should reduce the number of candidates in comparison to two-round majoritarian systems—is that plurality systems should produce more *loyalists* and two-round systems more *FWIs*. The evidence provided in this volume for this proposition is spotty; in some cases the system did produced results consistent with the theory, but in others party or contextual variables are more significant in explaining the emergence of the winning candidates.

A first case partially demonstrating the predicted role of the electoral system is Argentina, which now employs a two-round system (unless the first-place candidate has either 45 percent of the vote or 40 percent and a 10 percent margin over the nearest competitor), and as predicted, the country produced multiple candidates in the most recent elections. Interestingly, the multiplicity of candidates were not all outsiders or *FWIs* representing new parties; the top two vote getters in the first round were both from the Peronist (PJ) party—one a former governor from a small state and the other a former president. The two-round system thus influenced the number of candidates, and the loophole that allowed a single party to run multiple candidates was also influential in explaining the electoral process. A final variable, however, was the PJ's inability to impose a single candidacy, so although Menem could be considered a *party insider* at this time, party variables allowed the system to produce other types of candidates as well.

Brazil has employed a two-round system since 1989, and here again the system has generated multiple candidacies. In 2002 Lula won 46.4 percent in the first round and three other candidates earned at least 12 percent of the vote. Though the parties are not particularly solid entities (a party variable, perhaps with institutional roots), Lula and several of the others (two of whom had served in a previous presidential cabinet) would be considered *adherents* or *insiders* more than outsiders. In 2006 Lula was an incumbent, so reelection may alter the prediction. In that year just two candidates, Lula and Geraldo Alckmin, won a combined total of over 90 percent of the vote in the first round (Lula then won the second round with nearly 61 percent). Alckmin was not the best example of an *insider*, since he conjoined two parties for his election, the PSDB and PFL, but he clearly was more *insider* than *adherent* (and certainly not an *FWI*), given that he had been a founder of the PSDB (Partido da Social Democracia Brasileira, or Brazilian Social Democratic Party), in 1988, and later governor of São Paulo. Interestingly, the party with the largest delegation in the Congress, the PMDB (Partido do Movimento Democrático Brasileiro, or Brazilian Democratic Movement Party), did not field a presidential candidate. In sum, then, the outcome has not been fully consistent with the institutional predictions.

Colombia, too, has recently implemented a two-round system, and there is at least some evidence that this change contributed to the success of the current *FWI* President Álvaro Uribe. The new system arrived with the 1991 constitution and did not seem to have any immediate impact as the two main parties continued to battle for the presidency. But, as Taylor, Botero, and Crisp describe in Chapter 11, the traditional party candidates were increasingly pressured from the outside and three candidates received over 25 percent of the vote in 1998. When the Liberal candidate Horacio Serpa tried to consolidate party control over nominations, Uribe broke from the party and ran as an *FWI* under a new banner. His success in the first round in both 2002 and 2006 is inconsistent with the expectations of the theory; perhaps the recognition that he only needed to place second in the first round encouraged his candidacy.

Finally, Mexico, the one country in our sample that continues to use a plurality system, provides more limited evidence that supports the theory. Since 1988 the presidential elections have been reasonably competitive (with fraud playing an important role in 1988) and in each election there have been about 2.5 effective candidates for president, with each of the main parties running an *insider* or *adherent*. Plurality, therefore, has not reduced the number of candidates to two, but perhaps it has discouraged the rise of other parties.

Argentina, Brazil, Colombia, and Mexico give at least some credence to the theory about plurality electoral rules, but our other three cases generally belie the expectations. First, Chile, which also uses a two-round system, has defied the Duvergerian hypothesis by continuing to focus on two primary *insider* candidates. Perhaps the two-round system contributed to the strong showing of a third candidate in 2005 (the two main coalitions together won just 71 percent of the vote) in the first round. But the first round candidacy of Joaquin Lavín, a UDI *insider*, probably did not affect the second round result, as the *insider* Michelle Bachelet of the Concertación prevailed over Lavín's party's coalition partner, the RN *insider* Sebastián Piñera.

Next, although our two chapters on Uruguay clearly outline an important role for the institutional structure in that country, its new two-round system has yet to play a clear role in determining presidential candidate types. The Uruguayans implemented a two-round system recently to coincide with the new requirement of a single presidential candidate per party. This system, however, cannot explain the rise of its recent candidates, as most of them preceded the institutional change. As Buquet and Chasquetti explain, before the 1996 reform each party faction supported a different candidate. Since the reform the factional candidates have had to challenge each other in a primary, but there has been no marked change in the competitive patterns. Tabaré Vázquez won office in the first round of the 2004 election, and almost surely would have been the winner in a plurality election as well. He had competed as his party's candidate since 1994, rising in the polls with each election. More important for the theory is the fact that no important outsider candidates have risen to take advantage of the lower electoral plateau created by the two-round system.

All of these cases seem to suggest the following:

- The plurality versus majoritarian electoral rules and other institutional variables initiate the R&S process and push in an initial direction.
- The institutions vary in terms of how determinative (permissive or restrictive) they are.
- The party system variables pick up the path from the institutional push to direct the processes toward particular candidate types.

When the party system is solid—implying that voters are tied to existing and ingrained parties so that outsiders cannot easily attract voters to a new organization—the recent changes to majoritarian electoral rules have not produced multiple or successful *FWI*s. Over time, however, the incentives inherent in the two-round system could put pressure on the more solid party systems, as the Colombian case suggests. Perhaps, however, the plurality rules have a more determinative impact; Mexico's party system has not splintered, and multiple studies have suggested that the U.S. party system is sustained by its plurality system. A potential conclusion, then, is that plurality rules are more constraining (determinative) than are two-round systems. We lack a case, however, where a multiparty system has adapted a plurality system in order to test this proposition.

Context, Party Variables, and the Executives

Overall, the chapters on Latin American executives suggest that although institutions were influential in explaining candidate types, the striking fluidity of the R&S processes for executives also makes clear the adaptability of laws to fit the situation. For every country in our sample the recruitment pattern changed dramatically or the formal process used for the candidate selection exhibited a profound change for at least one major party or coalition in recent elections (Table 15.3). Most of the chapters also showed that in spite of responding to a singular institutional framework, each party employed different R&S processes. As a result, the authors highlighted the importance of non-legal variables, including party organization, candidate leadership, career experience, and social connections, as determinants of the executive candidate types. These results suggest that, at least at the executive level, the laws governing R&S procedures are not unchangeable structures, and that parties and candidates can choose substantially different strategies within one set of rules. The laws, then, are both flexible and generally permissive.

Though the laws are flexible and permissive, the chapters also confirm that party decisionmakers do take the institutional context into account. For example, the PJ could not have run multiple candidates in 2003 if there had not been a two-round electoral system. Similarly, Uruguay's double simultaneous vote allowed multiple candidates from each party to compete for many years, and the recent imposition of legally mandated primaries forced clear adjustments in their parties' processes.

Still, even for these cases, analyses of electoral laws require significant contextual support to yield explanations of the R&S processes. The Argentine case requires that we take into account the fragmentation of the opposition that allowed the PJ to win in 2003 despite a divided vote, and explaining the Uruguayan case requires the analyst to consider the adaptation of the electoral

TABLE 15.3 Recent Changes in Executive R&S Systems

	Old System	Recent Election
Argentina	One candidate/party	PJ multiple candidates
Brazil	All parties had natural leader	PT ran primary
Chile	Elite agreement within coalitions	Concertación ran primary
Colombia	Two major parties dominated system	Uribe broke from traditional parties and ran successful independent campaign
Mexico	PRI president hand-picked successor candidate (*dedazo*)	PRI ran primaries
Uruguay	Double simultaneous vote	Legally mandated primaries for all parties

Source: Author's compilation.

law to existing factionalism (rather than the reverse) for the early years and the rising competitive pressures that led to the electoral system change of 1996. In short, by themselves, electoral laws are poor predictors of how R&S processes for executive positions would operate.

The central role of noninstitutional factors is evident in all the chapters on the executive. For Chile, the Concertación's primary that brought Ricardo Lagos to power was the result of the unique coalition dynamics in that country. Perhaps the 2000 Mexican election was the most dramatic within our sample, with the PRI's change to a primary, away from the *dedazo*—under which the incumbent president figuratively pointed his "big finger" towards his successor. But this shift in result and process was more in response to democratization pressures than to an institutional change. Moreover, Camp argues that the party then moved away from an open primary at both the gubernatorial and presidential levels for 2006 as a result of both costs and the role the primaries played in legitimizing losers and hence encouraging them to leave the party. Camp argues that the change to selection by party delegates shored up the PRI's ability to ensure *party insider* candidates at the state and federal levels.

Overall, then, the volume's authors agree that the institutional context cannot be ignored, but party-level variables are crucial to the analyses in every chapter. First, following the suggestions of Chapter 1, several of the chapters focused on party institutionalization or the degree to which voters are attached to extant parties, arguing that when parties are both organized and bureaucratized and seen by voters and candidates as providing the only realistic path to the presidency, candidates rise through existing party ranks, thus producing *party adherents* or *insiders*. In Mexico, for example, Camp notes that losers in the PRI primaries have been converted into successful PRD gubernatorial candidates. Similarly, Altman's discussion of Chile explains that Presidents Aylwin and Lagos, both *party insiders* had long extended careers in their respective parties, whereas Frei, whom he categorizes as a *party adherent*, came into politics much later in his career from the business world. Strong attachments to extant parties, however, do not guarantee against possible successful incursions by outsiders, as the success of Uribe in Colombia or Chávez in Venezuela attest. Further, in spite of Argentina's long-standing party tradition, Menem, a *party adherent–insider*, acted, at least at times, more like an *FWI*, often working against the legislature and his own party. Menem earned a hybrid classification partially because of his origins in the provincial leadership of the party, but also through his actions. In spite of sometimes working against the party, De Luca in Chapter 8 explains that Menem stayed with the PJ and became its recognized head, and thus an *insider*, by 1995. Thus, unlike an *FWI*, who might have formed a new personalist electoral vehicle, Menem helped to transform the existing party from within. In sum, the different cases show that strong partisan identification is but another node on the explanatory tree; it moves the R&S processes in a direction, but is not fully determinant.

Providing more nuance to this broad theory about electoral institutions and party context, De Luca argues that Argentine governors and presidential candidates are the result of an institutionalized party system and provincial control over candidacies. He then explains that candidacies are won after long provincial careers, generally within the party's organization. He also discusses the importance of the legal context, including the recent changes that created a two-round system for presidents, permitted (via a court ruling) multiple candidates for an individual party,[3] and allowed reelection. Reelection was also important to gubernatorial elections, and the electoral timetable (whether or not the gubernatorial and presidential elections were concurrent with renewal of the legislature) was also a variable in his analysis.

A second set of variables common to most of the chapters fits into the categories that we defined in Chapter 1: geographic organization, inclusiveness, and party organization. These are often—but not necessarily—tied to federalism (a legal or institutional variable), so we discuss these items together. Further, it is clear that these variables are not limited to impacting the executive; even in Chile, a nonfederal country, the politics of regionalism enter into Navia's discussion about the parties' regional strategies and the types of candidates that compete best in different districts. Still, we focus here on the role of party organization and federalism in executive R&S.

The central role of these issues is first evident in Power and Mochel's discussion of the "environmental characteristics of subnational political systems" (p. 229). Their analysis revolves around two issues: the privileged power of governors and differences across states that yield parties that are in some cases mere "instruments of oligarchical power" (p. 234) while in others the parties effectively organize and mobilize the electorate. The chapter on R&S for executives in Colombia relates a similar story, but tells it at the factional level. Taylor, Botero, and Crisp note that candidates with more clientelistic ties run best in the rural areas, while reformist candidates win more votes in cities. Moreno and Escobar-Lemmon note that there is a parallel system of R&S at the national and state levels; governors have only been elected since 1991 and already there is evidence of a proliferation of candidates. Further, Camp argues, democratization has vastly increased the importance of the state offices in the recruitment of federal officials, with President Fox as a prime example. He also argues that Fox's outsider and *adherent* status was the result of Mexico's federalist system, which allowed Fox as a governor to develop an electoral base outside of the capital city. Although federalism allowed Fox to emerge, Camp also finds that candidate type is a function of the selection system the parties have used. In 2000 the PAN chose a *party adherent*, Fox, through a primary, whereas the PRD and PRI chose *party insiders* through very different processes. The PRI used a primary to

---

3. The multiple candidacies could fit into either the party or legal boxes, as it was a party strategy backed by the court. The law was clear that each party could present just a single candidate. Further, although the PJ presented multiple candidates in 2003, it presented just one candidate in 2007.

resolve an important division in the party (and to move away from the traditional *dedazo*), whereas the PRD chose its standard-bearer by acclamation. Institutions and structures provide background for Camp's analysis, which largely examines the parties scrambling to create processes to deal with a new competitive environment. Still, the importance of the three-party structure and plurality rules (Mexico being one of only four remaining countries in Latin American that has not adopted a two-round system) are clearly influential.

The Colombian and Brazilian cases allow us to flesh out the interaction of party organization, federalism, and institutional variables in a bit more detail. First, Taylor, Botero, and Crisp argue that Colombia has had generally *insider* presidents, in spite of the same decentralized two-party structure also producing entrepreneurial legislative candidates (as described by Moreno and Escobar-Lemmon). This outcome supports the idea that institutions can allow for multiple outcomes and that R&S processes respond to multiple and sometimes conflicting stimuli. An important thesis in Chapter 11 is that the malleability of party statutes allows different types of candidates to emerge, and elites alter the rules to accommodate different candidates. Thus, when a potential candidate emerges who has worked with the party and perhaps has family ties to the incumbent or previous presidents, the leaders centralize the decision to facilitate the selection of this particular *party insider*. Alternatively, the *party adherents* that have emerged have been successful in seeking more decentralized nomination procedures that suited their needs. But in making the argument that the party rules do not constrain potential candidates, the authors also acknowledge the importance of other institutions; in this case it is the permissiveness of the electoral laws (including majority run-off elections, privately printed ballots, and nonconcurrent executive and legislative elections) that permits such easy rule adjustment. The changing party system is also a key variable in their analysis, as they suggest that the increasing urbanization of the electorate helps *party adherents* over *insiders*. This increasing urbanization has contributed to waning patron–client ties and party allegiances, and was thus important to the success of President Uribe, an *FWI*.

Power and Mochel explain that Brazil, not unlike Colombia, has produced a number of *party insiders* in spite of its loose party structure. The authors point to the importance of foundational elections as attracting *party insiders*, but it is notable that of the elected presidents, only the current and previous presidents (Lula and Cardoso) fit that category. Perhaps this suggests an improving structuration of the parties (see Lyne, 2008.). Power and Mochel also identify Brazilian candidates who fit each of the other presidential types. The *party adherents* and *FWIs* are the result of the country's weak party system and of the ease with which a candidate can form new parties, and they attribute the nomination of several *group agents* to the country's corporatist tradition. The authors also point to other institutional factors, including the timing of elections and laws on coalition formation (including Supreme Court interpretations), that shape the R&S systems for presidents, ministers, and governors. In the noninstitutional area, the authors discuss regionalism and the difference between catchall and ideological parties.

A subsidiary issue related to party organization and decentralization that was prominent in several chapters was the use of primary elections. Primaries are new to Latin America, but they are now common at both the executive and legislative levels. Although they have been used at the executive level in Argentina, Brazil, Chile, Mexico, and Uruguay, in most cases primaries are not nationally prescribed. As a result, in three of these five cases, only one major party or coalition has used them.[4] Primaries have also gained a foothold in the legislative arena in Argentina, Chile, and Mexico. Primaries entered into the discussions in a number of ways. Navia contends that the decision to use primaries in Chile has been consequential, in that low turnout can sometimes allow a small group of local militants to impose candidates who lack the "skills and appeal" (p. 107) necessary to win the general election. The potential of choosing poor general election candidates through primaries is also discussed in Buquet and Chasquetti's chapter on the Uruguayan presidency. Using a spatial modeling analogy, they argue that the primaries have led the parties to choose candidates who may be close to the median of their membership but far from the median of the country's electorate. The parties will all have to take full consideration of these issues now that the country has mandated primaries for all parties at the executive level. Finally, the lack of primaries played a clear role in the Argentine and Colombian elections of 2003 and 2002, respectively. First, De Luca explains how several Peronist candidates took advantage of a court ruling that allowed multiple copartisans to compete, which resulted in multiple Partido Justicialista candidates running against one another in the first round of the 2003 election. The effect was to hold a primary and the general election simultaneously. This resulted in two Peronists reaching the second round with just over 20 percent of the vote. The effect in Colombia, alternatively, was to produce its first president independent of the long-standing parties. In 2002 voters' long frustration with continuing violence that the traditional parties had failed to quell led to the emergence of Álvaro Uribe as a challenger to the traditional parties. Uribe could have competed for the Liberal Party's nomination, but apparently he decided that the party label had become more of a liability than an asset. Still, it is possible to sustain an argument that Uribe ran as an independent precisely because the party did not have a primary system.

Finally, similar to Moraes's discussion of legislators, Buquet and Chasquetti focus on the electoral system in explaining why most Uruguayan presidential candidates rise as faction leaders. Until the recent reform which mandated primaries, faction leaders (who gain that role by acclamation) for the two

---

4. The exceptions are Argentina and Uruguay. All parties were forced to use them in Uruguay, but in Argentina, the UCR (or Alianza) has used primaries consistently, while the PJ only used them in 1989.

"traditional" parties competed against one another and against other parties in general elections simultaneously. Under the new law, the parties hold primaries, but the factions still structure the vote. Key, then, is how the factions choose their candidates. The authors define two basic processes: the anointing of natural leaders or the designation of compromise candidates. Factional politics, an informal process, thus interacts with the electoral institutions in defining executive candidacies.

In sum, the chapters all show institutions as a beginning node in defining and explaining R&S processes, but then must add both formal and informal party and contextual variables to get to the root of what determines the R&S process and what types of candidates emerge. The processes are more variable than in the legislative studies, with the institutions perhaps less constraining. Overall, however, the authors do show how R&S influences the emergence of different types of candidates, which, in turn, influences the behavior of the elected executives.

Recruitment and Selection or Candidate Type as an Independent Variable

Our organizing principle in this volume is that R&S processes are not simply arcane details of a political system: they affect the substance of politics through their effect in determining who will (and who will not) govern the country. The thirteen substantive chapters provide ample evidence of this conclusion, identifying multiple ways in which R&S processes, acting through candidate or politician types, affect political behavior and the functioning of democracy. Specifically, the different chapters show that the presidents' and legislators' types affect campaign behaviors, interparty relations (coalitions), executive–legislative relations, mandate-reversals by executives, discipline of legislative parties, cabinet composition, and other aspects of politics. The chapter on gender shows the effect of gender on the types of legislative candidates that tend to emerge and on the executives' propensity to name women as ministers. The relative importance of each variable differs across our countries, and thus while the maintenance of the durable coalitions has been a central concern for Chile, the chapters on Argentina and Brazil stress federalism and the control by subnational leaders over resources.

Our country chapters were structured to focus on either executives or legislatures rather than the interbranch relations, but many aspects of political behavior are clearly influenced by the interaction of the these two governmental branches. Therefore in order to discuss R&S as an independent variable, Tables 15.4 and 15.5 summarize the placements of the executive and legislative types identified by the chapter studies and a few other illustrative cases (Bolivia, Venezuela, and the United States in Table 15.5). These tables allow several comparative lessons. First, although our authors identified a single predominant

TABLE 15.4 Executive and Legislator Types in Latin America

	President Types	Legislator Types
Argentina	*Party insiders* Alfonsín, de la Rua, Menem[a] *Party adherents* Menem[a], Kirchner	*Provincial-party loyalists*
Brazil	*Party insiders* Cardoso, Lula *FWI* Collor de Melo	*Entrepreneurs*, with PT as *group delegates* or *party loyalists*
Chile	*Party insiders* Aylwin, Lagos, Bachelet *Party adherent* Frei	*Party loyalists*
Colombia	*Party insiders* Lopez, Turbay, Betancur, Barco, Gaviria *Party adherents* Samper, Serpa, Pastrana	*Entrepreneurs*
Mexico	*Party insiders* Calderón; Zedillo and predemocratic PRI candidates *Party adherent* Fox	*Party loyalists* or *constituent servants*
Uruguay	*Party insiders* or *party adherents* All recent major candidates	*Faction loyalists*

a. De Luca labels Menem a hybrid *party adherent-insider.* He also discusses how the candidate changed from *adherent* to *insider* status.

legislative type in most countries, they identified multiple types of presidential candidates. If type matters for behavior, executive–legislative relations must therefore oscillate. Second, most of the executive cases fall into the two extreme types, *party insiders* or *FWIs*, though there are also a good number of *adherents*. The legislators also appear in all categories, but *party loyalists*, including the subtypes identified for Argentina and Uruguay, appear most commonly. Still, this conclusion bears examination, as several countries we did not examine would seemingly fit into other boxes. Venezuela would probably fit the pattern until 1998, with *loyalist* legislators and *insider* presidents. Since then, Chávez, the country's prototypical *FWI*, has enjoyed a very loyal supermajority in the legislature. Other countries display different patterns. Bolivia's Evo Morales could perhaps serve as a

TABLE 15.5 Combining the Typologies

Legislator Types	Executive Types			
	Party Insider	*Party Adherent*	*FWI*	*Group Agent*
Party Loyalist	Argentina[a]	Argentina[a]		Venezuela
	Chile	Chile		
	Mexico	Mexico		
	Uruguay[b]	Uruguay[b]		
Constituent Servant	Mexico	Mexico		
		United States		
Entrepreneur	Brazil	Colombia	Brazil	
	Colombia			
Group Delegate	Brazil		Brazil	Bolivia

a. Identified by Jones as provincial *party loyalists*.
b. Identified by Moraes as *factional party loyalists*.

prototypical *group delegate*, and at least his legislative followers could be categorized as *group agents*. The United States could provide another off-typical path. Recent U.S. presidents would fall into the *party adherent* category and though traditional literature (Mayhew 1974; Krehbiel 1993) would suggest an *entrepreneur* label for legislators, party loyalty has a greater effect on U.S. legislative behavior than would be presumed by our ideal type description of that category (Cox and McCubbins 1993). The U.S. legislators, therefore, would perhaps better fit under our *constituent servant* label.

The tables also allow a limited evaluation of the merits of the different combinations of executive and legislative types. A first presumption might be that combining *insider* presidents with *loyalist* legislators would be good for democratic stability. The chapters do provide some evidence for such a conclusion. Still, there is also evidence that other combinations are workable and success is not guaranteed in the top-left box. For example, though some experiences with *FWI* presidents have ended in scandals, coups, economic crises, and other disasters resulting at least in part from executive–legislative clashes (for example, Collor de Mello in Brazil; Fujimori in Peru) so have some governments led by *insiders* (for example, Allende in Chile, Pérez in Venezuela, Alfonsín and de la Rúa in Argentina). Perhaps, then, a key lesson from the study is that although the combination of candidate types defines key aspects of democratic functioning, it does not generally determine government stability—a conclusion that could perhaps be extended to the presidential–parliamentary debate. With an overemphasis on Chile in the 1970s, that long debate (Linz 1990; Valenzuela 1994; Mainwaring and Shugart 1997; Przeworski et al. 2000) centered on crisis situations and on whether the negative aspects of presidentialism were so destabilizing as to yield a tendency toward democratic breakdown. The cost of this focus was a neglect of how the Latin America's presidential governments managed the efficiency-representation tradeoffs that defined how they worked when there was no immediate threat of military intervention, as is the case across the region today. Our country chapters, by contrast, offer multiple insights about these tradeoffs and executive–legislative relations generally during what is now a long period when democracy does seem to be the "only game in town" (Linz and Stepan 1996).

Argentina

For Argentina, De Luca explains that the R&S process and candidate type have affected the presidents' cabinet decisions and executive–legislative relations. He categorizes Argentine presidents as fitting into the *party insider* and *party adherent* categories and finds stark differences in their behaviors. Alfonsín, a *party insider*, distributed cabinet posts to his copartisans and obtained the support of potential internal rivals through his distribution of different party and government posts. Menem, whom De Luca categorizes as a hybrid *adherent-insider*, appointed as cabinet members people in whom he had personal confidence, rather than long-standing activists in the PJ party. De la Rúa, an *insider*, did not fully meet expectations, owing to his commitment to his coalition partners and the economic crisis that he faced. As predicted, his first cabinet was carefully constructed to hold his coalition together, but fractures in the group soon led him to restructure the cabinet, and he filled it with personal friends and confidantes. Finally, De Luca characterizes Néstor Kirchner as an *adherent*, but one who has been more constrained in his ability to appoint a cabinet by pre-electoral deals.

With respect to executive–legislative relations, Alfonsín's *party insider* status gave him firm control of the party and facilitated dealings with Congress, where he could count on his own party's support and was able to deal effectively with the opposition. De Luca argues, on the other hand, that Kirchner and Menem have had more of a tendency to govern unilaterally, partly because of their status as *party adherents* rather than *party insiders*. Still, it is important to consider the legislative side of the equation, where, as Jones convincingly shows, Argentine legislators have loyalties to provincial-party bosses. The ability of presidents to build majorities, then, depends on the relationship of the president to these provincial bosses. Jones underscores the significance of provincial-party loyalty among legislators, underscoring its positive outcomes in representational terms, but also some of its drawbacks in terms of the ability of Argentine presidents to be able to rely on disciplined legislative contingents.

To summarize, although Argentine politicians generally fall into the *party adherent–party loyalist* box, it is not an entirely comfortable location and evaluation of the results is similarly hazy. Two issues complicate the placement and evaluation: legislators' loyalty to provincial leaders to some extent undermines the efficiency gains of a disciplined legislative party, but at the same time, the recent presidents' tendency to evade the legislature and use decrees undermines the overall role of the legislature. Still, though the categories may need refinement, the authors make clear that the politicians' type is an influential variable in explaining Argentine politics.

Brazil

As noted, Power and Mochel find that all of the types of presidential candidates we identify have emerged in Brazil, and all but the *group agent* type have acceded to the presidency, though President Lula da Silva could potentially fit that description. The authors provide evidence that presidents' postelectoral behavior tends to serve the groups that brought them to power, confirming the hypotheses we set out in the introductory chapter. With respect to presidential campaigns, Power and Mochel confirm that *FWI*s usually campaign by attacking established parties, and are erratic and unpredictable after elections. They point out that both Jânio Quadros and Fernando Collor de Mello ran by attacking the corruption of the sitting governments. Tellingly, however, neither one finished his term, leaving Brazil with two unelected presidents, João Goulart in 1961 and Itamar Franco in 1992. They go on to show that *group agent* candidacies have not been viable and that *party adherents* campaign in line with what is suggested in Chapter 1, stressing broad themes and downplaying ideology. Power and Mochel add a note of caution regarding *party insiders*. Because they must often forge pre-electoral governing alliances in a political system where this is at times quite difficult, their behavior on the campaign trail and in government has the potential to vary according to coalition exigencies.

On the legislative side, Samuels argues that, excepting those of the PT, party leaders in Brazil are particularly weak because they do not control access to the pathways to power, and they control few resources once politicians are treading that path. Although nominations are centered at the state level, as in Argentina, the Brazilian case differs because local state-party officials lack the carrots and sticks that Argentine provincial-party bosses wield. Therefore, incentives for pork-barreling are high and, as a result, party discipline is low. However, unlike *constituent servants*, Samuels notes, deputies engage in this behavior to build careers in state government. There is no organized "partisan" dynamic to pork-barreling, and national political parties do not control resource distribution to the extent that they do in other countries. Consequently, Brazilian presidents face a tough time in cultivating working legislative majorities. This is particularly the case when these entrepreneurial legislators are paired with *FWI* presidents, who tend to lack a core party contingent around which they can build a majority.

Since Lula was first elected in 2002, Brazil has presented an alternative pairing, with an *insider* president supported by *loyalist* legislators. His copartisan legislators, however, only account for about 20 percent of the legislature and thus he has had a situation similar to other presidents, where much of his support had to come from *entrepreneurial* legislators unaligned with his party. His strategy, similar to that of his predecessor, Cardoso, has been to bring other parties into his coalition. By building a partisan basis of support, the legislators perhaps continue their *entrepreneurial* activity, but now within a partisan context. Perhaps this is comparable to the U.S. situation—legislators have dual concerns of party (or coalition) and selfish ambition. The result is more reliable support than the president would have in the absence of the partisanship, but that support will continue to be contingent on particular circumstances.

This contingent support, perhaps, is what has driven a number of corruption scandals in Brazil and many other countries. The major bribery scandal of 2005 revolved around a scheme whereby legislators were paid a monthly stipend in return for support of the governing coalition. Perhaps cash should be another variable on our list of informal factors that can engender loyalty.

Consequently, in line with the analysis presented here, Brazil tends to oscillate among quadrants in the lower half of Table 15.5, with different types of presidents and consistently *entrepreneurial* legislative candidates—though again the PT legislators are exceptional with occasional *group delegates* among them. Tellingly, evidence from the Brazilian chapters suggest more troubled interbranch relations when candidate pairings move toward the *FWI-entrepreneur* combination, as evidenced by the disastrous governments of Quadros and Collor de Mello.

The PT's exception, still, is an important consideration, since the party has held the presidency since 2002. This change, however, has not led to dramatically different forms of politicking, as the party only holds about one-fifth of the legislative seats. Like his predecessors, therefore, President Lula has had to grapple with a legislature largely filled with *entrepreneurial* legislators from parties other than his own.

Chile

Table 15.5 places Chile into the two left columns of the top row, with *insider* or *adherent* presidents and *party loyalist* legislators. The Chile authors discuss two implications for behavior. First, Altman shows how the equitable distribution of cabinet posts among different parties of the coalition has contributed to the maintenance of the Concertación coalition. In particular, he shows that *party insider* presidents (such as Aylwin and Lagos) were much more likely to abide by party and coalition agreements than Frei, a *party adherent* who tended to appoint candidates more from his inner circle, in a sense violating coalition norms. From the legislative perspective, Navia underscores that *party loyalists* provide a high level of discipline. This discipline also reinforces the coalitions because leaders, including the president, have been able to compel legislators to toe the party line. Further, *loyalist* parties have also made it easier for the executive to broker agreements with the opposition, because leaders have been able to credibly negotiate as representatives of the full party. Thus, *insider* presidents and *loyalist* legislators have helped to generate solid coalitions that have facilitated governance in Chile.

This pairing could support a contention about the benefits of the upper-left corner of Table 15.5, because, as Navia explains, *party loyalist* legislators owe their selection and election to party elites, but they have lower incentives to serve constituents. What is more, he shows that because the executive often negotiates with party leaders, the role of the legislature as a lawmaking and representative body is undermined. Thus, although Chile's democracy is frequently offered as a model for other countries, that model includes only a limited role for the representative branch of government.

Colombia

Taylor, Botero, and Crisp find that three types of presidents have existed since the end of Colombia's National Front period: *party insiders*, *party adherents*, and *FWIs*. Evidence from their case suggests that candidate type matters in several ways. First, their findings regarding the cabinet behavior of Colombian presidents present an interesting and counterintuitive complement to the Chilean case in terms of the types of cabinet appointments they make. Specifically, the chapters on Chile and Colombia both show that where the *adherents* rely on their inner circles for cabinet appointments, the *insiders* reach out to the opposition. The explanation is that whereas the *adherents* must concern themselves with constructing a solid partisan support basis, the *insiders* are more confident in reaching out to the opposition. President Uribe, an *FWI*, has different concerns and has thus named ministers outside of the traditional party structures.

Second, presidential candidate type also matters for the type of voter each attracts. Taylor, Botero, and Crisp argue that *party adherents* and *FWIs* rely more on support in urban areas where they are less bound by patron–client ties. This pattern clearly influences more than just the support base of the candidates. It has clear impacts on the style of politics; since the urban candidates are generally chosen through more participatory procedures, it influences the form of party organizations and nature of representation.

These differences carry over to executive–legislative relations. In spite of the *entrepreneurial* legislators discussed by Moreno and Escobar-Lemmon, Taylor, Botero, and Crisp argue that the presidents have been able to generate support among their copartisans. Historically this has likely been facilitated by the existence of two large parties (as in the United States), but the Colombian system has devolved into a multiparty framework in recent years. Still, the authors show that patterns of bill initiation are dependent on the president's relationship with the legislature, which is based on the partisan composition of the legislature and the type of executive. Uribe has had great success, but the authors caution that if his personal popularity were to decline, relations with Congress would quickly sour. The suggestion that governmental efficiency is more reliant on the president's personal popularity when *FWIs* are in charge has long-term ramifications, given that Taylor, Botero, and Crisp conclude that the norm for executive types is moving toward that executive type and that the legislature, as a result of the new multiparty environment, will not likely offer the executive consistent support. This result may hold even if the new electoral system does reduce the system's tendency to produce *entrepreneurial* legislators independent of their parties (perhaps an unlikely prediction, in light of our conclusions about the limited effects of electoral systems).

Mexico

Throughout the period of PRI hegemony, which only recently ended, executive–legislative relations and coalition building were not a concern for presidents. *Insider* presidents were guaranteed a majority and efficiency was assured, though the powerless legislature surely hampered representation. With the transition away from PRI hegemony, there have been dramatic changes to the party system, R&S processes, and, as a result, patterns of executive–legislative relations.

Though the system is evolving quickly, the Fox administration does offer some intriguing clues as to the relationship between R&S variables and politics in Mexico. President Fox's status as a nonprofessional politician with few ties to his own National Action Party led Camp to conclude that Fox was a *party adherent*. Fox was hampered by the lack of a partisan majority in Congress, but his outsider status also became a hindrance. Camp argues that this status led Fox to surround himself with business people and party outsiders, which strained relations with his own party and stymied his legislative success. At the same time, his outsider status brought a new corps of personnel into government who brought experience from the business world as well as state and local government.

Since Camp argues that President Felipe Calderón, elected in 2006, and future presidents are likely to be *insiders*, a key question is whether that type will have more success in building coalitions. The Chilean, Colombian, and Uruguayan examples suggest that this might be so, though to this point the Mexican example suggests that *party loyalist* legislators will be wary of joining coalitions with presidents of opposing parties. This is particularly troublesome given Calderón's minority status and the high degree of interpartisan conflict that resulted from the 2006 election.

Uruguay

As Chasquetti and Buquet and Moraes stress, Uruguayan legislators and presidents are closely tied to their factions but also are embedded within a defined party structure. This results in faction *loyalist* legislators and presidents who are *faction* (as opposed to party) *insiders* or *faction adherents*. Together these chapters find that the types influence coalition patterns, legislative support of the president, and legislators' orientation toward constituents.

First, Buquet and Chasquetti evaluate the effect of presidential candidate types on cabinets. Though they find the evidence inconclusive, their analysis does suggest that the types of cabinets appointed and cabinet durability do depend on how presidents were chosen. "Natural" faction leaders have had somewhat more diverse, representative, and stable cabinets than the "designated" faction leaders. With regard to executive–legislative relations, though they are necessarily tentative about the strength of their conclusions, Buquet and Chasquetti find some confirming evidence that *insider* presidents are better able to rely on consistent legislative contingents.

Moraes's chapter on the Uruguayan legislature confirms this contention about support for the executive, showing that *loyalist* legislators have high levels of commitment to their factions in the legislature. His specific focus, however, is on the degree of constituency service Uruguayan legislators provide. He finds that party and informal variables such as intraparty competition levels and legislators' future political ambitions, more than the electoral system (here, district magnitude), drive legislators' propensity to spend more time on constituency service. Moreover, parties distinguish themselves with regard to this tendency, which again suggests only a limited role for the electoral system. In conclusion, Moraes argues that legislators evince behaviors consistent with the *faction-loyalist* label, but also take on some characteristics of *constituent servants*.

Gender

Finally, perhaps no variable embodies the interaction of informalism and institutions, or the role of R&S as both independent and dependent variables, more than gender, the subject of Chapter 14, by Maria Escobar-Lemmon and Michelle Taylor-Robinson. Chapters 2 and 4 also touch on the issue. On the institutional side Jones shows that quotas in Argentina had their desired effect, substantially increasing the number of female legislators. On the less formal side, Altman discusses President Ricardo Lagos's efforts to engage in an affirmative action program for female ministers. Escobar-Lemmon and Taylor-Robinson present a more detailed discussion of gender, both pointing out that quotas are sometimes ineffective (see also Baldez, 2007) and that informal and party variables as well as candidate type are also highly influential.

Escobar-Lemmon and Taylor-Robinson discuss the importance of candidate type, quotas, the electoral system, position of the parties on the left or right, and other variables in determining the extent to which women are elected to the legislature and represented in the cabinet. For our purposes, the central role of candidate type in explaining women's representation is key; they show, for example, that countries with *party loyalist* legislators place more women in the legislature, and that *FWI*s have appointed more women to the cabinet than other types (though this conclusion is based on a very small sample).

Conclusions

The recruitment and selection of candidates is a central component of the political process, and so defining the pathways to power yields important insights into the forces that drive political behavior. Studying these pathways as a dependent variable yields information about how institutions, context, and party-level factors interact to produce particular types of candidates. Determining the pathways requires identifying to whom politicians owe loyalty; as the studies in this volume show, different loyalties yield different types of candidates. Further, because politicians' loyalty drives their behavior, candidates' pathways to power act through candidate types to become an independent variable influencing political outcomes. The thirteen substantive chapters have given ample support to this broad conclusion, and they have also identified many specific relationships between the variables that drive the R&S process as well as the impact of R&S on political outputs.

Although central to the political process, R&S processes are difficult to define and explain—and their influence on political behavior and democratic governance is even more difficult to discern. Two factors complicate analysis of R&S systems. First, R&S takes place over a long period, without a clear beginning. Even the end of the process is foggy, as appointment to one position may be just the first rung on a long ladder. As we explain in our introductory chapter, it is not even possible to separate variables that are more pertinent to recruitment from those that pertain to selection. Second, R&S processes involve many behind-the-scenes operations that are difficult to study. We accept that these backroom decisions are taken in response to an institutional context full of incentives that motivate political behavior, but the variance in how politicians and parties react implies a need for any explanation to go far beyond institutional analysis.

As we emphasize throughout, although electoral rules and other aspects of the institutional context may be highly influential, they are just a first node on the tree of factors that influence candidate types. As a result, analyses can pick up the trail of candidates at different points and this has led our book's authors to highlight different aspects of R&S in their search for understanding and explanation. Camp, for example, starts with the impact of Mexican politicians' backgrounds to show how they are socialized into the party. Several chapters highlight the way electoral laws encouraged a particular type of candidate, and in other chapters the particularities of the parties seemed the most important of the variables. This was true of both the executive and legislative studies, though there was perhaps less evidence that the institutions directed choices for the executives. Still, as we have highlighted in this chapter, there is some evidence that plurality electoral rules may help produce *loyalists* and *adherents* rather than *FWIs*.

The chapters have also substantiated our claims that the R&S processes have important effects on political behavior. Here again the authors spotlighted a wide variety of behavioral implications, but most can be grouped into the general political outcomes we outlined in the introduction: campaign behavior, executive–legislative relations, the shape of coalitions, legislative party discipline, and the likelihood that executives will remain loyal to their party platforms.

A pathway to power is, of course, a shorthand variable that ties together many interconnected variables. Their multifaceted nature complicates analyses but studying pathways as dependent and as independent variables reveals the inner workings of politics.

References

Abranches, Sérgio. 1988. "Presidencialismo de coalizão: O dilema institucional brasileiro." *Dados* 31(1): 5–38.

Abrucio, Fernando. 1998. *Os barões da Federação*. Sao Paulo: Hucitec.

Agor, Westin. 1971. *The Chilean Senate*. Austin: University of Texas Press.

Agüero, Felipe, Eugenio Tironi, Eduardo Valenzuela, and Guillermo Sunkel. 1998. "Votantes, partidos e información política: La frágil intermediación política en el Chile post-autoritario." *Revista de Ciencia Política* 19(2): 159–93.

Alcántara Sáez, Manuel, and Flavia Friedenberg, eds. 2001. *Partidos políticos de América Latina*. Salamanca, Spain: Ediciones Universidad Salamanca.

Aldrich, John H. 1995. *Why Parties? The Origin and Transformation of Political Parties in America*. Chicago: University of Chicago Press.

Alemán, Eduardo, and Sebastián Saiegh. 2007. "Legislative Preferences, Political Parties, and Coalition Unity in Chile." *Comparative Politics* 39(3): 253–72.

Allamand, Andrés. 1999a. *La travesía del desierto*. Santiago: Aguilar.

———. 1999b. "Las paradojas de un legado." In Paul Drake and Ivan Jaksic, eds., *El modelo chileno: Democracia y desarrollo en los noventa*. Santiago: LOM.

Altman, David. 2000. "The Politics of Coalition Formation and Survival in Multiparty Presidential Democracies: The Case of Uruguay 1989–1999." *Party Politics* 6(3): 259–83.

———. 2001. "The Politics of Coalition Formation and Survival in Multiparty Presidential Regimes." Ph.D. dissertation, University of Notre Dame, Government and International Studies.

Ames, Barry. 2001. *The Deadlock of Democracy in Brazil*. Ann Arbor: University of Michigan Press.

Amorim Neto, Octávio. 1998. "Cabinet Formation in Presidential Regimes: An Analysis of 10 Latin American Countries." Paper presented at the Latin American Studies Association. Chicago, September 24–26.

———. 2002. "Presidential Cabinets, Electoral Cycles, and Coalition Discipline in Brazil." In Scott Morgenstern and Benito Nacif, eds., *Legislative Politics in Latin America*. New York: Cambridge University Press.

Amorim Neto, Octávio, and Fabiano Santos. 2001. "The Executive Connection: Presidentially-Defined Factions and Party Discipline in Brazil." *Party Politics* 7(2): 213–34.

———. 2003. "The Inefficient Secret Revisited: The Legislative Input and Output of Brazilian Deputies." *Legislative Studies Quarterly* 28(3): 449–79.

Amorim Neto, Octávio, Gary Cox, and Mathew McCubbins. 2003. "Agenda Power in Brazil's Câmara dos Deputados, 1989 to 1999." *World Politics* 55(4): 550–78.

Amorim Neto, Octávio, and Paulo Tafner. 2002. "Governos de coalizão e mecanismos de alarme de incêndio no controle legislativo das medidas provisórias." *Dados* 45(1): 5–38.

Aninat, Cristóbal, John Londregan, Patricio Navia, and Joaquín Vial. 2004. "Political Institutions, Policymaking Processes, and Policy Outcomes in Chile." Working Paper 521, Interamerican Development Bank, Washington, D.C.

Archer, Ronald. 1990. "The Transition from Traditional Broker Clientelism in Colombia: Political Stability and Social Unrest." Working Paper 140, Helen Kellogg Institute for International Studies, University of Notre Dame.

———. 1995. "Party Strength and Weakness in Colombia's Besieged Democracy." In Scott Mainwaring and Timothy R. Scully, eds., *Building Democratic Institutions: Party Systems in Latin America*. Palo Alto: Stanford University Press.

Archer, Ronald P., and Matthew Soberg Shugart. 1997. "The Unrealized Potential of Presidential Dominance in Colombia." In Scott Mainwaring and Matthew Soberg Shugart, eds. *Presidentialism and Democracy in Latin America*. Cambridge: Cambridge University Press.

Ard, Michael J. 2003. *An Eternal Struggle: How the National Action Party Transformed Mexican Politics*. Westport, Conn.: Praeger.

Atkeson, Lonna Rae. 1998. "Divisive Primaries and General Election Outcomes: Another Look at Presidential Campaigns." *American Journal of Political Science* 42(1): 256–71.

Avellaneda, Claudia N., and Maria Escobar-Lemmon. 2006. "Pork or Policy? Legislative Styles in the Colombian Congress." Paper prepared for the annual meeting of the American Political Science Association. Philadelphia, PA, August 31–September 3.

Baldez, Lisa. 2004. "Elected Bodies: The Gender Quota Law for Legislative Candidates in Mexico." *Legislative Studies Quarterly* 24(2): 231–58.

———. 2007. "Primaries vs. Quotas: Gender and Candidate Nominations in Mexico." *Latin American Politics and Society* 49(3): 69–96.

Barber, James David. 1972. *The Presidential Character: Predicting Performance in the White House*. Englewood Cliffs, N.J.: Prentice-Hall.

Bejár, Luisa. 2004. "Representación y disciplina parlamentaria en México: El marco partidista-electoral después de la alternancia." In Ricardo Espinoza Toledo and Rosa María Mirón, eds., *Partidos políticos: Nuevos liderazgos y relaciones internas de autoridad*. Mexico City: Universidad Autónoma Metropolitana.

Benton, Allyson Lucinda. 2002. "Presidentes fuertes, provincias poderosas: La economía política de la construcción de partidos en el sistema federal argentino." *Política y Gobierno* 10(1): 103–37.

Bernardes, Franco César. 1996. "Democracia concentrada: Estrutura do processo decisório da Câmara dos Deputados." Master's thesis, Instituto Universitário de Pesquisas do Rio de Janeiro: Rio de Janeiro.

Black, Gordon. 1972. "A Theory of Political Ambition: Career Choices and the Role of Structural Incentives." *American Political Science Review* 66(1): 144–59.

Blondel, Jean. 1985. *Government Ministers in the Contemporary World*. London: Sage.

Botero, Felipe. 2006. "Reforma política, personalismo, y sistema de partidos." In Gary Hoskin and Miguel García Sánchez, *La reforma política de 2003: La salvación de los partidos políticos?* Bogotá: Universidad de los Andes.

Botinelli, Oscar O. 1991. "El sistema electoral Uruguayo: Descripción y análisis." Working Paper Series 3. Heidelberg, Germany: University of Heidelberg, Political Science Institute.

Boudreaux, Richard. 2004. "Fox Pushes for Overhaul of Justice System," *Los Angeles Times*, 16 March, A3.

Brady, David, Kara Buckley, and Douglas Rivers. 1999. "The Roots of Careerism in the House of Representatives." *Legislative Studies Quarterly* 24(4): 489–510.

Bruhn, Kathleen. 1997. *Taking on Goliath: The Emergence of a New Left Party and the Struggle for Democracy in Mexico*. University Park: Pennsylvania State University Press.

Buquet, Daniel. 2000. "Los cambios que aseguraron la continuidad: Coalición, reforma, elecciones y después." In Instituto de Ciencia Política, *Elecciones 1999–2000*. Montevideo: Ediciones de la Banda Oriental.

———. 2001. "Selección de candidatos y fraccionalización partidaria en Uruguay (1942–1999)." Paper presented at the twenty-third Conference of the Latin American Studies Association. Washington, D.C., September 26–28.

Buquet, Daniel, Daniel Chasquetti, and Juan Andrés Moraes. 1998. *Fragmentación política y gobierno en Uruguay*. Montevideo: Facultad de Ciencias Sociales.

Burnham, Walter Dean. 1970. *Critical Elections and the Mainstream of American Politics*. New York: Norton.

Cain, Bruce, John Ferejohn, and Morris Fiorina. 1987. *The Personal Vote: Constituency Service and Electoral Independence*. Cambridge: Harvard University Press.

Calvo, Ernesto, and María Victoria Murillo. 2004. "Who Delivers? Partisan Clients in the Argentine Electoral Market." *American Journal of Political Science* 48(4): 742–57.

Camp, Roderic Ai. 1986. *Entrepreneurs and Politics in Twentieth-Century Mexico*. New York: Oxford University Press.

———. 1995. *Political Recruitment Across Two Centuries: Mexico, 1884–1991*. Austin: University of Texas Press.

———. 1997. "Technocracy a la Mexicana, Antecedent to Democracy." In Miguel A. Centeno and Patricio Silva, eds., *The Politics of Expertise in Latin America*. New York: St. Martin's Press.

———. 2002. *Mexico's Mandarins: Crafting a Power Elite for the 21st Century*. Berkeley: University of California Press.

———. 2003. "Mexican Attitudes Toward Democracy and Vicente Fox's Victory in 2000." In Chappell Lawson and Jorge Domínguez, eds., *Mexico's Pivotal Democratic Elections: Campaign Effects and the Presidential Race of 2000*. Palo Alto: Stanford University Press.

Cañas, Enrique. 1994. "La transición chilena en los años ochenta: Claves de una transacción exitosa en perspectiva comparada." *Revista de Ciencia Política* 16(1–2): 41–65.

Carey, John M. 1996. *Term Limits and Legislative Representation*. Cambridge: Cambridge University Press.

———. 2002. "Parties, Coalitions and the Chilean Congress in the 1990's." In Scott Morgenstern and Benito Nacif, eds., *Legislative Politics in Latin America*. New York: Cambridge University Press.

———. 2003. "Policy Issues: The Reelection Debate in Latin America." *Latin American Politics and Society* 45(2): 19–133.

Carey, John M., and Matthew Shugart. 1995. "Incentives to Cultivate a Personal Vote: A Rank Ordering of Electoral Formulas." *Electoral Studies* 14(4): 417–39.

Carey, John M., and Peter Siavelis. 2003. "El seguro para los subcampeones electorales y la sobrevivencia de la Concertación." *Estudios Públicos* 90(Fall): pp. 5–27.

Carey, John M., and John Polga-Hecimovich. 2006. "Primary Elections and Candidate Strength in Latin America." *The Journal of Politics* 68(3): 530–43.

Casar, María Amparo. 2000. "Las relaciones entre el poder ejecutivo y el legislativo: El caso de México." *Política y Gobierno* 6(1): 83–128.

Caul, Miki. 2001. "Political Parties and the Adoption of Candidate Gender Quotas: A Cross-National Analysis." *Journal of Politics* 63(4): 1214–29.

Cavallo, Ascanio. 1992. *Los hombres de la transición.* Santiago: Editorial Andrés Bello.

————. 1998. *La historia oculta de la transición: Chile 1990–1998.* Santiago: Grijalbo.

Cerruti, Gabriela. 1993. *El jefe: Vida y obra de Carlos Saúl Menem.* Buenos Aires: Planeta.

Chasquetti, Daniel, and Adolfo Garcé. 2005. "Unidos por la historia: Desempeño electoral y perspectivas de colorados y blancos como bloque político." In Daniel Buquet, ed., *Las claves del cambio: ciclo electoral y nuevo gobierno 2004–2005.* Montevideo: EBO-ICP.

Cintra, Antônio Octávio. 1979. "Traditional Brazilian Politics: An Interpretation of Relations Between Center and Periphery." In Neuma Aguiar, ed., *The Structure of Brazilian Development.* New Brunswick, N.J.: Transaction Books.

Colombia, Republic of. 1994b. "Law 130, of March 23, 1994." Bogotá: Consejo Nacional Electoral.

Colomer, Josep M. 2002. "Las elecciones primarias presidenciales en América Latina y sus consecuencias políticas." In Marcelo Cavarozzi and Juan Manuel Abal Medina, eds., *El asedio a la política.* Rosario: Homo Sapiens.

Comisión de Reforma del Estado. 2000. "Proposiciones sobre el financiamiento de la actividad pública." *Revista Estudios Públicos* 78(Autum): 375–550.

Comisión de Reforma del Estado. 2003. "Contratos y remuneraciones de altos directivos públicos." *Revista Estudios Públicos* 89(Summer): 279–411.

Coppedge, Michael. 1994. *Strong Parties and Lame Ducks: Presidential Partyarchy and Factionalism in Venezuela.* Palo Alto: Stanford University Press.

Coppedge, Michael. 1997. "A Classification of Latin American Political Parties." Working Paper 244, Helen Kellogg Institute for International Studies. University of Notre Dame.

Coradini, Odaci Luiz. 2001. *Em nome de quem? Recursos sociais no recrutamento de elites políticas.* Rio de Janeiro: Relume Dumará.

Corrales, Javier. 2002. *Presidents Without Parties: The Politics of Economic Reform in Argentina and Venezuela in the 1990s.* University Park: Pennsylvania State University Press.

Countries of the World and Their Leaders Yearbooks. 1980–2003. Detroit: Gale Research Company.

Cox, Gary W. 1997. *Making Votes Count.* Cambridge: Cambridge University Press.

Cox, Gary W., and Mathew D. McCubbins. 1993. *Legislative Leviathan: Party Government in the House.* Berkeley: University of California Press.

Cox, Gary W., and Frances Rosenbluth. 1996. "Factional Competition for the Party Endorsement: The Case of Japan's Liberal Democratic Party." *British Journal of Political Science* 26(2): 259–69.

Cox, Gary W., and Matthew S. Shugart. 1995. "In the Absence of Vote Pooling: Nomination and Allocation Errors in Colombia." *Electoral Studies* 14(4): 441–60.

Crisp, Brian, and Rachel Ingall. 2002. "Institutional Engineering and the Nature of Representation: Mapping the Effects of Electoral Reform in Colombia." *American Journal of Political Science* 46(4): 733–48.

Crisp, Brian, Maria Escobar-Lemmon, Bradford Jones, Mark Jones, and Michelle Taylor-Robinson. 2004. "Vote-Seeking Incentives and Legislative Representation in Six Presidential Democracies." *Journal of Politics* 66(3): 823–46.

Czudnowski, Moshe. 1975. "Political Recruitment." In Fred Greenstein and Nelson Polsby, eds., *Handbook of Political Science: Micropolitical Theory.* Vol. 2. Reading, Mass.: Addison-Wesley.

Dantas Neto, Paulo Fábio. 2006. "O carlismo para além de ACM: Estratégias adaptativas de uma elite política estadual." In Celina Souza and Paulo Fábio Dantas Neto, eds., *Governo, políticas públicas e elites políticas nos estados brasileiros.* Rio de Janeiro: Editora Revan.

Davis, James W. 1988. *Leadership Selection in Six Western Democracies.* Westport, Conn.: Greenwood.

Davis, Rebecca Howard. 1997. *Women and Power in Parliamentary Democracies: Cabinet Appointments in Western Europe, 1968–1992.* Lincoln: University of Nebraska Press.

De Armas, Gustavo, and Salvador Cardarello. 2000. "Del sentimiento a la razón: La estrategia discursiva de Batlle de abril a noviembre." In *Elecciones 1999–2000.* Montevideo: EBO-ICP.

De la Torre Castellanos, Reneé, and Juan Manuel Ramírez Sáiz. 2001. *Conservadurismo, sociedad civil y gobernabilidad, nueva grupalidades in Guadalajara.* Jalapa: Universidad Veracruzana.

De Luca, Miguel, Mark P. Jones, and María Inés Tula. 2003. "Partiti e primarie: La selezione dei candidati in Argentina." *Quaderni dell'Osservatorio Elettorale* 3820 (49): 59–95.

———. 2002. "Back Rooms or Ballot Boxes? Candidate Nomination in Argentina." *Comparative Political Studies* 35(4): 413–36.

De Riz, Liliana, and Jorge Feldman. 1991. "El partido en el gobierno: La experiencia del radicalismo, 1983–1989." *Working paper 64.* Buenos Aires: CEDES.

Desposato, Scott. 2001. "Parties for Rent? Careerism, Ideology, and Party Switching in Brazil's Chamber of Deputies." Working Paper, Department of Political Science, University of Arizona.

Díaz, Christopher. 2005. "Electoral Competition in Mexico and Career Trajectories of PRI Gubernatorial Candidates, 1991–2001." *Politics & Policy* 33(1): 36–53.

Diez-Mendez, Jordi. 2004. "Political Change and Environmental Policymaking in Mexico." Ph.D. dissertation, University of Toronto.

Dix, Robert. 1980. "Consociational Democracy: The Case of Colombia." *Comparative Politics* 12(3): 303–21.

———. 1987. *The Politics of Colombia.* New York: Praeger.

Dow, Jay K. 1998. "A Spatial Analysis of Candidates in Dual Member Districts: The 1989 Chilean Senatorial Elections." *Public Choice* 97(3): 451–74.

Dugas, John C. 2000. "The Conservative Party and the Crisis of Political Legitimacy in Colombia." In Kevin J. Middlebrook, ed., *Conservative Parties, the Right, and Democracy in Latin America.* Baltimore: Johns Hopkins University Press.

Duverger, Maurice. 1951. *Los partidos políticos.* México: Fondo de Cultura Económica.

———. 1954. *Political Parties.* New York: John Wiley & Sons.

Eaton, Kent. 2002. *Politicians and Economic Reform in New Democracies: Argentina and the Philippines in the 1990s*. University Park: Pennsylvania State University Press.

Eisenstadt, Todd. 2003. *Courting Democracy in Mexico: Party Strategies and Electoral Institutions*. Cambridge: Cambridge University Press.

El Tiempo. 1997. "Consulta liberal sería el próximo 26 de octubre," April 14; "Consulta es obligatoria: Tribunal de Garantías," April 22; "Liberales, dispuestos a llegar un acuerdo," December 8.

———. 1998: "Se abre debate jurídico por designación de Serpa," March 27.

Ellicott, Karen, ed. 1980–2003. *Countries of the World and Their Leaders Yearbooks*. Detroit: Gale Research Company.

Ellis, Melody. 2002. "Gender Disparity in Representation: The Effect of Preference Voting in Japan and Italy." Paper presented at the annual meeting of the American Political Science Association. Boston, August 29–September 2.

Epstein, David, David Brady, Sadafumi Kawato, and Sharyn O'Halloran. 1997. "A Comparative Approach to Legislative Organization: Careerism and Seniority in the United States and Japan." *American Journal of Political Science* 41(3): 965–88.

Epstein, Leon D. 1980. *Political Parties in Western Democracies*. New York: Transaction Books.

Erickson, Linda. 1997. "Canada." In Pippa Norris, ed., *Passages to Power: Legislative Recruitment in Advanced Democracies*. Cambridge: Cambridge University Press.

Escobar, Cristina. 2002. "Clientelism and Citizenship: The Limits of Democratic Reform in Colombia." *Latin American Perspectives* 29(5): 20–47.

Escobar-Lemmon, Maria. 2006. "Executives, Legislatures, and Decentralization" *Policy Studies Journal* 34(2): 245–63.

Escobar-Lemmon, Maria, and Michelle M. Taylor-Robinson. 2006. "How Electoral Laws and Development Affect Election of Women in Latin American Legislatures: A Test 20 Years into the Third Wave of Democracy." Paper presented at the annual Meeting of the American Political Science Association, Philadelphia, August 31–September 3.

———. 2005. "Women Ministers in Latin American Government: When, Where, and Why?" *American Journal of Political Science* 49(4): 829–44.

Eulau, Heinz, and Moshe Czudnowski, eds. 1976. *Elite Recruitment in Democratic Polities*. New York: Sage.

Fenno, Richard. 1978. *Home Style: House Members in Their Districts*. Boston: Little, Brown.

Ferreira Rubio, Delia, and Matteo Goretti. 1998. "When the President Governs Alone: The Decretazo in Argentina, 1989–93." In John M. Carey and Matthew Soberg Shugart, eds., *Executive Decree Authority*. New York: Cambridge University Press.

Figueiredo, Argelina, and Fernando Limongi. 1994. "Mudança constitucional, desempenho do legislativo e consolidação institucional." Paper presented at the eighteenth annual meeting of the Brazilian National Association for Social Science Research-ANPOCS. Caxambú, Minas Gerais, Brazil, October 16–19.

———. 1996. "Congresso nacional: Organização, processo legislativo e produção legal." *Cadernos de Pesquisa CEBRAP 5*.

———. 1999. *Executivo e legislativo na nova ordem constitucional*. Rio de Janeiro: FGV.

———. 2000a. "Presidential Power, Legislative Organization, and Party Behavior in Brazil." *Comparative Politics* 32(2): 151–70.

———. 2000b. "Executivo e legislativo na formulação e execuçao do orçamento federal." Paper presented at the annual meeting of the Brazilian Political Science Association. São Paulo.

Finocchiaro, Charles J., and David W. Rohde. 2002. "War for the Floor: Agenda Control and the Relationship Between Conditional Party Government and Cartel Theory." PIPC Working Paper 02–02. Michigan State University, Political Institutions and Public Choice Program.

Flisfisch, Angel F. 1992. "Parlamentarismo, presidencialismo y coaliciones gubernamentales." In O. Godoy, ed., *Cambio de regimen político*. Santiago de Chile: Ediciones Universidad Católica de Chile.

Friedenberg, Flavia, and Francisco Sánchez López. 2001. "Partidos políticos y métodos de selección de candidatos en América Latina: Una discusión sobre reglas y prácticas." Paper presented at the twenty-third International Conference of the Latin American Studies Association. Washington, D.C., September 26–28.

Fuentes, Claudio. 1999. "Partidos y coaliciones en el Chile de los '90. Entre pactos y proyectos." in Paul Drake and Ivan Jaksic, eds., *El modelo chileno: Democracia y desarrollo en los noventa*. Santiago: LOM.

Furtado, Celso. 1971. "Political Obstacles to Economic Growth in Brazil." In Claudio Veliz, ed., *Obstacles to Change in Latin America*. Oxford: Oxford University Press.

Gallagher, Michael. 1980. "Candidate Selection in Ireland: The Impact of Localism and the Electoral System." *British Journal of Political Science* 10(4): 489–503.

———. 1988. "Introduction." In Michael Gallagher and Michael Marsh, eds, *Candidate Selection in Comparative Perspective*. London: Sage.

Gallagher, Michael, and Michael Marsh. 1988. *The Secret Garden of Politics: Candidate Selection in Comparative Perspective*. London: Sage.

Gamboa, Ricardo, and Carolina Segovia. 2006. "Las elecciones presidenciales y parlamentarias en Chile, diciembre 2005–enero 2006." *Revista de Ciencia Política* 26(1): 84–113.

Garcé, Adolfo, and Jaime Yaffé. 2004. *La era progresista*. Montevideo: Editorial Fin de Siglo.

Garrido, Luís Javier. 1982. *El partido de la revolución institucionalizada: La formación del nuevo estado en México (1928–1945)*. Mexico City: Siglo Veintiuno Press.

———. 1993. *La ruptura: La corriente democrática del PRI*. Mexico: Grijalbo.

Garretón, Manuel Antonio. 2001. "La cuestión del régimen de gobierno en el Chile de hoy." In J. Lanzaro, ed., *Tipos de presidencialismo y coaliciones en América Latina*. Buenos Aires: CLACSO.

Gergen, David R. 2000. *Eyewitness to Power: The Essence of Leadership: Nixon to Clinton*. New York: Simon & Schuster.

Gillespie, Charles G. 1995. *Negociando la democracia: Políticos y generales en Uruguay*. Fundación de Cultura Universitaria-Instituto de Ciencia Política: Montevideo.

Giraldo, Fernando, ed. 2003. *Sistema de partidos politicos en Colombia: estado de arte, 1991–2002*. Bogotá: Centro Editorial Javeriana.

Godoy, Oscar. 1994. "Las elecciones de 1993." *Estudios Públicos* 54(Fall): 301–37.

González, Luis E. 1991. *Political Structures and Democracy in Uruguay*. Notre Dame, Ind.: University of Notre Dame Press.

———. 1993. *Estructuras políticas y democracia en Uruguay*. Montevideo: Fundación de Cultura Universitaria.

González Ruiz, Edgar 2001. *La ultima cruzada, de los Cristeros a Fox*. Mexico: Grijalbo.

Grayson, George. 2003. *Beyond the Mid-term Elections, Mexico's Political Outlook, 2003–2006*. Western Hemisphere Election Studies Series. Washington, D.C.: CSIS.

Greenstein, Fred I. 2000. *The Presidential Difference: Leadership Style from FDR to Clinton*. New York: Free Press/Martin Kessler Books.

Guido, Pablo. 2002. "En el 2014 todos seremos empleados públicos." Unpublished paper. Fundación Atlas.

Guido, Pablo, and Gustavo Lazzari. 2001. "Tasa de desempleo encubierto en las provincias." Unpublished paper. Fundación Atlas.

Guzmán, Carlos Enrique, and Ermicio Sena de Oliveira. 2001. "Brasil." In Manuel Alcántara Sáez and Flavia Friedenberg, eds., *Partidos políticos de América Latina: Cono Sur.* Salamanca: Ediciones Universidad de Salamanca.

Hagopian, Frances. 1996. *Traditional Politics and Regime Change in Brazil.* New York: Cambridge University Press.

———. 2002. "Economic Liberalization, Political Competition, and Political Representation in Latin America." Paper presented at the 2002 Conference of the Midwest Political Science Association. Chicago, April 25–28.

Hartlyn, Jonathan. 1988. *The Politics of Coalition Rule in Colombia.* New York: Cambridge University Press.

Hazan, Reuven. 2002. "Candidate Selection." In Lawrence Leduc, Richard G. Niemi, and Pippa Norris, eds., *Comparing Democracies.* Thousand Oaks, Calif.: Sage.

Hazan, Reuven, and Gerrit Voerman. 2006. "Electoral Systems and Candidate Selection." *Acta Política* 41(2): 146–62.

Helander, Voito. 1997. "Finland." In Pippa Norris, ed., *Passages to Power: Legislative Recruitment in Advanced Democracies.* Cambridge: Cambridge University Press.

Helmke, Gretchen, and Steven Levitsky. 2004. "Informal Institutions and Comparative Politics: A Research Agenda." *Perspectives on Politics* 2(4): 725–40.

Herrick, Rebekah, and David L. Nixon. 1996. "Is There Life After Congress? Patterns and Determinants of Post-Congressional Careers." *Legislative Studies Quarterly* 21(4): 489–99.

Hoskin, Gary. 1971. "Dimensions of Representation in the Colombian National Legislature." In Weston Agor, ed., *Latin American Legislatures: Their Role and Influence Analyses for Nine Countries.* New York: Praeger.

Htun, Mala. 2003. "Women and Democracy." In Jorge I. Domínguez and Michael Shifter, eds., *Constructing Democratic Governance in Latin America.* Baltimore: Johns Hopkins University Press.

Htun, Mala, and Mark P. Jones. 2001. "Engendering the Right to Participate in Decision-Making: Electoral Quotas and Women's Leadership in Latin America." In Nikki Craske and Maxine Molyneaux, eds., *Gender and the Politics of Rights and Democracy in Latin America.* London: Palgrave.

Hunter, Wendy. 2006. "Growth and Transformation of the Workers' Party in Brazil, 1989–2002." Working Paper 326, Helen Kellogg Institute for International Studies. University of Notre Dame (September).

Huntington, Samuel P. 1991. *The Third Wave.* Norman: University of Oklahoma Press.

Ingall, Rachael E., and Brian Crisp. 2001. "Determinants of Home Style: The Many Incentives for Going Home in Colombia." *Legislative Studies Quarterly* 26(3): 487–512.

International Institute for Democracy and Electoral Assistance (IDEA). Global Database of Quotas for Women. www.quotaproject.org.

Inter-Parliamentary Union. 1995. "Women in Parliaments, 1945–1995: A World Statistical Survey." Reports and Documents 23. Geneva: IPU.

———. 1999. "Participation of Women in Political Life." Reports and Documents 35. Geneva: IPU.

Jacobson, Gary, and Samuel Kernell. 1981. *Strategy and Choice in Congressional Elections.* New Haven: Yale University Press.

Joignant, Alfredo, and Patricio Navia. 2003. "De la política de individuos a los hombres del partido: Socialización, competencia política, y penetración electoral de la UDI (1989–2001)." *Estudios Públicos* 89(Summer): 129–171.

Jones, Charles 1994. *The Presidency in a Separated System.* Washington, D.C.: Brookings Institution.

Jones, Mark. 1995. *Electoral Laws and the Survival of Presidential Democracies.* South Bend, Ind.: University of Notre Dame Press.

———. 1995b. "A Guide to the Electoral Systems of the Americas." *Electoral Studies* 14(1): 5–21.

———. 1996. "Increasing Women's Representation via Gender Quotas: The Argentine Ley de Cupos." *Women and Politics* 16(4): 75–98.

———. 1997a. "Federalism and the Number of Parties in Argentine Congressional Elections." *Journal of Politics* 59(2): 538–49.

———. 1997b. "Evaluating Argentina's Presidential Democracy: 1983–1995." In Scott Mainwaring and Matthew Soberg Shugart, eds., *Presidentialism and Democracy in Latin America.* New York: Cambridge University Press.

———. 1998. "Gender Quotas, Electoral Laws, and the Election of Women: Lessons from the Argentine Provinces." *Comparative Political Studies* 31(1): 3–21.

———. 1999. "Electoral Laws and the Effective Number of Candidates in Presidential Elections." *Journal of Politics* 61(1): 171–84.

———. 2002. "Explaining the High Level of Party Discipline in the Argentine Congress." In Scott Morgenstern and Benito Nacif, eds., *Legislative Politics in Latin America.* New York: Cambridge University Press.

Jones, Mark, Pablo Spiller, Sebastian Saiegh, and Mariano Tommasi. 2001. "Keeping a Seat in Congress: Provincial Party Bosses and the Survival of Argentine Legislators." Paper presented at the 2001 meeting of the American Political Science Association. San Francisco, September 6–8.

Jones, Mark P., Sebastian Saiegh, Pablo T. Spiller, and Mariano Tommasi. 2002. "Amateur-Legislators-Professional Politicians: The Consequences of Party-Centered Electoral Rules in a Federal System." *American Journal of Political Science* 46(3): 656–69.

Jones, Mark P., and Wonjae Hwang. 2005. "Party Government in Presidential Democracies: Extending Cartel Theory Beyond the U.S. Congress." *American Journal of Political Science* 49(2): 267–82.

Katz, Richard S. 1986. "Intraparty Preference Voting." In Bernard Grofman and Arend Lijphart, eds., *Electoral Laws and Their Political Consequences.* New York: Agathon Press: 85–103.

Kenney, Patrick J., and Tom W. Rice. 1987. "The Relationship between Divisive Primaries and General Election Outcomes." *American Journal of Political Science* 31(1): 31–44.

Kellam, Marisa. 2007. "Parties-for-Hire: The Instability of Presidential Coalitions in Latin America." Ph.D. dissertation. University of California, Los Angeles, Department of Political Science.

Kenworthy, Lane, and Melissa Malami. 1999. "Gender Inequality in Political Representation: A Worldwide Comparative Analysis." *Social Forces* 78(1): 235–68.

Keynes, Edward, Richard Tobin, and Robert Danziger. 1979. "Institutional Effects on Elite Recruitment." *American Politics Quarterly* 7(3): 283–302.

King, Gary, Michael Tomz, and Jason Wittenberg. 2000. "Making the Most of Political Analysis: Improving Interpretation and Presentation." *American Journal of Political Science* 44(2): 341–55.

Kitschelt, Herbert. 1989. *The Logics of Party Formation: Ecological Politics in Belgium and West Germany*. Ithaca: Cornell University Press.

Koelble, Thomas. 1992. "Recasting Social Democracy in Europe: A Nested Games Explanation of Strategic Adjustment in Political Parties." *Politics and Society* 20(1): 51–70.

Koolhas, Martín. 2003. "Coaliciones de gobierno en Uruguay: 1990–2003." Ph.D. dissertation. Universidad de la República, Instituto de Ciencia Política, Montevideo.

Krehbiel, Keith 1993. "Where's the Party?" *British Journal of Political Science* 23(2): 235–66.

———. 2000. "Party Discipline and Measures of Partisanship." *American Journal of Political Science* 44: 212–227.

Laakso, Markku, and Rain Taagepera. 1979. "Effective Number of Parties: A Measure with Application to West Europe." *Comparative Political Studies* 12(1): 3–27.

Langston, Joy. 1994. "Why Rules Matter: The Formal Rules of Candidate Selection and Leadership Selection in the PRI, 1978–1996." Documentos de Trabajo del CIDE: Mexico, DF.

———. 2001. "Why Rules Matter: Changes in Candidate Selection in Mexico's PRI, 1988–2000." *Journal of Latin American Studies* 33(3): 485–511.

———. 2002. "Los efectos de la competencia electoral en la selección de candidates del PRI." In Carlos Elizondo and Benito Nacif, eds., *Lecturas sobre el cambio político en Mexico*. Mexico: Fondo de Cultura Económica.

Lanzaro, Jorge, Daniel Buquet, Daniel Chasquetti, and Juan Andrés Moraes. 2001. *Estudio de la producción legislativa en Uruguay: 1985–2000, poder legislativo*. Montevideo: Poder Legislativo.

Latorre, Mario. 1974. *Elecciones y partidos políticos en Colombia*. Bogotá: Universidad de los Andes, Departamento de Ciencia Política.

Laver, Michael, and Norman Schofield. 1990. *Multiparty Government: The Politics of Coalition in Europe*. New York: Oxford University Press.

Lawson, Chappell. 2003. "Introduction" in Chappell Lawson and Jorge Domínguez, eds., *Mexico's Pivotal Democratic Elections, Campaign Effects, and the Presidential Race of 2000*. Palo Alto: Stanford University Press.

Leal Buitrago, Francisco, and Andrés Dávila Ladrón de Guevara. 1990. *Clientelismo: El sistema político y su expresión regional*. Bogotá: Tercer Mundo Editores.

Leal, Victor Nunes. 1949/1977. *Coronelismo: The Municipality and Representative Government in Brazil*. Translated by June Henfrey. London: Cambridge University Press. Originally published in Portuguese in 1949.

LeDuc, Lawrence, Richard G. Niemi, and Pippa Norris. 1996. "Legislative Recruitment." In Leduc, Niemi, and Pippa Norris, eds., *Comparing Democracies: Elections and Voting in Global Perspective*. London: Sage.

Leuco, Alfredo, and José A. Díaz. 1989. *El heredero de Perón: Menem, entre dios y el diablo*. Buenos Aires: Sudamericana-Planeta.

Levitsky, Steven. 1998. "Crisis, Party Adaptation, and Regime Stability in Argentina: The Case of Peronism, 1989–1995." *Party Politics* 4(4): 445–70.

————. 2001. "An Organized Disorganization: Informal Organization and the Persistence of Local Party Structures in Argentine Peronism." *Journal of Latin American Studies*, 33(1):29–65.

————. 2003. *Transforming Labor-Based Parties in Latin America: Argentine Peronism in Comparative Perspective*. New York: Cambridge University Press.

Lijphart, Arend. 1999. *Patterns of Democracy: Government Forms and Performance in Thirty-Six Countries*. New Heaven: Yale University Press.

Lijphart, Arend, and Carlos Waisman, eds. 1996. *Institutional Design in New Democracies: Eastern Europe and Latin America*. Boulder: Westview Press.

Limongi, Fernando, and Argelina Figueiredo. 1995. "Partidos políticos na Câmara dos Deputados: 1989–1994." *DADOS* 38(3): 497–525.

Lindahl, Göran. 1977. *Batlle y la segunda constitución, 1919–1933*. Montevideo: Arca.

Linz, Juan J. 1990. "The Perils of Presidentialism." *Journal of Democracy* 1(1): 51–69.

Linz, Juan, and Alfred Stepan. 1996. *Problems of Democratic Transition and Consolidation: Southern Europe, South America, and Post-Communist Europe*. Baltimore: Johns Hopkins University Press.

Linz, Juan, and Arturo Valenzuela, eds. 1994. *The Failure of Presidential Democracy*. Vols. 1 and 2. Baltimore: Johns Hopkins University Press.

Llanos, Mariana. 2002. *Privatization and Democracy in Latin America: An Analysis of President-Congress Relations*. New York: Palgrave.

Loewenberg, Gerhard, and Samuel Patterson. 1979. *Comparing Legislatures*. Boston: Little, Brown.

Londregan, John B. 2002. "Appointment, Re-election, and Autonomy in the Senate of Chile." In Scott Morgenstern and Benito Nacif, eds., *Legislative Politics in Latin America*. New York: Cambridge University Press.

Lovenduski, Joni, and Pippa Norris, eds. 1993. *Gender and Party Politics*. London: Sage.

Luna, Juan Pablo. 2004. *Política desde el llano: Conversaciones con militantes barriales*. Montevideo: Ediciones de la Banda Oriental.

Lyne, Mona. 2008. *The Voters' Dilemma and Democratic Accountability*. University Park: Penn State University Press.

Mabry, Donald J. 1973. *Mexico's Acción Nacional: A Catholic Alternative to Revolution*. Syracuse: Syracuse University Press.

Magar, Eric, Marc R. Rosenblum, and David J. Samuels. 1998. "On the Absence of Centripetal Incentives in Double-Member Districts—The Case of Chile." *Comparative Political Studies* 31(6): 714–39.

Mainwaring, Scott. 1993. "Presidentialism, Multipartism, and Democracy: The Difficult Combination." *Comparative Political Studies* 26(2): 198–228.

————. 1997. "Multipartism, Robust Federalism, and Presidentialism in Brazil." In Scott Mainwaring and Matthew Shugart, eds., *Presidentialism and Democracy in Latin America*. Cambridge: Cambridge University Press.

————. 1999. *Rethinking Party Systems in the Third Wave of Democratization: The Case of Brazil*. Palo Alto: Stanford University Press.

Mainwaring, Scott, and Timothy R. Scully. 1995. "Introduction: Party Systems in Latin America." In Scott Mainwaring and Timothy Scully, eds. *Building Democratic Institutions*. Palo Alto: Stanford University Press: 1–36.

Mainwaring, Scott, and Matthew S. Shugart 1997a. "Juan Linz, Presidentialism, and Democracy." *Comparative Politics* 29(4): 449–71.

———. 1997b. *Presidentialism and Democracy in Latin America,* Cambridge University Press.

———. 1997c. "Conclusion: Presidentialism and the Party System." In Scott Mainwaring and Matthew S. Shugart, eds., *Presidentialism and Democracy in Latin America.* New York: Cambridge University Press.

Malamud, Andrés. 2005. "Winning Elections versus Governing: A Two-Tier Approach to Party Adaptation in Argentina (1983–2003)." Paper presented at the *XI Encuentro de Latinoamericanistas Españoles* (CEEIB). Tordesillas, Spain, May 26–28.

Manzetti, Luigi. 1993. *Institutions, Parties, and Coalitions in Argentine Politics.* Pittsburgh: University of Pittsburgh Press.

Marenco dos Santos, André. 2000. "Não se fazem mais oligarquias como antigamente: Recrutamento parlamentar, experiência política e vínculos partidários entre deputados brasileiros [1946–1998]." Ph.D. dissertation, Universidade Federal do Rio Grande do Sul.

———. 2001a. "Experiência política e liderança legislativa na Câmara dos Deputados." *Novos Estudos CEBRAP* 59: 153–71.

———. 2001b. "Sedimentação de lealdades partidárias no Brasil: Tendências e descompassos." *Revista Brasileira de Ciências Sociais* 16(45): 69–83.

Martín, Rubén Martín. 2001 "Fox, los empresarios y el nuevo bloque de poder en México." In Joaquín Osorio Goicoechea, ed., *Fox a uno año de la alternancia.* Mexico: ITESO.

Martínez Vázquez, Griselda. 2002. "La conformación de la élite panista, relaciones diferenciales de poder entre los géneros." In Dalia Barrera Bassols, ed., *Participación política de las mujeres y gobiernos locales en México.* Mexico: GIMTRAP.

Martz, John. 1997. *The Politics of Clientelism: Democracy and the State in Colombia.* New Brunswick, N.J.: Transaction Publishers.

———. 1999. "Political Parties and Candidate Selection in Venezuela and Colombia." *Political Science Quarterly* 114(4): 639–60.

Marvick, Dwaine. 1968. "Political Recruitment and Careers." In David Sills, ed., *International Encyclopedia of the Social Sciences.* New York: Macmillan.

Matland, Richard E. 1998. "Women's Representation in National Legislatures: Developed and Developing Countries." *Legislative Studies Quarterly* 23(1): 109–25.

———. 2006. "Gender Quotas and Legislative Recruitment: A Comparative Study." Paper presented at the Annual Meeting of the American Political Science Association. Philadelphia, August 31–September 3.

Mayhew, David. 1974. *Congress: The Electoral Connection.* New Haven: Yale University Press.

McCallister, Ian. 1997. "Australia." In Pippa Norris, ed., *Passages to Power: Legislative Recruitment in Advanced Democracies.* Cambridge: Cambridge University Press.

McCubbins, Matthew, and Frances Rosenbluth. 1995. "Party Provision of Personal Politics: Dividing the Vote in Japan." In Peter F. Cowhey and Matthew McCubbins, eds., *Structure and Policy in Japan and the U.S.* Cambridge: Cambridge University Press.

McDonald, Ronald H., and J. Mark Ruhl. 1989. *Party Politics and Elections in Latin America.* Boulder: Westview Press.

McGuire, James W. 1997. *Peronism Without Perón: Unions, Parties, and Democracy in Argentina.* Palo Alto: Stanford University Press.

Meneguello, Rachel. 1998. *Partidos e governo no prasil Contemporâneo (1985–97)*. São Paulo: Paz e Terra.

Meyenberg, Yolanda. 2004. "El PRD: La pugna por un nuevo liderazgo." In Ricardo Espinoza Toledo and Rosa María Mirón, eds., *Partidos políticos: Nuevos liderazgos y relaciones internas de autoridad*. Mexico City: Universidad Autónoma Metropolitana.

Mieres, Pablo. 1992. "Acerca de los cambios del sistema de partidos uruguayo." *Cuadernos de CLAEH* 62: 65–75. Montevideo: CLAEH.

Miller, Warren E., and Merrill Shanks. 1996. *The New American Voter*. Cambridge, Mass.: Harvard University Press.

Mizrahi, Yemile. 1994. "Rebels Without a Cause? The Politics of Entrepreneurs in Chihuahua." *Journal of Latin American Studies* 26(1): 137–58.

———. 1996. "¿Administrar o gobernar? El reto del gobierno panista en Chihuahua." *Frontera Norte* 8 (16).

———. 1997. "The Costs of Electoral Success: The Partido Acción Nacional in Mexico." Working Paper, CIDE. Mexico City: CIDE.

———. 2003. *From Martyrdom to Power: The Partido Acción Nacional in Mexico*. South Bend, Ind.: University of Notre Dame Press.

Molinelli, N. Guillermo, Valeria Palanza, and Gisela Sin. 1999. *Congreso, presidencia, y justicia en Argentina*. Buenos Aires: Temas Grupo Editorial.

Monestier, Felipe. 1999. *La fraccionalización en los partidos políticos uruguayos en tiempos de cambio*. Montevideo: FCU.

Montesinos, Verónica, and John Markoff. 2000. "From the Power of Economic Ideas to the Power of Economists." In Miguel A. Centeno, ed., *The Other Mirror: Essays on Latin America*. Princeton: Princeton University Press.

Montes, J. Esteban, Scott Mainwaring, and Eugenio Ortega. 2000. "Rethinking the Chilean Party System." *Journal of Latin American Studies* 32(3): 795–824.

Moon, Jeremy, and Imogen Fountain. 1997. "Keeping the Gates? Women as Ministers in Australia, 1970–96." *Australian Journal of Political Science* 32(3): 455–66.

Moreno, Erika. 2005. "Whither the Colombian Two-Party System?: An Assessment of Political Reforms and Their Limits." *Electoral Studies* 24(3): 485–509.

Morgenstern, Scott. 2001. "Organized Factions and Disorganized Parties: Electoral Incentives in Uruguay." *Party Politics* 7(2): 235–56.

———. 2002. "Towards a Model of Latin American Legislatures," in Scott Morgenstern and Benito Nacif, eds., *Legislative Politics in Latin America*. New York: Cambridge University Press.

———. 2002. "US Models and Latin American Legislatures." In Scott Morgenstern and Benito Nacif, *Legislatures and Democracy in Latin America*. New York: Cambridge University Press.

———. 2004. *Patterns of Legislative Politics: Roll-call Voting in Latin America and the United States*. Cambridge: Cambridge University Press.

Morgenstern, Scott, and Javier Vázquez-D'Elía. 2007. "Electoral Laws and Party Systems in Latin America." *Annual Review of Political Science* 10: 143–68.

Mustapic, Ana María. 1988. "Radicales y justicialistas frente al desafío de la renovación." *Plural* 10–11: 22–26.

———. 1995. "Tribulaciones del Congreso en la nueva democracia argentina: El veto presidencial bajo Alfonsín y Menem." *AGORA* 3(2): 61–74.

Nacif, Benito. 2003. "Policy Making Under Divided Government in Mexico." Working Paper 305, Helen Kellogg Institute for International Studies. University of Notre Dame (March).

Navia, Patricio. 2003. "You Select the Rules of the Game and Lose? Advantages and Constraints When Choosing Electoral Rules: The Case of Chile." Ph.D. dissertation, New York University.

———. 2004. "Modernización del estado y financiamiento de la política: Una crisis que se transformó en oportunidad." In Carolina Stefoni, ed., *Chile 2003–2004: Los nuevos escenarios (inter)nacionales*. Santiago: FLACSO.

———. 2005. "Transformando votos en escaños: Leyes electorales en Chile, 1833–2003." *Política y Gobierno* 13(2): 233–76.

———. 2005. "The Effect of Open Presidential Primaries on Partisan Vote and Election Turnout: The Case of Chile." Presented at the Annual Conference of the Midwest Political Science Association. Chicago, April 7–10.

Nicolau, Jairo. 2000. "Disciplina partidária e base parlamentar na Câmara dos Deputados no primeiro governo Fernando Henrique Cardoso (1995–1998)." *DADOS—Revista de Ciências Sociais* 43(4): 709–35.

Norris, Pippa. 1987. *Politics and Sexual Equality: The Comparative Position of Women in Western Democracies*. Boulder: Lynne Rienner.

———. 1997a. *Passages to Power: Legislative Recruitment in Advanced Democracies*. Cambridge: Cambridge University Press.

———. 1997b. "The Puzzle of Constituency Service." *Journal of Legislative Studies* 3(2): 29–49.

———. 1997c. "Introduction: Theories of Recruitment." In Pippa Norris, ed., *Passages to Power: Legislative Recruitment in Advanced Democracies*. Cambridge: Cambridge University Press.

———. 1997d. "Conclusions: Comparing Passages to Power." In Pippa Norris, ed., *Passages to Power: Legislative Recruitment in Advanced Democracies*. Cambridge: Cambridge University Press.

———. 2004. *Electoral Engineering: Voting Rules and Political Behavior*. Cambridge: Cambridge University Press.

Novaes, Carlos Alberto M. 1994. "Dinâmica institucional da representação: Individualismo e partidos na Câmara dos Deputados." *Novos Estudos CEBRAP* 38: 99–147.

Novaro, Marcos. 2002. "La Alianza, de la gloria del llano a la debacle del gobierno." In Marcos Novaro, ed., *El derrumbe político en el ocaso de la convertibilidad*. Buenos Aires: Editorial Norma.

Nunes, Edson de Oliveira. 1978. "Legislativo, política e recrutamento de elites no Brasil." *Dados* 17: 53–78.

O'Donnell, Guillermo. 1973. *Modernization and Bureaucratic Authoritarianism*. Berkeley: University of California Press.

———. 1994. "Delegative Democracy." *Journal of Democracy* 5(1): 55–69.

Ortega, Eugenio. 2003. "Los partidos políticos chilenos: Cambio y estabilidad en el comportamiento electoral 1990–2000." *Revista de Ciencia Política* 23(2): 109–47.

Osterling, Jorge P. 1989. *Democracy in Colombia*. New Brunswick, N.J.: Transaction.

Otano, Rafael. 1995. *Crónica de la transición*. Santiago: Editorial Planeta.

Palermo, Vicente. 2000. "Como se governa o Brasil? O debate sobre instituições políticas e gestão de governo." *Dados—Revista de Ciências Sociais* 43(3): 5521–57.

Palermo, Vicente, and Marcos Novaro 1996. *Política y poder en el gobierno de Menem.* Buenos Aires: Norma-FLACSO.

Panebianco, Angelo. 1988. *Political Parties: Organization and Power.* Cambridge: Cambridge University Press.

———. 1990. *Modelos de partido.* Madrid: Alianza.

Payne, Leigh A. 2000. *Uncivil Movements: The Armed Right Wing and Democracy in Latin America.* Baltimore: Johns Hopkins University Press.

Payne, Mark J., Daniel Zovatto G., Gernando Carrillo Flórez, and Andrés Allamand Zavala, eds. 2002. *Democracies in Development: Politics and Reform in Latin America.* Washington, D.C., and Baltimore: Inter-American Development Bank and Johns Hopkins University Press.

Pennings, Paul, and Reuven Hazan, eds., 2001. "Democratizing Candidate Selection: Causes and Consequences" (special issue). *Party Politics* 7(3): 267–75.

Pereira, Carlos, and Bernardo Mueller. 2000. "Uma teoria da preponderância do poder executivo: O sistema de comissões no Legislativo brasileiro." *Revista Brasileira de Ciências Sociais* 15(43): 45–67.

Piñeiro, Rafael. 2002. "Elección de diputados y fraccionalización partidaria en Uruguay (1942–1999)." Unpublished paper. Montevideo: Universidad de la República, Instituto de Ciencia Política.

Pinzón de Lewin, Patricia. 1987. *Los partidos políticos colombianos.* Bogotá: Universidad de los Andes.

Pitkin, Hanna F. 1967. *The Concept of Representation.* Berkeley: University of California Press.

Pizarro, Eduardo. 1997. "¿Hacia un sistema multipartidista? Las terceras fuerzas en Colombia hoy." *Análisis Político* 31(May–August): 82–104.

———. 2002. "La atomización partidista en Colombia: El fenómeno de las microempresas electorales." In Gutiérrez Sanín, *Degradación o cambio: evolución del sistema político colombiano.* Bogotá: Editorial Norma.

Polsby, Nelson. 1968. "The Institutionalization of the House of Representatives." *American Political Science Review* 62(1): 144–68.

———. 1983. *Consequences of Party Reform.* New York: Oxford University Press.

Polsby, Nelson, Miriam Gallagher, and Barry Rundquist. 1969. "The Growth of the Seniority System in the U.S. House of Representatives." *American Political Science Review* 63(4): 787–807.

Power, Timothy J. 2000. *The Political Right in Postauthoritarian Brazil: Elites, Institutions, and Democratization.* University Park: Pennsylvania State University Press.

———. 2001. "Blairism Brazilian Style? Cardoso and the 'Third Way' in Brazil." *Political Science Quarterly* 116(4): 611–36.

Power, Timothy J., and Mahrukh Doctor. 2004. "Another Century of Corporatism? Continuity and Change in Brazilian Corporatist Structures." In Howard J. Wiarda, ed., *Authoritarianism and Corporatism in Latin America, Revisited.* Gainesville: University Press of Florida.

Prewitt, Kenneth. 1970. *The Recruitment of Political Leaders.* New York: Bobbs-Merrill.

Price, H. Douglas. 1971. "The Congressional Career Then and Now." In Nelson Polsby, ed., *Congressional Behavior.* New York: Random House.

———. 1975. "Congress and the Evolution of Legislative 'Professionalism.'" In Norman J. Ornstein, ed., *Congress and Change.* New York: Praeger.

———. 1977. "Careers and Committees in the American Congress: The Problem of Structural Change." In William Aydelotte, ed., *The History of Parliamentary Behavior*. Princeton: Princeton University Press.

Prud'homme, Jean-Francois. 1995. "El PRD: Su vida interna y sus elecciones estratégicas." CIDE Working Paper. Mexico City: Centro de Investigación y Docencia Económicas.

Przeworski, Adam, José Antonio Cheibub, Michael E. Alvarez, and Fernando Limongi. 2000. *Democracy and Development: Political Institutions and the Well-being of the World, 1950–1990*. Cambridge: Cambridge University Press.

Putnam, Robert D. 1976. *The Comparative Study of Political Elites*. Englewood Cliffs, N.J.: Prentice-Hall.

Rabkin, Rhoda. 1996. "Redemocratization, Electoral Engineering, and Party Strategies in Chile, 1989–1995." *Comparative Political Studies* 29(3): 335–56.

Rehren, Alfredo. 1992. "Liderazgo presidencial y democratización en el cono sur de América Latina." *Revista de Ciencia Política* 14(1): 63–87.

———. 1998. "La organización de la presidencia y el proceso político chileno." *Revista de Ciencia Política* 19(2): 89–124.

Reveles, Francisco. 2004. "La coalición dominante en el Partido Acción Nacional: Líderes, parlamentarios y gobernantes." In Ricardo Espinoza Toledo and Rosa María Mirón, eds., *Partidos políticos: Nuevos liderazgos y relaciones internas de autoridad*. Mexico City: Universidad Autónoma Metropolitana.

Reynolds, Andrew. 1999. "Women in the Legislatures and Executives of the World: Knocking at the Highest Glass Ceiling." *World Politics* 51(4): 547–72.

Roberts, Kenneth M., and Erik Wibbels. 1999. "Party Systems and Electoral Volatility in Latin America: A Test of Economic, Institutional, and Structural Explanations." *American Political Science Review* 93(3): 575–590.

Rodríguez, Flavio Irene. 2000. "Detrás de un gran presidente hay un gran empresario." *Milenio* (August 14).

Rodríguez-Raza, Juan Carlos. 1998. "¿Cambiar todo para que nada cambie? Representación, sistema electoral y sistema de partidos en el entorno institucional." In Francisco Gutiérrez, ed. *Degradación o cambio. Evolución del sistema político colombiano*. Bogotá: Editorial Norma.

Rodrigues, Leôncio Martins. 2002. *Partidos, ideologia e composição social: Um estudo das bancadas partidárias na Câmara dos Deputados*. São Paulo: Editora da Universidade de São Paulo.

Rohde, David. 1991. *Parties and Leaders in the Postreform House*. Chicago: University of Chicago Press.

Rule, Wilma. 1987. "Electoral Systems, Contextual Factors, and Women's Opportunity for Election to Parliament in Twenty-Three Democracies." *Western Political Quarterly* 40(3): 477–98.

———. 1994. "Parliaments of, by, and for the People: Except for Women?" In Wilma Rule and Joseph F. Zimmerman, eds., *Electoral Systems in Comparative Perspective: Their Impact on Women and Minorities*. Westport, Conn.: Greenwood.

Rule, Wilma, and Matthew Shugart. 1995. "The Preference Vote and Election of Women: Women Win More Seats in Open-List PR." In *Voting and Democracy Report 1995*. Washington, D.C.: Center for Voting and Democracy.

Saiegh, Sebastián, and Mariano Tommasi. 1998. "Argentina's Fiscal Federal Institutions: A Case-Study in the Transaction-Cost Theory of Politics." Paper prepared for the Conference Modernization and Institutional Development in Argentina, United Nations Development Programme. Buenos Aires, May 20–21.

Samuels, David. 1999. "Incentives to Cultivate a Party Vote in Candidate Centric Electoral Systems." *Comparative Political Studies* 32(4): 487–518.

———. 2001a. "Money, Elections, and Democracy in Brazil." *Latin American Politics and Society* 43(2): 27–48.

———. 2001b. "Does Money Matter? Campaign Finance in Newly Democratic Countries: Theory and Evidence from Brazil." *Comparative Politics* 34(3): 23–42.

———. 2001c. "Incumbents and Challengers on a Level Playing Field: Assessing the Impact of Campaign Finance in Brazil." *Journal of Politics* 63(2): 569–84.

———. 2003. *Ambition, Federalism, and Legislative Politics in Brazil.* New York: Cambridge University Press.

———. 2004a. "Sources of Mass Partisanship in Brazil." Unpublished paper. University of Minnesota.

———. 2004b. "From Socialism to Social Democracy: Party Organization and the Transformation of the Workers' Party in Brazil." *Comparative Political Studies* 37(4): 999–1024.

———. 2006. "Source of Mass Partisanship in Brazil." *Latin American Politics and Society* 48(2): 1–27.

Samuels, David, and Fernando Abrucio. 2000. "Federalism and Democratic Transitions: The 'New' Politics of Governors in Brazil." *Publius: The Journal of Federalism* 30(2): 43–61.

Sánchez, Marco Aurelio. 1999. *PRD: La élite en crisis.* Mexico City: Plaza & Valdes.

Santos, Fabiano M. 1997. "Patronagem e poder de agenda na política brasileira." *Dados* 40(3): 465–92.

———. 1999. "Party Leaders and Committee Assignments in Brazil." Paper presented at the 1999 Annual Meeting of the American Political Science Association. Atlanta, September 2–5.

———. 1998. "Recruitment and Retention of Legislators in Brazil." *Legislative Studies Quarterly* 24(2): 209–37.

———. 2003. *O poder legislativo no presidencialismo de coalizão.* Rio de Janeiro: IUPERJ/UCAM.

Sartori, Giovanni. 1976. *Parties and Party Systems: A Framework for Analysis.* Cambridge: Cambridge University Press.

Sawers, Larry. 1996. *The Other Argentina: The Interior and National Development.* Boulder: Westview Press.

Schlesinger, Joseph. 1966. *Ambition and Politics.* Chicago: Rand McNally.

———. 1991. *Political Parties and the Winning of Office.* Chicago: University of Chicago Press.

Schmitt, Rogério. 1999. "Migração partidária e reeleição na Câmara dos Deputados." *Novos Estudos CEBRAP* 54.

Schmidt, Gregory D. N.d. "Is Closed-List PR Really Optimal for the Election of Women? A Cross-National Analysis." Unpublished paper, mimeographed.

Scully, Timothy. 1992. *Rethinking the Center: Cleavages, Critical Junctures, and Party Evolution in Chile.* Palo Alto: Stanford University Press.

————. 1995. "Reconstituting Party Politics in Chile." In Scott Mainwaring and Timothy R. Scully, eds., *Building Democratic Institutions: Party Systems in Latin America*. Palo Alto: Stanford University Press.

Seligman, Lester. 1971. *Recruiting Political Elites*. New York: General Learning Press.

Semana. 1997. "Complot contra la consultas." *Semana*, October 27.

Serrafero, Mario. 1997. *Reelección y sucesión presidencial: Poder y continuidad: Argentina, América Latina y EE.UU.* Buenos Aires: Editorial de Belgrano.

————. 1999. *El poder y su sombra: Los vicepresidentes*. Buenos Aires: Editorial de Belgrano.

————. 1994. "Minorities Represented and Unrepresented." In Wilma Rule and Joseph F. Zimmerman, eds. *Electoral Systems in Comparative Perspective: Their Impact on Women and Minorities*. Westport, Conn.: Greenwood.

Shugart, Matthew. 1995. "The Electoral Cycle and Institutional Sources of Divided Presidential Government." *American Political Science Review* 89(2): 327–43.

Shugart, Matthew S., and John M. Carey. 1992. *Presidents and Assemblies: Constitutional Design and Electoral Dynamics*. New York: Cambridge University Press.

Shvedova, Nadezdha. 1997. "Obstacles to Women's Participation in Parliament." In *Women in Politics: Beyond Numbers*. Stockholm: International IDEA.

Siaroff, Alan. 2000. "Women's Representation in Legislatures and Cabinets in Industrial Democracies." *International Political Science Review* 21(2): 197–215.

Siavelis, Peter. 1993. "Nuevos argumentos y viejos supuestos: Simulaciones de sistemas electorales alternativas para las elecciones parlamentarias chilenas." *Estudios Públicos* 51(Winter): 229–67.

————. 1997. "Continuity and Change in the Chilean Party System." *Comparative Political Studies* 30(6): 651–74.

————. 2000. *The President and Congress in Post-Authoritarian Chile: Institutional Constraints to Democratic Consolidation*. University Park: Penn State University Press.

————. 2001. "Chile: Las relaciones entre el poder ejecutivo y el poder legislativo después de Pinochet." In J. Lanzaro, ed., *Tipos de presidencialismo y coaliciones políticas en América Latina*. Buenos Aires: CLACSO.

————. 2002. "The Hidden Logic of Candidate Selection for Chilean Parliamentary Elections." *Comparative Politics* 34(2): 419–38.

Siavelis, Peter, and Arturo Valenzuela. 1997. "Electoral Engineering and Democratic Stability: The Legacy of Authoritarian Rule in Chile." In Arend Lijphart and Carlos H. Waisman, eds., *Institutional Design in New Democracies: Eastern Europe and Latin America*. Boulder: Westview Press.

Sin, Gisela, and M. Valeria Palanza. 1997. "Partidos provinciales y gobierno nacional en el Congreso." *Boletín SAAP* 3(5): 46–94.

Smith, Peter. 1979. *Labyrinths of Power: Political Recruitment in 20th-Century Mexico*. Princeton: Princeton University Press.

Soares, Gláucio Ary Dillon. 1967. "The Politics of Uneven Development: The Case of Brazil." In Seymour M. Lipset and Stein Rokkan, eds., *Party Systems and Voter Alignments: Cross-National Perspectives*. New York: Free Press.

Solari, Aldo E. 1991. *Uruguay: partidos políticos y sistema electoral*. Montevideo: Fundación de Cultura Universitaria.

Souza, Celina. 1997. *Constitutional Engineering in Brazil: The Politics of Federalism and Decentralization*. New York: St. Martin's Press.

Spiller, Pablo T., and Mariano Tommasi. 2000. *Las fuentes institucionales del desarrollo argentino: Hacia una agenda institucional.* Buenos Aires: EUDEBA-PNUD.

Stokes, Susan. 2001. *Mandates and Democracy: Neoliberalism by Surprise in Latin America.* New York: Cambridge University Press.

Strom, Kaare. 1990. *Minority Government and Majority Rule.* Cambridge: Cambridge University Press.

Studlar, Donley T., and Gary F. Moncrief. 1999. "Women's Work: The Distribution and Prestige of Portfolios in the Canadian Provinces." *Governance: An International Journal of Policy and Administration* 12(4): 379–95.

Taagepera, Rein. 1994. "Beating the Law of Minority Attrition." In Wilma Rule and Joseph F. Zimmerman, eds., *Electoral Systems in Comparative Perspective: Their Impact on Women and Minorities.* Westport, Conn.: Greenwood.

Taylor-Robinson, Michelle M., and Christopher Diaz. 1999. "Who Gets Legislation Passed in a Marginal Legislature and Is the Label 'Marginal Legislature' Still Appropriate?" *Comparative Political Studies* 32(5): 589–625.

Taylor, Steven L. 2002a. "Personal-List PR and a Single National District: The Political Effects of the 1991 Constitutional Reform on Senate Elections in Colombia." Paper presented at the annual meeting of the Public Choice Society. San Diego, March 22–24.

———. 2002b. "Rethinking the Colombian Party System." Paper presented at the annual meeting of the Southern Political Science Association. Savannah, Georgia, November 7–9.

Thacker, Strom C. 2000. *Big Business, the State, and Free Trade.* Cambridge: Cambridge University Press.

Thiébault, Jean-Louis. 1991. "The Social Background of Western European Cabinet Ministers." In Jean Blondel and Jean-Louis Thiébault, eds., *The Profession of Government Minister in Western Europe.* New York: St. Martin's Press.

Tommasi, Mariano. 2002. "Federalism in Argentina and the Reforms of the 1990s." Unpublished paper. Prepared for the Center for Research on Economic Development and Policy Reform project on "Federalism in a Global Environment," Stanford University.

Torcal, Mariano, and Scott Mainwaring. 2003. "The Political Recrafting of Social Bases of Party Competition: Chile, 1973–95." *British Journal of Political Science* 33(1): 55–84.

Tribunal Superior Eleitoral (Brazil). 2002. "Resultados das eleições gerais de 2002." Data file. Brasília: TSE. htpp//www.tse.gov.br.

Tula, María Inés. 1995. "La reforma electoral en los '90: Algunos comentarios sobre la ley de lemas en la Argentina." In Ricardo Sidicaro and Jorge Mayer, eds., *Política y sociedad en los años del menemismo.* Buenos Aires: UBA-CBC.

———. 2005. "Las nuevas tecnologías en los procesos electorales: Perspectivas y comentarios sobre la adopción del voto electrónico en la Argentina." In María Inés Tula, ed., *Voto electrónico: Entre votos y máquinas, las nuevas tecnologías en los procesos electorales.* Buenos Aires: Ariel: 15–39.

———. 1997. "Ley de lemas, elecciones y estrategias partidarias: Los casos de La Rioja, Santa Cruz y Santa Fe." *Boletín SAAP* 3(5): 3–26.

Tula, María Inés, and Miguel De Luca. 1999. "Listas sábana, preferencias y tachas: Algunas reflexiones a propósito de la reforma electoral en la Argentina." *POSTData* 5: 97–146.

Ungar Bleier, Elizabeth. 1993. "El Congreso postconstituyente: Viejas practicas con nuevo ropaje?" *Political Colombiana* 3(4): 9–25.

————. 2003. "Qué pasó en el Senado de la república?" In Gary Hoskin, Rodolfo Masías, and Miguel García., eds., *Colombia 2002: Elecciones, comportamiento electoral y democracia.* Bogotá: Ediciones Uniandes.

Valenzuela, Arturo. 1994. "Party Politics and the Crisis of Presidentialism in Chile: A Proposal for a Parliamentary Form of Government." In Juan J. Linz and Arturo Valenzuela, eds., *The Failure of Presidential Democracy.* Baltimore: Johns Hopkins University Press.

Valenzuela, J. Samuel, and Timothy Scully. 1997. "Electoral Choices and the Party System in Chile." *Comparative Politics* 29(4): 511–27.

Varela, Carlo. 1974. "The Electoral Processes Have Begun." *Review of the Economic Situation of Mexico*, produced by Banamex (June): 224.

Vernazza, Francisco. 1989. "Minoristas, mayoristas y generalistas en el sistema electoral uruguayo." *Revista Uruguaya de Ciencia Política 3.* Fundación de Cultura Universitaria, Montevideo.

Waisbord, Silvio. 1985. *El gran desfile: Campañas electorales y medios de comunicación en Argentina.* Buenos Aires: Sudamericana.

Weingast, Barry. 1979. "A Rational Choice Perspective on Congressional Norms." *American Journal of Political Science* 23(2): 245–64.

Weldon, Jeffrey. 2005. "Institutional and Political Factors for Party Discipline in the Mexican Congress since the End of PRI Hegemony." Paper prepared for the conference, What Kind of Democracy Has Mexico? University of California, San Diego, Center for U.S.-Mexican Studies. San Diego, March 4–5.

————. 2006. "The Spring 2005 Term of the Mexican Congress." Mexican Congressional Report Series. Washington, D.C.: Center for Strategic and International Studies.

Wessels, Bernhard. 1997. "Germany." In Pippa Norris, ed., *Passages to Power: Legislative Recruitment in Advanced Democracies.* Cambridge: Cambridge University Press.

Weyland, Kurt. 1993. "The Rise and Fall of President Collor and Its Impact on Brazilian Democracy." *Journal of Interamerican Studies and World Affairs* 35(1): 1–36.

Willis Otero, Laura, and Aníbal Pérez-Liñan. 2005. "La evolución de los sistemas electorales en América: 1900–2004." *Colección* 16: 47–82.

Wuhs, Steve. 2006. "Democratization and the Dynamics of Candidate Selection Rule Change in Mexico, 1991–2003." *Mexican Studies* 22(1): 33–56.

Yaffé, Jaime. 2005. *Al centro y adentro: La renovación de la izquierda y el triunfo del Frente Amplio en Uruguay.* Montevideo: Librería Linardi y Risso.

Index

Abranches, Sérgio, 77, 228
Abrúcio, Fernando, 229–31, 234, 236, 240
Agor, Westin, 373
Agüero, Felipe, 246, 253
Aguilar Zinser, Adolfo, 311
Alcántara Sáez, Manuel, 356
Alckmin, Geraldo, 221, 235, 384
Alessandri, Arturo, 245, 249–50, 260, 381
Alfonsín, Raúl, 4, 6, 44, 200, 206–8, 216, 348, 394
Alianza (Argentina), 53, 55, 202, 208
Alianza Nacional Popular ANAPO (Colombia), 129, 277, 283
Alianza Nacionalista (Uruguay), 169
Alianza por Chile (Chile), 92–93, 96–98, 100, 102, 105, 109–10, 113, 116, 242, 244–45, 250, 252, 255, 258–60
Alianza Progresista (Uruguay), 319
Allamand, Andrés, 99, 118, 246, 250
alliances, 4, 31–32, 36, 161, 200, 223, 225, 233, 239, 321, 324, 395
allocation of seats and allocation formula, 43, 96, 98, 105, 121, 321
Altman, David, xi–xii, 116, 208, 265–66, 348–49, 387, 396, 399
Álvarez, Carlos "Chacho," 208
Álvear, Soledad, 252, 263
Ames, Barry, 6, 77–78, 80, 90
Amorim Neto, Octávio, 78, 228, 334–35, 350
Antioquia (Colombia), 122, 275
Antônio Carlos Magalhães (ACM), 237
Arana, Mariano, 319
Archer, Ronald, 126, 128, 131, 280
Argentina, vii, ix–xi, 6–7, 26, 41–44, 49, 51, 54, 66, 71–74, 88, 190–95, 198, 201–2, 205, 351, 362, 383, 392, 394–95
Arrate, Jorge, 117
Arriagada, Genaro, 248, 263
Asamblea Uruguay, 173, 319
Aspe, Pedro, 305

Astori, Danilo, 173, 319, 326, 329
Atkeson, Lonna Rae, 327
Australia, 264
authoritarian regime and authoritarian state, vii, 144, 147, 158, 242, 246
Avellaneda, Claudia, 141
avispa strategy, 126, 128, 141. *See also* list proliferation
Aylwin, Mariana, 263
Aylwin, Patricio, 106, 117, 241, 244–47, 253–54, 257–58, 262–63, 267, 269, 352

Bachelet, Michele, 241, 244, 251–52, 255, 257, 261, 263, 269, 385
backbenchers, 77–79, 89, 91
Baja California del Sur (Mexico), 297
ballot, ballot access, and placement on the ballot (Argentina), 51
ballot, ballot access, and placement on the ballot (Brazil), 79, 82–86, 89
ballot, ballot access, and placement on the ballot (Chile), 99, 103, 110, 112, 116, 243
ballot, ballot access, and placement on the ballot (Colombia), 120, 127–28, 135, 141, 273, 277–79, 289–91
ballot, ballot access, and placement on the ballot (Mexico), 146–48, 151–52, 159, 161, 297
ballot, ballot access, and placement on the ballot (Uruguay), 168, 172, 175, 320
ballotage, 243, 320. *See also* two-round electoral systems
Barco, Virgilio, 274, 278, 281–82, 284
Barros, Enrique, 246
Batlle Berres, Luis, 318, 332–33, 335, 338–39, 342
Batlle Ibáñez, Jorge, 319, 334–35, 339–42
Batlle y Ordóñez, José, 318, 330

Benton, Allyson Lucinda, 47
Bernardes, Franco César, 87
Berreta, Tomás, 332, 338, 342
Betancur, Belisario, 274, 277
bicameral congress or legislature, 356
Bilbao, Josefina, 263
bill initiation, 140–41, 273, 283,
    285–87, 397
binomial plurality (Mexico), 161
binomial system (Chile), 96–97, 99,
    261, 268
Black, Gordon, 6
Blancos (Uruguay), 172, 174, 180,
    319, 329
Boeninger Commission (Chile), 261
Bogotá, 130, 275, 277
Bolivia, 4, 243, 353, 372, 379, 391–93
Bordaberry, Juan María, 319, 332, 335,
    339, 342
Bordón, José O., 214
Botero, Felipe, xii, 132, 349, 384, 388,
    397–98
Botinelli, Oscar O., 168, 171
Bravo Mena, Luis Felipe, 156
Brazil, ix–xi, 3–4, 6, 27–28, 71, 73, 76–78,
    80–88, 90–91, 176, 218, 220, 223–24,
    229–30, 232–35, 238, 240, 242, 262,
    264, 336, 351–51, 355, 359, 362, 364,
    372, 376, 380–82, 384, 386, 392–95
Brizola, Leonel, 221, 224, 236
Bruhn, Kathleen, 158–59, 161
budget and budget amendments,
    48, 89–90, 191, 219, 264,
    306, 354
Büchi, Hernán, 244–47, 250, 254,
    258–59, 381
Buenos Aires, 43, 193, 201–2, 206,
    209–11, 214
Buquet, Daniel, 164, 168, 171, 174, 184,
    197, 318, 322, 333, 354, 385, 399
Burnham, Walter Dean, 28
business organizations and support, 35,
    153, 175, 246, 249, 253, 259, 303, 309,
    312, 387, 398
Busti, Jorge, 213–14

cabeza de lista, 63, 65. See also head of list
cabinet and cabinet composition, xi–xiii,
    3–4, 25, 31–34, 36, 60–61, 63, 66,
    68–69, 74, 179, 182, 190, 204, 207–11,
    216, 228–30, 236, 239, 242, 246, 252,
    256, 261–64, 268, 270, 273, 284, 287,
    294, 296, 299–301, 314, 317, 334–36,
    346, 348, 351, 353, 361, 367, 391,
    394, 399
cabinet-party congruence, 334–36.
    See also Rice index
Cafiero, Antonio, 209, 214
Caiado, Ronaldo, 224
Cain, Bruce, 119, 178, 180
Calderón, Felipe, 6, 296–97, 299–300,
    305, 312, 314, 382, 398
Calvo, Ernesto, 47, 192
Camargo, Affonso, 238
Camp, Roderic Ai, xii, 6, 8, 292–93, 301
campaigns (Argentina), 47–50, 63, 74,
    190, 195, 206–10, 216, 375
campaigns (Brazil), ix, 76, 80, 84–85,
    221, 224, 229, 231, 233, 395
campaigns (Chile), 242, 256–61, 269
campaigns (Colombia), 133–35, 273, 280,
    282, 290–91
campaigns (Mexico), 146, 152, 159, 294,
    302–4
campaigns (Uruguay), 169, 172, 325, 327,
    330–31
campaign contributors and campaign
    finance, 7, 16, 24, 29, 47–49, 79, 84,
    89, 291
Campeche (Mexico), 161
Canada, 166
Cañas, Enrique, 245
candidate profiles, 146–47, 151
candidate selection vs. political
    recruitment, 8–9
candidate typologies, 12, 17, 26, 29
Canelones (Uruguay), 176
Capital Federal (Argentina), 42, 45, 48, 215
Cárdenas, Alberto, 313
Cárdenas, Cuauhtémoc, 158, 297, 382
Cárdenas, Lázaro, 153, 298–99

Cardoso, Fernando Henrique, 221–23, 226, 228, 239, 382, 389, 396
career paths, 41–42, 66, 155, 160, 163, 177, 192, 212, 273–76, 279, 290, 371. *See also* progressive ambition; static ambition
careerism, in Brazil, 79–80, 85–88
Carey, John M., 6, 12–13, 27, 77, 88, 97, 105, 119, 165, 176, 253, 329, 348, 373
Carrió, Elisa, 202, 204
Casar, María Amparo, 145
Castañeda, Jorge, 307, 311
Catamarca (Argentina), 191
catchall parties, 229, 231–33, 239–40
Caudillos, 108, 147, 196
Caul, Miki, 350
Cavallo, Ascanio, 245
Cavallo, Domingo, 67, 202, 204, 208
centralization, 14–15, 17–18, 24, 99, 148, 176, 231, 235, 275, 300, 371, 382
challenge and challengers, 49, 77, 100, 105–6, 116, 120, 128, 130, 134, 142–43, 145, 148, 161, 173, 184, 196, 198–200, 212, 220, 235, 241, 256, 271, 280, 322, 326, 350, 366, 368, 378, 380, 382, 390
Chamber of Deputies (Argentina), 42–44, 46, 51–53, 56, 58, 66, 72, 191, 204
Chamber of Deputies (Brazil), 77, 85–87, 218, 228, 235
Chamber of Deputies (Chile), 93–94, 96–98, 100–102, 105–8, 110, 115, 250
Chamber of Deputies (Colombia), 121, 124, 134–35, 138
Chamber of Deputies (Mexico), 145, 150, 152, 156, 158, 160, 300, 355, 359, 374
Chamber of Deputies (Uruguay), 167, 175, 183
Chasquetti, Daniel, xii–xiii, 164, 169, 174, 197, 318, 322, 331, 333, 354, 381, 385, 390, 398–99
Chaves, Aureliano, 224
Chávez, Hugo, 380, 387, 392
Chile, vii, ix, xi, 3, 28–29, 59, 73, 79, 92–93, 96, 98, 106, 111, 113, 115, 208,

241, 243, 247, 253, 256, 264–65, 269, 317, 336, 348, 351, 354–55, 372, 379, 381, 386, 390, 392–93, 396–97
Chubut (Argentina), 51
Cintra, Antônio Octávio, 220–21
clientelism and clientelistic practices, 47–49, 76, 180, 189, 191–92, 195, 216
closed-list systems, x, 5, 11, 13–14, 23, 73, 81, 29, 106, 121, 131, 142, 163–64, 171, 178, 180, 183, 345, 346–47, 355, 358–59, 361, 367, 375. *See also* open-list systems
coalitions (Argentina), 193–94, 198–202, 208, 216, 394
coalitions (Brazil), 82–83, 220, 225, 228–30, 389, 395
coalitions (Chile), 3, 92–93, 96–100, 102–3, 105–7, 109–17, 241–48, 250, 256, 258, 260–66, 268–70, 373, 379, 382, 387, 391, 396
coalitions (Colombia), 133–34, 288
coalitions (Mexico), 147–48, 158–59, 398
coalitions (Uruguay), 166, 168, 173–74, 318, 323, 399
coalitional presidentialism, 228
Collor de Mello, Fernando, 221, 223–24, 229, 238–39, 352, 362, 392–93, 395–96
Colombia, x, xii, 3–4, 27, 71, 73, 119–27, 129–42, 171, 176, 264, 271–77, 279, 281, 283–85, 287–91, 317, 349, 352–55, 358–59, 362, 364, 372, 376–77, 379–81, 383–90, 392–93, 397–98
Colomer, Josep, 328–29
Colorados (Uruguay), 174, 180, 319, 329
committee and committee assignments, 72, 75, 87, 106–8, 112, 114, 150, 154–55, 157, 162, 176, 373
competitive elections and primaries, 51, 54–57, 145, 197, 292, 301
competitiveness, 124, 189, 194, 216, 288, 316, 327–28, 374
Concertación and *Concertacionistas* (Chile), 92–98, 100–110, 112–13, 115–16, 208, 241–48, 250–52, 254–55, 258–63, 265, 269, 348, 385–87, 396

concurrence of elections, 25–26, 30, 194, 220, 223, 288–89, 382

Conservatives (Colombia), 119, 122–27, 129–30, 134, 137, 277, 282, 290

consociational democratic model, 262

constituent servants, viii, xiii, 10, 12, 20–22, 73–74, 81, 97, 99, 102, 105–6, 113–15, 132, 136, 140–41, 146, 183, 351, 355, 358, 367, 372–75, 378, 393, 395, 399

constituents and constituency service, 5, 9, 11–14, 17, 20–22, 48, 51, 72, 74, 105, 115, 124, 128, 131, 142, 153, 158, 280, 314, 378–79, 399

constitution (Argentina), 34, 191, 196, 212

constitution (Brazil), 219

constitution (Chile), 113–14, 246

constitution (Colombia), 121, 125, 275–76, 278–79, 290, 384

constitution (Mexico), 145, 148

constitution (Uruguay), 165, 167, 176, 178–79, 181–85

continuismo, 27

Coppedge, Michael, 356

corporatist representation, 224, 231

Corrales, Javier, 42, 209

Corrientes (Argentina), 45, 191, 215

corruption, 224, 234, 243, 282, 395–96

Costa Rica, 26, 80, 88, 317, 353, 356, 359

coup, 226, 246, 318–19, 336, 393

Covas, Mário, 224

Cox, Gary W., 22, 71, 79, 91, 121, 125, 164, 166, 176, 379, 380, 393

Creel, Santiago, 311

Crisp, Brian, 119, 176, 178–79, 349, 388–89, 397–98

Crottoggini, José, 330

Crottoggini, Juan J., 326

Crusius, Yeda, 235

Czudnowski, Moshe, 6, 165

da Silva, Benedita, 233

da Silva, Luiz Inácio, 4, 221–22, 224, 383, 395

Dantas Neto, Paulo Fábio, 234

Davis, James W., 6, 164

Davis, Rebecca H., 346, 348–50

de Amézaga, Juan José, 332, 338, 342

de Herrera, Luis Alberto, 169, 319, 338

De la Madrid, Miguel, 300, 306–7, 362, 365

de la Rúa, Fernando, 6, 44, 190, 192, 198–99, 202, 207–8, 215–17

de la Torre Castellanos, Reneé, 311

De Luca, Miguel, 43, 47–52, 190–97, 203, 253, 348–49, 381–82, 387–90, 392, 394

decentralized nominations, 82, 85, 119, 141, 144, 150, 162–63, 379, 389

dedazo, 28, 386–87, 389

Democracia Avanzada (Uruguay), 319

Democratic Pole Party (Colombia), 291

democratization and transition to democracy, 143, 230, 242–43, 245–46, 253, 259, 269, 300, 304, 326, 353, 374, 378, 387–88

Derbez, Luis Ernesto, 304

Desposato, Scott, 87

Dias, Álvaro, 238

Díaz, Christopher, 140

Díaz, José A., 209

Diez-Mendez, Jordi, 311

dissident, 5, 27, 29, 32–34, 124–26, 131, 280, 318

district and district magnitude, 11–13, 17–19, 21, 42, 77, 121, 125, 177, 179–80, 373, 380

double simultaneous vote (DSV), x, 164, 168, 196, 316, 320, 375, 386

Duhalde, Eduardo, 44, 190, 206, 210

Dutra, Eurico Gaspar, 221

Duverger, Maurice, 4, 26, 325, 384

Eaton, Kent, 42

Echeverría, Luis, 306

Ecuador, 26, 372

effective number of factions, parties, and candidates, 168–70, 223, 325, 327–28, 332, 334

Eisenstadt, Todd, 158

electoral calendar and electoral cycles, 221, 242, 251, 263–69, 273, 278, 317

Electoral College, 191
elites and elite arrangement (Argentina),
  7, 49, 51–53, 196–97, 200, 203, 375
elites and elite arrangement (Brazil),
  78–79, 89, 223, 230
elites and elite arrangement (Chile),
  92, 96–98, 100, 102, 105–7, 111–12,
  115, 241–42, 244, 250, 252–53, 373
elites and elite arrangement (Colombia),
  129, 271–72, 274, 276–77, 290, 389
elites and elite arrangement (Mexico),
  151, 294–95, 299–302, 305–10
elites and elite arrangement (Uruguay),
  165–66, 172, 322–23, 326, 336
Ellis, Melody, 347
England, 308
Entre Ríos (Argentina), 191
entrepreneurs and entrepreneurial candidates,
  viii–x, xiii, 10, 12, 22–23, 71, 76–82,
  85, 88, 90, 97, 99, 102, 110, 113–14,
  119–20, 124, 127, 129, 131–32, 134–35,
  139–42, 321, 346–47, 351, 355, 357–60,
  372, 376, 378, 393, 396–97
Epstein, David, 143
Erickson, Linda, 166
Errázuriz, Francisco Javier, 244, 247,
  254, 256
Escalona, Camilo, 107
Escobar-Lemmon, Maria, x, xiii, 141,
  265, 348–51, 361, 363, 367, 376,
  388–89, 399
Espacio 90 (Uruguay), 319
Echegoyen, Martín, 332, 339, 342
Eulau, Heinz, 6, 165
Europe, vii, 304, 306
executive-legislative relations, x, 4–5, 9,
  25, 93, 114–16, 364, 368, 392, 394,
  397–99, 401

faction adherents, 317, 323, 332, 335–36,
  399. See also party adherents
faction insiders, 316–17, 322–24, 330, 332,
  334–36, 381. See also party insiders
faction loyalist, 127, 164, 167, 183, 351,
  354, 375, 399

factionalism, xiii, 3, 161, 181, 183,
  375–77, 380, 387
Federal District (Mexico), 147, 159,
  160–61, 298
Federal Electoral Institute (Mexico),
  313–14
federalism and federal systems
  (Argentina), 42, 74, 192, 375
federalism and federal systems (Brazil),
  77, 81, 88
federalism and federal systems (Mexico),
  x, 143, 148, 150, 374, 388
Feliú, Manuel, 248–49
Fenno, Richard, 373
Ferejohn, John, 119, 178, 180
Fernández Crespo, Daniel, 332, 335, 338,
  339, 342
Ferreira Rubio, Delia, 209, 340
Figueiredo, Argelina, 77–78, 87, 90, 239
Figueroa, Carlos, 263
Finland, 166
Finocchiaro, Charles J., 77
Fleury Filho, Luiz Antônio, 236
Fontaine, Arturo, 246
Formosa (Argentina), 191
Foro Batllista (Uruguay), 169, 174, 319,
  340–41
Fortuna, Adm. Hernani, 224
foundational election, 377, 389
Fountain, Imogen, 348
Fox, Vicente, 4, 157, 214, 292–94, 301,
  309, 352, 382 83
Foxley, Alejandro, 247
fragmentation and fragmented party
  system, 77, 277, 333–34, 386
France, 308
Franco, Itamar, 224, 238–39, 395
free-wheeling independents, viii, xii–xiii, 32,
  34–35, 204, 224, 229, 233–34, 237–38,
  240, 253, 273–74, 276–77, 283, 286,
  288, 333, 349–50, 352, 362–63,
  365–66, 380–85, 387, 389, 392–93,
  395–98, 400–401
Frei, Eduardo, 106, 244–45, 247, 249,
  253–54, 256–57, 263

Frei, Francisco, 263
Freidenberg, Flavia, 355–56
Freire, Roberto, 224
Frente Amplio (Uruguay), 168–69,
    173–74, 180–81, 183, 317, 319, 326,
    336, 376
FREPASO *Frente País Solidario*
    (Argentina), 44, 63–65, 67, 70, 198,
    201, 204, 208
Frota, Gen. Ivan, 224
Fuentes, Claudio, 96
Fujimori, Alberto, 393
Furtado, Celso, 89

Gabeira, Fernando, 224
Galán, Luis Carlos, 131, 272, 274, 278,
    280, 282–83
Gallagher, Michael, 14, 143–44, 164–66
Gamboa, Ricardo, 252
gamonales, 128, 131, 142
Garcia, Hélio, 237
Garotinho, Anthony, 224, 233,
    236–37, 240
Garotinho, Rosinha, 236
Garretón, Manuel Antonio, 263
Garrido, Luís Javier, 147, 158
gatekeepers, 8, 16, 28, 85, 346–47
Gaviria, César, 274, 278, 281–82
gender gap, 347
gender quota legislation, 66, 84, 345,
    350, 355–56, 359, 367
Genoíno, José, 235
geographical organization, 14, 17–18, 23,
    27, 96, 290, 382, 388
Germany, 166
Gestido, Oscar, 332, 339, 342
globalization, 228, 304, 306
Godoy, Oscar, 247, 259
Goicochea Luna, Emilio, 304
Gomes, Ciro, 224, 229
Gómez, Álvaro, 27, 277, 290
Gómez, Laureano, 127
González, Luis E., 168, 171, 318, 322
Goretti, Matteo, 209
Goulart, João, 221, 224, 395

governability, ix, xiii, 5, 8, 20, 36–37, 77,
    220, 368
governors and governorships, 8, 14, 28,
    42, 44, 47, 49, 52, 54–55, 63, 65, 71,
    90, 135, 145–50, 163, 189–221, 223,
    225, 229–40, 242, 264, 288–90, 294,
    298–300, 308–12, 382, 388
Grayson, George, 296, 312
Green Parties. *See* PV
group agents, viii, 25, 30–31, 34–36, 224,
    323, 352, 367, 372–73, 380–81, 389,
    393, 395
group delegates, viii, xiii, 10, 12, 17, 20,
    22–24, 97, 99, 102, 113, 127, 131, 231,
    351, 367, 372, 376, 393, 396
Guanajuato (Mexico), 299–300
Guimarães, Ulysses, 224
Guzmán, Carlos Enrique, 232

Hagopian, Frances, 185, 234
Hales, Patricio, 108
Hazan, Reuven, 8, 14–15, 143
head of list, 63–64, 135–36. See also
    cabeza de lista
hegemonic political system, 111, 143–45,
    147–48, 153, 327
Helander, Voito, 166
Helmke, Gretchen, 6–7
Hierro López, Luis, 174, 329, 341
Hirsh, Tomás, 261
holder's keeper right, 105
Honduras, 26
Htun, Mala, 348, 350, 361
Huenchumilla, Francisco, 107
Human Development Index, 356–57,
    361
Huntington, Samuel P., 352
Hwang, Wonjae, 47

ideological parties, 220, 229, 231, 240,
    253, 390
ideology, 20, 23, 32–33, 36, 71, 140, 153,
    159, 225, 233, 258–60, 284, 293, 318,
    331, 365, 395
inclusiveness, 15, 18, 28, 34, 289–90

incumbents, 7, 27, 79, 82, 85–86, 88, 97, 99–100, 105–6, 108, 110–11, 113, 117, 140, 194, 220, 235–36, 347
independent candidates, xii, 27, 98–99, 103, 107, 109–10, 243, 272
indigenous groups and parties, 35, 134
Ingall, Rachel, 119, 178
insider proxies, 234–37, 240, 382. See also oligarchical proxies
institutionalization, 35, 76, 190, 192, 212, 216, 231, 290, 323, 336, 387
institutionalized party system, xi–xii, 189, 216, 279, 388

Jacobson, Gary, 135
Jalisco (Mexico), 313
Japan, 79, 86, 166, 308
Jocelyn-Holt, José, 107
Jones, Mark, ix–xi, 26, 41, 43, 47–52, 58–59, 67, 70, 88, 197, 203, 223, 332, 347–48, 355, 361
Juárez, Carlos, 213, 215
judicial branch and Judiciary, 66, 313

Katz, Richard, 168
Kellam, Marisa, 350
Kenney, Patrick J., 327
Kenworthy, Lane, 356
Kernell, Samuel, 135
Kirchner, Néstor, 6, 44, 190, 210–11, 216–17, 355, 394
Kitschelt, Herbert, 166
Krauss, Alejandra, 263
Krehbiel, Keith, 78, 393
Kubitschek, Juscelino, 224, 239

La Rioja (Argentina), 191, 209
La Violencia, 126
Labastida, Francisco, 293, 297–98
Lacalle, Luis Alberto, 169, 319, 330–32, 334–35, 340–42
Ladrón de Guevara, Andrés Dávila, 119
Lagos, Ricardo, 116, 241, 245, 248, 250–51, 253, 257, 260, 269, 383, 387, 399

Langston, Joy, x, 88, 145, 355, 374, 378–79
Larrañaga, Jorge, 331, 341
Larrañaga, Luis Alberto, 169
Lavandero, Jorge, 106
Lavín, Joaquín, 28, 244, 250, 254, 260–61, 385
Lawson, Chappell, 293
Leal Buitrago, Francisco, 119
Leal, Victor Nunes, 240
legal variables, 4, 8, 10–15, 17–23, 26, 29–30, 73, 80, 82, 93, 96, 273, 279, 288
Lerner, Jaime, 238
Leuco, Alfredo, 209
Levitsky, Steven, 6–7, 47, 192, 210, 213
Levy Algazi, Santiago, 307
ley de cupos, 359
ley de lemas, 197
Liberal Party and Liberals (Colombia), 4, 124–25, 127–30, 137–38, 276–79, 281–82, 288, 390
Lichtinger, Victor, 312–13
Limongi, Fernando, 77–78, 87, 89–90, 239
Linz, Juan J., 36, 393–94
list proliferation, 119, 124–26, 129–42. See also Avispa strategy
Lista 15 (Uruguay), 319
Lizurume, Jose Luis, 51
Lleras Restrepo, Carlos, 127, 277–78
Lloreda, Rodrigo, 274, 277, 281–82
logistic regression, 268
López Michelson, Alfonso, 127, 129, 131
López Murphy, Ricardo, 202, 204, 208
López Obrador, Andrés Manuel, 6, 162, 298, 314, 381–82
López Portillo, José, 352, 362, 365
Lovenduski, Joni, 350
loyalty, vii, 5, 8–9, 11–17, 21–29, 35, 42, 49, 74, 96–98, 102, 106, 113–17, 127–28, 131–32, 155, 167, 184, 197, 228, 373, 377, 394

Mabry, Donald J., 153
machine politics and party machines, 50–51, 71, 75, 194, 196, 206, 208, 234–37, 245–46, 272, 375

Maciel, Marco, 229

Madrazo, Roberto, 297, 381

Magalhães, Antônio Carlos, 234, 237

Mainwaring, Scott, 36, 76–77, 80, 96,
    189, 192, 220, 223, 229, 231, 253, 290,
    317, 327, 393

Malami, Melissa, 356

Malamud, Andrés, 197, 207

Maluf, Paulo, 224

mandate reversals, 25, 391

Marenco dos Santos, André, 88–89

Marín, Rubén, 213–14

Marsh, Michael, 6, 14, 143–44, 164–66

Martens Rebolledo, Ernesto, 312

Martínez Trueba, Andrés, 332, 335,
    338, 342

Martínez Vázquez, Griselda, 313

Martínez, Gutenberg, 107, 263

Marvick, Dwaine, 6

MAS *Movimiento al Socialismo*
    (Bolivia), 372

Matland, Richard, 345, 350, 356

Matthei, Evelyn, 248

Mayhew, David, 22, 177, 373, 393

McCallister, Ian, 166

McCubbins, Matthew, 22, 71, 79, 91,
    164, 166, 176, 393

McGuire, James W., 192, 213

media and media access, 159, 224, 234,
    240, 330, 354

median voter, 328

Mendoza (Argentina), 191

Menem, Carlos, 4, 6, 44, 190, 200–202,
    206, 209–11, 214, 216–17, 355, 383,
    387, 394

Mexico, viii, x, xii, 4, 6, 26, 28–29, 82,
    88, 143–63, 292–15, 351–53, 355,
    358–59, 365, 373–74, 378–80,
    382–90, 398

Meyenberg, Yolanda, 158

Michoacán (Mexico), 161

Mieres, Pablo, 318

militants, 7, 14, 32, 107–8, 145, 152, 154,
    156–57, 159–60, 163, 173–74, 244,
    247, 329, 379, 390

military regime, 226, 230, 243, 245–46,
    258–59, 263

Miller, Warren E., 28

Minas Gerais (Brazil), 235, 237

minority party, 123, 147, 355–56

minority presidents, 32, 36, 356, 365

minority seats, 123, 160

Mixed Electoral System, x, 145, 355,
    359

Mizrahi, Yemille, 152–53, 293, 302–3,
    313, 315

Mochel, Marilia G., xi, 218, 382,
    388–89, 395

MODIN *Movimiento por la Dignidad y la
    Independencia* (Argentina), 43, 193

Moncrief, Larry F., 350

Monestier, Felipe, 171

Montecarlo simulation, 181

Montes, J. Esteban, 96

Montevideo, 176, 180, 319, 326

Moon, Jeremy, 348

Moraes, Juan Andrés, x–xii, 127, 164,
    317–18, 320–22, 333–34, 354, 375–76,
    379, 390, 399

Morales, Evo, 392

Morales, María Antonieta, 263

Morelos (Mexico), 161

Moreno, Erika, x, 119, 376, 388–89,
    397

Movimiento de Participacion Popular
    MPP (Uruguay), 173, 319

Movimiento Nacional de Rocha, 169

MPF *Movimiento Popular Fueguino*
    (Argentina), 53, 55, 193, 203

MPN *Movimiento Popular Neuquino*
    (Argentina), 44, 53, 55, 193, 203

MRL *Movimiento Revolucionario Liberal*
    (Colombia), 280

Mueller, Bernardo, 87

Mujica, José, 173

multi-list strategy, 121, 123. See also
    avispa strategy

multipartism and multiparty systems,
    vii, 6, 34, 83, 90, 96, 102, 228, 230,
    265, 268, 333, 385

municipal government, 48–49, 66–67, 70, 74, 82, 85, 90, 154, 157, 218–20, 238, 247–49, 265, 278, 281–82, 320
Murillo, María Victoria, 47, 192
Mustapic, Ana María, 192, 209

Nacif, Benito, 145
name recognition, 11, 99, 108, 134–35, 139, 140, 142, 177, 230, 247
National Front (Colombia), x, 120, 126–28, 130–31, 139, 142, 273–74, 283, 287, 353, 377, 379, 397
Navia, Patricio, ix, 15, 92, 96–97, 115, 253, 373, 388, 390, 396–97
negative binomial regression (NBR) model, 129, 179, 181
neo-liberal policies, 211, 246, 305
neopanistas, 153, 156, 293, 303, 313
Neuquén (Argentina), 51, 193
Neves, Aécio, 235
Neves, Tancredo, 221
NGOs, 311–12
Nicaragua, 26
Norris, Pippa, 6, 8, 14, 16, 144, 164–66, 178, 345–46, 348, 350, 356
Novaes, Carlos Alberto, 87
Novaro, Marcos, 44, 53, 209
Novoa, Jovino, 248–49
Nuevo Espacio (Uruguay), 319
Nuevo Léon (Mexico), 312
Nuevo Liberalismo (Colombia), 131, 280
Nunes, Edson, 225–26, 230

O'Donnell, Guillermo, 36, 228
oligarchical proxies, 230, 234, 236–37, 240, 382. See also insider proxies
oligarchical states and oligarchical systems, 233–34, 236–37, 240, 382
Oliveira, Ermicio Sena, 232
open-list systems, 6, 11, 13–14, 21, 23, 81, 83, 97, 132, 346. See also closed-list systems
operación avispa. See Avispa strategy
opinion polls and surveys, 211, 244–45, 247, 252, 261

Opus Dei, 308
ordinary least squares (OLS), 136, 179
Ortega, Eugenio, 96, 253
Ortega, Ramón Palito, 202, 213, 215
Ospina, Mariano, 127
Otano, Rafael, 245

PAC Political Action Committee, 16
Pachakutik (Ecuador), 372
Palermo, Vicente, 77–78, 209
Palmeira, Vladimir, 233
PAIS Partido Amplio de Izquierda Socialista (Chile), 107
PAN Partido Accion Nacional (Mexico), 143–45, 147, 151–57, 159–63, 292–95, 297, 299–300, 302–5, 311–13, 315, 351, 355, 374, 379, 388
Panama, 26
Panebianco, Angelo, 166, 172, 325
Paraguay, 26
Paraná (Brazil), 238
parliament and parliamentary government, vii, 6, 167–68, 173, 179–80, 182, 184–85, 348
participatory procedures, 272–73, 397. See also inclusiveness; primaries
Partido del Sur (Chile), 249
Partido Democrático Trabalhista PDT (Brazil), 224, 233, 236
Partido Nacional (Chile), 246, 249
Partido Nacional (Uruguay), 168, 180, 317, 324, 327–31
party adherent, viii, xi–xiii, 25, 31–35, 190, 204, 206, 210–13, 216–17, 224, 252–53, 256, 258–60, 263–65, 268–70, 272–88, 293–94, 313, 316–17, 333–34, 336, 349, 352, 354–55, 362–66, 380–84, 387–89, 392–98, 401
party affiliation, 81, 99, 132, 137, 232–33, 264, 266, 315
party boss, 47, 58, 70–75, 88, 147, 196, 209, 230, 234–37, 382, 394–95
party discipline, ix–xi, 5–6, 10, 22, 24, 34, 41, 78, 90, 114–17, 127, 129, 145,

151, 167, 184, 233, 253, 317, 326, 329,
  333–34, 377–78, 391, 395–96, 401
party identification and partisanship, xi,
  3–4, 15, 19–20, 28, 32–35, 76, 134, 137,
  159, 235, 180–81, 183, 225, 273–74,
  280, 291, 323, 371, 377–78, 387, 396
party insider, viii, xi–xiii, 3, 25, 29–36,
  115, 146, 151–52, 190, 198, 204,
  206–8, 210, 212–13, 216–17, 224–25,
  228–30, 234–35, 237, 239–40, 252–56,
  258–65, 268–70, 272–85, 287, 293–94,
  296–97, 300, 313, 316–17, 322–23,
  329–36, 348–49, 352, 362–66, 380–85,
  387–89, 392–99
party loyalist, viii–x, xiii, 10, 12, 19–22,
  32, 37, 42, 71, 73–74, 76, 79–80, 92–93,
  96–100, 102, 105–6, 110, 112–17,
  140–41, 146, 150, 152–56, 161–64, 221,
  232, 346–47, 351, 354–55, 357–61, 368,
  372–76, 378, 383, 392–99, 400–1
party registration, 99, 109, 130, 145,
  147, 243
party switching, 15, 32, 81, 84, 87, 233,
  237
party variables, 4, 8, 10–12, 14–15, 17–21,
  23, 25, 28–30, 32–34, 36, 53, 55,
  73–74, 80, 82, 93, 99, 120, 126, 189,
  273, 278, 289, 337, 382–83, 386, 399
Pastrana, Andrés, 274–75, 277, 281–83,
  286, 290
path analysis, 11–12, 26
patronage and patron-client practices, ix,
  10, 16, 21–23, 28, 33–35, 47–50, 71,
  74, 89–90, 135, 157, 189, 191–92, 195,
  216, 219, 236, 272–73, 287, 347, 354,
  375, 389, 397
Payne, Leigh, 224
Payne, Mark J., 29
PCU Partido Comunista de Uruguay, 173
PDC Partido Demócrata Cristiano (Chile),
  92–95, 100–109, 112, 116, 245–48,
  250, 252, 262–63, 266, 268–69
peasant groups, 23, 35, 372
Pereira, Carlos, 87
Pérez Yoma, Edmundo, 263

Pérez, Carlos Andrés, 393
Pérez-Liñan, Aníbal, 355
Peronism and Peronists, 43, 189, 192–94,
  197, 200, 204, 207, 209, 211, 213, 390.
  See also PJ
personal vote, 10, 13, 20, 22, 24, 72, 77,
  90, 119, 134, 146, 178–79, 183,
  373, 377
personalism and personalistic style, 76,
  173, 208, 232–34, 269, 324, 376
Peru, 27, 393
PFL Partido da Frente Liberal (Brazil), 84,
  223–25, 228–29, 237, 384
Piñeiro, Rafael, 168, 171, 180
Piñera, Sebastián, 244–46, 248, 252, 255,
  381, 385
Pinochet, Augusto, xi, 96, 245–46, 257,
  259, 379
Pinzón de Lewin, Patricia, 119
Pizarro, Eduardo, 119, 124, 131, 291
PJ Partido Justicialista (Argentina), 7,
  43–47, 51–53, 55–58, 63, 65, 67–71,
  189, 192–94, 196–98, 201–14, 216–17,
  383, 386–87, 390, 394. See also
  Peronism and Peronists
plebiscite, 245–46, 258
plurality races and seats, x, 43, 145, 150,
  152, 154–55, 160–61, 163
PMDB Partido do Movimento Democrático
  Brasileiro (Brazil), 84, 223–25, 228,
  232–33, 236–37, 384
Poisson model, 179
Polsby, Nelson, 14, 28, 79
pooling votes, 97, 119, 120–23, 137, 197,
  323, 376
popular approval and popularity, xii, 43,
  106, 114, 158, 162, 244, 250, 283, 286,
  288, 294, 326, 398
popularity, xii, 43, 106, 114, 158, 162, 244,
  250, 283, 286, 288, 294, 326, 398
populist leaders and parties, 5, 11, 15, 23,
  29, 34, 47, 85, 129, 140, 142, 150, 178,
  195, 210–11, 224, 229, 246, 249, 310
pork-barrel politics, ix, 47, 49, 89–90,
  139, 189, 191, 195, 216, 349, 395

poverty, 219, 259, 293, 315

power brokers, 6, 16, 128, 131

Power, Timothy J., xi, 76–78, 219, 224–25, 382, 388–89, 395

PP *Partido Popular* (Brazil), 84

PPD *Partido por la Democracia* (Chile), 92, 94–95, 100–105, 107–9, 112, 116, 118, 247–48, 250, 266

PRD *Partido de la Revolución Democrática* (Mexico), 143–45, 154, 158–63, 297–99, 314, 351, 374, 378–79, 382, 387–89

preferential vote system, 176, 347

presidency (Argentina), 44, 189, 190, 193–94, 197, 204, 207, 210–11, 380

presidency (Brazil), xi, 87, 220–25, 229, 239, 395–96

presidency (Chile), 3, 242–43, 253, 256, 262, 264–65

presidency (Colombia), 4, 271–91, 384

presidency (Mexico), 155, 294, 297, 304–5, 308, 313–14

presidency (Uruguay), 168, 176–77, 182, 317, 319–20, 322, 325–26, 330, 390

presidentialism and presidential systems, vii, 228, 242, 262, 393

Prewitt, Kenneth, 6

PRI *Partido Revolucionario Institucional* (Mexico), xii, 143–45, 147–51, 154–55, 157–59, 161, 293–95, 297–98, 301, 309, 312, 315, 353, 355, 372, 379, 382, 386–88, 398

primaries (Argentina), 48–52, 54–57, 74, 196–97, 200, 203, 206, 375

primaries (Brazil), 223, 232, 240

primaries (Chile), 92, 106–9, 111–12, 116, 241, 244, 250, 373, 390

primaries (Colombia), xii, 127–28

primaries (Mexico), 145–46, 151, 157–59, 162–63, 297, 387

primaries (Uruguay), 165–69, 172–75, 183, 327–29, 331, 337, 386, 390–91

principal-agent model, 176

prisoner's dilemma, 325, 327

PRN *Partido da Renovação Nacional* (Brazil), 223–24

progressive ambition, 11, 14, 59. *See also* career paths

progressives, 89

proportional representation, x, 19, 42, 77, 81, 96, 119, 121, 145, 164, 265, 321, 355, 374

prospective voting, 34

protests, 158, 206, 261

provincial party loyalists, 74, 351, 354, 372, 392–93

PRSD *Partido Radical Social Democrata* (Chile), 92, 100, 102–3, 105, 109, 251

Prud'homme, Jean-Francois, 158–59

PS *Partido Socialista* (Chile), 92, 100, 102–3, 105, 107–9, 116–17, 246–48, 250–51, 266

PSB *Partido Socialista Brasileiro* (Brazil), 224, 232, 236

PSD *Partido Social Democratico* (Brazil), 224

PSDB *Partido da Social Democracia Brasileira* (Brazil), 84, 223–25, 232, 235, 372

PSU *Partido Socialista de Uruguay,* 173

PT *Partido dos Trabalhadores* (Brazil), 6, 81–84, 89, 223–25, 232–33, 235, 240, 351, 372, 376, 395–96

PTB *Partido Trabalhista Brasileiro* (Brazil), 84, 224, 232, 236, 372

public sector, 191, 301, 303, 310

Putnam, Robert D., 165

PV *Partido Verde* (Brazil), 224

PV *Partido Verde* (Chile), 255

PV *Partido Verde* (Mexico), 151

Quadros, Jânio, 221–22, 224, 227, 238–39, 301, 395–96

quality of democracy and representation, vii, 36

Quércia, Orestes, 236

quota, 66, 84, 89, 121–23, 261–62, 345, 347–48, 350, 355–56, 359–61, 366–67, 399. *See also* gender quota legislation

Rabkin, Rhoda, 96

Radical Party (Chile), 109

Ramírez Sáiz, Juan Manuel, 311
Ramírez, Juan Andrés, 329, 340–41
rank-and-file, 154, 276
recruitment *vs.* selection, 8–9
reelection, 10–11, 14, 18–19, 21–22,
    24–25, 27, 32–35, 52, 54–58, 66, 71,
    73–74, 82, 85–88, 96–98, 100, 103,
    105, 109–10, 115, 117, 134, 145–47,
    157, 160, 177, 179–82, 184, 191, 194,
    197, 200, 210, 212, 220, 225, 231, 235,
    236, 251, 275, 279, 289–90, 323, 374,
    378, 380, 382–84, 388
reforms and reformers, xiii, 31, 33, 36, 92,
    112, 120–22, 131–32, 142, 147, 153,
    157, 180, 207, 210, 228, 243, 260–61,
    272, 278, 280, 294, 316, 330–31
regional factors and regionalism, 221,
    234, 299, 388, 390
Rehren, Alfredo, 262, 264
religious groups and religious
    organizations, 23, 35
remainders and remainders allocation,
    121–22, 132
residency requirement, 81, 375
retirement, 180, 185
retrospective voting, 34
Reutemann, Carlos, 213–14
Reynolds, Andrew, 347–48, 350, 356
Rice Index and cohesion scores, 78, 333
Rio de Janeiro (Brazil), 233, 234,
    236, 237
Rio Grande do Sul (Brazil), 234–35
Rodrigues, Leoncio, 89
Rodríguez Raza, Juan Carlos, 125
Rodríguez Saá, Adolfo, 190, 192, 196,
    202, 206, 214
Rohde, David W., 71, 79
Roriz, Joaquim, 238
Rosenbluth, Frances, 164, 166
Rousseff, Dilma, 239
rule of law, 314
Rule, Wilma, 347, 350
runoff elections and run-off systems,
    29, 169, 219, 389. *See also* two-round
    electoral systems
rural districts and vote, 129, 272, 281

Saiegh, Sebastián M., 42, 47, 49, 58, 67,
    72, 114
Salinas de Gortari, Carlos, 157
Salvador, Allende, 256–57, 339
Samper, Ernesto, 274, 278, 281–82, 364
Samuels, David, ix, 6, 59, 76, 78–82,
    84–86, 88, 90, 176–77, 212, 219–20,
    225, 230–31, 233, 376, 378, 395
San Luis, Argentina, 191, 196, 214
Sanguinetti, Júlio, 169, 319, 330, 332,
    334, 335, 340, 342, 352, 381
Santa Cruz, Argentina, 48, 191, 210
Santa Fe, Argentina, 191, 214–15
Santiago, 98, 107–8, 117–18, 215, 255,
    307, 311
Santos, Fabiano, 87–89
São Paulo, 83, 234–36, 384
Sarney, José, 221–22, 234, 239
Sawers, Larry, 42
Scandinavia, 348
Schlesinger, Joseph, 79
Schmidt, Gregory D., 347
Schmitt, Rogério, 81
Scully, Timothy, 76, 96, 189, 192, 253,
    290, 317
seat allocation, 96, 98, 105, 120–21
Segovia, Carolina, 252
selectorate, vii, 5, 21–22, 30, 74, 164,
    166–67, 233, 237
self-nomination, 5, 21–22, 30, 74, 164,
    166–67, 233, 237
self-selection, x, 15–16, 18, 23, 28, 82,
    126, 128, 171–72, 321–22, 347
Seligman, Lester, 6
Senate (Argentina), 42–45, 56, 59, 71–72,
    191, 204, 212
Senate (Brazil), 225, 236
Senate (Chile), 93, 95–96, 100, 102, 104,
    106–8, 110, 115–16, 256
Senate (Colombia), 121, 135–36, 276
Senate (Mexico), x, 145–56, 158–63,
    300, 374–75, 379
Senate (Uruguay), 168–69, 173, 175–82,
    320, 325
seniority, 7, 32, 80, 180–81
Seregni, Líber, 176, 326, 330, 339–40

Serpa, Horacio, 274, 279, 281, 290–91,
    381, 384, 392
Serra, José, 191, 229, 235, 339
Serrafero, Mario, 191, 200
Shanks, Merrill, 28
Shugart, Matthew S., 6, 12, 13, 26, 36,
    77, 119, 121, 125, 165, 280, 327,
    347–48, 373, 393
Siaroff, Alan, 348
Smith, Peter, 88
SNTV (Single non-transferable vote),
    119–21
Soares, Glaucio Ary D., 220
Social Democratic Party (Brazil),
    223, 384
Social Democratic Party (Chile), 92, 109
Sourrouille, Juan, 207
Souto, Paulo, 237
Souza, Celina, 237
spatial modeling, 390
Spiller, Pablo T., 42, 47, 58, 67, 70,
    72, 191
static ambition, 59, 86. See also career paths
Stirling, Guillermo, 331, 341
Stokes, Susan, 27
Studlar, Donley T., 350

Tafner, Paulo, 78
Taylor, Steven L., 271, 349, 384, 388–89,
    397–98
Taylor-Robinson, Michelle, xiii, 140,
    265, 346, 348–50, 352–54, 356, 358,
    360–64, 366–68, 399
technocrat, 208–9, 219–20, 226, 228–29,
    237, 246, 250, 258, 260–63, 269, 294,
    302, 307, 382
Terra, Gabriel, 199, 318
Thiébault, Jean-Louis, 350
Tlaxcala (Mexico), 297
Tommasi, Mariano, 42, 47, 49, 58, 67,
    70, 191
traditional politics, 234, 240, 260
Tupamaros, 173, 319
Turbay Ayala, Júlio César, 127, 277, 352
turnover, 85–88, 97, 139, 267
two-party system, 27, 119, 332–33

two-round electoral systems, 327, 380,
    383. See also ballotage
typology, viii–ix, xi, 9, 11–12, 17, 23–26,
    167, 206, 210–11, 223, 234, 242, 252,–73

UCEDE Unión del Centro Democratico
    (Argentina), 193–94, 210
UCR Unión Cívica Radical (Argentina),
    43–47, 51–53, 55–56, 58, 63, 65, 67,
    70–72, 189, 192–94, 197, 203–8,
    212–13, 216
UDI Unión Demócrata Independiente
    (Chile), 92, 102, 109–11, 118, 246,
    248–50, 252, 260
UDN (União Democrática Nacional,
    Brazil), 224
UDR (União Democrática Ruralista,
    Brazil), 224
UP Unidad Popular (Chile), 256
unitary systems, viii, 19, 22, 28, 32, 35
United States, iv, vii, 3, 6, 27–28, 33,
    71–72, 80, 86, 87, 166, 218, 298,
    304–7, 378, 391, 393, 397
urban base and urban electorates, 272,
    280, 318
urbanization, 89, 272, 281, 287, 389
Uribe, Álvaro, 4, 132, 274–75, 279, 284,
    286, 288, 290–91, 362, 364, 381,
    383–84, 386–87, 390, 397
Uruguay, viii, x, xii–xiii, 3, 28, 73, 88,
    127, 164–79, 181–84, 197, 316–25,
    327–38, 341–42, 351–55, 358, 362,
    372–73, 375–76, 379–81, 385 86, 390,
    392–93, 398–99

Valdés, Gabriel, 245
Valenzuela, Arturo, 36, 96, 393
Vázquez, Tabaré, 28, 168, 174, 177, 313,
    319, 326, 329 32, 334, 340–42,
    380–81, 385
Venezuela, 4, 26–27, 29, 264, 317, 359,
    375, 387, 391–93
Vernazza, Francisco, 171
veto and veto power, ix, 16, 89,
    92, 98, 106–7, 131, 173, 190, 209
veto player, 42, 114

Villarzú, Juan, 263
Volonté, Alberto, 330, 340–41
vote threshold, 109
vote-getter, 224, 231, 323, 383
voting discipline, xi, 114, 164, 184–85
voting sheets, 320

Walker Prieto, Ignacio, 117
Weldon, Jeffrey, 145
Wessels, Bernhard, 166
Willis Otero, Laura, 355
women in politics, 345–46, 366
working class, 305, 309, 311

World Bank, 304
Wuhs, Steve, 182

Yaffé, Jaime, 173
Yucatán (Mexico), 313

Zacatecas (Mexico), 297
Zaldívar, Andrés, 116, 247, 250–51
Zedillo, Ernesto, 294, 300–301,
    304, 306–7, 311, 362, 364,
    380, 392
zero-sum game, 100, 184, 266
Zumarán, Alberto, 324, 330, 340

About the Contributors

David Altman is Associate Professor at the Political Science Institute of the Catholic University of Chile and Editor of *Revista de Ciencia Política*. He works on comparative politics with an emphasis on executive-legislative relations in Latin America, the quality of democratic institutions, electoral systems, and direct democracy. His work has appeared in *Electoral Studies, The Developing Economies, Party Politics, Democratization, The Journal of Legislative Studies, Política y Gobierno, Nordic Journal of Latin American and Caribbean Studies, International Review of Public Administration, Revista de Ciencia Política, PS-Political Science and Politics*, and *Revista Uruguaya de Ciencia Política*, among others.

Felipe Botero is Assistant Professor in the Department of Political Science at Universidad de los Andes in Bogotá, Colombia and Editor of *Colombia Internacional*, published by the same institution. His research focuses on legislative institutions and electoral and party systems in Latin America. In his recent work he analyzes the factors that explain political career decisions and duration in the region. He has published recently in *Revista de Ciencia Política, Brazilian Political Science Review, Colombia Internacional*, and *Legislative Studies Quarterly*.

Daniel Buquet Corleto is Professor of Political Science at the Instituto de Ciencia Política of the Universidad de la República in Uruguay. His main academic focuses are party systems, electoral systems, and electoral reforms in Latin America. He is also a consultant in the area of public opinion and elections and a political analyst with frequent appearances in the media. His recent articles have been published in journals and books in Spain, the UK, Sweden, USA, Chile and Uruguay.

Roderic Ai Camp is the Philip McKenna Professor of the Pacific Rim at Claremont McKenna College. His special interests include Mexican politics, comparative elites, political recruitment, church-state relations, and civil-military affairs. The author of numerous articles and twenty books on Mexico, his most recent publications include: *Politics in Mexico, the Democratic Consolidation* (Oxford University Press, 2007), *Mexico's Military on the Democratic Stage* (Praeger, 2005), *Mexico's Mandarins, Crafting a Power Elite for the 21st Century* (University of California Press, 2002), and *Citizen Views of Democracy in Latin America* (University of Pittsburgh Press, 2001).

Daniel Chasquetti is Assistant Professor of Political Science at the Instituto de Ciencia Política of the Universidad de la República and Editor of *Revista Uruguaya de Ciencia Política*. His main academic focuses are party systems, electoral systems and governmental coalitions in Latin America. He is also a consultant in legislative affairs and political analyst with frequent appearances in the mass media. He is the author of the book *Multipartidismo y Coaliciones de Gobierno en América Latina,* and co-author of *Fragmentación Política y Gobierno en Uruguay: ¿Un Enfermo Imaginario?.* He has written several articles in books and journals published in Uruguay and abroad.

Brian F. Crisp is Associate Professor of Political Science at Washington University in St. Louis. His research on Latin American democracies has been supported by the National Science Foundation and Fulbright. In addition to *Democratic Institutional Design: The Powers and Incentives of Venezuelan Politicians and Interest Groups* (Stanford University Press, 2000), his recent work has been published in *The American Journal of Political Science, The American Political Science Review, Comparative Political Studies, Electoral Studies, Legislative Studies Quarterly,* and *The Journal of Politics.*

Miguel De Luca is Professor of Government in the Department of Political Science at the Universidad de Buenos Aires. His primary research interests include governmental institutions and processes, political parties and electoral systems, and local politics. He has published several journal articles and chapters on the functioning of Argentine democratic institutions.

Maria Escobar-Lemmon is Associate Professor of Political Science at Texas A&M University. Her research focuses on the increased opportunities for citizen participation and representation created by decentralization, the impact of electoral rules on personal vote seeking and career trajectories, legislatures, and women's representation. Recent articles have appeared in the *American Journal of Political Science, Latin American Research Review, Publius: The Journal of Federalism,* and *Policy Studies Journal.*

Mark P. Jones is Professor of Political Science at Rice University. His research interests lie in the comparative study of democratic institutions, with recent articles appearing in the *American Journal of Political Science, Electoral Studies,* and *The Journal of Politics.* Current research includes a study of the evolution of partisan politics in Texas over the past forty years, an analysis of inter-party dynamics in the Argentine Congress, and an examination of the combined impact of gender quotas and electoral laws on the election of women in Latin America.

Joy Langston is a Professor of Political Science at the Centro de Investigación y Docencia Económicas (CIDE) in Mexico City. She specializes in political parties in Mexico and has published in such journals as *Comparative Politics, Party Politics,* and *Comparative Political Studies.*

Marilia Mochel is a Ph.D. candidate in the Political Science Department at the University of Pittsburgh.

Juan Andrés Moraes is a Ph.D. candidate in political science at the University of Notre Dame and Professor at the Department of Political Science at the Universidad de la República in Montevideo Uruguay. His primary research interest involves political institutions and legislatures, political parties and political economy. He is the coauthor with Daniel Buquet and Daniel Chasquetti of *Fragmentación Política y Gobierno en Uruguay: ¿Un Enfermo Imaginario?* and coeditor with Diego Aboal of *Economía Política en Uruguay: Instituciones y Actores Políticos en el Proceso Económico*. He is also the author of several papers published in Uruguay and a forthcoming article in *Comparative Political Studies* (with Frances Hagopian and Carlos Gervasoni).

Erika Moreno is Assistant Professor of Political Science at Creighton University. She focuses on the roles and interactions of democratic institutions, including political parties, executives, and unelected branches of government in nascent and consolidating democracies. Recent articles have appeared in *Comparative Political Studies, Electoral Studies, and Legislative Studies Quarterly*.

Scott Morgenstern is Associate Professor of Political Science at University of Pittsburgh. His primary interests involve Latin American politics, with emphases on executive-legislative relations, electoral systems and political parties. He is author of *Patterns of Legislative Politics: Roll Call Voting in the United States and Latin America's Southern Cone* (Cambridge University Press, 2003) and co-editor of *Legislative Politics in Latin America* (Cambridge University Press, 2001). His work has also appeared in *Comparative Politics, Comparative Political Studies, Party Politics, The Journal of Politics, Electoral Studies*, and *Legislative Studies Quarterly*.

Patricio Navia is a master teacher of global cultures at New York University and a researcher/professor at the Instituto de Investigación en Ciencias Sociales at Universidad Diego Portales in Chile. He has published on democratization, electoral rules and democratic institutions in Latin America. He is a columnist at *La Tercera* and *Capital* magazine. His most recent book coauthored with Eduardo Ángel is *Que Gane el Más Mejor. Mérito y Competencia en el Chile de hoy* (Random House, Editorial Debate, 2006).

Timothy J. Power is University Lecturer in Brazilian Studies and a Fellow of St. Cross College at the University of Oxford, where he is also a member of the Department of Politics and International Relations. His research interests include political parties, elections, and executive-legislative relations in Brazil, and he recently co-edited (with Peter Kingstone) *Democratic Brazil Revisited* (University of Pittsburgh Press, 2008). From 2004 to 2006 Power served as president of the Brazilian Studies Association (www.brasa.org), and he is currently an Associate Fellow of the Latin American and Caribbean Research Project at Chatham House.

David Samuels is Associate Professor of Political Science at the University of Minnesota. He specializes in Latin American politics and the comparative study of political institutions, with particular emphasis on Brazilian politics, electoral systems, political parties, legislatures, and federalism. He is the author of *Ambition, Federalism, and Legislative Politics in Brazil* (Cambridge University Press, 2003) and articles that have appeared in *Comparative Political Studies, Comparative Politics, The Journal of Politics, The British Journal of Political Science, The Journal of Democracy, Latin American Politics and Society*, and *Legislative Studies Quarterly*.

Peter M. Siavelis is Z. Smith Reynolds Foundation Fellow and Associate Professor of Political Science at Wake Forest University. He specializes in Latin American politics, with a particular emphasis on election systems, political parties and legislatures. He is the author of *The President and Congress in Post-authoritarian Chile: Institutional Constraints to Democratic Consolidation* (Penn State Press, 2000), and articles that have appeared in *Comparative Politics, Comparative Political Studies, Latin American Politics and Society, Latin American Research Review, Party Politics, Política*, and *Revista de Ciencia Política*.

Steven L. Taylor is an Associate Professor of Political Science at Troy University in Troy, Alabama. He is the author of *Voting Amid Violence: Electoral Democracy in Colombia* (University Press of New England, forthcoming).

Michelle M. Taylor-Robinson is Associate Professor of Political Science at Texas A&M University. Her work focuses on the representation of women as well as the comparative study of legislatures and how the performance of legislative institutions influences the prospects for democratic consolidation. She is co-author (with Gretchen Casper) of *Negotiating Democracy* (University of Pittsburgh Press, 1996) and has published in journals such as the *American Journal of Political Science, Journal of Politics, Women and Politics*, and *Electoral Studies*.